THE ILLUMINATION CODEX

MICHAEL GARBER

MICHAEL GARBER

Printed in the United States of America
First Printing 2021
First Edition 2021

Second Edition

ISBNs:
Softcover 978-1-959561-01-9
eBook 978-1-959561-02-6

10 9 8 7 6 5 4 3 2 1

THE
ILLUMINATION
CODEX

Table of Contents

ACKNOWLEDGMENTS..9

DEDICATION AND INVOCATION 11

GUIDANCE FOR READING THIS BOOK 13

ABOUT THE AUTHOR 19
    Awakening to the Quantum Reality 19

NEW EARTH ASCENDING VISIONARY CREED.................29

GATEWAY ONE: Ascension Initiation
    Keys for Higher Evolution.. 33

    ONE: The Shift of the Ages..35

    TWO: Earth School Orientation....................................46

    THREE: The Human Experience 56

    FOUR: High Alchemy of the Soul 70

    FIVE: Awakening in the Matrix.....................................79

    SIX: Universal Laws of Creation 92

    SEVEN: Ascension and Descension Cycles of Consciousness.............. 103

    EIGHT: Ascension Symptom Care.................................110

    NINE: Shifting to New Earth 117

GATEWAY TWO PART ONE: Quantum Origins
    Keys for Ancient Cosmology... 137

    TEN: Quantum Origins... 139

    ELEVEN: Star Family Legacy 167

    TWELVE: The Earth Experiment 182

    THIRTEEN: The Human Experiment........................... 193

    FOURTEEN: Lemuria and Atlantis 212

    FIFTEEN: Atlantean Cataclysm 229

    SIXTEEN: Inner Earth 252

    SEVENTEEN: Ancient Egypt.......................................259

    EIGHTEEN: Holographic Earth & Planetary Grid 280

NINETEEN: Avalon & Jaguar Shaman 293

GATEWAY TWO PART TWO: Cosmic Christ Transmissions
The Ministry of Light 303

TWENTY: Jesus and the Ministry of Light 305
TWENTY-ONE: Protector of Jesus...............................323
TWENTY-TWO: John the Beloved................................332
TWENTY-THREE: Mary Magdalene.............................344
TWENTY-FOUR: Jeremiah: Disciple of Jesus 371
TWENTY-FIVE: Through the Eyes of Jesus 381
TWENTY-SIX: Esther the Essene 394
TWENTY-SEVEN: Melchizedek, David, Jesus..............423

GATEWAY TWO PART THREE: New Earth Transmissions
Future Timelines of Gaia.......................................435

TWENTY-EIGHT: Starseed Phenomenon....................437
TWENTY-NINE: Starseed Transmissions 444
THIRTY: Making the Transition...............................454
THIRTY-ONE: Main Wave Event 463
THIRTY-TWO: City of Light....................................471
THIRTY-THREE: After the Shift...............................477
THIRTY-FOUR: New Earth Civilization 494
THIRTY-FIVE: Family of Light Blessing....................507

GATEWAY THREE: Path of Awakening
Keys for Transfiguration 513

THIRTY-SIX: Path of Illumination 515
THIRTY-SEVEN: Taking Refuge in the Ideal..............523
THIRTY-EIGHT: Path of Nondual Knowledge 529
THIRTY-NINE: Spiritual Ethics 536
FORTY: Meditation 543
FORTY-ONE: Koshas: Layers of Being......................552
FORTY-TWO: Annamaya Kosha: Physical Body..........559
FORTY-THREE: Pranamaya Kosha: Pranic Body 568
FORTY-FOUR: Postures for Channeling Light.............589

FORTY-FIVE: Planes of Human Consciousness...................................595

FORTY-SIX: Superconscious Mind 610

FORTY-SEVEN: Bliss Body and Unity Consciousness 619

FORTY-EIGHT: 5D New Earth Consciousness....................................624

GATEWAY FOUR: Chakra Yoga Discourse
Keys for Higher Consciousness.. 631

FORTY-NINE: Wheels of Light...633

FIFTY: Root Chakra: Grounded in Being 636

FIFTY-ONE: Sacral Chakra: Divine Creatorship 649

FIFTY-TWO: Conscious Relating & Sacred Sexuality.......................658

FIFTY-THREE: Solar Plexus Chakra: Divine Willpower....................677

FIFTY-FOUR: Heart Chakra: Divine Love..683

FIFTY-FIVE: Throat Chakra: Conscious Communication.................692

FIFTY-SIX: Brow Chakra: Divine Vision... 700

FIFTY-SEVEN: Crown Chakra: Divine Limitlessness 706

FIFTY-EIGHT: Ascension Chakras 712

GATEWAY FIVE: Laying of Hands
Reiki & Beyond 719

FIFTY-NINE: Reiki: Laying of Hands 721

SIXTY: Pillars of Embodied Light Reiki......................................733

SIXTY-ONE: Hand Placements: Self-Healing.....................................738

SIXTY-TWO: Facilitating Healing for Others......................................747

SIXTY-THREE: Manifestation of New Earth Prayer 768

GATEWAY SIX: Ascension Lexicon... 771

Recommended Reading 791

Support Our Initiatives...793

ACKNOWLEDGMENTS

I bow in humble recognition of the One Light of Consciousness, the Source of my being and the source of all knowledge and wisdom. I give gratitude to the Supreme for dreaming me into existence and allowing me to have the conscious experience of life and the crafting of this codex.

I bow in love and gratitude to my dear beloved partner Ron Amit, a true gift of the Divine, for all the many ways he supports me in my life. I am blessed beyond measure to have such a brilliant master of love, compassion, and divine service to walk this earthly life with. Thank you for all that you do, seen and unseen, to amplify joy and higher consciousness for me and all beings in the Cosmos. I love you across all space, time, and dimensions.

I send gratitude to my friends and clients who have brought forth the lost stories of Creation through their Illuminated Quantum Healing hypnosis sessions. Thank you for being the powerful Light beacons that you are!

I send deep gratitude to my many modern scribes who assisted me in the transcription work. Thank you for helping me capture these incredible client stories so that the world can remember our cosmic divine heritage.

Bless all the beings, seen and unseen, who have helped me craft this material so that you, the reader, can be nourished on your path of Ascension. May you, the reader, be blessed infinitely and discover the highest truth of your being. May ascended consciousness, liberation, and divine unification be yours in this very life!

DEDICATION AND INVOCATION

This book is dedicated to the infinite expressions of our Oneself, for the celebration of our many incarnations, past, present, and future, and the lessons we have learned throughout eternity. May these words and the energy they carry be a potent force for awakening for all seekers of Unconditional Love and divine Truth. May this transmission support the reactivation and restoration of humanity's divine blueprint upon planet Earth and accelerate the realization of our eternal unity and oneness with all of Creation.

Let us join in prayer, honoring and sending gratitude to the Supreme Intelligent Source of Creation, the omniscient, omnipotent, omnipresent, transcendental Divine Source that is our True Nature.

Let us honor and send gratitude to the higher Light realms and the beings of Light who guide and protect Creation's evolution. Let us honor and send gratitude to our star lineages and those who support us from beyond the Earth. Let us receive your love and blessings now as we remember our cosmic ancestry and our role in the higher evolutionary plan for Creation.

Let us honor and send gratitude to our Earth Mother and her many dimensions and manifestations of Life including the animal, plant, bacterial, fungal, protozoan, mineral, crystalline, and elemental beings who contribute to her dynamic, regenerative biomes. These writings are offered as salve and balm to heal and bless our beloved Gaia, our Earth Mother and Divine Sister. May her waters be pure, her soil rich, her air clean, and may all beings, seen and unseen, within her living biofield know lasting peace forever and ever.

Let us honor and send gratitude to the wisdom and guidance from the seven directions of East, South, West, North, Above, Below, and Within. Let us call back our soul fragments scattered through time and space so that we may anchor ourselves HERE and NOW in this eternal moment of infinite potential to witness the unfolding manifestation of the Divine Plan.

Let us honor and send gratitude to the elements of Earth, Air, Fire, Water, and Ether that create the foundation of our evolutionary experience in form. May the Light of Consciousness awaken swiftly in each of us as we remember our True Nature beyond names and forms.

Let us honor and send gratitude to our ancestors and the many souls who have shared their light upon the Earth. Let us send special thanks to those who dedicated their lives to passing on the Mysteries and sacred knowledge of the Divine so that we may NOW stand at this Grand Turning of the Ages, with the support of all who have come and all who are destined to live upon this great Earth.

I call forth the full remembering of our divinity and the weaving of a new story of harmony and peace for all of Life upon the Earth. May we shed our stories of limitation and suffering and step forward into a new era as People of Light, cosmic co-citizens, and ambassadors for the Living Light of Creation.

Hallelujah! Jai! Aho! Blessed Be! Amen! And so, it is! Om!

GUIDANCE FOR READING THIS BOOK

The Illumination Codex is a multidimensional library for the path of Ascension. It is holographic by nature as each chapter contains a multitude of keycodes to activate ancient cellular memory and trigger multidimensional awareness and higher consciousness integration. As you read the material, your Inner Being will offer flashes of insight and higher perception into your awareness to assist you in healing, spiritual activation, and cosmic remembrance. I recommend using a highlighter, journaling your process, and using other resources to research and enhance your understanding of the topics presented in this book.

A major influence for this material comes from my work as a past-life regression hypnotherapist using the methods we have codified into a technique called Illuminated Quantum Healing (IQH). While in a deep hypnotic trance, my clients experience other lifetimes and other planetary civilizations and communicate with advanced intelligent species from beyond the Earth and Earth plane. The information contained in this book is a summary of my understanding of all that I have learned through my clients as they journeyed to the ancient past, probable timelines of the future, and higher planes of Light. There are many transcriptions of IQH sessions included in the book for you to have your own unique interpretation and multidimensional experience with the material.

This book contains a diverse collection of spiritual information from a variety of wisdom traditions that I have studied in my life. These writings are my own interpretations and understandings of these different concepts that have helped me in my awakening journey and do not necessarily speak for the lineages themselves. This presentation of information is meant as a collection of keys to unlock the wisdom that is already encoded within you. None of it is meant to become dogmatic as consciousness revelation and ascendency will open us continuously to higher and higher truths and understanding.

I confess that I share this transmission as a fellow traveler on the path of awakening. I have my own limitations, my own egoic nature, and my own struggles. I am capable of error and ignorance just as any other person. This presentation of information is what I have found along my path which has triggered awakening and helped me on my path back home to my Self. My prayer is that this book will become deeply meaningful for you and be a guiding light back to your own liberated being.

While reading this material, you may come across something in the text that triggers something within you that is uncomfortable. Maybe it is words that I use, perspectives that I share, or something else that may bring up resistance, judgment, anger, guilt, and so on. This is a wonderful opportunity to investigate the origin of the reactive mental and emotional patterns that create such experiences. The origin may come from earlier stages of your life or previous lifetimes. Use this as an opportunity to reconcile those parts of your consciousness through spiritual inquiry and self-study so that you may realize deeper states of wholeness and clarity.

This text is intended to activate 'gnosis,' a direct experience and knowledge of the divine presence within and around you. I do not recommend blind faith in any concept or religious doctrine. The information in this book is not meant to be treated as religious dogma that cannot be questioned or developed further. It is meant to be utilized to unlock the truth that lives within your very being. I am not writing this intending to change people's beliefs or convert anyone. I am simply relaying the summary of my life's research on the quest for spiritual truth. If something from the material does not resonate as truth in your heart, release it and move on to the next part of the transmission. Use the philosophy and information in this text to stimulate your expansion and the embodiment of YOUR deepest truth and to strengthen your relationship and innate connection with the Divine.

Another thing to mention is capitalization. You will notice that there are words that are not normally capitalized in other books and sacred texts that are capitalized in this text. My intention behind this was to add spiritual dimensionality to words that describe qualities or names of the Divine.

Typically, when I speak of light in this book, I am speaking about higher-dimensional, intelligently-encoded subtle energy and not conventional light from a light bulb. When I speak about "energy," I am speaking about subtle energy which exists beyond the visible light spectrum for most people. Many are becoming sensitive to subtle energy (i.e., multisensory, intuitive, psychic) and are developing the ability to sense and perceive this energy through extrasensory perception. All of humanity is evolving towards being able to perceive and interact with subtle energy and higher cosmic intelligence and consciousness.

The use of the term consciousness fluctuates throughout the book and can mean different things. When I speak of pure Consciousness I am speaking about your True Self as Source Consciousness, the Absolute, the Eternal Witness of all Creation, pure Awareness and Existence itself. Other times I will speak of consciousness as in variations of the mind such as unity consciousness or separation consciousness. All forms of consciousness, all experiences of the mind, borrow existence from the One Light of Consciousness and you are that!

I tried my best to organize this text in a way that can be read from front to back like any regular book, but it can also be read any way you feel intuitively called to read it. Part of the reason for the size of this codex is because it is difficult to explain one part without understanding many other components. In my effort to answer all potential and probable questions about ascension, I wrote everything I could on this multifaceted, multidimensional topic.

As you make your journey through this material, there are three stages to help integrate the information and use it to fuel your awakening to your True Nature:

Stage One: Listening (*Sravana*) As you read or listen to the material in this book, allow it to penetrate deeply and work with your inner philosophical understanding. Listen deeply to your Inner Being for there will be flashes of insight and knowing that emerge within your inner consciousness space.

Stage Two: Reflection (*Manana*) Try your best to understand the information contained in this book through self-inquiry and inner philosophical pondering. I am not asking for you to blindly believe any of this transmission. Think of this information as an active hypothesis. You do not have to believe it, but you can reflect over the information and see how it applies to your life.

Stage Three: Integration/Meditation (*Nididhyasana*) As you take in the words in stage one and convert the words to knowledge and understanding in stage two, you move into conviction and integration of knowledge in stage three as you crystallize and embody the Self-knowledge of "I am Pure Consciousness." As you go about your daily life, use the knowledge you have gained to interrupt habit and conditioned thought and re-direct your mind toward the Light of Consciousness that you are.

Gateways of Entry

Besides reading front-to-back or intuitively hopping around, I have created six gateways for you to enter the presentation of the material. I have created one large book that has all of the Illumination Codex material and separated the material into separately published volumes to make the information more digestible. The Gateways are as follows:

GATEWAY ONE: ASCENSION INITIATION: KEYS FOR HIGHER EVOLUTION gives an overall understanding of Ascension, reincarnation, universal law, and a theoretical and philosophical framework concerning Cosmic Evolution. This is an excellent place to start if you are open and eager to learn about these subjects and awakening, you may want to start in Gateway Three.

GATEWAY TWO: AKASHIC DATABASE contains a wide variety of Illuminated Quantum Healing session transcriptions describing key figures and events in the history of Creation, galactic history, ancient planetary history, and probable future timelines of New Earth from clients in hypnotic visionary states. This is a suitable place to enter the material if you already have a general understanding of multidimensionality, galactic civilizations, and the process of personal and planetary ascension. This gateway is conveniently separated into QUANTUM ORIGINS, COSMIC CHRIST TRANSMISSIONS, and NEW EARTH TRANSMISSIONS. If you find yourself resistant to those ideas and are new to these subjects. I recommend developing a meditation practice parallel to reading this material as the transcripts are deeply activating on multiple levels.

GATEWAY THREE: PATH OF AWAKENING: KEYS FOR TRANSFIGURATION is an in-depth collection of spiritual and philosophical wisdom to support personal, relational, and planetary healing. If you are in the beginning stages of awakening or moving through a deep healing process, you may wish to start here so you can develop your consciousness and prepare your mind and body for higher level initiation into the Mysteries.

GATEWAY FOUR: CHAKRA YOGA DISCOURSE transmits deeper

insight into the themes and physio-psycho-spiritual domains of the vortices of life force and perception called the *chakras*. Each section transmits valuable information to understand the common distortions in these processing centers and how to activate and reconcile each center.

GATEWAY FIVE: LAYING HANDS: REIKI & BEYOND is a full manual for learning the art of the laying of hands for healing. The manual clearly describes all the stages, steps, and practices to perform powerfully transformative hands-on-healing sessions for yourself, others, and even in groups. This manual would be acceptable for any Level 1 and Level 2 Reiki course.

GATEWAY SIX: ASCENSION LEXICON is a glossary of commonly used words to describe the process of awakening and ascension. These definitions act as keycode activators to unlock deeper meaning and inner wisdom. Many words used in spiritual/ascension circles are convoluted and sometimes lose their impact because they are misused or misunderstood. I may use words in a way you are not familiar with, or I may use words differently than you. I tried my best to make a glossary with foundational vocabulary to assist with understanding the material. You may wish to read the ASCENSION LEXICON before journeying through the main text of the book.

Bless you on your personal path through this material. May the light in your heart guide you with ease and grace on your journey of initiation with *The Illumination Codex*.

Awakening to the Quantum Reality

In the Summer of 2016, I was given a book that forever changed my life's direction called *The Three Waves of Volunteers and the New Earth* by Dolores Cannon. This book was a huge catalyst in my spiritual awakening. Reading the text stirred something deep within me and resonated profoundly with my heart's truth. The book's pages sent waves of energy down my spine as I began to awaken to a higher consciousness reality and remember my purpose for being born upon the Earth at this time.

Dolores Cannon was a world-renowned hypnotherapist specializing in past-life regression. To understand the power of regressive hypnosis, we also need to understand the workings of the mind. The mind can be separated into three categories: the conscious mind, the subconscious mind, and the superconscious mind.

The conscious mind is the ego/personality part of the mind. This active part of the mind uses limited information from the environment and past experiences to make decisions and take care of the body.

The subconscious mind is the recording device of our mind. It records incredible amounts of information at every moment. We easily pull data from the subconscious when we think about something from our past as we access memory.

Deeper in the subconscious, sometimes called the unconscious mind, we have unconscious memories and information, including societal conditioning, painful traumas from this life that are too painful to remember, and memories from other lifetimes. Even though this information is not in the conscious mind, it silently influences our day-to-day experience as reactive emotional momentum, called *samskaras* in Sanskrit, from past events which overlay and filter our experience of the present moment. These subconscious patterns are like applications running in the background of smartphones that quietly drain the processing speed and battery, silently influencing processor speed and functionality.

The superconscious mind is a higher mind capacity that gives us access to intuitive information, extrasensory perception, non-local consciousness, creative genius, universal connection, and access to divine consciousness. This part of the mind is mostly undiscovered and underdeveloped in most of humanity.

Dolores created a unique method of hypnosis, Quantum Healing Hypnosis Technique (QHHT), that opened a doorway to the client's subconscious mind to explore other lifetimes and realms in Creation. When I use the word "quantum," I am speaking to the fabric of Consciousness, the multidimensional unified field of Creation. When clients are in these hypnotic states, they tap into the part of their consciousness that is nonlocal and connected to All That Is. This includes access to other lifetimes, other realities and dimensions, and other intelligent consciousness forms (i.e., higher-dimensional light beings, telepathic extraterrestrials, etc.). Through this experience, clients came to understand another perspective and origin of self-sabotaging and limiting beliefs that were playing out in this life and the core mental/emotional patterns that create illness and disease.

During her sessions, Dolores started to contact a part of her clients' consciousness that seemed to have endless knowledge and wisdom. She called this aspect of her clients the Subconscious or the SC. Others have called this the Higher Self, the oversoul, superconsciousness, or the cosmic consciousness. I prefer the term Higher Self and superconscious mind and go into great detail of how to activate and evolve superconsciousness throughout this text. While the information was limitless, the SC/Higher Self would only answer questions in a way that was appropriate for the client's learning path and honored their free will. When working with the SC, both Dolores and the client described powerful healing energy in their bodies and the treatment room. Clients often reported instantaneous healing as they were transformed from the inside out during the session. While this may seem too good to be true, there are countless documented and measurable occurrences where clients received lasting miraculous healing through these types of sessions.

When she would work with the Higher Self, this higher consciousness identity and supportive Light team would speak through the client as a collective consciousness as if the client were speaking in third-person perspective about themselves. "We are always guiding her. We wish she would follow her intuition more." and "We are beginning to use white light to heal this now." are common examples of how "They" (i.e., SC/Higher Self) express themselves and heal the client during the session.

The healing work is always done with unconditional love and honors the free will and sovereignty of the client. If instantaneous healing was not "appropriate" for the client's growth and spiritual maturation, "They" would suggest what steps the client should take to heal themself. Slowly, over many years, Dolores's work expanded as "They" introduced more components to the healing process so that she could evolve her work and teach it to others.

The Three Waves of Volunteers and the New Earth was one of nineteen books written by Dolores Cannon before her transition out of physical life. Each book contains transcriptions of client sessions describing detailed events from other lives while using her Quantum Healing Hypnosis Technique (QHHT).

Awakening to the Starseed Volunteer Mission

After several years of working with clients worldwide, Dolores noticed a pattern of clients describing a massive galactic and higher dimensional mission to raise the vibration of the planet and shift it into a new reality called the New Earth. The book describes how countless numbers of advanced spiritual beings from distant star systems, and even other universes, volunteered to incarnate on the Earth with a mission to raise consciousness on the planet and assist with this grand transition.

The New Earth is a higher frequency Earth reality that exists in a higher dimension than we are in now. Clients describe a large-scale plan initiated by Source Intelligence (God) to reset life on planet Earth back to the original template of a harmonic environment thriving within diversity. Parallel to this, Dolores's work described a shift in human consciousness from a duality-based mindset to a heart-centered, multidimensional consciousness and a less physical body of light.

The First Wave Volunteers were born beginning around 1945 through the 1970s. They were like a stealthy reconnaissance mission. First on the scene. First to patrol and feel out the collective consciousness vibrations. First to introduce the higher consciousness perspectives to the masses. Many had a difficult and lonely time since there were not many other humans in higher, love-based spiritual consciousness on the planet at the time.

The Second Wave Volunteers were born around the late 1970s through

1990s and are channels for higher spiritual energy and divine wisdom. These souls came in with a higher level of intuitive gifts and are often extremely sensitive to energy. Many are hands-on healers, musicians, vocalists, yoga teachers, and so on. They are space-holders who transmit a new frequency out to the field of Earth, bridging the old ways with the new ways and consciousness of New Earth.

The Third Wave Volunteers, the younger generations, are builders and innovative geniuses in science, spirituality, technology, and so on. They are divinely inspired visionaries that will build the New Earth. They are radical lovers and shine bright with crystalline eyes and have achieved high consciousness levels in other lifetimes. Some of these souls have never had a physical incarnation or have come straight from Source as new souls with pure Light and no karma.

I have been told all the children born at this time are part of this Grand Mission. They are pure souls, evolutionary masters, here to build the New Earth. More is written about the Starseed Mission and phenomena later in this book.

As I was reading Dolores's book, I felt I was reading my own story. I felt the truth in her words. Suddenly so many things made sense about my life. I finally had answers to why I felt so different from others in my community and family. I understood why I felt other people's emotions and could tell what people were thinking. It all started to click together. I was so excited to share the book with Ron, my husband and co-founder of New Earth Ascending, who also deeply resonated with the material.

At the same time, we were beginning to work with an Australian musical group as dancers for their "Return of the Bird Tribes" tour for their album by the same name. Something about the term "bird tribes" caught my attention, and I started to research it. I found the book by the same name, written by Ken Carey, in 1988 that describes a prophecy of high spiritual beings returning to the Earth at a time of spiritual renewal.

Many cultures describe times when culture-bringing beings would come from the heavens or from across the waters to bring technology and information to humanity throughout history. Thoth went to the Egyptians, White Buffalo Calf Woman went to the Native Americans, Quetzalcoatl went to the Aztecs, the Seven Sisters of the Pleiades went to the Aboriginal people of Australia, beings from the Sirius A and B binary star system went to the Dogon people of Mali; and many other stories exist in many other cultures. Carey's book described when these beings would come again during a time of spiritual awakening on the planet.

I was receiving information from multiple directions and was going through a massive realignment with my soul's purpose as I became aware of this greater story and mission. Ron and I went to an arts festival in the desert of Nevada called Burning Man. While we were there, a couple excitedly recognized us as "twin flames" and asked us which star system we had come from. "We are from Sirius. Where are you from? Orion? The Pleiades? Sirius?" she asked. The concept of "starseeds" and "twin flames" was new to me, and I did not know what to say. I saw a special sparkle in the couple's eyes and felt that I should do some research to understand more about it.

After some research and some magical synchronicities, Ron convinced me that we should do the QHHT training and certification process. I was super resistant to learning it because of deep religious programming and egoic structures that made me doubtful of the truthfulness of the work. I was familiar with reincarnation but did not necessarily believe in it. Eventually, I gave in to Ron's suggestion and took the QHHT course.

Evolving Beyond QHHT

In the early stages of practicing QHHT, Ron and I were guided to start doing the sessions online to share the technique's power with as many people as we could. This method was not permitted by the organization because Dolores did not believe it to be safe and her organization does not permit it still. Dolores was an elder and this type of technology was new to her, whereas the younger generations are much more comfortable interfacing with video conferencing.

We have been told by the Higher Consciousness that there is nothing to fear, and NOW is the time to spread these healing methods across the world in whatever way is possible. To honor our lineage and teacher, we stopped using the name QHHT and started experimenting with different names as our way of practicing quantum healing evolved beyond our initial training.

Online sessions are just as powerful as in-person sessions and are often more comfortable and affordable for the client. It is completely safe to facilitate sessions remotely, and we have had countless powerful sessions that have been facilitated in this way. Dolores's organization does not allow adaptation of the QHHT technique. Its practitioners need to perform the method exactly how Dolores taught and not add any modifications or outside techniques. While it is important to protect the work's integrity, this rigidity does not permit the work to expand to its full potential. We are in a time of expansion and evolution, and we must always be open to the transformation and progression of all methods we currently use or risk leaving them in the past as everything on the Earth is evolving.

Another topic that caused us to evolve beyond our initial training of QHHT was the organization's strict denial of negative spiritual attachment and what felt like shaming those who believed in this common experience. Ron and I and other quantum healing practitioners discovered that certain psychological, emotional, and physical imbalances were being created by pervasive energies that did not belong to the client's energy field that had somehow become attached to the client. This includes spirit attachments, curses from past lives, and implants from nefarious beings to name a few. QHHT did not provide us with appropriate training to work with these serious complications. If it were found out that a practitioner had adopted these practices and still operated under the name of QHHT, practitioners could be removed from the QHHT directory.

Many practitioners have reported spontaneous visitation from Dolores through clients under hypnosis where she has encouraged practitioners to follow their intuitive guidance and continue to develop the work through experimentation just as she did when she developed QHHT.

We were inspired greatly by other quantum healing practitioners' extraction methods and crafted our own approaches to clearing pervasive energies and spirit attachments. The reality of negative thought-forms, negative extraterrestrial implants, and entity attachment is too big to ignore, considering so many cases are emerging, not to forget the thousands of years of wisdom and extraction practices passed down by Indigenous peoples and various wisdom traditions.

We never assume that someone has an entity just because they suffer, and we do not bring it up in our intake interview. Once the client is deep in a hypnotic trance, we ask the Higher Self if there are entities or attached energies. If the answer is yes, then we ask questions to understand how this occurred and if the client has anything to learn to release negative attachment. From there, the Higher Self can immediately extract the energy and take it back into the Light for healing. It is all extremely safe, insightful, and benefits all who are involved. We have found that, often, the revelation of spirit attachment or implants will not occur unless the practitioner asks and gives permission for a scan specifically for attached energies. Ron and I believe this is because of the honoring of the free will of the entities involved in the experience of attachment.

In my opinion, to continue to deny such experiences is a disservice to the clients who come to us seeking answers and healing. All practices and traditions can become dogmatic if we do not allow the evolution of thought to take us into new frontiers of consciousness. These are evolutionary practices, and we need to be constantly open to shifting our paradigm so that we can offer the best guidance and support with the changing of times.

Once we started offering quantum healing sessions online, clients started coming to Ron and me from all over the world. Not only were the sessions powerfully healing and transformative for the clients, but we were also going through a rapid transformation as we learned about ancient stories and galactic events from the perspective of souls embodied at those times. While Dolores taught that many people had "potato-picking lives," simple lives with simple themes, it seemed that almost every session of mine had to do with the New Earth Mission, powerful events from the ancient past, and future timelines of Earth.

I soon realized that I was getting a theme and timeline in my sessions. The timeline given to me via my clients describes how Creation came into being, ancient galactic history, the seeding of life on Earth, the rise and fall of ancient civilizations, the true teachings of Jesus through the eyes of people that were closest to him, information about the transformation of the human body to a less dense body of Light, and the evolution of the Earth into the higher frequency reality of New Earth. In less than a year, I went from a reincarnation skeptic to believing that anything is possible, and that the multiverse is more incredible than we can even imagine!

Illuminated Quantum Healing

After years of practicing and evolving how we do this work, Ron and I have created our own quantum healing method that incorporates all that we have learned on our path. This includes facilitating sessions online to reach as many people as possible to assist in this Great Awakening.

Our training method acknowledges spirit attachment and teaches our facilitators how to perform negative spirit releasement. We teach yogic psychology, holistic wellness concepts, and energy healing methods to ensure the practitioner has a thorough understanding of human consciousness and how to lead the client through the ascension process using multiple IQH sessions and mentorship programs. We call our method Illuminated Quantum Healing. IQH can be learned in live classes or through our online course offered on our social network Source⊙Energy.

Illuminated Quantum Healing (IQH) is a personal transformation method for multidimensional holistic healing and consciousness development. IQH incorporates energy healing, meditative practices, yogic philosophy, and hypnosis skills to reconcile limiting subconscious patterning and integrate instantaneous multidimensional healing and wisdom from one's Higher Self.

I am deeply honored to be a part of this work. I am so blessed to have an opportunity to work with such incredible people and energies. Each session that I facilitate nourishes me to the core, and I have the sublime opportunity to observe miraculous instantaneous healing and transformation in my clients. After witnessing the infinite potential of quantum healing hypnosis, I firmly believe that we can ascend beyond all states of illness and disease and that we have infinite support to move beyond the shadows of our past and become a new People of Light.

Getting to the New Earth involves a process of spiritual growth and purification. To transition with the Earth, it is required that we raise our vibration to match the accelerating frequency of the Earth as it changes. Mostly, this is about releasing fear and negative karma. I have written this book as a tool to use for your spiritual awakening and transformation that many are calling Ascension. This is my gift to humanity to help make the process easier and explain different components to cultivate a deeper understanding of this Grand Shift to New Earth and our newly evolving Lightbody.

Spiritual awakening and ascension are available for ALL people no matter what they have done in their past, current economic status, gender expression, sexuality, religion, etc. There are as many paths to the New Earth as there are humans on the planet. No one religion holds the keys or the way to heaven. The power is within YOU!

To support the global ascension process, we have created New Earth Ascending. New Earth Ascending is a non-profit, faith-based organization focused on global ascension and establishing heart-centered, sustainable communities and educational centers around the world.

Alongside Illuminated Quantum Healing (IQH), Ron and I have created other pathways of support for the global ascension process:

1. Embodied Light Reiki Training and Certification

2. New Earth Ascending has three levels of Reiki certification to train people how to channel divine light for healing. These trainings honor the lineage and teachings of the Usui System of Natural Healing while also infusing evolutionary concepts and practices that go beyond standard Reiki training.

3. Online courses for awakening and ascension are available on our private social network Source⊙Energy. The courses include philosophical exploration on several models of spiritual growth and alchemical practices to support your healing, awakening, and ascension. These courses include meditations, holistic wellness education, breathwork, lightbody activation and more. These courses lay foundational understanding for beginners and move through a progression of intermediate and advanced practices and knowledge.

4. TransformOtion was created to support the embodiment of one's Higher Self using dance, somatic movement, yogic practices, meditation, imagination, and energy healing. This fusion of practices helps to purify and repair the physical, etheric, and mental bodies so that one can move beyond perceived limitations into boundless rhythm and flow. Through this interweaving of multiple disciplinary paths, we integrate physicality with transcendental ecstatic play while cultivating a deep connection with and trust in the body's wisdom.

These ideas and concepts can be used for personal embodiment and activation or infused into performance art to create powerful alchemical experiences for the performer and the audience. This fusion of high art and spiritual transformation creates a multidimensional experience for all who are within the field of performance energies.

5. Source⊙Energy is a social network exclusively for those on the path of ascension to connect and share inspiration as we manifest and build a New Earth. We invite all souls who feel aligned with New Earth to join this network and add your unique energy and love to this community. Source⊙Energy serves as a pathway of social interaction and is the home of our online courses and training.

6. Children are our future. Youth inspiration and enrichment programming is in development to assist the spiritual activation and consciousness mastery of the youth. NEA is dedicated to creating harmonic environments and rich educational programs to guide youth to connect with cosmic intelligence and embody their divine nature and mastery as they build the New Earth.

Ron and I have dedicated our lives to supporting this Grand Transition. We stand alongside all of you as humanity awakens to its True Nature and becomes a People of Light in the heavenly reality of New Earth.

New Earth Ascending is dedicated to assisting people to realize their divinity and manifest that truth in every aspect of their life. For more information about New Earth Ascending or to contact Michael, please scan the QR code below for a list of resources and links, or visit *www.newearthascending.org*. Be sure to check out our courses including the Illuminated Quantum Healing practitioner course.

New Earth Ascending is a registered 508 (c)(1)(a) Self-Supported Non-profit Church Ministry with a global outreach. We greatly appreciate your support as we create new systems, communities, and schools for the development of the New Earth civilization. If you would like to make a tax-deductible donation to support our mission, please go to:

https://donorbox.org/donationtonewearthascending

Scan with a smart device camera for more information!

NEW EARTH ASCENDING
VISIONARY CREED

We acknowledge the sovereignty and equality of all levels of Creation and support the liberation of all of Life from cycles of suffering. We believe in the power of divine sovereign creatorship endowed to us by God/Source and dedicate our life to Light and Love in service to All. We believe in conscious participation, empowering everyone to activate awakening in themselves and their community.

We recognize free will and surrender our will and desires to the higher will of the Divine. We believe in divine timing and practice trust, patience, and tolerance as we witness the unfoldment of the perfection of the Divine Plan. We believe in the potency of empowering prayer, meditation, and ritual as tools for communication with the Divine for the culmination of spiritual light and divine wisdom. We believe everyone has a direct connection to the Source and no intermediary is needed. When we come together in fellowship, prayer, and devotion, we amplify the light of each individuals' loving intention through our unified, heart-centered consciousness.

We seek to uplift all groups and communities so that we may celebrate our unity, diversity, and wholeness. New Earth Ascending is non-competitive and embraces an ecumenical relationship with all religions and wisdom traditions. We believe in interfaith and inter-spirituality, acknowledging the teachings of Light, Love, and Wisdom in many traditions, philosophies, and cultures. We believe that no single religion holds the keys to the Kingdom of God and the blessings of redemption are available to all people through their unbreakable innate connection to the Godhead.

We believe in the Law of Oneness and that all of Creation emanates from one Divine Source that has both masculine and feminine principles. As we heal and balance the divine masculine and divine feminine principles within us, we embody the divine androgyny of Source and Nature as a harmonic synthesis of Spirit and Matter.

We believe that humanity and planet Earth are going through a rapid physical and spiritual transformation called by many as The Ascension or The Event. We believe this process to be part of a higher evolutionary divine plan guided by the Source of Creation and legions of beings working for the Light. This evolutionary process is multidimensional and is beyond the standard biological evolution spoken of by modern science.

We believe that we, as humanity, are awakening to our spiritual Self and are becoming a heart-based, unity-focused species with higher, multidimensional awareness, which some call Christ Consciousness, Cosmic Consciousness, or 5D Consciousness. We believe this transformation's power is happening through our divinely designed and curated DNA as the physical body transforms into a less dense body of Light with tremendously expanded multidimensional abilities.

We believe that Planet Earth, the sentient being of Gaia, is going through a similar restoration process and will soon transform into a revitalized higher dimensional planet, which many are calling the New Earth. Earth changes, weather events, crumbling institutional structures, frequency fluctuations, and astrological phenomena are all signs that we are nearing that shift into the next Golden Age, where Heaven and Earth become one and all systems of control and limitation will fall away.

We believe that we are supported by benevolent higher dimensional, subterranean, and extraterrestrial beings that work in harmonic collaboration with the higher evolutionary Divine Plan of Source. We believe that soon humanity will be consciously reunited with these benevolent beings and serve the higher evolutionary plan of the Light and Love of Source as cosmic co-citizens of the Multiverse working as one Family of Light in service to all of Creation.

We understand that the pathway of Self/Source-Realization and Ascension is comprised of self-study, self-practice, self-discipline, and steadfastness. We practice self-care and self-purification to clarify our Light. We acknowledge and value the acceleration of this process when we practice together in groupings of two or more in fellowship and worship.

We strive to grow in awareness and focused attention, practicing mindfulness in all areas of our lives to grow as conscious, heart-centered creators. We choose to focus our life positively with faith and knowing that Life is evolving in perfection following the Divine Plan of the Supreme Source.

We believe in the power of intention. We practice nonviolence and non-harmfulness in intention, thought, and action. We strive to release all forms of judgment and dual thinking. We honor the sacred heart's radiant potential and believe loving compassion and understanding to be The Way. We practice the heart-centered qualities of gentleness, reverence, loving-kindness, and forgiveness as pathways to reconciliation to emulate the eternal grace of Source and our Earth Mother, Gaia.

We see that Truth is alive within each of us, and we practice inner reflection to grow in discernment for what energies are resonant with our inner Source and our path. We practice benevolent truthfulness, honesty, straightforwardness, and vulnerability to embody and vocalize our deepest truth.

We value and practice transparency and accountability, believing in the opportunity for spiritual growth through spiritual partnership with our community members. We recognize one another as divine mirrors, reflecting to us where we are in our vibration, beliefs, and intentions.

We practice sacred sexuality as an alchemical tool for Divine Union and Ascension. We strive to purify our intentions and desires to align with Higher Love and authentic connection. We believe in heart-based self and consensual mutual pleasure to unite body, mind, and spirit so that we may deepen in our love and authentic connection to our Divine Self, our partner(s), and Creation.

We practice contentment, acceptance, appreciation, and gratitude for our life's many blessings and lessons. We practice non-attachment, non-possessiveness, non-stealing, non-excess, and sustainability, for all we need is given to us through our alignment with our Creator Source and our connection to our Earth Mother. We practice stewardship and sustainable selfless service, acknowledging our responsibility to take care of the world around us and within.

We practice sacred commerce, investing our resources, time, and energy towards the greater good and sustainability of our community and planet. We believe in reciprocal energy exchange and strive to do so when able. We practice generosity, hospitality, and charitability as reflections of the abundance of the Universe.

We strive to embody and emulate these spiritual principles to manifest the complete liberation of all beings from cycles of suffering and to assist this Grand Transition into the New Earth.

Bless us all!

GATEWAY ONE: ASCENSION INITIATION

Keys for Higher Evolution

This section describes the higher evolutionary pathway of the transmigrating soul and the purpose of incarnation and Ascension. It also includes a presentation and exploration of Universal Law and a description of the progression of consciousness through cosmic evolutionary cycles.

ONE

The Shift of the Ages

Humanity stands at the brink of unprecedented transformation, a gigantic quantum leap in consciousness that has been foretold by many prophets in many cultures throughout history. This is the Omega phase, the ending of a grand experimental cycle where all the karma of Earth and humanity will be reconciled as the Earth is transformed into a higher light spectrum reality commonly known as the New Earth. In unison, humanity is going through its own transformation process to become a civilization of Light, divine beings in sophisticated bodies of Light who operate from a liberated and expanded multidimensional consciousness.

Ascension was brought into the collective consciousness of humanity through the teachings of Christ Jesus, also known as Yeshua ben Joseph, the Master of Light for Planet Earth. This rapid transformation process is supported by leagues of benevolent extraterrestrial and ultraterrestrial beings that form a Hierarchy of Light that serves a higher evolution following a Divine Plan established by the Source of Creation. As humanity and Earth ascends, we will be consciously reunited with the Hierarchy of Light and the Star Nations and live as cooperative cosmic citizens united in a higher consciousness reality.

In my attempt to describe the indescribable, I will mostly refer to the Supreme Consciousness and all its functions as the Source of Creation or simply Source. For me, this term accurately describes what many commonly call God. Some traditions have different names for Source in pre-manifestation such as *Ein Soph* or *Brahman* and another term for God with manifested attributes like *Ein Soph Or, Ishvara,* or *Logos.* For simplicity, I will simply use the term Source to speak for both the transcendental and manifested expressions of the Supreme Consciousness. Many people have turned their backs on the Divine and religious institutions because of the pain and suffering created by dogma, sexual abuse, hypocrisy, religious wars, and oppression. Each person carries a unique definition and set of internal images and emotions evoked by the word "God." While some people believe in a higher power of some kind, others reject the idea of a god-man in the clouds punishing and judging the world for their sins. Some can at least recognize some type of higher connection to nature. Some have decided to have nothing to do with spirituality and the divine and choose to stick with modern versions of science and what they can sense through their five senses.

The dualistic philosophy of Samkhya speaks of Source in terms of *Purusha* and *Prakriti. Purusha* is the pure consciousness, the Seer of Creation. *Purusha* in the human is the Self, the *Atman*, the pure Source within that observes this bodymind and this universe. *Prakriti*, Sanskrit for Nature or Creation, is everything in manifestation, everything with a name and form. This includes all universes, all dimensions and realities including the higher "heavenly" light dimensions, and our concept of God.

Prakriti can also be called *maya*, a Sanskrit term commonly translated as illusion or magic. Source through its power of *maya* projects this entire universe including the bodymind complex you find yourself in. When people say only Source is real and everything else is false, an illusion, it is because all names and forms borrow existence from the Eternal Source, the Pure Consciousness that you truly are.

Maya not only projects names and forms into creation but it also veils the True Reality. A classic example of the power of *maya* is when a person sees a rope out of the corner of their eye and mistakenly thinks it is a snake. *Maya* has veiled the true nature of the rope, so one sees a snake. At the most fundamental level, the Absolute level, neither the snake nor the rope exists. It is Source using its power of maya to project a whole reality which includes the rope which one confuses as a snake, a dream within a dream, within a dream.

Another classic example of this is water which comes in many names and forms. Whether we call it an ocean, a glacier, fog, or mist it is all water. All these objects with different names and forms borrow existence from the water. In the same way, all is Source appearing as universes, planets, individual plants, animals, good people, evil people, energy, and emotion. Yet all of it borrows existence from Source, the pure Consciousness which you are.

One of the purposes of *Prakriti*, of *maya*, is to test the Seer's ability to perceive the True Source that is behind all manifestations. *Maya* arises, abides, and dissolves in an ever-changing landscape pulling our senses and awareness in every direction. *Maya* seduces us and ensnares our consciousness in the pull of sensory experiences and deepens our misidentification with our bodymind, distracting our attention from our True Nature. We falsely believe that all we see, touch, taste, smell, feel, and think is real and become enamored by the dream of reality, overlooking our True Nature. It is a game we play with our Oneself. A game of forgetting and remembering who we truly are as Pure Consciousness.

Our perceived reality is like a distorted funhouse mirror that bends, shrinks, and accentuates the reflected image. The thing with a funhouse mirror is that most people can keep the awareness that what they are seeing is not real. In a physical body, it is much harder to stay aware that only Source is the true reality and that all the rest is smoke and mirrors. It is our own complex inner reality that is projected and outpictured, distorting and hypnotizing our mind into emotional intoxication and spiritual amnesia.

In physical life, the initiate is tested in their ability to stay laser-focused on the true reality of Divine Love in the background of all experiences and to invite what is normally in the background of experience into the foreground so that the "face of God" is all that one perceives.

Sometimes in my hypnosis sessions, a client returns to the Source. Typically, they describe the environment as being a bright warm light and that they feel so loved. They say that many other beings are there and that everything feels so good there. Sometimes they say something like, "We are many, but we are all one." I ask them how long they have been there, and they often respond with something like "There is no time here." or "What do you mean? We have always been here." I usually let the client experience this for a few minutes to deeply remember the love they came from and truly are. Often clients are crying tears of joy as years of trauma and struggle begin to melt away through the power of union with Source. It is a powerful and beautiful thing to witness.

Interfaith dialogue recognizes the threads of harmonic commonality found in religious and spiritual texts, philosophy, humanitarian beliefs, and science. As humanity awakens, many realize that there is a common foundation in all these traditions and viewpoints of what "God" is and the meaning of Life.

As we move forward on the New Earth timeline, we can release our wounds from religious dogma and be open to the teachings of Light and

Unconditional Love inherently found within the sacred texts from ancient cultures and world traditions. We can drop the dogma of dead religions focused on fear and condemnation and find the indwelling of the Living Source Within and claim our divine inheritance.

When I speak of Creation, I am speaking of the holographic Multiverse. The Multiverse has been described by several different mystical philosophies and esoteric wisdom traditions using different terms to describe the various planes and subplanes of reality. They all seem to agree on one plane that is the substratum of all the other planes, the plane of the Absolute, Source, or God. From this Absolute Reality all other planes and subplanes emerge. Another level of reality is the Transactional Reality of Relativity, the realm of phenomenon where the Light of Consciousness interacts in different forms with varying frequencies and polarizations interacting in varying planes of light density. This level would include the physical plane we are in and the higher experimental light dimensions. Another level is the Reality of Illusion such as mirages or the reality we experience in our dream states which appears real until we are in our waking consciousness.

Just like in lucid dreaming where the Dreamer awakens in the dream, another level of awakening can happen during our waking consciousness. When the soul is ready, spiritual consciousness begins to stir awake and higher knowledge leads their consciousness out of entanglement with the Transactional Reality towards the realization of the Ultimate Reality which is both imminent and transcendent. God-Source is both beyond the knowable universe and the Universal Principle which pervades all realities, realms, planes, and dimensions. This is what Christ meant when he said to go within to find the Kingdom of God. All that you seek is already within, yet you must seek it to find it.

All of Creation exists within a continuum of ascending and descending movement patterning to and from the Source. Divine Light flows from this Source out into many levels and layers of Creation, universes within universes, existing in various states of light density. Within these multidimensional experimental zones of Light exist a multitude of species, physical and nonphysical, in various states of evolution with each plane of Creation working in symbiotic relationship within a unified field of Source Consciousness. As the light descends in frequency, we arrive at the physical dimension, the material plane that our universe exists in. Light descends from the higher dimensions and is projected through one Great Central Sun of this universe which pulses evolutionary coding through a vast stellar "modem" network of fixed stars. Each Central Sun broadcasts multidimensional light coding to evolve each "theater of evolution" in accordance with the higher plan of the Divine.

Eventually, we arrive at our Sun, the central star of our solar system, which emanates all the intelligent coding for the evolution of countless levels of life forms and celestial bodies in our solar system. Even each planet in our solar system is connected through a web of subtle energy pathways that support the other celestial bodies. Everything, including each individual human, is connected within this web of evolutionary communication and complex multidimensional configuration.

At the beginning of Creation, the Divine Intelligence sent out parts of its Oneself to create, learn, and explore. When I use the word "soul," I am speaking of the individual lightbody essence, the conglomerate of subtle bodies, that has been sent into the realms of Creation to learn and create with free will. This part takes on lessons and karma as a way of learning and growing as it ascends back towards the realization of its true origin and true nature which I refer to as the Source within, the Atman, the Witness, or pure Consciousness.

The soul is immortal, has lived many incarnations, and will release the physical body upon its death experience and continue its evolutionary journey in other forms. The soul is a portion of what I call the oversoul, which is a higher density form of your consciousness that exists beyond this physical dimension of reality which you will be consciously reconnected with as we shift into the fifth dimensional (5D) also called 4th Density, New Earth reality. The oversoul is like a quantum information storehouse of all the information collected from all of its many soul aspects which have lived myriad lifetimes throughout eternity.

The Hindu traditions describe the journey of ascension as *jiva* (personal self) as it awakens to Atman (Source within) or Brahman (God/Source), experienced as Eternal Existence, Eternal Consciousness, and Eternal Bliss. The Kabbalistic/Jewish traditions describe it at the journey of the *Nephesh* (soul) that is matured into *Neshamah* (sovereign soul or Spirit-soul Synthesis) through the ministering Spirit (*Ruach*). The Buddhists describe it as an awakening to the Buddha within. The Hare Krishnas describe it as the path to Krishnahood or Krishna Consciousness. The Christians call it being "saved" and following the path of Christ. The New Age community calls it ascending to Christ Consciousness. Each of these beautiful traditions and philosophies describes the same ascension process and the same spark of the Creator within all of us that has taken on karma to learn and grow through a process of God-Realization.

While there may be differences in practices or conflicting philosophies in some of these traditions, there is a beautiful interweaving of them all that can give us keys and insight into the greater tapestry of Creation. There are infinite philosophies, infinite practices of devotion, and infinite pathways of Ascension back to the Source. All of these wisdom traditions lead to the same Source, the same Love, the same Light. If you are reading this text, you can rest assured that you are on your unique path of Ascension.

Throughout this book, I will speak of intention and consciousness in terms of service-to-self negative polarity (STS), and service-to-all (STA), positive polarity, which some call service-to-others (STO). Religions speak of "good" and "evil" with a charge of judgment. The problem is everyone has a different definition of what those terms mean.

Service-to-self (STS) consciousness is when we serve our false self, our ego, often at the expense of others. The negative polarity in our consciousness is all about me, me, me! Individuals in the negative polarity are concerned with self-preservation and the accumulation of external power. Negatively polarized consciousness manifests as passive aggression, selfishness, greed, pride, domination, control, egoism, and so on. Individuals and groups that are negatively polarized are often also called "dark," "evil," or tyrannical as the fullest expression of negative polarity is consciousness cemented fully in material reality and is void of higher spiritual intelligence and empathy.

Service-to-all (STA) consciousness is a mindset of honoring and protecting the expansion, freedom, and joy of the world around you while respecting your own inner being, sovereignty, and alignment. Positively polarized consciousness manifests as gentleness, benevolent truth speaking, healthy boundaries, forgiveness, devotion, and all other attitudes and actions of harmony and stewardship. People holding a high level of positive polarity consistently act altruistically and from a place of loving compassion and spiritual unity. Individuals and groups from the positive polarity are often called "good," "holy," and "light," as they reflect the benevolence and goodness of the Divine.

This concept speaks to something deeper than action and points to the underlying intention that drives thought, speech, and action. Someone may appear to be positively polarized, service-to-all, but in actuality is using nicety to manipulate others or protect their ego-self. Conversely, someone may be judged as "negative" because they say something that stirs up chaos but, in actuality, are doing so because of their commitment to truth and goodness. Look at what happened to Jesus. Even as "the world" projected hatred and judgment on him, his actions were for goodwill.

We all hold consciousness that is of both sides of polarity. As we begin to awaken, we begin to transform our negative polarity into positive polarity by aligning with our deepest truth and the unity of the compassionate heart. We move from an STS, negatively polarized, expression into an STA, positively polarized embodiment of righteousness, unconditional love, and spiritual sovereignty.

Earth has been an experimental zone for the full spectrum of thought, from the evilest and most negatively polarized to the most sublime and pure expressions of consciousness. That experiment is ending as the negative polarity, the service-to-self consciousness thought-forms, will no longer be permitted in the New Earth reality. So now we see all of those ways we have hidden from our True Nature coming to the surface to be reconciled by compassion and noble action. Those shifting to the 5D New Earth consciousness are those who are making the polarity switch and raising their overall vibration. Truly, unconditional love and unity consciousness is the way to the New Earth.

The Event

For some time now, highly charged photonic waves have been broadcasting from the Great Central Sun of our universe, pulsating from central sun to central sun carrying streams of divinely encoded evolutionary energies that are revitalizing and renewing all that they touch. These Light information pulsations are awakening the consciousness of humanity from the duality of polarized consciousness towards the awakened and liberated higher consciousness that many are calling christ consciousness, cosmic consciousness, or oversoul consciousness. Christ consciousness is not only for those of a mainstream religion. This consciousness is available to all people who choose to live a life of unconditional love and unity. It is the pure Light consciousness of the Universe, and it is your birthright to realize this capacity in yourself as a liberated being of Light.

Space Weather and the Schumann Resonance

Some of these evolutionary energy events are being picked up with modern technology. Solar events like solar wind, coronal mass ejections, and solar flares bring major upgrades to the planet. I have noticed that when the solar wind reaches 400 km/sec, I start having headaches, chest tension, dehydration, and emotional sensitivity. The higher the solar wind speed, the more amplified these symptoms are. When solar wind speed reaches 600 km/sec or higher, I am either wiped out, emotional, need lots of water, or I feel like I am riding a wave of bliss and insight. Everyone handles these energy waves differently and there are simple self-care practices and protocols that you can implement to help the integration process. These are mentioned later in the book.

Another measurement to watch is the Schumann Resonance. The Schumann Resonance measures Earth's atmosphere's electromagnetic frequencies found in the cavity between Earth's surface and the ionosphere. The lowest frequency mode and fundamental Schumann Resonance is 7.83 Hz, followed by harmonics of 14 Hz, 20 Hz, 26 Hz, 33 Hz, 39 Hz, and 45 Hz (rounded numbers for the sake of simplicity). It has been found that when the wave size or amplitude of these frequencies increases, we may experience direct effects on our electromagnetic fields causing fluctuations in our emotions, cognition, cardiac system, and consciousness. I have been following an online Schumann Resonance monitor associated with the Tomsk State University in Tomsk, Russia for the last few years. I have noticed a direct relationship between fluctuations of the Earth's frequencies and my own mental, emotional, etheric, and physical experiences that I call ascension symptoms.

It should be noted that sensitive people worldwide also report "ascension symptoms" even when the measurable frequencies (space weather and Schumann) are not present. I believe that these energies are coming from a source that humanity does not have measurement technologies for at the time. This can include friendly spacecraft, distant planets and stars, and other sources, including the Photon Belt. Earth will be passing through the Photon Belt for around another 2,000 years, which will dramatically accelerate the ascension processes. These light waves are building in intensity and potency gradually changing all of life as we know it on the planet.

We cannot even imagine the world we are about to awaken to from our current consciousness level. Each wave awakens another group of souls on the New Earth trajectory and begins their healing, activation, and divine embodiment process. Those who have awakened before the rest of humanity will experience "The Event" as a series of waves and upgrading energies that gradually lead us into higher and higher consciousness. For others, they will continue in the lower dimensional consciousness until they experience a wave that awakens them to their higher consciousness as the planet makes its ascension into the New Earth reality. All of this was designed pre-incarnation and we are watching the timings play out.

There are many people who build up a lot of emotion expecting a major solar event that instantly awakens and changes the Earth. This may or may not happen as the many timelines and probabilities play out. In some ways, the Solar Flash has become a "savior program" for many. In truth, all experiences arise within the Light of our own Self. We are the Solar Flash! We are the Divine Plan in action!

After these energy waves leave the Sun, they make contact with the biofield/aura of Earth. After the energy passes through the Earth's electromagnetic fields, the energies enter our biofield and begin to enter the tissues and cells of our body. These energies carry intelligent coding that is evolving every cell of our body to a less dense bioluminous body of light. Human DNA is evolving beyond the typical two strands to a fully activated and revitalized 12-strand system. We are returning to our "Adamic" form, the original divine human blueprint.

Each energy wave brings in new ascension symptoms as the whole human body and consciousness system is upgraded. Every individual is unique in this experience. Many report headaches, cold-like symptoms, hot flashes, ringing in the ears, vivid dreams, burning in the chest, digestive system issues, detoxification symptoms, emotional purging, and more. I talk more about these symptoms and ascension symptom care later in the book.

It should be noted that not all of humanity will be making this transition. These plans were made before incarnating and are not the polarized judgment narrative propagated by world religions. This is part of the Divine Plan, and all souls are playing a part in the great story that is unfolding. Those who will not be transitioning will not be receiving the upgrades to their genetics and will start to deteriorate in health and transition out of the body.

There is nothing "bad" about this. They have simply fulfilled their life plans and will transition out of the body to support the ascension from the spirit side and/or prepare to incarnate again in another form, either on Earth or another planet/realm where they can continue their soul's evolutionary pathway. Physical death is not final. We are immortal beings who have lived many times and will continue to evolve and serve Creation through many more forms in the future.

The Unveiling

Apocalypse is a Greek word meaning "unveiling," "uncovering," or "revelation." This implies that what was once hidden is to be brought into the light of awareness. We see this in the unfolding of events around the world as the unconscious shadow is being brought to the surface to be cleared. In the coming months, we will see more political scandals surfacing and the unveiling of travesties that have been committed over time and kept hidden from the public.

Turn off the Television: Tune into Your Inner Being

Repeatedly in my hypnosis sessions, it has been suggested to turn off the news stations, put down the smartphones, and tune into the presence of Gaia, the Divine Source, and our own Inner Being. The gateway to this new Light Kingdom (Queendom if you prefer) of New Earth is through the electromagnetic field of your own heart and your innate connection to the Grace and Light of Source. Ascension requires us to grow in our capacity to love unconditionally and transform our physical, etheric, and mental bodies through transformative practices and purification. This is what Christ meant when he said to "clean thy robes" to prepare for the next "garment of Light."

This book serves as a guide to illuminate the Ascension pathway and initiate the reader to the Higher Mysteries and Laws of Creation. It aims to explain our origins from the eternal Source and provides a summary of the story of Creation as it relates to cosmic, galactic, planetary, and human history. It gives a futuristic perspective of the revitalized higher dimensional Earth post-Ascension that describes what the New Earth will be like and how humanity will live upon the Earth and with the Star Nations and Hierarchy of Light.

There is a detailed description of the stages of Ascension as it relates to the evolution of the planet, human biology, and human consciousness.

The reader's consciousness is guided into an experiential relationship with their Lightbody, and spiritual energy practices are given to activate, heal, and upgrade the human subtle energy body in preparation for the next "light garment" and higher consciousness reality of 5D New Earth.

TWO

Earth School Orientation

The Earth School, a term I first read about in *Seat of the Soul* by Gary Zukav, is an evolutionary playground for advanced souls from all over the multiverse. The multiverse is made of many universes, or universities, where souls project their consciousness into various forms to evolve and learn in many worlds and environments. Each planet is a separate school within the larger university with its own unique dynamics at play. You are an eternal being who has lived many lives in many forms, quite possibly on multiple planets, each one bringing its own unique lessons as you journey on the path of God-realization, the path of realizing yourself as God in form. As a seeker of knowledge and truth, you eventually discover that which you seek is seeking you, and, in fact, you ARE that which you seek.

This ancient mystery school, the Earth School, is a master school and has everything that a soul will need to achieve unprecedented growth, expansion, and mastery. For humanity, the course work is mental and emotion-based and is full of challenging twists and turns to make your journey unique and exciting.

Free Will

You have the freedom to choose your evolutionary journey. You are free to choose your thoughts, beliefs, and actions. You have a choice to be in service-to-self or service-to-all. As you grow in awareness of your inner realm, you have the choice to be a slave to fear or to transform your intentions and beliefs to align with spiritual truth and unconditional love and become a powerful Divine Creator in service to the higher evolution of consciousness.

Let us visualize a branching off of spheres of consciousness that extend from the original sphere of Source, a family tree of Light. Each sphere branches out to another smaller sphere as the limitless Light of Source is stepped down to other spheres of consciousness. Eventually, we would come to what we call your oversoul.

The oversoul sends out parts of its essence to experience different lifetimes. Your soul is one part of a grouping of souls that have experienced and are experiencing many lifetimes simultaneously. They have acquired vast amounts of information that are merged within the consciousness of the oversoul. It can be likened to the shape of a hand where the center of the palm is the oversoul, while the fingers are the individual soul aspects that merge with the center of the palm.

You As a Soul

I have chosen to use the word soul primarily in the book to describe the immortal individual lightbody that moves from the higher light dimensions into physical bodies. It takes on limitations and karmic lessons so that it can know itself but is not impure or unholy. The impurities lie in the different layers of the lightbody such as the mental, emotional, etheric, and physical layers which are reconciled through spiritual practices.

While the English language can use the word in a variety of ways, both poetic and technical, I have tried my best to use the term specifically and with intention. When I am speaking of the True Self, I am speaking of the highest identity of the individual which is the pure Consciousness, Source itself. While there seems to be many beings, many souls, there is truly only One Light of Consciousness, your True Self.

At a certain point, your individual soul came into being. As a soul, you possess the ability to incarnate into different life forms to experience Creation and grow spiritually. You have lived many lifetimes and have learned many lessons in many forms. Some lifetimes are on the Earth, and some are likely in other forms in other planets, star systems, and universes. Many souls have been bound to Earth's negative karmic lessons for many lifetimes, experiencing the same cycles of suffering over and over, similar to a student who fails a class and has to repeat until passing.

As we come into the Earth life, we pass through a veil of forgetfulness (avidya/ignorance) and lose conscious memory of other lifetimes and the knowledge we gained from those lives, and we begin to fall under the spell of the seductive quality of the world of form, believing it to be real and that we are separate from The Divine.

Human babies are extremely vulnerable and fragile and are dependent on their caregivers to give them all their basic needs. Since we forget our connection to Source and our spiritual Self, Earth life is extremely challenging as we innately struggle to remember the truth of who we are. The light that we came in with often begins to fade as we become enamored with the illusion. We quickly absorb and adopt the limiting beliefs of our family and culture and quickly forget the light that we are.

Because of our spiritual amnesia, we begin to create a false self, an egoic identity structure that we piece together from the thought-forms and programmed conditioning that are available in our environments and experiences. Because of this amnesia and the chances of developing negative karmic patterns, only highly advanced souls choose to come to the Earth School.

Understandably, we get stuck in loops and karmic cycles, having to see the same themes and scenarios play out again and again until we have done enough research to understand, integrate, and choose the appropriate direction that aligns us with Higher Truth.

It should also be mentioned that many new souls are incarnated on the Earth directly from the Source having never had previous incarnations here. This is an experiment being implemented to assist the planetary ascension. These beings bring bright, fresh energy to the Earth. They have no previous karma and have a higher baseline vibration because of this. This helps to raise the overall vibration of the planet. These souls can also have a difficult time here on Earth because of all of the density held by humanity at this stage.

Soul Family

Soul family are souls that incarnate together, again and again, to help each other along their path of spiritual growth. Sometimes we play certain roles in one lifetime and switch in the next. We have scheduled rendezvous with different soul family members that activate us on our path of remembering. Sometimes it is pleasant, but often the initiations are painful and activate wounds within our consciousness that want to be healed through spiritual and emotional work. This "clashing," whether physical or psychological, is essential as it reactivates unprocessed energy for integration, spiritual insight, and assimilation of wisdom from life experience. Often the closest soul family member decides to play a "villain" in our story, or they may bring conflicting situations for us to learn from and have the experiences that we need to evolve.

Spiritual Council: Your Light Team

Prior to incarnating from the spiritual realms, you sit with a council of other light beings to design your next incarnation. These light beings, your council of guides, are highly developed spiritual beings that guide you through your incarnations. Some have lived human lives. Some have lived in other star systems that you are connected to. Some are Ascended Masters and angelic beings that no longer need to incarnate to learn and now mostly stay in the higher realms to guide and support the evolution of Creation. These spiritual allies are non-judgmental and eternally patient. They are behind the scenes coordinating rendezvous with other important people on your path and guide you through situations using signs, synchronicities, internal promptings, and other experiences.

Contracts

Before incarnating, you meet with your council of guides to create your contract for the next incarnation. This higher plan for your life is where you decide what emotional themes you will explore and which experiences will initiate you into deeper wisdom in that life. You decide the parents that will give you the conditions and genetic coding that will form the foundation for your life. In doing so, you are aware of the culture, spiritual and religious affiliations, sex, economic status, geographic location, etc. Each of these categories are like sub-classrooms, filters that we get to experience our unique human life through. I often chuckle when I hear someone say, "I did not choose this!" when, in fact, they are the ones that envisioned and signed the contract!

All is designed and planned, pre-chosen so that you have optimal conditions to grow. In truth, we have no one to blame for the conditions of our life but our own self. Suffering is not a divine punishment but fertile grounds for tremendous spiritual growth through contrasting experiences.

Each lifetime's experiences and knowledge feed into and support the other lifetimes as the soul advances through various consciousness stages. In fact, all of us have lived many lives in preparation for this Grand Transformation of Life occurring on the planet NOW!

Primary Guide

Everyone has a primary guide who stays with them for the duration of their lifetime. The other members of your council are skilled in the areas you are studying and have wisdom to share. Sometimes, these guides shift partway through a lifestream when someone shifts into a different area of learning and needs different guidance.

Once we incarnate, our guides communicate with us in many ways, mainly through our Inner Being. You are constantly receiving transmissions and signs from your team and Higher Consciousness. Learning to listen to your internal guidance happens naturally as you begin to tune into your inner experience, emotions, variations in thought quality, and so forth. Learning to quiet the mind is essential in learning how to communicate with your individual team of Light.

The uninitiated individual, a person who is not spiritually awake and aware of the other realms and the Family of Light, is mostly unaware of the guidance that comes to them. As you begin to awaken, you will notice increasing signs, synchronicities, and symbolism that seem to lead you down the Higher Path. Your guides speak to you through the matrix by sending these messages. They work with other guides of the souls who are beneficial for your path and growth and help to coordinate rendezvous opportunities through impressions broadcast into the thought and emotional fields of a person to offer the opportunity to follow the intuitive guidance.

It is up to each of us to discern what signs come from our guides, felt through the heart, and which come from the duality-based ego. Guides will not interfere with our free will, and their guidance is always loving and never fear-based, although they can transmit a strong impression if the timing is important or urgent. Your guides can see opportunities and events coming down your timeline before you experience them. Your guides will repeatedly send you the same information until you get it. If you miss it, rest assured that another opportunity will come to you as your team coordinates another chance to learn that lesson or take that step. When you receive the guidance, acknowledge it, send gratitude, and follow the guidance.

Non-Emergency Divine Intervention

For non-emergency assistance from your guides, you must ask. By asking from the heart, a simple prayer for divine assistance gives your team of guides permission to work in more areas of your life in more profound ways. As a sovereign creator, you have the authority to grant this permission. Simply ask for divine assistance and trust that much is happening behind the scenes already to assist your growth and healing.

Some may be open to light beings but may be closed to the idea of having guides from other worlds. The opposite is also true. If you have not, invite your entire team to be with you to assist. Ask your star lineages to assist you. Ask your Inner Earth family to assist you. Ask your angelic light being team to assist you. Welcome your entire lineage, past, present, and future to assist you on your great Mission.

There is great love for you out there, but they cannot interfere, and they will not approach until you have opened yourself to be reconnected. Intend that only the highest beings of Love and Light can work with you and open yourself to be reunited with your Family of Light! We have created the *Quantum Launchpad* course to help you grow in multidimensional awareness and develop your relationship with your Guidance Team.

Exiting the Earth School

When a soul finishes a lesson in the Earth School, it graduates to the next appropriate course of study. When a soul is finished with all that it came to experience and grow through, it is time to leave the body and continue the evolutionary pathway.

Multiple exit plans or physical death experiences are agreed upon depending on which way the life progresses. Many people exit earlier because they run their bodies out of vital energy and accumulate so much suffering because they do not learn their lessons which manifest as illness, disease, and suicide. Therefore, it is important to do spiritual practice to maintain the vessel as you explore your coursework.

As the incarnated soul approaches an exit opportunity, it decides whether to make adjustments to its approach towards life and remain, or else exit and continue its evolutionary path in another form. We can see the physical death experience as a graduation event. When a person leaves the Earth School, this means that they have learned all that they could in this life or have accomplished their life purpose and must continue the eternal path of soul evolution. Truly, you are an eternal being and no one really dies.

Stepping Out of the Body

When clients review the physical death experience of a previous incarnation in the IQH sessions, they are immediately relieved as they transition out of the body from the physical Earth realm and into a parallel spiritual plane of Earth that people call the Astral Plane. If others are around the body as they transition, the soul often wishes them to release the sadness because they feel so good now that they have left the body. For the most part, souls are greeted by a loved one who has already transitioned or a guide or spirit animal, something they trust as loving, and they are whisked away into the Light for healing and rest in the higher light dimensions. In some wisdom traditions, they describe different processes of this transition phase but in my sessions, it always seems much simpler.

There are times when a soul does not continue to the Light. Maybe they died suddenly or were heavily sedated and not aware that they left the body. Maybe they fear punishment from God because of fear-based religious beliefs. Maybe they have "unfinished business" and want to stay close to the physical plane to accomplish what they wanted. For whatever reason, some souls or portions of someone's essence such as etheric and astral debris do not transition and linger in the lower astral realm close to the physical Earth plane.

Spirit Attachments: Implants

There are varying opinions on whether it is the entire spiritual emanation that sometimes stays behind or only some etheric and astral debris that remains. To avoid making a blanket statement either way at this time, I can only confirm that sometimes some part of a lifestream does stay behind and can be problematic for my clients if the debris becomes attached to the client. Once removed, the problematic conditions fade away instantaneously or over time.

Many people are surprised to find out in hypnosis sessions that they have other energies attached to their systems that do not belong to them. Negative spirit attachment can happen when a person is in deeply traumatized or depressed states, habitually uses drugs and alcohol, or has in some way invited the energy into their system because of loneliness or another reason that weakens their energetic field. Disincarnate souls and/or parasitic astral thoughtforms use this as an opportunity to attach to the host and live out their "unfinished business." They feed off the light of the host and torment the consciousness and emotions of the person by creating self-sabotaging, obsessive-compulsive patterns. Often, the way the spirit died or illnesses they had when they died begins to redevelop in the host body. This is why energetic hygiene is crucial for every person to learn to maintain clarity and sovereignty in their vessel.

There are times that malevolent extraterrestrial beings install "implants" in a person's physical or subtle energetic bodies to track or limit the consciousness of the host body. Not all beings are in support of free will for humanity and seek to control and limit human consciousness and the restoration of our DNA. Most of the time, as I dig deep enough into the subconscious of the client, I find that on some level, the client unconsciously invited the experience to support their growth in some way.

Many beautiful beings on the planet assist with spirit transition and implant extraction in these cases. I have done it many times while clients are under hypnosis. We ask the Higher Self how it got there, how it affected the human, and what they have learned through the experience. We call in light beings, often Archangel Michael and Archangel Raphael, or a guide or loved one to assist the extraction. Every soul must go into the Light to continue the evolutionary process. When I help them transition, there is a huge relief, and they often wonder why they waited so long to rejoin their Family of Light. The effects are felt instantaneously by the client.

This is not to say that one should automatically blame negative extraterrestrials, entities, or curses for the conditions of their life. It is an opportunity to reclaim the sovereignty that you lost through your unconscious creation patterns. It is up to you to heal the parts of your consciousness that allowed such an experience. To release the resentment for such an "attack," send gratitude to the being(s) for creating conditions for optimal growth and release them to the Light. You can call on Jesus, the archangels, or any other ascended Light-consciousness being to assist you with the extraction

Some people, even after an entity extraction has taken place attract another entity attachment soon after because they have not effectively repaired their Lightbody or because they continue to enact the same patterns that caused the interference to begin with. It is up to the individual to repair their bodies and fortify their consciousness to maintain a clear vessel.

There Is No Hell

As mentioned before, there are resting places and healing temples for a soul to be refreshed and clarified once it returns to the higher light realms. After the soul is recharged and revitalized, the soul communes with its council of guides to review the previous life. This is done with grace and is never from judgment. During the review, plans are made, and preparations begin for the next life.

Every soul is welcomed back into the Light of Source. Never once during any of my sessions has a client gone to Hell or seen the "devil." These are fear-based, dogmatic control systems generated by superstition and tyranny to enslave humanity and feed off its fear. Even the most terrifying souls are received with grace and allowed to reflect, heal, and grow. Nothing is judged. The worst of the worst are simply recycled back into the Light for new creation. It is all part of the eternal evolution of Creation within the Divine Plan of Source.

I have heard of a place in the higher dimensions created for and by the souls who feel they deserve such a place. A "hell building" was created for them to play out their distorted belief systems until they decide to finally release their attachments to negative polarity and exit their self-inflicted hell matrix. The client said all who pass the building send prayers and loving intentions, inviting the souls to rejoin their beloveds in celebration of Eternal Life. How else would our Family of Light tend to those are suffering?

Some will reject this idea because on some level they still operate out of the belief of a fear-based reward and punishment system. We all contribute to perpetuating this system each time we act out of fear or teach a child to be afraid or ashamed. We see sin and darkness in the world because it still exists within the collective of humanity. We remove the "evil" from the world by removing the distorted, limiting, fear-based beliefs within our own consciousness first. Then we can assist others in liberating themselves from their own hellish creations.

We must stop blaming Satan, the devil, the Cabal, the negative ETs, the governments, and so on for the suffering on this planet. We have all played a part in adding to this horrifying imbalance that we see upon the Earth. In some way, we have all given some level of our creative power away and have allowed our bodies, minds, and planet to be corrupted and polluted. It is time to reclaim our light and reclaim this world through fierce love and unwavering focus. No savior will fight this battle for us. We ARE the second coming of Christ upon this planet, and we are the Children of God who will tip the scales and reclaim this world in Truth, Love, and Light!

Let it be so! Let it be NOW! Let it be in pure love!

THREE

The Human Experience

W hen a body is born, the physical body is given a soul. Newborn babies come in with fresh Light, fresh from the Source, and inspire joy in those around them as they emanate this pure Light and Love. I have had clients experience themselves as the consciousness of the sperm racing towards an egg surrounded by other sperm. Most of my clients who experience the birthing process in an IQH session see themselves with their guides preparing to come into a physical body as the embryo forms within the mother. Periodically they "pop in" to check on the development of the embryo or to feel into the environment the mother is experiencing to start to feel the sensations of physicality. However, the soul needs to be in the body by the time the body takes its first breath.

Sometimes being born holds such an intense trauma that it affects that incarnation for a long time. Coming from realms of Love and Light into a loud, cold, and sterile hospital room and all the procedures quickly done to a baby leaves an imprint with that child that stays with them for a long time, possibly several lifetimes. I had a client with shoulder injuries from where forceps gripped her shoulder as she was born. She recalled the scene with full detail. By re-experiencing the origin of the pattern, she released the imprinted effects of the trauma from her body and associated mental patterning and began to heal instantaneously as the pressure and pain released from her shoulder, neck, and head.

Entering the Earth Matrix

Human bodies are bio-transducers, organic machines for receiving, transforming, and emitting subtle energy. When a child is born, it immediately begins to absorb data from its environment. Sensory information like sounds, smells, physical sensations, and the emotional thought-form vibrations of those in the birthing space begin to inform and develop the mind of the new human. We are dropped into the simulation, and we begin to download data immediately.

Souls entering a new physical life need sacred high-frequency environments to enter the Earth plane. While some souls may choose a traumatic birth experience to learn a karmic lesson of some kind, these souls deserve to be received with love and calm energy to honor their passage from the higher light planes to the Earth plane. They are like sponges absorbing all the new information through their senses. When a child is young, we can protect their pure energy and vulnerable minds by creating harmonic environments for them to come into their own brilliance. They should be masters of their bodies and minds and fully aligned with their Inner Source. They should be guided into their multidimensional mastery so that they can be all that they came to be!

Termination of Pregnancy

Part of the draw for spiritual beings to descend into a human body is the vast experience that can be had through physicality. Some babies decide partway through the birthing process that, for whatever reason, the conditions are not right for them to fully incarnate. Earth life is dense and can be too intense for some. Some souls choose to stop the incarnation process during labor or a few days after birth, deciding it is too harsh or that merely being born was enough to complete their contract for that life.

From a higher perspective, some people manifest a pregnancy as an alarm alerting them to bring more conscious awareness to the state of their life's conditions or to change the direction of their lives. This is a nexus point for all parties involved as to which path they want to follow. Sometimes the choice is between allowing the pregnancy to continue or terminating the pregnancy. There is no judgment for women who choose not to carry their pregnancy full term. Everything comes down to intention. Will the person use this as an opportunity to follow a higher path or use it to continue with the momentum of their previous attitudes and perspectives? Everything is held with perfect love from Source and is seen as a learning experience for the souls involved.

A pregnant woman came to her IQH session to connect with the soul that wished to incarnate. The woman had decided that she was not ready to bring new life into the world. Through hypnosis, she connected with the consciousness of the unborn child to explain that it was not time. The next day the woman had a powerful experience during the medical procedure where her guides surrounded her and an angelic light-being form of a young girl came to share that she would be her daughter in the future. The experience was full of love and grace.

Source's Love and Grace is unwavering. We, as humanity, place our own ideas of morality and judgment onto choices and expect that the Divine would hold the same harshness that we do. Where we stumble, we have the opportunity to grow in humility and grace. Each choice is an opportunity to learn and listen to the higher guidance of compassion.

Even if there is no judgment from above for having an abortion, abortion often creates suffering. To avoid such suffering, we can learn to discern our life choices and live a noble life. Our bodies yearn to be treated as holy temples for the indwelling of spiritual light. To end the suffering related to sexuality, it is important to honor the act of sex as a powerful, sacred container for spiritual transformation and pleasure. As we come into higher consciousness and practice sacred sexuality, we will move beyond needing to manifest experiences like abortion to learn through suffering. Tragic experiences of sexual trauma are echoes from our past, often originating in past lives. Victims of violations such as these likely have a set of beliefs about themselves and fears that they hold that draw such terrible experiences into their lives. While it may seem cruel to say, this has been demonstrated over and over again in the quantum healing sessions.

In the Earth School, we often learn through suffering. Deep spiritual practice and healing will help the person understand the nature of their suffering to avoid subconsciously recreating the experience in the future. Remember this is a school of karma and it is through suffering and the redemptive power of love and higher knowledge that we break free from endless cycles of trauma.

Domestication and the Human: The New Gods of our Reality

When we are first born, we seemingly get everything we need from our parents or primary caregivers. They are responsible for feeding, clothing, and keeping us safe. They appear to be the source of love and resources, the god and goddess of our own personal reality.

These seemingly omnipotent beings can bless us or curse us at will. We learn to obey the gods and give them what they want so that we can continue to be in their graces and receive their blessings. They are the law of the land, and we learn quickly that it is best not to question their authority or knowledge. At this point, we are young and small, and we learn that there are limitations to our power and that we are dependent.

Part of our awakening process is the repatterning of our identity in connection to our biological parents. They were, fundamentally, our entry point into the Earth School and laid out the necessary conditions for the themes we would explore in this life. Emotional courses not completed in our family of origin play out in our other relationships as we grow older.

When we look at human behavior, we can separate consciousness into a few archetypes or "parts" that regulate how we process life events and relationships.

One archetype is the Child, which is made up of the spontaneous joy and intuition found in the innocence of childhood. The Child can also be a Wounded Child which has difficulty processing big emotions like when children have emotional meltdowns and fears related to authority figures and the stressors and desires of life. The Adaptive Child is the immature part of our consciousness that we created to protect our Wounded Child by rebelling against opposing forces or by changing our feelings and behaviors to fit in.

The Parent archetype is a fusion of all of the authority figures of our life, especially our birth parents. This parent can either be loving and supportive or critical and threatening.

The Adult is the mature part of our consciousness that handles life with a mature and rational attitude. The Adult is responsible for regulating the needs of the Child and the authority of the Parent.

We are constantly jumping between these archetypal vantage points. When someone is in their Child, they can inspire the Child in another, bringing more spontaneity and joy into the interaction. Meanwhile, the Wounded Child can bring out the Critical Parent or Adaptive Child in another. The Adult mediates between the two so that we do not stay in our Child and avoid the responsibilities of life and lets "bygones be bygones" by cultivating openness, practicality, and understanding to move forward in life without staying in the critical perspective of the Parent.

Our true parent is Mother Father God, the maternal and paternal emanating qualities of Source. Instead of spending our lives trying to fit into the karma of our family identity and ancestral trauma, we can rise above this and synchronize with our True Parents. As we emulate and embody their Love and Wisdom, we truly become Children of God. We can listen to all of our different "parts" and mature and integrate them into a cohesive unity and rise as Children of the Most High.

This idea of multiple "parts" to our personality expands when we start to factor in mental patterning stored in our subconscious from our personalities and experiences from other lifetimes, personality traits passed down through our ancestry, as well as flashes of insight and thoughts from our higher consciousness identities. We are each a collective. We are not one personality but a multidimensional, multifaceted conglomerate of many parts.

Some of us were born with siblings who are also doing what they can to receive affection and resources from the adults. At some level, a competition ensues. We begin to learn the human experience of scarcity consciousness as the attention of our source of love and resources is divided amongst the siblings and activities of life.

Our "family of origin" sets up the dynamics of how we relate to the rest of the world. Much healing is needed by all of us concerning our family of origin and our ancestral lines. Each new life is an opportunity to bring fresh light into the family tree to soothe ancestral trauma and evolve beyond the momentum of ancestral karma. We all took on our portion and it is up to us to fully heal our lineages through our own transformation.

We are like erasers being born into the Earth matrix with a frequency of love and a heart filled with devotion. A fresh chance to grow light! Advanced souls incarnate into the darkest regions of the human drama to bring Light and Wisdom and to transmute generations of shadow and distortion. These beings are fierce angelic souls who will use their liberation from suffering to serve humankind by transforming their suffering into wisdom.

Developing Your Matrix Character

Learning how to use the body takes time. It takes months to learn how to roll over, crawl, sit up, and eventually walk and run. This is vastly different from our spiritual body that can change form and fly! From the moment we are born, we begin to absorb the conditioning of the world through our senses. We are taught that this body is "me" and that it belongs to a family, a religion, a race, and a nation. We are given a name, gender, and an identity based on our body and cultural customs and learn that the body is subject to harm and, eventually, death. We begin to cling to physical life and our body and believe that this is all we are.

The world around us and our experience in it leaves its mark on our physical body. All of this is encoded into the muscles, into the breathing patterns, habitual holding patterns, intonation of our voice, eye patterning, fascial grid, and all the way into the cells and DNA. Everything is recorded and translated onto the body. This is how we take on family traits and hereditary illnesses, social posturing habits, accents, biases, preferences of our community, and so on.

The Human Language

The human family that we were born into has a particular language to describe its experience and share information. These words are made up of collective agreements of what each word means. With those also come individual agreements of what the individual uses the words for. Definitions for commonly used words like "love," "god," "good," and "bad" are all understood differently by different people and social groups. The meaning of words even changes over time from generation to generation.

Words carry power and intention that transform consciousness. Every word we speak or think ripples subtle information across our consciousness, affecting every level of our mind, body, and spirit. As we create sentences, we weave spells that crystallize and focus our NOW experience and draw forth a reality that matches the vibration of our inner and outer dialogues.

Many of the words in our language and how we use them are rooted in negatively polarized consciousness. When we speak half-truths, curse at someone, or intentionally use our words to cause harm, we immediately lose life force energy. We poison ourselves with our own words and thought patterning.

As we become more aware, we can feel the words' vibrations and use language that supports restoration and unity. We can develop a new vocabulary to describe our awakening life experience and use our words, thoughts, and intentions to create a new story of our personal and collective future and reverse the spells we have placed on ourselves through our distorted thoughts and words. Let us be dream-weaving wordsmiths of the New Earth and create a magical reality through every thought we generate and every word we speak!

Cultivation of Belief Systems and Belief Structures

As we learn the language of the land and the emotional and mental associations with each word, we also begin to take on our family and culture's belief systems. As we imprint the association and emotional patterning associated with the word, these become our beliefs.

The adult humans told us what our name was, what their name was, and told us our relationship to them, and what that means. We believed them, came into agreement with it, and adopted the information as truth. We learned the agreed-upon names and labels and applied them to everything in our experience. We began to narrate the story of what we were experiencing through these predetermined definitions and associations, and we programmed our consciousness to perceive things in a certain way.

As we grow, our human experience is programmed through beliefs passed down through family, society, and various institutions. These beliefs are reinforced by other programs and reward/ punishment systems. When we are "good," we get affection. When we are "bad," we get punished. Some lessons we learn through traumatic experiences leave deeply embedded thought-forms and beliefs in our subconscious, operating mostly in the background of our awareness. For example, if we were bitten by a scared dog as a toddler, we may have a subconscious belief that all dogs are dangerous.

You can think of these subconscious beliefs like applications on a smartphone, silently draining your power, speed, and proficiency from your device. Once we become aware that there are open programs no longer useful for our path, we can use various tools to "close them down," so that we can use the power of our awareness to perceive life clearly without the distortion of limitation.

Ego/Personality

When most people think of who they are, they think of their personality, thoughts, and physical body, the bodymind complex. They identify as their past experiences and behaviors, thoughts, family identity, national identity, age, sex, gender, religious identification, and so on. All these experiences are temporary and contribute to developing the personal egoic identity structure. Some people consider the ego to be "bad" when, in fact, the egoic identity structure, when entangled in the conditioning of the world, is made of positive and negative qualities. When I use the term ego, I am referring to this limited egoic identity structure. We can use spiritual practice to mature our consciousness beyond limited identification into universal I AM presence. We can make friends with the wounded part of our egoic identity structure and use higher knowledge and wisdom to bring our consciousness into appropriate perception and the realization of our higher consciousness identity.

The lower egoic identity structure is developed by us to protect our light and being, preserve our identity role (self-image), and keep the body from suffering or death. The conditioned ego, the separate self, is mostly made of protective, fear-based limiting beliefs. This is the part that thinks it can be "good," "bad," "sinner," "holy," and so on. The ego is concerned with protection, the accumulation of power, and self-preservation. The egoic identity structure creates hierarchies of importance and power and gives value to certain experiences over others. The illusion is so real that most people do not look beyond this level of identification.

Some religious institutions threaten people with eternal damnation or punishment from God if you begin to question and think of yourself as being any more than a lowly human, a servant, and a slave who is stained for eternity. This belief system feeds that shadow aspect of our personality and traps us in cycles of suffering.

Each of these identities (e.g., boy, son, husband, American, etc.) within their respective communities comes with certain beliefs and agreements of how a person should behave, think, and feel. These agreements are reinforced by reward and punishment systems to enforce the programs. This is a duality-based system, and it is what humanity has been operating in for thousands of years. Even the Godhead is seen through this duality program and is portrayed as a vengeful punisher. One must be "good" to get to Heaven or else spend eternity in Hell. This is a control system that is out of alignment with the ever-loving Divine Parent.

When most people refer to "I" or "me," they are likely speaking about their body-mind complex, their psychophysical self. The Buddhists break the bodymind complex down into five *skandhas* or five aggregates. This includes the physical form (body), feelings and sensations, perceptions and recognitions, thinking processes, and our mind-consciousness. All of these are subject to change. They arise for some time and dissolve, yet there is another part that witnesses all of these manifestations and changes occur. This is your True Self which is ever free, perfect, and whole. It exists beyond all names and forms. It is beyond all worldly identities, labels, and beliefs, yet we quickly cover it up in our early life through mental conditioning and the hypnotic power of the experience of being in physical form and taking on the spiritual amnesia of humanity. Regardless of our awareness of it, this pure existence consciousness is always there shining in the background of our experience.

Relationships

Relationships in the 3D consciousness are about control and power. What many people consider to be "love," with a lowercase "l" is a self-satisfying control system where both people expect the other to behave a certain way to win affection. From the seemingly limited supply of love and sensory gratification, we behave in ways to manipulate our external reality in an endless search for fulfillment and happiness. As we start to awaken to life's interconnectivity and begin making choices for the Greater Good of All, we begin to transform our relationships through higher expressions of unconditional love and heartfelt understanding. We begin to cultivate a richer inner life as we cultivate self-love and compassion for others. We begin to release the control programs from our own consciousness and empower others to be their own source of joy.

Emotions

Our emotions are our guidance system. They let us know what we like and what we do not resonate with. If we do not have the skills to work with emotions in a healthy way, our emotional realm likely tortures us in endless cycles of clinging, aversion, desire, and fear.

In our pre-awakening phase, our inner desires and our outer expressions do not match. We may be afraid to show our true emotions and may become deceitful out of fear of rejection or ridicule. Sarcasm, denial, avoidance, criticism, niceties, and aggression may be used to maintain a false sense of security and public image. We may repress, restrict, and reduce the expression of inner desires, judging them as "good" or "evil." In doing so, we develop a false sense of value. Self-aggrandizement, self-pity, and self-loathing are all symptoms of a degrading spirit as we play pretend and maintain our self-image.

In an immature consciousness, we may have specific conditions for us to show love and compassion. Our relationships may have different levels of honesty, authenticity, and transparency to manipulate the other person to do what we want and maintain our outward appearance. We may silently beg for approval and validation from those with whom we relate and unconsciously audition people to play out our own inner world's subconscious roles.

In the belief that fulfillment comes from our external world, we may become territorial and hoard items and money to stockpile our external power. Consumerism is fueled by the misperception that true joy and power come from our external world's conditions. There is no end to this appetite, and continuous accumulation of wealth and materials will never fill our inner void.

Many people have monotonous lives, avoiding the mystery of uncharted paths because they learned to "go with what they know" to maintain happiness and power because it is "safe." This primitive animal instinct keeps them unevolved and immature in their own emotional, mental, and spiritual growth, having to never face any new challenges or reflections.

Some people develop superstitious beliefs in their attempt to control life. They may hope that if they do "this" or "that," they will earn God's Love or get a ticket to Heaven, or at the very least, avoid misfortune. Each of these beliefs keeps us in states of shame, judgment, and powerlessness. These beliefs cut us off from the experience of God's Love, the fullness of the Self, that is always available to us. Let us learn to drop deeper than the mind and the limited conditioning of the egoic identity structure to feel the deeper part of ourselves that is always in connection with the Higher Power so that we may learn to work in unison with universal law and rhythm to create beyond our perceptions of limitation.

Society

As we zoom out, we can see how separation consciousness and lack mentality are outpictured in our collective societies. We can begin to see how systems of control based on fear and misidentification are at the core of all mainstream institutions and hierarchies. In the denial of our interconnectedness and inherent connection to the Divine, we have created systems of enslavement, domination, and oppression.

Across the globe, an elite group of extremely wealthy and powerful people forms a web of shadow control over the life and consciousness on planet Earth. Some may call this the "Deep State" or the "Cabal." In the time of this writing, this horrific system of abuse is beginning to be exposed as much of the world is beginning to awaken to the truth of what is and has long been occurring here.

The main instruments of mind control are the media, medical, and education systems. News stations and media networks use the problem-emotional reaction-solution pattern to steer the human collective into coerced consent and voluntary compliance with the service-to-self agenda of the elite and corporate interests. Mainstream media and smart devices have been used to induce people into an almost constant hypnotic trance and suggestibility. This takes less than a minute's worth of focus on a screen. Subliminal messaging and hypnotic suggestions are scripted into the video media programs, popular music, and advertisements to keep humanity at a certain bandwidth of consciousness.

The use of plant medicines and psychedelics was an integral part of my own "hacking" out of the matrix. I have an intuitive feeling that one of the reasons cannabis was cultivated on the planet was to assist us in freeing our consciousness from the mind control grid. Plant medicines, entheogens, and psychedelics are powerful tools for "breaking the matrix connection and can be used respectfully and safely to encourage consciousness expansion. The Controllers have created smear campaigns and legislation to keep these medicines from the people out of fear of what humanity would do when their mind has been set free.

The education system is used to program consciousness with a controlled narrative about history, mathematics, science, social behavior, and ethics. When the human collective reunites with the Star Nations and

Family of Light, we will get a much more advanced education that will make the current education system completely obsolete. What humanity clings to and calls science currently will look like baby blocks when compared to what the advanced intelligent beings from the stars and light dimensions use.

The "sick-for-profit system" uses genetically modified food, toxins introduced to the environment from chemtrails and industrial agriculture, toxic pharmaceutical drugs that remove symptoms but do not holistically heal, fluoridated water that corrodes the cognitive and nervous systems, onslaughts of vaccinations for newborn babies, and other means to keep people sick while charging money for the cure. Banking systems keep high interest rates so it is extremely difficult to get out of debt. This is especially true if you do not have health insurance and have to pay out of pocket for medical care.

Follow the money. Who profits from endless wars? Which families benefit from the mining and sales of fossil fuels? Who owns the central bank of your nation? As you follow the trail, it eventually narrows to a small group of people who control the entire planet for their own benefit, yet even beyond them in the higher dimensions exist forces that influence these dark masters. These service-to-self forces are being removed from the Earth, with the assistance of many great beings of light and advanced star nations, to liberate the planet and restore it to the paradise it was designed to be.

Many of the religions of the world propagate dogma based on damnation, impurity, and judgment. They deny our divinity and claim to be the only pathway to the Divine. These institutions enslave humanity, repressing and controlling the consciousness of the masses with fear and lies, and keep humanity from ascending to Higher Knowing. They take divine teachings and distort them to fit their agendas. If these institutions do not confess to their abuse of power, they will be left behind in the changing times as all who carry service-to-self consciousness will no longer be able to sustain life upon planet Earth as she transitions.

We are more than a biological machine having a temporary life. We are immortal, divine beings of light. The richness that we seek and the power that we desire are found by creating a rich inner life and relationship with our Higher Nature and Source. Ascension is the tool to lift us individually and collectively out of the cycles of suffering that we have created on the planet and move us into a culture that honors life as sacred.

Instead of being a culture focused on accumulating external wealth and power and avoiding physical death, we can be a culture that celebrates eternal living and the equality of all expressions of life. We can move beyond the misperception of separation and embrace the truth of our Oneness and Unity in the Light of Source.

Wheel of Karma: Samsara

The purpose of reincarnation is for the soul to be perfected by unconditional love and compassion and to grow in our relationship with the Divine. What we do not complete in one life, we will complete in the next. This continues endlessly until the individual soul has learned all the lessons offered through physical life.

Samsara is a Sanskrit word for the endless cycles of reincarnation, the Wheel of Karma, created by the loops of distorted thinking and the suffering mind. We step off the Wheel of Karma through practices of Ascension. We step out of the reincarnation loop by maturing our consciousness with spiritual knowledge and wisdom and reaching for the Light of the Divine. We avoid endless cycles of needless suffering by honoring our divinity and choosing thoughts and actions that support a Greater Good for All.

Humanity, as a collective, chooses to live in a hellish reality based on misidentification, distorted relationships, and the culmination of external power. Terrifying wars, destruction of ecosystems, extreme poverty, illness and disease, overflowing prison systems, unstable weather patterns, and humanitarian crises are all symptoms of collective denial of our divinity and the avoidance of the right relationship with our True Source.

Liberation includes releasing a victim and slave mentality. It is not the Church, the Archons (nonphysical controller entities), the Cabal, the Anunnaki, your parents, your lover, the government, and so on that is to blame. These are conditions for you to free yourself from the tyranny of thought. Wipe the mirror clean of illusion so that you can see the face of the Divine shining back at you. All is Self, all is God in manifestation seeking itself through the illusion of multiplicity and ignorance.

It is up to each of us to heal our inner world, push the upper limits of our consciousness, and ascend into the glory of our True Nature. If we want to see Heaven on Earth, we must refine our inner reality and open the pathways for the indwelling of Divine Light in our being. As we liberate our light from the enslavement of our distorted beliefs, we become way-showers for the rest of humanity to free themselves from the tyranny of thought, thereby dismantling the power of the controlling forces.

As we awaken to the Higher Love of the Higher Power, we become an extension of the Higher Evolution, and we begin to emanate the Love of Source out into the world. As each soul awakens to the Light of the Divine, they join the collective radiance of ascending humanity and begin to pull all of Earth life out of the shadows of fear and negative karma and into a brighter future and the dawning of a New Earth.

FOUR

High Alchemy of the Soul

Alchemy is the practice of transforming energy from one form to another. Alchemy is commonly understood in stories of turning water into wine or simple metal into gold. High Alchemy, the alchemy of the soul, is the transformation from mundane consciousness to the discovery and embodiment of one's True Divine Nature. This process activates and accelerates as the Mysteries of Creation and Laws of the Universe begin to be revealed to the honest seeker of Higher Knowledge and Wisdom of the Divine.

All alchemical processes need a container for transformation. The alchemical container for high alchemy is mindful awareness. Mindfulness is the practice of bringing our life's gross and subtle manifestations into the light of our awareness. Nondual awareness is the ability to see beyond the illusion of duality and see with the eyes of loving awareness. The spiritual alchemist uses mindfulness to observe limiting beliefs and patterns to refine distortions and misperceptions with compassionate understanding and spiritual knowledge.

Divine Embodiment

As we awaken and transform our worldly conditionings and limited thinking, we begin to embody the Light of our Divine Nature. Divine embodiment is a process of spiritual evolution where we give form through our beingness to higher spiritual virtues and anchor the Light of our True Nature into our human form. Every moment we can use self-inquiry and self-reflection to understand the origin of our thoughts and actions and what fuels our intentions in life. From this vantage point, we can discern which intentions, words, and actions are a reflection of our pure consciousness and which impulses come from our unprocessed trauma and worldly conditionings.

Manifestation

Manifestation is the process of bringing nonphysical energy into physical creation. Our life circumstances are a manifestation of inner experience and the intentions we carry, many of which are buried in our subconscious mind. As we awaken, we reclaim our powers of Divine Creatorship and become deliberate creators. As we take our power back from our subconscious limiting beliefs, we begin to attract higher manifestations at increasing speeds.

The magic behind manifestation is vibration. When our dominant vibration is high, our mind is fortified by love and higher truth and we attract more of what we want and experience synchronous events as we begin to see how the matrix of Creation works. When our vibration is low and our mind is infiltrated by distorted perception, we experience little to no synchronicity and attract manifestations that reflect those limiting beliefs and unprocessed traumas which create our inner distortion.

Our intention, our inner resolve, drives and motivates our path of creation. As we start on our awakening path, we become aware of our inner experience and refine our beingness into its highest golden nature and expression. We begin to manifest higher and higher creations and draw forth our own version of Heaven on Earth.

The Journey of a Thousand Miles Begins with One Step

The hero's journey is a framework of spiritual evolution found in many stories of beings who have pushed the upper limits of their consciousness and abilities to reach a higher state of exaltation and freedom. This is a path of initiation where a being departs the old ways to pursue higher knowledge, wisdom, and experience.

The hero or heroine's journey consists of three stages:

1. The Departure where the initiate leaves the known world and crosses the threshold into the unknown.

2. The Initiation phase is where the initiate must face challenges and grow into a higher version of themselves.

3. The Return phase is where the initiate, having been transformed into a new expression of themselves, brings the mystical elixir, the wisdom of their experience, back home to be used as a force of healing and transformation for the good of all. Let us look more closely at each phase to understand the mystical journey a bit deeper.

Departure: The Call to Adventure

All quests begin with a call to adventure, an inner yearning to journey beyond the horizons of what is currently thought or experienced and be initiated into higher awareness and understanding. It takes surrender and trust to follow the initiate's path and truly "Know Thyself." To choose awakening means to release attachment to all you have known and identified as. It takes nothing short of bravery to awaken.

Many hear the call and are afraid to leave the mundane behind, hoping to snooze for "just five more minutes." This is likely due to fear, a sense of duty or obligation, insecurity, or any other limiting or self-sabotaging beliefs that keep people from taking a leap of faith into uncharted territory. Some people will live in perpetual states of suffering for long periods of time because they do not believe they are capable or worthy of the change and growth they desire. Awakening is a choice that is constantly asking to be renewed as we become increasingly more aware of our inner realm, actions, and the repercussions of those actions on our life.

Awakening means taking full ownership of the circumstances of our life. Many would rather stay in a victim mentality of negatively polarized consciousness than accept that their life circumstances have been chosen and created by them, mostly unconsciously, for the purpose of spiritual growth. Many would rather stay in their story of suffering and "play it small" than take brave steps to make new choices and face the void of the unknown. Many hear the call, but only the brave embark on such a mysterious journey of high alchemy.

An Honest Prayer

On some level, the consciousness of the individual petitions the Godhead/Universe/Light/Spirit to show them the truth, and they send out an honest prayer or plea from the heart. This reaching for something higher is a crucial step in the initiation process. This prayer comes when one has experienced enough of the issues that have manifested from protecting the ego and personality. All the ways of "going it alone" have become exhausted. Often the emotions have become so painful that a person humbles themself and calls out from their heart to be shown the Truth, to be shown The Way.

From here, Spirit begins to work with the consciousness of the being to mature it to a sovereign, divine embodiment.

Supernatural Aid

Once the adventurer decides to accept the call to journey into the unknown, a seemingly serendipitous event occurs where a guide, physical or nonphysical, appears to point the initiate towards the higher path. Maybe it is someone who has information or resources that point to more wisdom and keys to unlock the mysteries. Maybe it is a dream or vision that activates the person and encourages them to seek out more information. Maybe it is a series of signs and synchronicities that are hard to ignore. I highly recommend watching the movie, *The Matrix*, which has many keys for awakening. The supernatural aid in this movie is when Neo, the main character who questions the nature of reality, receives a message that the Matrix is real and is invited to a meeting where he can learn about the truth of the reality matrix he is trapped in.

Threshold Guardians

The Threshold Guardians are the forces that attempt to keep the adventurer from following their path. Maybe this shows as relationships that try to control you or sow seeds of doubt, shame, guilt, or fear for desiring to expand beyond what is currently known, accepted, and experienced. Maybe it is the journeyer's limiting, self-sabotaging belief structures that keep them from taking the step towards a new way of life. These are just obstacles on the path of mastery and the initiate must truly trust their path and intuition and believe they are worthy of receiving the benefits that growth brings. If they succumb to the inner shadow or the pressures of the outer world, they will inherently experience more limitation and suffering until they follow the call. Once they affirm that they are ready and forge onward on the path less traveled, the magic of transformation can truly begin.

Initiation: Crossing the Threshold

Every person has a unique story to share about how they began to awaken. Every one of them is beautiful and powerful in its own way. Maybe it was gradual, maybe it was sudden. Maybe it was gentle, or maybe it was traumatic. Maybe it was practical. Maybe it was mystical. Everyone who begins to awaken has some initiation experience that points them towards a higher destiny pathway and a higher consciousness reality. These events, people, and experiences activate within them the desire to "know thyself." Slowly, the layers of misidentification peel away as they begin to deprogram their consciousness and ascend out of the limited cultural programming, ancestral trauma, and personal identifications, aversions, desires, fears, and attachments.

When one decides to seek the Mysteries and higher consciousness and steps beyond the default paradigm, they will be tested to measure their commitment to their sovereignty and awakening path. Some people may be threatened by new ideas and unusual behavior and try to lure the new traveler back into the old world, their old character, and limited egoic identification. This is just a test for the initiate, an opportunity to trust their inner guidance and inner knowing and take action towards their higher ideal expression and true liberation.

Trusting one's inner voice of wisdom and reason is the foundation for the path of spiritual growth. Awakening involves honoring the inner voice of Spirit and releasing habits that give our power away to outside authority. Heaven/God is within each of us, softly guiding us towards everything we have ever wanted. We are always being presented with the same option: acknowledge and follow the presence and guidance of the divine felt within or follow "The World" and outside authority. One leads us to salvation, the other keeps us in cycles of suffering and endless reincarnation cycles.

Mentorship: A Guide to Show the Way

As we begin to awaken, we start to look, consciously or unconsciously, for a teacher or mentor to guide us to higher truth. All good teachers, true teachers, point us back to the power we have within our beingness, to the "teacher that lives within." These mentors are role models for qualities that we want to mirror and embody. It is important to keep in mind that all beings are equal, and we risk disappointment when we put our teachers on pedestals. Many "spiritual teachers" on the Earth plane will reveal their own shadow as we move further along the ascension pathway. There are many teachers and spiritual leaders who use spiritual knowledge and their influence as a teacher to fulfill service-to-self agendas. Hidden agendas are hard to hide in an increasingly telepathic and intuitive culture. All of us are subject to our humanness and all hidden agendas will eventually be brought into the light of awareness.

Once we have learned all that we can from one teacher, we move to the next teacher. We are meant to use many teachers in our life path, and we limit ourselves by devoting ourselves to one teacher or guru. In truth, everyone and every life circumstance is our teacher.

The message that we received through clients is that "They," the spiritual beings that tend to the development of Earth and humanity, have coordinated it so that there will no longer be one source of divine wisdom and prophecy on the planet because the "Savior" and "Guru" templates cause people to lower in vibration and give their power away. Instead, "They" are spreading the dissemination of spiritual information and insight across the globe through many people to keep a higher balance. Anyone or any group that says that they are the savior or that only they know the divine truth is likely using this to generate fear or manipulate people for their service-to-self agenda. The true teacher lives within, and no outside authority supersedes your innate connection to the Divine.

Initiations: Trials and Errors

Each relationship and life circumstance is a course in spiritual growth, an educational alchemical container for transformation. The coursework involves understanding our emotions' hidden meaning and bringing more awareness to our thoughts, habits, beliefs, and actions. As we move through a course, we experience certain conditions to stimulate the potential for spiritual growth, consciousness expansion through trials and tribulations, and the insight these experiences bring. Every moment is ripe with the potential for deeper awareness and spiritual growth as one begins to consciously transform into higher consciousness. If we do not learn the lesson, it comes back around again in another circumstance or another relationship.

Helpers along the Journey

At certain points in the initiation phase, helpers appear on our path to encourage our growth and expansion. Sometimes it is pleasant and sometimes the relationship is challenging. As we awaken, we start to see our relationships as catalysts for spiritual growth. We begin to grow in our awareness that what we judge or fear in another reflects our inner world. Many people leave one relationship, only to manifest and recreate the same circumstances in another relationship. When you are in a spiritual relationship with another, you see the other as an ally for spiritual growth. As we shed the victim mentality and take authority over our experience as Divine Creators, we see that the biggest villains in our life, especially the characters involved in the most painful experiences, served as powerful activators for massive healing and consciousness expansion. It is up to each of us to cultivate a compassionate heart so that we can tend to our wounds and realize the deeper teachings of our traumas.

Growth: New Skills

Each challenge in our life is an opportunity to grow spiritually. We can use alchemical practices to transform our stagnation, stored trauma, and limiting beliefs. We can read literature that inspires higher thought and understanding. The more we use our skills and acquired knowledge, the better our life becomes and the more automatic and integrated the new understanding becomes. Questions lead to more questions as we come to a deeper and deeper understanding of our True Self. True nourishment is that which feeds our soul and sets us free.

The Abyss: Ego Death & Spiritual Rebirth

The Dark Night of the Soul is a spiritual crisis period for an awakening initiate as their old identities and beliefs go through a death process. This is a deeply transformative phase as the light is seemingly stripped from the world. Deep churning, pain, doubt, fear, and grief often color the experience of this Dark Night. The Dark Night of the Soul finishes as the initiate discovers the light within them and begins to embody a higher expression of themselves. Rising like the phoenix from the ashes, they emerge with deeper insight and wisdom. Miracles are simply a shift of perception from fear to higher love and unity. When we release our addictive thinking towards fear and discover the source of safety and abundance found within, we begin to access our power as divine creators and limitless beings.

Final Changes

Once we are finished with one course, we move into a higher-level course to achieve a better understanding. We see this outpictured in the changing of relationships, jobs, homes, and so on. Often, right before our "graduation," a final test, a final opportunity emerges to see if we are truly ready to move into the next level of consciousness exploration. We are meant to change and grow. Some people may have a difficult time accepting that you act differently or have new boundaries. While it may be uncomfortable, this is simply a test to see if you are truly committed to embodying your deepest truth or if there are still places in your consciousness where you get hooked into old patterns that need to be reconciled before you can be fully anchored in your new embodiment. It is in this phase that the initiate receives revelations that illuminate the mind to higher truths that liberate their consciousness and create a higher perspective of their life. Finally, the sword is pulled from the stone, and victory has been achieved! Now the victorious adventurer can begin their quest back home.

Atonement: Reconciliation

As we awaken, we may find that we have harmed someone else when we were caught in the illusion of our ego or a less enlightened state. It is important to make amends and reconcile with those we may have wronged. The best way to make amends is to transform your limiting beliefs and stored trauma that caused the suffering. From this place, you can approach the situation with the intention to relieve the suffering of others. Reconciliation involves healing the hearts of all parties involved and coming to a deeper understanding. To love others as we love ourselves effectively, we need to first love ourselves unconditionally. Grace is available for all, no matter how terrible the action is.

Ho'oponopono is a Hawaiian healing practice for reconciliation and forgiveness. It can be translated into four steps and phrases: "I am sorry, I love you, please forgive me, and thank you." When we say "I am sorry" to another, it shows that we have thought about our actions and see that we have potentially caused harm to another. We say "I love you" to let them know that we release the fight and want positive solutions for all involved. When we say "please forgive me," we invite them to be a part of the healing process. They may also want to confess their role in the issue. We say "thank you" because we have come to a deeper understanding of how this opportunity provided nourishment for our growth.

We do not need the other person to forgive us to release ourselves from feelings of guilt. That is our wound to heal. When we do our part of the work, we release our part of the karma with this person and can truly stand in sovereign support of the other's growth. We can do this process for loved ones far away and even those who have traveled beyond the physical world.

A Gift from the Universe

When we complete our missions, there is often a gift from the universe for persevering through challenges. Maybe it is a physical item, an opportunity to share your new skills or talents, or some other blessings of abundance from the universe. Facing your inner shadow is tough work! Being sure to thank God/the Universe for blessing you will open the pathways for even greater blessings!

Return Changed

"We only keep what we have by giving it away." is an adage from 12-step programs that perfectly describes the final stage in the cycle of the hero's journey. As we learn to make peace with our inner distortions and transform into the limitless nature of our Divine Self, we stand as emanations of Higher Understanding and Higher Love. We broadcast this frequency into the world through our very being. We then carry within our essence a healing elixir, wisdom that can be shared with those who seek a higher truth. It is our responsibility to humanity to share our spiritual insight and discovered gifts. Our heroic characters from humanity's history were pioneers, rebels, visionaries, and artists who pushed the upper limits of what was thought possible to achieve the seemingly impossible.

From their new heights, many have borrowed strength and inspiration to walk their own path of initiation. Each of us carries these extraordinary potentials within us. Each of us can be pioneers of consciousness that help to unshackle the collective of humanity by first taking the shackles off of our own self.

May these words shared here fuel your path of liberation, your own hero's journey, so that you can bring back the wisdom you have discovered within and share it as medicine for this world.

FIVE

Awakening in the Matrix

A s we begin to awaken to the Light and Love of Source, to the Light of our soul, we awaken within the dream we call life. This awakening process is called Ascension. During this process, we question everything we believe. We begin to sort through all our internal rubble to uncover the Divine Self that lives within. This process begins our exodus from the mundane mainstream consciousness and initiates us into the Mysteries of Creation. We "save" ourselves from our karma and mental trappings by reaching for the Higher Knowledge of the Divine. This reaching for higher understanding is crucial to begin the process of awakening and ascension.

As a new initiate, we begin to notice the programming in the people and world around us. The illusion loses its luster; the games we used to play and roles we used to act out do not interest us as much. Many of us have felt completely alone as most of the world is focused on the material reality and egoic preservation and not the spiritual quest. They are asleep within the dream. This is perfectly fine as every soul designs a time when they will begin to awaken to their divinity and the Higher Realms of Light.

This awakening process is well on its way for millions of people around the world. What once was only available for the mystics, sages, and spiritual masters throughout time is available for all people who desire to grow in Light and Love and evolve into higher, heart-centered consciousness. Can't you feel the quickening of transformation occurring in your own life and across the planet? While some look at the conditions of the world and see destruction, others look and see a healing crisis as all of humanity faces its karmic shadow. Nothing can stay hidden anymore and all will be brought into the Light as we shift into New Earth reality.

Quantum Physics is now beginning to measure that the multiverse is conscious and interconnected through a unified field through principles such as quantum entanglement and nonlocality. We are beginning to measure how matter is affected by our consciousness and how all of life is connected in a symbiotic relationship. These advancements will continue to accelerate as humanity's consciousness expands and ascends as we connect to a higher consciousness reality through the upgrading technology of our bodymind complex.

Everything Is in Support of Your Awakening

You are the writer, director, and main actor of your dream. How you think and what you think about changes your reality. Your environment is constantly rearranging to match your intentions, vibrations, and desires. Whether you know it or not, the entire universe is conspiring in your favor for your victory in awakening to your Divine Self. Even in the moments of your deepest pain when you feel that you have totally fallen from grace, you are still building massive momentum towards attaining your ascended self-mastery. Every experience is valuable, and every experience carries nourishment and spiritual wisdom to fuel your awakening. This journey is about YOU and your willingness to unconditionally love every part of yourself and extend that radiance out into the world.

Different Levels of Consciousness

In the Ascension community, we speak about humanity's ascension in terms of "dimensions" or "densities." There are likely other models to describe this transmigration process of our consciousness and this world into the higher consciousness reality of New Earth. Some say that Earth is moving from third density to fourth density and that humanity is becoming a fourth-density collective. Some say Earth and humanity are moving from the third dimension through the fourth and into the fifth dimension. I understand and find value in both ways of describing the process. I will summarize both perspectives from my understanding to provide a framework for the discussion of Ascension.

The first time I heard of ascension in terms of "density" was through a somnambulistic client who described the creation process of the multiverse and the evolutionary pathway of Gaia and humanity. This client's Higher Self referred to the Operation Terra material that the client had read that activated his awakening process. The material is said to have been channeled from the Heavenly Hosts and is strikingly similar to what has been channeled through the quantum healing sessions. I recently read parts of the Operation Terra material that speak about the differences between density and dimension. Here is a much simpler summary of that information infused with my own understanding and experience.

When we think of ascension in terms of changing "density," we are talking about shifting the material reality's particle structure by increasing the vibration of the material. This is understood easily by water's transformation from ice to liquid water to water vapor. As more energy (i.e., heat) is applied to the material, the density begins to shift from solid matter to a vapor that you cannot necessarily see but can feel.

We can think of the shift from Third Density to Fourth Density as shifting bandwidths of reality, similar to Dorothy from the Wizard of Oz where Kansas is seen as a black and white film reality and Oz is the bright technicolor reality where magic is real and anything is possible. We are shifting to a whole new "program" of a harmonic Earth reality that is beyond anything we can comprehend from our current vantage point.

In Third Density Earth, our current Earth, we experience the physical world in the three dimensions of space: height, length, and depth, in a linear experience of time. As we start to awaken, our experience of time begins to shift and become nonlinear as we tune into the unfolding of eternal time.

In Fourth Density, we have the previous four dimensions as well as the Eternal Quantum Consciousness and experience ourselves as extensions of the Oneness of Creation. This moves us out of linear thinking and linear time experience into multidimensional awareness experienced through nonlinear holographic consciousness.

Another way to think of consciousness evolution in terms of "densities" is to think of different complexities of consciousness forms. In First Density, we see inanimate objects such as fundamental energy, elements, gases, stones, and minerals. In the Second Density, we see organic animate forms like microbial life, plants, and animals. In Third Density, we see physical beings such as humans with their individual consciousness and intellect. In Fourth Density, in terms of human consciousness evolution, we see individual consciousness operating in universal consciousness which gives humanity tele-thought communication with Earth, the Earth kingdoms, nonphysical and nonlocal beings, and Source. There are other densities beyond Fourth Density, but I do not feel they are necessary to explain for this book. I am sure that there are many ways people categorize and describe "densities," but this is a simple enough theoretical model to understand what people are talking about when they speak of consciousness evolution in terms of "densities."

Humanity, in its current form, cannot experience Fourth Density because we have a Third Density body. Christ Jesus (Yeshua ben Joseph) brought the template for the Fourth Density human back to humanity through his ascension processes and soul mission. His birth, life, death, and resurrection laid the foundational template to restore humanity and the Earth to its original divine blueprint and perfection. Humanity's transformation from the Third Density human body to the Fourth Density Adamic human template is already underway and experienced as ascension symptoms as our DNA is returned to the perfected divine human template.

Now let us shift to another way that people commonly look at this Ascension process in terms of dimensions which is the most commonly used and understood framework for understanding the process of Ascension.

3D Consciousness: Slave Mind — Living in the Material World

In 3D consciousness, we perceive ourselves as a single point in the world, cut off from everything else. We are ignorant of our higher consciousness identity as a divine being and create a false self based on cultural programming and societal structures. This ego is fear-based, operates in survival mode, and can be quite animalistic in its expression of self-preservation, domination, and control.

In 3D consciousness, we perceive life in linear time via the five primary senses through the untrained mind's duality. Life is seen as finite with a string of events that follow each other, seemingly unrelated. We can have a "slave mindset" and "victim consciousness" and give our power to the world outside of us. From the 3D perspective, our biology decides our destiny, and we see ourselves as victims of our past and enslaved by our genetics, culture, and economic status. It is a "me versus them" reality that focuses on controlling the physical elements of life to feel safe, secure, and powerful.

All the Earth issues at this time, all the imbalance and shadow, stem from this core wound, this belief that we are disconnected from the Divine. This suffering and misinformation have been amplified by distorted religious teachings that use shame and guilt to control the consciousness of that religion's followers. As humanity awakens to its divinity, all imbalances will fade away as we return to the truth of our Oneness with All That Is and rise in our embodied consciousness as divine beings of light.

4D Consciousness: Initiation of Light and Vibration Stepping into the Magical Reality

As we awaken, we move from 3D consciousness into the initiatory passageway of the Fourth Dimensional Consciousness. 4D Consciousness is like stepping into a world of magic. The matrix of Creation begins to speak to you as signs and synchronicities begin to emerge on your path. It is like the background comes to the foreground as you begin to sense the spiritual and mystical significance in your life. Events seem to be interconnected as you begin to see the patterns of the matrix reality. This is where an ascending consciousness begins to recognize universal laws like the Law of Attraction — "that which is like unto itself is drawn."

The initiate begins to take inventory of their internal experience and find higher compassion to transform and alchemize the inner realm of their consciousness. The seduction of duality begins to fade away as Unconditional Love begins to show The Way. The default belief systems of the collective consciousness born from limitation, trauma, and unconscious karmic programming, begin to lose their power over our consciousness. We begin to awaken within the dream of Earth and reclaim our sovereignty as Divine Creators with free will.

The Higher Self is a term used by spiritual circles to describe the part of our consciousness guided by Divine Love and Wisdom which maintains an unbreakable connection to the Higher Realms of Light. For the sake of this text, the Higher Self is described as this mature part of our consciousness that is always seeking harmony and works for the betterment of All. It expresses through flashes of insight, intuition, inner knowing, discernment, ethical action, and universal compassionate connection.

To transition from 3D to 4D and beyond, one begins to become curious about the Divine and their connection to the Higher Worlds that exist beyond the five senses. Through this curiosity, the Mysteries begin to be revealed to the seeker. The seeking initiate begins to follow the internal "still small voice" and moves into higher states of enlightenment. Some call this inner guidance the Holy Spirit, their Higher Self, or their soul. In truth, there are a few Higher Selves, higher consciousness identities, which exist in higher and higher light dimensions connecting to the Source. This is reflected in the physical world through the pathways of connection from humans to the solar system, the galaxy, super galaxies, and the Great Central Sun. As above, so below.

This Higher Self consciousness, or the illuminated, mature part of our consciousness, guides us away from our False Self, egoic identity, into our higher exalted True Nature. As we release the limited lower mentality of the ego and collective default belief structures and step more and more into our sovereign power as divine creators, we begin to merge with a higher consciousness that can perceive beyond the visible light spectrum and open to information from Higher Light Realities and Consciousness.

In 4D consciousness, we begin to awaken to the subtle energy universe of spiritual light and subtle vibrational frequencies and begin to consciously and/or unconsciously activate and repair our Lightbody. Our empathetic nervous system begins to activate as we begin to sense and feel subtle energy fields within and beyond our physical form. There are many schools of thought on the study of the human subtle energy systems which each have their way of accessing, manipulating, and reconciling the energy systems.

This energy system can be activated, cleansed, and strengthened through spiritual practice and proper diet to prepare it for its transformation into the next "light garment" of the perfected divine human template with fully activated and repaired 12-strand DNA.

For this process to complete, all vibratory fields, every atom of the human body, is to be brought into a state of sustained coherence and harmony which naturally occurs through the integration of ascension energies, focusing one's life on spiritual values and love, and eating a proper diet that is free from toxins.

5D Consciousness: Cosmic Christ Consciousness — Moving into Miraculous Reality

The oversoul is a higher aspect of our consciousness beyond the psychological, neurological, and physiological process of our human self, existing beyond the physical nature of reality. Once we awaken and repair our Lightbody through diligent practices and spiritual growth processes, we begin the process of linking with our Overself consciousness and the overlay of the Overself Lightbody. This process was demonstrated publicly by Christ Jesus (Yeshua ben Joseph) and is written about in the *Tibetan Rainbow Lightbody* teachings and the *Lightbody Ascension Teachings of Ancient Egypt*.

Fifth Dimensional (5D) consciousness, Overself Consciousness, or Christ Consciousness can be described as the perspective of reality experienced as the eternal unfolding of heavenly and miraculous phenomenon witnessed through loving nondual awareness. When humanity ascends to and maintains 5D Consciousness, we will be completely aware of our connection to All That Is. We will no longer experience the lower emotions of fear and suffering. We will instead maintain loving awareness and the deeply profound and embodied knowing of our interconnectivity with all of Life.

Oversoul Embodiment: Multidimensional Awareness

In 5D consciousness, we are fully immersed in our body's ecstatic blissful awareness as an avatar for the higher consciousness of our oversoul. The oversoul consciousness contains all the wisdom and experiences from our other lifetimes. Each soul emanation returns with life experience after each incarnation and merges with the total wisdom of the oversoul consciousness. Once we completely "dock" with our oversoul consciousness, we will have access to all the knowledge and wisdom from our current life as well as other lifetimes in our oversoul's collective experiences and legacy.

Wayshowers are those who have been developing their consciousness, moving out of the standard 3D consciousness into 4D consciousness to shine as planetary ascension leaders. They have continued to push the upper edges of their spiritual development so that they may guide others along the path as the masses begin to awaken. These beings are great Cosmic Masters who are proficient and experienced in moving planets and species into their next evolutionary phase. These lightworkers have lived lives as master healers, cosmic frequency technicians, quantum space engineers, architects of reality, angelic light warriors, Ascended Masters, goddesses, oracles, and quantum consciousness pioneers and have come from all regions of space-time and beyond to assist humanity and planet Earth. All of the best are here upon this Earth, and surrounding it as well, to welcome the dawn of this new day!

The Three Stages of Spiritual Awakening

The journey to New Earth involves surrendering to unconditional love and learning to live in harmony with Creation. This involves striving to "know thyself" and awaken to the redemptive power of compassion, forgiveness, and understanding. Through healing and spiritual processes, one activates and maintains the Higher Love vibrational perspective of their Higher Self and opens themself to the Higher Mysteries of Creation. Through our desire and efforts to grow and mature in our love and appreciation of the Divine, we begin to embody that love and become honorable, cooperative co-citizens of the cosmos.

This awakening and ascension process can be broken into three segments of *purging, activation,* and *embodiment.*

We are healing and releasing all the limiting beliefs, stored trauma energy, and toxins from our physical body and subtle bodies during the purging phase. As this old energy leaves, we move into the activation phase. We become more in tune with subtle energy, our Inner Being, and our spiritual gifts during the activation phase. As we move into higher thought and follow our guidance from our Inner Being, we embody the presence of our Higher Self, our radiant Divine expression of pure Light.

This process is accelerated by spiritual practices that purify and unite the body, mind, and spirit. A "practice" is anything that we repeatedly do to accelerate our healing and transformation consciously. Homeostasis is our body's natural ability to return to perfect balance and health. Homeostasis, perfect balance, is the natural state of our body. We can use spiritual practices to support our systems back into balance, health, and coherence.

Spiritual practices align us with our Higher Self and anchor us into multidimensional presence. We can be simultaneously aware of our physical, etheric, emotional, mental, and spiritual processes at any given moment. As we bring more mindfulness to these processes through our practice, we are more likely to be aware of them in other areas of our lives to consciously make choices that align with our highest path.

Conscious embodiment practices help us to grow in our capacity to be conscious and present in our bodies. Physical practices like meditation, yoga, qi gong, walking, dancing, running, or somatic practices like Feldenkrais or Pilates bring our awareness to the present moment as we train the mind to focus on the subtle processes of our body, mind, and energy. These meditative practices help us slow the mental processes down to feel more grounded, centered, and present in our subtle energy field and our life.

Cognitive therapies, reading of self-help and sacred texts, journaling, and other practices bring more mindfulness to our mental processes so that we can become aware of limiting perspectives and train our minds into higher thought patterns and habits. Breathing practices help us clear old energy from the body, train our minds to the present moment, and bring fresh energy into our body to support natural, vital flow in our systems.

There is an infinite number of practices available to soothe your system and align you with your Inner Being and higher consciousness. They do not have to be "spiritual" to be effective. What matters is that we have activities that we do consistently to help us gain positive momentum in the direction of our higher goals and aspirations to holistically embody our Higher Self.

Beyond bringing mindfulness to all these processes and finding coherence in the body, it is vital to have an openness and desire to connect with the Higher Consciousness Reality to make this evolutionary leap of Ascension. Rejecting the Divine or holding animosity towards the Divine closes the crown and heart chakras which connect us to the evolutionary energies. The opening to and development of a closer relationship with the Divine Consciousness opens the pathways for Higher Light to saturate the human bodymind instrument with a higher evolutionary coding. This moves the human body's biology out of patterns of decay and entropy into a Higher Evolution of Eternal Light and Eternal Living. As this Higher Light enters the biofield, it enters the cells and DNA. It begins to repair the building blocks of the organic material so that the full brilliance of one's consciousness can express through the physical body's genetics.

Shifting Paradigms

In the default model of civilization, power is something outside of ourselves, and we see ourselves as separate from everything else. We are limited to our five basic senses, only able to prove and believe in things we can see, touch, taste, smell, hear, and measure. We have created a whole civilization based on controlling our external world to feel powerful and secure. This is a devouring power that is opposite of the true nourishing and life-affirming power of the Divine. The New Earth paradigm invites us to perceive the world through energy and our Inner Being's guidance. We discover that the power is within us, and we had it all along. Even if we cannot see the connection, we can feel that all of Life is interconnected and One.

Spiritual awakening, the ascension pathway, is an ongoing process of shifting paradigms. When you change the way you look at things, things will change the way they look. We can see this shift happening not only on a personal level but at all levels of civilization. Having forgot our True Nature, everything we have created in the 3D matrix was created from an inverted, limited perspective and misidentification. Everything we have thought to be true and everything that we created from that limited perspective will shift as we transition to the New Earth higher light spectrum reality.

When paradigms are shifting, it is normal for us first to reject new information that contradicts our current paradigm, our current way we interpret reality. Eventually, we may come to accept some part of the new perspective, even if we are not ready to fully accept the totality of the new paradigm. Eventually, we become more and more accepting of the new perspective's components, gradually embracing the new beliefs and new ideas. There is no going back to the old ways from that place, and we move forward in life with a fresh, updated framework of understanding.

The New Earth paradigm is absurd to many people and likely sounds insane and based in fantasy. It does not matter if everyone believes in extraterrestrials, Ascended Masters, or even God, all at once. It makes sense that most people would reject these concepts at first since most reject their own divinity and light. Instead of focusing on getting people to believe in the abstract and foreign concepts, we can focus on guiding people into their hearts and allowing the Higher Love to show The Way. This is why Jesus and the disciples focused on the heart as an access gateway to the Absolute Reality of the Higher Realms of Light.

We are each like a baby bird about to hatch. From within our egg, we believe that the world is only the inside of our egg. As we crack through the illusion and break free from the shell, we realize that the world is so much bigger than we could have ever imagined from our previous perspective.

As we shift into New Earth, the new consciousness, and the repaired and upgraded Lightbody, all the systems based on the old paradigm must fall away and be replaced by creations made from the new paradigm of our individual and collective expanded consciousness. This means a complete transformation of how we relate to ourselves and the world. This also means that every part of society, our governments, financial systems, medical systems, and educational systems must have a complete overhaul to match the new paradigm.

As this world decays and the New Earth emerges, many will fight to keep the old ways alive. This is futile as every atom of life on Planet Earth will be reset and revitalized through the powerful undulating Light emanations from the Great Central Sun. The potency of these transformative divine powers is amplified by the compassionate efforts of our extraterrestrial, ultraterrestrial, and positive subterranean allies joined with the thoughts, prayers, and actions of awakening humanity upon the Earth.

YOU are here on Planet Earth, our beloved Gaia, with a BIG purpose! You are here to awaken to the truth of who you are, an aspect of Source, a Divine Being. Through the process of this realization of your Divine Nature, you become a conscious bridge between Heaven and Earth, a walking prayer, and an ambassador for the Light of Source. You are the bridge between the Higher Heavenly Light Realms and Earth! This process is about you bringing all your shadows into the Light to be healed and growing in your capacity to allow the Love of Creation to flow through you and illuminate this world.

Self-Initiation Prayer

Moving into the higher consciousness is a personal choice made by an individual who desires to know the Mysteries and truly "Know Thyself." Different traditions have different ceremonies or rituals for initiation into the Mysteries. I invite you to enact your own ceremony that is deeply personal and a symbol of your personal exodus from the mundane world into the Hidden Mysteries. You can create your own or follow this prayer I have designed.

1. Set up a ceremonial and sacred space for yourself. This may include lighting some candles and turning the lights down low, maybe burning incense or diffusing your favorite essential oils. Some people prefer silence or light, ethereal music. You can create an altar with symbols and pictures that represent Higher Love and the Divine. Let your intuition and creativity guide the way.

2. Sit with yourself in quiet, mindful awareness and connect with your

heart by bringing your hands to a prayer position or by resting the hands on the heart center. Gently extend and equalize all the breathing stages: inhalation, pausing, exhalation, and pausing to calm the mind and bring it into the present moment.

3. With your intention, welcome the Light of the Divine to be with you. Imagine, sense, and feel this Light completely surrounding you. Invite your spiritual guides, angelic light beings, and loving ancestors to be with you. Feel their love as they gather around you. This may be the first time you have ever consciously reached for them, yet they are always with you and always shining their love upon you. Since this is a free-will planet, you must ask for them to work with you. Once you have initiated communication and connection, they will be able to work with you in a much more expanded way that is beneficial and appropriate for your path. Simply intend to connect and trust that the connection has been established.

4. Use your voice to make a statement and declaration to the Universe/ Source/Family of Light that speaks to your decision to follow Unconditional Love and the Light of Truth.

Beloved Father Mother God, Source of my Being, Light that I am:

- I choose now to awaken in my consciousness to the Truth of Who I Am.
- Open my eyes to the Greater Love Light and the Higher Mysteries of Creation.
- Open my heart and show me The Way of Eternal Peace, Eternal Life, and Eternal Light.
- Awaken and reform my DNA and make my body an instrument for the indwelling of spiritual Light.
- Let me be a lamppost for the seekers of your Grace and Wisdom so that all may find liberation from cycles of suffering.
- Let my words and actions dispel darkness so that I may be a luminary in this world and beyond.
- I surrender my personal will to the Higher Will of the Divine and choose to live a life guided by Unconditional Love in service to the Greater Good of All.
- Infuse my consciousness with higher vibrations and the power of awakening and ascension.

- Let me commune with the Family of Light and Star Families so that I may be a bridge for many worlds of Love and Light and an extension of the Higher Evolution of Creation.
- Activate my full potential as a realized Divine Being and help me be a powerful Light Force in the liberation of all beings from cycles of suffering.

Let it be so! Let it be Now! Let it be Love!

5. Take some time to sit quietly and feel the vibrations and sensations of your Inner Being. You may even feel inspired to dance or sing a song to celebrate your initiation. When you are finished, continue with your day and trust that you have activated your sacred path of Ascension.

SIX

Universal Laws of Creation

You are a powerful creator with the ability to manifest your own Heaven on Earth. You can break free of karmic cycles and create the life you truly desire. You need to be aware of a few rules to get the most out of this Game of Consciousness. Once you understand and apply the rules of the game, you will launch yourself on a much easier path of creation. The origin of the teachings of these principles/laws (on this planet) can be found in the ancient texts of Hermetic Philosophy and other occult and esoteric schools of thought who received these teachings of universal knowledge from the higher realms and higher consciousness beings from beyond the Earth.

Below I have described a summary of my understanding of some of the basic Hermetic philosophical principles that have helped me on my path of High Alchemy, the alchemy of consciousness. I highly recommend the classic text *The Kybalion* by Three Initiates if you wish to journey deeper into Hermetic philosophy and further activate your mastery in alchemical multidimensional creation.

Law of Divine Oneness (Law of One)

All is One, and One is All and everything is in THE ALL. Everything is Source. All of Creation comes from one Source. All of Creation exists in a continuum of descending movement from and ascending towards the glory of the primordial Source. Nothing is above or below in value. Nothing is separate, and all of Life is connected in a symbiotic relationship in the Unified Field of the One Source. Nothing exists outside of the One Supreme Source. In fact, the Advaita Vedanta philosophy would say "All is not, Source IS" as all names and forms appear within Source.

The One Being manifests itself in the illusion of multiplicity. In truth, there is only one of us here! We can use the appearance of multiplicity or duality to understand the deeper wisdom of the Oneness of All and to truly "know thyself." Every time we choose to see beyond the illusion of separation, we reaffirm the Truth of Unity and Oneness of what appears to be many but is truly ONE. The mantra of "I AM THAT I AM" opens our capacity to experience the Oneness. This same mantra is found in other languages such as "*Eyeh Asher Eyeh*" in Hebrew and "*Aham Brahmasmi*" in Sanskrit, which both translate to a similar meaning of "I am the all-pervasive, vast, limitless Supreme Source."

- If all is THE ALL and The All is One, is there anything in Creation that you consider "outside of God?"

Law of Mentalism

"Watch your thoughts, they become your words; watch your words,
they become your actions; watch your actions, they become your habits;
watch your habits, they become your character; watch your character,
*it becomes your destiny." —*Lao Tzu

Everything in creation is a product of the Infinite Eternal Mind of Source. The Multiverse is within the mind of the Supreme Source and is continuously evolving through the evolution of divine thought. From the simplest evolution of subatomic particles to the most complex orchestrations of cosmic events, all is happening within the mind space of Source Consciousness.

This universal law is mirrored in humanity's capacity to dream, imagine, and evolve thought into new creations. As we think, we create. Thoughts are a manifestation of our vibration. When our overall vibration is high, we manifest enjoyable thoughts of inspiration, insight, and joy. When our vibe is low, our thoughts drag us deeper and deeper into our story of suffering.

In the words of Abraham-Hicks, "a belief is just a thought you keep thinking." Most beliefs are programmed from our cultures and upbringing, and many are based on doubt, fear, and control. Our beliefs are our Book of Law, and we use our Book of Law to discern, judge, criticize, and evaluate our experience. As we grow in awareness, we can consciously choose how to shift our thoughts in a more positive, life-affirming direction and rewrite our Book of Law. Spiritual awakening and self-mastery involve deprogramming these limiting beliefs and aligning our thought processes with Universal Truth and Wisdom.

Emotions show us the quality of our belief systems and how we process energy information from the world around us. If we experience negative emotions, we are processing the energy and information from our experience through limiting beliefs and possibly unprocessed trauma from the past. The Law of Attraction magnetically attracts a similar situation into our NOW moment to retrigger the unprocessed energy so we can process the information correctly and mature our consciousness.

If we experience unpleasant emotions and situations, we can turn inward to find out what within us is drawing this experience into our reality. *How have I created this? What is my part? How are my thoughts contributing to this situation? What belief am I holding that is out of alignment with my soul? What can I learn?*

Each thought and word spoken is a spell that we cast on ourselves and our environment. Are we working with white magic or working with shadow magic? Are we giving power to our light or power to our suffering?

- If THE ALL is Mind and Creation is mental by nature, what are you doing to guide your thoughts toward higher thought patterning that aligns with Divine Knowledge and Divine Creatorship? (e.g., meditation, reading sacred texts, mindfulness practices, forgiveness work, etc.)

- How can you deepen in awareness of the parts of your consciousness, shadows in your personality, which are self-sabotaging or limiting? What steps can you take to reconcile those "parts" to clear the mind of negativity and align it with higher truth and coherent thought patterning?

Law of Correspondence

As above, so below, as within, so without. The microcosm is a reflection of the macrocosm; the reverse is also true. What you experience outside of you is an out picturing of your beliefs and emotions of your inner experience. What is happening in the physical dimension reflects what is happening in the astral dimensions. What is happening in the astrological alignments reflects what is happening within our inner progression and transformation and so on. All of these reflections and presentations can be utilized for high alchemy to "know thyself."

- Where can you take more responsibility for the conditions of your life knowing that what happens around you is in some way a reflection of what occurs within your mind?

Law of Vibration

All of Creation is made from Light and Vibration. Everything moves and vibrates in circular patterns. Everything is energy, and nothing rests. These pulsations of energy are the building blocks of all phenomena of our reality and beyond. Different aspects of Creation have different vibrational rates (frequency) that give them a unique vibrational signature. Physical objects, feelings, thoughts, and sensations all have their unique frequencies.

Distorted energies, limiting beliefs, and unprocessed trauma are entropic. They take away vital life force and creative vision and move us into a downward spiral of decay, a lower vibration. Source Energy, the Ein Sophic Light, is the highest, purest form of Love and Light energy with the highest vibration. It is the energy of centropy, harmonic evolution, and balance. When we align with life-affirming values and beliefs, we begin to put out a higher vibration. When we cultivate a Source-driven intentional life, we live longer, happier lives, and everything and everyone around us benefits from that vibration as we become an extension of the regenerative energy.

Our vibration and energy signature are constantly in flux due to many forces that affect our vibration. The food we eat, the environments we are in, the people we are around, the thoughts we think, and even our simple intention in each moment create immediate shifts in our vibrational output. As we become sensitive to subtle energies, we begin to grow in discernment of what we attach to and what we release that is not serving our higher aspiration of self-mastery.

- Knowing that all manifestations on all planes of Creation are vibrational, how can you use your will, the power of focused thought and intent, to raise the frequency of your manifestations? What actions can you take to clear out and reconcile lower vibrational energies to raise the frequency of the bodymind complex, your environment, and your manifested experiences?

Law of Perpetual Transmutation

There is the saying that "the only thing constant is change." Everything is in a constant state of change and evolution. Nothing stays the same. All experiences arise, abide, and dissolve in a continuous state of transformation. We, and everything in the universe, are constantly receiving, transmuting, and transmitting energy. We see this in the cycles of the breath, the stages of our life, the change of the seasons, and so on. Everything is meant to evolve and transform. Everything is evolving in a constant dance.

This is good news for someone who is experiencing something negative and painful. Having faith and KNOWING that everything will change eventually is sometimes all that is needed to shift someone from a low-vibrational, limited perspective to a higher, more enjoyable state.

- Where do you hold fixed judgments or negative internal images? Where do you hold yourself or others in limitation? Where are you static or holding yourself back from evolving? How can you use this Law to allow thought to evolve beyond its current preconceived notions and assumptions and into openness and higher understanding?

Law of Polarity

Everything in Creation has an opposite. Everything in the physical, mental, and emotional realms has a dual opposite. There are two sides to every coin. There are two ends of a stick. Everything is, and it is not. For every problem, there is a solution. We know what we do not want because we know what we do want. Life is full-spectrum so that each side of the polarity can be understood more deeply by the opposite expression. In truth, the opposites of anything are truly the same but with varying degrees of polarity in expression which is interpreted through different points of perspective. What is a blessing for one person may seem like a curse to another. What is enjoyable for one may be uncomfortable for another.

The book *A Course in Miracles* defines a "miracle" as a change in perspective which fundamentally is a change of polarity in our understanding of a situation. We can consciously respond to uncomfortable or negative situations by reaching for higher, positively-charged thinking that empowers us as architects and manifesters of our reality.

Humanity has the choice of being in service-to-self (negatively polarized) or service-to-all (positively polarized). This polarity plays out in the realm of our personality when we behave in a way that serves our egoic identity or from a place of altruistic action that honors all of Life.

- Where do you hold negatively polarized perspectives (i.e., judgment, resentment, pessimism, aggression, etc.)? Using the power of mental alchemy, how can you move up the vibrational scale towards mental neutrality or more positively polarized perspectives (e.g., inspiration, empowerment, sovereignty) that are rooted in nonviolence and compassionate understanding?

Law of Relativity

It is what it is. Nothing in life has any meaning except for the meaning we give to it. Nothing is good. Nothing is bad. It just "is" until we filter our experience through our belief systems, compare it to other experiences, and project meaning onto it.

- How do you project meaning onto people, places, and events? Good? Bad? Holy? Loveable? Unlovable? Damned? Evil? These judgments, interpretations, and biases are reflections of your consciousness.

Law of Rhythm

Everything moves and vibrates in rhythms and patterns. We have seasons, anniversaries, heartbeats, weather patterns, music, life cycles, and so on. The Multiverse can be imagined as an orchestral masterpiece of symbiotic rhythms and patterns, with each sphere of creation having its own set of tones and layers within the symphonic composition of the Multiverse.

When we become aware of rhythms and patterns that are out of tune, out of harmony, we can shift our intention and attention and consciously choose to focus our energies in a way that establishes new rhythms and patterns that support balance and flow. When our negative rhythms are brought into the light of our awareness, we can practice patience with ourselves and our manifestation and use spiritual wisdom to guide us into a new rhythm. This begins a spiral pattern of change that diffuses the backward pull of the negative, entropic thought-form energy. Over time, with consistent influence from our practice of aligning with spiritual wisdom, we move forward into a new rhythm that builds more and more momentum in a positive direction.

- What are the triggers that take you into cycles of suffering? How can you use mental neutrality (Law of Polarity) to "step off the wheel" and create a new response and a new outcome?
- How can you align with Earth's rhythms and the astrological movements in a way that is intentional and sacred? Sunrise? Sunset? New Moon? Full Moon? Solstices? Equinoxes?

Law of Causality: Cause and Effect

Every cause has an effect, every effect has a cause, and nothing exists outside of this universal law. These words describe the interconnectedness of phenomena in manifestation across the physical, etheric, mental, and spiritual planes.

"Luck" and "chance" are words that are describing where one does not understand the cause. The concept of "luck" is a superstitious belief based on the limited consciousness of the Higher Order. Nothing happens by chance but occurs because of infinite inputs from infinite chains of events from the physical, etheric, mental, and spiritual planes which all lead back to Source, the original Cause to all effects.

Newton's Third Law of Motion states that there is an equal and opposite reaction for every action. There is a cause to the effect, and nothing is happening by itself. Every intention we carry and thought we think creates a response in one or more planes of Creation.

This law is sometimes called the Law of Karma. Karma teaches us responsibility, not morality. Responsibility can be defined as the ability to respond to our manifestation in alignment with the greater good and light of our inner Source. It is often mistaken as a morality system of good and bad. This perspective of karma is a duality-based control system that distorts the Eternal Love and Light of Source. There is no judgment from the higher realms, only grace and support in evolving to higher states of glory.

- Are there areas of your life that you have begrudgingly accepted that they will not change? Do you feel powerless in relation to the will of the government, your spouse, your boss, financial state, your family karma? How can you step off the wheel of karma, the wheel of suffering and ignorance, and take back your power as a sovereign creator? How can you be an agent of change in your own life and community?

Law of Gender and Divine Androgyny

Everything in Creation contains masculine and feminine qualities and attributes. This manifests on all levels and planes of Creation. Feminine energies are associated with receptivity, creativity, reflection, magnetism, and so on. Masculine energies are associated with action, willpower, electricity, and assertiveness. When the feminine qualities overpower the masculine, we may get stuck in receptivity and reflection without taking action. When the masculine energies of our personality and consciousness are strongest, we may act too quickly without considering and envisioning our options. Divine Androgyny is the balance, union, and harmony of masculine and feminine principles in our consciousness. As we heal and integrate all parts of our Divine Masculine and Divine Feminine qualities, we embody the Love, Power, and Wisdom of Source.

The Law of Gender in terms of the physical sex of a human is seen in both male and female bodies and reproductive systems. In terms of gender, we have many expressions of masculine and feminine genders in male, female, and intersex humans. Many starseeds and the new children coming in have spent lifetimes as androgynous beings and find it restrictive to try to fit into a polarized system. Our species is a kaleidoscope of gender expressions that should be acknowledged and celebrated!

- Can you identify the masculine and feminine traits of your personality? Are there any areas of your life where the polarity of these principles is imbalanced? Are there areas where you need to be more reflective, nurturing, intuitive, sensual, or still? Are there areas where you need to be more direct, firm, structured, or goal-driven?

Law of Abundance

We exist within a unified field of energy that is endless and eternal. What we experience within that field is a projection of our own beliefs and perspectives. When we are experiencing lack, we are in a state where we have cut ourselves off from the limitless field of Creation and the Higher Power. As we refine our vibrations and update our understanding of Creation, we begin to allow more of the higher manifestations of ease, gratitude, patience, trust, and love into our experience. As we open to the Higher Love of Source, we begin to work with the power that creates universes and begin to shed all ideas of limitation and lack.

- Where can you acknowledge and affirm abundance NOW in your life? Count your blessings. Make a gratitude list.
- Where are you experiencing lack in your life (e.g., finances, relationships, opportunities) and how can you use mental alchemy to manifest higher levels of abundance?

Law of Attraction

Like attracts like. We attract into our reality that which we are a match to vibrationally in a process called manifestation. What we manifest is an indicator of where we are in vibration and belief. The universe gives us exactly what we ask for energetically in our dominant and consistent vibrations, intentions, and beliefs. Along the path of manifesting the higher aspirations, we attract into our reality experiences that show us subconscious beliefs that are out of alignment with our desired manifestation. When we experience the manifestation of something unwanted, we can bring awareness into our subconscious beliefs and limiting patterns to upgrade our perspectives and overall vibration which creates the potential for higher manifestations within the hologram of our reality.

Our desires and emotional investments in our thoughts magnetize experiences into our reality. Earth is a dense environment filled with contrasting experiences, some wanted and some unwanted. Desire is necessary for creation, or else we would simply rest in stillness and never accomplish anything more. Some desires satisfy our false self, and some satisfy our higher calling. Some desires are from an attempt to overpower and devour, and some desires honor free will, connection, and spiritual growth. There is nothing inherently wrong with desire, yet we should grow in awareness of where that desire emerges from and the intentions behind it.

- How can you use the power of your mind to generate positive momentum towards your desired goals? Spend time visualizing and feeling the emotions of your desired outcome as if it is already received. Feel the power of this pre-matter creation and trust that the universe is assisting you in creating this outcome. Conjure your future reality in the NOW by using the power of spoken word to describe how you are bringing this dream into reality while simultaneously holding the internal image of it already manifested.

Law of Resonance

Everything within an environment entrains to and evolves toward the dominant vibration. Every person has various vibrations happening simultaneously within their experience. While we may have a vibration of love in our hearts, we may also have a vibration of fear that reduces our overall vibrational frequency. If we want to be in a higher vibration, it is vital that we clear and reconcile our lower vibrations to align with wholeness, joy, and freedom.

The power behind manifestation is subtle energy and vibration. As we grow on our path of mastery, we become powerful deliberate creators. The Law of Resonance shows that we can transform our lower energies so that our dominant vibration is high in frequency and aligned with Love and Wisdom. The Law of Attraction draws into our reality that which we are a match to so that we can understand our vibrational output and do the work to raise in vibration.

Those who deny the existence of their shadow and try to be "positive vibes only" spiritually bypass their suffering. This only perpetuates more experiences of suffering because they still hold lower vibrational attitudes in their subconscious. When someone decides to consciously do "shadow work," they can refine their overall vibration and manifest more of what they truly desire in a faster process. This path may seem more painful, but it requires less effort over time and eliminates unnecessarily prolonged cycles of suffering. Illuminated Quantum Healing makes shadow work easy to do, enjoyable, and even one session can process a lot of the self-defeating patterns that cause suffering and illness.

Law of Compensation/Reciprocity

What you give, you get back. What you sow, you reap. What goes around comes around. What is important here is if the action is born from love or fear. What you give in love with the vibration of abundance comes back as love from the universe, possibly through another person, place, or experience. What you give out in fear, doubt, and scarcity will always come back as a reflection of that energy. In karma yoga, the path of service and altruistic action, everything is to be done in service of life without expectations of reward. You simply perform an action with love in your heart for the sake of doing it, not because it somehow benefits you now or in the future. That being said, selfless service is one of the best ways to cancel negative karma.

- Are there areas in your life where you are primarily acting for self-serving benefit where you can instead take the approach of selfless service and altruistic action?

Law of Action

This law describes how we must act on our dreams and desires to bring them into reality. Newton's First Law of Motion relates to inertia and states that an object will stay at rest or in motion until it is influenced by another force. Your input is essential for you to get what you want from your life. To manifest our higher aspirations, we can apply consistent intention, thought, speech, and action in the direction of that aspiration. Nothing changes if nothing changes, and we are the creators of change in our reality.

Newton's Second Law of Motion relates to momentum and states that acceleration is parallel and directly proportional to force. The more you consistently practice a new way of thinking, feeling, and acting, the more momentum you pick up and the faster that change will happen. You can further accelerate your growth by being surrounded by a community of those who are excited about and interested in your growth.

- Where can you grow in disciplined focus and consistency to achieve your goals and manifest your dreams?
- What are your gifts, talents and strengths? How can you use them more dynamically in your life to manifest your highest destiny and serve the greater good?

As we practice acknowledging and applying these Laws of the Universe, we begin to form our life into a higher expression. We can step out of mundane biological evolution and endless karmic cycles and live in a world of magic and alchemy. We can become conscious extensions of Universal Law and evolve out of the ordinary into the extraordinary. We can use the Universal Laws to unshackle ourselves from creations born from habit into a visionary path of artistry and deliberate creation.

SEVEN

Ascension and Descension Cycles of Consciousness

All of life is in a constant state of evolution. Forms come into existence for some time and then they evolve into something different. Nothing is static. Within this dynamic flow of evolution and devolution exists patterns and cycles of change, evolutionary rhythms that guide manifestation in an eternal dance. Imagine the gears of the clock with many different timings of revolutions all contributing to the grand turning of time. Each segment of time is a container for certain processes to occur that affect the All. Let us look at the cycles of change on the planet and how human consciousness evolves through these interrelated time cycles.

Day and Night

Gaia, our beloved planet Earth, spins around its axis, creating our perception of day and night. We have limited hours of daylight during this creation cycle to activate our intentions and work towards our goals. As day fades into night, we begin to unwind and prepare for sleep so we can rejuvenate for our next segment of creation. Each day is a new beginning on our path of learning and expansion.

Four Seasons of the Year

Earth spins around the Sun creating the seasons of spring, summer, autumn, and winter. We can see this as one giant breath cycle of the Earth as life explodes into growth and slowly fades into stages of hibernation and decomposition before beginning the cycle all over again.

Spring in one hemisphere is like the Earth's inhale as life bursts into creative flow as the Earth's surface is warmed by the Sun and the hours of the day grow longer. Seeds are planted, and inspiration gives birth to new creative projects and ventures.

During the summer segment, we tend to the seeds we have sown and use the fire of the long summer days to put consistent action into our creations. This is a time of exploration and community as everyone comes into the Sun for fun and creative play.

We finalize our creative projects during the autumn segment and begin to harvest the fruits of our labor in preparation for winter. This is a perfect time to trim back the decaying parts of ourselves that inhibit our creative process.

As winter approaches and daylight hours shorten, we retreat inward for contemplation and meditation. This is a perfect time for dreaming and visioning what we want to create in our next journey around the Sun.

The Great Year: Precession of the Equinoxes

The Precession of the Equinoxes, or the axial precession, is the third movement of the Earth. It travels with our solar system around a Central Sun, commonly thought to be Alcyone in the constellation of seven stars commonly known as the Pleiades.

Different cultures and groups have different ways of measuring the Precession of the Equinoxes. It is commonly agreed that this cycle takes approximately 26,000 years. As the Earth moves around this spiral, the Earth's north and south celestial poles seem to make circles against the darkness of space as the spheroid shape of the Earth is pulled on by the magnetic force of the Sun, causing a "wobble" in our rotation. Moving just like a giant gyroscope, this wobble slowly changes our seasons' timing and the alignment of the Earth with a North Star. Our North Star changes during the wobble, alternating between Vega and Polaris in cycles of 13,000 years. Earth is currently aligned with Polaris, but it will align with Vega in the constellation of Lyra in the future.

The Precession of the Equinoxes is segmented and measured by the Sun's timing during the Vernal Equinox in the Northern Hemisphere as the Sun seemingly travels backward through the 12 zodiac constellations. Within the Great Year, each astrological age or Great Month, rises and falls in a timeframe that lasts approximately 2,166 years.

The 26,000-year cycle can be looked at as 13,000 years of waking up, called Ascension, and 13,000 years of falling asleep in consciousness, called

Descension. The Sanskrit traditions segment the Great Year into four eras called yugas, which describe the Golden Ages of Consciousness (*Satya Yuga*), where perfect Unity and Divine Paradise exist on the Earth. These Golden Ages slowly begin to erode as humanity's consciousness begins to deepen into sleep (*Treta* and *Dvapara Yugas*). War and pestilence begin to cover the Earth, and shadow invades humanity's heart and consciousness. Disease and degradation devolve us until we reach the apex of a Dark Age of Consciousness (*Kali Yuga*). Slowly, the spiritual sun begins to rise in humanity's hearts as consciousness begins to wake up and remember its divinity as humanity ascends through the Dvapara and Treta Yugas to shine in the full glory of the Age of Truth, the Satya Yuga.

Dark Ages and Descension Cycles

Ascension leader Gigi Young made a wonderful video summarizing the shifting of astrological ages that inspired these next summaries. She has a wonderful way of describing esoteric knowledge in a simple way.

During the descension cycles, darkness and distortion begin to infiltrate human consciousness as we move into The Forgetting. Wisdom gives way to rational thought and, eventually, ignorance as we become completely devoid of spiritual light and higher consciousness. During this time, humanity needs to put forth great effort into spiritual growth as the veil begins to thicken and distort our perception of the Divine. During this time, our commitment to the Light is tested as we endure trials and tribulations, accruing negative karma and a "pain body" from repetitive cycles of suffering and delusion. Higher consciousness connection gives way to fear and superstition, and individual spirituality becomes dogmatic religion as we forget our True Nature and believe God to be outside of ourselves.

In descension cycles, times of The Forgetting, we see an increase in the shadow of our consciousness as the exalted masculine and feminine parts of our consciousness begin to decay from the absence of spiritual light. The Divine Masculine energy begins to distort and overpower the Divine Feminine. The Goddess and Divine Feminine archetypes lose their value, and the Godhead is typically seen as male. Emotions and intuition lose importance to analytical thinking and science as humanity moves from the unity of the heart to the duality of the mind. The feminine energy in men and women is repressed and oppressed. Disease, famine, and war begin to spread across the Earth as our collective inner world is outpictured in Earth's reality. As the world darkens spiritually, nobility decays into political corruption as unity crumbles into domination and trickery.

During these times, spiritual truth is only taught to the elect, and many noble people dedicate their lives to protecting the Divine Feminine in all forms during these dark times. We can look to the most recent Dark Ages to see the burning of sacred books, the witch trials, slavery, and even God being externalized and personified as a vengeful, jealous man who destroys those who do not obey him. It is during these times that advanced spiritual beings from the higher realms incarnate to protect the sacred teachings as humanity moves through these times of density.

Golden Ages and Ascension Cycles

At the end of the Dark Ages, the spiritual light begins to build as we begin to remember our divinity, and the transformative power of ascension begins to awaken in our hearts and consciousness once more.

During ascension cycles, we see a rise in the Divine Feminine within humanity. Spirituality heightens as people begin to connect with the Divine through the development and resurgence of ritual and spiritual practices. The veil thins between the physical and spiritual realms, and we can access Spirit with increasing ease. Healing practices are cultivated and shared to heal the karmas and disease developed through our unconscious conditioning and habits during the Dark Ages.

Ascension cycles move us towards a matriarchal society where we begin to acknowledge the Feminine Aspect of Source, the Goddess, the Holy Spirit. It is at this time that we see a softening in the masculine energies, and the feminine energies begin to rise in the consciousness of humanity as we remember our purity and divine identity. On the New Earth, we will live in balance with the exalted expressions and union of Divine Masculine and Divine Feminine working together towards higher and higher harmony.

Matriarchal societies highly value emotions and intuition, and spirituality tends to focus more on cycles of the Moon and the fertility of nature because we see ourselves as part of the cosmic and Earth rhythms. This is a time of nurturing and the return of "white magic" that inspires harmony and unity. Women begin to find their voices and fill positions of leadership, leading humanity back to their hearts. Men become more compassionate and noble. Spiritual light begins to pervade humanity's consciousness. The Divine Masculine begins to heal and return to balance, and all gender expressions begin to walk together towards common goals of peace and balance.

During these high times, creativity and sensuality flourish as we tune into our creative, divine power. This is a time of discovery as we release the Dark Ages' shadows and move into higher experiences of radiant glory and opulence.

Astrological Ages

Each ascension and descension phase takes on the qualities of the zodiac sign that Earth and our Sun align with during the Spring Equinox in the Northern Hemisphere. We can look at the high points and low points of society during various periods of civilizations to understand what astrological age we were in at that time.

The birthing of each new astrological age challenges the practices and beliefs of the previous age. Each transition tests our ability to adapt to the shifting tide. This is when the "wheat is separated from the chaff" as revolutions and uprisings emerge from the shift in consciousness, and old ideas are tested by visionary thoughts of the dawning of the new astrological age.

We have been in an ascension phase for some time now and are shifting out of the Age of Pisces symbolized by the symbol of the fish connected to Christ Jesus's life and into the Age of Aquarius, the beginning of our next Golden Age as the redemptive power of the Holy Spirit is dispensed throughout the Earth to return Earth and humanity to the original divine blueprint.

The Age of Aquarius

The sign of Aquarius is the sign of the Water Bearer pouring consciousness and life-giving water onto Earth's soil. As we shift into the Aquarian Age, we are starting to see a rise in humanitarian efforts as we begin to think globally and holistically. We see a rise in visionary and futuristic creations as our imaginations burst with creativity. There is a deep drive for transformation as humanity rejects ideas of limitation and control. We are becoming independent and empowered creators, rebellious against the stagnant and controlling ways of the past. We are beginning to see rapid technological progress on Earth and a growing desire to travel amongst the stars. There is a strengthening of inner discipline as we begin to actualize our visionary dreams and ideals by refining and unifying our body, mind, and inner Source.

During this time, we should question everything we have believed to be true. While the expansion of ascension can be exhilarating, we need to exercise prudence to discern what beliefs and societal structures truly support our highest aspirations as individuals and as collectives. As we transition out of the Piscean Age and into the Age of Aquarius, many shadows will come up into our conscious awareness that have been hidden in our individual and collective unconscious memory. This will coincide with the revealing of the efforts by the negatively polarized groups and individuals who wish to keep humanity from awakening to our True Nature. There will come a time where these control systems will no longer be able to work their dark magic on humanity's consciousness and full disclosure will occur. Humanity will see how we have been kept in the dark of ignorance by the controlling elite cabal systems and from there, we will create a New Earth with true freedom for all!

Photon Belt

Another influence over planetary ascension is what is called the Photon Belt. It has been mentioned a few times in sessions, but I have not yet asked many questions specific to it. I will give a brief summary of my understanding of it based on the research I have done online, comparing it to what has been said in sessions.

The Photon Belt is said to be a band of radiation encircling the Pleiades. As our solar system travels around Alcyone, it intersects this band of light two times. The last time the Earth crossed the Photon Belt would have been in the times of the ancient lost culture of Atlantis approximately 13,000 years ago. When we pass through the belt, all distortion is brought to the surface to be purified by the Light. It takes approximately 2,000 years to journey through this multidimensional light field. Crossing the threshold is an initiation to see if we are ready to release all our shadows and ascend to the next level of experience. In Atlantis, we did not make the mark which caused us to implode on our own consciousness. Humanity still wanted to "play God" and live out of integrity. So, humanity had to start our consciousness development all over again. More of this is discussed later in this book.

We started traveling through this band of light around 2012 and will continue through it for the next 2,000 years. Every shadow will be purified and the "wheat will be separated from the chaff" as only those who can raise their frequency will continue with their current physical life. I have been assured many times that humanity and the Earth WILL make it this time and that the Earth will ascend into her Fourth Density form taking with her all who have aligned with this ascension pathway through the love and openness in their hearts. Truly, humanity's heart is currently being weighed against the Feather of Truth!

The Age of Aquarius ushers in the beginning of our next ascent into the Golden Era, and it comes with many challenges as we are forced to choose between adaptation or decay. Each of us gets to choose between truth and divinity's upward spiral or to continue down the death spiral of entropy and ignorance. Not a single person on this planet is insignificant, as we all play our role in contributing to our collective future. No one knows the exact details and chain of events that lay ahead of us, and probabilities and timelines of events are constantly in flux. It is up to each of us to ignite the fire of our inner Source and walk through this collapsing paradigm into the next Golden Age of Gaia.

Other cycles exist beyond the Precession of the Equinoxes as infinite alignments and patterns play out as the myriad of galaxies, stars, and planets spiral around the Great Central Sun of this universe. As humanity moves into the Age of Aquarius, we are about to complete a much larger cycle that culminates with a Grand Reset of Life on planet Earth via the Great Solar Flash. Humanity is about to take a quantum leap in consciousness and rapidly ascend to the greatness seen in the glorious Golden Age of Lemuria, the purest high-consciousness civilization that existed upon the Earth.

All karma must and will be balanced as we manifest New Earth and become a People of Light!

EIGHT

Ascension Symptom Care

Lightbody ascension practices are found in many ancient cultures, especially in India, Tibet, and Ancient Egypt. The systems focus on transformation by refining the physical, vital, emotional, mental, intuitional, intellectual, and spiritual bodies so that a being embodies Divine Light and their Divine I AM Presence. As we clear our lower energies, we make way for the Light of the Higher Realms to descend into our physical vessel so that we radiate Light and Truth out into the world.

In the past, once an initiate reached a high enough vibration and the highest level of enlightenment they could reach in the body, they would consciously shed the body to continue learning in the higher realms in their Lightbody. Sometimes they would go into a trance and consciously leave the body, or some highly advanced initiates who could control the frequency of their cells would spin them faster and faster until they shifted beyond the visible light spectrum into the higher realms as their physical body dissolved into thin air. Yeshua ben Joseph (Jesus) made this ascension process popular, but it has also been documented and written about by other cultures, especially the Egyptians and Tibetan Buddhists.

What is different about our upcoming ascension is that we will be transforming our physical body into a lighter form and taking it with us into the next dimension of consciousness and reality. What was once only available to select initiates through arduous purification and healing practices in secluded temples and monasteries is now available to all people committed to compassionate heart-based living and have done the work to raise their overall vibration.

As we prepare for Gaia's transformation from Third Density Earth to Fourth Density Gaia, our DNA is being restored back to the Adamic form, the original pristine human Lightbody. Many alterations have been made to the human DNA throughout humanity's time on Earth, and we are in a purging process of all the distortions stored within our multidimensional genetic structure and sequencing.

These distortions are the product of genetic implantation from other star races, ancestral memory, mental fields absorbed from the collective thought patterns, toxicity from our environments, damage from the cataclysm of Atlantis, and more. As these ascension energies move through our system, they clear any blockages we have accrued so that we can hold more light. This can appear as cold/flu-like symptoms, increased body heat, heightened intuition, foggy mind, dizziness, chest pain, digestive issues, vivid dreams, emotional purging, paranormal experiences, ringing in the ears, dehydration, and more.

Below is a list of guidelines to support the ascension and Lightbody activation and recalibration processes. This is not meant to be "medical advice" but speaks to common experiences held by myself and others in the global ascension community.

If you feel that you are unhealthy and at risk for serious health concerns, please see a medical professional. I highly recommend seeing a medical professional who treats clients holistically. Western medicine is trained to focus on symptoms. Eastern medicine and holistic healthcare professionals are trained to look for root causes and treat entire systems to bring the body back into homeostasis.

Meditation: Calling in Light

Meditation is a crucial step in this process. Developing self-awareness helps you discern what is best for your path so that you can release what no longer serves you. Meditation practices that utilize conscious breathing are some of the best tools to ground your energy, clear out stagnant energy, and revitalize your personal energy field as fresh life force enters through the breath. Visualizing clear, bright light moving through the body helps raise the body's vibration and transform dense energy into a more refined and clear energy signature. Let the sunshine in!

Dehydration

Many health problems stem from chronic dehydration. Drink plenty of fresh spring water to hydrate the tissues and cells of the body. Municipal water sources often contain chlorine, fluoride, or other chemicals that poison our bodies and mind. Adding trace-mineral hydration salts to your water helps the water absorb into the cells. Also, consider taking a "cell salt" supplement to support healthy cellular function. Adding magnesium to your hydration practice will also help with discomfort in the chest/heart region when assimilating the energies. This will also help with headaches and anxious feelings.

Silica Supplements

It has been recommended that we all take silica supplements to support our body's transition from being carbon-based to a crystalline, silica-based Lightbody. This will help with achy joints, cognitive functioning, and more.

Essential Oils and Plant Medicine

Nature knows best. Herbs and plant extracts work with our body's cells and consciousness to bring our systems into homeostasis. This includes medicines like psylocibin, cannabis, hemp, kava, and other plant allies to help us soothe the ascension process and connect with higher intelligence for healing and transformation. Of course, intention and safety are important for all medicine journeys. Keep it sacred!

High-quality essential oils that are certified pure and organic safely work with the body's cells to support the body's natural ability to heal itself. Some oils can be taken internally, and most are safe for topical and aromatic use. Check with each oil's health and protocol guidelines to understand how to use the oil safely and properly.

When using topically, consider using a vegetable/nut-based carrier oil to help spread the essential oil across the skin. If an essential oil is applied topically and causes irritation, dilute and clean with a carrier oil. Do not use water as this drives the essential oil further into the tissue.

Detoxify the Body

Physical symptoms include a variety of detoxification symptoms as toxins are released from the body. You may notice a diet change as the body craves fresh, organic fruits and vegetables and less meat. There will not be meat or killing of any kind when we shift to the New Earth consciousness.

Everyone should follow their own guidance about what nourishment their body needs at any given time. Periodic fasting can help the elimination process as well as eating a naturally detoxifying diet. Eating fresh greens fills the body systems with biophotons, light particles to support healthy system functionality. Switch to natural, organic products versus products with toxic chemical ingredients to reduce your organs' toxic load. You may feel guided to do a cleanse regimen like a liver cleanse or kidney cleanse, or a heavy metal detox to help the body eliminate toxins.

Cellular Oxidation

Radiation from cosmic energies, solar events, 5G radiation, and other energies puts stress on our body's cells. Increase antioxidant intake and supplements that promote cellular health and reverse the effects of oxidative stress.

Alkalize the Body

Reduce the body's acidity to reduce inflammation and support the body's natural ability to heal itself. This includes eating a mostly "sattvic" diet or a "yogic diet" which is simple and free from processed ingredients and synthetics. Practices like drinking apple cider vinegar, fresh lemon juice, or citrus essential oils help to break apart and eliminate toxic build-up in the body.

Detoxify People, Places, and Things

Spend less and less time around people that are vexatious to your system. Find like-minded people who are loving and gentle to spend your time with. Avoid places with highly charged energies when you are feeling extra sensitive. Many find that they need to spend more quality time alone or with their pets and limit their social interactions to focus on their own healing and expansion. Declutter your home to free up stagnant energy. As within, so without!

Rest and Sleep

Listen to the body and honor when it is asking for rest. At times, the body will need much more rest and sleep as it adjusts to the shifting frequencies. Sometimes, you may not be able to sleep because of the rush of plasma entering your field from the ascension energies. Be gentle with yourself. Natural sleep aids, teas, and herbal supplements help the body stay in deeper sleep to feel refreshed when you awaken. Chamomile and lavender can help you prepare for a deep night's rest.

Get Into Nature

Nature has a grounding and centering effect on our consciousness and nervous system. Take frequent trips into nature away from people, pollution, and technology. "Earthing" or walking barefoot on the ground helps to ground pent-up energy in your nervous system, leaving you feeling grounded and clear. If you cannot stand on soil, you can stand on a layer of sea salt to ground your energy. Use a container to stand in so that you do not make a mess!

Ringing in the Ears

The electromagnetic fields of the Earth and the planetary grid will be unstable in the process, as will our own energetic field. The ringing of the ears is common for people at different times as waves of plasma enter the Earth. Some people find themselves to be extra sensitive to Electromagnetic Frequencies (EMFs). Many devices and crystals (e.g., shungite) are available to help reduce the negative effects of EMFs on the body and consciousness. It is suggested that we take as much time as we can to get off our devices, out of range of Wi-Fi and cell towers, and immerse ourselves in the regenerative field of Nature. Return to the wild and wonderful!

Headaches, Dizziness, and Cognitive Functioning

These energies affect our minds as we shed lower beliefs and upgrade the brain's anatomy and cognitive functioning. This could manifest as states of confusion and feeling sensations in the brain, including headaches, energy movement, and pulsations.

Dizziness and headaches can be a sign that you need more water and need to ground excess energy. Consciously ground the energy through intention and meditative practices or walk barefoot on the earth. Increase water intake and rest until the dizziness subsides. Add hydration salts, trace minerals, cellular salts, and silica supplements to support the process. Essential oils like peppermint and lavender help soothe head and neck tension to alleviate pressure in the head.

Digestive System Issues

The digestive system not only processes food to create energy, but the solar plexus digests subtle energy for a variety of processes. Many find that their digestive system is either over or underactive at different times. I recommend using a natural digestive supplement, digestive enzyme supplement, or laying of hands to support the healing process. Essential oils like ginger and peppermint help support healthy digestive processes.

Low Energy and Fatigue

Sometimes, no matter how much you rest, it may not feel like enough. Using invigorating essential oils can boost the mood and increase focus. There are many natural food supplements to use to boost energy like cacao, maca, and spirulina. If you use caffeine, I suggest using tea, especially yerba mate, versus coffee to reduce acidity in the body. Essential oils like peppermint and citrus oils help to lift the mood and focus the mind.

Soaking in Water

Water is a powerful tool to use to ground and clear energy. Find natural sources of water to swim in or soak your feet. Take baths with natural salts and minerals added to the water to help clear and restore. Adding your favorite essential oils, candles, and soft music or recorded meditations helps amplify the bath's healing effects. Frequent showers also help to reinvigorate the senses and clear your personal energy.

Emotional Triggering and Heart Activation

Collective, ancestral, and individual trauma stored within the body's systems and DNA are being reactivated and cleared. Many experience this as a deep churning in the heart, fatigue, vivid dreams, and more. Aromatherapy is one of the quickest natural ways to soothe emotions.

Increased Intuitive Abilities

Intuition, psychic gifts, and multidimensional awareness are increasing rapidly as our lower energies clear out of the chakra and subtle energy systems, creating an expanded empathetic nervous system. To avoid unnecessary suffering and psychic attack, one can cultivate a strong and clear subtle energy system and grow in heart-centered discernment and energetic hygiene.

Vivid and Prophetic Dreams

Many are experiencing vivid dreams as their subconscious works out limiting beliefs and unprocessed trauma in their dreamtime. Some dreams are teaching dreams where people experience themselves in learning environments practicing new skills. Some are healing dreams where people report miraculous, rapid healing often conducted by extraterrestrial beings or higher light beings. Some people are reporting meetings with other souls in their soul group, where Ascension topics are discussed. Some people are reporting that they are being brought aboard spacecraft and introduced to galactic beings and receive updated intel on Earth changes and Ascension information.

Some people do not have any dream recall during the ascension process because the information being discussed in the dreams would keep them from playing out the role they need to in their regular human life. Some people have even traveled to the New Earth or future timelines where they get to experience life after humanity and Earth have ascended.

Each person is different in how they handle this process. Do not judge yourself based on how others are handling it. Also, one minute you can be fine, and the next minute have an emotional purge and a headache. Let the process happen. Make a practice of nourishing yourself.

This process can be intense, but it comes with great benefits! Thank you for facing your shadow and aligning with Truth, Knowledge, and Wisdom. You are so brave!

NINE

Shifting to New Earth

We are now at the final moments before this Grand Shift. From a higher perspective, we are being divided between positive polarity collectives and negative polarity collectives. This means that some are awakening to a higher love within, and others are maintaining a duality-based consciousness and will continue a downward spiral of entropy and destruction, eventually exiting the planet through physical death.

Over the coming years, people will be moving on the planet to the places they have decided to be for these final events leading up to the Main Event Horizon and shift in consciousness. Those who are awakening are beginning to find others who are awakening. Much of this has been happening on the internet, and more and more events and gatherings will be happening across the world as people come together in One Heart. What a cause for celebration as we all begin to see the familiar Light in one another's eyes and awaken to the game we have been playing with ourselves since the beginning of time.

Not everyone is meant to continue with Earth and ascending humanity into this next Age of Light. Their souls will continue their maturation process in other incarnations on other planets where the Third Dimension exists or whatever dimension best serves their growth. Some of these embodied souls are seen as the "villains" and "traitors" that will catalyze and amplify the desire to awaken in the hearts and minds of those who are choosing Love, Light, Unity, and Harmony. The villain archetype is crucial for Ascension. We see this character in Set from Egypt for the resurrection of Osiris and in Judas for the ascension process of Jesus. Each awakening soul is invited to play the role of Collective Messiahship and share the good news of Ascension and the Higher Mysteries so that those who hunger for Truth can be set free from the entropic thought patterns of service-to-self, ancestral trauma, and negative karma.

It is wise to remember that "everything is not what it seems" in this school of illusion. Everything is happening for a Divine Purpose. We are invited to stand as pillars of Unconditional Love and broadcast the messages of New Earth. For those who have ears to listen, let them hear the "good news" of what is to come. Let us all reveal the thought processes and beliefs that have created our own inner tyrant and an inner adversary so that we no longer need to see it outpictured in our reality. Let us choose peace. Let us choose harmony. Let us choose unity. Let us choose Ascension!

Prophecy

Anyone who does intuitive readings can tell you that their prophecies and intuitive understandings are based on energy at that particular moment of the vision or reading. Free will gives us the ability to choose a higher timeline by releasing density and making higher choices. With so many volunteers and support from galactic beings and the higher realms, we have moved beyond much of the death and destruction that has been foretold by prophets and seers of the past. Even modern prophecies are subject to change as we are constantly shifting between probabilities of how this will all play out.

Every action you as an individual or we as a collective make shifts us into different timeline potentials for the unfolding of The Event. Our job is to maintain the highest vibration and the highest vision for the highest potential outcome so that we can guide our collective experience into a more harmonious unfolding. The power is in our hands, minds, and hearts. We can come together as a collective and use the power of focused attention and loving intention to guide us all into peace and unity. The power and potency of positive and empowering prayer holds the keys to manifesting our most desired outcomes. While some cataclysmic events are necessary for this shift to occur, we can avoid unnecessary suffering by coming together in unified prayer. Together, we can create a powerful prayer field to influence weather patterns, seismic activity, and harmonize collective emotional experiences to avoid events that could cause massive suffering and transition to a higher timeline of experience.

There will be those that will stay focused on the doom and gloom narrative that is widely accepted and propagated by world religions. By focusing on the darkness and suffering, they will likely create that experience for themselves on their personal timeline. We, as the human collective, do have the ability to collapse timelines that no longer serve us. We have a choice. It is the same choice that there has always been — between unconditional love and surrender to the Divine Plan or else live in fear, judgment, and inner turmoil. Even when chaotic events are happening around the world, it is up to us to hold the highest outcome in our vision and be unwavering in our ability to hold the Light.

Discernment and False Teachers

Discernment is of the utmost importance at this time. When the energies are high, so are the emotions. Many wild and misleading ideas will be shared amongst the collective. It is up to each individual to grow in the power of discernment to feel what resonates as Truth within them. If a message generates fear or panic within you, walk away from that material. Many religious leaders, government officials, and spiritual teachers will have their shadows brought into the light where they have abused their power, especially those who have claimed to be the voice of God. This includes the ascension community! It is important not to put any human on a pedestal. We are all subject to shadow. Instead, place your faith in your Inner Light and the unfolding of the higher evolutionary plan. For the most part, I have stopped listening to most spiritual teachers and have instead invested time learning to listen to my own internal guidance and the study of sacred texts to grow in my own spiritual capacity. Follow your heart. It knows the way. The mechanics of discernment are taught later in this book in the section about the *vijnanamaya kosha*, the Intellectual Wisdom Body.

Many Are Exiting the Earth School

Once a soul has aligned with an exit plan, no outside force can stop it from exiting. Many people will leave their bodies during these events per their design before entering this life. Every contract has to play out, and a balance must be achieved. As these souls go through their physical death experience, they will support us from the "other side." Another reason people die is that they take their fear and karma out of the Earth realm, which increases the collective vibration of Earth.

As the shadow systems and shadow players are revealed to the masses, many will have to face the fact that they have supported these systems unknowingly and in doing so have supported systems that have killed countless people. I was told that when the truth comes out about the cancer industry, many will be outraged because of all the loved ones they lost from cancer and other illnesses that could have been saved if the controllers had not created the conditions that cause cancer and repressed the healing technologies and medicines. Many people will have to face the fact that they ridiculed us "new agers" and "conspiracy theorists" who were right all along. Disclosure of the shadow system will cause people to have heart attacks from a broken heart; people will kill one another in rage; many will commit suicide or die from psychosis because they cannot live with the truth.

Some people will not be able to hold the vibration of these high energies and die suddenly or quickly decline in health because they have not shed dense energies and will not evolve. Some souls decided they would leave the Earth School as a group, possibly in a natural disaster or casualty of violence. During these times, we will need one another to support each other through the natural grieving processes. This is another reason why we need more people with a higher perspective of death and the afterlife, as many will be looking for answers.

Not everyone is meant to ascend into the New Earth. Some are meant to have simple lives and exit this world for the next journey throughout the cosmos. Ascension involves reconciling judgment within us for those who seem not to be "waking up" or seem to be following the false narrative presented by the controllers. They are offering us an opportunity to release polarized perspectives and be open to nondual understanding. Even the most "evil" people are offering us bitter medicine to grow into deeper compassion and clarity. This does not mean that we condone the actions that cause harm, it just means that we do not have to hold hatred, judgment, or contempt towards them. Every single being here on the planet is serving this great awakening whether they are conscious of it or not. All is Source; all is the One Being experiencing itself in myriad forms and polarities for the purpose of truly "knowing thy Self."

Much grief will sweep through humanity during these next stages. They are the most difficult to bear and many will experience intense grief. Grief is a powerful emotion. It carves deep into the heart and seems to stay around for eternity for some. We can use the power of High Alchemy to use grief as a powerful tool for transformation. I invite us all to use the pain of what is to come to launch us into our sovereign power to reform our reality. Use it to become a voice for the Earth and for those who have suffered under the tyranny of these shadow systems. All of this ends when humanity stands in its power and says ENOUGH!

Rapture

This is a complex multidimensional topic because I have only heard of this a few times. This type of event is not connected to any religion. Since it is a common question, I will share what I have learned through my sessions.

The first point to share is that there will not be a mass disappearance of bodies as depicted in some modern Christian interpretations. The main way of departure will be from people leaving their bodies through physical death as they finish their contracts. This is not a judgment. It is simply part of the plan as they have only agreed to live through so much of the process.

One other type of departure I have heard of, but only once, is the departure of some starseeds. I have heard of two major departures from the planet for souls from other star systems who volunteered to incarnate on Earth as humans to assist in the Great Awakening. Some starseeds are only on the planet to help energetically until a tipping point occurs in our collective consciousness. Once that marker is reached, one large group of people will be taken from the planet, followed by another group a few months later. I have been told that there are twelve "New Earths" including this one that we are all currently on. Each of these planets will be home to different humans and life forms. I do not know much about the other planets as much of my sessions have been focused on the shift of Gaia/Terra from the Third Density to the Fourth, aka the Fifth Dimension. From my understanding, there will be considerably fewer people living on the planet once it finalizes its shift.

In my second meeting with the Council of 24 Elders, I was shown how I would have the capacity to jump between realities or embodiments. It seemed as though I would be able to be in one embodiment in 5D New Earth and then "flip myself inside out" to be in the 3D Earth reality to assist in some way as if I would be living in both realities simultaneously. I still do not completely understand what was shown to me, but I thought I would write about it in case it is helpful for someone. Part of the intention with this book is to have the book printed in physical form so that it would be available for people if timelines split into different experiences of The Event.

It is common for people to question if they are going to "make it." This question is rooted in fear and insecurity and deserves time for reflection and healing so that you can embody the higher love of your Divine Nature. No one is "left behind" which means that you are exactly where you need to be, and Source is with you always. Trust in the process and stay present in your heart.

Potential Timelines of War

As part of the design, service-to-self forces will likely destroy one another as they war against each other to control the planet. War, battles, protests, revolts, riots, and other such events are likely to happen as we get closer to the launch point of the main event — the pulse of Light from our Sun via the Great Central Sun.

This experience of war is for those who agreed to such an experience before incarnating. There will be places of peace and places of conflict. Those who exit the Earth School are simply done with their life contract and will continue to their next incarnation in whatever level of spiritual growth is appropriate for them. The wars and destruction serve as a contrast for those who are awakening to anchor us into knowing that Love and Peace are truly The Way.

True and lasting peace, the Heaven on Earth reality is not possible in the third dimension. This true peace and harmony are found in the fifth-dimensional consciousness. Until then, conflict and duality remain as karmic contracts play out before 5D consciousness fully manifests across the remnant of humanity upon 5D Earth.

My understanding is that there are a few different groups of service-to-self consciousness that are fighting for control of the planet and humanity. The overlord structures coordinate events to create a crisis and suffering and then offer a solution to manipulate people to follow their agenda (problem-reaction-solution). This bait-and-hook method of mind control hijacks the goodwill intentions and actions of the unaware who unknowingly follow the mainstream narrative because they feel that they are helping the situation. Coordinated power outages, food and supply shortages, and other false flag events are planned to create fear in humanity. Those who are connected to their inner truth and higher consciousness connection will be able to see these events for what they truly are, while others will not as they are still under the spell.

This dark initiative is powered through psychological manipulation tactics used through subliminal messaging and suggestion using the trance-induced state created by watching a television or screened device. Phrases are repeated by global leaders, politicians, and other influential people to implant the overlord-approved narrative into the listeners' consciousness which subconsciously programs them to follow the nefarious agenda. The war on consciousness and the battle for dominion over Planet Earth and humanity is real and we are watching it play out in real time.

Collapsing of the Old Systems

All of society's systems are being forced to shift with this energy or crumble to make way for the new. Governments, financial institutions, religious institutions, judicial systems, educational systems, and so on have been used to keep humanity in the lower consciousness and enslaved through various methods. All of these systems will be reconciled over the next years. This is especially true of the collapse of the financial systems which must dissolve so that the Cabal-run control systems that depend on currency to fund their dark projects will run out of financial backing. Humanity will no longer "chase the dollar" to create their worth or security and will instead realize their inherent worth and source all that they need from the quantum field and Gaia.

Governing systems will shift towards councils of representatives who will be selected based on spiritual resonance. In the New Earth, everyone will perform the role that is most in alignment with their soul's path. No more slave jobs! The old system of economics will give way to a quantum-based financial system.

Earth Changes

Parallel to our ascension symptoms, Gaia is going through her own clearing process before she shifts into her higher, lighter form. Volunteers on the surface and galactic beings have been assisting this transition by helping Gaia transmute some of the dense energy built up over millions of years. Seismic and volcanic activity, massive storms, and abnormal weather patterns are likely to increase as the planet's energies and toxic areas are cleansed. This is like a cat or a dog that shakes and shimmies after it gets injured. This natural movement is mirrored by the Earth as Gaia releases her pent-up energy.

Gaia is a powerful and sovereign being. She permits humanity to live upon her and go through the karmic lessons necessary to remember our higher consciousness identity and unity with All. What we see happening with the Earth in terms of climate change is a reflection of the imbalance within us. She is incredibly patient with us. She could shake us all off in a heartbeat if she wanted to! The Controllers have been using the "save the Earth" narrative to convince us to give up our freedoms and to pay more money to fill their bank accounts. If we truly want the Earth to be clean and clear, it is the global elite control systems that need to be dissolved so that the land can be freed up. It is the greed born from service-to-self consciousness that needs to be eradicated. I imagine that the Controllers will use the Earth changes to further their narrative but those who know, who are connected to Spirit and our Earth Mother, will know what is truly occurring.

Crustal shifts, pole shifts, and water displacement will reorient the planet's surface as has happened in previous resets (Lemuria and Atlantis). This will reveal lost temples, lost technologies, and lost artifacts that will remind humanity of its galactic legacy. I was told that the Galactic Federation is working with the tectonic plates to balance the plasma of the core of the Earth to open up telepathic communication with Inner Earth civilizations such as Telos, Agartha, and other civilizations who have been keeping ancient records and protecting advanced technologies from the times of Lemuria and Atlantis specifically for these times. While many humans have already been communicating with Inner Earth beings, physical meetings will begin soon.

I have heard of many big fires around the world as well. I share this information cautiously because I know that we can create the future that we want. It all comes down to the collective consciousness intention and what we have agreed to in our soul contracts before incarnating. Again, I have been told that much of the destruction has been averted already and that Earth changes will not be as severe as once prophesied.

This is a natural process, and there is nothing to fear. You are always where you need to be. If you feel safe, you are safe. If you follow fear, you have the potential to create that outcome. It is up to us to become aware of our fearful tendencies and refine them through Higher Knowledge and Faith. Trust that you are being guided to the right place for the right timing of these events.

It is wise to have some supplies available if power outages or other events occur. Having a few weeks' worth of food, water, and basic supplies can be useful if supply chains are cut off because of these shifts and changes. There are potentials for communication systems and power supplies to go down at different stages. I am told that around this time awakened people will have developed a level of telepathy that will help us communicate without the need for these systems. I am told the Earth changes will begin after the big disclosures have started and sometime after the "illusion of food shortages" and power and communication system failures created by the Cabal. One sign to watch for is the birds. I imagine that before the major Earth changes start, the migratory pathways will be disrupted for birds and other animals like whales and fish who use the electromagnetic pathways to navigate across the Earth.

Safe Havens and New Earth Communities

During this Grand Shift into the next era, safe havens will need to be organized while society goes through its transformation. Some clients speak about schools and centers of education where people will gather soon while various events and changes are happening worldwide. The centers will be high-vibrational environments where people can heal, connect with one another, and support others as people continue to be drawn to these vortexes. We have heard mostly about the first City of Light that will be developed in the Pacific Northwest. This community will be a place for us to create a reality that is "off to the side" from the chaos of the crumbling world. I am not sure exactly how it starts to be manifested, but I have heard that eventually this higher dimensional, etheric, crystalline city that many starseeds see in dreams and meditation will be anchored to the Earth realm. The fires in that region are clearing out the old templates held by the land and the people that need to be released to make room for the new. Many of us have this shared dream of living in healing communities because we designed this plan before we came into the Earth School. Ron and I are excited to be a part of catalyzing that collective dream and manifesting this New Earth community.

Experimental Injections

The rollout and use of the inoculations for Covid-19 are playing a significant part in the Ascension. It is an introduction of a major catalyst that will mean different things for every person, every family, every nation, and the collective story of humanity. Each of us has a unique path, and they are all part of the divine coordination of this ascension event.

In the Bible, the "End Times" prophecy speaks of the "Mark of the Beast" being implemented to control humanity. According to the prophecy, those who do not have the mark would not be able to buy or sell. This control structure sounds remarkably similar to what is happening with the inoculations for Covid-19 and the planned "Vaccine Passports" beginning to be implemented by different governments around the world. While some of the world believes the mainstream media narrative, many see this as an attempt by those in service-to-self consciousness to control and manipulate humanity. Hopefully such an experience of tyrannical control never comes to full manifestation.

The information coming through many quantum healing hypnosis sessions is that these inoculations will negatively affect the health of many people and the worldwide push for vaccination is intended to initiate humanity into another level of overlord control, moving us towards a one world tyrannical government structure. While all of the vaccines will cause issues globally, the bigger issue has to do with the negative fallout from the mRNA gene therapies. At the writing of this book, there are already global reports of myocarditis, pericarditis, rapidly growing aggressive cancers, pulmonary embolism, and sudden death. Anyone who speaks out against the Covid-19 narrative is censored, deplatformed, or silenced. I have a feeling we are just beginning to see the tip of the iceberg in terms of the long-term effects of these injections.

In my sessions, it has been described how the service-to-self forces are using the injections to broadcast low-frequency thought patterning into the injected people, causing a distortion in their minds that lowers their vibration. Something in the injections also connects the injected person to a massive Artificial Intelligence network that extends beyond this planet that tracks the people who have been injected. The signal strength of the AI technology weakens at around six months which is part of the reason for additional booster shots. It was shared that individuals have the ability to recode the AI technology and use it to broadcast light frequencies back into the AI network to assist in the dismantling of that system.

Just because someone took an injection does not necessarily mean they cannot ascend or will get sick. The human body can transmute ANYTHING! That is part of the magnificence of human design. We can overcome every entropic pattern and transform it into the highest light. Although, I certainly would not want to test that capacity on myself! Every time I have asked, there is not yet a technology on the Earth that can reverse the negative fallout, but many physical and subtle body detoxification protocols are being downloaded by lightworkers to assist in detoxification and repair. We have been told that the IQH sessions will assist with this in the future.

It is necessary to have a high light quotient and be in outstanding health and cohesion to transmute this negative technology. Detoxification protocols should be followed for the physical and subtle bodies to clear out the negative components of the injections. The people who have taken these injections must hold no resistance to the divine and clear their various bodies with whatever means necessary. If you have taken the inoculations and wish to clear them from your system, I want you to know that I believe in you and your capacity to turn this situation into something that feeds your spiritual growth and catalyzes your process of liberation. We are here to assist!

Many people have turned from the Love of Source and do not take good care of their bodies and have not awakened to the higher Light. They are going to have the most difficult job transmuting the negative effects of the inoculations and many will leave the planet.

For some people, taking the inoculation is a sign that they are still hypnotized by the narrative that is being pushed on them by the Controllers and are unawakened or just in the beginning stages of awakening. Some will take the inoculation because they have meditated on it and fully trust that this is part of their divine pathway. They are not doing it from lower ego reasons but because of divine guidance. Some will not choose to take the injections because they prefer the organic immunity of the human body and do not want to take any risk.

Now we are at the waiting and witnessing stage as we watch what these inoculations do to humanity. For some, it will be part of their exit plan from the Earth School. As I said, not everyone is meant to ascend. Some are meant to have simple lives and transition out. Many will be born in new bodies on New Earth or continue in other schools. For some, it will be a catalyst for major awakening. For planet Earth, it begins the crumbling of the "sick-for-profit" system and the rising of the people against the forces of darkness and control.

The hardest part for those taking and not taking is not to judge or go into states of fear. Even the inoculations are a test to see if we follow the *maya* into the suffering mind or if we stay in loving conscious awareness. This does not mean that we should not speak out against tyranny and injustice, yet we can let our voices be heard from a place of true empowerment and nonviolence. One who is united with their True Nature is more powerful than one thousand who are not. Together, we ARE THE WINDS OF CHANGE!

Another challenge is that during this bifurcation of consciousness, the Great Divide, most of the people that have taken the inoculations are in a different consciousness that will be difficult for ascension-focused people to be around. Our reality may be offensive to them because we are not under the spell of the mainstream narrative. It is a two-world split. We live in completely different realities side by side. The Old Earth consciousness and the New Earth consciousness occupy the Earth at the same time. I suggest finding your people, those with the Light in their eyes! Those who are on the path of seeking spiritual wisdom and spiritual knowledge. These are the ones you will build the New Earth with!

Artificial Intelligence and Microchip Implants

It is wise to exercise extreme caution when creating Artificial Intelligence as this was already an issue in our past in Atlantis. No matter how tempting, we should not allow any person or group to install microchips or AI technology on or in our human bodies. Our human body is extremely powerful, and the controlling powers will likely attempt to use these types of technology to suppress our awakening. No matter what promises are made, or conveniences may come from integrating the technology into our body, I suggest avoiding such hybridization and transhumanism while humanity still operates in 3D as hijacking is still possible and highly probable. The organic technology of our own human body is capable of telepathy, bilocation, astral travel, telekinesis, levitation, channeling higher consciousness beings, and so much more, and there is no need to give in to the allure of the promises made by Big Tech and other influential powers.

Healing

Energy medicine is the way of the future. One client described being in a safe haven community when global events were in chaos. She described a beam of light emanating from the center of the community that people who were awakening could see and travel towards to find the community. On the grounds of the community were many lightworkers with visible light emanating from their hands. She described Arcturian beings teaching advanced healing practices to humans and medical beds that rapidly heal people at the cellular level.

As the human consciousness opens, we will receive more information through channelings and hypnosis sessions like Illuminated Quantum Healing. We have tremendous amounts of information stored within our Akashic Records, our soul's memory bank. Illuminated Quantum Healing and the other quantum healing hypnosis modalities will be of great support during these next stages to help those who are ascending and to ease the suffering of those who are destined to exit the Earth realm.

Shifting to New Earth Relationships

Individuals are now finishing their karmic contracts in preparation for what is to come. Many people are finishing up karmic relationships and moving into supportive soul family relationships. Instead of the past's power and control techniques, these relationships are supportive, cooperative, and empower individuals to be their own Sovereign Self. Many are reporting that they have left the patterns of karmic romantic relationships of the past and are meeting their Divine Mirror or Twin Flame. More is spoken about twin flames, spiritual partnership, and sacred sexuality in the Sacral Chakra section.

What a relief to be in the presence of others who are genuinely loving and share the same energy signature. In these relationships, we can feel "HOME" through this highly resonant vibration. These beings are familiar to us, and we feel quickly in tune with one another with a depth that cannot be explained by how much physical interaction we have had in this life.

For some, this includes moving to a new home or geographic location, changing careers, or even being in a void space as it is not so clear what the next steps are. The void space is a natural part of this process. Rather than forcing action, it is best to meditate and reflect until you feel divinely guided and inspired to make a choice. Trust that you are being guided every step of the way.

We can look at spiritual relationships in four categories. I cannot remember the origin of the teaching, but I remember the four categories:

1. *Spiritual Teachers and Mentors.* These people embody and exemplify the consciousness and achievements that you aspire to.
2. *Spiritual Friends.* Those at a similar level of spiritual development. Your energetic frequency is similar, and you easily find resonance.
3. *Spiritual Acquaintances.* This type of friendship is where we often feel like mentors more than equals in terms of spiritual growth.
4. This last category is made of those people who are either unawakened and have little to no commonality with us or who could bring harm.

Many people get caught relating to level 3 and level 4 types and feel they are always helping others without reciprocation or feel that they are misunderstood and often get hurt. We should spend the majority of our time with the first two categories to fuel our expansion!

The Unveiling of Technologies and Knowledge

Throughout Earth's history, information has been suppressed and many powerful technologies have been hidden from humanity. This includes artifacts hidden by the Vatican, the Crown, shadow government projects, and secret subterranean programs. Some of this repressed information has been kept by service-to-self, and some has been "lost" until humanity was ready to remember the lost knowledge. In the coming years, these technologies and lost wisdom will return to humanity as we continue the transition to the New Earth reality.

Family of Light Reunion

Many countless spaceships and lightcraft are surrounding the planet at this time that are cloaked using advanced technology. More and more UFO sightings are happening all around the world. Many of these ships exist outside of the standard visible light spectrum. As we raise our vibration, more will begin to see them with their physical eyes or sense them with their inner eye.

Contact is beginning to increase around the planet between humanity and higher consciousness beings. Many people are experiencing apparitions of light beings or extraterrestrials. Many are experiencing them in their dreams or have begun channeling information from these other consciousnesses. The rekindling of relationships between humanity and the higher realms is beginning and will continue to increase. Soon, governments will start to disclose the truth of extraterrestrial visitation in preparation for the reunion of humanity with the Star Nations.

Soon, we will see lightships and spacecraft in our skies as the Star Nations and Hierarchy of Light return to the Earth to usher in the New Era. These beings will teach humanity advancements in Spirituality and Science and teach humanity how to be Cosmic Citizens as we collaborate and interact with many cosmic species and Beings of Light. Inner Earth life will go through a resurfacing process as the vibration rises. While some of these beings may have gotten used to Inner Earth, many are excited to stand with humanity in Unity and Love once more.

The New Earth will be a galactic meeting place for many races from the stars. Many advanced species will come here to share their knowledge and wisdom with humanity and one another. They will bring new plants, new animals, new songs, and new ideas. It will be a cosmic renaissance with everyone sharing from their hearts to uplift all of Life. With no more negative polarity upon the planet, everything will be done in service to the greater good and we will all sail beyond the horizons of everything we have ever conceived, known, or experienced.

While I am writing this book, the news stations have started disclosing more footage of UFOs. I wonder why they are showing this now? Is it truly to disclose what has been intentionally hidden from humanity, or is there a darker agenda behind it? The Controllers may push a false narrative of "threat" from ETs to use emotional manipulation to get humanity to give up more of its freedom. The nefarious ET presence has been here and has played a massive part in the control of humanity and the Earth. The Controllers will try all they can in these final stages to incite fear and separation. I have never heard of a threat of negative ET invasion; however, I have heard through documentaries of shadow project initiatives to stage an ET invasion, but I am assured that the craft we see in the skies are our allies and star family who are here to assist.

New Humanity

Fourth Density humanity of New Earth will not age in the way that we do now. Children will mature into adulthood but will not age beyond that until their soul has completed its mission and has aligned with an exit trajectory. There will be no illness, no suffering, and humanity will have complete freedom of life to create and play. If there are imbalances, clients describe healing beds that use crystalline technology, frequency, and sound to amplify wellness at the cellular/quantum level.

Earth will have fewer seasonal changes and less harshness in weather, and the whole of the planet will be in balance with incredible peace. Earth will return to the "vacation planet" status where no negativity exists, and peace and abundance are experienced by all. The emotional/mental body of humanity will be completely reset, and the lower astral planes will be cleared of distortion and negative entities. This will mean no more tormenting dreams, no more resentment, no more negative internal voices, and no hijacking of consciousness. People will understand one another and be connected through the heart and through telepathic communication with nothing to hide and plenty of love and connection to share. Not only will we share telepathy with one another but also through telepathic communication with Gaia herself and all of her kingdoms of Life. We will not possess the land because we clearly recognize Gaia as our Divine Sister and Earth Mother who provides us happily with all that we need. We will truly be a community of Light experiencing God's Kingdom upon the great cosmic garden of New Earth.

I have had a few powerful experiences where I was shown through vision and through my own body how the body and DNA will evolve into the new form.

I was taken into my body and DNA to show the gigantic mess that has become our DNA. Thousands upon thousands of years of ancestral trauma blocks our DNA. Even our unconscious and trauma-ridden words send entropic vibrations into our cells and tissues which lowers our vibrations in all our systems. Toxins from our food, water, and environment clog and distort the free flow of energy throughout our body. No one on the planet, at this time, has had a fresh start. We all are operating from significantly poisoned and damaged instruments on some level.

The new DNA is clean, clear, and perfectly reset to the Adamic DNA template. This gives the Light of our Divine Nature the freedom to broadcast through our DNA without being distorted or limited. This perfected DNA will open a wide array of abilities that are normal actions from our pure DNA but will seem miraculous from our current consciousness vantage point. We will be able to fly and bilocate to other points on Earth and beyond. Our new, bioluminous instrument will channel divine energy and intention to work harmonically with the consciousness of Gaia. We will be merged in unity consciousness and work symbiotically with all levels of life on the planet to maintain the harmony of our renewed paradise home. We will be able to work with the technology that is the consciousness of Nature and purify the waters, instantly raise forests up from the soil with our heartfelt intentions and psychic gifts. We will work harmoniously with one another as cooperative communities in celebration of Eternal Life and our reunion with our Family of Light.

In the times of Atlantis, we allowed Artificial Intelligence to be created outside of balance and Natural Law. Artificial Intelligence can be a dangerous creation, especially when being created by humans in the third dimension. We should avoid any type of inorganic alterations to our DNA and body before this shift. This includes microchips and inoculations that will be encouraged or even forced upon humanity by controlling forces. While I have heard of people in future timelines who were integrated with AI and microchips, it was way after we had shifted to the higher consciousness.

Housing on the New Earth

When clients visit future timelines of Earth, they describe a vibrant Earth with more color and light. They describe a beautiful aroma as all the waste and pollution has been removed with the support of the Hierarchy of Light. People commonly describe that many people will be living in tree house communities and dome structures. I assume that the energy is much better above ground, and one client shared that in Atlantis, she used a tree as a dimensional transport. Trees are a bridge, just like humans, to higher realms of existence. Some people describe domes and healing temples where sound healing and other spiritual training are conducted. These homes are intimately connected to Nature. One client described vines growing in her home, offering their fruits for her to eat. Another client said that if one were hungry, they could reach towards a tree branch as a flower transformed into an apple for them to eat. Another woman described going off into the forest to deliver a child alone. As she lay by a waterfall, plants, animals, and nature spirits came to her to assist her in pain-free birth.

Estimated Timelines for these Events

Please keep in mind that there is nothing to fear. All is in the hands of Source and Gaia as we make this transition. We are about to move into the big revelations of information which will cause a tremendous amount of emotional turmoil as people put the pieces together and understand what has been happening on the planet. I have heard that eventually a powerful energy wave will cause a split in dimensions, some ascending and the rest will play out the end of their contracts on 3D Earth as they have agreed to before incarnation. After the main event pulse, dramatic Earth changes will occur. After this stage the building up of new systems will take place as we establish harmony in the New Earth civilizations.

There are many timelines possible for this play-out. I am giving dates very loosely with zero attachment to those dates. I have heard through a few clients that much of this Grand Transformation of Life will occur by around 2027-2030 with at least two major energy events occurring before then, possibly one in 2022/2023 which will awaken many to their soul purpose. The Shadow Controllers will not be able to hold humanity down any longer as millions awaken simultaneously. We will be, and already are, an unstoppable Force of Light!

That means that we will be in a constant process of major multidimensional transformation over these next few years and mainstream society will be quite chaotic as all is revealed and transformed. We cannot even imagine the world we are about to manifest. Even as the world seemingly turns dark, I offer you these next transcriptions and visions of the future to help you stay focused on what is ours to inherit.

As we walk through the shadows of this collapsing reality, know in your heart of hearts that you are walking towards everything you have ever wanted and more. Keep your eye on the prize! I am assured over and over again that there is no turning back and that on all timelines Ascension happens. We will be victorious! Don't give up before the miracle!

Now we journey into the Akashic Database!

Akashic Database
Gateway Two Part One: Quantum Origins
Keys for Ancient Cosmology

This section contains a wide variety of Illuminated Quantum Healing session transcriptions describing key figures and events in the history of Creation, galactic history, ancient planetary history, and probable future timelines of New Earth from clients in hypnotic visionary states. I recommend developing a meditation practice parallel to reading this material as the transcripts are deeply activating on multiple levels.

TEN

Quantum Origins

These next chapters take you throughout all of time and space, from the beginning of Creation and into future timelines upon the Earth. I have woven together incredible stories from several clients from various sessions done all throughout the world over a period of five years. This story was given to me piece by piece, allowing time for me to integrate the multidimensional information which included me dismantling many layers of conditioning from my family and culture of origin. If you have challenges assimilating this information, I totally understand as I went through various stages of resistance throughout the process of receiving these incredible stories.

The delivery of the material in this book is to take you from the macrocosm to the microcosm, from the greater cosmic story to the hidden mysteries available in your very own life. I also make an effort to describe the core unity of all wisdom traditions and religions that speak of the one Source of Creation in an effort to unify the individual hearts of humanity as one. I will try my best to the best of my ability to answer the Great Mystery which inherently involves the questions of "What is the meaning and purpose to life?" "Who am I truly?" "What is God? Is he/she/it real, and if so, what is my relationship to him/her/it?" To explain my understanding of these age-old inquiries, I will start where all good stories start, in the beginning. I will start with explaining my understanding of a few concepts and then we will dive into the holographic records of time and space!

Trinitized Unification of Mother Father Child

When I was a teenager, I was tormented and confused by my religious training. I felt that there was much more to understand when it came to God than what I was receiving in my Methodist upbringing. Jesus taught that the "truth shall set you free," so I prayed to God and Jesus to show me the truth so that I could break free from the bondage of dogma and truly understand the Mysteries of the Divine. I prayed for the truth to be revealed to me and soon after, I was guided through inner messaging to stop going to church and began to seek out sources of information that could point me to higher truth. My research of the Divine took me into Buddhism, Vedic traditions of India, Gnosticism, Hermetic Philosophy, Reiki, and many other fractals of wisdom and philosophy as I tried to understand the Great Mystery and to heal myself. My understanding is constantly deepening, evolving, and expanding as I continue to contemplate on the Divine within and the Divine without.

Of all the books I have read regarding spirituality, I have found that the *Pistis Sophia*, an ancient Coptic Gnostic text translated and with commentary by Dr. J.J. Hurtak and *The Book of Knowledge: The Keys of Enoch* by J.J. Hurtak to be the most impactful texts for me in understanding the dual and trinitized principles of the Godhead. I have also been deeply nourished by the Eastern traditions of yoga and tantra which have helped in the cultivation of my own divine light by balancing the polarities within my own being.

Different traditions place different genders on the Supreme Source and some genderize and separate the different functions of the Godhead. In English, we lump it all together and call the Source of Creation and its different functions, God. This word is ambiguous and convoluted as everyone places different limitations and restrictions on what God is and what God is not, and where God is and where God is not. For some it is a word that brings joy, mystery, and inspiration. For others it brings suffering, irritation, and anger.

Some people anthropomorphize the Supreme Source as a Divine Father or a Divine Mother. Neither really felt completely right for me when I thought I could only choose one or the other. What I have come to understand is that the Supreme Source is a unification of both the Mothering and Fathering Principle. What I have come to accept is that the Divine Parent is beyond definition and concept, yet all definitions and concepts are manifestations within the Supreme Be-ness that is the Supreme Source, and that there are infinite pathways and infinite practices of devotion that lead to the realization of that Supreme Source. Whether it is called Moksha, Nirvana, or Salvation, they all lead to the same Source of All and the truth of who we are as Children of God.

It is common for people to humanize the Divine Parent, thinking the Supreme is a man or a woman, yet this is still a limitation and a concept born from human thinking. The reality and function of Source is much more comparable to an open-ended quantum computer system than to a humanoid being sitting in the clouds judging humanity. Source is androgynous, containing both masculine and feminine principles, which we may describe as Divine Androgyny. Source is paradoxically masculine, feminine, both genders, and neither. That which we refer to as the Source of All Creation is unknowable and beyond all concepts, names, and forms. Source is paradoxically transcendental and yet omnipresent while also being impersonal and personal to each of us. It is through this experience of duality that we are able to understand nonduality and the inherent oneness of Life.

Heiros Gamos is a Greek term meaning "sacred marriage" which describes the harmonious unification of the Mothering and Fathering Principles. It is also common to use this in reference to the ceremonial sacred merging that occurs in a deeply connected sexual union between two partners creating a multidimensional experience that bridges the material reality with the spiritual. In modern times, this could describe the unification of the Divine Masculine and Divine Feminine polarities in our subtle energy field which leads to God-realization (hatha-raja yoga) as our human self awakens to our Divine Self. Whether it is from the perspective of the microcosm of the individual or the macrocosm of THE ALL, this interplay of the Divine Masculine and Divine Feminine can be found on all levels of Creation.

God in terms of the Divine Masculine polarity or Fathering Principle could be considered the transcendental, administrative, and unmanifest potential of Creation. The Fathering Principle is beyond all forms, names, and definitions, yet paradoxically contains ALL that has been, is, and will ever be. The Masculine Principle is Consciousness. "He" is the Seer and Knower of Creation, the Indwelling Witness that pervades all of Creation. The Kabbalistic term for God is Ain Soph (En Sof), which can be translated as "limitless" or "no-thing" as it is the unmanifest potential of Creation existing before any concept or manifestation of "other." Each of these definitions describe the infinite, timeless, unmanifest nature of the Divine.

If the Masculine Principle is the Infinite Eternal Mind of Creation which holds the unmanifest potential seed forms and plans of Creation, the Mothering Principle is the creatrix, the cosmic womb which births all names and forms. She is the Cosmic Priestess whose intuitive wisdom and evolutionary forces guide Creation through its many steps and stages within the architecture of the Grand Design! Our beloved planet Gaia perfectly demonstrates the Divine Feminine Principle of regeneration, nurturance, and harmonic balance as she abundantly gives her grace and support for countless levels of Life. When we lay hands, we inherently use the Divine Feminine emanations, the Holy Spirit Shekinah, to regenerate and heal.

The Goddess archetype goes by many names in different traditions, some demonstrating the Goddess in her exalted embodiments and some in her chaotic and tormented expressions. She has been called the "Goddess of a thousand holy names" and many highly developed spiritual beings have incarnated on the Earth to demonstrate the many expressions of the Mothering Principle. The Divine Feminine expressions of Shakti, Pele, Yemoja, Isis, Quan Yin, and Holy Mother Mary each emanate qualities of the Cosmic Mother to remind humanity of our Divine Inheritance as Children of the Divine.

When I asked in sessions how to describe the concept of the Divine Parent to others, the client's Higher Self said that the Fathering Principle is like a human father that travels off to work and we do not see him very often, but he sends us everything we need and visits us from time to time. While the Mother Principle is like a human mother who tends to our every need as we grow and mature.

Some people have a hard time connecting with God in terms of the Fathering Principle because of religious wounding or trauma with men. People in this category tend to have an easier time connecting with the energy of the Goddess because the Mothering Principle is easily accessed through connection to Gaia, Mother Earth. Some have a hard time opening to either because of trauma and difficulty in their relationships with their human mother or human father. Our human parents are temporary experiences while our Cosmic Parents are eternal. For wholeness and balance to be fully achieved, we must reconcile our relationship with both principles by reparenting our consciousness and aligning it with our higher cosmic lineage.

Awakening to our True Nature is awakening to our own Daughtership or Sonship and realizing ourselves as Children of the Most High, progeny of the Limitless. Each of us are seed points who have seemingly departed our Divine Home and taken on the appearance of individuality and multiplicity, having clothed ourselves in many forms with many names as we matured our consciousness enough for God-realization. Paradoxically, we are simultaneously the seeker and that which we are seeking. We are the Child, the Mother, and the Father; the devotee and the Divine; the One and the many.

As we cultivate our divine radiance, we are inherently evoking, balancing, and integrating the Divine Masculine and Divine Feminine principles within. We become extensions of the synthesis of Divine Intention and Divine Evolutionary Force realized in individuated form as awakened Children of God. From this trinitized unification, we naturally tend to the Garden of Life around us and uplift all of Life into elevated states of balance, luminosity, and harmony. This was the original intention of the divine human synthesis upon planet Earth and what we are returning to during this ascension process.

The pathway to God-realization could be broken into four pathways. One is through the Divine Masculine Principle with the focus of awakening to the transcendental, that which is beyond names and forms, existing beyond the physical dimension. Another path focuses on the Divine Feminine Principle, finding the Divine Presence in all of life which eventually awakens us to the transcendental realms. This path is recommended for those who have challenges with the Fathering Principle as the redemptive power of the Divine Feminine, which some call the Holy Spirit, will soothe the consciousness of the aspirant and open it to other facets of Mother Father God. Another path of God-realization is cultivating the Divine Presence within by reconciling and unifying the Divine Masculine and Divine Feminine principles within one's own being to embody Divine Androgyny and come into Divine Self-realization. Yet another path of spiritual awakening is spontaneous awakening to the divine which will certainly happen for many with these ascension waves. Even within each of these categories are infinite pathways to Divine Union.

The ancient Vedic teachings instruct us to first use discernment and self-inquiry to discern and realize that we are not this limited bodymind complex but truly eternal beings of Light. From there, we can see that all of Creation exists within the One Consciousness Reality, or God. From there we begin to realize that all experiences arise, abide, and dissolve within our very Self and we ARE that One Light of Consciousness. We are eternal God Consciousness having a finite experience through the appearance of this bodymind and physical time space dimension.

All streams eventually lead to the ocean. Whether you focus on one path or utilize the wisdom from combining multiple paths, they all lead to the same experience of God-realization and the claiming of your divine inheritance as a Child of God. Find your personal path of devotion that illuminates your soul. Seek out the knowledge that sets you free from bondage. Do all that you do selflessly while meditating on the Divine. Let yourself come ALIVE with your spiritual expression!

The power of God-realization has been exemplified by Yeshua ben Joseph (Christ Jesus), the Buddha, Krishna, and other divine avatars who have come to Earth to demonstrate the capacity of humanity to awaken to the Higher Consciousness Reality. Trust in the teachings of the masters who have walked before you. Follow by their footsteps as you walk your own path up the holy mountain of Ascension.

For simplicity, I combine both the Divine Masculine and Divine Feminine principles into one term, Source. Source is the pure consciousness of the Multiverse, the Eternal Mind, a quantum supercomputer that contains the holographic matrix of Creation. Source is omnipresent, omniscient, and omnipotent. Source is that from which all is born, exists, and dissolves back into having never truly left. It is the indwelling witness of its masterpiece, eternally watching itself cycle through the illusion of separation. This play of Light and Vibration, the Game of Light and Consciousness, is called Leela by the Sanskrit mystics. In this Cosmic Game, God is both the Seer and the Seen, the Witness and the Creation, the Light and the Dark. All is Source and All is One and "*tat tvam asi*," thou art that!

Elohim: Creator Gods

This initial explosion of Source Intelligence began to form the first essences of individual consciousnesses, which eventually formed into the first beings of Light, the Elohim, which was described as the First Creation in a session with a somnambulistic client named Matan. The Elohim, androgynous beings of Light, were created in the "likeness and similitude" of Source and were given free will to create and tend to the Garden of Creation, also called the Multiverse, or what Jesus Christ (Yeshua ben Joseph) refers to as the "Father's House of Many Mansions." These first Lightbody creations gave individualized aspects of Source the ability to craft, explore, and evolve its creation from within it.

If Source is the grand landscaping contractor of the Cosmos, the Elohim are the workers who go out and tend to the Garden of Creation. These Creator beings began with the simplest forms of frequencies, color, and atomic life and began to create, through shared group intention, larger and more complex light and sound vibration fields like stars and galaxies. From this divine play between forces, entire universes — worlds within worlds and realms within realms — came into existence throughout time and space with infinite levels of consciousness forms in eternal, perpetual stages of evolution.

Creation exists on an arc of descent from and ascent back to the pure Light of Source. With the support of the Elohim, Light emanates from the Source and is solidified into form to use for Creation. Creation exists within a feedback loop of information that always returns to the Source. As life ascends back into higher light forms, the Eternal Mind of Source integrates the information and pulses out the next waves of evolutionary energies to harmonically evolve Creation. This divine play of birth, existence, death, and recreation; and forgetting and remembering, is a game we play with our Oneself, ever striving towards harmony, realization, unity, and oneness.

Transcript: The Story of Creation

Here is a session transcript from a client named Matan as he describes the first stages of the beginning of Creation. Matan is a somnambulistic client, meaning his personality goes into the background in a "sleep state" and he "becomes" the consciousness he is regressed to under hypnosis. When I brought him up from hypnosis, he had no recall of the session information that went for approximately 2.5 hours.

As you read the transcripts, I will use "M" for when I (Michael) am speaking, "R" for when Ron is speaking, and "C" for when the client is speaking. I will use "HS" for when the client is channeling their Higher Self and will note when clients are channeling other higher consciousness beings. I have italicized all information that came through the client. Any added commentary from me is in the default font style.

C: *In the beginning, we were all together as one in what you would call a "space" of nothingness. There once was nothing. There really was nothing. But within* that nothingness, all was contained. This is the space of nothingness which contains all beings. This is before any light has been put forth throughout all of Creation. This is a place you would call the "soup of Creation," where all possibilities and probabilities play out and come into manifestation. Where what you would call your "thoughts" were passing through all of us as One. We are a collective of a whole of all Intelligence. This is a "time" where there is no time. This is where it all started.

We were all there. We all had an individual intelligence. All souls do before they are created into an individual soul. There is an intelligence to each soul within the consciousness that is the Creator, which we all are. In that nothingness contains all light, all knowledge, and wisdom of the Creator. So, to convey this message to understand in simpler terms, it is like seeing a cell, and within that cell, there are tiny little particles, and each of those tiny particles is moving within that cell. These are intelligences, individual ones, that end up being individual souls of the Creator. We are giving you a picture of how Creation came into being. This is so you can come into your own understanding of it. So once there was nothing, absolutely nothing, and within that nothingness contained all of the little particulates that moved within that consciousness of that cell.

Then over a period, vibrational forces came into being where the vibration of all of us being together started vibrating at a very high frequency. The vibrational frequency of that cell rose faster and faster. As this happened, there came the point where the first Light of Creation came into beingness.

Light was first created, and within that Light were the individual souls that would be pushed out into Creation to be created as light beings that would then be created into other lifeforms, or we should say entire realms were created. The first Light of being came into Creation, and we were all there. Every being was there. We were all one. Vibrating.

There came the point where the frequency of the light that was created from the vibration of the individual particles...we must convey it this way so that you can understand it...the light was created from all of you, and then a vibrational frequency rose. It kept rising and rising until it got to a particular point that it had to be shot out. Once the light was created, all of our beingness came together and shot out into all of Creation. This is where individual souls made out of Light came into being. This is where your galaxies came into being. Your universes and planets came into being. And from that, the first group of

Soul Creators. We are all seed points in this. This is where we ALL BEGAN.

M: Tell me more about this process of creation.

C: There are many aspects to it. Many. There are infinite aspects in which individual souls became these seed points. Where parts of Creation came into creation in First Creation, such as the first group of Creators.

M: Tell me more about this first group of creators.

C: They are the individual souls that came together as the first beings that were first created by Source in Creation. They are the ones that came in as the first group to manifest creation throughout Creation. Where planets stem from. Where universes stem from. Where whole galaxies stem from and other realms. We feel there is a lot of information that you are asking of us, and we ask you to feel free to go ahead and do so.

When I asked Matan to describe the space he was in, he described dark, empty space with stars and galaxies forming in the distance and he described his feeling state as serene. When I asked about his form, he said that he did not have a form yet; he was simply intelligence that was beginning to form, and he was aware that other individualized intelligences were forming around him. As he came into his first form, he described his first Lightbody.

C: Form! I see my first form. I am a light being.

M: Tell me about that being.

C: I have hands. Arms. Legs. In the shape of the form with all of that. I can fly.

M: That sounds fun. Are you a male form or a female form?

C: At this point, I have not come into the physical form, but I am formed.

M: What kind of things do you do in that form?

C: Help to create more colors. Spirals. It is through space. More than one space. Several groups of us come together at times to help form planets.

M: Tell me about that process. It sounds fun.

C: We all come together in harmony. All the other beings. And they're of Light. We don't have to speak. We don't have mouths yet. We're exchanging energy through thought to create. And we go from one place to the next to help create more planets. They are beautiful.

M: You said, "help." What are you helping? Who are you helping?

C: The other beings. So, we come together in groups through thought to manifest a form of a planet. And through the matrix, it manifests. It's just there. This is the beginning. The very beginning of a planet.

M: So, you start it out as a thought? A collective thought? And it manifests within that thoughtform? That structure that you created together?

C: Yes, and what we wanted to put into that planet. A theme.

M: Tell me about that. Tell me about the theme of the planets.

C: There are many. They all are different. It depends on what universe you are in. This universe that I see...I just see a round shape. It's of a planet, but I cannot make it out yet. The collective came together to form this planet into a beautiful planet. Peace. There is such peace on it. There are no living beings on it yet. It's still forming into its physical manifestation. It's beautiful to be with all the others. We are all one. Creating.

Negative and Positive Polarity Consciousness

Of the original Light Being Creators, the Elohim, some were given positive polarity consciousness and were created to be in "service-to-all." These beings used their power of Divine Creatorship and Source-endowed free will to create within Source's Divine Plan of open-ended eternal evolutionary creation, which continuously evolves into a higher and higher harmony.

Some of the original Creator Beings were created to be in "service-to-self," negative polarity consciousness. Sometimes these beings are called "Fallen Elohim," although this term does not accurately describe these beings' intention, function, and higher purpose. These beings are aspects of Source Intelligence that were permitted to create based on the illusion of separation from Source, the illusion of multiplicity and duality. This gave the creation process, the Game of Consciousness, a bit more edge and an element of surprise that Source could experience through its Creation. These beings did not "fall" in the way we might think but were permitted by Source to operate in this way to fulfill a divine purpose of creating a contrast, which is a necessity for evolution.

Throughout the multiverse, various forms exist created by the forces of positive and negative polarity consciousness. Positively polarized consciousness (service-to-all) strives towards unity and cohesion. In contrast, negative polarity consciousness (service-to-self) seeks to overpower the Light and be the "god" of its own creation. This is all a game as Source is both the "good" and the "evil," the shadow and the light playing with itself in this eternal Game of Consciousness. Nothing can ever truly fall from the Oneness of All That Is.

Transcript: Fallen Ones and the Interlopers

The topic of the Fallen Ones or the Dark Forces has come up with many clients. Here is a transcript from a session where the client's Higher Self talks about the Fallen Ones.

M: Thank you. So, I have a few questions about the information given today and one of them has to do with the fallen ones... I would like to know more about them...where they came from and...yeah, let's start with that.

HS: The Fallen Ones are a spark of Source energy. They are beloved by the Beloved One, by Source Energy itself...the Creator. Always beloved these ones, no matter what they do, no matter where they go. They have taken to lust and power when looking upon the Earth...and seeing its beauty...all of its beauty. The beauty that is inside, the beauty that is outside, the beauty and the beings on the planet...all of the jewels that sparkle. They were very much attracted to them, wanting to be a part of, wanting to have, possess. Wanting to dissolve the power, so it is all their power. Wanting to usurp the energy to be within it, unto them...instead of leaving the Earth with its own power to grow and flourish.

These beings were in consumption and filled with the lust of this power. Desirous of more and more. So, they hoped to be able to take the Earth easily, but there were those in the heavens that saw their plight and challenged them. They were warned and threatened that they would no longer be welcome on the planet if they went down to steal...to usurp all these beautiful jewels that were not theirs. They did not believe this was true. They thought that everything they could see must be theirs because they could see it, but their eyes were bigger than their hearts. Their hearts could not hold all the beauty that was on the Earth, so they tried to take it for themselves.

M: You said that these beings were a spark of the Creator...and I've learned of the first creation, the Elohim, and I'm wondering how do these fallen ones relate to the Elohim...to the first beings of Light?

HS: They are the same. They all wish to fight for what they believe they are deserving of. They feel they are better than others, they are greater than others, they are purer than others. But they have not looked in the mirror, and they do not know the true nature of life. So, they had to be challenged, and they had to fall.

M: So, my next question is…if all things are Source, then what is the divine plan for beings like the Fallen Ones? What's Source's relationship to this?

HS: On a deeper perspective…it is not hard to understand the laws of duality because it is…seems so unfair, but those that have fallen also have a function to bring coherence and enlightenment to those that are not fallen…to those that they have fallen upon. So, the ones that have been fallen upon must see the truth of what is real and not real, what is true and is not true…must learn to discern with their heart and see the truth of who is who. Who has dark intentions, who has light intentions?

And what does that mean? We can all learn from the Dark. We can all learn from the Light. Sometimes Dark needs to be there so the Light can stand up to its fruitful potential and become even brighter through the transition. And in the enfoldment and in this process, the dark ones can become enlightened also if they have such a propensity for changing…for indulging in this beautiful light…for experiencing the other half of the Dark or the other half of the Light. Because they truly coexist. They do coexist with each other. One cannot live without the other. One encourages the other, even though one may be filled with hate, and one may be filled with love.

M: I also learned before about beings that inserted themselves into the original blueprint of planet Earth and the name that was given was called the interlopers. What are the relationships of the Fallen Ones to the Interlopers? If there is one.

HS: These Interlopers are those who wanted to experience all the incredible things that are going on on this planet. There is so much diversity and so much drama and so much color and energy to experience. People wanted to experience this. Many, many, many beings in the universe want to experience this right now on this planet. They're not bad; they're not good. They just want to experience and be part of it. They want to be part of history. And the Fallen Ones just see them as just another being that they can use if they have anything to give. So, it's just another being that has come to the planet.

M: Do you know where they came from? What's the origin of the Interlopers?

HS: Originally, they came from deep space. Very, very deep space, which is a different dimension...actually, it's through portals. So, they have come from another universe through a portal, but they had heard of this acute, incredible, pristine planet in this particular universe. It's like someone might hear of a drug...these days on the planet...oh, you haven't tried this drug? If you go over here, you can experience it. If you try this, you can experience it. So, it was almost like a drug they had to experience...they had to try it. It was just too delicious and too intriguing and mysterious. They had to find out about it. There are many beings like that on the planet right now...that are coming through many different dimensional portals that are just vying for a space here.

Transcript: Fallen Consciousness and Luciferian Agenda

Krissa is another somnambulistic client that I have worked with several times. She has an amazing ability to fully incorporate the consciousness of her other incarnations, her oversoul, her monadic consciousness, and even her archangelic aspects. When working with her, powerful energy vibrations pulse through my body. Sometimes it is hard to focus because so much energy moves through my body during the session. Waves of energy clear my energy field as powerful revelations are channeled through the client. Here is a transcript from a session where I was curious about negative interference in human consciousness.

M: The other question that I had is about the...because things are being brought up in the collective about 'satanic ritual' and 'Luciferian Agenda.' And that also gets put in with the word 'Satan' or the 'Devil.' And so, I would love to hear the higher, more cosmic explanation of 'Luciferian,' 'Satanic,' and the 'Devil.' How do those words interact? What do they mean?

HS: The gods, goddesses, and such we understand, they have an archetypal significance, yes? The archetype...it is said that some, many, or maybe even all of them do exist on a different dimensional level, at the Monad say.

There are many ways to tell this story and many ways to interpret this story, but just as the great avatars, the Buddha, Jesus Christ, Meher Baba, and others such as Zoroaster, also known as Ahura Mazda, these avatars came to hold the post of Source on the planet. Other beings, in the terms 'Satan,' 'Lucifer,' have held the post of dark polarity in this 3D game of polarity that we are in.

Some use 'Satan' and 'Lucifer' interchangeably.

The way I understand it is 'Satan' is more of an archetypal concept, if you will, and 'Lucifer' being the archetype of the fallen angel, probably based on a real being that existed, that still exists dimensionally. The details of that may not be so important. Yet the trouble is humans. There are human beings on this Earth right now who affiliate with this Satanic church or the Church of Satan, and they are not doing anything wrong. They are not doing anything evil. They are not doing anything against the fundamental laws. They are not doing anything that we would consider harmful or bad. And yet there are others who have perverted the Church of Satan to suit their purposes.

And I can't emphasize enough how much negative ET interference latches on and hijacks that, just like they latch on and hijack fundamentalist law. Just like they hijack Scientology. Just like they hijack the Mormon fundamentalists and, yes, the ugliest and most fundamentalist parts of the Christian church. They've hijacked any and all of those. It's just that certain ones like Satanic groups were more ripe for that because they were already in the shadow; they were already out of the mainstream. And yet we know even the Catholic Church is implicated and there are certainly ties, like an underground bridge, between the Catholic Church and the Satanic. This is human and [negative] alien interference.

The Luciferian agenda, I think of this as the fallen consciousness. Not just a schism, separation, and longing for Source, which is indeed the primary wound of humanity, or at least the illusion of separation. They're turning their backs and denying Source Consciousness and saying, "nothing matters." It's really extreme nihilism without heart. [They think] "Nothing matters. It's all a simulation. It's just all pursuit of pleasure and power and I can do whatever I want. It's just all a game. So, none of it really matters." And this is also a main port of entry, this type of consciousness, this Luciferian consciousness, for negative alien interference to take hold and has been for many, many, many years. What better avenue for a negative being to take hold than 'nothing matters,' 'I don't give a shit,' disconnecting from the heart.

From a shamanic perspective, disease happens when aspects of our soul that we need to be a fully functioning being and really fully occupy this vessel gets split off, or when things that aren't supposed to be here come in. It originates with trauma. It all originates with shock. It is where it originates in the physical body and of course it can be from other lifetimes and previous generations.

Everybody would do well to study forms of shamanism because they have a very simple and elegant way to explain the problem. It's not 'Satan' or 'Lucifer,' it's people who have taken these archetypes and distorted it to the lowest common denominator.... [negative] alien interference. I mean that's the type of food that they want.

M: How does that work? The ET interference? And the feeding and harvesting and influencing?

HS: It works in a number of different ways, but the main way it's worked is etheric implants. We've removed a lot of that from Krissa. The implants are not...if you did an x-ray on her you would not see it. It's in the fourth dimension, it's etheric. And she probably has more in there to clear. And the thing is that we can't clear all of it at once because her contract just isn't written that way. There are things she has to do long hand in order to fully live out her purpose. That's all we can really say about that for now.

M: So, there are the etheric imprints. Something that's been talked about in the Pistis Sophia. J.J. Hurtak calls this fallen Elohistic consciousness. Like distorted service-to-self programs that have been permitted in this third dimensional universe...

HS: It's free will after all.

M: Can you explain to me how that consciousness affects humanity and how we can liberate our own consciousness from that?

HS: Yes, absolutely. It perpetuates the disconnect from Source, and that splits us off from our soul essence and really creates enough room in our bodies and energetic field for interference to come in. And a lot of times that happens when we've given permission when we're too young to remember, when we're not conscious, but if you imagine from the very Source...how big do we want to go with this? What can Krissa's nervous system handle is more like the question. We can talk all night about this, but we don't want to keep you two from sleeping.

Imagine just in the known universe, there are unknown...but we won't even go there...there's a cloud of Source consciousness. You could call it Ein Sof, the Source. There's the desire to know oneself through separation and individuation. So, splitting off into two. The original Elohim. And splitting off from there, further and further, on the arc of descent away from Source. Descent down and down through the dimensions, finally, third dimension. We could talk about Orion as one of the earlier experiments with duality, polarity, third dimension, war.

This happens to be part of the game, what souls sign up for in Earth School. To play with polarity. Well, sometimes the game is played with loaded dice and for a number of years this fallen consciousness has shown up in various ways and gained power through extraterrestrial interference. So, they are the cheaters in the game. Those are the ones that come in and say, "Oh, we see this Monopoly game, but we want to see what happens if we sneak in here and give these people extra money and extra hotels." We're saying this in a way that Krissa will understand but that others will too. "We're going to sneak in and give these guys — the service-to-self — extra money and extra hotels to see what we can get out of this."

They gain a large amount of energy from the victim-persecutor cycle. And so, by loading up the decks of those in that service-to-self, that fallen consciousness... you see the essence of that fallen consciousness is turning the back away from Source and God, and saying no. It's just like a child saying "You don't want to play with me, well, I'm going to take my toys and go home. I didn't want to play with you anyway, and I'm going to go away like you don't even exist." It's that low. And that's not to diminish the level of power some of these individuals have, but it really is such a wounded consciousness. "Oh, I'm getting rejected from heaven, well, fine, I'm rejecting you first. I don't even think that you exist. I'm turning my head and looking the other way." Do you see how this parallels the individuals looking the other way, "La la la, we don't want to hear it; we don't want to hear it." You see?

The refusal to see and hear and acknowledge truth. That cuts off a lot of power. They go horizontal out to the world of form to other people and "What can we get?" and "What can we use?" rather than going vertical. The cross. The symbolism of the cross must be seen and discussed. The horizontal plane is to other people and the world in form. The vertical plane is what goes to Source. Only through that can we access and really, really open the heart. Which is an infinite, self-renewing source of power in the human being. The torus field generated by the heart.

None of these 'service-to-self' beings have a lot going on in the heart center. They have the 'below-the-belt' chakras running the show, so to speak. And they might be clever, they might speak well, but that's mostly because of implants to be honest. Their lower consciousness is running them. It's really kind of gross. It's almost like the Borg in Star Trek; it's like that.

M: How is it that these 'service-to-self' ET groups give humans

resources? Some people say the bankers and the CEOs and the Rothschilds and the Rockefellers are Reptilians that are working with the negative ETs and that's how they get their money and power. Is that true and how does it work?

HS: *Well, there are certain things that are locked in etheric vaults not to be revealed until the timing is right. What I will say is this: that archetypal story of selling one's soul to the devil. People don't really know who the devil is, it's a consciousness. But there have been a number of these groups, and yes, some of them are Reptilian and some of them are not. The Greys don't even register on that scale; they are not that smart. Even the taller greys, they don't have an organized and focused attention on Earth that way. They're blocked; they can't really do much with Earth right now. We're talking about something much more intelligent that exists between third to sixth dimension. And some of them are Reptilian and some of them are on the Earth in reptilian form, mostly underground.*

What I want to say about it for now is the idea of selling one's soul to the devil in exchange for money, power, resources; the origin of this is with this fallen consciousness and the negative ET groups that have helped to keep and perpetuate that consciousness. And unfortunately, the Law of Attraction works for nefarious purposes as well. Things like dark magic. These tools are really decreasing in potency as the Light is being shined on it. These things thrive in shadow and there's been such a high light quotient on the planet for some time now that my guess is the dark magicians are finding it's harder and harder to harness and manifest the level of power they need — really force, rather than power, I would call it. The level of force they need to accomplish what they want to accomplish because let's just say that they have less access to the fuel and less cover of dark under which to do the deeds.

The Forces of Light

Source as the Higher Mind of Creation has hierarchies, legions of highly evolved light beings that tend to the Garden of Creation. These forms of consciousness have been given different names by different cultures. I generally use the term "Light Beings" to describe higher consciousness beings that are Service-to-All. They are constantly radiating Light, Wisdom, and Unconditional Love into Creation to support harmonic evolution. At times, members of this elite armada of Light incarnate or descend from the higher realms into the physical dimension to teach and help a species or civilization evolve. Sometimes they appear as divine apparitions and sometimes they take on physical incarnations.

To simplify this Hierarchy of Light, or *dhyan chohan* in Sanskrit, we start at Source; the next step down are the Elohim, archangels, and angelic kingdom — the eternal architects of Creation. The next level down includes oversouls, Ascended Masters, higher consciousness species who have evolved beyond negative polarization, and soon to join is Ascended Humanity in the Fourth Density body and Fifth dimensional consciousness.

Many ancient and Indigenous cultures speak of light being visitation, where wise, divine beings appear and deliver messages of Love, Wisdom, and Unity to humanity in its darkest times. These eternal beings are omnipresent and exist outside the confines of time and space. We find them in the ancient Tibetan culture, Hebrew culture, Christianity, Hinduism, Islam, and more.

IQH sessions regularly have visitations from beings like Archangel Michael, Archangel Raphael, Archangel Metatron, and other higher consciousness beings from the higher light dimensions and other star systems. When this happens there is a noticeable shift in vibration even when I am doing the work remotely via video conferencing. Their words are imbued with healing energies that go straight to the heart of the listener. When I asked when they would all be returning, they said "We have never really left and that it has only been the fall of human consciousness that has caused a perceived separation." These beings are very much here with us on the inner planes to assist us. We just have to open our consciousness to them and ask for their divine assistance.

Extraterrestrial Life

During my hypnosis sessions, I have learned of many different star-being races and astral beings and how they have influenced Earth life and humanity since the beginning of the Earth experiment. Some of these species have had a positive or neutral effect on Earth life, and some have had a negative influence on Earth life because of nefarious service-to-self agendas.

All these interactions serve a Higher Purpose for the unfolding of the Story of Creation. Remember that all of life exists in arcs of ascent and descent. One group in a lower consciousness provides contrasting situations for a group in an ascending consciousness to create conditions for growth and the maturation of consciousness.

While there are likely countless groups that have been assisting Earth and humanity, some of the most common include Pleiadians, Sirians, Lyrans, Andromedans, and Arcturians, which humanity has named because these civilizations exist in the constellations with the same name from our perspective on Earth.

There are infinite levels of life in the multiverse, many Gardens of Creation. I have heard of underwater civilizations on water planets, civilizations of pure light, extraterrestrial communities that live in treetop dwellings, robotic Artificial Intelligence worlds, and giant spacecraft that contain ecosystems for a wide variety of life forms to thrive. Many intelligent species from these star systems are humanoid, meaning they have two arms, two legs, a torso, and a head. Some resemble more of a Lightbody, whereas some are hybrids of animals or insects like feline beings or locust-like beings. Some have a loving presence, and some are more analytical and practical, with little to no emotion.

Beyond the physical dimension exist different planes of existence that are nonphysical which ascend in vibrational frequency to the Source. Each dimension is like its own universe containing a variety of different beings with various levels of consciousness. The Vedic traditions speak of *lokas*, planes of existence that each have their own consciousness forms. The Pistis Sophia, a Coptic Gnostic text, also speaks of Jesus's ascended Lightbody form traveling up through the light dimensions and bringing the Christ Light to other planes of existence beyond the Earth to assist in liberating those realms from the Archons (see Ascension Lexicon). It is so fascinating to see how the ancient sacred texts have so many crossovers with these modern-day quantum healing sessions.

When people speak of the "astral realm," they are speaking of nonphysical reality, the Light dimensions. When we are dreaming, we travel through the astral realms in our astral body, our consciousness body, to learn and do other spiritual work. We also use this consciousness body when doing remote healing or remote viewing, giving us the ability to "tune in" to something nonlocal. Everyone has this ability and there are many ways to practice astral traveling and astral projection.

Astral traveling happens mostly unconsciously for the majority of people, although some have the ability to be conscious of this process, and there are many stories about this available with a simple internet search. People often report a silver cord that keeps them tethered to their physical body so that they can safely return. I have been told that there are other planets in our solar system that we cannot see because they exist in higher dimensions that we cannot see from the 3D consciousness. When we transition to the Fourth Density body, we will see this universe much differently.

Many ancient civilizations speak of contact with intelligent beings that came to Earth at different times throughout Earth's history. Indigenous cultures and wisdom traditions speak of extraterrestrial beings that delivered teachings of science, agriculture, writing, healing, and so on to aid humanity in raising consciousness and knowledge. Often, the stories speak of beings coming from the sky in clouds, spacecraft, or across the waters bringing higher consciousness teachings and messages.

It is important to emphasize the existence of a myriad of biological and higher dimensional species beyond the Earth in various levels of consciousness spread throughout Creation. The number of evolving species in Creation is infinite. As humanity awakens and embraces the truth of life beyond Earth and beyond our current visible light spectrum, we open our species to being reunited with the infinite species of Creation and begin the process of becoming conscious co-citizens of the web of life throughout the Multiverse.

Galactic Federations of Light

Within our galaxy exist groups of benevolent Star Nations working with members of the Hierarchy of Light that have joined to form a galactic fleet that some call the Galactic Federation of Light and the Ashtar Command. The Galactic Federation of Light supports the Higher Evolution in the physical universe. They work with DNA, test planetary and solar environments, transmit evolutionary programs of light from stars to planetary systems, transport resources, introduce technology to species, project evolutionary thoughts and love vibrations into consciousness fields, and so on. Collected information is sent to councils of Light Beings and Source to make adjustments to Source's evolutionary plans for Creation so that Creation evolves into greater harmony and balance.

There are many varieties of ways that the Family of Light supports evolution throughout Creation. Cultivating and maturing a planet's ecosystems is a stage-by-stage process that is precisely calculated using advanced science and alchemy cultivated over trillions of years, further than we can imagine, stretching back to the original architects of Creation. Light beings and extraterrestrial beings working with Source work together to introduce new species and life forms and help them along their path of evolution.

Councils

Each region of the universe is a unique testing ground for various creation components to interact and evolve. Just like a science experiment, different components are put into place and observed as they interact and evolve. At times, different elements of the experiments are manipulated, enhanced, reduced, altered, and so on to observe how the forms interact and evolve with the new conditions.

Various councils exist in the higher realms and physical universe that watch over and govern Creation. These beings are like the "hands of Source" moving throughout Creation to tend to various evolutionary fields and experimental zones. There are countless councils in Creation. For example, there exists a council for each planet that oversees the evolution of the planet. Each galaxy has its galactic council that oversees all of the other councils and evolutionary processes for that galaxy. Each universe has its own council that oversees the evolutionary phases in the totality of this universe.

The Council of Elders: Universal Council of Light

I have personally experienced and communed with a group of Cosmic Elders that shared with me that they are the originators of all cultures. This Universal Council of Light are the council overseeing all councils, administering the Divine Plan for all levels of Creation. Occasionally members of this council take on a physical incarnation for ground-level work and to experience their masterpiece from within.

My meeting with them was activated through a plant medicine journey that was beyond anything I had ever experienced before. The medicine opened my psychic perception, creating a spontaneous astral projection into a realm of pure white Light. This experience is mentioned later in this book. The first time I met them, I just knew they were "Elders." The second time I encountered them psychically, they shared more about who they were and that I would be working with them much more intimately in the future.

Each of these Elders carries a unique wealth of wisdom and knowledge that they share with the evolving cultures and species throughout the multiverse. Per their request, I have created a quantum hypnosis journey to meet them to receive guidance, healing, and wisdom. This is available in our Quantum Launchpad course.

When humanity awakens to the 5D consciousness, we will be reunited with the Star Nations and the Family of Light and receive monumental amounts of information and advanced technologies to propel humanity into an advanced civilization that no longer has disease or poverty. Healing technologies, free energy devices, and higher science and spirituality will be shared with humanity to assist us in our quantum leap of consciousness. In truth, the sharing has already begun through transmissions like *The Illumination Codex*.

Transcript: Theaters of Evolution

This next client describes herself as a being of light who travels from planet to planet to assist the evolution directed by Source. As she came into the scene, she described a beautiful valley full of wildflowers. I asked her to describe her emotions and senses and to describe more of this place.

C: *Everything is in harmony here. The animals, the plants, the land, there's so much diversity and so much complexity, and it's all in this beautiful harmony — this perfect balance. It's so gorgeous, alive, and radiant.*

M: **It sounds nice there. I want you to look down at the ground and see if you can see your feet.**

C: *No, there's just plants around me. There is no path. I'm just being there...floating there. There's a lot happening around me. The insects are buzzing; the butterflies are fluttering; everything is alive and well. There's this beautiful positive energy, and I'm just soaking it all in. And I'm analyzing it. I'm kind of melding my energy with the energy all around me to understand if any areas are out of balance. Also, to understand how in balance it is. I'm experiencing it...looking, smelling, feeling...but it's more like I'm experiencing it on this energy level. I'm looking for positive energy and expansion and growth. And I'm looking for any areas of contraction or negative-type energy so that I can fix it.*

M: How do you fix it?

C: I would meld myself with the negative energy, and I would bring positive energy into it. It's like when you're making a cake, and you've got the ingredients a little bit wrong. It's like you taste it, and then you figure out what ingredients are missing, and then you add those ingredients. It's like that on an energy level. I bring in what's needed to balance. I bring energy from Source into the molecules to help them get back into balance. But there's nothing that's needed here. It's all in perfect harmony. I feel this huge sense of love and satisfaction.

M: Tell me what happens next.

C: I drift along the valley. I am basically exploring all over this planet to see if there are any areas of concern. I am touching base to see how the planet is doing, and if there is anything that it needs on its surface. This is a carbon-based planet so it needs water and oxygen, so I'm making sure everything is in balance so that it can continue to grow and thrive and develop. So, I'm just floating over the valley and then up and over the mountains. Gliding along with my energy expanded out all around me, searching for areas that feel like they need attention, but everything is seeming pretty good. I've gone up and over the mountains, and I've dropped down into another valley, and there's a bear in this valley. High life forms. I'm going to go over and look at this lake. There's fish.

M: Are you always on this planet?

C: Oh no, I'm just checking in. This is one of many planets that I check on or am working to create.

M: How do you choose which planets to go to?

C: I go to the planets with the most needs. Basically, Source will tell me the order, the priority, and it's usually based on critical stages in that planet's development. For this one, there is kind of two roles I have. I am actually helping Source to create the planet by actually going and helping mature to the next step... helping them evolve. There's a steep curve at the start, kind of like with children on Earth. At the start, they are very needy; they need a lot of input. They need a lot of help and assistance, but as they get older, you have to back off and just let them evolve on their own. So, this beautiful valley of this planet I'm visiting now...I'm just touching base and checking up to make sure everything is as it should be. There are no surprises. Nothing that needs attention. Just touching base...that's because it's a more mature planet. It's doing really well; it's evolving beautifully. But it's important to check up on them, to make sure nothing happens in the meantime...like an asteroid that would introduce new materials and things and outside input that would actually halt the perfect progression, evolution, that's going on. And it would taint it or take it in a different direction. So, I'm just touching base with this one, which is kind of like having a vacation.

M: It's an easy planet that's doing well?

C: Yeah, it's doing well, and I get to enjoy just experiencing the fruits of my labor. It is such beautiful energy...the energy it has and the energy I have are blending together so harmoniously. It's like this gorgeous synchrony. It feels wonderful for me and the planet.

Transcript: Earth's Evolutionary High Council

This client found herself with a group of beings who announced themselves as the council that oversees Earth's evolution. The client was in between incarnations and was planning her current life.

C: The one being representing their group is saying I am going to represent their essence on Earth this next time and so I agree to that; that's fine because this group is very loving and supportive and uplifting. And they work very quickly but very resourcefully. So, I agree to that. And they're trying to debate if I will be male or female. I am just waiting. I am pretty open to any, whatever.

M: While they're deciding that maybe you could tell me a little bit more about this council. You said there is one human there?

C: There's just one human. This human comes in my visions as my spirit guide but introduced himself as Jesus, but he looks like...what's that wizard from Harry Potter? He's got a long white beard. But he says it's Jesus, but I know he's a representative of the collective consciousness. Christ-minded consciousness.

M: What about the rest of the council members. What can you share with me about them?

C: There's one that looks like a rock, like an earthen being, and he's of the 'Sha?' And then the others are very luminous. Like a white, thin illuminated white being, but very opalescent. They are beings of...Sirian. And the being that I will be part of will be of the Pleiades. Pleiadian blue. They will help the Sirians. The Sirians are serious. And they can't...they struggle to work with the humans because they are devoid of emotion, mostly. So, the Pleiadians agreed to assist.

M: What did your council decide?

C: They are still deciding. They are taking forever (giggles) to me! I am ready to go! They said why I am there they can't say, but I have a feeling they are planning for my life now. But they can't divulge any other information.

M: And what will you be doing in that next life? Do you know the intentions?

C: They said I'll be doing a high level of lightwork, and they will be able to assist if I ask, if I call them in. And it's going to take me quite a while in this life to realize this and what I should be doing. And once I do, I will be assisting the collective consciousness to move and shift to a higher level so that I will be able to spread these to others so that it webs outwards and it connects to other students, of other teachers, creating a Christ-minded web across the Earth. I am going to be planted in a certain area so as to help that area vibrate higher and collectively to help the shift.

I am going with the Pleiadian member because they said if I am representing, coming in as an aspect of their essence, I will need to have more knowledge embedded in me. So, the council adjourns, and they have agreed on what my lifetime will be. And so, the Pleiadian is taking me to this, like a white room, the walls are kind of like opalescent, and everyone is floating in the room. So, I am kind of like just standing, hovering, just my essence.

There are five beings around me. They are holding hands in a circle, and they are beaming information into my essence and when they do their foreheads, in the center, start to illuminate a golden color that infiltrates me with this vibrant and joyous energy. It is so fulfilling and wonderful.

I am just seeing and feeling DNA spirals and different alterations to that. And little snippets. It's almost like I am looking at cells through a microscope, separating, changing colors, alteration to the cellular structure, and being embedded with information. And then they're done.

I am going to go back to Council and then we'll all approve what's going to happen and then I'll go in. Now I'm in front of Council but the Sha has to scan me with his eyes. He's checking what I was coded with to make sure it was appropriate. It's like checks and balances. He says everything is wonderful. He

*reaches out his energy to touch mine and he's in charge of sealing the template.
So, he seals the template of what was loaded into me and now I was processed.*

M: What else can you share with me about the Sha?

*C: He says that he has the information, the original template information, and his
people hold it on the Earth plane so that we can remain stable in the human
genome. He approves and seals any template alterations.*

M: How else do the Sha support humanity?

*C: They hold space on and under the Earth. He says when people say, "the spirit of
Gaia," that's him. But also, they will stand in different places, and sometimes
people will see them, or sense a large, heavy energy. And that's not a negative.
It feels heavy because that's of their people. And they have a lower vibration,
and that's not in a bad way.*

*He says he gets frustrated when he hears humans talk about "a high
vibration" all the time. He wants us to know that the low vibration is assisting
us as well to seal in templates and that. Not a low vibration equating to a
negative energy, but you need all of the frequencies to create the song.*

**M: So, if I am hearing you correctly, you are saying that vibration
and polarity are different. That someone can be of a positive
polarity but still be of a lower vibration?**

*C: Not for humans. Not in the human being itself. With him and his entities, yes.
Sometimes if you are feeling a heavy energy in a room, or outdoors especially
(they are rarely indoors), just to acknowledge it and that that's okay. Some
people will perceive it as negative. He says that sometimes my people will be
standing outside, and humans will try to clear us. But they need to be there. It's
funny because he says, we don't clear anyway (laughing).*

**M: What were the Sha's original mission on the planet? What was
their beginning mission here?**

*C: We needed to lay a foundation and be the first vibrational frequency to arrive
and be laid down and to be the holders of the original human template — the
Christed mind. The original template. And be keepers of it. We hold it deeply
within us so that it is protected and there is no other entity that can interfere
with it. They can assist and it's up to our people to prove or disprove it and we
also are to hold space on top of the planet as well so that other astral families
can assist us when we observe vibrational shifts are needed. So, we are satellites,
so to speak, in human terms.*

M: The first time that I heard of the rock beings it was a ceremony

with a few other beings and they were taking, what the client described as, a citrine crystal, and then holding this ceremony and then the citrine and these rock beings were absorbed into this planet. And at the time they said this was the beginning of the Earth. And I have never really heard anything else about it. I am wondering if this feels connected and true. Or if there is something else you would like to correct?

C: *Very much so. That is our primary stone, but we are also keepers of all the others. There are other things that have come upon Earth. There is one green stone. We needed assistance because we were in a vibrational shift, and we were struggling and one of the astral families assembled us a new stone that came from outer space. That was the start of when the plan was laid out for the shift that we're experiencing now. But yes, that's very...we did...we were the creators of the Earth.*

R: We wanted to know about the creation of the first humans on the Earth.

M: There are talks about human beings coming from Lyra being seeded onto the planet. I also know that there were times when humans were more in a Lightbody. Some call it the Adamic seed. I am wondering about the first time the humans were brought to the planet. What their bodies were like. What their consciousness was like?

C: *When the families first collaborated, they were brought in their essence form. We needed to train some to do basic survival things. I am seeing four or five brought in at first. And then as they were able to thrive more were brought in. And they were brought into a denser jungle location where there would be plenty of vegetation for them to live off of. And fresh water. It almost seems like the Christian version of the Garden of Eden.*

M: So first they came in in more of an essence form, like a Lightbody?

C: *Yes.*

M: And then how did it become more dense? What was that process? Moving into physicality.

C: *The Families of Light worked together with the Sha to create the human body. We manifested it. We were able to manifest the thoughtform into matter. And we were a main aspect of that, and the human body needs to be heavier to stay here on Earth.*

Although it may have been able to be a bit lighter in the beginning, but we were the facilitator of that and that is why it's heavy.

Age of Expansion

As we can see, there is a system of higher evolutionary intelligence that is beyond the standard biological and geological evolution models accepted by mainstream science. Each domain within Creation is tended to by these benevolent forces, evolving each domain towards higher and higher harmony. Once the Earth and humanity have been liberated from the grips of the negatively polarized controllers, there will be an unprecedented revelation of technology, science, and philosophy to bring humanity into a new frontier of consciousness.

ELEVEN

Star Family Legacy

Here is more of Matan's story from the perspective of his oversoul describing the Elohim, and the creation of the first male human form on a planet his group created named Aiden. When I tried to search for it on the internet to see if anyone else has written about it, I only came across the boy's name Aiden which is the name of a Celtic sun god which I thought was nice synchronicity. In the session, Matan meets another Elohim in a male human form named Leo who is his divine counterpart. Coincidently, in this life, Matan and Leo are gay males again!

Transcript: The First Male Form

HS: The planet Aiden is a planet that Matan and Leo's Beings first created, where they started creating their first forms, and they came through as male. With that, they started creating other forms (material creations) with it. They came to form the first male forms when they were light beings. We must bring to your attention: everything is created in spirit first before it is manifested in a solid, physical form. Matan and Leo's souls had a job, and it was brought through the Creator, to bring on first male forms. Through their unveiling process, they were shown how their Being came into Creation and how they started creating together. This is a big part of their beings, of who they really are.

This goes back to the first incarnation on the first planet that they were created on. This is the planet, what you call Aiden, and it consists of men. There are different themes throughout creation on different planets. There are some that have much diversity through them as your Earth planet. There are some that are just the same beings. Going into your other cosmic families, such as your Greys or Tall Ones, Tall White Ones — they all look alike. They're all the same. So, there was a planet that was created that was all of the human male forms. There are female planets of the same too, and then there are planets that came together to intermix them together.

Your current Earth that you live on is a manifestation of other star systems. Many planets came to this planet to bring the creations forth. This planet, as it is ascending, will be the pearl of this galaxy. It will be the garden planet of the galaxy that will home the diversity of life forms throughout all star systems in this galaxy.

M: What types of intentions were put into creating the first male forms?

HS: Pure love. Pure love. The male form originally is pure love and gentle. He is not what you see in your now upon the planet. Actually, quite the opposite.

M: How did males interact with each other?

HS: Very lovingly. They did not compete; they cooperated. They were fully conscious of one another, living in full consciousness. You must know, there are other planets that have just males on them. There is a vast spectrum of planets out there in this universe and other universes that have themes to them. Some just have male forms on them. This has been spoken of through other people of your world. You must remember the vastness of creation.

R: Was the male form brought to this Earth before the female, or...

HS: Yes, we are telling you this is the truth. We are part of that. And there were others that were part of that with us.

R: What was the first civilization that was created upon this planet?

HS: Well, we can take you back to the time of Lemuria. That is still, within your world, still folklore, but Lemuria is a very true civilization that did exist. But there were others that came even before that.

M: Before we go to these other earlier civilizations, I want to ask more questions about the original male form. How did the male form replicate in those early times, if there was not the opposite sex?

HS: They did not have to actually reproduce in the way you do in your world. It was more energetic, yes. There is physicality in other worlds where males can actually reproduce and bring on another male form.

M: So, what was the process like when it was simply energy?

HS: Two males coming together energetically with love, which they are already, and intent of creating another form. And then it was reproduced.

M: Was it reproduced in the body of one of the males?

HS: In some worlds, yes. In certain planets, yes. On others, no.

You must note that the male forms on other planets do not look like yours.

M: What's different?

HS: They are more pure. They are pure humans. They don't have the mixing you have in your world.

M: When you speak of mixing, do you mean galactic races?

HS: Yes. Meaning that they are not hybrids. They are a pure human male.

M: We were wondering what the purpose was for the homosexual man or the homosexual woman? Is there a story there?

HS: There are themes to planets. Many themes. Some themes aren't the same form. Where they all come collectively together and separate from the collective into the same form. Then they choose within that consciousness of that form what they want to create, how they want to live within the creation, their roles, their personalities. It's a very beautiful thing.

M: Gay people have had a really hard time on this planet.

HS: Matan carries answers to that. We were all once the same, which we all really are. That is the cosmic joke of it. We take on so many forms, but there are first forms in Creation. There is an order in Creation when things are manifesting. Matan helped with the creation of the gay male. He was also shown about the gay human woman. Or what you would call gay in your world. It is just the same forms interacting on a certain level for an experience. This is what they have chosen, but it is a big part of Creation. This planet has been backward for some time now. For when it was first formed, there were the first forms of the same, that looked the same, that grouped together. Then came other forms that were different that came together. Then it branched out from that.

M: So, you are sharing with me...maybe I am getting this incorrectly, at first there was the same gender, the same sex together and then it was opposite?

HS: Yes.

M: Then we started creating from that? Creating other life forms? Creating other humans?

HS: Yes. That is where humanity has gotten things wrong.

M: Tell me about the first humans.

HS: They were gentle. Very gentle. They did not know violence. Then, an energy came in and created something where they fell from grace, and there are ones of us that decided to depart. There are ones that decided to stay. Oh, things got all scrambled up. Too much. Too many differences. So, he left the planet with other beings. He did not die.

R: In the Jewish Bible, there is a story of Adam, the man that took his

rib and created the female. Can you share your perspective about the creation of the female and human life on Earth?

HS: There are other beings that came in to help create the female. Once the female was created, then there was a force that came through, that chose to manifest them on the Earth plane. It's not as everyone thinks, through the rib of Adam; that is a metaphor to be used. We must remind you, there have been many civilizations on this planet that go back further. Everyone has questions pertaining to the story of Adam and Eve. There is some truth to this. Yes. As there are many gardens on this planet that were created when it was first created.

R: Can you set the record straight?

HS: We want to give you clarity on this without confusion. As you know of Lemuria, that time was a special time on this planet. When Lemuria was created, in the time of Atlantis, those were civilizations on this planet, but there were others too. There were many gardens and things set into Creation. So, when you have your souls that speak of the Adam and Eve story, there is truth for them on their soul path for that. In the manifestation of Creation, it's part of the Creator putting that set forth in Creation.

M: Yes. So, there were more creations before Adam and Eve?

HS: Yes. A lot more...many, MANY!

Ancestral Genetic Lines of the Milky Way

In one of my sessions, I learned of a group called the Carans or Carians, said to be the oldest species in the Orion constellation, who were described as an ancient negative polarity, service-to-self species who travel the universe in search of planets to plunder and species to control. When I did an internet search about them after the session, I read a few different descriptions of this group that had similarities to the sharing my client gave but also some differences. I had a slight hesitancy in sharing this data as I like to get information from several sources to verify the information. I have decided to include this information because I received it from a client that I trust deeply. I wonder if they even call themselves by this name. I decided that the archetype of progenitor and the intentions put into their genetic creations and experimentations was the important part of the story.

Receiving this information was a profound experience for me that opened up my mind to a more expansive understanding of the ancient Milky

Way history. I'm sure there is much more to learn and understand and more clarity will come as we move down the Ascension timeline.

These service-to-self beings would be described as reptilian in appearance and created what is commonly called the Draconian species which are from the constellation of Draco; the Draconians eventually created what is commonly called the Reptilian race. The Reptilian genetic coding was later permitted by Source to be inserted into the human genome as a way of expanding their genetic line in this region of space. The Reptilian DNA is what gives humanity the ego so that it can have individual consciousness, competitiveness, and the drive to protect itself.

The Carans, which are never up to any good, created the Draconian race by merging the highly intelligent and spiritual expression of the dragon DNA — yes, they are real — with the primitive intelligence of the dinosaur DNA. Dragons are defenders of the realms and "rule over" entire regions of space by tending to the energetics and protecting their territory from invaders. The Carans basically wanted to create a dumbed-down dragon that was self-serving and very powerful. This Draconian species would be an army that would rule over the region of Orion for the Carans. From the perspective of these cold-hearted rulers, the more species they can control, the more power they have which is a complete inversion of power of true creator beings that are working in unison with the Divine. The client's Higher Self said that at a certain point the Draconians ruled over 800 species in the Orion constellation.

The Draconians were described as having reptile-like features, wrinkly faces, and protruding spikes on their face with stocky bodies. They have a high frequency and high consciousness capacity like the dragons but with a primal, instinctual consciousness like the dinosaurs. Even though these beings operate at a higher consciousness, I was told Eighth Dimensional, they lack an emotional body, which makes them purely analytical and focused on the next steps in their agenda with no emotional hang-ups. Although, it was said that the Draconians do have a touch of feminine energy to them and that they do have a capacity to grow in love. The beings that created this species were curious about what would happen if a being were given a high consciousness but had no reference of cause and effect, no empathy. This is unlike humans who are mentally preoccupied with how people relate to them on an emotional level. These Draconians are more goal-oriented without the duality that comes with emotions. This type of service-to-self consciousness is quite different than humans on the Earth who do things, as backward as it may seem at times, to acquire more love and emotional safety. This does not mean that the Draconians are not connected to the Divine; their connection is just felt differently than a heart-centered species who consciously choose to work towards a greater harmony for All. Both polarities exist to create dynamics for interaction and evolution of consciousness.

Eventually, the Draconians created a more commonly known race called the Reptilians as a lower-dimensional expression and hybridization of the Draconians. While many humans on the Earth in modern times hold a negative perspective of the Reptilian race, I have had several clients who regressed to lifetimes of living as a Reptilian or a Draconian as their soul wanted to experience being on the "dark side," or the other side of the conflict, for the purpose of spiritual growth and knowledge. I was quite surprised to learn that the Reptilian races have the capacity to grow in love and compassion and ascend in their own consciousness. Clients described Reptilians who carry love in their hearts, have loving families, and have their own evolutionary process to awaken to higher love. We are quick to pass judgment on beings from our limited perspective from not having the bigger story. I find that once we hear the other side of the story, we often grow in understanding and compassion. Even in human history, we see examples of people and groups of people committing terrible acts believing that, in doing so, they were protecting their family or nation.

Lyrans, from the constellation of Lyra, are Earth humanity's ancient ancestors and the first humanoid species in our region of space. The Lyrans also seeded Earth with the first humans using 144,000 oversouls from the Lyran lineage. I have heard of pure Lightbody forms and angelic beings, as well as hybrid humanoids that have arms, legs, and a torso like humans but are mixed with feline genetics. We can see some of these beings in the Ancient Egyptian statues from when these beings visited the Earth in the past.

Long ago, much longer than humans can comprehend, an intergalactic war began between beings from the constellation of Orion and beings from Lyra. Factions of beings in service-to-self consciousness from Orion attempted to take over the Lyran civilization for their own gain. This intergalactic battle was a war over resources and consciousness. The Reptilians not only wanted to take over the Lyran system but wanted to infiltrate and control the Lyran consciousness through mind control tactics and energy devices. It was one of those wars that went on for so long that many forgot why they were even fighting and there were many casualties on all sides.

This story causes a lot of judgment against Reptilian beings, especially because some Draconian/Reptilian ancestral lines have been using these same tactics against the people of Earth. It was shared in one of Ron's sessions that it is two ancient Reptilian family lines that have been controlling humanity for thousands of years. This is the tyrannical force and distorted consciousness behind the mainstream institutions like the Vatican, the banking systems, sick-for-profit industries, and other institutions that keep humanity in poverty, race wars, and mind control. That being said, the power has always been in humanity's hands to stand in sovereignty or give in to outside authority and tyranny. Jesus is called the "Redeemer" because he came to show humanity the pathway out from the slave mindset so that we could break free of these shadow controllers.

The Reptilian race has mostly evolved beyond service-to-self into a service-to-all consciousness and is supporting humanity now in our grand transition. Some will have a hard time releasing the charged narrative about Reptilians because they hold polarity and victim consciousness within their being and do not have all sides of the story. All characters have played a role in the unfolding of our galactic story to assist the expansion of galactic collective consciousness. That being said, it is suggested to use discernment through the power of the heart when engaging in communication with any beings to ensure that they hold the highest intentions for the engagement. This applies to physical interactions as well as astral and psychic interactions.

The Lyran home planet was described as a beautiful paradise teeming with life. Technology was used by the Orion group that destroyed this paradisaical Lyran planet. The loss of this planet is still felt within the heart of the souls of those who had lifetimes on the destroyed planet. Many humans that were souls incarnated as Lyrans when the planet was destroyed still experience high sensitivity to radiation and electromagnetic frequency pollution. Their etheric DNA, the higher dimensional form of DNA, still holds significant radiation from this cataclysm.

Transcript: Destruction of Lyran Civilization

The following session is from Krissa, a somnambulistic client. Krissa's consciousness began to fade away as I asked for more information. As this happened, the feline Lyran aspect of her Oversoul began to incorporate fully through her vessel. When this happened, Krissa said her consciousness was "floating" around in the background and could sometimes hear what her body was communicating but it was not coming from "her." It became emotional as her Lyran aspect began to cry over the loss of her beloved home planet.

C: *I'm walking on a white, stone path. There's a quality of the light that is far more brilliant and I'm wearing a long, white garment with sandals on. It's not the same kind of solid matter that is experienced on Earth in the third dimension. I see now there are beautiful, white stone buildings that are luminous and iridescent in color. Almost an ivory-colored stone building, and I keep hearing the words: Orion, Orion.*

M: **Let's get a little bit more familiar with your body. You said you were wearing this white material and sandals. Become more familiar with your body and describe it to me.**

C: *This is amazing. I'm a beautiful being of feline fur and body, very tall, coverings of the feet. Sandals for the feline feet and the walking on two feet like a human. There's a piece of me that is so scared to see this because it feels like home. I feel like my heart's going to break. It hurts so bad. I can do it; I can do it.*

I am about to deliver the sad news to the elders, the other Lyran elders. I'm an oracle. I'm so old and my physical body isn't as strong as it used to be. I'm thousands of years old in this body. I have foreseen and others have foreseen various timeline possibilities, that beings from the Orion system are not to be trusted; they will ruin our world. We will be at war, but it has not yet come to pass, that a critical tipping point has come into the consciousness of myself and other seers where we must report the findings, and it grieves us very greatly. It grieves us to do so because we did not want...we spent our lives trying to shift the consciousness away from this outcome, away from this tipping point. Yet we have failed and all that we see before us will crumble and we must leave now.

I feel the shadows of many, many lifetimes in this world. Forward and backward, I feel my consciousness stretched between twelve dimensions. And when it is thus, an even higher angelic emanation harkening back to closer to the origin of Source consciousness itself. I see that all is well. I see that all is well, yet the part of me that deeply loves this world and all that it stands for feels that it will break and shatter and that a thousand lifetimes of tears won't be enough to grieve it adequately. There's so much to hold, so much to say, so much to do and express. I am tired. I am ready to do this final piece of my work and let this body pass, pass beyond the threshold again.

M: You were saying that there were beings from Orion that aren't to be trusted? Is that true?

C: They're walking through a cycle that is a world not so different from the Earth at the present time you see, with lessons of contrast and duality. Lessons of separation and greed and wanting to define that there is a...all beings exist on an arc of ascent and descent. Predictable cycles of emanation from Source. Lower than Elohim and angelic emanations and then Ascended Masters and things like this and into the body; this is from an Earth point of reference. So, this cycle of emanation on the arc of descent is going from the Oneness, that Source Consciousness, to various emanations moving down the dimensional levels. The arc of ascent is what the Earth is on now. At the moment of time Orion had been on an arc of descent and it still existed in dimensions six through three, you see what I say, they had descended, and they were on an arc of descent having to iterate fully the division, the "us and them," the hatred, the wanting, the greed, the destruction. They had to do this, you see, that was part of what that world was meant to learn and teach. So much could be said about this, yet I have seen that I will have lifetimes helping them back up the arc of ascent. I don't want to. I would choose not, yet the larger piece of me knows that it is part of my soul's path, and I will accept it gladly.

M: I'm wondering what we would call that group here on the Earth? Do we have a name for this group?

C: All of the names that have been said on Earth don't really fully express that this was a FACTION of beings. A large faction. But a faction of beings that gained traction. Some were humanoid. Some Reptilian. Many Reptilians were not of this ilk. There are many Reptilians that are positive or neutral. We would say these words are an oversimplification, but we say these words for our purposes, you see. But there were a number of, you see, humanoid beings, reptile beings that were part of that lower denominator of consciousness that had to iterate out polarity to its extreme. Do you see?

M: I understand, yeah.

C: And people use the word here Archons. They use the word like a vampiric, a very draining like enslavement. Words like...um... creating a trick around to harvest and utilize lower vibrational energy for their own purposes. This was part of the situation. They want to do that to Lyra. They want to do that, but we will leave. They can have the buildings, the container; they can have the planet as much as it grieves me, but they will not harvest; they will not enslave; they will not hijack our consciousness. We will leave and we will build anew. And then my soul will incarnate in another star system for the purposes of helping to elevate. This is a cycle of ascent and descent, yet it is part of a bigger plan. A bigger, divine order.

In the journey of rediscovering the nature of self as creator gods and goddesses, we must first see our power to create entropy, destruction, despair, and annihilation collectively. And then relearn the power to create life, to create connection, to create elevation, ascension. So, this was a downward arc in the Orion system; they are not for the most part...they are back. They have ascended from that.

Everybody that I love and care for deeply is inside a spaceship ready to go. I don't want to go to Vega as I want to die here, and now my body is so close to expiring you see. But they, they do not trust; they're not ready to let me go. My children, my grandchildren. The priests and priestesses and seers that I taught and mentored. And I'm so tired and they're putting me in this spaceship, and I rest and wait for the process of propulsion to go; body drops into a stasis while this happens, folding space and time like an accordion. Folding into a pocket of altered gravity, you understand. Travel. So tired... The individuals listened; they mostly almost all listened to us, and we know it is the correct information to leave and go re-establish the Pleiades. We know this will come to pass; it will be well. I'm dying.

Transcript: The Oracle of Orion

Here is a client named Tina that regressed to a lifetime as an oracle in the Orion civilization. As the oracle, she would sit in a room far from the influences of other beings and channel information that would help the Orion group during the great war. In previous sessions, she shared about the black cube and black pyramid technology that is installed on planets for harvesting negative energy for nefarious technology and deeds. They describe the black cube in Mecca and the black pyramid in Las Vegas as being part of this negative extraterrestrial energy harvesting network. The client also mentioned a solar flash event that is similar to what we will experience here on the Earth as we ascend. I took some time to ask about the cause of the Orion Wars.

C: So, the technology of the black pyramids came from somewhere up in that Orion's belt. They would fight the same way that, say you have two people who, like maybe the Jews and Palestine, like fighting to the death. It's a tribe like that. So, you have these tribes. And they would fight to the point where they would obliterate each other, their whole DNA line, just total annihilation. And what would they learn from that genocide? They did this for millennia, back and forth, back and forth, back and forth. So, what changed them was that their sun 'burped,' and it blew open a bunch of third eyes at once. It 'burped' them open... It's more like gas; it's more like a belch and it burped, and it blew the tops off some people. Their physical body popped off; their top popped off. They don't look quite like us. But their top popped off. And this changed them.

The war was over technology. It was so long. I mean, you think of the Hundred Year War, the War of the Roses, a multi-generational war, a war that went on so long that nobody can remember why it started. You just remember, you just don't like that other side. Nobody can remember why. So, that's because nobody can remember why. We're going to get over it now.

M: So, the humans now are ending that collective war by finding peace with themselves?

C: Yes. And so that war that was started in Orion is coming to an end now. Like it was always on the end date. It's been ending, but the actual period at the end of the sentence will be like, the end. Period.

M: And how is the war from Orion...how does that influence the war that's happening here on Earth?

C: So, the tribes from Orion, the tribes from Earth are the descendants of the tribes from Orion. So, in some ways, some of those people, they would just destroy things, just totally obliterate them. So, in order to escape their technology, they had to come. Some of those tribes came to Earth to start the tribes here. This might sound controversial. I don't want to make anyone upset. So, even if it isn't actually able to be proven that the DNA is from them, they carried the codes in a way. Or the incarnation codes to incarnate. So, you were talking about Abraham and his sons and the tribes of Abraham. He was holding that [coding], you know, and then King David and all of that. And you look at those old kings and they held a higher frequency than the average person on this planet. And that was true. You might today, if you met them, it wouldn't maybe feel that different because more people are higher on the ascension. But back then there weren't that many people that had higher thought.

So, what happened? There was almost complete genocide in Orion. The oversouls of the Twelve Tribes wanted another chance to try to work it out. And so, it's almost like we were talking the other day about "the most impossible thing." Is it peace in the Middle East? It's not that impossible when you think about it, because they all come from the same tribe, in a sense, back, back, back, back, back. But the original argument had to do with those black pyramids and the original argument was over power and technology. One group thought they were better than the other group and then tried to get domination and power over them. And then that didn't work. And then they had the 'burp' and then that changed them. And then after that, things were different, but they wanted to test it. It is a test. It's a test of energy to see if they can come together. The test of energy is if those oversouls can split apart into twelve tribes and see if they can come together.

So, they did all this before on another planet, almost destroyed it, right? Some of them escaped. Some of them didn't. Some of them started over. Then they did it again somewhere. So, you have the Orion wars. So, you have a lot of battling, different battling factions. So, you have invading tribes coming and basically ripping down the culture of another existing planet. It was gnarly.

M: What about the Orion civilizations and how they interacted with the Lyrans, with the cats?

C: Well, that's what she's seeing is the cats are ripping her out of the temple. I see lions that are taking her out of the temple, like RIPPING her out of the temple. But she's the oracle so she doesn't see well. That doesn't make sense. She doesn't physically see well. I mean, she may be blind as the oracle. So, she can't see them, but she can smell them. And so that lion smell. Why did they do that? I think they ripped the oracle out because the oracle, they thought, was what was giving away their secrets or giving away their next move. They could see their next move. She could see the next move. It was strategic. It was a military strategic thing. They were angry. I want to call them lions, but the Lyrans were angry. So, their technology started to outpace their human...not their humanity...but what makes you compassionate or what makes your empathy. So that it's almost like you would say, like in a sci-fi movie where an AI would take over something like that. It was sort of like that. So that the frequency that was given off, like when we were talking about the brainwaves and how certain frequencies are given off and that's what creates the ascension. The theta waves. The waves were being manipulated. That was one of the weapons going back and forth. They were blasting each other with different brainwave weapons.

So, the Lyrans showed up and they cleared everybody out. Just killed everybody. This is a long time ago. The Lyrans are not like that now. I mean, everybody's passed this, people are past this now. This is billions of years ago. A lot of time. I'm seeing 2.4 something. Million? Billion? It's a long time ago. It's a long time ago.

M: Well, when people speak about Earth being under the control of Dark Forces, is that connected to this Orion war?

C: So, because those planets went through their ascension, the frequency of the biology couldn't hold lower frequencies like war and hate and things. But Earth was still compatible with that. I mean, it's not as much now as it was. So that's the difference. You know we've shifted; we shifted things here. And so now the frequency won't hold things. That's why all this stuff is coming to the surface. For millennia, we've had child abuse, but now we're angry about it and taking to the streets about it. That is the same. It's just now the frequency...when we go through our ascension here, then things won't be able to manifest here. They'll go somewhere else; they'll go to the next...and it's not...I mean, I know it feels very, like right and wrong, because I'm not saying that it's right to have murder and abuse. But I'm just saying it's part of the duality. It's part of this ascension process as far as it creates a catalyst for another planet to go through what you've gone through. But there won't be a great war again. I know people think things are getting worse, but there won't...

The war that you're in now, and you're in war right now, is very covert, like COVID covert. COVID is not a disease. It's the name of the war. So, your war is just not obvious to you. And that's part of what the dark side likes about it. Because then they tell you, you're not at war. What are you talking about? You're not at war. You're crazy. But you're not crazy. You're at war. It's a war. And so, there's so much happening behind the scenes, you know, on all levels. And so, it's good because victory is coming; victory is coming soon.

More Intergalactic Races

Another group that I heard about was the Aldebarans from the constellation of Taurus which is close to Orion. One of these beings was described as a black-blue-skinned humanoid, with brown hair, and electric blue eyes. This species is a highly intelligent, family-oriented, loving species. These peacekeepers worked with the Pleiadians and the Lyrans to push back the Reptilian group during the Orion wars and stop the destruction.

Many of the ascension wayshowers had incarnations on both sides of the conflict. Some played the villain, and some played the victims. This karma balanced on Earth now is the finalization of the greater galactic karma reaching back billions of years throughout our Milky Way galaxy. The way it was simplified to me was that God was like "You cannot keep destroying everything. All of you go to Earth, incarnate as humans, and settle your issues." So, it seems like that is the task for humanity, to release our perceived differences and our various self-serving agendas and come together as one family in one heart.

Beings who could escape Lyra before the cataclysm spread throughout the galaxy as refugees looking for a new home. These beings seeded new Lyran outposts in the areas of the stars Sirius A and Sirius B, in the Canis Major constellation, the Andromeda galaxy, the Pleiades star cluster, and maybe other regions. These beings were received and cared for by different intelligent species living in those systems. These star races shared healing technologies and began to create hybrid species using the Lyran DNA.

Besides the Lyrans, Pleiadians, and Sirians, our allies include the Arcturians from the star region of Arcturus in the Bootes constellation. I have also heard of the Blue Avians, which are blue, bird-like humanoid beings. I have mostly had clients regress to Blue Avian lives at the beginning of the seeding of Earth and the beginning stages of New Earth development. Maybe part of their purpose is using their ability to fly to watch over new experiments and report back to the higher councils how the progress is moving along.

I have also heard of "the Greys" who were permitted to experiment on human DNA to create hybrids for the seeding of other worlds. Although, I heard that they are not permitted to do these experiments anymore because it got too out of control. Most of the time, "abduction" is an experience that has been agreed upon by the soul before incarnation. Many starseeds are taken aboard spacecraft to have DNA repairs or updates to their consciousness to support the ascension. Even if the mainstream news and governments push the story of a threat of alien invasion, we must remember the negative ETs are already here and control the mainstream narrative. The positive ETs are here as well, and they would never allow a negative ET invasion at this stage of the ascension.

I have had clients describe civilizations in many other regions of space, including even more distant star systems and other universes. This universe is teeming with intelligent life with many advanced species who have existed for trillions of years and likely more. Humanity (on planet Earth) is still quite young when we compare our species with the other star races and planetary systems' legacies. When we shift to New Earth, our star brethren will return and teach us many new things to advance life on planet Earth. We have so much to look forward to!

TWELVE

The Earth Experiment

Over a long time, Earth's physicality was formed and eventually infused with its own soul essence. Earth, our beloved Gaia, is a living, breathing sentient being of Light. Beyond her physicality, she has a soul with an evolutionary destiny pathway and plan, just like you and me, that is per the Divine Plan of Source. The soul of Gaia had other lifetimes leading up to a graduation phase where she was initiated into a higher level of soul ascension that meant that she was ready to hold life. Many cosmic beings gathered on the planet's cooling surface after the volcanic phase to perform a grand ceremony where Gaia infused herself into the planet as life-giving water was poured across the surface to bring life.

Transcript: Activation of Gaia

This next client takes us to the beginning of the seeding process to a grand ceremony to activate the Life of Gaia!

C: *I'm wearing all white and there's a golden room around. It feels like a sacred space. And there's water. There are people in robes bathing and steam and flowers. It smells really beautiful. Incense.*

M: **Are you alone there or are there others with you?**

C: *It's full of people and people are laughing. Music playing. I see that someone is playing a harp. It's a celebration. It goes outside. Again, a long environment. It goes as far as a football field. I'm at the top of this waterfall again. It looks like Pangea before everything changed. I'm back to the beginning of the planet. We're all here at the beginning for the birthing of the planet, and the birth of the planet comes when the waterfall came into this planet. We earned it. The planet has the badges. She earned this. Gaia was a young woman once. She earned this ability, and the Gods blessed her.*

M: **You were saying that Gaia needed to do some things to earn her badges. Tell me what that means.**

C: *I'm saying that she had earned them and that's why she became a planet. And that's why she got to be our mother. What an honor it is for her. To have come so far in the universe to have gained the trust of the stars and all of its people. All of the sacredness and all of the things that are here in Gaia. We're like a treasure box. We are this special thing, and we have no idea how sacred we are. How special we are. Gaia trained for a long time to be strong enough to hold us on her back. Running through obstacles and shooting arrows. Warrior. Many lifetimes Gaia lived before she was able to be strong enough to hold this. I see Gaia is a true daughter of the Creator.*

Transcript: Beginning of Earth

This dear soul is the one who brought me into the world of Quantum Healing by following his intuition and sharing *The Three Waves of Volunteers and the New Earth* by Dolores Cannon with me. This session still teaches me something new every time I read it. It truly is a living transmission! This client describes himself as a being that I now understand to be one of the Sha although he never said that term in our session.

C: *I guess it's like magma all around me. Like a planet full of fire and different craters...not craters, but like how on Earth when it dries out it cracks; it's like that except in between all the cracks is red magma.*

M: Is there any plant life there?

C: *There's no plant life. There doesn't seem to be life. I seem to be a kind of rock figure. Like a...I'm like a little humanoid rock. I'm like gray and brown stone. Four toes and like a stone for the lower part of the leg. A little joint. Bigger stones for thighs. I don't see any genitalia, but there's a butt. Kind of a round belly.*

M: Do you have anything in your hands?

C: *On one hand, I have...my right hand I have a violet crystal. In my left hand, I have two blue stones that look like sapphires.*

M: What do these stones do?

C: *They're glowing. Across in the distance, there's a yellow, looks like a spire, a pyramid, shining really brightly. It actually looks like...it's like a soft, white glow is coming off of it, and it's hardening the ground. It's bringing life. And plants. And water.*

M: What do you do with most of your day?

C: *I think I have been surveying the growth of the planet.*

M: So, you are a steward there? Caretaker?

C: I think so.

M: How did you get there? Were you born there?

C: I think I am. Yeah. I'm manifested from the planet. It's giving birth to life.

M: So, what would you like to do next?

C: Well, I think I need to go over to the spire with the crystals. Standing in front of it. It's very tall. It's a giant citrine crystal. Sticking out of the earth, actually goes all the way through it. I'm there with other beings like me. We all have crystals of different, varying colors, and we're putting them onto the citrine crystal.

M: What does that do?

C: It activates it. I think we've been waiting a very long time to do this. And we've all gathered there; we're putting the crystals into the citrine. Citrine's dissolving.

M: Is this a good thing?

C: Yes. The planet's calming. It's a feeling of love (begins crying). It's a very positive feeling. The crystal is being absorbed by the planet, and we're going in with it. We're dying. And this is what we came here to do. I'm being drawn to the center of the planet. We become the planet itself. And it's starting to grow life. Volcanoes are erupting. The shimmering, yellow glow is going again; it's disappearing. Planet's starting to spin. I can see it going around its sun. All the giant crystals are coming out of the planet.

M: And what do these crystals do?

C: They're sending beams of light out into the universe, in all directions, in all colors.

M: Where do these beams go?

C: To different solar systems. It seems that everything's getting drawn in. Getting closer and closer and they explode to come together and explode. Everything's shattering into a million crystals. Looks like a nuclear explosion, except it's a rainbow crystal. Flowing outward in a disc.

M: What happens to these crystals next?

C: They're getting sucked back into a core. It's Earth.

Creating Planets

Once a planet moves beyond the volcanic phase and begins to cool, a web of mycelial species, fungus, is put on the surface to lay the foundational grid of life force energy. The mushrooms act as a neural pathway to pulse vital energy across the planet's surface so that other, more advanced biological forms can be introduced and connected through the network. This network bridges with the greater pathways of Light connecting all of the planets, stars, galaxies, and beyond to the Source. From there other life forms can be introduced.

Over long periods of time, millions upon millions of years, Earth was tended to, nurtured, and matured by the support of ultraterrestrial and extraterrestrial beings working together with a unified vision directed by Source Intelligence. A theme was chosen for the planet of "seeking harmony within diversity," and many varieties of species and DNA were brought to Earth from many different areas of the universe to interact, grow, and evolve in the paradisiacal and diverse environment of Earth. These cosmic scientists watch and observe the planet allowing the magic of evolution to unfold within the grand Earth experiment, occasionally visiting the surface to check on their precious creation.

Transcript: Young Earth

Here is another transcription from a session with Matan speaking about the seeding of life on Earth.

M: How was early civilization created between the animals and the plants and the beings of the planet?

HS: When the planet was brought into creation, many plants and animals were brought from other planets, through other star systems. Not everything originated here. Other planets have been in Creation much longer than this Earth. This Earth of yours is new still, but at the same time old as time progresses. Not as old as other planets in your star system. Many other beings from other planets have brought many things to contribute to this planet. Is this making sense for you?

R: Yes.

M: How many other planets were sourced from for these creations here?

HS: Several. Several. If you knew how many beings were actually in this part of your universe, you would be amazed. And they are around this planet, not everyone can see them. At times people can, and at times people can't.

M: Tell me about how human beings came to be on this planet. Early human forms.

HS: You must know that humans of this planet came from other planets. The human form came from other planets, other star systems. There are humans in other star systems. You are not the only humans.

Transcript: Overseeing the Beginning of Earth

This next client was taken to a lifetime at the beginning of the Earth Experiment. The client described her body as having lizard feet with three toes that were webbed together. She was not wearing clothing but remarked about iridescent, green-blue scaled skin, and long, thin legs. She described herself as slightly androgynous but leaning more towards masculine expression. She felt younger but a bit flat in vital energy as though her body was not meant for the Earth's environment. The top of her head came to a crest like a mohawk that went over the top of the head and faded as it descended the spine. Her face had a pointed beak with eyes that were oval-shaped under a heavy brow. She held in her hands a defense weapon that resembled a harpoon or arrow. She wore a necklace with a medallion that denoted her rank.

As she looked around herself, she described a desolate lava field with little vegetation. The land was dark; the sky was dark; and the scene felt "moody." On her left side, she saw and felt the ocean and all around her wrapped the black lava field. She had a sense that she was guarding, protecting, or keeping watch.

She lived alone in her "watchtower," a structure made of crystalline material and simple rock that was formed into several intersecting diamond shapes framed with wood. There was a hole in the ground where she could acquire fish from the ocean which she ate raw.

M: I want you to see what you do with most of your time in that life. What do you see, what do you do?

C: Ok, now I am seeing... Well, the first thing that came to mind is a fire — a light. I am a fire or a light. I am the guardian of that fire.

M: What's the significance of this fire?

C: It feeds down, through the land, into the center of the planet. It's a representative...I can't think of the right word. Flame vibration. Emissary? Of the planet. I protect it. I keep watch over it and protect it to make sure it keeps emitting its vibration.

M: What is this vibration used for?

C: It constructs things. It slowly...it gives, it informs step-by-step the biological processes that existing organisms respond to. Allowing them to...not just mutate and grow but embody and contain the foundational information they need to exist on the surface and support what will then come next.

M: So, it's a very important energy there.

C: Yes. It comes from the heart spring.

M: The heart spring of what?

C: The Earth.

NEXT SCENE: BROADCASTING FLOWERS

M: Where are you?

C: It's like a texture is all I'm seeing. Like a sloping blue shape of...not blue, blue-ish...it's like elephant skin or something like that type of texture, but it's so strange. Everything is soft. I am in dark. If I reach out to touch or lean into the structure like it's a hill, it's squishy. It has a softness to it.

M: Let's zoom out so we can get a bigger perspective on it. What do you see as you zoom out?

C: A flower. A purply, bluish flower. And so, from where I just came from, my awareness was inside of it — pushing against the petals.

M: Why were you inside of this flower?

C: This is the same veins into the heart space of the planet; it's the same access. The flower center has the same light.

M: What does it do for you to connect with the flower this way?

C: I'm just happy that they're multiplying, broadcasting, and becoming. They are torchbearers, in a sense, of this vibrational frequency, replicating and sending out higher and wider. I feel proud and happy for it. This is why growing things are attracted to growing things. All tapped into the essence of vibrational encodement.

M: What kind of codes are coming from this flower?

C: That's what is interesting. They're so many transmissions that we're not even necessarily aware of.

M: What's the function of these transmissions? You can share a few of them.

C: This particular flower informs. It has to do with way of being, growth, and openness. It has something to do with openness. This balance of...it's like the Tao, the balance of fire and water. The growth, the reaching, the striving, and the receptivity. Ebb and flow. Allowing. They kind of hold...it's holding that Light of the Tao, of perfect balance. And they're all, if I zoom further up, there is so much communication. It's so striking. There's a world of transaction — the giving and the receiving. It's a group effort. Each one holds a thread of this heart flame, and together it's a group effort to make it larger and more spread out. By making it thinner and wider. As they communicate with each other, they're informing each other as well. They're not singular. They have become, in a sense, their own self-protectors, but they don't need to protect anymore because of that network. It's self-evident, I want to say. It is. It cannot be bothered.

M: What was the purpose of that life?

C: Foundation and formulation. Helping just maintain and steady the foundations of creation of this place. And tending to the formulation, not creating, but it's almost like gardening. Where things need to be just pruned or tended a little bit, keeping things on track. This was almost like a lab lifetime. It was like honing, testing and honing, fine-tuning.

MEETING HER COUNCIL OF GUIDES

C: There are four entities, nonphysical. Patches of light, they're light basically. There's just all darkness, not a room. Half of the entities on the left, there are four in front of me. The two on the left are quiet. The two on the right are more involved in this. The two on the left feel more...they all feel cosmic, but the two on the left feel less concerned with matter. The two on the right are the bridge between spirit and matter, more creation-oriented in a physical sense. I just see them more invested in whatever this is; they're more involved.

M: What's being discussed there? What's happening in this group?

C: The idea or the agreement is being made around incarnating in some kind of physical form in order to... The dialogue is around the physical form in order to be involved directly in the physical creation. Through obviously an energetic source and impulse, that's where everything comes. There is something about it that, for me, feels unusual or foreign to do that, but there is something necessary about being in the body with this distribution of this heart vein — light source.

M: What's unique? Why must you be in physical form? What was needed?

C: It's also to see how it affects the physical bodies. I think I am culturing DNA in my own body as well. I am experiencing them watching this for other life forms. In the proximity to guarding that flame, or sitting with and being around that flame, I was also...am also...going to be receiving the pure encodement of the planetary body so that life can be on it. There are the DNA and the cellular structures. There has to be some cultivation of dense body tissue in order to be a dense planet. There have to be access points in those structures for non-density as well, for this pure energy to move and cleanse and clear this cultivated physical tissue and DNA and cellular, nervous systems.

M: So, once you cultivate this DNA, once you gather all this information to make the changes, what will this DNA be used for in the future? How is it used?

C: This is somehow interwoven into what becomes different life forms on Earth. In particular, the different races of beings who are meant to hold space for the physical life forms and be the custodians of the physical life forms, and continually be integrating spirit into the cellular networks of themselves and the structures around them. Like the flowers we were looking at, everything is resonating and vibrating with everything else. There is never a moment when there isn't information moving between cellular structures. Anything, everything that is the planet and life on the planet is emitting cross-coding frequencies. They are needed to be...like labs where this movement of energy through different types of tissue and structures was not quite tested but tried in different ways. The way the structures work isn't quite... The network initially was supposed to be more open — even with the concept of density. It's slightly muddied, or more blocked.

M: What caused it to be muddied or blocked?

C: There is some kind of contamination. Like too much involvement somehow. I'm not super clear. There was more involvement very early on that gave a thicker...I keep saying "cellular structure," so I guess it's cells. Everything should be slightly more porous ideally, but it went forward with the thicker structure. Just in hope it could be alleviated at some point along the way. There are continued moments in time where there is an alleviation and then thickening. It goes back and forth a little bit.

M: I want you to see what was causing that initial disturbance. You said there was involvement earlier on. Do you have access to what that was? What do you see there?

C: Totally, my area of focus I can feel, but there's some kind of a wave. Not a liquid wave but a wave pushing in from outside very early on. That wasn't part of the plan. It's almost like catching a cold. That kind of infection, something came from outside. Outside what was the initial idea. I see it.

M: What does it look like?

C: It looks like a darkish cloud, but it just feels like it doesn't fit. It feels like when two people don't get each other — it's the kind of discord. That this powder, this thickness, this vibration...it's essentially a vibration but pretty powerful infiltration of a vibration that doesn't have anything to do with the existing what was created. What was created is stronger and bigger than this...it feels like a virus to me.

M: How did it affect the planet? What did it do once it arrived?

C: In this analogy, it's like when the body is fighting something that doesn't belong there. The planet begins to do that too because it doesn't belong there. And so, in this early moment — early, early, infantile stage of things, the template of conflict is seeded because it's trying to evict this disharmonious vibration. Disharmony becomes a part of the story, and then the next part of the story is how to harmonize out of disharmony, at every level.

M: So, it sounds like this energy affected all layers of evolution on this planet.

C: Yes.

M: What was being done to balance this, from your perspective?

C: You can see how from within the Earth's core-essence, there is still this overwhelmingly huge web of life that functions perfectly, even in its chaotic states. It's in the perfect state of balance. And so, it, oh...there's continued amplification from the core through these kinds of veins of energy through to the surface. It's from the inside out that it's healing itself. It's so similar in what is called the "New Age," the conversation is always that if you want to heal something, you go inside and heal from the inside out, the same principle. The same. The self-realization of one's own core of light amplifying from the center through to the surface and radiating outward to cleanse and clear the whole space around.

HIGHER SELF CONVERSATION

M: Wonderful. So, out of all the lifetimes you could have shown her today, why did you show this particular life?

HS: To give her a sense of her place in the order of things. How she fits into *structures of creation. How she is involved when sometimes she doesn't think she's involved — a sense of being in life.*

M: The next scene you showed was with her exploring this big flower and the network of energies that come from the Earth's core up through these flowers into the atmosphere. Why did you show this to her?

HS: This is most especially for the sensation of the beauty and the joy of creation. Of the nucleus of love in all living things. That there is an open point of any living thing that can be connected with, that is connected down into this vein of heart-based but Source-based energy. It's the still point in anything out of which life, love arises. Also, we wanted to connect her with that so she can experience that kind of soft love all around her wherever she goes. She's been feeling disconnected often.

M: What are some ways she can tap into that connection there?

HS: Well, spending more time in nature. It's a cliche, but not just spending more time in nature but consciously opening to what she's now experienced as this portal in anything living that's around her. Plants are easy because they are rooted. They are not moving; they are patiently waiting to be tapped into. They love to share these codes, this energy, this Source point. It's part of their sacred service.

M: There is often this talk about the experiment, or the test, what is happening here on planet Earth. What was the intention of this experiment?

HS: Bringing life to the planet. The intention was to create a sphere of great biodiversity, very specified. A wide range of energies and vibrations that are more specific than many other places, than any other places. And how they can exemplify Oneness by existing in the same place together as a web of life. Again, this idea of separateness but connectedness. Specificity, but universality. The extremes, but the paradox of those extremes being the same thing. Life existing in this way and self-actualizing, self-realizing in such a place. The potential for growth of consciousness in the one is amplified with this type of experiment. And for the sake of design, the beauty of so many different things in one place is astounding.

M: I would like to know some more about this energy that came in that influenced the Earth's environment. How can we work with transmuting this energy here on the surface?

HS: One way of working into raising our vibration as representative of the core of Gaia is in re-establishing, or if it is established — deepening, a reverential relationship to the planet. Beyond simply appreciating its beauty, which is wonderful, and its creatures, but also to get deeper tuning in — anchoring into the core energetically — opening as a clear channel to radiate, as if you were a flower, this Source energy that is foundational in the core of Gaia. There are obvious habitual things around diet and environment, and these are very important. But a practice where even a small amount of time is taken each day to open from heart space as wide as possible while holding a deep anchor into the center of the Earth and broadcasting. Become a channel for pure Light. It seems small but would actually do a lot.

Gaia's Theme

The Earth Experiment was originally intended to be the creation of the Gem of the Universe, a Master Garden of diversity. From the physical forms to the subtle vibrations, Gaia is a massive record of cosmic intelligence. Hopefully, these pages will inspire you to connect more deeply with the sentience of Earth. She has much wisdom and love to share!

THIRTEEN

The Human Experiment

My clients have described various civilizations on the Earth that have been lost in history, with whispers of their existence still held in mythological stories. A few clients describe amphibious humanoid beings that swam in the oceans who eventually came to the surface and learned to breathe air during the time of the dinosaurs. A few clients have regressed to lifetimes where they were part of a cooperative force of star nations establishing observation stations on the Earth to organize the seeding of life on the newly developing planet. Huge "arks" descended upon the Earth to drop animals into the various ecosystems that were being crafted by extraterrestrial and higher dimensional beings. Star relatives brought medicinal plants with unique frequency signatures from different star systems to plant them on the new time capsule of the universe, our shining Master Garden of Gaia. Many gardens were created within the experimental zone of Earth to see how much diversity could be introduced while maintaining harmony and balance between all biomes. Sometimes, the clients' descriptions were so outside of my understanding that I had difficulty integrating the new information into my perspective of Earth history.

While all of this is so common for me now, I had to release a lot of my judgments, programmed belief systems from my culture, and assumptions to grasp the massiveness of what was being shared with me over four years. If you are having trouble with these new ideas, I totally understand, as I, too, had to deal with cognitive dissonance and my limited perspective of reality to be able to expand with this new data. We know so little of what truly happened in Earth's billions of years of history. So many records and artifacts have been lost due to war, ignorance, colonialization, and time. To truly begin to comprehend our history, there needs to be openness to new information that contradicts the history taught to us by our cultures, religions, mainstream media, and institutions. The Indigenous peoples and the Mystery Schools hold some of the ancient lore of the Earth, yet so much has been lost, hidden, and distorted through the turning of time.

At a certain point in the seeding process, there was a decision by the

Galactic and Higher Councils to introduce an intelligent species to Earth. A variety of types of human beings with different types of gene expressions were introduced at various times in multiple "gardens" to see what types of genetics would mature well in Earth's environment. The story of Adam and Eve is just one story describing how new species are introduced. It is not the only story of "first humans." The Hebrew genetics are newer but not the first. We see now in human genetics a mixture of many genetic implantations and experiments over the many thousands of years of humanity's existence on Earth.

Many Indigenous Earth peoples speak of their connection to the stars and the Star People. Many Indigenous believe that the root of their genetic lineages, culture, and lore comes from the Star Nations. Our star families observe our experimental zone of Earth and assist in our maturation and awakening process within the limitations of Universal Law which states that they cannot directly interfere with our maturation process or override our collective free will. They can, however, bring new teachings and new ideas to help us along our path of remembrance and ascension. At certain times, human DNA was permitted by Source to be altered by different star races, for example, the Pleiadians, to help our maturation and move us into higher consciousness. The human genome has been called the "galactic cookie jar" that everyone has had their hands in over what was said to be a period of 365,000 years of human genetic experimentation. This experiment is coming to a close, and soon we will be restored to our original pure human-soul synthesis form.

The organic technology of the *christ-alline* human being, in its purest form, is meant to channel the collective consciousness of the Masters, of the Great Illumined Ones. We have the ability to be in the material universe while also being channels of the pure Light of Source. Our genetics are infused with the genetics of all the greatest races of the Cosmos. We have keys hidden within our genetics that give us the ability to access eternal life, eternal knowledge, infinite power, and eternal bliss. This has made some groups jealous and envious, and much harm has been done to humanity and to the Earth to suppress our abilities and ascension. This has all been training for us to do what we are doing NOW in this era. We have the ability to completely transmute all of the entropic shadows upon this Earth and reclaim this planet as a Planet of Light!

Transcript: Anunnaki — Nibiru

Now we start to look at the human genome experimentation upon planet Earth which begins with the introduction of the Anunnaki. The Anunnaki are space gods described by the ancient Sumerians, Akkadians, and Assyrians. Many of the "gods and goddesses" of ancient Earth are truly space beings with higher consciousness and expanded abilities. There is much fear and judgment around the Anunnaki on planet Earth and I hope to update humanity's understanding of the Anunnaki and their past and present involvement with Earth. Here is a summary of a client's session who experienced a lifetime as an Anunnaki.

When the client went to the next "appropriate scene" in an IQH session, she saw herself on a red, rusty planet that felt hot, which she internally knew was from imbalance on the planet from the collective greed and overuse of artificial intelligence which was killing the planet. The client described a sandy surface and advanced technology that was used to harvest energy from the universe and local stars. The greed of the civilization and the technology they used had overtaken their world, leaving the planet barren and stripped of resources. Not only was the atmosphere and surface of Nibiru stripped of resources but also the reserves of energy and materials from deep within the planet which caused major distortion in the organic flow and balance of life.

When she described her own form in that scene, she immediately sensed that she was inside of a robotic body, an intelligent, nanotech, smart armor around her soul essence. She later described herself as pale-skinned but that it was more etheric than it was physical. The metallic casing felt indestructible, yet she was aware that she had to sacrifice some of her trust and faith in Source to be able to use this protective armor. The armor gave her the ability to extend her life span and gave her other skills and power which she used to mine precious metals and harvest energy from the energetic grid of the planet. She described the planet as a higher density planetary body when compared to modern Earth, existing in a different bandwidth of energetic frequency.

As she looked around this dying world, I asked her if her planet had a name and she said with surprise, "Nibiru!" This higher density world has been verified in other sessions about Nibiru that say it is part of a system of celestial bodies that pass through our solar system every so many thousands of years but exists in a higher density/dimension that we cannot see with our third-density form.

She described her home as pyramidal-shaped and advanced technologically. Her home used power from the Sun and ley lines for power, as did the whole civilization. When home, she would remove her robotic layer covering her form. She described a crystalline, liquid-light substance that she would ingest for sustenance. She described the members of her family unit as emotionally independent, free from the codependent family dynamics found in humanity. There was an interdependence, no sense of ownership, as each member was considered an equally powerful creative being.

I moved her forward to the next important scene from that life and she was shown her role in the Anunnaki council at the time when the group decided to manipulate humanity.

C: *I see the council, our council, our decision to enslave humanity... (cries). Oh my God...*

M: **Breathe into these emotions and breathe into these thoughts so that you can understand it, so you can express it, and describe it to me. Tell me about this decision on this council.**

C: *It was like (crying)...it's life or death. It's our species or theirs. We're...at that point it wasn't...because I can look at it from the NOW perspective. I didn't...we didn't know humanity would...it would look like it does in the present time that we're in, but...*

M: **So, what's being discussed amongst the council? Tell me about it.**

C: *Well, we've been taking resources from Earth and it's not working to heal our atmosphere. The minerals aren't aligning with our plan the way we thought. It's not... 'cause it's not organic, the same organic elements, so we can't patch up our home. We took from Earth to patch up our home and then when we realized it wasn't going to happen, we always had Plan B to move — who wanted to move to Earth; some went to Andromeda. The ones that chose to go to Earth chose to, out of their own pain, take advantage of a less evolved species. And a way for us to fully be able to survive on Earth because we're from a different density, we had to...we had to splice, we had to share the DNA, we had to disrupt the organic evolution of the beings, the primitive beings of Earth.*

M: **When you say that you're in a different density, explain that to me.**

C: *Our physical form vibrates at a higher resonance, so a higher density; so, at the human eye, we can only see 30 frames per second, so if you're looking at us and we're 60 frames per second, you can't pick it up with your human eye. The density in which humans vibrate is such a lower frequency that they look solid, that you're a solid structure. We can phase through time; we can phase through dimensional walls; we can time travel — that is a higher frequency of a higher frequency being; so in order for us to dense down to...be with gravity, oxygen, and to organically survive, we have to adjust our frequency.*

M: And how do you adjust the frequency? How did you share DNA?

C: *By breeding with humans, by sharing DNA. How was DNA shared? Because I see it kind of as splicing. I don't so much see it as like an Anunnaki having sex with humans. It didn't create that way. It's very...it's such an advanced looking thing. It's like I'm seeing DNA strands. I see, it like...it looks like a syringe pulling our DNA from one being and putting it into another. So, it looks...I'm seeing it's like an injection as a medical procedure. But there is also a consciousness, it's also through the consciousness as well.*

M: And how did this sharing of DNA affect the human? What was it like before and what did it become after?

C: *Well, we like to believe we were doing them a favor because they weren't very advanced. So, by sharing our DNA was allowing the expansion of things they had never thought of, such as sourcing energy out of the ley lines. The humans were very primitive, very...you know...just focused on their grooming, their shelter, and their food. There wasn't a lot of like...thought.*

M: I understand that. And I'm wondering how this transaction was introduced to the humans. Was this a free-will choice? Was it something that was agreed upon in some way? You can see this now.

C: *I wouldn't consider it agreed. I would consider it manipulated, free-will agreement. I see just sharing the smallest amount of technology — the small amount of ease and excitement in life is easy to sell or to get a species to want more.*

M: So, there were promises made or little gifts given to sway them into wanting more?

C: *Yes and handing over power. I'm really seeing jump through time, 'cause I can see humans when they're really primitive, you know, kind of like a monkey, to having more knowledge to...then I see the advanced species of like Lemuria and how our DNA is a part of that experiment as well, so it's a really...the advancement...it's really interesting...*

M: Very good. Would you say this timeframe is before or after Lemuria?

C: Way before.

M: Very good. What do you see happening there now? What are you watching?

C: I was just observing. It's like monkeys running around and they're unknowing of anything beyond them. Which is interesting to think about, because it's taught now that there is nothing beyond humans now, so it's like that mentality has carried through in some aspects. And I'm talking about the very beginning beings before any advanced race was introduced. And I also hear that when Anunnaki were experimenting there were other experiments happening on Earth at the same time, so...

M: What kind of experiments were going on then?

C: Other species using the resources, other species, especially the Draconian species using...changing the structure of the human DNA as well. Looks like they were experimenting as well, but it almost looks like it's on the other side. Like the Anunnaki were on this side of the planet, totally different agendas.

M: Very good. And what was different between the Draconian and Anunnaki agendas?

C: We were trying to source Earth material and they were trying to source energy from human bodies, from the actual beings. So...I'm not going to say it's more twisted, but it feels like it.

M: I'm wondering why you showed the scenes from the Anunnaki today? Why was that brought forth for us?

HS: The Anunnaki are clearing their karma. So many Anunnaki are asking for forgiveness for their souls, asking to be forgiven from the human race. They have, you know they went...they started this to save their planet, then to save their species, and then it snowballed into this really dark space and the majority of the Anunnaki were there, and they are done serving the Dark and they're ready to serve the Light. They've set down their swords. They're setting down their nanotech; they're setting down their protection; they're setting down their past. They're ready to serve the Light and they've agreed to move forward with the evolution of humanity in an organic matter.

M: So wonderful. I know people are curious about what the pass-by

experience will be like, or if that will happen in our lifetime?

HS: What do you mean? The pass-by?

M: The pass-by of Nibiru.

HS: Oh. It's interesting because there is...two different stories but I see Nibiru as being already gone and there's this shadow energy of it still in place. Yes, yup. There will be a decloaking of it, so it'll...the awareness and the truth and remembrance of it will come but I don't see it as an actual physical space that can be gone to, and I don't see it as something that's going to crash into Earth or crash into the Sun, which is stuff that has been told...because there are timelines of course where that plays out, and that played out, but that's not what's playing out in this reality.

Transcript: Tall Hairy Ones Watching over Humanity

This client regressed to a lifetime of a tall, red-haired humanoid on the Earth about one-and-a-half times the size of a modern human. The being was benevolent and lived for thousands of years. The being watched humans being introduced to the area and watched humanity cycle through many needless wars. When I had the client go back to when the humans first arrived, she described a group of extraterrestrials that arrived at the planet by spacecraft.

C: I see them moving. I don't call them people because they have longer legs and shorter torsos than the people look now.

M: What do you call them, or what do they like to be called?

C: I am hearing a word that I don't want to just assume because I have heard this word before. A-nun-nak-eye [pronounced in this way] – Anunnaki.

M: Ok, very good. Well, tell me what's happening, what you notice about them. Describe everything to me.

C: Well, I see kind of like a dark blue-purple, almost shimmery, scaly-looking skin, but it's like if it moves, it can change color from different shades of blue and purple like it almost looks like it could be holographic, but there's also form to it. It's like it can be less dense and then more dense. I am not afraid of it because I am part of this land, so I am just curious.

M: Do you have any connection to these beings?

C: I place my hand up just to see, and I see it place its arm up to show that it doesn't want to threaten me.

M: And how many of these beings are there?

C: I am focusing on one but there's more behind it. I do sense some sort of ship or thing in the sky that it came from. Really, really big — way bigger than me.

M: What does it look like?

C: Like...I think it is referred to as disc-shaped, like it's circular but wider than it is tall and it's symmetrical — the top and bottom are the same, almost the same, almost the same size. But it's pretty massive, but I didn't see it at first. It's like it was just there, but then it just...now that I am paying attention to it; it is easier to see. It's all very...it's not something that you can just look at and see right away. You have to wait patiently, then you see it kind of move. And that's how you sense it and notice it because it can blend in and hide very well, but just like the beings.

M: So, what do you see these beings doing now?

C: Taking samples of the ground and plants. It looks like they are studying things. They don't look like they are here to just have fun; they look like they are working. They have business to take care of. I can't really see their faces because it blends in so well with their skin. I almost feel like it's something that they just change about themselves when they go somewhere new, almost like a protective, holographic body that they just change form into so that if they need to hide — if they need to do anything they are safe in this form, but they can change form kind of thing.

NEXT SCENE:
INTRODUCING HUMANS TO ENVIRONMENT

C: I am looking at somebody lying on the ground with dark hair, and they are unconscious. It looks more humanlike, pale skin, and this being...one of these beings are reviving it, to see how it adapts. They...everybody is curious to see if this works. It looks like a woman. Black hair, and they are...I feel like they are telepathically trying to help her wake up; they are making intentions and speaking to her telepathically to get her to start breathing. There! The mouth opened. She is still living, but they are helping her learn to breathe. Now I see her eyes open, but she doesn't see any of these beings around her. She is not looking at them; she is just looking at the bushes and the ground and the sky. It looks like she thinks she is all alone, and she is just trying to figure out where she is almost in a panic state...but she will know; she will be ok.

She tries to get to her feet and starts to back up and hide in some bushes and rock because there is a natural sense of fear coming from her, because she doesn't know where she is, and I think she just feels like she is safer to hide. It could be really...that would be really frightening to not know where you are. I feel bad for this woman.

M: Yeah. So, what happens next?

C: I still see these beings on the ground just standing there observing, but I can't see her anymore. I know she went undercover, but it looks like they are going to give her some time and leave on their ship and come back and see how she has made it. And I am not sure if she saw me. I don't think she did. But she doesn't come my way. I am aware that she's there. I don't go and try to communicate with her because I feel that would hinder her ability to take care of herself. She needs to focus on getting food and getting herself feeling safe and secure before she can nullify that fear.

NEXT SCENE: MORE HUMANS ARRIVE

C: That woman looks a lot dirtier than when they first brought her. Her hair is pretty wild and ratty and messy. She...it is almost as if when they brought her here, she was part of a test. She looked like she was well cleaned and taken care of. And then she just didn't know what to do so she's not wearing any clothes, but she did find a way to feed herself. She is cutting up a fish with a sharp stone just on the side of the water on a big rock. But she does look like she is reacting more like an animal, but I think it's because that's what she has observed, and so that is what she has learned from what is around her. But she does seem like she is a little bit on edge almost; she is always watching around her to make sure she is still safe.

M: What happens next?

C: She is eating and making sure she has food. She doesn't think about future plans; she only thinks about surviving, so she is very limited in her...I don't say limited in her quality of life because that's not fair for someone to say who knows this, but she could be experiencing more, but she only knows how to be surviving.

M: Yeah. That's understandable.

C: And she needs more; she needs to meet more people like her so they can help each other and learn and start to feel...start to feel safe and secure, and resting and relaxing.

M: So, what happens?

C: So, I do feel like these beings that brought her here are bringing just a couple more in her area. There may be more in other areas, but beyond that, I see another little boy, a man, but they don't do this near her. They do it a bit further away, so that they can meet each other naturally.

M: So, they bring another boy and a man?

C: Yeah. Now I need to focus on that part and leave her for a moment. They...they have the boy and the man together because I think they do want to see this succeed. They don't want to just...they want to see if they can manipulate how people can live. So, they don't have any heart connection to these beings, but they want to see this succeed for their own learning to study. And they do the same process where these humans can't see them. This man looks more...he doesn't look as...he looks slightly different than the woman. He looks like, I don't know the proper word, but I would say the word is Neanderthal. Like he looks more ape-like. Like a bigger mouth, bigger nostrils but still similar to the woman so that she feels that they are similar and not be afraid of each other. Then the man is still somewhat slender but just more strong. And the boy is similar to the man in appearance. They don't recognize each other...like they don't know each other, but they feel a bond that the little one can trust him. And he is just very thin, and they hope that the two will meet.

I do see them looking at each other...like they did come to meet each other, but the woman is kind of circling around him. She is trying to figure him out, but she is also careful not to...she is assessing whether it is threatening, but the man is not really afraid of her because he is slightly bigger and like most all animals, they can sense if something is going to bother them or not.

They watch each other a lot. He is watching how she is feeding herself. They can't talk to each other, but they can watch how they do things, so she's taking water from the river and cutting up her fish, and he's observing and learning from it. And she's not...she's not nice to the boy yet. Like she doesn't take on a mothering role right away, but she just kind of looks at him. But the boy isn't afraid of her. And so, they just keep watching each other and see what each other do and just become more comfortable in each other's presence and survive next to one another, but they are not hurting each other, so that is a good thing.

I see they're working together now. They sleep in the same area, and they built an upside-down L shape out of some pieces of some large branches, so there's one big branch that stands up straight and then another one tied to it. And they are using that to hang meat off of. I think to dry out the skin and stuff. I see three pieces of animal...small animal, but it seems like the skin is drying out. So, it looks like they are beginning to come up with ideas, and instead of just eating fish, now they are eating from the animals that are around them and working together to survive. That's cool that they came up with that.

I am being shown like the sun going and going and going. Like the sun's up, the sun's down. I am being shown like the passing of time. And the hair on these beings is a lot longer. They all have black hair. It just seems like this is working. This is good.

M: Is it still just the same beings, or are they multiplying at all?

C: I am still only seeing those three.

NEXT SCENE: ARCTURIAN DNA ENHANCEMENT

C: I'm seeing like a different color of blue being...a little bit shorter; it's like a light blue this time, and they are walking through forests and bush. And these beings are different than the ones...than the other beings that were here, and I think they are trying to find the humans that are here. It almost looks like a search party, like sticking their nose in other people's business. They...I am hearing like the phrase "conflict of interest." These beings want to kind of take over what the other ones started. Like they are trying to take advantage of the progress that somebody else did and they want to do; they want to see what they can do with the situation. And they...it's like stealing somebody else's ideas, stealing somebody else's work, but they want to see what they can change.

M: Where do these beings come from?

C: I am just supposed to say what pops in my head, right? Because I am hearing two words: one I am hearing — Arcturus, and Nebulae — those are the two words I am hearing. I don't want to overthink it.

M: So, these Arcturians want to... What do they want to do with the humans?

C: They want to adjust them. I am seeing like a syringe or a needle, but I think that is to make it so that they aren't aggressive or combative. And I think they are taking them on to their ship and likely giving them DNA... just a little bit of a DNA change, but not so much that it's noticeable, just to help them understand a little bit more so that they can learn things with a broader understanding.

M: **How does it affect them that they are able to do that? What does this change in the DNA do to them that makes them see a broader perspective?**

C: *I don't think they want them to be so animalistic — not that being animals is bad, but they, I am trying to think of how to say this, because they can see where this can lead to if it is not helped. They want to shift it in a slight way so that they can form maybe some of their own thoughts in a more pure way.*

Transcript: More on Nibiru and the Anunnaki

Here is another transcription from my work with the somnambulistic client named Matan whose Higher Self is one of the original Elohim creators.

M: **We were told about a celestial body that might be passing the planet, and we want to know about it.**

HS: *Are you talking about these asteroid bodies that are passing the planet. Is that what you are talking about?*

M: **We are talking about Nibiru.**

HS: *This has come up many times. It depends on what path you are on. We must remind you that not everyone is on the same path to the same next Earth. There are many destinations playing out all at once.*

M: **Can you share about the Anunnaki?**

HS: *The Anunnaki go back to the ones who came through at a time with a purpose, a divine purpose. They are a significant group of souls. There has been much information given to many about the Anunnaki. You have heard the term "large people" or the "tall ones" as skeletons have been found of them. They are connected to the Anunnaki. This is what has been shown to people many times, but your governments and your media will not show this. They want to keep you in the dark.*

M: **Are the Anunnaki a benevolent race?**

HS: *We would like to share with you that they aren't malevolent in the way that you think. They did have malevolence towards human beings. During their time on your planet, in your millennia back towards the beginning, they came in for a purpose — that they must come in to do what they needed to do here with the assistance of humans of the planet of that time. We are seen in that time as gods, but we are just like you.*

M: **Some say humans were slaves to them. Is that true?**

HS: There is some truth to that, yes, but not as malicious as everyone thinks. These were agreements of people that came through as humans of this planet that they would serve the "tall ones," your Anunnaki group, to help them do the things that they needed to do, that they were mining during that timeline.

M: Will the Anunnaki come back?

HS: It has been said that they will make an arrival. Yes.

M: Is that something that we need to worry about?

HS: No, you must remember that they evolve as well. So just know, let fears go pertaining to the Anunnaki. Remember it is Source, soul groups, all playing out the parts that they are guided to play out that they have agreed upon with Source. People who keep bringing up these old scenarios need to let go of their fears and let all of the past go.

Transcript: Enslavement of Humanity

Another session with Tina as her Higher Self describes the Anunnaki race and their involvement with humanity on planet Earth.

M: I would also like to know about the history of the Anunnaki in our galaxy and also with the Earth.

C: Yes, so the king that we showed her first (a king in the ancient civilization of Ur), he wasn't an Anunnaki. But he was a modern representation of the ancient Anunnaki at that time. In their culture, they believed the king was a descendant of those beings. They weren't really gods; they were just advanced beings that had different biology. So, they came down; they look different. They look like gods because the people were like, 'Whoa.' Imagine if a tribe in Papua New Guinea is seeing a helicopter or something come down; it's that kind of difference in technology. Like going from mud hut to Japanese bullet train.

M: Some people think the Anunnaki were our parents in some ways. Is there any truth to that?

C: Well, a lot of times humanity's been sort of used and abused as a slave race, as "loosh" (food for dark forces), as energy for other people. The power structure of the time was different then. The setup was...I don't know about parents; they feel more like celebrities. I don't know how to explain that. More like a celebrity. Someone who's just like you who just had a different path, but like, it seems fake. I don't know. There's something very farcical about it. But I don't know about parents, but they were definitely, when we were talking about...you know...adjusting the brainwaves that come down. They were doing that. They could do it en masse. They could hold everyone. They can hold 30,000 people's consciousness and intention because they could do that with their third eye. It's like telepathy. But they could actually send out a pulse of energy that would almost entrance, get everybody's attention, control everybody. They were almost like lemmings or if you ever see little kids watch TV. It's like that, enchanted. They could do that; they could do that to groups.

M: I've seen that happen with different public speakers and things that are able to hold people's attention that way. Hypnotizing them in a way.

C: Yes. So, imagine that, but like a thousand times more. Because imagine that it's a public speaker, but they're seventeen-feet tall and have glowing wings. And it looks like...you know...the only way you could describe it is it looks like a bird head, but that's not really what it was. You know what I mean? Like that. Yeah, because a lot of the ancient descriptions of what you see are just based on the context of the person living at the time. So, it's not necessarily an accurate description — it's not necessarily wrong; it might be a symbol for something else.

M: Yeah, for sure. Were they physical beings or energetic?

C: Yes, they were physical and energy. Yes, they were ascended beings, but they were physical. But that's what made them appear to be gods is because they had their Lightbodies and their physical bodies together, working together, and they could do things that were metaphysical. So, whether that's producing water from...they could tap the Earth with a staff and water would come out in the middle of the desert. They could use plasma, like lightning in a way they could start...they could use the lightning; they could draw the lightning out of the earth; they could draw it out. And that was very scary to the people, you know, before electricity. I mean, it can be scary now, but especially before.

Nibiru Collision Course Cancelled

There are many groups on the internet and people that are waiting for the return of Nibiru to our solar system. What I have been told is that Nibiru is more of a spaceship and not just a planet and that its orbit can be altered by its inhabitants. It has been shared that, contrary to some people's beliefs, Nibiru will not be in a collision course with Earth. What was shared with me was that humanity had seemed to have "passed the need to have a planet fly on a collision course towards Earth to get humanity to start praying to God again!" I laughed quite hard at that statement! Although, I have also heard that if people continue to generate the fear of such an event, they may create it for themselves on their personal timeline of this ascension event.

It is preferred by our galactic relatives that humanity liberates itself from the clutches of overlord/victim consciousness upon the planet and return to unity without direct extraterrestrial involvement on the surface. They are doing much from behind the scenes to assist us in this process including incarnating as humans to assist from the ground level.

At this point in our human history, we can release the old stories and see everything from a higher perspective. Everything is part of the Creator's plan for evolution. We perceive these races as negative when we observe through the lens of polarized 3D human consciousness. From a higher perspective, humanity's interaction with these races has helped us mature our collective consciousness through the experience of duality and chaos. The great majority of beings from these races have evolved to the point that they are no longer a "threat" to humanity and support humanity's ascension. It is important to emphasize that our "adversary" is not a person, an institution, or a culture. Service-to-self consciousness in a person or collective consciousness is the devouring force that causes chaos and suffering in the cosmos. As "evil" as it seems, it serves as a contrast to create conditions for exponential consciousness expansion.

There does seem to be a connection with Nibiru and what has been called the "Three Days of Darkness" where the Sun is covered by Nibiru, or some other celestial body or spacecraft, as it passes our sun. It has been described that as it does this, a rapid acceleration in DNA evolution will result, creating thousands of years of evolution in just three days. This scenario has played out in a few sessions, but I am not completely clear if this is something that everyone will experience — only certain individuals on certain timelines — or if the DNA changes will happen in another way. "They" do not want to give us the whole plan because it would be like giving the answers to our great test.

Transcript: Star Family from Sirius

I met Zoey on the beach in Thailand. We instantly had a strong connection. Meeting her was like catching up with a dear friend. After a few days, we decided to do a session with the intention of knowing what our connection was from the past. I asked for her to be shown a lifetime that she, Ron, and I were together. She had very little knowledge about extraterrestrials and really had no idea what a "starseed" was. The information she received was quite life-changing for her!

C: It's like black matter and stars, and I can see the Moon. It's a peaceful state, but I don't know how I'm there. There is black matter and stars everywhere. It seems like it is outside in the universe. I see the Earth from the top.

M: How wonderful. How does she look?

C: She looks white and blue. It looks very icy...ice. I think we are waiting for the Earth to get flooded. The Earth will be all water. We will wait for this to happen and then go back after. We are observing from the stars and observing the Earth. But there is no time at the same time, so there are no thoughts. We are waiting, but we are not really waiting. We are just observing with no feelings. I think we are nothing. Just one with everything. The Earth is all ice and water, and what I get is this ice will melt, and it will go all water on the planet. It's going to start over again — the planet itself. So that's when we will go, to start over. We will start over from the beginning, and we're going to help in that.

M: What causes the ice to melt?

C: I see the Sun. The Sun is very close to the Earth and looks very fiery. I can see waves around the Sun going. That's what I can see.

M: When you said we were going to start over again, what was the Earth like before the ice?

C: I see it was very primal, a lot of fighting, killing, and wars. It was nothing more than this. Very close to the animal life. Yes.

M: Was it humans fighting?

C: Yes, it was humans. I think we want to bring something new. I think we want to show them something more than this. We want to connect Earth to our planet. What I get is Sirius, but I don't know if I can see it.

M: What do you mean by connecting with it?

C: The intelligence that we have already and how they can connect with the whole solar system, the whole universe, all the universes, the whole cosmos, how they can connect, and how to go away from this primal animal life and hate because that's very much suffering. I very much want to show them how to be light beings. We are light beings, and they are not, but it seems like we are going to mix with them and transform them.

M: Tell me more about that. How will you mix with them?

C: I see now that we are blue. It's very strange. It's like blue blood something...blue...ah! I see the feet. It's weird...it's like I can't think of any animal like this...um, dragon or something feet. Very weird. We are blue and we look like a mix of alien and...it's very strange. It seems like we can travel and that we have a machine attached to our back and we can disappear and reappear. My energy is nothing; it's like light. My body is blue, grey, these astral colors...it feels Earth, very earthy, very different than our planet. I feel the Earth is very...we don't have ground; we live in the air mostly. It's very different. Now I just touch the ground and we need to make something there. We need to start creating something there and teach these humans how they can connect with the rest.

How can we mix with them? We have the blue blood; they have red blood. How we are going to mix it without, not in a sexual way; we're not going to have sex with them, it's in a different way. How we can help this planet. This Earth needs to be evolved and needs to align with the rest of the solar system. That's the only way to do it. Otherwise, it's going to keep destroying itself all the time. It doesn't help us because we are all connected. We need the Earth to grow on a spiritual level. This will help the rest of us to evolve even more. It actually blocks us from growing further. We've come here to help.

M: How did humanity and Earth not evolving block you from evolving?

C: It's not really blocking...as we are all the same consciousness. First, we have to help the ones that are not so evolved as us and then we have to, in terms of expanding more, be on the same path. That's what I get.

M: Tell me what's happening next.

C: It's very basic fire, and they're naked. They look like monkeys, but their energy feels very primal, like food...survival, they're in survival mode. And we are not alone. There are not just three of us; there are more beings like us that came — a lot of people that came. I see myself like...I wear this jacket that looks like pyramids on the shoulders, and it's so strange.

M: What do the pyramids on the shoulders do?

C: It's like silver-white color. I don't understand. It's a very weird being. I can't see the face, but I feel it's good intentions, good energy. I feel the body, I have this blue body. I feel it's light. The body is like super astral and super light. How are we going to mix with these people? I can see them from above and go around, and we have to create something for them, like a religion. We will have to create something that they believe in us superior beings so they will follow what we say to them. So that's what we're going to do next — work with them, show them the Light, show them how to be infinite beings and how we are similar, and we are not at the same time. They can be like us, but we can't be like them. We're coming from a different lineage, but we want to help. We have very beautiful hearts; we come to help. We don't want to kill them or enslave them. We want to help. The women are more interesting; they look very sweet and more approachable, so I think we're going to start with the women. They look very motherly; they're most afraid of us, but they are the ones we will approach. Maybe with the babies, we will start something. Start trying with a few babies, we will mix the blood.

M: How do you mix the blood?

C: Let's see... What I see is I'm holding a baby, and I'm passing...so the baby seems heavy and earthy on my hands. I'm putting my hands on it, and the baby becomes stars all over the baby, and the baby becomes blue light on top of the baby, and I think that's how I mix it. It kind of activates and gives the energy to the baby somehow. The baby looks different; the eyes look different. It looks like big, rounded eyes.

M: How does the baby respond?

C: Does nothing. Just stays there.

M: You say the humans can be like you, but you can't be like the humans. Why is that?

C: It's different. We're coming from a different star, Sirius. It's different. We don't have a body; we've never had a body. Humans have a body. We move into the bodies. I see myself in the Transformers movie outfit that can take me anywhere. Transforming from one place to another. I see myself in space and then going straight into sitting next to the fire with these humans. No time experience. Humans will never understand that. It's different, but that's what our purpose is, to make them like us. It's basically to make them like us, but they're not now. This is the purpose of the universe expanding, evolving.

M: So, you'll help them be more like light?

C: Yes.

Human Initiated Contact with Star Family

Humanity has been assisted since the very beginning by our extraterrestrial relatives. In fact, WE ARE EXTRATERREISTRIALS!

These advanced intelligent races have been permitted to assist us at each major junction of our development and only when we were ready. As we, as humanity, open our minds and our hearts to our cosmic and celestial lineages, we send out a signal that we are ready for the next stages of collaboration. Contact has already begun for many people through dreams, channeling, and seeing crafts in the sky. There are many people around the Earth that are initiating extraterrestrial contact to welcome in this next family reunion. I highly recommend checking out the work of Dr. Stephen Greer and his CE5 protocols for initiating contact with Star Family. The key to initiating this reunion is an open heart, loving intention, and the desire to connect!

FOURTEEN

Lemuria and Atlantis

The first human, high-consciousness civilization on the Earth that was described through our hypnosis sessions is the ancient civilization of Lemuria, sometimes called Mu, which is commonly understood to have existed in the area of the Pacific Ocean which is now underwater. The remnants of this continent are the Hawaiian and Pacific Islands, and the Indigenous of those locations are said to be descendants of Lemuria. For some reason, not many clients regress to Lemurian lives, and we only get snippets of information. When I asked, "They" (the higher consciousness collective that guides humanity) said that humanity is not yet ready for the full story, and it will be revealed later. I will share a summary of what I understand to be true.

By the time of Lemuria, many varieties of human beings were introduced around the planet in many "gardens." In a way, Earth was a farm or laboratory to grow the perfect human that was able to be in the physical dimension but connected to higher aspects of consciousness in higher densities. This is where we see the introduction of the Adamic human form with the fully activated 12-strand DNA.

The Adamic form was a perfect biological creation for high beings of Light to incarnate, a way to experience the physical dimension. Each strand of DNA gave the human the ability to call in higher bandwidths of energetic knowing and higher consciousness access reaching all the way to Source. Superhuman abilities like manipulating the elements with intention, telepathy, telekinesis, astral projection, bilocation, stargate/merkaba transportation, and other abilities were embodied by the Adamic human. This new human was incredibly powerful and beings from other star systems and densities sought to exploit and control this new being.

Lemurian civilization revered the power of the Divine Feminine. Earth was still in its original Fourth Density form and people describe Lemuria as having a blueish tint. This could also be because of the water element which was central to the Lemurian culture and was used for healing and powering the civilization. We lived in opulence, abundance, and did not want for anything. Humanity was much more technically advanced than we are today as much was downloaded from the higher consciousness access and through relationships with other star civilizations.

Even with this "Garden of Eden" archetypal society, a shadow consciousness seeped into the Earth and human consciousness. I have had a few clients describe a dark cloud (service-to-self/fallen consciousness field) entering the Earth which began to infiltrate human consciousness. One negative influence was a meteorite that brought disease to the Earth for the first time. Yet another negative influence was other star races that brought distorted belief systems that corrupted humanity's hearts and minds.

I was told of five original races of humans living on different continents but operating as one consciousness with the Earth. Each nation was entrusted with the teachings of one of the five elements — their own piece of the elemental puzzle — to maintain the balance of the Earth. Each group started to be afflicted by these various influences and began to fall away from the initial template of perfect harmony and unity which caused the whole of the Earth to be in imbalance. This started the descent of human consciousness as humans adopted the overlord mentality similar to what was described on Nibiru but done in a more "feminine" presentation. As the imbalance accelerated, it was decided by Gaia and the Higher Realms to end the experiment which was done through cataclysm and natural disaster. Many beings went to Inner Earth, taking with them advanced technologies and sacred information which would be hidden and protected until the shadow was cleared from the Earth.

When an experiment is ended, the guardians of the experiment always save some of the experiment to be used for seeding the next. This is demonstrated in the story of Noah and the Great Flood. Noah and his family were not the only ones saved. Indigenous peoples have stories of the Great Flood and fleeing their homeland by way of water, looking for a new home as their continent sank beneath the ocean.

The Atlantean Era

The next civilization that was focused on was the lost civilization of Atlantis, which is generally connected with the Atlantic Ocean on land that used to be above sea level. Although, Atlantean and Lemurian civilizations were completely capable of travel across the globe. I imagine there were civilizations and different projects happening in many places on the planet in those times. During this time of high consciousness, we developed extremely advanced technology. Earth was a cosmic hub, with many galactic beings visiting. These visitors included extraterrestrial races that were service-to-self that aimed at suppressing consciousness to control the Earth and humanity.

During the time of Atlantis, humanity began to experiment with DNA, manipulating it and creating it outside of natural law. We began to use technology to induce states of separation consciousness and distort Earth and celestial energies. Artificial Intelligence was developed, and controlling powers suppressed human consciousness. Even with galactic and angelic support, these experiments spiraled violently out of control. All of this built up to a major cataclysm that included a massive explosion of a large tower, which was being used to limit humanity's consciousness. This sounds very similar to the story of the Tower of Babel.

Humanity spiraled rapidly down in consciousness, causing a major collapse in cellular structure and reducing our DNA from twelve active strands to only two strands of DNA, and most of humanity perished. Due to this deterioration, we descended from a much higher consciousness into a significantly lower consciousness, which we have been climbing up from for thousands of years. We lost our conscious connection to the higher realms and dimensions, wisdom from other lifetimes, and many abilities, including telepathy.

Alongside humanity's fall in consciousness, the explosions caused the planet's consciousness grid to collapse and fall from the Fourth Density into the Third Density. The Earth suffered greatly, and the water began to rise over the continent of Atlantis as the Earth started to change. When everything settled, the guardians of Earth decided to try the human experiment again and inserted human species into various timelines and began to reseed the Earth.

Transcript: Holographic Library of Atlantis

This next client named Eric went back to the ancient civilization of Atlantis into a great library of multidimensional records.

C: *There is a large crystalline dome in a sphere, up into the atmosphere and it protrudes down into the ocean as well. There are also crystal chambers down into the ocean. The actual city is a three-dimensional sphere that contains higher dimensional frequencies. There are crystal pyramids and buildings and also very fine softwood, like sandalwood, structures all in and around and inside of the crystal buildings and structures. I am being led to the very center of the circle, where there is the largest pyramid that is massive and giant and holds the generators that are the key to all the energetics of the city. It powers all of the resources and holds all the information and also is a transmitter into communications with higher dimensional star systems and galaxies.*

I see my body. I am wearing a purple robe with gold flame in the stitching over it. It has the fire at the waist and a flare around the cuffs of my wrists. I can see my hands, delicate, soft. I have long, red, blondish-red hair and an elongated face. I am very tall, slender body.

M: Do you feel male or female?

C: *I feel like both.*

M: Do you have anything else on your head or any other jewelry?

C: *I have a small gold band around my forehead, it has an emblem. It looks like a half-moon with a star and two or three other smaller stars around the half-moon. It's etched in gold on my forehead. It actually feels etched into my forehead. I see gold, simple lacing around the back of my head. It feels like it's sacred somehow; you can't take it off. There is also some kind of metal, maybe it's called...or something similar... a transductive, magnetic device that amplifies my brainwaves so that I can direct energy in different ways and frequencies. Dissolving matter and bringing energy into matter, slowing down time and space, etc.*

M: Very good, what are you doing here as you look around this place?

C: *I am in the library, or the chamber, or the storage of intergalactic information, and I am moving into the antigravity field where I am able to float up into different mobiles. It's a very, very high, very large room. Very high ceilings. The ceilings are crystal. They absorb the sunlight and transmit it to produce the perfect temperature and space for antigravity. The books are holographic and are not read, but energetic resonance and signatures are absorbed into the system and then expanded so that the knowledge becomes immediately downloaded or uploaded or activated within the consciousness of the person who is activating the information. I am at the top. I am reading about the seeding of the human race and the cycles that they are to go through. There is complete knowledge and understanding of the imminent destruction in different cycles that we will go through in human society and the loss of all information. And diving deep there is a softness, an acceptance of it, but it is many, many millennia away. This is the height of Atlantean civilization. The height of the last Light Age. There is very little if no suffering or illness in this existence here.*

M: **Why don't you tell me about your reading for the time we are currently alive in.**

C: *It is a time where the majority of people upon the planet are imprisoned. They believe that they must struggle and fight in order to deserve a semblance of love or nourishment that already has been a birthright. The fear to release such a reality is at its highest. It's like humanity is standing at the brink of a cliff looking down and just becoming aware of their imminent peril. Just that moment of rushing toward that cliff and stopping, but not even knowing there is a huge crevasse. A canyon there. And that in those moments where everything seems to slow down, milliseconds really, when you realize I've come too far. Now there is a great divide, and I cannot go back. I cannot stop myself from falling, and I am going to fall. And the fear is the greatest that it could be. And inevitably there is a surrender as there is no way to stop themselves and the fall takes place. But when the fall happens, they simply step into another form of matter, lighter and invisible. It holds them. And the changes shall be swift, the destruction swift, the rebuilding swift. Faster than anyone can imagine. New forms are taking shape already.*

M: **How is this form taking shape? What is forming this?**

C: *Those that are awakening to the truth and their memory, and they have come to be again. Holding these literal structures in their matter and form and through their radiations, they will create a new magnetic field that activates magnets inside of people who are afraid. It calls them forth, summons them, in a way that is impossible for them to deny. They are called forth into the field. And more ideas and more brains join together in a solution; solutions begin to pour forth from the inner records that we already have and hold activated, and then everyone takes their role and place and begins to revolutionize the foundational systems of humanity. Environmental issues will be solved. The Earth, of course, will shift and change her face so the ecosystems can rebalance. This will take a lot of time; however, the memories of how to access weather control will become very swift and move so that the places that new humanities and systems are beginning to form shall be protected from the rest of the Earth's shifts and changes. The political system will be completely dead as it is known of now, and a new system of leadership shall emerge where people are much more responsible for their own inner ecosystem, which then naturally harmonizes in collective communities that can (concurrently) reach out and out in greater and greater harmonies. Resistance will still have its function, but it will be valued accordingly, and therefore pain will be experienced in much of a different way. For it is valuable only in the way that it expands awareness of their capacity to bring forth the Light that is meant to spread across the globe. In this new way, there will be many years, as it seems, of further division and deterioration and yet these new models and systems will swiftly take form. Those that resist this, and resist the magnetic pull, will be leaving the body.*

M: Very good. Is there anything else in that book that is important for today?

C: The absolute knowing that there is nothing to which one can worry about.

Transcript: Mer-people, Gathering of the Tribes

The next client, Lenora, initially came into the scene as a human male who was carrying a lantern and walking down a cave-system trail deep into the Earth. She had a sense that she was going on an adventure. I suggested that she move forward on the path until she arrived at where she was going to learn and explore.

C: It's blue and luminous. There's water. I am breathing underwater.

M: You're breathing underwater? (Yeah). What do you see as you go through this water? What do you experience there?

C: Feels good to be here again.

M: Yeah. Sounds very relaxing. What do you do when you swim through this water? What is your purpose there?

C: It feels like I'm remembering, like a limitless possibilities kind of feeling. Like I'd forgotten that I can do this.

M: Must be nice to remember your limitlessness.

C: Yeah, I forgot that I could do it all alone and I forgot that at any moment when I turn the corner my friends are all still there.

M: Tell me more about that.

C: There's a whole community of people under here. We've lived here before. And there's a whole magical world under this water.

M: Describe it to me.

C: It's this really advanced place. Oh my god, the consciousness is so high. I can feel it in my cells and my buzzing. I just see this straightness in everybody. The fluidness of their body. The straightness of their vertebras. I don't even know if that's a spine. These creatures they... We are with fins too. They look like mermaids!

M: You said they have fins? *(Yeah).* Where do they have fins?

C: These like tail, like from their feet would be. It is like something that would help them move even more in the water. They are so beautiful and sparkly. And it's just like the creation of it is so smart for the movement, but they still have arms.

M: I want you to look down at your body and see what your body looks like now that you're there.

C: I have it too!

M: What does yours look like?

C: Oh my gosh it's so nice. It's sparkly. Everything is. Because we are underwater everything is kind of a blue tinge. Like blue shiny, elegant, thin, beyond any fish fin I have ever seen. It is like it can move in any direction. It's not limited by like, a bone or a spine or anything like that. It is like I could do anything with this fin.

M: Show me around this beautiful civilization. Take me with you and describe what you see and sense and feel.

C: Mmm. Interesting, because I am seeing and noticing that there's still gender. Like there's still the men and there's still the women. And there are still the little kids. And it is so neat because, well it's almost like this center place where I am. Where there is like a hustle and bustle of beings, people, entities, whatever we are calling [those] that are here. And it is like there's this harmony. We are like building... It is just lots of energy and movement in this part. So, I don't know where we live. Or if we just live like this, but this is what I'm seeing right now.

M: Let's go and see the place that you live when you're there. Go to the place where you live, where you rest. Tell them what you see. What do you see there?

C: Oh neat. So, there's like, woah, there's like some cave of some sort. Cave isn't really the right word, but it's like some sort of organic, natural maybe coral structure that... but it's not hard like that. It's comfortable to rest. To be there and rest. But it is not like I really need my own home. It is like we all have this big home. It is a different concept. It is just like a sweet place to rest. I am definitely a woman. I'm definitely one of these creatures, I definitely feel feminine. I definitely have this feeling that I, that I am a woman of some sort. So, we have these little nooks for resting.

M: How about the relationships of the beings that are with you? I want you to see those people that rest with you in this place. Describe them to me as you look around.

C: Like this feeling that we are actually really and truly all one being. It's really, you know when the one next to me starts to feel something like he's getting sleepy, it brings the other ones into that same feeling. So, it's like this really deep empathy that we all share. Like we are all so the same being and so connected in this way. It is also like I just feel love. The feeling is that I do not know if there is any danger.

M: What do you eat for nourishment? Do you eat anything? See yourself doing what you do now for fueling yourself, for nourishing yourself. Tell me what you see there.

C: It is almost like a prayer circle. It is like a circuit like a wheel but horizontal and we all sit on this wheel together. Maybe not all of us at the same time but maybe like eight of us or nine of us and we all sit together on this wheel contraption thing, and we just sit there, and we recharge on it like it's just like, the energy just is like a whole new wave of buzz. Oh, wow! That is really nice!

M: Allow it to recharge you. Welcome it into your body. Tell me what it is like to be recharged by this experience, what does it do?

C: Ohhhhh Wow. It is a lot of really good energy. It's like oh wow, it's like this pulse. A buzz. Warm and electrifying but stimulating but subtle. It's like the energy of the pure water that surrounds us. It is bringing us back to that exact structured state. It structures all of the water in us. It just brings us back to total perfection. That's all.

M: How blessed you are to have this supply of energy and community.

C: Wow!

M: I want you to see now what you do with most of your time. Tell me what you see. What are you doing there?

C: Seems like we are mostly always together with the others. It is like where we are wanting to figure something out together. Like we came here to learn. What we are figuring out together is how to create the highest feeling of structure between our fields. So, what we do is we swim. One of the things we are doing right now is we are swimming around each other in this pattern. It is like we are seeing how close together we can be but still have some space apart and we are feeling, we are really tuning into the energy that gets created in our collective field. So, if I am a little bit further away, I notice that I am closer to someone else on this side, and then there's someone else above me that's a little bit further away.

So, we are all weaving in this really cool way that there's like spaces in between us and we're playing with the spaces in between us to feel what harmony feels like. We know what harmony feels like and what that buzz feels like because we have those devices, we have those machines, and so those are these amazing tools that I do not even know who created those or where they came from, but this amazing device reminds us of this perfect feeling.

We are remembering how to weave with one another while we are swimming and flowing in this way so that we could actually recreate with our bodies that same exact sensation. We are getting more sensitive at the same time, and we are learning a lot this way. It feels like that is just one of the many things that we do.

M: Well, let's see what else you do. Let's move to another activity. Another scene where you're seeing what you do there. Move to that next scene and tell me what you see.

C: Okay, so besides movement that was a question I had are we always moving? Besides movement I see. I see also this like really powerful, almost like you could call it a "temple space". Yeah, this space where... Then we sit. We sit in this way. It is so interesting for this part. It doesn't really feel like we have fins anymore. Maybe we don't need them.

M: Tune into that and tell me what it's about.

C: Yeah. There's still a sense of gravity. I definitely still feel like we are on the floor of the temple and we're kneeling together. We're all facing the same direction. We're not in a circle. Some practices are facing each other and feeling the energy that way and right now we are kneeling, and we are all facing, yeah, the same kind of like "spot". We are all on this floor together. We are kneeling in this meditation. What we are doing in this meditation, well, it all feels kind of similar, right? It all feels like there is the same goal. It is like the concentration of this energy in our individual. We focus a lot on this collective and we are still in this collective. But in this collective, it's like clearing. Where all of the energy that [has been individually cultivated] gets to come back into our own spaces. Our own body. Almost like we're creating a prism. Like each of our bodies, we are creating individual prisms. Oh, I am seeing it more clearly now. Oh, when we sit down, we are creating a perfect prism with our bodies. Our physical bodies do not look like that. But that is what our energy is doing. It is creating a perfect prism. Then this prism with the individual strengthening of our individual light, we're creating this really, really... It's a rainbow! Each person has an individual color in this prism. So, this reflects upward. When we refine it more and more, when we sit for longer and get even better at our practice, the prism creates this one frequency. This one stream of light is blasting upwards. It is a powerful light that we can create together.

M: **When this light travels up, where does it go?**

C: *Wow!*

M: **What do you see there?**

C: *Whoa. We are connecting to a different planet.*

M: **Tell me about this connection. What do you see there?**

C: *It is like this little blue planet that's surrounded by a bunch of other planets just in the middle of space. Wow! It feels so good to feel the connection with a planet that far away. It feels like, we are charging up this little cold planet. That is what it feels like.*

M: **So, you all combine your rainbow prism light to direct it to this planet to regenerate it in some way?**

C: *Yeah, exactly. We are bringing it back to life. Like it's gone cold and kind of dormant. But like, yeah, exactly.*

M: **What happens when you send this light to this other planet?**

C: *It's an alive thing, which is, it was just so nice to feel because there's this communication. When we're blasting the little planet with our prism, I'm noticing that there's a relationship. That it isn't... It's alive too, even if it's subtly alive right now. It's like it's still bringing its energy and grace and gratitude back to us and there's like this network that we're opening up between it and us so as we're blasting it with prism light it's also reflecting it back to us and strengthening our abilities. Wow!*

M: **That's so lovely. Why has your community decided to help this planet?**

C: *It is our mission. Yeah, we chose to do this.*

M: **Wonderful. So, you decided to help like it was time to help this planet?**

C: Yeah, well, I think it's because it feels like because we've done this before to a lot of different planets. So, it's like we knew we were closer... We were the closest in the ability to harmonize and know our mission and to do this. It is kind of what we do. Yeah, it's kind of what we do. It's not just this planet. That is what our team does. We can bring these things back to life and we know how to do it. And so, yeah, that's what we're doing.

The next scenes that we looked at were of a different embodiment, a body of Light. She would take her love and wisdom to different planets and galactic systems to hold a high vibration of love and higher consciousness to assist other systems in their elevation of frequency.

WORKING WITH THE HIGHER SELF

HS: She's been wanting to know what her role is. She's been wanting to... She's been needing lately a sense of empowerment and so I felt like it would be empowering for her to know who she is. She's felt disconnected from that part of herself.

M: Why does she feel disconnected?

HS: Her infiniteness. The advancement of the soul she came in with. She has fallen into the innocent human spell and deeply forgotten that she came from the higher realms and that she serves a very large purpose and yeah that there is... That there is grace in all of this. There is no way that she could ever do wrong.

M: Thank you for sharing that with us I know she really wanted to know what her soul purpose is on this planet at this time.

HS: A beautiful innocent sweet wondering inquiry. She is here to bridge this infiniteness with this humaneness at this time on this planet. And everything she does, it's so beyond one thing or you know... She gets caught up in that sometimes of what is this one thing to practice or what is this one art form or... And it is so much more beyond that. It is bridging that infiniteness. This totally deep initiatory path with everything she does and breathes life into, onto this planet and into this body that she has been gifted and given and chosen Herself. That has been a big one for her in this lifetime. It is new for her. It is new for her to be in a physical body at all. And then flesh and blood. It is her divine path. I think what she really needs to know is that it is not a limitation in the sense that there is suffering in this. It is a chosen limitation. A limitation is not even the right word. This is her divine purpose.

This might sound more simple than anything, but the divine purpose is bringing everything she has learned and known, and embodying it into this vessel so that she can be that bringer of total harmony and peace in everything she does. To share the infinite knowledge, she knows of the interconnectivity of all life and the importance of the structure and the harmony and the grace and all of this that she is being shown today. That sole purpose is so simple and so huge at the same time, but so natural for her.

M: **Where does she have a struggle with allowing that infinite beingness to come through? What gets in her way?**

HS: She thinks too much. Yeah, she gets into some places that can extract her away from that connection. Then there is the opposite too. It seems like the top and bottom of her body like when she's feeling connected to the infinite, the mind can or the brain or upper chakras can kind of shut down and yeah, close off to the connection. And when she is in that total connection of the upper realms, which she came in knowing she can forget how to bring it to the Earth again, but this is what she came in to learn. This is one of the main things that she came in to learn is how to masterfully hold experience. Master that total connection.

She does have the potential to fully not come back into incarnation. There does not need to be. Even knowing that. She knew that. She knows that. So, this is her trial or initiation or her big thing to learn. It does deeply have to be with continuing to remember this soul's purpose is bringing the divine into everything and sharing it. It is not just enough to come into her and into her heart. It is to share it with the others into the world with the different beings here and to share those really high vibrations here with many, many, many, many, many beings on a very large scale.

M: **She said she feels like there's a block between her upper chakras and her lower chakras.**

HS: Yes. Yeah, this is one of her main inhibitions or fears is... There's fear. I noticed. I noticed this. Yeah, when I look at it in her body it looks like this sad little girl around her Solar Plexus area. And she's kind of curled up into a corner into a ball. And it is like this fear of totally allowing the vibrancy of her soul into this body. She remembers in herself, a lot of persecution and torment and suffering and rape and pillage and violence and lots of intensity in her cellular memory, around being a woman and not being able to shine her full glory and her full power, and that imprint has not fully been cleared. It's something that is inhibiting her even though she consciously can know her power and her beauty and her Grace. There's still an entity of being that is not allowing her to fully blossom and ground and root and be her full, enlightened, self-embodied.

M: And so, what does she need to learn now so that she can release that being and open up these pathways for creation? Bring her brilliance into the physical world.

HS: She needs to learn that she's doing everything exactly right. And there's never been a moment where she wasn't.

M: What's nice for her to hear, tell me more about that.

HS: Everything since her birth, to where she is now. And forever beyond, before that. Everything has been divinely guided by grace. And she has always been with me (Higher Self). She never walks alone. She cannot make a mistake. She thinks that she makes mistakes a lot. There is a judgment or self-criticism or something that limits her internally and it's just a matter of starting to paint, starting to sing, starting to speak to others about what she knows. Starting to write about what she knows. She has so many art forms that she loves and that she masters and she just yeah, it's just time to start. And I see too that there is even, there's a fear in her around even just starting.

M: What can you share with her now so that she can light that fire and get it started?

HS: What I want to share is that it is safe here now. You have made it to a place where you know, this bubble of light, you exist within. You know that you exist now in a time and a place in your level of consciousness. No matter what is going on around you that you are always safe, and you are always protected fully by the grace of God, by divinity. So, there is no actual fear. Fear was the illusion. The prosecution was the illusion. You have learned a lot from these ones, these are old lessons that we can now clear out of your system. These are old things that were traumatic to you for many lives. For much time. Or even just imprints, whether you live them or not. They are not yours. They are not yours. They were yours, maybe to grow from. Yes, we are grateful for the lessons. Those old stagnant energies and entities are not actually relevant to this lifetime anymore. So, we can, and will erase and delete those old programs. Those fears of rape, torture, and abuse. Because they do not actually exist, and cannot actually exist in the state of consciousness that you exist in. So, this feeling of being afraid of these old entities and old beings and old pathways is actually the only thing that is keeping them around. Because they cannot actually get to you anymore. You have transcended that. Once she really knows and embodies that, then she will know in her root and her womb and everything that it is safe to drop in and it is safe to feel the inspiration come through her, and it is safe to act upon that inspiration that comes through her. It is safe to share the inspiration that comes through her. Everything that she is wanting to shift in her life will heal naturally as soon as she starts to allow the immense amount of inspiration that wants to come through her to actualize on this planet.

M: Wonderful. She wanted to know about her purpose on the New Earth.

HS: It has a lot to do with the level of integrity that she was tapping into of the very specific, very aligned, very pure soul she has. And that her journey is to the purpose, the purpose is to share with others, this very specific journey, and to share with others. [She is] also to bring the clan back together. There's actually like a tribe or a clan, that she's actually reconnecting, rekindling from different star systems and bringing them together and reminding them of these Essene ways and these ancient practices that she will continue to cultivate and is remembering in herself that are very specific to her lineage. Her purpose is really this big world bridging, bringing the clan back together. It is a very specific mission, and it's not one that she's willing to get thrown off of. Even if there have been moments in her life where the compromise felt safer, easier, like this very big. Yeah, this very big purpose of educating the mystical ancient ways and bringing the children up in ways of magic and initiation and this bardic, magical way of being and knowing and eating and treating things very specifically.

M: Was there anything else you would like to share with her about the transition to the New Earth?

HS: I think what I want to share is that it won't be easy. She knows that easier isn't what allows her to grow anyway. There's always grace, and she is with her clan. With her chosen, the people she chooses to surround herself, the breadcrumbs she chose... She chooses to follow. It will be peaceful, and graceful. For many, it won't be that way. There will be a separation and consciousness split. That will happen. It is happening. And she is divinely guided and will continue to be. As she continues, there's a listening that's needed, and she's doing that. There's an alignment that's needed. She's doing that. As she is continuing with her new practices, with her old practices, with her remembering, with listening. With everything she's doing with reconnecting to nature, it's going to be just continuous. Yeah, her psychic abilities will expand. Her brain will transform into full-body intelligence along with many others. The whole entire genetics will upgrade within her cellularly and within many and within anybody who is ready for the full upgrade. It is just a matter of staying in this alignment and continuing to follow the pleasure and the joy and continuing to create and show the magic.

There is no need to fear this shift for anyone really. Everyone did choose before they incarnated if they were going to have a really tragic time, or if they were going to have a really graceful time and many are choosing... Many are going to die. Many are going to have a really struggling, suffering time. Many light beings [awakened humans] will get pulled into the darkness into the abyss of that dark energy that they may mistake for truth. There's nothing wrong with that. There's nothing scary about that. There's nothing bad about that. There's nothing evil about that. They are souls incarnated and that was what they chose to learn in this incarnation so that they could come back in the next iteration and build the New Earth with us.

So, the New Earth will exist here on this planet, with our mother Gaia, and all of her children will be here with her. It's just a matter of if it's this incarnation for them or the next. But it's soon. The amount of Light on this planet is larger than it has ever been before and the tipping point is very near, and she sees in her vision of the New Earth and in her future in this lifetime, the full iteration of that life. And so, it is the feeling of its nearness that is in her heart and also guides us to continue building in really authentic and compassionate and loving and integral ways.

M: Thank you so much for sharing. It sounds like there's going to be a continuing division of consciousness splitting off in different ways. And also, some repairs happening to the genetics. So that sounds like we'll be changing the bodies a bit, can you share more about that process?

HS: Yeah, so, those, there's an upgrade that is needed for us to sustain a higher frequency, a higher level of consciousness which is now going to be existing on the entire planet and is continuing to exist on the entire planet and will keep growing. It looks like the machine is more fine-tuned. Like the apparatus of the human body will become more and more, feels like liquid light, like plasma. Like we will be more water and more light and we will, with that, be in a more, like our all of our consciousnesses are coming together. And we are realizing and remembering that we work better and more efficiently in this deep, deep cooperation.

Our bodies will transform in the ways that they need to in order for the energetics of the energies to pass even more cleanly between each other to have the electrical impulse. The being that we are becoming as one entire human species or beyond human species. The superhuman species, this one consciousness. Our bodies will need to be more malleable; we will need to detoxify deeply.

This is why the path of the Essenes has always been very deep in this soul. The purification process of fasting and meditation and clearing our consciousness and being kind to everyone. Even getting to the point where we love everyone that we thought was evil, or we thought was an enemy, all of those things are now dissolving into the truth of us cooperating into a really cohesive, coherent structure. This has been our goal all along on this planet. This is why we came here, all of us. This has been what keeps ringing really true is that the way that we do complete this mission is by each individual, one of us, coming into ourselves so fully allowing the soul embodied in its completion, and really getting clear on what our specific tribe is. What our specific genetic frequency is, what our specific clan is, and what our specific values are. What are those specific things for each individual? Then we will know where our perfect piece is to fit into this puzzle.

That is how harmonization does and will happen when each of us stands true, and continues to stand true to those values, even when it looks like the rest of the world is going crazy or thinking the opposite of us or whatever pressures there may be. And there will be because we are very high-level advanced beings here on this planet. Every single one of us, no matter how far we fall from that in this experience, we are all very, very high-level beings in this experience. We all have the capacity to remember our core values and because of that, we all have the capacity to be completely teetered off from that and to the opposite extreme where we have no idea where we are, who we are, what our values are, and what matters to us. And so that is the pressure of the evolution that is bringing us into the fullest alignment with what is true to us.

Nobody is right or wrong in their beliefs, it's just a matter of what is deeply, deeply true. All of the false beliefs will fall away when we get truer and clearer and clear. Then we will find that we do have a very similar belief. As we do come closer and closer and closer to unity, we cannot keep eating the animal. We just cannot, they are part of the ascension process. And the ones that do, it *just feels like they need to keep coming back and remembering again, that they're part of the choir, and that they're essential in this process as well. And they have an equal opportunity. We are the ones that allow these other lower consciousness beings to evolve.*

M: That makes sense, yeah. I am wondering about the area that she's in and the region that she said. Can you share about the community there and the evolution of that region?

HS: There is a coming together of tribes into this part of the world. That is learning how to, on a microcosmic scale, do what we are to do on a larger scale. Where we are in the process of learning how to be one body, and how to cooperate. The fires that were experienced here, were a big catalyst to this cooperation, this willingness to help one another. This pandemic that was just experienced, was also another big opening and opportunity for people of all different kinds to come together and remember that we are all one kind and cooperate together.

There is a spark of potential that exists in this part of the world. As far as physical, and natural disasters ago, it feels very unknown, depending on how well we harmonize and remember the magic that we actually do create and the impact that we do have on the weather. Specifically, we do have the ability to make it rain. The karma of this area is asking us to come together and become more magical, to step into our abilities. Coming together, going into a deep trance, and going into meditation together as a collective, because it's not for one person to do. We can do it! We can, in this part of the world, stop this natural disaster that happens every season. We can make this a more tropical climate that is simpler and more natural and more comfortable for us all to live in without fear of something coming in to take our houses and all of this fear.

We actually are asking to embody love more, to embody our magic more and to come into harmony more, and to start doing these sacred practices together. To set up times, centers, and places where we actually remember these things together and actually take action on doing these things together. And so, there are masterful people here. And it is also just a matter of how are we going to do it? Can we do it? Are we going to do it? How much time does it take? Are we going to? Who is going to get these groups together and start making the magic happen?

FIFTEEN

Atlantean Cataclysm

Here is another section of the work with Matan that talks about the lost civilizations of Atlantis and Lemuria.

M: So, what caused the fall of Lemuria?

HS: It was a group effort; it wasn't just one. The civilization reached a point where they became so advanced that they were abusing it.

M: In what ways were they abusing it?

HS: Their power. Just like in Atlantis, the power was abused. So, when it got to a certain point, all that could happen was the fall. They were hurting the planet.

M: What civilizations were before Lemuria?

HS: There have been many.

M: Can you share with us some of what these other civilizations were like? Maybe even their names?

HS: There was a time when there were just animals on the planet and it was a beautiful garden, and then other beings brought other things from your star systems from other planets. Then there were times when your Lyrans were coming and bringing humans to this planet. If you know of the Lyrans, they are human, just like you. They are your ancestors.

R: Are the Lyrans some of the first humans on the Earth?

HS: They are one, yes. If you were to see them, you would be in awe. They are beautiful. They are not as dense as you are.

M: I've heard of some Lyrans being connected to a lion hybrid.

HS: Yes.

M: Can you tell us more about the different types of beings in the Lyran star system?

HS: There's many. There are us humans, and there are ones that do not look human like we do. We are also connected to the Pleiadian star system, as you call it, as there are many beings on that star system as well. As we are part of that star system as well.

M: So, after the Lyrans brought the human being to Earth, what kind of civilizations came next?

HS: Other star beings started showing up, and they were curious. Ones from the Sirius star system started showing up. There were ones that were not human; they looked more like dinosaurs of your world during that time period. They were not dinosaurs in the way of being dinosaurs; they are what you call reptiles. Some of them are self-serving, and some of them are not. This is where the fall of this civilization started happening. The insert of the mixture of your races started to happen. There were once very tall beings upon your planet as well, and they started intermixing with the regular humans. Have you seen pictures in your world of the tall beings?

R & M: Yes.

HS: They started intermixing with the regular humans, but this was not part of the plan. They were not supposed to do this.

R: Where did they come from?

HS: They came from another world.

R: Is there a name for their planet?

HS: All that we can call it for you right now is from what you call Planet X. Are you aware of this?

M: Yes, can you tell me more about Planet X?

HS: There is a lot going around on your planet right now about Planet X. Prophecies about what's going to happen and when. We say to detach from that. Whatever people want to believe is what they're going to believe. There are timelines that people are on that pertain to that.

M: Can you give us a truthful summary about this planet?

HS: This is where your tall ones came from. They are still very much part of this world but not in the way they used to be.

M: How are they still involved?

HS: They can be seen in your skies. They have their own ships that they use, but they are not malicious like they once were. They once enslaved your people.

M: So, what is the next interaction with this planet and Earth?

HS: That is something that is still in manifestation. That is hard to tell and give you anything exact because there are so many possibilities and probabilities playing out in this moment. We don't want to misdirect you.

Transcript: Fall of Ancient Civilizations and Master Builders

Here is a session with a client named Tina who described ancient Earth history and the rise and fall of ancient civilizations.

M: Now, what about Earth's early history? In the early civilizations? What was going on here in our...you know...pre-written history? Can you give us a summary of how that went down?

C: Yes. So, there was much...can't tell if it's four and a half or five different starts or advance starts. By 'advanced civilization,' it is not the right word for it because maybe it's not. If you think of your society of today as being advanced, it's not the same. Just like in Orion, where the technology outpaces the consciousness. They created some unstable Earth...I don't know if they created it, but they were definitely a factor. Because the Earth reflects the humans, and the humans reflect the Earth.

M: So, what was the first civilization? Can you share with us about that one?

C: Yes, I see lots of large stones that are cut, really precise angles. Lots of stone buildings. It was very important to...this, this one that I'm looking at now had libraries, like information libraries. It's hard to say; they're like tablets, but they kind of look like they're glowing in a way. Or like glass. But I'm not sure why they would have glass tablets. Ok, so there are glass tablets. And there's writing on the glass tablets; they glow; the writing is kind of glowing, like an iridescent glow. And you can pull them up and look at them. And then you can take them, and you can enter them into machines as well. They're records of the universe. Some of them did come from Orion. Some of them actually have come from very, very old. They hold the keys to the information. And all of this was, you know, always it's just a test of energy. So, we're running the test, right. And what happened was the technology just outpaced their decisions to use it in a way and then the waters came. So, what happened, the waters came up. So, it just started slowly at first, but then like whole, like if you could train the ocean down. And maybe the planet was colder then? And maybe more water was in ice?

M: Is that what you're seeing there?

C: I'm seeing a big chunk of ice, but it's almost like it goes all the way from on the South Pole. But a lot more frozen. But it's almost like off Africa; parts of Africa are frozen, and parts of Australia are frozen.

M: So, what caused the ice to melt?

C: The technology got hot; they were using it to heat the water. Why were they doing that? Were they creating energy with the heat from the water?

M: Was this civilization human or were they another species?

C: No, they were human. They're definitely human, but it wasn't as many people as it is today. And I know we know that. The population was maybe 50,000 people total. So, a civilization is at best between 150 to 100,000 people; it is not a lot as far as what you're used to now. But working with those tablets, and it's just created some Earth changes, but if you could see underneath the ocean there's so much left even some of it was reclaimed. Some things were built here before it was really inhabited. They're not necessarily human but other types of spirits, individuals, came here to build these structures. So, the Master Builders, I don't know much about them, but they travel the universe building things, or they did; they travel many universes, these Master Builders are big. And they can build sacred geometry sites that are very ancient and very old. And then those sites can be used by many cultures over a long, long time. They could be inhabited and then just forgotten about then inhabited again, but not necessarily by the people who made them. And the second inhabitants will leave maybe more archaeological records. Their pots or whatever. So, it's hard to date how old these things are because multiple different generations or different inhabitants of different civilizations have come in and inhabited the same space.

M: So, these Master Builders built some structures on the planet, and then eventually, the planet became inhabited? And they were able to use those structures for different things?

C: Yes. And a lot of it's still hidden; a lot of it hasn't been found, or it just sort of got covered with trees in the jungles of like Thailand or where the jungle would eat...or like Brazil, or where the jungle, the Amazon, would just sort of engulf an ancient ruin. But now, they have special cameras that can go through water and look at where ancient roads would be, or a shipwreck would be, or something like that. They can see that now. And so, there's so much that happened before, before, and before. So, there are three "befores." So, you have maybe your history up until, I don't know the civilization, like the Byzantine. You go back a little further, maybe, I don't know, 10,000 BC, I'm not sure. And then that's civilization. But then before that, there were all these parts that were forgotten about that would happen for a while, and then it kind of just decayed. They would try it again. And each time there was an intervention, but the soup just wasn't quite right. You know? The soup is right this time.

M: I'm wondering...the humans that were there when the library had these glass tablets. Were they in similar bodies to us now? Or were they different? Can you explain?

C: Their bodies were different, but they're similar in some ways. I feel like they *could breathe differently, maybe through gills or something. I know that sounds weird, but they process oxygen differently. There was more oxygen on the planet; there were a lot more plants, a lot more oxygen. The air was different, the air tastes different. I would say their head, I don't know, it feels like it splits open and there's more of a higher brain coming in, higher so looks like their brain swells right there. So, their skulls are shaped differently. I would say they're kind of humanoid, but they're definitely different in some ways.*

M: Let's learn a little bit more. Tell me about the civilization after this one of the libraries and the glass tablets. See those images now, those cultures, and tell me about them.

C: So, after that, it's hard to say what happened, but that culture fell. And people were back to cavemen again. I see the cavemen again. Living in caves, more "of the Earth." Like the Native Americans. They kind of all got away from that knowledge. It was totally forgotten about.

M: Just see an image of what happened to cause that shift in consciousness. You can see that image now. Tell me what you see.

C: It's hard to describe. I see water where water was not before. There was arguing about what to do about it. Not everyone has the same ideas, and the population was dwindling. Isn't that interesting? They were struggling with fertility issues, but I think that was Gaia's way of expressing it that was the end of that. First people just didn't have, or just didn't have as many children, then the procreation just didn't happen the same.

M: So, the water started to rise and what happened?

C: And the water rose. So, they were really attached to those ancient builders' structures. And so, the technology, the library with the tablets, it's full of water. And so now they couldn't get the tablets to work. I don't know what they did with them, if they tried to take them and move them and then rebuild a new machine to...I think by this point it's the end of this civilization. So, in the beginning, the tablets could be read; they didn't have to be read by a machine. But by the end, they have lost that ability.

M: Let's go back to see how they lost that ability. Back to see how they lost that.

C: They became too dependent on the technology.

M: Let's learn about what happened after humanity went into this caveman phase. How did that progress? What do you see happening there?

C: I see a lot of fighting amongst themselves. It's a lot more basic; people don't live as long. People die of accidents, like falling off a cliff or getting hit by a rock or something. Or disease. Or lack of food. That's a big one. People starve; a lot of people starved at that time. A lot of lack of food. And then what brought us out of that is that, what brought us through, was the star intervention, the star mothers that came by next would be after that. I think that would be more of the Indigenous connection with the star people, to bring us back. And so, the biology back then could only take so much...this has been an experiment that's gone on for so long because the biology changes so slowly.

But this is interesting because your biology now is doing it on its own without having to be manipulated or messed...now it's almost like when you learn to ride a bike. At first, your father's holding the back of your seat, you know, and then he lets go, and now you're pedaling. So now you're beginning to pedal on your own, which means you're creating the momentum of the Ascension. Instead of it being an external catalyst, it's an internal catalyst. It's a very good sign.

M: So, what happened after that, you know, evolution from caveman to starting to move up? What was the next evolutionary stage?

C: Well, then you sort of get into the time history that you know. But even before that...so when the technology started to outpace the consciousness, and then the waters came, and then the tablets were gone, and then we went back to cavemen and then we started reconnecting with Gaia, Earth. It was a restart to connect you, to ground you back into the planet. Ok, so that we ground you back, get you back in there, and then open up your third eye again. So, you have to make sure that you remain grounded while your third eye is open. That's part of it, it's not just to get your third eye open.

M: So, what was the civilization that had the crystals? Is it what we would consider as Atlantis or Lemuria or something different?

C: Yes, yes, you would consider it one of the Atlantis [civilizations]. There were a few that have that same...it's sort of like how when flight was given to the planet, the gift of flight that several people like the Wright brothers, and then the group in France; there were several people working on it at the same time. Or radio. Like eight people invented the radio at once. It's the same with that. Same thing. So, what was the question?

M: I'm just wondering... So, it seems like we were talking about

Atlantis and maybe haven't heard about Lemuria?

C: *Right. So, the flood. The flood stories, and so there are several cultures that had that same experience, where their tech began to outpace their...Lemuria is a little different because that was a very pure start of things. That's more of the Garden of Eden story. And the Earth changes that affected the Lemurians were sort of more natural over time, where the stuff that affected the Atlanteans, they had more of a play in it. Self-induced.*

M: So, what caused the shift between the Lemurian to the Atlantean timeline? There were Earth changes, but what happened?

C: *So, I, from the perspective that I see, the Lemurian culture was only supposed to be for a certain time period, like, you didn't get reincarnated in that culture over and over and over and over and over again. It was like, everybody kind of went through once. Most people went through once, I would say, maybe some of the leadership was there for lifetimes, but everybody went through once, and then you carry that code into the whole planet. So, everybody's gone through Lemuria at some point, like everybody, and then, you know, everyone who's working on the Light side has gone through that type of life there because it was extremely pure. And it was connected to the star mothers up in the Pleiades, Pleiadian star mothers. And so, because you could get direct Pleiadian DNA imprinted. Every lifetime you have, you collect in your personal...your soul's record, your crystalline record, your...you know, the cave that keeps the records. It's not...it is a physical place, but it's also not a physical place. It's hard to explain, but every time you live your life, you're putting down an energetic stamp that retains on your soul that is eternal. And so, everyone who is on Earth right now had to go through Lemuria to receive that Pleiadian mother energy and that connection to the Pleiadian mother energy in order to accomplish the ascension that is happening right now. So, you had to go through Lemuria to get to now.*

M: I don't know much about the civilizations before Lemuria. Do you know anything about that to share with us today?

C: *It's really hard to see like the timelines of one, which one was first? I would say that, you know, Lemuria was a very ancient civilization from a long, long time ago. And then after that, then came a couple of the Atlantean stories, there were a few... So, there was one, sort of off the coast of...it's hard to say because the ocean is different now, but the Atlantic Ocean used to look very different. It used to have different islands that were bigger islands, not big like Australia, but big like the Philippines, maybe even bigger, but that type of...big enough to see. There was one that was up off the coast of Spain, maybe in that area somewhere, Africa, Spain, up high off Africa. There's one down somewhere between, off the coast of South America, kind of between, south of Florida, south of all that off there. And then there's another up towards Japan and then I feel like there's maybe one more too that was in the South Seas. That one might be the one with the tablets.*

M: What about America's history because they're seeming to discover a pyramid in St. Louis, possibly a pyramid in the Grand Canyon. What were the civilizations like here on the North American continent?

C: So, the water was in a different place before and it moved quickly. It used to move a lot faster, where things would freeze and unfreeze quicker. So, the Grand Canyon was cut quickly, it wasn't cut slowly over time. I mean, quickly, I don't mean like, in a matter of days, but I mean, for geology, geology is slow. So, for geology, it was quick, how fast the ocean was cut there. Yes, they were just like the ancient...you'll find Ancient Builder, they're going to find ancient stuff on North America. And so, they're not going to be able to explain it with the paradigm of history that they have now. It's going to look so technically advanced. It's like, they can't explain it that way. But the Native Americans used to have the history, but they've been eradicated. Their stories have been eradicated, but the history was in their stories of how the ancient pyramids on North America, and the ancient other structures, like the round, they look like sundials, but they're not. They're more like energy conductors. And they're all over too, but they haven't been found yet.

Transcript: The Great Cataclysm of Atlantis

As the scene opens up, my client Carrie describes a society with residential pyramid structures surrounding a massive, dome-like epicenter. She is in a female body around the age of 50-years old (same as her body in her life as Carrie). She is wearing a mid-thigh-length, translucent dress, a multi-pointed star necklace touching her thymus area, and a crown made out of organic, living material. She is holding a palm-sized ankh in her left hand. Her occupation is a doctor who makes house calls. I asked her to move to the next important scene in that life.

M: What do you see there?

C: It's a tree. It's a tree I go to often. It's my dimensional transport. My name is Kasha. I use this tree for dimensional transport as I'm not a physical doctor. I do dimensional work.

M: Where do you travel?

C: This is like my parallel Earth, and so I go to the material Earth a lot. I do most of my work on the material Earth. I also do some...this seems sci-fi...do something in space. Like a satellite system or something.

M: Look around does anything else call your attention?

C: Well, as I was saying that I instantly bilocated to this space thing that's metal. It's kind of cold feeling; it's not my favorite environment, but I do a lot of work there. I do some advising. There's also some soul work.

M: Are there other entities there when you're in that space?

C: Yes. It's an intergalactic thing. Apparently, this is a place where intergalactic decisions are made.

M: Decisions about what?

C: When you ask what I do there, I see myself sitting in a large room. It's almost like I'm not part of the discussion, but I'm monitoring for integrity. So, it's not a physical doctor's work, but they call me Doctor Kasha.

M: So, Dr. Kasha, what else do you specialize in?

C: Frequency work. Frequency networks.

M: How do you do this frequency work? Tell me the processes.

C: It's telepathically in this room, so I am in this room. I am there to measure integrity, and...

M: What do you mean by integrity?

C: Whether people are coming from the heart-space or truth as they speak. For me, there is an internal alarm that goes off when the truth is not being spoken. There is a switchboard that I operate telepathically to those who are on this panel. It's connected to my monitoring system within, and it lights up for everybody — even the people speaking. It's like a way for them to monitor their own level of integrity.

M: Is there anything else within this space that's calling your attention?

C: There is a horseshoe-shaped table where this panel is talking. They're representing their leagues.

M: Is there a name for their leagues?

C: *It's like their nations. It's almost like a United Nations thing but in this horseshoe-shaped...I keep wanting to say enclave. There's a golden-yellow ball that's pulsating in the middle of the horseshoe.*

M: And what does this ball do?

C: *It's some sort of energy source. It's Source intelligence. It's like citrine.*

NEXT SCENE: GREEN PYRAMID GENE MANIPULATION

C: *I keep seeing a large hand, almost representing the Hand of God. It's pointing to a tower that is outside of the society. There's a platform on the tower, and the hand keeps pointing to that as if it has something to do with potential danger. I think I'm in this lifetime in a society where it would seem futuristic to us, but it's very old. I think it's that lifetime where I did something terribly wrong. I wasn't meaning to, but there was a great deception. It has something to do with the Artificial Intelligence.*

M: So, let's travel to that tower. We've now arrived at the tower.

C: *Ok, I've seen this before. The tower pulsates with a light all up and down that is an odd color green. It's not the evolutionary green that we see. I would call it an alien green. It's a signal. And the platform it's on is not very big, but it seems to be red. It doesn't seem to be a light. It seems like it's a...I'm not sure what the material is. It's not wood. It's not metal, but it's red. And there's a green beam the same color as the antenna that's connecting to a huge green pyramid, same color green, off in the distance where it's receiving a signal from. And then that signal goes into the society. It's not good. It's controlling their minds.*

It's keeping them from experiencing their full humanity — the senses and the free-will mind. It also creates a cage environment of the heart. It is very unpleasant, and I have a lot of trepidation going up to this tower.

M: Tell me what you're experiencing.

C: *A lot of conflict. I know about this tower and about this signal, but I also know that interfering or shutting it off or interrupting the transmission would have devastating effects.*

M: What do you want to do next?

C: *Well, in hindsight, from my human perspective, I would do the same thing all over again. It's already been done. And that is somehow interrupting that signal, but many people die. There is a lot of blame that goes around until the truth is known, but that's not for a long, long time. The truth is not known for a LONG time.*

M: Do you know the truth?

C: Well, yes. This seems crazy, even to me. So, this is a time where the human genome has been completed for a long time — thousands of years at this point. There were many, many thousands of years where the human being was learning of itself and engaging at multidimensional capacities and capabilities. So, there are really ugly-hearted beings that are not from this galaxy that have been very upset about the human genome and this new experimental being. They're not part of the twelve-dimensional splicing. They're very angry about the power of the human being. They see it as a threat. They've made many attempts to enter the Earth dimension, and they keep getting bounced off of some sort of field. I don't know how it happened, but that field became weak, and this other galactic race was able to enter. This beaming of the pyramid and the transmission towers, they were able to infiltrate the human race. From the inside.

M: How did they do that?

C: This is why Jesus had to come from the inside.

M: Very good, trust all of this. You're doing great. So, tell me more about this race. How did they affect the humans? Are they still affecting them?

C: Ok, so they somehow...this was the first group to mess with the human genome. And they were the ones that did the initial — they cut it in half first so that we were only six-dimensional beings and overlaid, somehow, they got into the human genome on the inside of the human being. I don't know how they got in some kind of tone or signal or frequency that was able to splice in. And they began influencing from inside the human genome with their own splice of dimensional influence. They could signal outside this galaxy to their home through the human being.

M: So, they used the human beings' abilities?

C: Yes.

NEXT SCENE: THE SHA

In the next scene, Carrie was shown an elevator that went down into the Earth to a subterranean community of the Sha. She described them as the original Shamans of the Earth. She described them as her "tribe" that she reported to once in a while for intelligence briefings and Lightbody upgrades. She would place a device over her head that would enhance Source energy in her subtle bodies and reconcile any distortions in her genetics from the negative AI technology and genetic splicing. She shared that the Sha are connected to Mt. Shasta and Shambhala and other sacred places and civilizations of the Earth.

NEXT SCENE: THE CATACLYSM

C: *Well, I've seen this before, and now I realize what lifetime it's connected to. I did have something to do with that; there was a team of people — scientists. They had to do with the shutting down of that transmission signal. And a lot of people did die, but now I want to say to myself, "Did they really die, or were they already dead?" as far as the human interaction. It was almost more robotic at that point because of the first big attempt at the AI becoming the human. So, there was a huge explosion. I've never been able to determine if it was just there or if it was all of the Earth, but that green light was gaseous as well. And it was almost like affecting people invisibly. It was sustaining the AI programming somehow. It feels gaseous to me, and somehow, I was involved in a covert operation with direction from the Sha. The Sha were the saving grace. They've always been the saving grace of the Earth and the Earth people. They are the keepers of the human race.*

Yeah, so the explosion threw me into the water, and when I originally had the vision, I woke up hanging onto a log. It was my first experience with those kinds of human emotions. Great grieving sadness, sobbing, sobbing, sobbing...guilt and shame, and fear. It was my first experience. And as I am hanging onto the log, I am looking back at this peninsula where society was, and it's totally on fire. The green pyramid has been destroyed. The signal is no longer active. There are many bodies floating in the water. I see a being sitting on a huge boulder. Kind of like the thinking man, but in the original vision I had years ago it was Michael the Archangel crying. And the first thing I said was, "I didn't know angels could cry." And the sword of Michael was not blue, it had lost its Light. I asked why he was weeping, and he said now the human race will suffer for eons and they will know this pain. So that vision came to me years ago and now I see what it was connected to. But I don't know; I don't feel like I died in that lifetime. I just remember that being the end result of the explosion or the attempt to disconnect from those outside beings being able to look at us all the time, and it was successful for the most part. There are still some strands of signals, very few, and they're very thin, but there is still some observation of the human race. Malevolent — it's not good.

FINAL SCENES: HUMANITY'S CYCLES OF WAR

We learned that the client was part of a covert mission initiated by the Sha to destroy the tower and stop the hijacking of human consciousness and genetics. The session continued by showing the client having multiple lifetimes as a human on the Earth. The lifetimes were a mission given to the client by the Sha to go to the surface and observe the next stages of evolution. She watched war after war and felt tremendous sadness that she felt was God's sadness for humanity and its choice to choose war again and again.

This current Ascension Event is a reconciliation process for the damage humanity and other species have done to Earth and atomic life. This is a restoration and redemption plan to right all of the shadow that has infiltrated the Earth over its billions of years of existence. The experiments are coming to a close, and a new era is beginning where humanity and Gaia will be restored to their original divine templates. You could say that it is not a "new" Earth but a restored vintage masterpiece with some enhancements!

Transcript: Star Family Assistance in Atlantis

This next client named Nicole came to me wanting to understand why she felt tremendous guilt. She used all of her skills to try to release it but could not find the origin. We had no idea this storyline was going to present itself!

When Nicole looked at her feet, she noticed that they were webbed, and she wore sandals. She could not tell if she had a particular gender or sex but definitely was not human. She wore armor made from a material not of this Earth. She had a belt around her waist and held a sword in her hand. When she saw herself from an outside perspective, she described herself as something of a reptilian-feline hybrid with green-brown scaled skin, strong bone structure, and a thin body and described the scene as having a moonlight glow.

M: What are you doing there, in this desolate place?

C: It feels like I am searching for people.

M: What happened to those people?

C: *There was a lot of destruction and war. I'm just looking for people and not seeing any life. It's a very panicked feeling. I was to be strong and hold together, but I am realizing that this world as I know, it has ended. In that, it is not there any longer.*

NEXT SCENE: HOME IN THAT LIFETIME

C: *It's a very highly evolved civilization. I see lots of towers. It's interesting; it looks so primitive in some ways, but the feeling in my body is that I don't like being there.*

M: Why don't you like being there?

C: *The destruction. Knowledge is being used in a way that is destroying the civilization. People are dying. Lots of aircraft moving around. There's lots of energy; there's too much. Too much. I can see it. Where I live is a hut, and I am trying to keep the solitude in my space.*

M: What is a way knowledge is being used in a harmful way? What's happening there?

C: *It's so fast. It's so fast, and people are misusing what was to be used for healing in ways to advance society and turning it into a place of destruction. Energy being misused. The knowledge is being put into robotic entities and not human soul entities. They are wanting to take over this civilization and misuse the knowledge of energy.*

M: So, like Artificial Intelligence is starting to take over? Starting to fight back? Is that what you're saying?

C: *Yes, there are hybrid humans. Angelic beings, people are coming in trying to save this civilization by incarnating, and it is lost. I feel myself losing my people. It's very painful because there are beings without souls using power to...I am just being a seer and seeing these things and not knowing what to do but seeing that this civilization is ending.*

M: When you said there are angelic beings and others incarnating to help? How does that work?

C: *I can see them coming in. Streaming in, almost from different planetary systems. Different realms. Most of them are from my soul family. This is the Atlantis era. It's very dark. Very dark.*

M: Let's see what else is going on. Let's see what you do with most of your time.

C: *I am around a fire. The word "war" comes up. So, people come into my hut, and we talk, and the words "peace" come to mind. They ask me questions to see, as a seer. So, I mostly see, but there are times when...and we all have wings on our backs. There are times, though, when we must go out and fight. And that is not comfortable.*

M: When you say that you have wings, what do they look like?

C: Big, huge wings. They are hidden. They are hidden during war, during the opposition. But within the family, these huts are very, very large, within the family the wings are exposed. It's a very bright yellow light, almost a native essence. Native American essence. Star people, star family, hybrid human.

NEXT SCENE: PYRAMID AND COUNCIL OF LIGHT

C: I'm in front of a grey pyramid; it's metal, and I'm holding my hands to it. It is probably thousands of times larger than my body. It almost looks like a receptor. There is a ball at the top of it.

M: What are you doing here at this pyramid?

C: Feeling the energy. It feels like I am trying to download information to slow down the...I just keep getting I am trying to figure out a way to slow down the energy coming into those who will do things that will harm. I'm asking for answers. I am asking what the souls are doing. The robotic souls. I get zapped. I am being almost zapped by it. It knocks me back, and it affects me in the way of feeling helpless.

M: Why would it do that? Why would this energy zap you like that?

C: I am the opposition. I am the opposition. Almost like there is a robot not wanting... There is technology overriding heart and soul. It's disheartening me as a healer and a seer. I feel helpless in that, but I have to be a leader and very strong.

M: So, what happens next?

C: I keep pacing. I go back to my hut, and I am pacing. The Council of Light is coming in, and I don't have the answers. It almost feels like we have to submit to the end of that civilization. I just keep trying, willing, in the hut — willing, maybe we can will something out of this, but there is almost this feeling of the end.

M: What does the Council think about this?

C: They look disheartened, very disheartened.

M: Who is on the Council? Do you know their names?

C: I recognize them from...they don't look like they're from the time I'm in. They have white robes, and their auras are very bright. They have wings. I keep seeing them streaming into this civilization. It's not enough.

NEXT SCENE: WORKING WITH HIGHER SELF

M: Why did this happen in this reality? Why did Atlantis go down?

HS: Because people wanted to go beyond their limits. They wanted to do things that were destructive. They were operating from a place of ego and greed, and it was numbers and the political influence. The power became the center of this place, rather than how it started, which were vibrational downloads from the stars and healing and a very, very wonderful star tribe council of seeing what could be done with energy. Then it got into the wrong hands, and many great souls incarnated to help. It couldn't be done.

M: What eventually caused the collapse of Atlantis? You can show her without it bothering her. What was it?

HS: It was an explosion. It looks like a tower. Lots of power going through, surging through, and an explosion.

M: And then what happened to everything?

HS: No vegetation, but it began to do that many years before. It was happening twenty to thirty years in advance. The vegetation was dying. It became very grey. Very grey.

M: You know, in modern times, we began to think that things changed with the crust or the waters. What happened? We can't find Atlantis anymore.

HS: No, I see it was above. It was pre-Earth. A continent that is more of a star, many different types of light beings were on this continent. It is not linear. There are remnants, but it does not feel of-the-Earth. It feels above the Earth.

M: Like a dimension?

HS: Yes, absolutely.

M: So, when this explosion happened, what happened to the people who were alive at that time?

HS: Some went back to their original planets, which was good for humanity. There were some very malevolent beings. Then others went into the angelic realm. Those in Atlantis are very, very technology savvy and hold that ancient knowledge. Nostradamus, many incarnated into different lifetimes to teach.

Most just perished or went back to their planets.

M: How did Earth manage to begin to populate again?

HS: People were birthed into different times. So, Earth showed up, and people were born into different times. Egypt. We had the Celtics. Those, many of them, had Atlantan knowledge. And so, they were put onto the Earth plane, the third dimension. Atlantis felt more ninth dimension; it's difficult to describe in a linear way. It's more of a realm, the different realms.

M: So, humanity was brought back, just in different realms within the Earth's existence?

HS: Yes. The third dimension.

M: Interesting. Where else were they put besides what would now be the UK and Egypt?

HS: Jerusalem, Southern France, Cairo, many places...yes.

Transcript: Escaping Atlantis

Here is another transcript segment from the somnambulistic client named Krissa who shared a bit about the end of the Atlantean civilization

C: Mad panic, everybody. Running. Fire from the sky.

M: What kind of fire from the sky?

C: It's like a volcano erupting. Looks like red fireballs and it also looks like it's coming from above. It's just a sickening deep crack of sound and kind of on top of a pyramid in a temple space of some kind. People are running and going crazy but I'm just numb. Like totally numb and resigned to it. Let's get it over with. I'm so sick of this. My heart's been broken, but it's almost like I've used magic to make myself not feel anything.

M: Look down at the body that you are in. Look down and describe to me what you are seeing. What do you see there?

C: A woman in long, white robes with another color, blue. My hair is in intricate different kinds of braids; it is long down my back. There is part of this temple that connects to the water. I really do healing work with the Merbeings, too.

M: Tell me about the work you do with the Merbeings.

C: Well, they would come up through the water; the temple would connect into the water, and they could come through this level, like a hole at the end of the water. There is this whole level like canals and waterways at the bottom of the temple and places they could sit partially in water and lay people in healing beds, in crystal, and I learned their ways of healing and it was a lot about sound, vocal sound, and oh my gosh, it's almost overwhelming. I'm so sad that it's gone (crying). I don't know what happened to any of them.

NEXT SCENE: THE DESTRUCTION

M: What's happening?

C: I'm really sick. There is a boat, and we are going somewhere else. I haven't had enough water, but that's not why I am sick. I could pull the frequency of water from the zero-point energy field, but my heart is broken.

M: Tell me about what happened to your heart.

C: When everything got destroyed. When it all fell down and no matter what we did, it wasn't enough to balance out the wrongs that were being done. I just put a layer around my heart so I wouldn't have to feel it, but then I didn't have the will to live anymore. Going on this boat ride I just got sicker and sicker until...

M: What was happening that was so bad? What wrongs were being done?

C: There was a perversion of the power to use sound to control people to be almost like slaves, slaves for Atlantis. And they would use these learning centers. They're really all just disgusting ways of controlling people, and it was almost like it was hypnotism of the lowest common denominator to just make them work harder and harder. Almost like an amphetamine, it would just make them work and work and work, and it was not of the heart. It was service to self. It was these people in this group and my skin would just crawl seeing some of them on the street. They were trying to use the beautiful, God-given powers and the crystals — crystal technology and sound technology. They were using it to harm people and do negative experiments. And they were hurting the Merpeople, and they were trying to make beasts, like bad beasts. And it's not, it's not natural. They were doing hybridization. And it just was so...I don't really understand how they got so much power, but they did.

M: I can see why you'd want to close your heart because it all tumbled down. That makes sense to me.

C: I let myself feel it right now. I just feel nauseous. It's so awful. So awful. I don't even know how many people died right then and there in this series and sickening cracks and explosions, and I don't even know what... I don't even know where they all came from. But I did know this. I did know that with so many wrongs, it would be made right somehow, even if it caused hurt and destruction.

M: Yeah. So, you just allowed yourself to fade away?

C: It's so sad now that I see how...without my working heart field, how quickly I just faded away and gave up in that life. And I was only powerful when I was feeling unable to feel. So, I just became a shell of a person like hardly even responsive. In shock. I was just in shock.

Transcript: Restarting the Earth Experiment

Now we will explore a session with a client named Veronica. Veronica's first scene she was regressed to was on a different planet, and she described herself as a tall and hairy being similar to Bigfoot or Sasquatch. These beings have shown up a few times in my sessions and seem to operate at a higher dimension than what humans can currently see. On the other planet, these beings lived together in caves and were benevolent. The planet was in a binary star system, and one of the suns was passing by the planet, increasing seismic activity and heat (sound familiar?). The species was preparing to make an exodus from the planet to look for another planet that would support the life of their species. (Did they come to Earth?) She was then taken to a great library (Akashic Records) and shown her angelic Lightbody form, pink in color. She was then shown another life that explains what happened after Atlantis.

Veronica was shown a gavel dropping, a decision being made to start over again. She described pyramids and a building with a ball on top of it, and everything had been covered in sand as if the deserts of the Earth tossed sand back and forth, covering the previous civilization so that only the tops of the previous structures could be seen.

NEXT SCENE: HIGH COUNCIL MEETING

C: A big light overhead. A table. A big, round table and there's a bunch of us there. Some of them are different colors, but there's a lot that look like biblical characters...like the long hair and robes and stuff. But others are like fish or dolphins and different colors, and we're all around this table. There's this big, bright light...

We're talking about all the things that have happened... There's like a...like a praying mantis sort of thing, and it's kind of upset. And it's got its arms... its elbows on the table, and it's asking us, "Now what are we going to do?" And everybody's talking. And it's like a wave of energy...like running around the table.

M: What is this group of people in charge of?

C: I want to say, creation...like different aspects of it. Different places.

M: So, what's being discussed?

C: I came back, and it was like a failure. We didn't make it work, and that was why everything was covered over. And there was a lot of sadness, too. They...it is kind of like the light overhead shines brighter, and it's like it's..saying something, but not in a voice.

M: What is it saying? You can connect with it telepathically.

C: Start anew.

M: Start anew? How would you start anew?

C: There's a place. It's green, green, green. It's got water...like the Garden of Eden, how you would imagine it...it's beautiful. It's like, start there...well, these beings don't know what to do. How to start.

M: So, let's talk about it. What's decided?

C: That light is showing us this place, and everybody's mind has this picture of this beautiful, beautiful place. And we start but it's a joint effort. Everybody's got their hands in there. Ah. It's...and there are animals, and the plants are beautiful, and then they start putting people there again. But there's something like swirling in front of the people...they can't... I don't know what it is...like energy? But they can't see it. They can't get past it, or they can't see past it.

M: What's the purpose of this swirling energy?

C: It limits them. They can't see things that they should be able to see.

M: And why was that put there?

C: It's almost like, not physically, but kind of energetically, it's almost like poking out their eyes. Like they can't see. Like it made itself into a cone and so they just live kind of like...like animals almost. They just kind of exist. They always have this cone of energy covering their face. I can't describe it. It's like a cone, but it's almost as if it was poking out their eye or something.

M: Do you have a name for this new creation you are making...this new planet?

C: I think it's the Earth, but it's like the start.

M: The very beginning?

C: Yes. Or not the very beginning because there were others before.

M: So, you're going to create a new creation there?

C: *They're just...they're people, but they're so like...so blind. There's like this vortex of energy in front of them, but they just...it's like as [if] it were like a giant chakra spinning, spinning, spinning in front of them and they can't move past it. I don't know why it's there because they're...they're like animals.*

M: Well, what happens next?

C: *I see a light. Like two...two snakes like swirling up a post. Like the medicine symbol.*

M: Caduceus.

C: *Uh-huh. The two...and they're different colors. There's one...almost like browns and one that's like golds, so they're not that different. And they're like...swirling up that post...I see that...and then like...they get, the post, the cane or whatever, taps these people on the head, but they're still just like animals. Like it taps them, and that chakra thingy goes away, but they're still kind of rooting around as a pig would.*

M: What caused this double serpent to tap them on the head?

C: *I feel like they were too blind, and they really couldn't do anything. And they were really just like rolling around in the dirt and just eating...like rooting around. And so, it came, and it tapped them on the head. And it did take away the light cone thing...but it's...but they're still not changing very much.*

M: Yeah. What happens next? Are there male and female humans there?

C: *Yes. And there's just more of them. They are created. There's just more of them. They just kind of appeared...like they were just put there, fully grown.*

M: Who put them there?

C: *Some of these beings, but it's almost like they keep trying to fix things and they're just doing like...they're not doing the right thing. They live together...they're walking upright now, at least. They're humans. They start to leave that area and they go out into the desert again. They're just...they think they're alone.*

M: They don't know that you're watching.

C: *Yes. They don't know. And they're just surviving. And they make things, but they just are surviving. They don't know that even if they're doing not the best job, that somebody is helping them and somebody wants them to...they don't listen.*

M: Well, what do you see happens next?

C: It just keeps growing, and they keep procreating and expanding. Civilization, I guess, is expanding. They're not the only ones. I just saw other places on the Earth that there are like these small, little groups, but they're just living and surviving.

M: Well, now I want to go back and find out what happened to the pyramids? What caused that last creation to...not work out? Let's go back to that time and tell me what happened.

C: They were... They're just not good people. They were strong. They were tall and strong, and they could do a lot of things, but they were just...their energy was just...ugly.

M: Were they human beings?

C: Yes, but like more...they were like taller and brown skin and really, really beautiful. There's one that I'm looking at. He looks like how we would think of a pharaoh. He's got this all-gold headdress on. It's a bird. They can see the energy and stuff, but they don't listen.

M: Let's learn some more about this culture.

C: They've created these pyramids, and they're huge. They're huge, and they've got crystals on the top, like shooting up at space. It's like they do it even jokingly. They put their two fingers under it and move it along but it's all mental. It's all mental. For them, it looks like they're little pyramids, like they're not that big. I don't know how big these people are, or maybe they can change their size. It looks like this pharaoh-looking person got really big, and the pyramid was like up to his knee, but then he was small again, normal again. And they...the Earth's like dry and they don't care. They're in a desert, but they can make plants and water and stuff like that. But they don't care if the Earth is dry. And then it...it all starts to go. The sand, like in an hourglass, that's how it starts moving like (makes swishing sound), but they're getting recycled, like a garbage disposal. And they're lost. They're thrown around. They're just done. They're just gone like a garbage disposal. It threw the sand all around as if nothing was as powerful. I'm watching this. I'm this pink, marble-looking angel, and I'm just watching it, and it's... they're just gone. Like the Titanic. That's what it looks like. Just getting sunk.

Pre-Matter Manifestation

There are checks and balances to this higher order of evolution. If experiments get too far out of control, the experiment is reset. I am told that the current phase of the Earth experiment will manifest as the New Earth reality as it has already occurred in the pre-matter energy fields in the higher dimensions. Now, we are watching the play out of the energy as everything falls into place for the singularity event of the solar flash. Even if it seems as though everything is in chaos, this is necessary to reconcile karma from the past to pave the way for the New Earth energies to arise. May it be so!

SIXTEEN

Inner Earth

Before the cataclysm of Atlantis, many intelligent beings went into the Earth for safety. These beings used cave systems and dimensional portals to take themselves deep within the Earth to build civilizations. When clients go to Inner Earth, they describe peace-loving civilizations and beings that modern humanity considers mythological. Some even say that at the core of the Earth is another sun!

There are many varieties of species living within the Earth. Some clients have described being elven beings who eat bioluminous food. Some beings occasionally come to the surface to assist humanity, but most choose to stay within the Earth, where there is no smell of pollution, war, or radiation from our technology. These beings are sending waves of love to us here on the surface as well as prayers for our remembering and healing so that we may all live together one day in peace. Many volunteers upon the Earth at this time have had or are simultaneously having lives in Inner Earth civilizations.

Transcript: Crystal Caves of Inner Earth

This next section is from a session with Krissa. Take a journey with us to Inner Earth!

C: *It's a vast beautiful cave. Crystals. Some are clear. Some have a blue or purple tint to them. It's very beautiful.*

M: **What else is there in this vast, beautiful cave?**

C: *Gosh, it's dwellings. It almost looks like something between dwellings for an Ewok in Star Wars and elves from Lord of the Rings. It is built into the stone, glowing crystal garlands, and they have a sun and sunshine down there. This feels really homey and comfortable to me.*

M: **Look down and describe your body for me.**

C: *Bare white feet of a child. Soft garments. It's pretty warm under there. Flowing garment and I am holding a homemade kaleidoscope. It's actually for identifying the properties of different gems and crystals.*

M: **So, you use it to identify the different qualities of the crystals?**

C: *Yes and decide what is this crystal. It's kind of a learning one for kids. Kind of like on the crust of Earth right now a kid could have a chemistry set that still works. But this isn't one of the really advanced ones. It's to help me learn. I'm just fairly young there.*

M: **Are you male or a female. Do you have a gender of any kind?**

C: *It's kind of hard to say.*

M: **What does your face look like? What does your upper body look like?**

C: *It's beautiful. It's masculine but very androgynous, so I think I am a male but with long black hair. My skin is almost shimmering gold and copper.*

M: **What are you doing there? What is happening?**

C: *There are a lot of tales. The older ones...Atlantis fell. A lot of work is being done to preserve the ways. They are teaching us the Law of One. The Law of One is this great governing principle that allows ultimate love and compassion with a high understanding that we are all one. That what you do to others, you really do to yourself. There are these beautiful priests and priestesses that work with crystals for healing. Maybe that's how they created our sun.*

M: **Tell us about this sun. What is it like?**

C: *It feels like it is more at the core than it is above. Warm, nourishing, allows food to grow. I only eat fruit, really. Maybe there is a grain of sorts. Vegetables, but we mainly eat fruits. That is most of our food.*

M: **Do your people call themselves anything? Do you have a name for your community?**

C: *Is it Agartha? Agartha. My father is a priest. He is so kind and loving.*

M: **Ok, tell me about your father. You said he is so sweet and so nice and that he is a priest. What kinds of things does your father do as a priest?**

C: *Oh, he is healing. There is so much shock and trauma and sadness over the loss.*

M: **Can you share with me what happened?**

C: *Yeah. I wasn't there but what they told me is that this other group was making a perversion of our powers. They were trying to get control. They were focused on material gain. They created these ways of mind control through sound, making people almost like slaves. They created beasts. chimeras, combining beasts on Earth. They only thought these existed in mythology, but they were really making them.*

M: **So, what happened?**

C: They were trying to be God. They were trying to...they were not creating in alignment with Source. They were creating out of alignment with Source. So, what happened was that the ones from the sky, the ones from the sky, the Pleiades, they saw what had happened. They helped some of us. Not me, I wasn't born yet. Helped my father and mother get to different places. We are under a great mountain. They helped them get to different places with crystals and created a massive...I can't say earthquake, flood, or explosion, but all of those things could have been the result of this. But it was this magnetic or so...I see where you call the Bermuda Triangle...why do planes and ships disappear there? There was a magnetic disturbance created and wiped everything out, but there is still a big crystal. There is a still a big crystal under water there, and you know who is working with it now?

M: Who is working with it now?

C: It's these beautiful beings, these whales and dolphins. God, humans have no idea how powerful they are and what they are doing for us. They are helping to clear it. I am showing. I wish I could show you telepathically what I am seeing. I am seeing this great pyramid crystal under the water with a big crack. This healed more and more, transmitting light codes. When it is healed, there is a great benefit to the Earth and humanity.

M: Is there a way we can help it heal today?

C: The work is already done but you can send all the positive energy and light to these whales and dolphins. They do so much for us, and we have no idea. We can send them our gratitude.

NEXT SCENE: RESURFACING PROJECT

C: Pleiadians came again. They are underground with us. They are saying that the time of contact is near. I'm afraid, somewhat afraid, but it will be. It is set. We are to come up and join the other humans on the surface. Work together. The Pleiadians have said we are working on their ascension. It's from the pulses of Light from the Great Central Sun. But also, there are so many different ships around the Earth right now. If you only knew. We are surrounded by ships. Can you see them?

M: I can feel them sometimes.

C: Yeah. They are every day working with these...I don't know the word, beautiful, beneficial extraterrestrials, angels, which really are extraterrestrial beings. There is Metatron.

M: I'm wondering what the plan is for resurfacing. Do you know what the plan is and how it is going to work?

C: Let's see. It starts with a very small amount that is already on the surface. It is showing me in your life, in this woman's life, you already know some of them. Some of our people who have been scouts. Maybe that's the word. Living on the surface. And sometime, and we don't know exactly when, the call will be given for these scouts to reveal their true nature, and then more will come upon the surface. There will be an exchange system of sorts where some will go down into Agartha and you will see how we have been living there and understand more about the crystals. This is the Atlantean...there is more than just Shasta under there. There are other places. Even Brazil. Even Bimini Islands. Other places where the crystals are held. Humans from the surface will be brought under and shown how to work with them. New technologies for healing, beyond what you ever thought possible. But it's already started. That's what you must know. You and this woman will be shown people that you interact with, that might have a special quality about them, could be one of us already.

M: Very good. Is there anything else that wants to be shared about the Pleiadian plan of resurfacing?

C: The best you can do right now is believe and hold high consciousness for planetary healing. You are doing the right things by what to eat and how to care for yourselves. You will be shown so much more really. We have your back, so to speak.

Transcript: Human Discovery of Inner Earth

Gaby came to me at a point of transition in her life. She was shown two lifetimes. The first was of Lady Guinevere in the lost civilization of Camelot. She was a mystical woman who sang to the land and spread magic and light everywhere she went. She described Sir Lancelot's sword being real and metaphorical as he was learning to retrieve the sword of truth from his own inner being. I moved her forward to the next scene and we arrived at a different lifetime in Inner Earth.

M: What do you see there?

C: Blue. Flowers. A little garden. It's hard to tell. Everything is just blue. Grass — things are shining. There's a lake. Horses. But everything is blue, it's very funny. Like fluorescent blue, not blue. I'm blue. My feet and my arms and my...everything is blue. I shine. My head shines, shining dots. Shiny stuff. No gender.

M: I want you to see the place that you live in that lifetime. What do you see there?

C: Like a sunrise, like an ocean; it's very strange. Now it's morning but I feel it's inside. I'm inside. Inside the Earth!

M: You're inside the Earth?

C: Yeah, under the Earth.

M: Do you call this place anything?

C: Yeah, it has a name. I can't pronounce it. A-S-T-H, Astharia, something like that. It has the sound THH. I see Astharia or something like that.

M: Very good, what's happening now? What do you see?

C: Butterflies, things flying in nature. And an ocean. And a sunrise. Very funky colors. It's like a rainbow sunrise. Let me see... Yeah, I feel laughter. There are other species, not only these blue ones, but it's also funny. There are big ones that are tall and there are these fairy-looking things. And there are lots — lots! And they are so happy. Everyone is happy. Everything is easy. There's not much to do but just be happy.

M: And you said the sun is coming up? How does the sun work there?

C: It goes...I was asking the same question because this is very strange. There are stars, but they look like crystals. And then the sun is like in the middle, in the water. It comes...I can't explain. I mean, it's just there.

NEXT SCENE: PRAYING FOR THE OUTSIDE

C: There is a gathering of us. We talk; we pray; we hold hands. We join.

M: What are you praying for?

C: Up. Outside. I just know it's not well, but I don't know more. I don't know much about it.

M: But you're praying for those on the outside?

C: Yeah. Someone said they don't know how to have fun! And I couldn't believe that. I...we were laughing because we couldn't understand. It's just weird. Then we pray. It's fun. It's okay. And we love them very much. Some of us wish to share, but we don't know how because they don't believe. They don't see. They don't know. They don't know how Earth works.

M: How does Earth work?

C: It's alive. It's a being. And we talk with it. We communicate with the ecosystems. We all, all of us, live. They think they're alone. They think they're very, very lonely. That makes me sad. But they're not alone — never — how can they be lonely? This is a lie. They believe lies. And they make them real. And then they can't escape because no one tells them it's a lie (laughs/cries). Someone has to tell them. And they will understand little by little. Because they can't see. If they don't believe, they can't see. You have to first believe, and then it will be revealed, and then you will see us and other stuff. Because outside there are also many beings. Outside beings will interact, but they seem like they can't see them. Humans can't...they forgot all of the beings inside of the human body. Their heads...their bodies are dirty. They're very polluted. They need to clean the body. Then they will start remembering because the truth is always there. It's calling. It's always calling like "hello," but when they clean themselves, they can hear better. And when they hear, they will see. When they change their beliefs. And then we can meet! Yes. They say we will meet them very soon. I'm so excited.

NEXT SCENE: HUMANS VISIT INNER EARTH

C: There's a big light. There are humans! Not many — not many, there's just a few. Just a few were allowed to enter because they believe. And they can see. And we share with them. They're very happy; they can't believe their eyes (laughs). It is a man and a lady. There are some guys; they look very dirty. Like a lot of beards. They came on like an expedition or something; they were walking for days. They look dirty. I think it's funny. We serve them, and they want to stay. We serve them something; they're hungry. I don't understand hungry much, but...

M: What do you eat there?

C: Light. They eat plants and berries. Sometimes I eat berries. They are nice. They said, "I knew it, I knew it." He wants to stay also because people wouldn't believe him, but he also wants to go out and tell. But they wouldn't... I think some of them went back and some of them stayed. They help now with Earth inside. But not outside, they don't believe. And it's okay. It's okay.

NEXT SCENE: FLYING OUTSIDE

C: I think I am flying.

M: What do you see as you fly?

C: Earth from outside in the cities.

M: How did you get outside?

C: I wished it.

M: What do you see as you fly around?

C: Cities and pollution. Ah, I'm just so excited. This is going to end. All of this mess, it looks very messy. Little houses and grey...it's all just going to go. These buildings and this dirtiness, it's gone. It's going to be wiped out somehow. I'm just so excited. Everything around tells me it's going to go. It has to go now. It's like there's this choir of angels, and this energy is like drums...it's chasing all of this away. It can't remain anymore. It's about to crumble. It can't hold itself anymore. Everyone is so excited. I'm just flying...I like to sing with them, because the more we sing with them, the quicker it will just crumble. Like a cookie. It's fun!

Closing Statement

Our subterranean relatives have been holding massive amounts of love and positive intentions for our awakening. When the resurfacing begins, they will share great healing technologies with us and lost knowledge. Make sure to include them in your prayers too!

SEVENTEEN

Ancient Egypt

Our last great Golden Age was in the time of Ancient Egypt. This age can be seen as a massive evolutionary step in restoring humanity and planet Earth to its original divine intention. I was told of seven beings who visited seven locations around the world to teach for seventy-seven years to raise certain civilizations in consciousness. This was when writing was spread throughout humanity so that we could evolve to higher thinking and understand the symbolism of written language.

During this Golden Age, humanity was assisted by different beings from the stars and higher light dimensions. People gathered in the temples of Egypt to study the alchemical ascension arts from many masters who either walked upon the Earth at that time or were available in the inner planes of the initiates. Journey with us now as we unlock the mysteries of the pyramids and travel to the ancient Egyptian times of high alchemy and magic!

Transcript: The Time of the Rising

This client came to work with Ron. Immediately upon entering the first scene, Ava's intonation and accent changed. The session is full of amazingly detailed information. Every time I listen to the recorded session, I feel energy move throughout my body, activating my DNA and subtle bodies. The following transcript is just a small section of the material Ron and his client have produced. I am sharing a tiny portion of the information because I felt it was an important part of the Earth story. Ron and his client worked together several times and are working on their own book which will be released soon called *The Songs of Remembering*.

When Ava came into the scene, she saw and felt that she was being pelted by sand in a sandstorm. As the storm cleared, the pyramids of Egypt were revealed. Around her, she could see and hear people talking and animals moving about. When she looked down at her form, she began to incorporate more of this character and her intonation and pronunciation began to change. She described that she was covered in robes because she did not have a physical form, she was in Lightbody form. The robes she wore were a precaution taken because if humans saw her in her true form, they would be afraid.

Since this session, we have learned more about the "I." They are extensions of Source who watch over us, tending to our evolution and growth. They came again after the bombs were dropped on Hiroshima to get a feel on the ground level of what was happening on the Earth. They returned on February 22nd, 2017, as the next wave and stage of DNA transformations began for our ascension.

C: *It is the time of the rising. It's the time of the Light. It is the time when Heaven and Earth become one. The pyramids have been finished. They are energy vortexes. They amplify and communicate. They help us amplify the bridge so that we can ascend. So, we can bring the next iteration of human. It's time to bring Light down, so that they may evolve. For we cannot interfere, but we can bring new ideas. We can bring Light. Upgrade. It's time for the upgrade. Next level.*

R: **Will you share with me the building of the pyramids, how has that been done?**

C: *Well, I don't know how to describe it so that you would understand. Perhaps an analogy might work. It seems as though there is a weaving of the stories of the matrix. As I said before, there is a weaving, and there is an amplification through the group work. There is a collective consciousness of our wills that we can weave stronger. And so, we weave the matrix of Earth, and therefore, we draw the stones into existence, and we place them. It is easiest to do this in sections, for Earth is dense. Slow building, but easier in a group. We could make it all in one piece, it is possible, but there must be The Forgetting. If we built it in one single piece, not only would that take longer and much more energy for many more of us would need to combine our will, but in the future, they will not forget, because they will not be able to explain. Therefore, the pieces make it seem like it could be built by man. In the times of The Forgetting, we cannot leave symbols of The Remembering. Too much, their brains would explode. Cannot, not yet, not time now.*

R: **Wonderful. You mentioned now it was the time of awakening now that the pyramids were complete?**

C: *Yes, awakening to the next level but not ready for the full awakening, too much, they can remember now, but in the future, they must forget again. It is a cycle of remembering and forgetting. It goes in waves. These beings are in a time of remembering; they know something is going on, but they don't fully understand. They cannot see us; they cannot see our forms. Their brains would EXPLODE. They would not understand our form yet. Not time yet.*

R: Wonderful now "I." Describe what is happening now that the pyramids are finished.

C: We collect our will telepathically into the center deep, deep inside. And there is a stone, not stone, a material, we bring in from another dimension. We sing it into Earth now, but it will not stay. Too powerful this, not stone, material, liquid, solid light, all at the same time. Hard explain to you. It does not make sense in three dimensions.

R: Okay, what is the purpose of this material?

C: It amplifies the bridge between worlds so that the upgrade can affect larger populations, instead of the slow way of genetic implantation. Genetic code implantation takes millions of years to spread throughout the gene pool, but this method is actually much faster. We are able to open the gates between other dimensions and upgrade the DNA of multiple beings at once. It is for the shift of all humanity, for there are multiple pyramids around the Earth. We work in conjunction, all together in teams to amplify all around the planet at once.

R: So, it's amplifying the whole planet and all the beings on the planet?

C: Yes, the whole planet is being upgraded.

R: Where did the energies come from that are going into the pyramids and around the planet?

C: From the...from other dimensions, from light dimensions. This time it's a combination of Fourth, Fifth, and Sixth. It is a trifecta to work with the DNA patterning and increase a certain percentage up from before. We want to be careful.

R: So, what is happening there now?

C: People are gathering, for they sense in the time of The Remembering, there is a sense that it is happening, there is gathering, but there is also...it does...only those on the edge of remembering will come, but it will eventually affect the whole planet once they come online with the gridlines. There are gridlines around the globe, and it is like pressing the acupuncture points of a person. It is the same. Once all systems are online, then the whole system gets an upgrade. It does not matter if they come or not, but some remember, and some come.

R: So, it's about to be activated?

C: We are planning, yes, it is beginning. We are beginning the preparations. I must be here to oversee. It must be very precise. The amount of material and the amount of will entering and the amount of bridge open to other dimensions. I must calibrate with the team, in the different parts around the globe, to make sure we have an even transmission. It's extremely important that it is calibrated correctly, or else we can create explosions and earthquakes and volcanoes. We are trying to avoid that and keep stillness on the planet. It is very precise work.

R: Thank you so much for your precise work. Can you tell me about the team members, what are their names?

C: Names, not important, light beings, manifest in smaller bits, all "I," but manifest in small bits in the robes to hide their true form. It is an illusion. Not embodied this time. Not incarnated. It is One Mind, One "I" that divides and is the overseer in each of the locations around the globe.

R: How many locations are there?

C: Scanning. There are, I believe, there are thirteen. There are more that are smaller; there are thirteen major nodes and many more smaller nodes around the world to help to send out the ripples farther out into the world, especially in places where there are higher concentrations of humans. There are thirteen main nodes. There are many more smaller nodes. Not sure how to count in numbers, because many of them are quite small. Seeds really. There are the secondary nodes, and then there are the tertiary nodes, only one atom thick — infinite numbers, like grains of sand.

R: I understand, thank you for this information. Will you share with me about the thirteen main places? Where are they located on the Earth today?

C: Various locations. For example, we [now] know about the ones in Egypt and the ones in Bosnia and the ones under the ocean near Japan. There are some in what you now call Central America. There are some that are now covered in the fault lines. They have disappeared. There are some in Siberia. There used to be one in Antarctica; that one is still there. Yes. The North and South Nodes have not been discovered under the ice. It has not melted yet, so we have not found those yet. I think though they are developing new technology and are able to sense them now. They are placed randomly — not randomly, wrong word — opposite of randomly, precisely placed for balance but appearing random.

R: Very good. What is the name of the era that this awakening is happening? Is there a name for this era on the Earth?

C: It is the time when we introduce writing. When time of the mind grows to understand the written word, so we are introducing that into the consciousness beyond that of just the mystics. We have taught the ceremonial leaders about language and writing, but it is now time for the rest of the world to begin to understand the pictorial, the symbolism of language into written form.

R: I see. How long does it take to build the pyramids in Earth time?

C: In Earth time, I believe the pyramids were built by another team. I only oversaw from the other dimension. Once the pyramids were finished, I came. I offered the schematics; it is hazy, because I witnessed from other realms. I believe it took many Earth generations to build, but yet at the same time, it was almost immediate. It is very confusing to describe this, because they manifested not in the way you would think. Not like with building blocks one at a time where you are stacking them like you would a normal building in this time. It was a slow materialization of nothingness. Therefore, they were not there, and then they were all built. One atom at a time, spaced out, and then they were woven together. So, it was like a wide net at first. So, they almost sort of just appeared. But it took a long time to materialize in Earth time, but it was instantaneous. It was very quick. From my perspective.

R: Yes, I understand. Can you describe what is happening from within a pyramid?

C: The pyramids are the augmenters. They take the material, and they hold the vibration, so as the songs of the materials are growing brighter in the Light, then they need a container so that they do not EXPLODE. We must match the density of Earth with the density of the other dimension. Therefore, it is like a translator. So, they are the translator for the transmission — you might call them something like a radio wave, but not radio wave, it is a light transmission.

So, therefore, the pyramids are like the...what do you call those, collectors, those energy collectors from the large arrays that focus the waves in order to send them far out into space. It is a similar concept, except the opposite, in where the energy must be matched. The large vibration of the ascension energy must be matched with the Earth dimension density. Therefore, it is a net that is weaving third-dimension reality (3D dimensionality) with the larger dimensional light frequencies so that it can be a bridge. So, therefore it is like the transmitter, the augmenter, and the bridge holder. It is like the bolts that hold the bridge into the Earth.

And it also connects the bridge into the sky. So, it is an energetic transmission network center, and it also holds the material and allows that material that is not used to be held in the third dimension. It gives it a chance to breathe, so it has certain portals to allow the energy to move throughout the pyramid so that it does not EXPLODE. There is an opportunity to experiment with the pathways to see if we can find a more efficient way of working with this material in the third dimension. As this is always an experiment that is developing and growing over time, we are always exploring how to better and more efficiently work these grids. For this does seem to be a lot of work to create this augmentation system, and therefore, we are trying to create a more efficient pattern.

However, this strangely simple and complex idea is the best idea our team has come up with in order to amplify the awareness mentality of the entire planet without causing any major explosions. So, it is both a grounding rod and an amplifier. It is all sorts of things all at once and difficult to describe to you in the third dimension.

Transcript: Building of the Pyramid and the Original Alchemist

This next client named Michaela came to me at the beginning of my years of doing quantum healing hypnosis. I had the pleasure of working with her three times. On the second meeting, we were both surprised by her arriving at the top of the Great Pyramid surrounded by many advanced spiritual beings for the placing of the capstone. We were taken through a montage of scenes showing what occurred in the pyramids, the function of the capstone, and how its magical, alchemical technology was removed for safekeeping for when New Earth was fully realized and activated. Somehow, the recording did not record. I lost the whole transmission. You can probably understand how shocked and heartbroken I was. A year or so later, we met up again to re-explore that lifetime to get more of the story for the book. Here is what we discovered!

M: All right. What do you see there? What are the first impressions that come to mind?

C: It's the pyramid. It's a large pyramid and I can see it surrounded by just lots of green trees, river. It's not like a desert. It's like all green and lush. They're huge.

And it's showing me the top of the pyramid.

M: What do you see when you look at the top of the pyramid?

C: It's like a separate piece. It's like a tip of the pyramid, but it houses like a large egg-shaped crystal. It seems to change color. I see it white and then emerald and then like a rose, very yellow.

M: So, the top of the pyramid is crystalline and has different colors shining from it?

C: Just the crystal. Yeah. And then it's like the tip of the pyramid is kind of like opal-like looking...sheen to the bricks like they're so polished. It's like a cap. It's a cap that houses stone. The Philosopher's Stone.

M: So, what does this stone do?

C: Many things, that's why it has different colors. Those different colors are like just the different energies and then they're funneled and used for different purposes. Like healing, knowledge, time travel.

M: Become aware of yourself. What do you see when you look at yourself?

C: They are man's feet in sandals like open-toed, leather sandals; robes of a brownish-burgundy color; robes with long sleeves, many pockets, many pockets in the sleeves. I am like the original alchemist (Thoth).

M: Are you carrying anything or holding anything?

C: A staff. A staff — wood, polished, not fossilized but maybe petrified? Yeah. And it's been through some kind of process, and it's alive somehow. It has a consciousness, this staff, because of a process, an alchemy process that I put it through. So, it's imbued with consciousness power connected to my own. Yeah, it's like a caduceus with a crystal, and when you stamp it on the floor...I see myself holding it and bringing it down, like Lord of the Rings, you know, the great wizard, when he stamps down the staff and says, "You shall not pass." It has that kind of feeling to it. You could stamp it down and the ground would shake. You know, it would clear out energies, clears out lower frequency or unwanted, you know, negative entities or energies. It's like a blast, you know? It's something you see in a movie. That's how they experience it, like if a bomb went off and you had the air rushing at you, it just clears it out like a bomb.

M: Yeah, sounds very powerful. You said you had a bunch of pockets in your sleeves. What was in those pockets?

C: Um, oh, alchemical elements. Tools. So almost like where you'd get the idea of Merlin the magician. It's tied to that archetype as well. See, the original alchemist is not a magician, per se. They have an understanding of the archetypal properties of elements. It's a spiritual amalgamation; it's not a physical process. They use physical elements, but it's a spiritual understanding of the archetype of frequencies of these elements. And you understand the natural laws of their processes with each other. Those processes you take within yourself in a spiritual way, which can be named as the amalgamation of mercury with sulfur to create salts. Crystallization. This is the spiritual process that we are capable of interpreting. It sets us above all, many, above the animals; the gift to mankind is the ability to understand these concepts and with understanding and spiritual knowing it can create enlightenment and crystallization.

M: Makes sense. Thank you. What are you doing there at the pyramid?

C: I'm a curator.

M: Tell me more about the curation process. What are you curating?

C: There's many objects of spiritual technology. Artifacts, ancient tools passed down from the Old Ones. I know everything about these. I keep them safe, keep the knowledge. I also search to increase the collection and add to it.

M: That make sense. When you're saying, the "Old Ones," describe them to me. Who are the Old Ones?

C: The original angels. The Nine. The original bringers of Light. They brought knowledge to this planet.

M: Good. Have you ever got to meet them?

C: Hundreds and thousands, eons...original architects. I have a kinship to them. So, there is as you say, know them, like as your soul knows, but to say meet them — not in the current state from which I'm speaking.

NEXT SCENE: MOVING BACK IN TIME

C: I'm a young boy, seven-years old. Dark hair; dark, dark brown eyes; skinny arms; skinny legs; happy, healthy.

M: What's happening there? What are you doing?

C: The priests have come. I have shown evidence of reincarnation. I am able to remember who I am. So, they have come to visit with me and speak with me. They perform these tests, but they know they don't even need to do the tests; it's so obvious. I don't speak to them like a seven-year-old boy would. I can tell them who I am and am already so full of knowledge.

M: What kinds of things do you share with them about who you are? What kind of tests do they do?

C: There are objects. A feather, some kind of like silver-engraved tool. Choosing my possessions from previous incarnations. Some of their items are misrepresented, as in not what they believe or were told that they were. So, I correct them on the origins of the objects that they perceived to be belonging to the past incarnation. Some were correct and some weren't. I was a great teacher…and I keep seeing the Emerald Tablets.

M: Tell me what you see.

C: Green stone and a chisel in my hand. I can hear it again, like almost feel it, tap tap.

M: So, they're testing you to see if you can get these things correctly. It sounds like you're passing?

C: Yes, putting them to shame. Well, I must leave my family now, which is hard for my mother. I must be like almost something for her that I am not, as in a small child. Because I am but I am not. But for a mother, no matter how much a child grows they are always a small child. So, the empathy and compassion I feel for my mother and the loss that she will experience, I do feel sad. But I am not reacting in a way that a normal seven-year-old boy would be leaving his family because it's just something I've always known I would do. I don't have the same tumultuous emotions. So, I sort of have to play a bit the part for my grieving mother, to be that boy for her, but now it is time to go.

NEXT SCENE: COMING INTO MANHOOD

C: I am thirteen. They are crowning me, but not like royalty. Well, that's hard to say. It's hard to stop other people from idolizing, which is the difficult thing.

M: What's happening on this ceremony day?

C: They're placing a golden, embroidered cloth around me, around my neck, the slim piece, not a full cloak. I have robes and then they're placing this strip of embroidered, gold cloth, like a golden garland crown.

M: You said they're idolizing you. Why is that?

C: Not all of them. There, man is just prone to, you know, to idolize that which they wish to be.

M: Why did they want to be you? What makes you so special?

C: My abilities, my demonstrations of knowledge and power in one, so young to just be born that way. I can move objects. I can perform miracles. It's just that I have an understanding of the natural laws of this universe into a spiritual level. I have DNA that is fully activated, like Mozart, born a small child and just playing the way he did with perfection, effortlessly. How does that make people feel? They feel many ways about it. The movie Amadeus gives a good depiction of worship and envy.

M: So why are they crowning you now? What is the ceremony commemorating?

C: Manhood. The full embodiment of my higher self. They make much ado about nothing. But I am still young, so I let them perform their rituals; I'm still learning. They want to put me on a pedestal and there are many years that I spent getting back down off that pedestal they keep trying to put me on, to keep trying to teach that what is within me is within all.

M: That makes sense. What do they call you there? To hear your name. Someone will yell it out now.

C: Ishmael. Which is funny; it's like Michaela, Ishmael, which is similar to the Michael energy that we share as well (referring to me, the facilitator). You see we are many things. We are many archetypal energies, wonderful combinations and equations. So, even in those past realities, I had an understanding of my own adaptability. I am many things; I am all things; and yes, I had a clear recollection of the source of my archetypes, that is all...simply, that I could remember. We all contain this. So, I would keep trying to teach the humble principles of the alchemy.

NEXT SCENE: PLANNING THE PYRAMID

C: I was the architect of the pyramid. I am back now to where we started.

M: Tell me about what you're learning about the architect.

C: I see me drawing out all the plans, the numbers, the equations, and on how I knew these things. Yes, yes. I wasn't just working with humans. After thirteen, that ceremony, they came for me in the ships just like a sun, a ship like a sun. And that was why it was so silly, their little tests, because they had already come for me. They were just performing rituals for themselves. So I went; I went with them for a time, for many years, and went through spiritual training, changed form somewhat, and then came back to construct the pyramids.

M: And so, when you say you went with them, who's them? And see them and describe it to me.

C: *I just see light. Beings of light, ships of light, colored light. They're fractal-like forms and patterns. They're like angels, higher dimensional beings.*

M: And they took you on this ship with them? Where did they take you?

C: *Through the Sun. Home. Arcturus, they say.*

M: What kind of training do they do with you there?

C: *It's hard to explain...kind of understanding how reality is formed. Working in different dimensions. I'm just seeing a lot of patterns, like sacred geometry. I'm seeing like all these equations, like color-coded bars. It's hard to conceptualize in this reality the way because it was like another dimension of learning, and so, it's outside of time. I just see this rapid experience of building; it's trying to show me so many things at once. It's like it's showing me Legos as a kid, I don't know. And then these like, it's showing me the sketch doodle thing I had when I was a kid (current life). Where it's like the circle and you put your pen in, it forms the geometric patterns, you loop around and around (Spirograph). Yeah, creates all these circles. Do you know what I mean?*

M: You were saying that you also changed form while you were there. Tell me about that process.

C: *It's a crystallization to the DNA. Much of what we are expecting to experience with the DNA activation happening now on the Earth.*

M: Like is going to happen in this life?

C: *Yeah, well, not for all, but yes, that is the goal, this activation to the next level of evolution.*

M: So, when you came back, what did you do? Be there now, tell me what you see happening.

C: *Moving these just massive, massive stones like just in the air, forming them and placing them. Everything has this like sheen to it.*

M: Does anyone assist you with this?

C: *There's like a ship, a light ship above, and I feel like they are like amping up my powers, you know, like I'm a conduit. They're definitely adding a lot of power to perform such a massive task. It's a lot, it can be a lot of work to do one of these huge bricks, right? Never mind doing a whole pyramid. So, they help focus energy, staying in a certain state, they just magnify all that, amp it up.*

M: So, the pyramid is being built, did they share with you the intention of this pyramid? Who gave you the idea to build it?

C: *The ones who came from me, the angels, the original angels.*

M: **What is the purpose of the pyramid? Why did they have you build it?**

C: *A magnifier to teach, to heal, to set the journey. It's a huge source of power. It lifts the frequency of the planet. It makes it easier for those who don't have my abilities to like, pierce that veil. It puts them in a higher state. It makes it easier for everybody else to learn and do.*

M: **That makes sense.**

C: *So, it heals, it teaches, gives love, allows for communication, purification. There is a massive amount of knowledge in the crystal. It's like the natural laws. All of them. All of them are clear cut in this crystal, haven't been messed with, haven't been inverted or bogged down with dogma. Just the clear-cut, simplistic truth to every last detail, the natural laws and elements of this universe.*

M: **Before we were allowed to see the ceremony of when this whole thing was completed, I'd like for you to go to that ceremony now. Describe to me what's happening there. Be there now and tell me.**

C: *A large crowd all gathered around, thousands. Colorful, colorful material all around, just flags blowing in the wind. Many priests as it's being lowered into place, just the crystal. It's all open at the top. And we're setting the crystal in place, like into its housing, and then lowering. We all leave the top and the capstone is lowered and placed. And cheering all around, applause, celebration. A beam, a beam of light purple — light, vibrant purple, from the top up to the sky. I feel like it goes all the way through, down through the crystal, down into the pyramid. Deep down.*

M: **So now that this capstone has been placed there on the top, what will this do now?**

C: *Well, you can feel, it's like the air is thick like rose water. Like it's this energy, I'm trying to compare it to like water that's like silk that smells like roses. The air has this thickness to it, like this sensual, just love, and like gliding through, you know, a pool of bliss. The air is thick with it. It almost has like a rose-purply-rosy color to everything, the Light. Rose-colored glasses. I just want to say, like seeing through rose-colored glasses.*

NEXT SCENE: EXITING THAT LIFE

C: *I'm watching my funeral.*

M: **What happens, how did you pass?**

C: I chose when to leave my body. I feel like I lived a few hundred years, and I was done. My body does not look that old though. I didn't really age. And I'm just like floating above watching everybody go through the rituals.

M: And from that perspective, you can understand the purpose and the meaning of that life.

C: Well, it was to leave a record behind. Leaving a record behind and setting in place aspects for the storyline. Markers, nodes in time. It's part of what I learned. We work through time; we leave points that require a conclusion. Like points in the plot of a story. We participate in building it, but it was also leaving records and teachings behind not just for that time. [for future timelines that we would incarnate and continue using the tools and sacred knowledge.]

M: So, what is the storyline of Earth from that spiritual perspective? What is the storyline for Earth and humanity?

C: Ascension always. Elevation. Always growth, expansion, enlightenment. Always higher, higher, higher. It never stops. The torus, always evolving. It's just turning itself inside out once again.

M: So, in modern times the capstone is not there. Can you show her? What happened to the capstone?

C: Stolen.

M: Tell me about it. What do you see happening?

C: But they didn't get the crystal because I took it away. Well, this was what we talked about before. When they came there was a big rush; they're coming; they're coming; we are not protected. Because living in this peace and love [believing] "No, people don't steal; they don't hurt; they don't take; they give." We are not a society that is in defense of itself, and unfortunately, there has been an erosion. They did leave, these higher beings, and it has left us open. They're coming to take what is ours and to use our power for their own.

M: Who are these higher beings?

C: Anunnaki. There's good and bad Anunnaki, polarities and everything. So, these are ones still working within hierarchal dominance; they want man to fuel and feed them. They are not looking to fuel and feed man; those are the polarities. One side wants man to ascend and to grow and release; receive; experience their full, true capacity. The other wants to harness it for themselves. So, we are removing your Christos [the consciousness technology of the Great Pyramid]. It is time; it is part of the story. And going in a large, like box or chest, gold, but actually very little adornment. It's kept very humble. I have come back to take it away. Confusing, well, it's confusing because, you know, I die, but I didn't really die. And I left, but I came back and took form, basically took form as my old self to retrieve it.

M: And how did you do that? How are you able to take form? Let's see the process now.

C: You create a template. Understanding the geometry, sacred geometry, you create a template and then you attract protons, like magnetics. It adheres to the template that you create. I'm explaining this very simply, just kind of showing, like magnetic slivers. They're showing me like if you were to draw a symbol like you know, the Metatron's cube or sacred geometry, and then you magnetize particles, the building blocks of life, they get stuck to it. And then they just build. You just take form. You can take any form you want if you understand the templates and how to draw them, and then you just magnetize them, and then it takes form. You could literally make anything in the palm of your hand if you have this knowledge.

Transcript: The Life of Goddess Isis

This next session is with a client named Nicole. When Nicole came into the scene, she described a beautiful clay and rock temple filled with radiant sunlight. Many people were around being creative, and music played in the background. I had her look down at her body and describe what she saw.

C: Wearing beautiful, golden sandals, white robe, beautiful necklace...beautiful necklace and symmetrical jewelry, gold jewelry on each wrist...showing the divine feminine and masculine inflow. Symmetry is very important. Then going up, wearing crystals, gold necklace with crystals, blue malachite. There is some obsidian and a red stone. Just a very comfortable garment.

M: What about on your head? Do you have anything there?

C: Yes. It is a sphere, but what it does is emit energy so that others can download the energy that is in the sphere and feel that beautiful healing. It's a headpiece, and it was put there by Thoth...Tehuti. He and I work a lot together in downloading and receiving energy. It is representative of life, the life force and inner journey, a mirror. He infused the headpiece before he put it on. I have women also who helped me put it on, but he infused it with a mechanism that can enlighten and awaken others faster than the use of hands. So, it's a downloading, teacher sphere. It is a very heavy piece, but I like to have my crown covered, my crown chakra. It is a very, very sacred space, and I like to receive directly from the Divine so no energies coming in other than that of the Divine and so the headpiece is a purifier of energy coming in, as well.

M: Wonderful. Do you have anything in your hands or in your arms?

C: Yes, I have a golden staff sphere and a top that has a beautiful bird...just the head of a bird, but a beautiful bird. There are a lot of wonderful energies that come from that totem.

M: How did you get something like this?

C: I was gifted, as I was a child.

M: Were you aware of its lineage? Where does it come from?

C: My mother. That my mother also symbolizes, is a symbol of a white heron. That being at the top of the staff was very important.

NEXT SCENE: LEARNING FROM THOTH

C: It's nighttime. We all go to our places and receive energy. It's my favorite time of the day. It is a time where I get to feel the oneness within and I am commencing with other philosophers, other astronomers, other beings that are coming to me to teach me in order for me to teach others. I like the quiet. This lifetime is very quiet. It is...there are energies of Tehuti, who is the Great Alchemist. He holds the Emerald Tablets. He holds so many soul embodiments, such as Melchizedek, Nostradamus...many, many incarnations of beings. He has many soul essences. On my end, we connect through, not words, but energy, philosophy. I feel Nostradamus. I feel the numbers. I feel the Mother Mary energy. I am more of the transmuter of the energy. Tehuti is the astronomer download. It is a very great kinship healer. Healer, friendship, as he and I have created magic, and that is what the time was about...it's about magic. Creating what is unseen from knowing...from a "knowing"...you must believe it to see it, and that was such a great and useful tool and is now a tool that is being reintroduced. The tool of manifestation.

NEXT SCENE: HOLDING THE LIGHT

C: In the temple. Sitting next to my partner in front of people. He has something in his hands. A gold staff. It looks like a snake. Actually, it's not a snake. It's a lion on the top of it — a lion's head. It keeps the energy away. It's a protector. He keeps it facing the people.

M: So, what are you guys doing there in the temple?

C: Guiding.

M: How do you guide?

C: Energy. The priestesses have their hands out to receive the energy. I am sitting next to my partner. My hands are facing the people. I'm not saying much.

M: How do the people look?

C: They're all in white. They're barefoot. It feels like worship, an initiation. It's before the underground.

M: What happens there?

C: The actual underground school where there isn't worship, but there is the inner knowing of finding God within. I keep getting the word Thoth.

M: What about him? Is he there?

C: Yes, he is the information. He's holding a tablet of information that I also received a lot of knowledge from, the Emerald Tablet. And Thoth is important. He's just showing the tablet. He says to bring in the bird knowledge. Use bird medicine. Very important — it's a way to open the heart chakra. Pretend the soul is in flight but hold steady to the Earth. He keeps pointing his hands at me, so it feels like we don't speak a whole lot; we just exchange energies and downloads.

NEXT SCENE: SITTING UNDER THE STARS

C: It's beautiful. Up high. It's got a white bed, and I have many women there working, and they keep it beautiful. They keep it together for me (gentle laugh). I like it at night. Most of the time I channel the stars for healing properties and study astrology. Tonight, I am connecting with a wizard.

M: What does the wizard teach you?

C: Alchemy.

M: Does he have a name?

C: Melchizedek — sacred geometry.

M: What kind of things do you learn from him about sacred geometry?

C: Everything's interconnected. It's the magic of manifestation. The light frequencies pull energy. So starlight is a very good time to manifest. I sit at night by the pyramid and hold my hands up. I sit in a receptive position with legs crossed. My palms are facing upward, resting on my lap. That's how I get my downloads.

M: So, you just open yourself to the stars?

C: Yes.

NEXT SCENE: SITTING WITH THE COUNCIL OF RA

M: I want to learn about the people that you live with. Let's go to a time where you're all sitting together for a meal. Be there now. Tell me what's going on.

C: It is joyful. There are eight chairs. Everything is stone. And we're all wearing white, and there's a lot of gold.

M: What do you look like?

C: I have very green eyes, dark hair. I have a headdress on and lots of paint on my face.

M: Tell me if there's anyone sitting there at the table with you?

C: It's a tribe of people. The women are on the left, and the men are on the right, and my partner is across from me, so I'm at one head of the table, and he's at the other. There are three on one side and three at the other. I'm at the front, and my partner's at the front.

M: What's your connection to these people?

C: Council.

M: What kinds of things do you see over?

C: The Egyptian people.

M: What do they call you in that council?

C: Council of Light, but I also hear the name Ra.

M: What do they call your body and your person in that lifetime? Can you hear that?

C: Isis (she pronounced as ee-sis).

M: Is there anything else you would like to share?

C: Animals. There is knowledge in the animal. There was a lot of esoteric wisdom drawn from animals. They played a very important role in guarding the temples, so I am very close to my animals.

M: How would you gain esoteric information from the animals?

C: They are a part of our totem. They are a part of us. They are our soul family as well. They are the guardians. They have the power of presence. They have the wisdom of the unseen. As for Tehuti, the Bird Tribe carry within their totem a bird essence. He, as well as I, knew that whether you had the totem of a swan or a heron or an eagle or any sort of bird, it was a true honor to have that in your totem. Others had felines; others had cows; and others had dogs. These beings we do not consider less than us. They weren't even animals. They were teachers. We did not own them. The priesthood is getting together. The high priestesses are coming in. It is a beautiful gathering. Some queens do not enjoy these gatherings. I enjoy them. There are souls from different star systems coming to this planet to learn. There are people coming from different areas from Earth to learn from this temple.

M: What kind of things will they learn?

C: Manifestation, instant healing, vibrational frequencies, healings, downloads. They are learning the esoteric art of alchemy, the meaning of existence. They are learning philosophy. They are learning many things.

NEXT SCENE: DEATH OF OSIRIS

C: There's chaos. People are running. Not sure what they're running from. I'm standing at the front looking out.

M: You're in front of what?

C: The temple. Yes, there's...(breathing) I'm just getting the word disbelief. Hathor and I are turning to each other and are holding each other, holding energy to send out to other people. The council is sending energy out.

M: Why are they sending energy out? What's going on there?

C: Unrest. Something is missing.

M: What's missing?

C: A leader.

M: What happened to the Pharaoh?

C: Killed.

M: Who would have done such a thing?

C: His brother. Set.

M: So, what are you doing now?

C: Praying. Holding the energy among sisters and brothers, but the people don't understand.

M: So, you hold this energy, and what happens next?

C: *Get guided to go.*

M: **Where will you go next?**

C: *Find the Pharaoh.*

M: **Ok, so tell me what happens next?**

C: *Go to the Nile. See he's dead. Thoth is there, and we guide in the manifestation of magic, of burying the energies of the Pharaoh.*

M: **Tell me how you do this?**

C: *Intention and the Emerald Tablet.*

M: **The Emerald Tablet is part of it?**

C: *Yes, it's a big part of it.*

M: **And so, you connect with the Emerald Tablet?**

C: *And magic and manifestation happens. It's the unseen, the unknown — letting the manifestation happen — magic happens. His Earth body is done, but he's resurrected, and all of the work that we've just done worked out for the Pharaoh. He's living but in an ethereal body.*

M: **How are things with the people?**

C: *They want revenge.*

M: **Revenge against whom?**

C: *Set. I don't agree. It's not worth the energy.*

M: **What do you think would be the right choice — the highest choice?**

C: *Having an heir.*

M: **Like a child? So, what happens?**

C: *Yes. Thoth says it could be done through the ethereal body, that I could have a baby, and the people will calm.*

NEXT SCENE: CELEBRATING WITH THE COUNCIL

C: *There is a council meeting. There is a council. It is almost a celebration happening.*

M: **What is the celebration about?**

C: *My son. He is becoming the king. Everybody is dressed up in a very proud... There are many people who will be influenced by him. We keep walking through the tunnels, and everybody's hands are up. We are speaking without words. At the end of the tunnel, we go into a beautiful, beautiful room where there is a table...a long table where all of the brothers and sisters sit, and a celebration happens. Many, many, many nonphysical entities, as well as my sister. There is my husband, who is there. There are three chairs on the left, three chairs on the right. The front end has beings across the table.*

M: What do you call your husband? What is his name?

C: Osiris. It's interesting. We are each wearing different headpieces that represent our specialties. Yes, there is one with a snake on the top of the head. The snake is the conqueror. It is the infinity sign, but the conqueror of ego and emotion. It is a sign of royalty. A lot of us are wearing some sort of snake jewelry, but I see that headpiece very clearly.

M: So, a snake, and what else? What else is on that headpiece?

C: It is gold and black. It looks like the sphinx...what the sphinx looks like. Only certain people can go near the knowledge that is in the sphinx, and the Gnostic knowledge is there as well. It is very much tied into Jerusalem and the Essenes. It is a sign of knowledge —The Keeper of Knowledge. There is a lot of laughter and joy, and the energies are so comfortable that there is no trying. My son is to the right of me, and he is now able to wear the wonderful eye makeup that is announcing him as a part of the spiritual council. It's very bright and light and joyous and fun.

Hathor is also somebody that I go to often to laugh and enjoy. She is the bringer of laughter and dance. Dancing is very, very huge in raising the vibration of energy. In Egypt, there was a lot of dancing and celebration. Movement. There was knowledge of movement. There were schools but knowing that we were all there as Christed beings, as Source consciousness, as Bird Tribe, Star Tribe members, it was a very fun time to experiment with vibrational frequencies and being in human form.

My child is being crowned. I see his crown — I see the back of his head. He's eight or nine. Horus. He's taking over. People are rejoicing. It's a sacred time. He has his father's staff. He's wearing a white robe to his knees, and he's barefoot. He is being adorned with things, and the people are sending beautiful energy to him. The sky and the Earth have finally come together.

M: What do you mean by that, "the sky and the Earth have finally come together?"

C: Merging the Sun energy and the Earth energy in my son. He's just walking forward. We're sitting again in the same temple and its [an] initiation.

M: How do they initiate young Horus?

C: Adorning him with things. Also, he's given the visions and that is how the sky and the Earth are merged. He is opening up to the visions that he's ready to see.

NEXT SCENE: TRANSITION OUT OF LIFE

C: I see the sky, and I'm on my bed. It's Sekhmet to the left, Hathor to the right, and my son is there. I feel very, very honored. I feel very empowered and rested and I can see that I am older, and the sisters would also help keep my room, keep my temple, my room upstairs. They were my best friends; they were my maids, and it is time to transition. It is very, very peaceful. No one is crying. It is not the mourning that we do here on this Earth plane. It's just as natural as birth, going into a new realm, ascending. It is something that can be done while living as well.

Many people in modern times have a draw towards Ancient Egypt because they lived lives there in preparation for this modern life. Let us reawaken the temple magic of Egypt and celebrate our eternal spirit. Let us each become a pyramid of Light upon this planet and beam the frequencies of Remembrance out across our beloved Gaia. It is time to remember our ancient codes of Ascension!

EIGHTEEN

Holographic Earth & Planetary Grid

Sacred Geometry is the foundational template of Creation formed by harmonic structures of Light and Vibration. Everything within Creation is formed using this divine coding and language.

Earth exists as a holographic field of overlapping connective pathways of light and sound formed in sacred geometric design. Flowing telluric currents of electromagnetic life force pulse information and evolutionary coding across the vibratory field that we call Earth. These pathways have been called different names by the ancient Indigenous and wisdom-keeping cultures of the world, such as ley lines, dragon lines, songlines, and dream tracks. Along these subtle energy lines, we find rivers, lava flows, mountain ranges, currents of weather patterns, and pathways of migratory animals. All of life is connected in symbiotic relationships through these etheric, vibratory highways of subtle energy.

Pyramids

One of the biggest mysteries is the pyramids that are being found all over the world in areas like Giza, Bosnia, Mexico, Guatemala, Australia, Indonesia, St. Louis, the Grand Canyon, and off the coast of Japan under the ocean.

In the ancient days, the Builder Races from the stars and higher realms built pyramids and star technology structures upon the Earth to support healthy, progressive evolution across the biomes of Earth. Thirteen major pyramids around the world create a system that receives, converts, and transmits evolutionary coding across the ley lines connecting with pyramids, temples, stone circles, and other sacred sites across the planet built by several generations of humans and nonhuman beings.

These pyramids line up with other pyramids and energy pathways in distant star systems as part of a fractalized information superhighway interconnecting all of Creation back to Source. Three main star points that our planetary grid system connects with are in the constellation of the Pleiades, Orion, and the star system of Sirius A and Sirius B. The global pyramid system acts as a bridge for the higher light dimensions to infuse Earth with higher evolutionary coding to evolve the entire matrix of Earth.

The building of these structures was systematically coordinated and developed in particular timelines and areas of the Earth in preparation for these times we are living now. They had to be created in a way that humanity would believe that they could build them on their own using manual labor. I have pyramid building stories from the Inca, the Olmecs, and a few from Ancient Egypt that all describe the stones of each of those pyramid systems being moved into place using forms of telekinesis, materialization, alchemy, and divinely inspired harmonic geometric design. I do believe that humans tried to build them on their own at later times, but the architecture is noticeably less precise and stable.

I am told that the capstone will be replaced fully when we are in the New Earth frequency and that the energetic structure of it is being put in place now as we prepare for the next stages of Ascension. This will put what was described as a "gel" over the grid of the Earth to assist our ascension. This will help with telethought communication and regulate the electric influxes that are occurring from space weather, the Schumann Resonance, CERN, and other causes. This will help with cardiac health and the psycho-emotional purges from the influxes.

More and more pyramids and star technologies will be found in the oceans, frozen within the ice, underground, and in other hidden places in the coming years. I am sure this will accelerate as public disclosure of the truth of extraterrestrials increases. Each of these "discoveries" is timed for when humanity is ready to receive such revelations at each stage of the ascension process.

Sacred Sites

At certain points within Earth cycles, higher levels of energy pulse from the planetary grid. Full moons, new moons, solstices, equinoxes, and other celestial alignments mark shifts in the global vibrational signature. New energies come into the planetary system and pulse through the planetary grid and vortex points to support harmonic evolution across the biomes of Earth. These time markers are potent opportunities to implant intention into the planetary grid to affect collective consciousness and planetary evolution.

The ancient Indigenous and wisdom cultures had various methods of connecting with and manipulating these pathways in practices that some call geomancy. Sacred sites like temples, stone circles, sundials, and megalithic structures were built by ancient people along these pathways or at intersection points where subtle energy pathways converge and pool, creating swirling vortexes of Light information. Ancient priests, priestesses, shamans, and initiates would gather at the sacred sites and power points to communicate with and travel to other realms, anchor prayers and blessings for their communities, share gratitude for the Earth, and manipulate weather patterns, among many other uses.

In ancient times, temple priests, priestesses, and medicine keepers would clean and clear the sacred sites. These ancient initiates knew the power of the sites and regularly held ceremonies and sacred rituals to amplify divine energies and intentions. These sites serve as multidimensional portals, where you can access information from other realms. Large communities held ceremonies and celebrations at the turning of the seasons and during astrological events to anchor their prayers of love and awakening and transmit their intentions to the higher realms and ancestral lineages.

During the Dark Ages, much of this was forbidden, and many died because of their sacred work. There are groups of people in every period — some sisterhoods, some brotherhoods, some a mixture including nonhuman higher intelligence species — which met at these sacred sites to initiate, activate, and clear energies. Many of us have been called to do this work on the Earth now. During my travels to sacred sites worldwide, I have had incredibly powerful experiences where higher dimensional energy poured through my crown and radiated out into my energy field. During these powerful transmissions, I have received insight and wisdom for the next stages of my life and self-healing in parts of my being that I could not access before visiting the site.

The Druids and pagan traditions of the UK, Ireland, and Europe have extensive systems of ley lines and sacred sites. I have had some of my most powerful experiences along the Apollo/Athena ley line, which is sometimes called the Archangel Michael ley line. This line of energy runs from Skellig Michael in Ireland through the tip of the UK, France, Italy, and Greece and passes through Mt. Carmel in Israel, where one of the Essene mystery communities was located.

The ancient wisdom traditions and Indigenous cultures are stewards of the planetary grid and have been in service to maintaining harmonic exchange across the system for thousands of years. The history of colonization can be seen at these ancient sites as dominating forces have condemned native spiritual traditions and built over their sacred sites with their structures and enforced new dogma on the people.

The esoteric knowledge around the amplified ability to manifest during certain gateways is known by both positive and negatively polarized groups. As we approach major holy days and astrological alignments, fear and chaos-generating events are coordinated by negatively polarized groups who wish to hijack the opportunity for expansion to keep humanity in the lower consciousness states.

The awakened people of the world are invited to anchor in heart-centered intentions and visions during these times to amplify unconditional love and unity with the Divine and this blessed Earth. As carriers of Light, we are invited to anchor divine presence upon the Earth and to project visions of peace and wholeness during these gateways while those who are not awakened are likely to be swept into the entropic mind control trap set up by service-to-self groups.

The war on consciousness is real, and it has been happening for quite some time. Wars over land and resources include the fight for power over the grid of consciousness. There is a major stargate in Iraq that souls exit the Earth plane from on their way back to Source. Another major vortex is in Jerusalem at the Temple Mount, the land of Megiddo, and around St. Catherine's Monastery in Sinai where Moses is said to have received the Ten Commandments. One session showed the connection of the black cube in Mecca which is said to transfer siphoned energy from Earth to Saturn to be used by nefarious star beings. Many vortex sites are owned by institutional Christianity that broadcast distorted teachings of Jesus, Mary, and the Disciples from these powerful sites, programming fear, shame, and condemnation into people's hearts and minds, thus suppressing consciousness and making humanity slaves through their perverted teachings. Clock towers were used to keep us programmed into linear time versus eternal creative experience. Military complexes have been built on the sites, pulsing fear and war mentality into the field. One of the grossest energy vortex sites I have been to is the Pentagon. Cell phone towers built along these lines pulse harmful electromagnetic frequencies across the planet, creating a cage-like environment for our hearts and minds.

For example, I have visited many sacred sites along a ley line that travels from the UK to Denmark that many call the Mary Magdalene line or the Michael-Mary line. At one site close to Copenhagen, I stood looking west down the ley line pathway, looking at the miles and miles of church steeples that were built on the line. The ground that I stood upon contained two ancient ceremonial burial grounds desecrated by decades of public executions. Next to me, on the same piece of land, stood a military tower with various broadcasting devices attached to it and a cellphone tower broadcasting cellular signals. This is just one example of how convoluted the grid has become.

When Jesus and Mary walked the Earth, they traveled to many grid points to anchor in new codes and dismantle the "dark matrix" established by service-to-self beings. These beings overlaid the "fallen consciousness grid" over the Earth grid which used the inherent dual nature of third-dimensional consciousness to their advantage. This saturation of "fallen thoughtforms" was used to hijack human consciousness by overpowering the mind and subtle vibrations to keep people in endless cycles of reincarnations. Many starseeds have been completing the work on the grid since the first wave arrived starting in 1945. As the starseeds move about the planet, they create a new grid for Gaia's energy to be cleared and act as lightning rods for new energy to come in. Much of this work is done unconsciously as starseeds are called to travel to different locations around the globe to shine their love! Thank you starseeds for taking on this grand mission!

One of the most recent technological attempts to suppress consciousness is the global installation of 5G satellites, Wi-Fi routers, and smart meters. It has been said over and over again in sessions that these frequency devices are not good for humanity. It is advised to detox the body of heavy metals, get into nature more frequently, move away from 5G towers, turn off Wi-Fi broadcasting systems, and turn off the smartphones as much as possible. These attempts to control human consciousness are futile as we are now ascending to a consciousness that cannot be affected by these measures. Over the coming years, all of these harmful systems will collapse as the new harmonic structures are put into place. We will take them down!

Interacting with the Planetary Grid

At this time, many are being called to different sites and ley lines worldwide to either receive codes or play some part in the restoration and reactivation of these sites. As the planet's energy ascends in frequency, these sites are emitting beautiful energy that can be interacted with. Many beings want to be on or near Earth just to feel these new energies! It is like an orchestra of musical spheres toning the songs of New Earth! I highly recommend traveling to the places you feel called to travel to. You never know what magic that land has for you.

We interact with the planetary grid primarily through the Earth Star chakra and our heart center. In this way, we are connected to the life force of Gaia and all information from her past, present, and future. Each moment, we act as a bridge between the higher realms with the planetary grid. Starseeds and lightworkers are moving across the globe, cleaning and clearing the grid consciously and unconsciously as part of their divine service in this life. This is why many of us prefer not having a solid home base and choose to travel the Earth and visit sacred and beautiful places.

When traveling to a sacred site, I feel that the site begins to work with your consciousness before you arrive. Often, Ron and I would have some type of argument as we drove to the site. Unknowingly, subconscious lower energies were being cleared to prepare us for the sacred grounds. As we traveled to the sites, often repeating number sequences (e.g., 11:11, 1:44, 2:22) and other synchronicities would happen en route to the site.

Before entering a sacred site, it is important to ground, center, and tune into your energy field. Some of these sites are quite powerful. Sometimes I would get dizzy or disoriented, or manically joyful. Each site is unique in its energetic offering. These ancient sites have often become popular tourist sites with a cacophony of etheric, emotional, and mental, energies congesting the site's vibratory field.

When at the site, I recommend starting with a meditation to connect more intimately with the energies. We are often barefoot at the sites so that our nervous systems and energetic pathways interact with the site's matrix without being hindered by shoes. Simply ground, center, and drop into a place of absolute stillness.

I have experienced a full spectrum of events when it comes to these sites.

Some are so congested and dense from tourists that I did not want to stay long. Other sites were like stepping into another world while high-frequency energy pulses through my body and floods my energy field. Each experience is unique and beautiful in its own way.

Many sacred sites of major historical importance are treasured and adored by the people who protect them. Many sites belong to Indigenous people. These sites should be treated with the highest respect. While traveling to Australia, an Aboriginal man explained his hostility towards people visiting his tribe's region because of uranium mining and the defacing of important ancestral sites. In many places, it is suggested to get permission from the lands' custodians before entering a sacred site. Whatever you are guided to do, do it with love in your heart and respect.

Leaving an Offering

While many people leave items at sacred sites as an offering, I find this eventually becomes a mess of wet and weathered items polluting the site. Plus, depending on the stewards of the land, offerings could be seen as disrespectful, vandalism, or littering. I once met an Aboriginal man who said he would try to get my visa revoked if I even chanted on the land!

I suggest leaving something energetic. Sing a song, dance a dance, shine your love, or some other activity that brings the energy of joy and gratitude into the vortex of the space. Simply coming with heart-centered intention and an open heart is more than enough to show your gratitude for the site and Spirit. I honestly feel the best offering to give is your silence, your listening, and your loving presence. Just BE there!

Transcript: Andromedan Builders of Incan Pyramids

Here is another session transcript from a somnambulistic client named Krissa. It took me some time to comprehend the massive story that was unrolling because there were so many plot twists! I did this session back in the beginning days when I practiced QHHT. There are several topics in this one session that were shocking and new for me. Looking back years later, I am seeing several opportunities to get more data. I am always hungry to learn more about all of these lost and hidden stories.

C: *Beautiful valley, but I'm in pain in my neck because someone's tied a rope around my neck. I hate them.*

M: **Tell me what else you're seeing there. It won't be uncomfortable. You can just allow that to be more comfortable now as you tell me what's happening there.**

C: *It's getting more comfortable. These men are there. They're not like us. They have these animals and spears, and they see that I have magic or power. I'm a woman, but I'm really, really tall. Taller than them. They're scared of me. They have a rope around my neck, and they're pulling me going somewhere, and I don't know where.*

M: **What's it look like around you? What kind of place are you in?**

C: *There's a jungle; there's a river. There are our buildings of stone. Oh... I see I'm here, but I'm not from here. This is...we call it South America now.*

M: **Why don't you look down at your body and tell us what you notice about your body. You said you're a woman.**

C: *Yes, pretty much. The people I'm with are small and brown, and I'm tall with red hair, and I'm very white, and they know that I came from a ship. They're not afraid. They put me as a sage, or a wise woman, a wise medicine person. I'm not a regular human. I'm having a hard time remembering where I came from exactly, but I know that when I think about it, I'm sad. I want to go back (begins crying). I want to go back (continues to cry). I don't like these humans that much. Why did I have to do this?*

The Spanish and Portuguese came, and they want gold. They're killing people, and they want to keep me. They tied a rope around my neck, and they're putting me on a boat. I can't help the people who are getting hurt. I'm planning to kill myself.

M: **Before you do that, you said you have powers. What kind of magic do you have?**

C: *I can put my hands on people and pull their sickness out of their body. Transform it and heal them. I can wave a...oh, I'm seeing it now...(laughs). I can wave a geometric light grid around their body.*

M: **What does this light grid do?**

C: *It can be for healing and protection. It can be around a place. Oh, I can see something interesting. There's a lot of places those Spanish people didn't find. One kind of this grid thing can make a place cloaked into invisibility, not totally, but less likely to be noticed. That's nice. Wow. Oh, I can see what's happening...*

People who are getting killed let fear overcome them. They're not staying in these temples that I made. I told them if you stay in there...I went out there and let myself be captured as a distraction. I'm taking the heat on purpose. I'm trying to tell the people to go back into those stone temples that are protected, but they run out in fear, and that's why they're getting killed; it's the fear. I'm trying to tell them, "No. Stay in the frequency of love, and you'll be protected. Go into those refuges that we made." But they're doing the best... They don't know. They're just really scared. It's terrible what's happening. These people are Spanish, and they don't even think they're human. They're treating them like nothing, like animals, and even animals shouldn't be treated this way. It's disgusting. And they're just looking for gold and resources and slaves. And I don't know what they're trying to do with me, but they are scared of me. They have a metal ring around my neck.

M: When you say you built these temples, how did you build them?

C: It's the sound. Oh, there are others like me...I can see them now. I'm not the ultimate master of building in sound, but some of them can do it with sound and harnessing those powerful tools that use crystals and sound. And the builders in my race set these, but I set the grid protection around them. They can move stone with sound and crystals. They can really do it. I think they can lift and levitate these... Oh, I see, I just showed somebody to put a capstone on using only the power of your mind.

M: Do you all call yourself anything?

C: Oh...Andromedans.

M: Andromedans. And what about the people you're with? These shorter people. What do you call them? What do they call their tribe?

C: I'm being shown that today we call it "Inca." There's another group I encountered, the Toltecs. Very wise, very beautiful and wise. But I was mostly with the Inca.

M: Ok. Tell me what's happening now.

C: I'm on the ship, and we're going...and they think that they're really going to get a lot of money from me because I'm different and have these powers. But they're keeping me below, out of the sun. All I eat is fruit. I live on (fruit) and sun. They're giving me this weird paste. It's disgusting. But I could go for a very long time without eating food. I'm not very worried. It's uncomfortable. I realize I could take my own life, and I was almost planning it, but I saw another way.

M: What's the other way?

C: *I saw that I could create a storm and shipwreck, but I found compassion for them, and I decided not to do it. I decided not to create a shipwreck and a storm. I decided to trust. Not the humans...and that's okay. But I decided to trust myself and my people that whatever happens, that nothing will happen that is beyond my capacity. So, I'm on the voyage, and I'm kind of smiling now. I have dropped deep into a meditative state. Almost like stasis. I'm glowing.*

M: What are you doing when you're in this state? What is the purpose of it?

C: *Energy conservation and union with love and Source. Something like the connection to receive downloads from the mothership. It's not just a ship, it's a center of love and community. That ship feels more like home than anywhere on Earth. I can see the whole ship. It's like I can directly connect in that state. My brainwaves are so slow. I'm a pure channel.*

M: What was the purpose of you coming to the planet? The Earth?

C: *I did volunteer for it. Elevation. Illumination. Laying groundwork. Setting some foundations of a conduit for more light, higher consciousness to come in. This particular group was one of many that were focused on from a number of groups. I'm seeing another ship with beings from many star systems that I've lived in. I just see my body morphing and changing like a big fast forward. It doesn't matter how I looked in these different places and different bodies. At the core, it's the same being, and it's a really loving, ancient being, and we were setting up elevated consciousness on the planet. There has been so much, what we would consider human, [that] had influence from other planetary systems, but the Andromedans were on a council and Galactic Federation, and some of us are real masters of healing, sound, energy, color, and light. We were setting up civilizations with the knowing. I didn't get to help them become adept before this interference with the conquerors, but wow, they had the potential to learn. These humans have the potential to learn...and it brings joy. They do have love. They can feel so much love.*

NEXT SCENE: DRUIDS

M: What's happening?

C: *I made a big escape. Someone was trying to hurt me to get information. They don't understand the information. They didn't believe me, and so I made myself nearly invisible, and I was able to sit in stasis to the point where the physicality of my body was not as solid anymore, and I slipped right now off the shackle on my neck. They were so shocked and confused. It was almost funny. They couldn't believe it. They couldn't believe it, and some of them really felt like idiots, and too bad! But I got away...I'm seeing a boat, but where is it going?*

M: You're on the boat now?

C: This is a different boat though now. I got passage somewhere else. Okay...it's colder and very green. The people there...

M: What about the people there?

C: Oh...there are some who are very wise and intelligent. I'm seeing the stones, plant medicine, and they know a lot about the celestial bodies. There's a group.

M: What do these people call themselves? You can hear this now.

C: They said a word in old Gaelic and said the modern word is Druid. I'm doing something with a crystal where I look through it with my eye, and I can look at a woman and tell her who she should mate with, have children with, to fortify her bloodline. I'm stewarding the development of these people. Wow, I really have this open connection with the ship now, and these people know that I came from the stars, and they also are fine with it. Some people were very open back then...my mind is moving so fast; I need to slow it down a little.

M: Tell me what's happening as you experience it.

C: I'm teaching these people and learning from them. And there were beings over there before. I know them, Pleiadian beings...Lyran ancestor. I've had lifetimes there too. So much more emotional than the Andromedans. We can be passionate but years of refinement.

M: So, the Lyran beings are more emotional?

C: Yes, but very, very wise. The ones who are emotional...there are these younger strain of Pleiadians who once Lyrans were. I'm seeing the Pleiadians...I don't want to say factions, but some are more evolved than others. I don't want to be rude, but some are more evolved than others. Some of them have a more feline look, but they aren't a feline being, per se. They're just a little intense, a different frequency. But the Druids have a deeper understanding, and I can see that some of these people...

I can see this is now called Wales, and some of these Welsh people ended up in Australia, and this bloodline really took root down there. When I sit in stasis and connect to the ship, I'm reminded that most of my mission on the planet is just being exactly who I am. Not trying too hard to do any one thing because I would get sad sometimes. What happened in South America made me very sad. But that I was doing my purpose just by being and carrying a frequency not native to the planet but really loving, beneficent, elevating. Not so much about doing but being.

M: What makes Wales such a location for everyone to gather?

C: It seems like the veil is thinner there for some reason, and there is a powerful crystal aspect in the land.

M: Tell me more about this.

C: Jesus. There are two things. The bloodline of Jesus ended up in Wales at some point. I can see that glowing, like a thread through the land, yellow-gold, white-gold...beautiful...Christ bloodline. But then, some crystals from Atlantis ended up there. The word Avalon keeps coming up... What is that? I can't see what it is...(exclaimed). I saw something funny! Merlin is real. He's a real person!

M: What else are you seeing there?

C: Tower on a hill. No...that's somewhere else. Gosh, I'm seeing grid lines lighting up, connecting to powerful spots.

NEXT SCENE: CHRIST BLOODLINE

C: I'm holding a little baby. The baby was having trouble feeding, and they brought the baby to me. I'm a healer. This is in a similar place. The baby's skull bones and spine... I can place my hand on them and make subtle adjustments. The flow of the fluid, the baby is healed; I hand him back.

M: How do you work with this energy? How do you bring it in?

C: I open a portal at the top of my head. I quiet the mind and the senses, and it flows out through my hands. Oh, my gosh... this is a child very close in the lineage of Christ. I'm supposed to support this lineage. It's showing me something. Jesus Christ was from a ship. Oh my...

M: Tell me what you're seeing as you see it.

C: I almost want to cry...how wonderful. The star of Bethlehem was really a ship!

M: Tell me about it. What do you see there?

C: Beautiful, advanced Pleiadian ship of Light. And it wasn't that the baby...that's how Mary got pregnant. It was time. Everything we did before...it's showing me multiple lifetimes of setting the stage so that such a baby could be born right at that time. The divine...everything is so misunderstood.

M: Set the record straight. Tell us what we need to understand.

C: *All of our enlightened masters and deities are examples of beneficent, loving extraterrestrials who have come to elevate us. To elevate us! That's the salvation! And Christ was a living embodiment and example, but when he said, "We will do all of this and more," he meant it. He meant that humans will reach the point of being able to do things like he did, like I did when I was living on the earth closer to my Lightbody form. We don't need to feel so limited by the heaviness and density now. This planet has so many seeds of Light from different extraterrestrial races that are here to benefit us. Yes, there have been negative influences, but what I'm seeing now is...it's not even worth talking about. It's so inferior now that it's not even worth talking about — the negative races and negative influence — because there's so much light that's about to reach a critical tipping point. And the fact that I held in my hands a baby of the lineage of Christ and he just needed a little adjustment in his spine...sometimes our spine things are just not flowing quite right through that channel, through that energy channel. I'm moving my spine now. There! Sometimes all it takes is a little adjustment to keep flowing properly.*

M: So, what are you seeing now?

C: *I'm seeing myself growing old in that lifetime. I had to look human enough in that body, but I was quite old.*

M: How old did you live to be in Earth years?

C: *A little bit over 200 Earth years in that lifetime. I'm going off into the woods, and there is not a death experience that happens. What I'm seeing is that...it's so crazy. I'm sitting at the base of a big tree. I'm cozy and warm, and I'm going into a deep, deep meditation. The energy of the tree, I can see it now, is wrapping around me and through me, and I'm becoming lighter and lighter. I've been still for weeks and months. The body, the vessel, shrinks down, and there is an explosion of Light upward. And my consciousness is gone, back to the Source, just in this glowing, peaceful light. The tree helped carry me home. It's so beautiful.*

Closing Statement

This session has many keys to unlock lost knowledge and trigger cellular memory for awakening. Hopefully, I will get to work with this client again in the future to research more of this storyline. Many components of this story are revisited through other clients in later transcriptions that are in this manuscript.

NINETEEN

Avalon & Jaguar Shaman

A few clients have gone back to the lost matriarchal civilization of Avalon. They describe a highly psychic community that honored the Divine Feminine principle of the Godhead. The Avalonians worked with the fairy and elemental realms and were very connected to the Earth's living waters. As the shadow consciousness of the world descended on the region of Avalon, the Druids helped to fight against the intruding forces. The Avalonians decided it would be best to ascend to a higher dimension and assist from the higher planes.

Transcript: Journey into the Mists of Avalon

As Gaby came into the scene, she describes herself as a female wearing a blue, hooded dress with a golden cord around the waist. She is standing in the forest, holding a round magical object in her hand that resembles an eye that illuminates her inner vision. She has a strong connection to the trees that surround her and feels that they are "holding space." She lives in a temple space illuminated by crystals in a community in nature. Joyful children are running about having fun. The community eats lightly, mostly fruit. She spends most of her time swimming, meditating, and connecting with a tree. She also spends a lot of time sitting in deep meditation and quiet presence with other community members in a sacred circle.

C: *I am human. A woman. I am sitting with children, teaching. I feel that I am teaching everybody, and I am channeling and connecting to the Source. All these kinds of tools. Two kids, I feel that they are girls.*

M: **What kind of place are you at? Look around at your environment and describe it to me.**

C: *It's a temple surrounded by water. It's beautiful, kind of like an antique Roman temple with white stone and with lots of light. And I see water all around. It's very peaceful. Light.*

M: **So, you're teaching the children in this temple?**

C: *Yeah, and I see the women walking around. We are all in blue. It's a blue skirt and a blue dress with large sleeves around the arms. It's very soft and beautiful.*

We are all barefoot.

M: Do you have a name for this temple?

C: The only thing coming is "Avalon." I feel that I am hosting a circle of women.

M: Describe to me what is happening there in the circle of women.

C: It's how we communicate and how we discuss and see how we can serve best. It's very flowing telepathically. Everyone is sharing what is important that needs to be said and being heard in return. I feel there is something with the outside world.

M: What's happening in the outside world?

C: I think we feel what is coming. There are men outside, Druids, that we can communicate with, and they are the ones who are witnessing and are immersed in it.

M: What are the Druids communicating to you?

C: That our past is ending. Our time is ending. They do their best, but they're saying there is a disconnection now and they can't hold it anymore. They are asking for our help.

M: And what will you do?

C: That's why we are in a circle. We are putting our energies together to send light and love.

M: Tell me about that process. How do you do that?

C: By intention. We have our third eye open; that's why we have the symbol on our forehead.

M: Describe the symbol to me.

C: It's a moon, the crescent moon, holding the third eye. So, it helps focus and direct...

M: So, you sit together and focus your third eye somehow? How do you do that?

C: Yeah...from the divine. We are all connected to the Divine. And then, through the third eye, we hold the Light in the middle. This Light ball which works with Earth. And the Druids are able to receive, to channel, but not the human.

M: Why not humans?

C: They're closed, and it's okay. It has to be.

NEXT SCENE: HEALING WATER

C: I can't feel my legs. I see water. I feel like I am paralyzed until my knees. Maybe I'm in the water. Yes, I am in the water.

M: You're in the water, wonderful. Describe it to me. What's around you?

C: I don't remember the word in English. It's not cloud, mist. Fog and mist.

M: So, you're in the mist. Why are you in the water?

C: (Sighs) We need to. We have to leave. It feels this way to live is not safe anymore. The energy isn't safe anymore. We can't hold the Light anymore. There is much darkness. I see fire. I feel like it's destroyed what we've built. Our safe temple has been destroyed. Humans. They don't understand. They don't understand what they are doing. It's sad. We are grieving. We can't do anything anymore. It's another time. We were all connected to Mother Earth, to the trees, to the water, we were one. It's nothing now.

M: Times are changing?

C: Yes, and it needs to happen. It's okay. We have done everything we could. We have learned what we needed to learn. Our time has passed. Now, I feel it's in a body now. We need to learn through the body. It's hard. It has to be to come back. I think we have become too light, not enough in our body. We need to go back to the beginning to learn to be in the body. We are leaving peacefully now. To the Light.

M: So, you're going into the Light now?

C: Yes, but it's not death. We keep doing what we're doing, but from another place.

M: Take me with you and tell me what's happening as it happens. Describe it all to me.

C: I dance with the water. I am going through the water.

M: You are going through the water? How does that process work? Tell me how it happens.

C: I feel like the body had to emerge slowly. That's why I couldn't feel my legs. But now (pauses)...it's hard to describe. We're all going in at the same time. Kind of going through a wave.

M: And everyone is doing this together? How does it feel to do this?

C: Light.

Transcript: Life of Goddess Rhiannon of Avalon

The client named Norah describes herself barefoot with a long, white dress and cape on and she called herself Rhiannon. She lived in a forest cottage with her horse and had a healing bed with crystals that she used for her healing work with the community which she called Avalon. She described the birth of her child who was born with a crescent moon on her forehead just like her mother. This marked them as Priestesses of the Goddess who carried the Light teachings upon the Earth.

In this next scene, she is with a group of women in a secret, invite-only meeting at Stonehenge, working with the magical energies of the Moon. The women are setting up for a sacred ritual honoring the Goddess.

C: *There are only thirteen of us. The older women are setting up. Some of us are going to receive. Mmm. We're receiving something tonight on this full moon. I'm not sure of what yet. Someone is placing a wreath, or a headpiece, on me. It's made of flowers. And she just handed me a crystal — an amethyst crystal. She's asking me to hold it during the ceremony against my heart. She kissed both of my cheeks. There are thirteen roses.*

M: **What does the number thirteen symbolize for you?**

C: *It's a sacred number of the Goddess. We celebrate thirteen moons, thirteen cycles of the Divine Feminine, to honor our bodies. We honor our cycle [menstrual]. We honor emotion. We understand that with the moon we can release the emotions and honor them at the same time. It's healing.*

M: **Do you often meet in this way?**

C: *We meet on the full moon and new moon. We're all healers. We all have healing abilities. Many of us bring something different, and we honor each other. We teach each other so that we all can learn from one another.*

M: **What healing abilities do you work with?**

C: *There's a white light coming out of my hands. And my heart — the energy is gold. It is to heal. It enters through my crown and goes through my body. Others use herbs and can create potions, elixirs...elixirs they're saying...elixirs. Some balance energy. There are those that "see." So, they bring what they see for whomever, and in their knowing they know what needs to be done, and then they send them off to those who can do the appropriate healing. So, we all work as one.*

M: **So, everyone gets to use their unique gifts to work together.**

C: *We are one. We don't separate ourselves. We are the energy of the Divine Feminine in individual form on Earth. We come together, and we share all that we have been given and all that we know. And we pass this on, if we have daughters, we pass on this knowledge. We are not the only group of thirteen.*

M: **What other groups are there?**

C: *There are other sisters that do this as well. I'm seeing three groups. They come from far. They use the same grounds. They don't have it there — the ground is very sacred. It's a connection point. There is, below, what looks like a crystal cavern or maybe a mine. It's very high energy and high frequency. We know it's there — others don't. The sun and the moon energize the area. It almost looks like the crystals are a battery, and when the energy of the moon comes in, the full moon, the energy shifts. And you use that energy for...I'm seeing twenty-four hours; you have twenty-four hours to use this energy of the full moon. It cleanses those of us that do this work (sigh of recognition). This is a cleansing ritual. It's because we work with others and we remove their illness or injuries or density, we have to remove it from our own selves. The full moon does that in this particular space. Ah! It's amethyst below us. It's very healing. That's why it's sacred. The Sun is out. It charges through the Earth, and it reaches the crystals. There is a way to get to the crystals, but only a few know how.*

M: **How do you access the crystals?**

C: *There is an opening...this is not the same place where the original stones were. It's been moved. To access from where we were.*

M: **You said they moved the stones to access more of the energy?**

C: *No, this is the original place where we're at now. They were moved...they're not in their original place anymore in this time.*

M: **So how do you find the access pathway for the crystals?**

C: *There is a drop-down cliff that is all stone. We know where it is. You have to be small to get in. It's on the side, what they're showing me, it's on the side of this stone ledge or mountain. And there is a path at the edge, it's very narrow, and we walk it. And there's an entrance, but only...you would have to be a woman. It's too small for men; they can't get in. They've tried. So, a child can get in, or a small woman. We go in sideways. You don't even know it's an entrance to anything; it's very well hidden. We turn ourselves sideways and we push against it, and we slide in (sigh). There is an energy there as well, where when you get to a certain point if you are not pure of heart you will not be allowed to enter. It's beautiful in there. We perform rituals there.*

LAST SCENE OF HER LIFE

C: *They're telling me I don't leave in illness. I leave in the Light. I chose to pass on the knowledge to her today. After I pass the knowledge on, I'll step into the*

Light. So, I won't be there.

M: Will your physical body experience death?

C: No.

M: How does this process work?

C: It is our choice to leave. As eternal beings, we can step into this Light. It's an activated Light that comes from above when we are ready. It's done when we step into it.

M: Well, when you're ready, you can step into this Light.

C: I told my daughter I will see her in the Light one day. It's purple, just like the amethyst.

M: Purple Light?

C: Yes. I am being lifted. The Light is taking me straight up. It is gold. My body is just traveling...it is stopped.

M: Where did you stop?

C: Home.

M: Home, mmm. What does home look like?

C: It looks like the sky.

M: Are there others there?

C: I'm stepping out of the Light. Yes, there are many here. It is a celebration when you go home. You may choose to leave the body and allow the soul to leave, but some of us just step entirely into the Light when we know our work is done. Mmm. There are many.

M: Very good. I want you to now be with your counsel of guides and other high beings. Be with them now and tell me what's happening.

C: Mmm, they are greeting. Saying "very well done." There are many.

M: What kind of space are you in?

C: I'm a room, and the table is round. There are twelve here. They are all wearing (chuckles)...they're wearing the same stuff that I see in meditations. It is like a white linen with gold at the collars. And a gold sash. It is very comfortable. Some of them have a long tunic with pants, but some of them just have a long robe. Some of them choose to wear an open collar and some of them choose closed. It is all white. The gold is around the collar, and the sash is gold.

M: What are the names of the beings that are there? In your counsel?

C: Many of them are masters. They are guides. Jesus is there. Mother Mary, Master Kuthumi (laughs), Melchizedek, Athena, Rowena. There's the mother, Isis.

They are saying, "Council of Light." They are the Council of Light.

M: They have important information to share with you. Connect with them and tell me what they share.

C: *What you set out to do has been accomplished. The process continues.*

M: What was it that you set out to do?

C: *To heal. Each dynasty is a culmination, an ascension process for humanity. It's gone both ways. They're showing a blueprint of Gaia. That's why the table is round, it covers the entire table. It's the blueprint of Her. It shows culmination points they are saying. It shows us dense points and points of light. It shows what needs to be focused on. Where the Light needs to reach. Where the healing needs to go. And why there are those of us that have to go. We take our beacon of Light there; we bring the codes in, and we anchor them. We anchor them under Earth, into the crystals. We spread this energy of Light until it reaches another that is doing the same thing. Until it covers the entire Earth. It's bringing back the Light of life force energy. It had been blocked. It was shut down because it was not of the Light. It hurts my heart (almost starts crying), what they did...*

M: What did they do? And who are they?

C: *The negative energy. The dark forces. They took our light for their own. They feed off of it. They feed their...(sighs)...it energizes a structure of theirs. I do not understand what they're showing me. They use the crystals. They use the crystals the wrong way. I am hearing nuclear fusion. Atlantis. They used the crystals the wrong way.*

M: Was the dark structure there in Atlantis?

C: *We had structures there we placed in the beginning. We used them in temples. The temples were mounted over highly energetic areas. We infused those crystals with the energy, the same way I did in that lifetime. We infused them in love and healing. There were other ones that were used as energy centers. They were batteries. There were certain ones that were batteries to power ships and to bring power to what we needed. But the others came and manipulated the power. They changed it.*

M: What did they do to change it?

C: *Dark magic. There became more of them than there were of us. They wanted the power for greed.*

M: What did they do?

C: *They took over the centers. They were able to manipulate the energy. Some...these beings are different; they're not like us.*

M: How are they different?

C: You can feel their energy. You can feel their negativity. I don't like it. It's making me sick. Ugh.

M: What happened there in Atlantis to cause the cataclysm? You can see it now.

C: It looks more like a nuclear war. It's...I see what looks like beings from ships, but not beings of light...beings of conductive energy, beings of negativity, beings that blow things up. They're blowing things up. Fighting on the ships. This isn't how it's supposed to be. It's not what we originally created in the beginning. It's not the same. It hurts my heart.

Conscious Death

The mysteries of ascension and conscious dying are sacred arts taught only to the highest initiates in different orders on and beyond the Earth. I have had other clients describe spinning their cells faster and faster until they became Light, ascending through pillars of Light, or consciously laying down to leave the body. This potential lives in ALL OF US. As we grow in our attention and tend to our Divine Light, the Mystery is revealed by the Master who lives within, and we awaken to our immortality.

Transcript: The Jaguar Prophecy

Another lost civilization that was brought through in an IQH session was a jungle culture that had medicine people who were able to shift into animal forms. The high priest of the culture could take the form of a powerful jaguar. This position was passed down to the fastest young boy in the tribe. The high priest carried a staff that could be cracked against the Earth to make the ground shake and the jungle animals ROAR!

C: There's a woman crying. She is in pain. She's about to give birth.

M: Why are you here?

C: I am singing. I have a rattle.

M: What are you singing?

C: I am calling in the jaguar. I am getting old, and there has not yet appeared a young man in our tribe who is capable of receiving the power of the jaguar.

M: What happens if there is no young boy?

C: *That is why I am calling the spirit into this child. The mother is in great pain. When she gives birth, it is not a human child. It is a baby jaguar.*

M: **What does this mean to you?**

C: *This was foretold by our people. For thousands of years, there has been a prophecy. When a jaguar child is born into the people, a new threat is coming.*

M: **What is the new threat?**

C: *When we hear of the men coming across the water, we must leave our cities because these men come to destroy us. We will go back to the jungle. Those who have not forgotten will survive. Those who can shift shall remain in their animal forms.*

M: **What else does the prophecy say? How long must you hide?**

C: *Thirteen. My people will not know the cities again.*

M: **What does the number thirteen have to do with this?**

C: *Thirteen cycles before our lands are free.*

M: **How do you measure one cycle?**

C: *It is where the sun rises on a certain day of the year. This moves over the years, but when it returns to the point where it shines its light on the pyramid, it is the beginning of a new cycle.*

M: **So, it will be thirteen of those before the freedom of your people again?**

C: *There will be freedom, or there will be the annihilation of all.*

M: **Tell me more about this prophecy. Is there more information, more to the story? You can even share the full thing if you'd like.**

C: *At the time the jaguar child is born, there will begin the great scattering of our people. The stories will arrive of strange men from the far waters. Men with hair on their faces. These men come to destroy our people and to take our land, and this cannot be prevented. At this sign, our wisdom carriers must train as many as possible. Transmit the wisdom and the powers and strengthen our connection with the jungle. The cities must be abandoned, and we must roam with the jaguars in the jungle. Many of our people have forgotten, and they will not survive. We shall remain in the consciousnesses of the jungle. These strange men will change many things. As we watch, we shall not recognize our land. And for thirteen cycles, we must wait. At these thirteen cycles, these men with hair on their faces will destroy themselves. If the land shall remain, we may emerge from the jungle and build our cities anew.*

Generation of Prophecy Being Fulfilled

While many may doubt these stories, I have come to believe that anything is possible and that I just need to open my mind to understand the bigger picture. In all these scenarios of collapsing society, the cause for these civilizations to fade into history was the rise of service-to-self consciousness where people abused power for their own personal gain. We are the generation that puts this struggle to rest! We are the ones who get to see the end of domination, overlord power structures, and heartless destruction born of ignorance of our True Nature. We are the generation that learns to walk and live in honor of all levels of Life. Let us claim our bodies, our communities, and this planet for the Light, and welcome in this new Era of Peace and Harmony!

Now, let us journey into the Cosmic Christ Transmissions!

Gateway Two Part Two: Cosmic Christ Transmissions

The Ministry of Light

TWENTY

Jesus and the Ministry of Light

One of my spiritual path's driving forces has been the search for the truth of the life of Jesus and the deeper meanings of his ministry. As a young boy, I could not fully believe the version of his life taught to me in church. Something did not sit right with my Inner Being. Jesus taught of unconditional love and the power of a loving God. When I went to certain churches I felt fear, condemnation, and judgment infused into teachings, and the congregations often felt dull and unresponsive. I was not blind to the fact that thousands upon thousands of people had suffered and died because of the Church's actions. I knew in my heart that Jesus's true story had been distorted since his ministry, and I began to search for truth. I knew there had to be more. I prayed and prayed to Jesus and God to show me the Truth.

As a young child, my grandmother taught me that I should not just read about the version of Jesus in the Bible but also develop a relationship with the Living Christ found in my heart. In the darkest of times in my life, I would retreat into my heart in prayer and ask for guidance and support. Without this connection, I would likely be another statistic of someone lost in the shadows of this world. Jesus has been my number one ally in my life. I invite everyone to release the religious dogma teachings and find the powerful love emanations of the Living Christ available in your very own heart.

My willingness to look beyond the approved teachings of the Church led me to Thich Nhat Hahn and his book *Living Buddha, Living Christ*. As many of you know, there is intense fear programming and shaming around reading spiritual books that are not considered "Christian." I read the book secretly, hoping that I would not be digging my way towards an eternity in Hell. Thich Nhat Hahn helped to encourage my maturing soul to find the interconnectedness between the teachings of the Buddha and Christ. I started reading many of Thich Nhat Hahn's books and started to bring my consciousness out of fear and into compassionate mindful awareness.

Much suffering has occurred across this planet over many generations because of the distortion of the story of Jesus's life and his ministry. Much suffering has been created in the name of Christ that was truly service-to-self consciousness seeking power and domination. Christ's core teaching, like Buddhism, is loving compassion.

Some of the most powerful resources I have found beyond my hypnosis sessions have been Dolores Cannon's books of *They Walked with Jesus* and *Jesus and the Essenes*. I have also felt strong resonance and activation with the channeled texts of *Anna: Grandmother of Jesus* by Claire Heartsong and *The Magdalen Manuscript* by Tom Kenyon. I have a deeper trust in hypnosis sessions because the client's conscious mind filter is removed by being in a deep trance. Even then, I still run the new information through my own heart to see if it rings true! Discernment and deep listening are crucial to anyone who is seeking Higher Truth.

Many of my hypnosis sessions included people involved in the Ministry, and their stories reveal a much more compelling story of the life of Jesus than anyone has ever told in any Sunday school lesson. While some may look for differences in the stories to debunk what is untrue, I have found more power in focusing on the themes and storylines from these various sources that are similar and consistent.

Here are some key points from my research into the life of Jesus that can inspire your path and offer healing.

Redemption Plan

Yeshua ben Joseph's life served as a culmination point in the Redemption Plan that has been initiated by many star nations and the Hierarchy of Light for thousands of years. Before his ministry, ascension teachings were only shared with and known by initiates in secret orders and mystery schools. He came to demonstrate the power of christ consciousness and the Truth of Eternal Life publicly. His body and life provided the redemptive vehicle for the reseeding of the Fourth Density coding for humanity and the Earth.

He foretold the changing of our physical bodies into Light bodies and the many changes that would come to the Earth during a Grand Shift, including the return of the Hierarchies of Light and our Star Nation relatives. Here we stand at this grand culmination point, and each of us has been invited to awaken to our divinity and hold the Light of the divine through this grand passageway.

The Prophecy of the Messiah

High initiates in various traditions shared the same prophecy of the coming of a Messiah, a divine being who would come to set humanity free from slavery. While many hoped that this savior was coming to overturn governments and control systems, he was truly coming to overturn the hearts and minds of those who were ready to free themselves from their suffering and karma.

The slavery mindset is the consciousness of humanity in the third dimension. Jesus came to be a wayshower of consciousness — to liberate the everyday person from slave mentality by sharing wisdom held by high initiates for centuries. It is said repeatedly in sessions that Jesus did not want to be worshipped. He certainly did not intend to be the head of a dead religion where people's consciousness and light are limited and controlled. His teaching was of ONENESS, not of hierarchy. While he played a massive role in the Redemption Plan, his life was meant to be a source of inspiration and a model for what a human can embody in a fully awakened consciousness. His life was not meant to be used to confirm our powerlessness or label us as "lower than" and eternally stained. He said, "You will do these things and more." because we ALL can ascend in our consciousness to achieve christ consciousness and claim our own Sonship/Daughtership as Children of God.

The Essenes

The Essene community on Mount Carmel (Nazareth) and Qumran (Dead Sea) were spiritual communities of initiates that lived in close relationship to Source and the Earth. Members of this community studied the secret mysteries of Creation. They were taught advanced meditation and psychic development from childhood. Children were taught how to materialize and move energy with their minds. Each young student was guided into their power and initiated into the sacred arts they were most proficient at. This included hands-on healing, astrology, astral projection, sacred geometry, telepathy, telekinesis, and even telepathic weather modification was taught to the young masters if it was appropriate for their soul's path.

The Essenes shared sacred scrolls and spiritual techniques with a wide net of mystery schools worldwide, including schools of thought from Egypt, the UK, Tibet, India, and more. Once a young student passed all the initiations and education in their home school, the students often traveled to other communities around the world to advance their studies.

Beyond Earthly resources, the Essene's high initiates were communicating with astral beings and benevolent star beings. These ascended beings would share knowledge and wisdom with elect initiates to be shared amongst the community. Many beings from many star systems would incarnate as Essenes to learn and protect the hidden arts of Ascension.

Yeshua ben Joseph and his family were members of the Essene community. From a young age, Yeshua was taught the Mysteries and advanced spiritual practices. He surpassed all the initiations and all the major schools at the time. There are stories in different cultures about his visitations, particularly in India, Tibet, Egypt, and the UK.

Essene Women

Women of the Essene community were equal to men on all levels of their society. They had full authority over their own life and were able to study, own a home, and even divorce if they chose to. This was quite different from the traditional values and perspectives practiced by the local Jewish people of the time.

Mother Mary

Mother Mary, a High Priestess of the Ancient Egyptian Mystery Schools and Mt. Carmel Essene, embodied the Goddess, the Divine Mother, and gave birth to a child conceived by the Light. A select group of high initiates in at least Egypt and Mt. Carmel knew about her soul purpose before the child was conceived. When clients have seen Mother Mary, they describe the Holy Mother with the presence of a cosmic queen, a powerful priestess, and a central force in Ancient Egyptian priestess training. She was a Master of

Light and Consciousness. She was a cosmic conduit channeling powerful energy from distant star systems like the Pleiades into the Earth to activate awakening across the planet. Part of her mastery included the high sacred art of Light Conception.

Joseph, Mother Mary's husband, was a simple man. He worked to provide for his family but was not directly involved in the miraculous world that his son and wife were. He gave Jesus the core teachings a child would need to grow into maturity. They would work together in Joseph's carpentry shop and had a deep love for one another. When Jesus was old enough, Joseph humbly took him to study with the other initiates knowing that his precious young son was destined for great things!

Light Conception

The ancient Egyptian story of Osiris, Isis, and Horus has described the sacred ritual of Light Conception long before the birth of Jesus. After the resurrection of Osiris, Isis conceived her child Horus from the Light Seed of Osiris through a sacred ritual. Through accessing the Higher Planes, the initiates of Isis were taught how to bring a soul into their womb with or without the seed of a man.

Mother Mary learned this ancient ritual to conceive the soul of Yeshua directly from the Divine. Her unwavering faith and crystalline body temple, fortified through arduous spiritual activation, made her the perfect vessel to bring forth the powerful Light force of Yeshua.

The Birth of the Messiah:
Star of Bethlehem

The birth of Yeshua was of extreme importance for the unfolding of the Divine and Galactic Redemption Plan. A rare celestial alignment created a "tear" in the 3D matrix creating an interdimensional pathway for advanced souls to enter the Earth Matrix. In my sessions, clients describe the Star of Bethlehem lightcraft/spaceship with many high beings from throughout the galaxy and higher light dimensions on board. When clients describe the birth scene, they describe powerful love vibrations emanating from the Christ Child. Even the animals in attendance played a part in creating a pristine energetic container for the arrival of Yeshua's soul. Soon after he was born, Yeshua was taken to live in a spiritual community in Egypt to protect his emerging consciousness from the conditioning of the world and to activate his spiritual gifts through training.

Yeshua grew up with the Essenes and in the temples of Egypt between the approximate ages of eight to sixteen. In his childhood, he was surrounded by initiates in constant prayer and spiritual study. Many around him knew what his soul purpose was, and many galactic beings incarnated to support his grand mission. They created a pristine high-frequency environment to protect his mind from being indoctrinated by human conditioning to keep him pure and strong for what was to come. One client described his laughter as a child filling the entire space as if the whole world could feel his innocent child nature. He spent a lot of time in silence, meditation, and spiritual development to maintain his connection to the other realms. A deep understanding of Creation was inherently encoded in his Inner Being and genetics. He wasn't necessarily "taught" but nourished so that he could embody the oversoul mastery he came in with. This high level of spiritual practice helped him maintain his divine alignment so he could be the powerful Light force he was destined to be.

Transcript: Yeshua Begins His Ministry

Around the age of sixteen, Yeshua left Egypt to begin to spread The Word and to start teaching the collective. Here is a client describing Jesus and his path towards completing his soul's mission upon the Earth.

C: *I see four camels. I see Yeshua on one of them, and there's four of them leaving. Just like to spread the word to start the mission, or...the mission had already started but to really get it out there and spread the word, to start their journey. No fear. He actually...wow! What a...like his lack of fear of death, like it's exactly what I was talking about in this temple, and it's a really bright reflection on humanity and this timeline of forced medicalization and stuff like that. He's such a role model and it doesn't matter... He knew who he was. He knew he was going to be crucified; he knew he was going to be hated and he was just so solid in his truth and his commitment to the Light, and his commitment to God, and his commitment to truth, and his commitment to the truth of who he is. 'Cause it's really difficult to carry a truth that...yeah, it's nice and safe when your community hears you and believes in you, but to leave that security, to go out into the wolves and try, you know, to teach the wolves English is a very, very honorable...something I very much idolize in this very moment.*

I see the heat. I see him sweating. I see him worn down. I see his hope. Like, it feels really hot on him, but I don't feel like it's...like the place he's at, I feel like it's symbolism.

M: Tell me more about that. So, he's worn down?

C: Yeah, like I said, there weren't very many beings of light like him, so the amount of hate versus the amount of love was just, you know...twenty to one. There just...

M: Sounds like it would have been really hard for him.

C: Yeah, and he was aware of this ending. He was aware of the odds. He was aware of all this. It's really interesting 'because I can feel his human aspect of it being really hard and him being tired, but I can feel his spirit, which was never tired, EVER! So, there's...I can see both aspects and very trusting, very willing to be a public symbol of...I'm going to say hate but being a public symbol of also not rolling over and being like "Okay, I'll stop being who I am. I'll stop trying to create peace in the world to save my human body." He was like not about that. The human body was just the experience in that NOW moment for his soul and he still connected to his soul that it never...that it didn't ever feel confusing to him.

Mary Magdalene

To know Yeshua and Mary Magdalene's true relationship, we can call into our awareness the path of Divine Partnership and Twin Flame souls. Yeshua and Mary met in their adolescent years. At the time, Mary was living in the chaos of the uninitiated world. Young Mary had a pure heart but was born into terrifying density. The collective consciousness at that time was negatively polarized and extremely low, steeped in fear and limitation. Society was patriarchal, and women were treated horribly. Tax collectors and religious dogma ruled the land, and the common consciousness was enslaved by fear and karma.

When Mary and Yeshua met, Yeshua was already very well into his studies and initiations. From the moment they met, he knew her as his Beloved, and her heart quickened in his presence. They spent sweet time in nature falling in love with one another as Yeshua shared the Mysteries with her. They practiced meditation and astral traveling together as he guided the Light of her True Nature out of the shadows of conditioned thinking and fear. Their innocent love illuminated both of them and propelled them on a rapid path of awakening and high alchemy.

Eventually, Yeshua and Mary made their way to Egypt, where Mary studied under the Holy Mother, Mother Mary, and learned the high priestess arts to become a priestess in the Ancient Egyptian Mystery Schools. Women gathered around Mother Mary to perform group rituals as they channeled divine cosmic energies into the ley lines of the Earth. They practiced moon rituals and womb magic and honored the esoteric power of their menstrual flow. Meanwhile, Yeshua and the other initiated men worked in the local communities to elevate the consciousness and protect the women while the women performed their sacred work.

Yeshua and Mary were Twin Flame partners united in marriage and in the light of their souls. One embodied the divine masculine, and the other embodied the divine feminine expression of perfected humanity. We cannot fully know one without knowing the other. We miss out on so much of the story without knowing the truth of Mary Magdalene and the Holy Mother. While Yeshua has received the global spotlight for his work on the Earth plane, it is Mary Magdalene who helped him fortify his determination and trust in his path and potential. When Jesus doubted his own abilities, it was Mary that comforted him back into his power.

Transcript: John the Beloved Comments on Mary and Jesus

John the Beloved, brother of Jesus and friend of Mary Magdalene shares his perspective of the dynamic relationship between Jesus and Mary.

C: *They were inseparable. They worked together all the time. When he laid a hand, she laid a hand. When he spoke, she curated the space, and when she spoke, he curated space. We followed her as much as we followed him. She also knew that she was reflecting an energy that was not quite time to be celebrated, but he celebrated her. We celebrated her through his example, but she also was celebrating him. They truly were one flesh. A mirror image. They would say that to us all the time; they both lived inside of everyone and that the masculine and feminine were not actually separate from one another. God is.*

Tantra: Sex Magic Alchemical Practices of Isis

When people describe Mary Magdalene in hypnosis sessions, they describe an exotic beauty with tanned olive skin, dark hair, and piercing eyes of love decorated with makeup in the style of Egyptian women. They comment on her captivating presence and her ability to fill a room with her powerful love vibration.

Mary Magdalene wore the serpent band of the priestesses of Isis around her arm as a mark of her path in the mystery school of the Temple of Isis. The Sex Magic practices of the Ancient Egyptian mystery schools and tantric traditions of India learned and practiced by Jesus and Mary were alchemical ascension practices done with a partner to clean the physical and subtle bodies so that one can access higher realms of consciousness existence. While making love, initiates could travel together in their light bodies and into Higher Realms of Light to study, heal, and expand in consciousness. The Egyptians saw these practices as divine technologies to access and embody the God/Goddess within.

Those who were not initiated into the sacred sexuality practices, regular people, would mistake this work as mere promiscuity and low morals because they see them through their cultural conditioning and limited understanding. Mary Magdalene was not an immoral whore but a powerful High Priestess of Alchemy and Magic. She was a master in her own right. Her wisdom and knowledge of high alchemy and tantric practices were instrumental in helping Yeshua develop the power of his Lightbody to hold the tremendous amount of Light needed to complete his public initiation on the cross.

Jesus and Mary were both practitioners of sacred sexuality and tantra. They used their sexual relationship to connect deeply with their Self, one another, and the Divine. This level of sacred sexual expression was not only shared between one another but shared with others to assist their awakening and ascension. I have had a client who described Mary and a group of women working together to cultivate erotic energy and sexual life force to heal from sexual trauma as well as a story of Jesus working with another man to help him move beyond his own sexual shadow and trauma. These two beings were masterfully empowered tantric practitioners who were completely liberated from religious and cultural conditionings. Many will read these words and reject them because of their own traumas and conditioning. Others will find these words comforting and liberating. We all carry sexual programming and wounding that limits our creative spirit and life force, and it is time for ascending humanity to peel away the layers of shame and condemnation and reclaim our soulful erotic innocence.

The Children of Jesus and Mary

I have not had a clear definitive answer to how many children Yeshua and Mary had together in my sessions. It ranges from one to four biological children that shared DNA from Yeshua and Mary. Jesus and Mary loved children, and many children would gather around them as they traveled and taught. At times, they would adopt children to take care of for some time.

When I asked about why there were discrepancies in the story regarding the number of children, I was told that the life of Jesus is presented differently depending on which timeline one is experiencing him through and there are infinite presentations of the life of Jesus and infinite ways the story played out and that we would benefit from expanding our understanding of holographic reality to understand the multidimensional presentation of his life.

The child most talked about was a girl named Sara. When four children are spoken of, clients describe two boys, one girl, and a perfectly balanced androgynous soul in a body with both sets of reproductive organs (an intersex, hermaphroditic human). This being was a prototype for future human generations. This was a genetic test to see if the new biology could handle such a highly evolved soul that embodied both masculine and feminine energies perfectly.

Sara is said to have been conceived through Light Conception by Mary just like Mother Mary did with Yeshua. The DNA from the offspring of Yeshua brought in an upgraded DNA signature. This DNA gave the body the ability to hold a higher light quotient than the other DNA signatures on the planet. People from this genetic lineage awaken easier and will develop psychic abilities faster than others. The offspring of Mary and Yeshua were protected by initiates. The new DNA signature was implanted into the collective gene pool through the following generations with the mixing of bloodlines across the planet.

Transcript: Rh-Negative Bloodlines

One somnambulistic client described the origins of Rh-negative blood types with this bloodline.

M: I'm wondering about this lineage of Jesus. What was the purpose of establishing a lineage?

C: Let me see... That lineage is one of the lineages, it could be the only one, but I think it could be one of the few people for whom the advanced skills are more acceptable. It's showing me copper blood, Rh-negative blood.

It carries light easier. Oh! Krissa has A negative. People can feed off light like a plant doing photosynthesis easier with Rh-negative. It's less dense; it's less earth-bound, crystalline. These people are heralds or will be evolving faster into what eventually the whole of humanity can be. So, these people can show the way and also help calm the fear because people get so fearful when things are changing. These people can show, "Hey, what we're going through isn't so bad."

And there are some individuals on the planet now who can subsist almost solely on breath, light, and maybe some juice. That's actually the evolving direction. Jesus's lineage seeded some humans on this planet with not only Rh-negative, but that's one of the strongest manifestations; it's just a less dense, less earth-bound blood type. It's a lineage of people holding the higher Light frequency.

Traveling and Spreading Knowledge

Yeshua and Mary traveled together to many distant places to share and trade knowledge. Yeshua's uncle, Joseph of Arimathea, also an Essene high initiate, was an extremely wealthy tin tradesman. He would purchase tin ore from his brethren, the Druids, in the UK and sell it to harbors in the Mediterranean and distant waters.

His wealth, seafaring ships, and connections along the various trade routes across the Middle East, Asia, and Europe gave the Essene community the ability to travel great distances. Yeshua traveled to Avalon (Glastonbury and Wales) to study with the Druids, India to study with the yoga masters, Tibet to study with Buddhist monastics, the Far East to study with the Chinese masters, and likely other areas. Often Mary was by his side. These two traveled to more places than we can imagine, all the while knowing that time was limited and there was much to do and share.

Large groups of people followed them wherever they went to hear the wisdom and knowledge they shared. They barely had time alone. While they were a healing presence, they also shook things up with their advanced ideas of a liberated consciousness. Often, they were weary and tired because they would flee from one town to the next under cover of nightfall because authorities were looking for them. This even included being arrested or detained because they were seen as radical and dangerous by power authorities.

Too often, I hear people using the life of Jesus as a whipping tool. One of the major issues that I hear people talk about is that Jesus did not charge for his healing. He gave it away, and so, as healers, we should not charge for healing services since it is not "Christlike." Jesus's ministry was funded and supported by his uncle. Yeshua, Mary Magdalene, and other disciples would ride on the various seafaring ships owned by Joseph to distant ports in Greece, Turkey, India, Britain, the Far East, and likely other distant lands to not only trade goods but to trade knowledge with other wise people. Jesus did not need to "charge" for services because he had a patron and many galactic and higher dimensional allies directly (and financially) supporting his path.

The Ministry: Spreading the Word

The disciples of Jesus extended beyond the core twelve. They were made of men and women from the Essene community and other followers who believed in the teachings of Jesus. Jesus and his disciples traveled together for a few years to teach Oneness and heart-based devotional living. They taught of the Light within and how to become a sovereign soul, free from the slavery of a conditioned mind and the Truth of Eternal Living. Even after his crucifixion and resurrection, many disciples paid the price with their lives as they continued to spread "the good news" of Ascension and God's promise of a New Earth.

Miraculous Healing

Essene community members were taught methods of natural healing and advanced energy healing practices. Jesus and the disciples traveled together, spreading The Word (Truth from the Higher Realms) and performing many healings across the land. These highly advanced spiritual humans could "read the soul" of the person to see the root cause of the illness. If it aligned with the individual's soul pathway and did not interfere with the free will of that soul's choice to learn through suffering, rapid multidimensional healing would be performed through psychic transmission, laying of hands, and other healing practices. When complete healing could not be done, natural herbal remedies were used to support the healing process and relieve suffering. This included frankincense, myrrh, and eucalyptus, commonly used and readily available in the Middle East.

One of the higher mystery teachings involved resurrecting the dead. I have had two different clients describe a scene in a temple where Jesus, Mary, and a few other initiates were present. They stood around a fire made of blue flames and began calling on the presence of God to reanimate a dead calf that lay on the floor. They describe a Light power descending into the calf, bringing it back to life. You can imagine what it was like to hear this story once. It was extra wild to hear the same scene described by another person a year later. These transcriptions are presented later in this manuscript.

Another client went to the lifetime of John the Beloved, brother of Yeshua. When John was just a young boy, he became sick with an illness that drained him of life force energy until he died. As he transitioned into the Light, he was united with his spiritual family and higher consciousness. He heard the voice of his brother Yeshua calling out his name, and the next thing he knew, he was back in his body in the tomb with Yeshua by his side shining a brilliant grin. Like many people with Near Death Experiences (NDEs), John returned with expanded consciousness and was invited to join his brother on his travels to be his scribe. John the Beloved eventually writes the original scriptures that would become the Book of Revelations.

I had a hypnosis session where a client described Yeshua kneeling over the body of a woman who had just passed. Yeshua connected with the soul's higher consciousness and coordinated an exchange with the body, a walk-in. As the tired soul of the body left the Earth plane, another fresh portion of the oversoul was invited back into the body to reanimate it. The body was resurrected with a new consciousness with a higher frequency to continue in service to awakening with the new vibration. Walk-ins are a common way for members of the Hierarchy of Light to embody for a short time to accomplish their work to support the Higher Evolutionary Design and Trajectory.

Judas: Devout Disciple of Yeshua

Those closest to Yeshua knew that at some point he would have to leave the Earth plane. Not everyone knew all the details, but they were told many times that those days would come. When asked who was most faithful, most rooted in nondual awareness, to do what was necessary to lead the authorities to Jesus, Judas volunteered. Yeshua and Judas both knew what needed to happen. Even though Judas struggled with his role after volunteering, his role was incredibly essential and blessed by the Divine.

In these modern times, we have many Judas characters in our human collective who, on the soul level, agreed to come into the Earth to play the role of the villain and move us into our own resurrection timeline. These souls will play out terrible actions that will assist the human collective in shifting out of their slave mind and into the power of the heart by creating conditions that inherently invite us to reach for higher wisdom and higher love.

Rites of the Sepulcher: Initiation on the Cross

The Rites of the Sepulcher performed by Jesus have roots in Ancient Egypt and Ancient Tibet. High-level initiates in these orders would use these practices to reverse the aging process of the body and access higher realms of Light and Wisdom.

During this process, the body would go into a state of dormancy and appear dead. Often these bodies would be stored in tombs or hidden caves for safety. In this meditative state, the soul traveled to higher realms while remaining tethered to the body through a chord of Light. Once the soul was ready to reenter the body, the tending priest or priestess would be notified psychically and begin working with the soul and body to help the soul integrate and reanimate the body. The soul would reenter the body with a tremendous amount of Light and higher coding that would regenerate the body's cells so that the body would reverse its aging process. Initiates could do this process repeatedly, extending their life by hundreds of years. Once the initiate was finished with their Earthly experience, they would stop performing the rites and allow the body to die. Many ancient traditions speak of this rite, particularly in the Tibetan mystery schools where young Jesus studied.

While on the cross, Yeshua remained tethered to his body as his soul traveled to the higher realms back to Source. In my sessions, many speak of his Lightbody emerging from the cross and the coordinated efforts by Joseph of Arimathea and others to move him to a close tomb paid for by Joseph. While in the tomb, the completion of the Rite of the Sepulcher was performed. When Yeshua's soul returned to his body, he brought the keys to our Ascension given to him by Source. He broke through the density of the Earth realm's dark matrix created by fallen thoughtforms and the influence of negative polarity beings and paved the way for humanity to connect again and collaborate with the higher realms. His body was transformed into the Christ Light body, and he was no longer limited to the Earth plane. At will, he could take his body to the higher realms and travel to other star systems.

This is what humanity is transforming into. This is our destiny! As he said, "You will do these things and more!" We are also passing through our own initiations to purify our souls so that the Christ Consciousness Light can move through our bodies. When this "Event" happens, we will no longer be limited to the Earth plane. We will be co-creators with the Hierarchies of Light and our Star Nation brethren. We will travel throughout Creation, tend to the many Gardens, and teach The Way of Light and Love.

Post Resurrection

Quickly after the crucifixion, many of those who followed Jesus and the Ministry were in danger from the authorities. Mary and other family members and disciples fled Israel to escape punishment and death. They met up with other Essenes and initiates who guided them to safety. Some of the group split partway and made their way to Egypt/Africa, and Mary, John, Sara, and others made their way to Southern France to a community of allies. For more information on these fractals of the Ministry, check out the Coptic Gnostic Christian and Saint Thomas Christian history.

After the resurrection, Yeshua continued to teach the disciples before finally ascending to the Heavens. For an account of his teachings, I highly suggest the *Pistis Sophia* translated by Dr. J.J. Hurtak.

Jesus was a human, just like you and me. Through yogic and alchemical practices, he realized his Divine Nature. His life is something to aspire to but not something that we should use to punish ourselves or perpetuate self-loathing or reinforce our slave mentality. His life is a perfect example of what human potential is. If you want to know the hidden mysteries, invite Jesus into your heart. Invite Mary into your heart. Invite the Holy Family into your heart. Ask them to show you the Christ That Lives Within You. Let them help you open your heart and teach you The Way of Love and Light.

Religions

The Word, the original religion of the Multiverse, is the pure Light, Love, and Unity coding of Creation. It lives within your very heart and has the power to illuminate and transform every atom of your being. In the ancient times of the high consciousness civilization of Lemuria, The Word was what we radiated into the environment of Gaia from our beingness. When the negative polarity was permitted by Source to enter the Earth realm, Truth, Light, and Love began to become distorted. In doing so, humanity's commitment to living a noble and righteous life has been tested for countless generations.

While there are certainly positively polarized religious leaders throughout time, religions, for the most part, have been used by the colonizing shadow forces, those in service-to-self consciousness, to distort spiritual teachings as an attempt to control human consciousness. This experiment in consciousness is ending as we reach the graduation point and the culmination of this Grand Redemption Plan, and all that is hidden will be brought into the Light.

Yeshua ben Joseph and the disciples of the ministry dedicated their teaching and their lives to uplift and empower people in their Divine Creatorship. They taught people that they held the keys to the Kingdom of Heaven. They taught Love, union with the Divine, and heart-centered living. Jesus did not want to be the center of religion but wanted us to find the Living Power of the Divine within us and all of Life.

Religion is something outside of the body and is part of the *maya*, or illusion, of Creation. It is temporary. It will decay and wither away. Some components of the *maya* of religion trap people in cycles of suffering such as messages of fear and damnation, while some of the *maya* of religions assist in the liberation of consciousness such as messages of higher love and images of divine beings that remind people of the presence of God.

From a reincarnation perspective, religious institutions are schools of evolution for a soul to experience itself through the lens of that religion's beliefs. There are many paths, and all paths are valid and lead to Source-realization eventually. Every drop of water eventually makes its way to the ocean. The illuminated Truth of the Love and Light of Source is found in all the world's wisdom traditions and religions. No one religion owns the way to Source.

Much of what modern Institutional Christianity teaches are teachings that have been distorted or fabricated to program and control people using fear, judgment, and punishment. The Spanish Inquisition and witch trials aimed to eliminate the mystery teachings, magical traditions, and mystical peoples of the world and convert people to their twisted version of Christ's teachings. This all served a higher purpose to catalyze collective humanity out of slave mentality. When we are finished with enslaving our consciousness, we will no longer need tyrannical external authority figures and institutions. All of the suffering has been an invitation to uncover the tyranny of the mind and open to the limitlessness of our being and Source.

The choice has always been left to the individual and to the collective of humanity to follow the truth within our hearts or follow a concept of God given to us by someone else. The externalized religions of the world reflect our collective denial of our divinity and power. Many Christians worldwide are leaving organized religion to cultivate a living relationship with the love of Christ that is free from dogma, shame, and fear. Simultaneously, people who have never involved themselves with a religion of any kind are using the teachings of Christ to improve the quality of their own life.

Jesus and the teachings of the Ascended Masters show us the way of Love and Unity. Jesus is quoted in the Bible as saying, "I am the resurrection and the life. The one who believes in me will live, even though they die." Jesus was speaking of the path of ascension. He was speaking about awakening to our divinity and the truth that we never truly die. He offered an invitation for the human collective to release the fears and slave mentality of lower consciousness and expand into new horizons of consciousness and unity. To "believe in Him" is to believe in the truth of ascension and the promise of God to grant ascension to our generation.

Feel into the essence of Jesus's teachings and feel the vibration of unconditional love that illuminates his words and speaks to your heart. Let this Light permeate every cell of your being and awaken the Divinity that YOU ARE. Drop the dogma and align with the great power and potential he embodied.

He asked his followers to follow in his footsteps and share the "good news" of everlasting life and this new age's dawning. We each have been given an invitation to awaken and serve humanity as ambassadors of Light and Unity.

The Threefold Flame of the Heart

The Threefold Flame of the Heart is the divine spark located within the central chamber of the heart's altar, the inner sanctum. The three flames represent three sublime virtues of a Christ-conscious being: Wisdom, Power, and Love. Wisdom is the application of the mind to Higher Wisdom and Divine Truth and the illumination that comes from the right use of spiritual knowledge. Power is seen as the right use of our willpower to be in service to healing and awakening others to the Christ that dwells within. Through our allowing, Universal Love works through us so that we can be instruments of selfless service for the Greater Good for All.

To be born again is to be resurrected from spiritual death by pursuing spiritual growth and the absorption of spiritual wisdom into your being. Through spiritual practices, we evolve beyond our animalistic, carnal nature into a spiritual human being of Divine Light, a divine-human synthesis. The path of embodying our Holy Christ Self involves loving ourselves completely, and in doing so, we emanate love to all we meet. As we dissolve the conditioning of our mind and surrender to the inner voice of love, we reveal our own Christhood.

It is up to each of us to cultivate a deeply personal relationship with the Unconditional Love and Grace of Source. The potential for attaining the Christ-Self, the Buddha-Self, or the Krishna-Self is available for ALL who wish to grow in Truth and Love. Bless us all!

TWENTY-ONE

Protector of Jesus

T his client came into the first scene of a vast golden desert with structures, temples, and pyramids. The client saw herself as a male human in his twenties wearing a white, shin-length robe with gold trim and a draping over his head. He was walking through a corridor with pillars and arrived at a feast with other people. Everyone's attention was on a "loud and boisterous" woman who was feeding everyone who he called Maria. Not much information was coming from this scene, so I moved the client forward to the next important scene.

NEXT SCENE: IN A TOMB

C: *I'm in a tomb, a pyramid, or temple...but it's deep, enclosed. There's writing on the walls, and there's something protected in the center. It feels like a pyramid. I'm scribing. I'm reading something off the walls. The history of this place...there's something that I'm trying to find out there, something coded there that I'm in search of. There are other people here, but I'm walking around, keeping to myself, and scribing the symbols that I'm seeing.*

M: **Why are you looking for this code?**

C: *It's connected to what I'm learning. It's something I'm being guided to learn. I'm leaving there, and I'm walking out into the bright sun. It's very bright outside. I'm going to some water, a river, and I'm releasing something down the river. They're like tubes of gold filled with paper. I'm letting them go and sending them somewhere. Something about a child. Whatever I'm sending down the river is related to a child, and I expect that someone will receive them.*

M: **What's important about this child that you are sending information down the stream?**

C: *This child is special. This child is a teacher, very wise, and there's something that I've scribed to be kept for that child. He's come to teach and to help us in this place understand what I was writing, what wisdom and information I was collecting. I've known he was coming.*

M: **How did you know he was coming?**

C: I have a teacher that told me what to do and told me about the child. I am a student of this teacher and doing my part.

NEXT SCENE: SEEING THE CHILD

C: I see the child now. He's young, maybe seven or eight. I'm there with his mother, and he's just playing. He's very quiet. His mother is watching our interaction. I've come to share what I know about him with her. She knows he's special, and she's grateful, listening, and observing him as am I. I share that he is going to play a really important role in the freeing of people and ending corruption where we live. He can see a lot more than most people can see. He can foresee things. He has the power to predict what is going to happen. He plays a very important role in the turning of the times. I tell her to not be afraid. He will have to leave, and he will be on his own path. I tell her to encourage him to be brave as well. The boy seems to know everything already that I'm sharing with his mother. He seems to understand.

NEXT SCENE: TURMOIL AND CHAOS

C: There's busyness and turmoil. A lot of chaos in the streets of this place. There are horses and chariots, a lot of shouting and commotion. It feels like a sort of political unrest; the people are upset about something — their leaders or hierarchical beings that have upset people. There's revolt. I'm observing the scene, and it's like I'm always collecting data wherever I am. Just being there, observing whatever is happening, but I feel calm. They're bringing up that boy. He's more grown now. I think they're trying to arrest him. They bring him out; there's a crowd of people. He's still quiet, and I don't know why they're arresting him. I think his power has been found out. I see some people in the crowd that I recognize that are also peaceful, and we meet eyes. There are also others like me that are peaceful and observing. It feels like we are anchoring Light there. And I observe the boy, he's now grown, he's more of a man. I don't fear because I know that he's always okay.

The people are watching the man get arrested, but he's up above them on a platform so they can see. He's thin. Healthy but thin. He has dark hair, long hair, and he's peaceful. He's not fighting back or speaking. There's a lot of people watching and shouting. It's like a very public display of arrest for some reason.

M: What color is his skin?

C: It's dark, but not black. Tan, olive-like skin. I feel this might be Jesus. It might be where they're choosing what to do with him. They've arrested him, and they're asking people what to do with him. People are shouting and this man, let's call him Jesus, they're accusing him because of his power, his clairvoyance. They ask the crowd and decide to crucify him. This is the scene. It's very loud, and there are many people. They're all turning against him. He's a healer and sees through the distorted powers that are in charge, and he speaks of that, and they don't like it.

They're taking him away. They're pulling him; his hands are tied. They're taking him away to have him murdered. He's been sentenced. There are some people that are really sad; they're crying and know it's not right. There are many others that are very angry, very aggressive people; most of them are following, it's like it's a spectacle of some kind. It's disturbing. People are very unkind. I stay behind and continue to follow and observe what's happening. I keep noticing the beings in the crowd that are aware of me, and I'm aware of them. We are there, but again, it's almost like we're invisible. We're quiet.

M: How do you know these people?

C: We all feel like we're not from Earth. We feel like angels, and we've come knowing our role here now. We are anchoring Light and observing and recording even just by our observing of what's happening.

NEXT SCENE: THE CRUCIFIXION

C: (Begins to cry) I'm there now where they've crucified him. It's a very sad day. It feels very sad...the land, the people, everything is sad. I see his mother and two other women; they're crying, and they don't want to leave. Many people have already left. They're there with him and don't want to leave. It's raining a little now; it's stormy. Very surreal. The energy is very surreal. I'm approaching his mother again. We don't speak words; we just communicate with our eyes. There are no words. She's very sad, but she's also very strong. I feel a sensation of really warm, tingling sensations in my shoulders and in my back. I'm there to help these three women come down the mountain, come down the hill, and care for them. It feels like the energy is very potent, and it's uncertain what will happen, and I want to make sure they're safe.

M: What can you tell me about these women and your connection to them?

C: I have a strong connection to his mother. I'm a protector of her. The other two women she's very close with; they're very special, and they were special to him. He asked me to protect them. They're all Mary. They have to move now. They're being guided to move...they may not be safe. The people in power, they want to control and know everything, and now that he's gone, they may want to control his family, people that knew him and knew who he was, who he is. So, they have to move away. There are many of us that are helping them move away. Take them to a safe place, for now; they've sort of been hiding. But we're not far from where his body will be because they want to stay close with him.

M: What is everyone talking about as you go into hiding?

C: There are not many words. There's a lot of communicating without words. As we move, we want to be very quiet, not because we don't want to be heard, there are many people out and about, but words feel limiting to what's happening, truly. I have been reassuring them that they're safe. A lot of people have left the mountain, and a lot of sorrow then comes. The commotion has gone, and it's like the family is left with the weight, and his body is put into the tomb, and no one seems to care anymore. The family is very sad. There are others that are close to him that come, gather together, and stay close. There were men that prepared the body. We didn't stay to watch. And they put the body in a tomb, but Mary wants to see the tomb, see the body. So, I'm agreeing to take them there. Yeah, this is when...

NEXT SCENE: GOING TO THE TOMB

M: What do you see?

C: We can't go there yet. We can't go there now, but I agreed to take them when it's right. The sun is out now; the weather has changed. It's hot. It's feeling very important that we stay hidden now. We walk to the tomb. For days we walk there. This is when we find the tomb empty. It's empty. There's the cloth there that he was wrapped in. The tomb is empty, and there is some panic. There's some fear and panic. This is when Mary wanders off, and she sees him. She's the first to see him. She sees his Lightbody. He has risen. She sees him, and she cries and screams. We find her, and she tells us she has seen him. She knew she would see him. She knew what would happen.

M: Which Mary is this that sees him?

C: This is Mary...not his mother, this is Mary Magdalene. His beloved. One of the Mary Magdalenes. It's very prayerful now. There's relief, and we are listening to Mary, what she saw. What she understands is to not fear that he is here, and they must move, and he is with them.

M: Are you all aware of how he was able to change into this Lightbody?

C: *He prepared a long time for this. This is what the initiates were preparing for and Mary specifically with Jesus — preparing for the Lightbody resurrection.*

M: What happens next? What do you learn?

C: *We learn that there are many things set in place for the family to move. To be safe, they will travel across the sea. They've prepared to go on a voyage now. To be safe, I will stay. I am staying. There are men in their family that take them to safety into a boat, and they go where they know they'll be safe. I don't know where they're going...they're going across the sea. I stay. I feel that my role has been fulfilled to let them go, and there is still a lot happening here that I have to stay here.*

M: What do you do next?

C: *I go back. I go back to the city where things are more quiet now, but there's a lot of...the energy is very unsettled here. That's part of my work here, to balance the energy. People are scattering away; people are going home, back to where they live. It just feels very unsettled in this place, so people are leaving.*

NEXT SCENE: WRITING THE KNOWLEDGE

C: *I am old now. I am old, and I am writing down many things — books, and books. Writing...I feel near the end of my time on Earth, and I am writing what I've experienced and what I know. My wisdom.*

M: Tell me about it. What are you writing?

C: *It's related to the wisdom and knowledge I was gathering in my younger years, and there are also predictions of what will come. I'm writing to help people understand what has happened in this time, around my family and my teacher and this boy and the life of Jesus and his mother. It feels important that I write everything down because I may not be living here much longer.*

M: I would like to know more about the history of your relationship with Mother Mary. Let's go back to the first time you met her.

NEXT SCENE: MEETING MOTHER MARY

C: *The first time I saw her was before she knew she would be a mother. I knew who she was. She was gathering water. I just observed her. I didn't speak with her* *this time; it wasn't time. I was even protecting her then, making sure she was safe and well. She was...she was happy and safe and very gentle. Very present.*

M: Let's move forward to the next time you saw Mary.

C: Now I'm with her when she knows she's pregnant. She's scared; she's crying. Again, she's crying, but she's strong.

M: What does she know about this pregnancy?

C: He was Light conceived by her. She was an initiate. A very pure being, very strong and devoted in her life, in her practice, and she was told she would carry a son into the world. She's scared because she doesn't feel ready. She doesn't know she's ready. There's a part of her that knows she's ready...she's human now, and she's scared. She doesn't know all of who he is yet. She knows he's special and important.

M: Can you share with me about Light conception and what you know about this process?

C: Yes. Light conception is very possible with devoted practice. Humans have forgotten. It's not possible with all, but with some. It is to be conceived by the energy of Light. This is why they called her a Virgin. It's that purity of Light to be able to conceive and that energy to be able to bring a physical being into form through the Light.

NEXT SCENE: THE BIRTH OF JESUS

C: I was there when he was born. It was so beautiful. The scene was so peaceful. There are a few people, many animals there, beings that could hold the frequency of him coming into form. There was a lot of Light there. Very peaceful. It was also somewhat hidden away, somewhat secretive. Not secret but protected. And there were many celestial beings present as well. So many celestial beings came for the birth. There were many starlight beings in the sky. It was a very bright night. The energy was very angelic, very light, as it had to be for him to come. Even now, I feel a spinning sensation; I feel a swirling of energy of Light. I feel the power of the energy that night. It was an energy that the Earth had not felt in a very long time. Mary is very happy, very at peace, very supported, which makes me happy.

M: Let's learn a little bit more. Can you tell me about this star in the sky?

C: The star of Bethlehem is his home. A ship. It did guide beings to this place; it was not just a star. It is a ship where Jesus and Mary came from, and it is present along with others and legions of angels and star beings. It was quite an event in the heavens.

M: Can you tell me more about how Jesus and Mary came from the ship? What do you know about it?

C: The ship...there are Pleiadian ties, but it is not just a Pleiadian ship. It is from beyond there, but it did travel through the Pleiades to come there as well.

M: How were Mary and Jesus able to get from that ship and into these bodies?

C: That is the Light conception. Yes, it's possible with the help of the energies and technologies of these ships, and from this ship, in particular. And with communication and connection with beings on the Earth, it is possible.

NEXT SCENE: YOUNG JESUS

C: I'm back to the time when he was seven or eight years old. I spent time with him then to make sure that Jesus was in a safe place and protected, but also that they were happy and well. It's important that they felt that at this time. Mary was well taken care of; they had a good community, and Jesus was very, very wise, very bright — learning a lot and teaching. He was very interested in what was happening in the temples, what was being taught to the people. He had innate wisdom about spirituality and what he was learning was the human way of things, what was happening here, and why and who was controlling and teaching. He did not fear. He was not capable of certain emotions, so he was very bold in his learning and his speech when he chose to speak. Often, he was quiet. Very sweet boy.

NEXT SCENE: JESUS AND MARY MAGDALENE

C: Now, Jesus is grown, and he has many people around him almost all the time, still teaching and healing. He's learning still...he's learning with Mary Magdalene. They see their role in each other's lives, and they're very devoted. They travel energetically together; they strengthen their energies together, and they teach this among a small group of them, family, what we call disciples. And he's healing many people. His presence is healing; he doesn't need to do much. His presence, everywhere he goes, is healing. He knows this, and he travels. He teaches as he travels.

M: How do they travel together energetically and strengthen their energies?

C: They practice mastering their physical body with the breath. Moving their energy together strengthens the Ka body, the energetic body. They learn from a long line of initiates, and Jesus learns much of this from Mary, Mary Magdalene. All three Marys and many others who are all family, they learn these practices, and it's just breath. It is physical with their bodies as well as with their minds; they go into their bodies; they breathe. They build the energy; they move the energy; and the more they do this, the more they do it easily and quickly. This strengthens Jesus for his path.

NEXT SCENE: THE CHRIST BLOODLINE

C: Children. There's a lot of children with him. There's a lot of children born at this time. Many people in their lineage, bloodline, in their family. He's teaching many children. There's much to be carried on. He knows these children will understand and carry. It's important that they carry codes and wisdom. Children come to him. Those that are meant to carry the codes know to come to him. Their parents bring them from all over.

M: Share with me about the bloodline and family.

C: This bloodline, they're all connected from the stars, from beyond here on Earth. They know each other from far back, from beyond, and incarnate many times to carry this wisdom and these codes. Oftentimes secretly, quietly to maintain the presence of this Light on Earth. There is a lot of corruption. There is a lot of hiding the truth, what we know now as religions, and it's important that this bloodline be carried, mostly quietly, and so it's time.

M: Who works with these children? How does he share this information with the children?

C: There is activation happening. He doesn't need to say very much. Spending time with these children is activating them, and they remember. Mostly it just looks like loving play, being in nature, and laughing and eating food together. Mostly he uses energy, not words.

NEXT SCENE: JESUS STRUGGLES

C: Jesus is struggling. He's not sick, but he's tired. Doubt, he's feeling his humanness; he's feeling tired and somewhat confused. These are the times that Mary strengthens him and reminds him. He has a deep respect for her and her wisdom.

She strengthens him, his body, and his spirit. There weren't many times that he fell to this lower vibration, but when he did, it was very important that she was there to strengthen him, and she was.

NEXT SCENE: RESURRECTED JESUS

C: This is where Jesus is resurrected. He has risen into his Lightbody. He's coming in and out now, space and time at will, and he comes in and out to assist. To visit. To visit his family, to visit only where it is truly important for him to be visible and present. To fulfill his path on Earth.

M: Tell me what's happening. What is he doing?

C: He mostly appears to his mother and Mary Magdalene and other Essenes. He continues to teach them to guide their path. He brings peace and continues to anchor peace. He's teaching them how to do it. It's done. He's teaching them his full experience now that he has resurrected, so they can know how to do this.

M: What does he teach them? How does he do it?

C: They have very strict, devoted nutritional practices. Water. Water is very important — healthy water. And using the breath and body as a tool for ascension. Knowing the body, knowing the technology of the body, which takes just practice. We know...his teaching is that we have the wisdom within us. It's just devotion and practice. Being healthy, healthy in our bodies.

M: What does he share about being the Way and the Light?

C: There's love. The way is love; it is. It is who we are, we know. It sounds so simple, but it is so simple. He shows that there is nothing that can hurt us or what he is saying...there is only love. There truly is only love, and when we are in our bodies, we experience this love, this ecstasy, this blissful feeling that is love. And the more we are in that place, the less allowed all other feelings are in our bodies.

We just need to practice being in love. It takes practice. It's not easy. Sometimes it's compassion, for ourselves too, for ourselves. He also teaches that the Way is living. Living in love, living as an example, living without separation, we have less separation as human beings. We are all connected; we are all one. He teaches to remember that. So much pain is caused by separation, by polarity, that's so created by man.

And greed, he teaches to give. Forgive. He teaches forgiveness, it all comes back to giving. Giving our love in all forms, in all that we have. The more we give, we receive.

TWENTY-TWO

John the Beloved

I first had the opportunity to work with Erik when I began learning quantum healing hypnosis. This is another one of those sessions where I felt like I was riding a bucking bronco of energy! It may have been the first session where a client experienced a lifetime in Atlantis, and it was the first time Jesus made a guest appearance!

As I moved Erik to the next scene, he began sobbing uncontrollably. The room began to rise in frequency, and I began to sweat. Something different was happening. As he began to talk, I had to consciously deepen my breath to stay focused. A lot of energy was moving.

C: *I am seeing something that looks like walking on sandy earth before the cross. My teacher is being hanged.*

M: **Who was your teacher?**

C: *Yeshua ben Joseph (begins to sob). Yeshua ben Joseph. Yeshua ben Joseph...*

M: **How does it feel to be with your teacher as he dies there?**

C: *Devastating (crying).*

M: **I want you to scan around and see if there is anybody who has more information for you there. Tell me what you're experiencing.**

C: *Angry.*

M: **What are you angry about?**

C: *That no one can see this beauty, that they are so afraid of their own truth that they had to destroy.*

M: **To destroy what? Tell me what you are hearing.**

C: *His Lightbody has emerged from the cross, and he is standing before me. My heart. His eyes. See the way I do see. Nothing is lost or destroyed; the flesh is but a temporary experience, and all experience is joyful to the consciousness that brings life into it. He says when you learn to stop looking for me, for the teacher or the love to save you, then you shall see what I see when I look upon you.*

M: **And what do you see when you look upon us?**

C: *Children learning to walk. Delightful in their stumble. Sweet in their ignorance, their curiosity. Innocent.*

M: **It sounds like you have a deep love for us.**

C: *(Deep crying)*.

M: **Yeshua, I would like you to help our dear friend here, and as you're visiting with us, today offer him some healing.**

Yeshua: Feed my sheep. Tend to my flock. Walk in the glory of my name.

M: **There is a lot of conflict in our modern world about who you were and the messages you brought, and what we should do to really be like Christ. Can you tell us what that is? What it's really like to be Christlike?**

Yeshua: It is like the most simple way to be. Everything complicated, and the perception of complication is no longer interesting. When it is accepted, it is a beautiful game, as an intellectual stimulus perhaps, to explore complications, but as we come to be addicted to the sense of value and worth that we believe comes from the complication of creating difficult and complex problems that require complex solutions and that garners the value and worth that allows us to seemingly assimilate a deserving, what we're begging for. When this interest, preoccupation, that the idea of value and worth through complication ceases, and the simplicity of the moment is unopposed in its majesty... That is what it's like to be Christ. A child of God that is the fullness of God that has been liberated from the connection and idea of pain.

That [Christ, a child of God] looks upon the Kingdom of Heaven on Earth with a single eye [nondual consciousness] and notices that even as the resistance believes that it is falling from heaven, that it is fighting against, rejecting its very nature, it is still hurtling its way home. When you learn to hear that one message, no matter what is spoken, that is when you find Christ.

I wanted to learn more about the story. Several months later, Erik and I worked together again to focus on the lifetime of John the Beloved. Here is what we discovered!

C: *We're walking along a river in the desert. Actually, I am seeing myself as a young boy. There's a caravan. It feels the whole family, like a lot of families, are filing into another city for the census. We're being counted. We're also going to be visiting another family.*

M: **Look down at the ground and tell me what you're wearing as you scan up the body. Tell me what you notice about the body you're in.**

C: *It's small. Small and maybe ten or eleven, and I'm wearing ankle links and a vest-like robe and an undergarment with sandals.*

M: How do your emotions feel?

C: Excited.

M: What are you excited about?

C: Getting to see my older brother. Yeah, he's going to meet up with us in Jerusalem. We're in the home of my father's brother, my uncle. There's a large wooden table with lots of people talking and waiting for my brother to come. He's been away in India and Egypt and other places studying. My uncle, my dad, and my uncle, but mostly my uncle, paid for him to go. So, we're just here to honor my uncle and to welcome my brother back and hear about his experiences. I love him so much. I've missed him, and he's been gone for a couple of years or so. I am anxious to see him.

M: You said that your mom and your dad and your uncle are there. Who else is there?

C: My uncle's wife and their children and my mother's father and her sisters and my one other brother and two sisters and some servant people.

M: Tell me what happens next.

C: He arrives.

M: How does it feel? What's it like?

C: His hair is longer, and he's smiling and hugging my father. They embrace for a long time, and then my mother. Then my brothers and sisters. We're just sitting on the floor all eating, and there's singing now. We're singing a very old Jewish song of homecoming, celebration, and the feast. He comes over to me and asks where I am, and I say, "Here I am." He picks me up. His hands are warm, and it feels like tingling throughout my whole body. He asks if I can feel it, and I nod my head. I don't know why exactly I have tears in my eyes (emotional).

M: Feel into it. What are those tears about?

C: I don't know. He says there's much for me to learn and that one day I will travel with him, and I will get to go on the journey too. He hugs me and kisses my mouth and says, "Let's enjoy the feast." and puts me down.

M: Does he share anything about his time from his travels?

C: The family is eager to hear about the exotic lands we had only heard about. He is really reluctant to share. He says that he found ancient civilizations and the ability to travel through time and that he can feel his teachers with him always. It sounds fantastical. Some of the women ask about not having to go to the temple in order to meet teachers. He is saying the teachers are within his consciousness. Then he is talking about food and the True Nourishment, that which is nourishing. Some of the people are laughing now, in a fantastical way. My mother and father are sitting on either side of him, and they feel proud, and they know. They are assured something is profoundly meant for him to be.

NEXT SCENE: JOHN BECOMES ILL

C: I'm sick. It's about five years later. I'm becoming a man. I've become ill, and they do not know what is causing the illness. I am sweating and trembling and vomiting. My body goes into seizures, and then I seem to go unconscious.

M: What is your experience during this?

C: Fear. Immense fear and anger. Mainly that I haven't seen my brother again in quite a long time and I've been waiting to get older for him to come for a visit again and to say it's time for me to go with him, and it hasn't happened yet. I am angry that I may be dying here, and I'm not going to be able to see him again.

M: I see why that would be upsetting.

C: My mother is with me. She is rubbing my cheek and my hand. She is very calm, with gentle tears. She's telling me to rest and be at peace. Be at peace. I don't want to; I want to fight. I want to stay. I want to see him again, but it's no use. Everything goes dark and black. I feel my body tightening, going hard.

M: What happens now?

C: I'm in the spirit plane with angels all around...watercolors, vibrant. I hear trumpets and horns and string instruments and singing. I feel large. There is intimate golden light as myself, in myself. This fabric that everything is, that the angels are a part of, and I feel I remember that the largest part of my soul essence had not yet entered John's young body and that it will soon re-enter. I can now see the tomb and see his body wrapped and laid in there. Such beautiful music and beautiful light. I watch the tomb open, and my brother enters. He's dressed all in white, and he lays his hands upon the body, and I am rejoicing. Praise. The very sound of the trumpets, I am the Light that precedes the angels' presence, and he commands my reentry in the body, reanimation, and I am aware and profoundly devoted. I, as the Breath of Life, reenter, merge, activate. "John!" He's commanding me to rise up to open my eyes. To stand. To walk. To speak. To praise. He leads me out of the tomb into the light. My sister, aunt, and mother are there, and they weep and gasp and shout. My brother calms them, then they rush over to me and are hugging me and splashing me with water.

My brother smiles and says it's time. He announces to them that I am to be by his side from now on.

M: Is anything different now that you are back in your body?

C: Everything is different. Now I know the truth of death and life. Now I know that everything is true and that there's no more waiting. No more confusion. No more anger, at least not in the way I felt it before. Now I feel ordained and devoted, curious, but also immensely powerful. Part of it is feeling chosen by or protected by or in the wake of his energy, and some part of me knows there's much left to be done, to experience, to unravel, to integrate in my own consciousness. In these moments after reawakening, I am very close in his energy, like an extension of his energy field. I am getting a glimpse of the authority and the majesty and the grace that he is, that I am, but that's been still perceived as bestowed upon me, not that which I am, like is in his energy. So simultaneous awareness of the truth of being and also the great leap of consciousness that very quickly was accelerated through the seeming death and resurrection of the body to the greater shift in consciousness beyond the body that simply symbolized how much, how many more rooms of this great palace (the multiverse) have yet to be explored or touched by my own personal vantage point. How glorious the journey is to become, to be. Yes.

M: Beautiful.

C: I go with him. We leave almost immediately. We join his other friends just outside of the city and continue to move on. I am to be the scribe recorder who writes many things down and to be an escort and to listen to everything. To not miss anything. Listen, listen.

NEXT SCENE: FEEDING THE MULTITUDES

C: There's a large crowd. We're handing out fish and bread. He's speaking. He's talking again about nourishment. He's saying to be nourished is to know wholeness, which happens through truly knowing hunger. That in the Kingdom of Heaven, it's impossible to hunger. In this physical dimension, when one knows that there is truly no hunger, then that which nourishes the body appears. The baskets are overflowing. We take a fish; we take a loaf of bread from the top, and it reappears immediately. The hungry are being fed. That is what we are to do to allow our hunger, our yearnings, to collapse and cave in on themselves and carry us to the depth of our awareness. The realization of wholeness, of completeness, of oneness. It permeates every cell out of the molecule; every aspect of mind is in the awareness of every thought, even in playing with the thoughts that involve distinction, division, separation, classification. And to be that which nourishes as a reflection of generous nature to serve.

M: How many would you say are around you?

C: Thousands.

M: What's the mood like there?

C: Gratitude. It's a symphony of gratitude. Praise.

NEXT SCENE: MEETING IN THE GARDEN

C: We're in the gardens a few days before the crucifixion. It's the most famous time when he called out to Judas and was preparing us for what was to come.

M: What's happening there?

C: It's actually very sweet. It's a very sweet moment; it's not so much out of the ordinary. He would often give us little hints about some things that were right around the corner, very playful — even here. So, it's kind of a sense of "Oh, okay, this is going to be coming up," but you know, he's essentially warning us of what he's been talking about. He's been talking about it for a long time. About the true essence of his nature, of our nature, of our preoccupation even with the projection of a physical form. Really inviting us to rewrite our perception of the body as a projection, an extension of consciousness that is not really tied to this life and death cycle as it appears. That is actually the mind, the identification of a servant mind, that is imprisoned — divinely so.

So, he's talking, and this has been one of the things that none of the disciples...this is one of the things that goes over everybody's heads, and they're just like, "I don't know. I don't know really know what you're talking about." And I am connected with that feeling, and I'm also...so he's kind of like playfully leading, "You know what I've been talking about...transformation of life, power, heaven." and now he's saying he's inviting us to, everything that I just said, see through a singular eye (nonduality) to behold the kingdom of heaven on Earth. To look with a singular eye, to be so anchored in nondual awareness and being that we can still engage in a game of polarity where there is a spectrum, where there is what appears to be a Light and a Dark — a positive pole and a negative pole. Dynamic charges. And there appears to be ecstasy and happiness and harmony and safety and also strife and pain and suffering and loss and cruelty.

And that in the space of mastery, in that he is bringing, all the value of all of those experiences are equalized and completely immortalized and integrated. There is no more delineation. He is essentially warning us that the scene is going to be challenging, gruesome, and difficult, but he is speaking of it in a way that it's just another day. It's just anything else. "I'm not going anywhere; nothing is really changing at all. You're still going to be able to feel me; you're still going to be able to hear me like you hear me." We would walk and we could hear him; it's almost like he had a microphone in each of our ears, but really it was he would speak, and we would all hear it in our heads, but it was so audible we thought we were hearing him in our ears.

And so...and then he, the Judas part, he actually asked which one of us is the most willing to... Gosh, what is he saying? He's saying, "the most willing to step into this resonance that I speak of now, the most willing to embrace or surrender or invite that which you would project onto as awful or wrong or bad?" And he steps forward. He is very loyal.

M: You're speaking of Judas?

C: Yeah. That is not his name. Very sweet, but loyal and a kind person. He had strong convictions. There was a part of him that is almost like he wasn't thinking on as many levels as some of the rest of us, but I think that's that beautiful dichotomy of why some people relate to this. He has a very intricate mind, and other people perhaps think of things more simply, but that doesn't mean that they're not, you know, still in an intelligence vibration. He was a simple man.

As he steps forward, Master confirms, "Of course it would be you." Of course, it would be you. And so, essentially, what he is saying is you'll know what to do; you must do it; you'll know what to do when it's time to do it; you'll know that it's my blessing.

And that actually this was a lesson for us as disciples because this is what we were to bring into the ministry. It was to embody — conscious divine beings, creators in the flesh. And that was the whole message. The Christ sets you free...the only begotten son...you shall not perish; you will have everlasting life. Everlasting life is the breath of Creation. Creation that we are, that we have at our disposal. This was an initiation into that. I'm getting chills through my whole body; it's the exact same initiation as is happening right now for us in this moment and in the work we are doing to create a space to usher people from prior paradigm enslavement way of thinking into claiming their divine inheritance on Earth — to seeing with that singular eye, to have nondual awareness be dominant. To live as a new human, which is the embodied awareness of the deliberate Creation. To take full responsibility for everything.

The initiation was like 'you are going to see them abusing me.' All this was telepathic; he didn't say all of this, and he didn't say this to Judas. But essentially what he was saying was everyone is going to look at you, and you'll be remembered throughout all of history as being the traitor, as being the one who betrayed, and basically what he is saying is, "You cannot betray me." You cannot betray what we are. You cannot betray the One. That's impossible. Everything that you are seeing, this is an experience, and it's just as valuable and just as beautiful as any other. It's perfect. And I'm not, whatever you think is happening to me because it's happening to this flesh, it's not happening to me, but it's an experience that I get to have through this flesh. And he is speaking of it almost in this fascination way, in that, who is willing to step up and be the one everyone projects their story onto that devalues them as a follower of mine? Well, you need to be the one who is most loyal, right? The most ardent student would be the one that would be willing to take all that, to be seen as the least amongst them.

And so that is why that was him. The rest of us had some measure of doubt; we needed to see more examples — more evidence, more everything. And then most of us were simply grappling with what was left of our humanness, and not knowing how to embark on a life in the time period. It's actually really similar to now, but different.

He said, "Go and tend to my flock." Go and be this ministry; he said it mainly to John and to Mary Magdalene and Peter and some other ones supported, but it was really John and Mary's ministry that they were to take leadership and then all of the other disciples to hold them. He is saying this very rapidly, so everyone was like getting it like, 'What? You are the ministry. You're the magic man.' He's like, 'No, this is this flesh. I live in YOU. This is YOU. This is YOUR Creation.' This is what it is. To go out and do that and still look at the world where it's like...this was when we were following in the glamour of this man performing all these miracles...that was easy, but to embody it in our own consciousness that was still vastly much more limited than him, we couldn't perform all these miracles in the same way. It was daunting. I remember feeling fear, scared, and feeling that he, you know, was kind of being coy about leaving us. I feel like everyone was kind of feeling that. It's such an interesting thing now.

In "hindsight" and really to relate to where I am at present to see him looking back at me with knowingness in his eyes and me knowing we could never be apart. Ever. We could never die. We would play together forever. And there is such immense freedom in that, and I can still feel the fear. I can feel the fear in my own body here; how am I going to be this new human?

NEXT SCENE: WALK IN THE GLORY OF MY NAME

C: *I am sitting with the other five on jagged rocks. His body has a glow to it, and it's clear, but not clear at the same time. We all touched it. We felt how solid it is, but also confused. The wounds are still apparent, but not bleeding. This skin glows. He's saying, "Walk in the glory of my name." "Feed my flock, feed my sheep." "Follow my command as it is your command." "Remain the Light and the Truth. Remember always." He's saying that we were lost, but that there will be more suffering and hiding and trials, but he was showing me that this was not so. Suffering is not so. That we each will embody his ministry, the ministry, the truth, in the glorious way. And then he disappeared. The image is gone, and I feel that tingling in my body that I felt when I was a young boy, and he would pick me up. And I feel it coursing through every part of my body. I can feel him touching me from the inside (crying). And I hear him give me a blessing. "March true. There's no law. There is no law."*

M: So, what will you do now?

C: *Leave this country. Leave the Romans. I want to go back to see my mother, but there is no time. There is a commotion, and then I am on a ship bound for Frankia. Someone is there, a soldier with us.*

M: Who all is with you on the ship?

C: *The Priestess (Mary Magdalene), my sister, and three children — his children. Fisherman and ships. And I see the flash with my Light, meditating, writing, and also running and being chased. Being in exile, but also deeply held and thinking much about how the world is crumbling and changing. That there will be a time, a similar time, and it's light and wisdom and memories written down. It will inspire another time, another place, another me. That his name, his beingness that emerges in the flesh as knowing.*

M: How is it there on the ship? What's the mood like on the ship?

C: *Somber. Quiet. Discreet. Sad.*

NEXT SCENE: DYING IN EXILE

C: I'm dying again. I'm older, not too much older — forties. In exile. I had gotten sick, and I'm with the scrolls, parchments, and things that I handed off. And I'm just lying there, just allowing and reading. He comes for me. The angels again, the trumpets, the colors. I allow it to consume me, and there's a flash of light. I'm gone.

M: Will you be returning to your body again?

C: No.

M: This is the end?

C: Yes.

M: What were the last years of your life like? What were you doing then?

C: Different houses in the countryside. Writing, keeping mostly to myself. Had to part ways with Mary and her children as they were taken to even deeper hiding places, disguised. I was caught by the Romans at one point, imprisoned, released, exiled, and then kept watch over. I mostly was quiet and peaceful and writing, and I was able to get some of the scrolls that I wrote to couriers and messengers and people devoted and surrounded around Mary and the kids too. To protect the lineage. Which really is, I told them, ridiculous because he lives in us. He lives in all. Too reactive in the mind, the flesh is not as important as that which animates it. But of course, you can't listen to that. The scrolls were handed to someone in that order. It feels like starvation, or not having food. It's ironic really when the message is so much about nourishment. Remembering when the food was plentiful and even feeling how I am very nourished in my awareness and in my writing. The food in my body was, I think it was the Romans somehow...I think I am in some kind of prison. It's not a traditional prison, but it's some kind of prison. They know where I am, and they control me. They are basically slowly poisoning me. Bad water, stale. Bad bread. My body died.

M: I am wondering if you were the one responsible for writing the book of Revelations? What we call that today in this present time.

C: Much of it. It was, of course, subject to additions and subtractions and other inspired writers. Also, other writers inspired with the human political agenda, but the essence of what I wrote is there. The essence of it is about the coming of a time, the coming of the days of another crumbling of structure. And of the resurgence of the one who knows of his message in the hearts and minds of [inner] knowing too. To usher in the great new era that he was merely a glimpse [of] even a millennia before.

M: When you say the one who knows, who are you speaking of? What are you speaking of?

C: Alpha and Omega. That which is. That which is called parent, father, mother. That which nourishes. That which is nourishment.

NEXT SCENE: THE BOOK OF REVELATIONS

C: I am writing in a stream of consciousness in silence, deliberately. Speak. I have a quill, ink. I intend to use it up, and they are nice enough to continue to give me paper and ink. They, I know that they feel, they laugh because they are going to destroy whatever I write. It doesn't matter. I might as well, but they know that the core of it is going to be sneaked out with this messenger person. Stream of consciousness. A lot of what I read back even to myself didn't quite make sense, but I could feel it's glow. I must admit much of it was beyond me. I didn't even quite comprehend a lot of the specific uses of words, but I know the feeling. The feeling was to claim and proclaim the great cycles and ages and the harmony, how everything fits together and flows in the great dance. By the end, I was at profound peace. There was nothing more to hide from or run from or figure out or know. It was just a profound unfolding and refolding and unfolding and refolding dance.

WORKING WITH THE HIGHER SELF

M: Out of what was shown today, why did you show these certain scenes?

HS: To illustrate the folly of the sense of battle, of loss. To illustrate the perfection and ordered timing to all expression. To convey being reunited, to convey reunion, with that which is. And with this legacy of discipleship, mastery naturally cannot be anything but unfolding perfectly. To remind the personalities of the body, of mind, and you and he and all who perhaps will listen to this voice, your voice, in the coming days to be infused in the sound of truth. To no longer see an adversary for the reflections are surely to come in greater and more powerful seeming form as your voice and this voice and our voice and those other voices infused with the message are to be heard in a greater and greater, more expanded light-sweeping way.

There is to be no adversary, only support, and a dissonance of sound to be invited. To [be] harmony again and for there to be allowed a negative contrasting space that further ignites. It is of utmost importance within your own consciousness, within your own polar energies, and within the mind in every single interaction of that which is seemingly oppositional that it is to be not so.

M: How can we work with that now to embody the truth that there is no adversary?

HS: To not allow the emotion to be projected inward and to follow it to its lowest common denominator, which is an essence of loss, rejection, abandonment, shame, and to allow these deeper emotions to be the master teacher. To be his teaching, a willingness to allow it to break us under the part that is clinging to its identity as less than, as vulnerable, as weak. To be in the living practice of constant annihilation and resurrection, of death and rebirth. To respond with awareness and intention, proactivity, in these moments.

Every single thing and expression is designed to support and encourage the expression and emergence of one's most authentic being. To celebrate in the oneness, the profound opportunity that physical existence is to express the diversity and infinite combination of that one that is, that which is, that which is nourishing. To celebrate in the apparent differences knowing that it is all but fun, you see. Solvent, transient experience. All the play.

M: So, in these times, there are many people that identify as Christian who have been reading and following certain words and languages of how this is going to go during this change. How do we deliver this message? What kind of language do we use that is inclusive to all people?

HS: To court the language as a beloved. To know that it is possible to speak with accuracy, creativity, and clarity. To simplify, to bring words into their most coherent formulation. To be intentional with the motivation behind why you share or speak that which you speak. To be clear in the invitation that it proves, and to whom it is provided unto. To simply remember, is it true? Is it accurate? Is it specific? Does it describe exactly the function of that which I speak, that which I speak into? Is it easily understood and creative? Creative meaning it simply does not piggyback on a concept that is already preconceived or pre-valued. And the ones that do are very intentional in that it is a bridge for something to be familiar enough to simply invite or excite a movement into what is even more accurately describing that which you are speaking into.

TWENTY-THREE

Mary Magdalene

Mary Magdalene is mostly unknown to the collective human consciousness. The Holy Bible says very little about her. What IS said illustrates a very different perspective of the Mary Magdalene I have come to know through these Quantum Healing sessions.

At the writing of this book, I have worked with three women who have regressed to the lifetime of Mary Magdalene. This is possible as each individual soul is part of a much greater pool of energy called the oversoul. Each client gives their perspective and translation of the scenes as they unfold. What speaks to me in all of these stories is the similarities found in each telling.

In one session, it was too intense for the client to witness the time of the crucifixion because of how traumatic it was for her. I believe that the beings who have been assisting me in writing this book sent me another "Mary" to fill in the missing data of the life of Mary Magdalene. Please enjoy these transcriptions as we explore the life of Mary Magdalene, divine partner of Yeshua ben Joseph.

I met Nikki at a sound healing session I was facilitating at a spiritual center that Ron and I owned called The Lighthouse in Ashland, Oregon. We instantly had a deep connection of the heart that I knew had to be from a past life. For months, I had a nagging feeling that I should reach out to her and ask her if she wanted to do a session. I found her number, called her up, and we found a time to meet up. As I was driving to her home, I had an intuitive feeling that I was going to be getting more of the Mary Magdalene story.

During the interview, Nikki mentioned that she wanted to explore this strong resistance that she had towards Jesus. She had no idea where it came from. She went to church as a young child but never really had any interest in Jesus, just an intense resistance. When I regressed her, she saw herself at the end of an ancient civilization and she was leading many people into a cave system to retreat to Inner Earth and escape the cataclysm and Earth changes that were coming.

When I moved her to the next scene, she started screaming and crying out loud. I was so surprised by the intense emotional explosion and asked her what she was seeing. "They are KILLING MY HUSBAND!" she screamed repeatedly. I tried to calm her down, but she was inconsolable. I received a flash of Christ on the cross in my inner space and asked her to tell me to describe what was happening to her partner. "They are putting him on a cross! Yeshua! My husband!"

At this point, I could not get much information out of her. I asked to speak with her Higher Self. Her Higher Self explained that she carried strong resistance to Jesus because she was still carrying the trauma from witnessing his crucifixion and that she still held resentment towards him for leaving her on the Earth. Her Higher Self shared that I would get more of the story and would work with her about five more times to get the full story.

When I brought Nikki up from trance, she was quite surprised by the whole thing. She had never heard of Mary Magdalene being the wife of Jesus. I asked her not to do any research or speak to anyone about this until we finished the research. This way we could trust that everything that came through would be pure. When I went to send her a copy of the recording, I was shocked to find that the recording did not save. This has happened to me a total of four times and is always during a highly potent session with a powerful storyline. In those moments, I trust that the experience was supposed to be that way, my eyes only, for some reason.

A few weeks later, Nikki and I met for another session. Working with Nikki was a bit of a challenge at times. When she went into trance, her eyes would roll back in their sockets, and she would twitch and jerk as waves of light frequencies rippled through her body. She often responded to my questions with fragmented words. She would slip into deep trance and Mary would incorporate into her channel very clearly and she would speak her inner thought process as Mary out loud. When Mary would run, Nikki's legs would run in place. It was fascinating to watch.

When Nikki came into the first scene, she saw herself as a little girl next to a wooden fence, a horse, and a man who was milking a cow surrounded by straw grass. She wore a black dress and could see her tiny bare feet. When I took her to her home, she saw a building made of long grey stones. When she was eating a meal, she sat with her father and mother.

She described her father as being skinny with dark hair and her mother with orange hair. Her mother was angrily moving about the space serving her and her father food, while her father sat in silence, preoccupied with reading. She said her home felt empty because everyone was always in their heads. It seemed as though her father was always scheming on how to make money to buy food for his family.

The next scene was Mary standing on a great stone pathway outside of what she described as a castle. She was plotting a way to get into the castle, beyond the wall, to try and see her father who had been arrested for stealing. She was considering using her neighbor's horse as a decoy to distract the guards from her real intentions.

NEXT SCENE: MEETING YESHUA

C: *A man speaking. There are so many people around him. He's speaking about God. That God is inside of us. There is Light inside. They're screaming at him. "Blasphemy!" He says the Light...there's Light inside, and that inside connects inside of ourselves. There is power inside of us. He says there is power inside of us. Some people are screaming. What is he saying?*

M: **And how do you feel as you watch them sharing this?**

C: *It sounds funny (laughing). We don't have any powers. We don't have anything (laughing). We barely have food. I can barely survive. The men in the castle, all the guards...it's disgusting what they say. They want us to stay sick and poor so they can be in power. They have all the power. We are being punished...punished. That's why we don't have anything. Don't speak up; don't say anything; hide. Don't dare speak up; don't say a word; hide (whispers)...hide yourself; hide yourself. All our lives...they're small...there is so much, so much...everybody down here is dying...dying...diseases. We don't have any money. We don't have any power. He says we have power (laughs). I wonder, what makes him think that? I'm curious about it (laughing).*

M: **What is it that makes you so curious about this message?**

C: *He looks so well...so well...almost very handsome.*

M: **You think he is handsome?**

C: *(Giggles) Yes. I don't know where he is from.*

M: **Does he share his name?**

C: *Yeshua.*

M: **What is happening now? What do you see happening there now?**

C: *I see a market...and arts...and people giving food, and I have a white basket in my hand...collecting.*

M: How old do you feel here?

C: Sixteen...seventeen (yawns). People are greeting me; I bow. I see that man again. He's talking again. Healing. Healing sickness. We can heal our own sickness. We can heal our sickness. My mother. His hands, his hands — people are saying his hands; he has healing hands. Healing people with his hands. I wonder if he can heal my mother. I can't...I'm not going to ask. I can't (laughs). I'm so scared...I'm scared.

M: So, what do you do? What happens next?

C: "Mary" (very loud voice) ...he says. He must know my name (in a loud voice). "Isn't your mother sick?" I'm trying to hide (whispers). I can't go anywhere. There's nowhere to go. I'm walking backwards. Running. Running...I'm going to get in trouble. I'm going to get in trouble...

M: Why would you get in trouble?

C: So scared of these people (body trembling). What if they find out that my mother gets well? They don't like this person (body shaking). First, I'll take care of her.

M: What are you doing now?

C: I'm home. Oh, my poor mother. She's got a fever. She doesn't look well. I will have to ask him to come to see if he can help her.

M: So, you're going to ask that man?

C: (Nods head yes) Maybe he can come and help her.

NEXT SCENE: DISBANDING HERETICS

C: People screaming, people are screaming. The men are coming through their houses. They are looking...looking for that man. They heard he is in this village; he's in this village helping people...telling people that they have power. That there is love, healing, and light and we have to be...and here we are and that's not ok (frantically). That's not ok. We cannot hear this heresy...neighbor's house...is he hiding in the house? (Thrashing and contracting the body like she's running and hiding.) I can't come in here and get in trouble... Oh, my poor mother. I have to help. Lock the door (whispers). "Be quiet." (She becomes very quiet.)

M: So, you're getting quiet. And what happens?

C: (Whispers) They're gone.

M: They're gone now?

C: Yes, gone.

M: So, what do you do?

C: I'm going to go out at night and look for him.

NEXT SCENE: MEETING JESUS AT NIGHT

C: I walk into the forest. It's a bright moon (yawns). I can see the path. It's calm. I have a long coat on to keep me warm and I am walking down a path. It's quiet. Trees. It's very peaceful. I hear a stream. I bend down on my knees and take a drink of the water. (She becomes startled. Body jumps off the bed a little).

M: What happened there?

C: There is a hand on my shoulder. It's him. It's him. His eyes are so blue; his eyes are so blue. He's so strong. I can feel his heart. It's so big and so strong. "Mary" ...he says my name. I'm speechless (laughs).

M: You're speechless? Why is that?

C: (Giggles) My whole body is shaking. I'm sweating. I'm like I know him...I know him.

M: You feel like you know him?

C: Yeah. He's looking at me. He's just staring at me (laughs). "I heard about your hands." (laughing awkwardly)

M: How does he respond?

C: He smiles. I'm blushing. He asks if he can hold my hand.

M: That's nice. Are you going to say yes?

C: Yes.

M: What is it like to hold his hand?

C: Amazing (smiles warmly). Amazing. There is so much power. So much Light. It feels like home. Safe. Warm. Still connecting. He's barefoot in the cold (laughing). We're walking. We're walking down the path towards the village. There is a stone path. We are walking up the stone path. We are looking over the mountains...looking down into the forest and the stars are so bright on this path. Where he is taking me. I don't feel unsafe. I feel very comfortable.

M: So, he's taking you somewhere?

C: Yes, to look at the stars and the moon. It's peaceful and we sit. He asks me if I need help with my mother. (Shaking her head and whispers) "Yes." He says, "You're scared." I'm seeing him watching me. "I asked for your name, and I know I can help you." They took my father and mother. They can do anything.

They don't like him. They were trying to get to him the other day in the village. He's been hiding. Yes.

M: What else do you talk about?

C: How does he heal these people? He tells me I can heal with my hands (starts laughing). That everybody has an inner light, the same as the stars. Open your heart, open your heart and it's all inside of you. No one has more power than the other. Not those men. No one. They can heal with their hands, too. Just believe it. I want to learn more. I want to learn this. "Sit," he says. "Be still and listen." There's a light coming from his heart. It's a shape. Triangles. Always triangles. It's so big and so bright. I feel like the light is filling my body.

M: What's it like?

C: It's so big and perfect. So much love. His hands are on fire. (Her body is shaking, and she sounds as if she is in a state of ecstasy.)

M: What are you experiencing?

C: So much joy and love.

M: What are you two doing there? Describe to me what you are doing?

C: I don't see anything but light. The light is gold. I don't even know where my body is. He let go of my hand (body is now calmer). He is just staring at me. He says pure, pure, pure, so pure. He says that to me. We walk down the hill. Big stones. Big stones.

M: Where are you heading to?

C: This is where he stays. It's stones. One is on the bottom, big one on the top. And there is one on the left and a little opening. He stays in there. He's bringing me inside (laughing).

M: Tell me as it happens what it's like.

C: Just a little cot, a little bed (laughing), a little mattress. And a fire, a small fire. There is nothing else in there. He's sleeping there. He says he meditates in here. He connects the energy from his Father. The sky, the stars, that's where the light comes from.

M: Where does the light come from?

C: Through his body, through his head.

M: Where is it before it goes into his head?

C: From the sky. When he closes his eyes, he sees light, and he feels connected to everything — everything that exists. There is no separation between anyone. Just love. We are one in this body. This body heals itself by connecting to this light. He says I can practice with him. I can practice. Okay. No one knows I am in here. Okay, I can heal my mother (smiles really big).

M: You were saying he talks to his father there. Did he share anything else about his father?

C: His father is not human. His father is in the stars. The vibrations of light and sound.

M: His father is the stars, light, vibration, and sound? Tell me more about that. Did he share anything else about it?

C: This earth has many, many, many stars. There are many stars around the earth. This is one. There are many, many, many stars. We are here to learn.

M: So, he was speaking about one star in particular? And that there are many? Are they all his father or just the one?

C: All of them. One creator of all things. Our Father, all of our Father.

M: Does he share anything about his mother?

C: She has the same name as me (laughter). His mom...was sent the Light. Humans need the Light; she believed in the Light. She wanted to receive it so everyone could feel it and share it with the world. She prayed that the Light would be within her, and that people could see it. She felt it...she felt it come into her body. She saw the gods and goddesses in a circle of light, blue light was actually a circle, and it came into her body.

M: What was that blue light?

C: Yeshua.

M: Where was that blue light before?

C: Pleaides...light beings (body arching and shaking). Vibration...so much vibration. It's so expansive. There is so much Light there. There is so much Light there.

M: What does that mean?

C: Tell me about it. Stars. Stars...lots of love...shining light...they talk to each other through their bodies...their vibration (her mouth was stretching). I have a lot of power (starts gesturing with hands and fingers and making swishing sounds).

M: What gives you this much power? You said you have a lot of power.

C: I feel the power in my heart.

M: What gives you this great power in your heart?

C: Love.

NEXT SCENE: CUDDLING IN THE CAVE

In the next scene, Mary and Jesus are cuddled up inside the cave. She feels Jesus's soft hand in hers while she strokes his hair. She comments on his smooth muscles and giggles. She shared that he tickles her sometimes and whispers in her ears how beautiful he thinks she is. Her smile is beaming from ear to ear as I imagine them wrapped up in one another's arms, staring deeply into one another's eyes, engulfed in teenage love. At this point, Mary is around sixteen or seventeen-years old. Jesus is just a few years older than her. The next scene is with them connecting and playing in Yeshua's cave-dwelling.

M: That's nice. What else do you do with each other when you are in the cave?

C: We hold each other's Light in our hands. We breathe (camera shows the fingers of both hands being held up) and imagine our bodies all different colors like a rainbow.

M: So, you fill yourself with this rainbow color? What else do you do?

C: We create. We create more dynamic energy, and we send it all over. All over...everywhere. We imagine healing, seeing all the people well, food everywhere, and peace. Everyone is taken care of.

M: That's nice. Does he share where he learned how to do these things?

C: He says to look in your heart. Relax, be still, and listen to the answers. I feel his chest against my chest.

M: That's nice. What are you doing there?

C: Breathing. Breathing in the Light. And we're pulling all the energy up to our chests and filling our hearts. Filling our hearts with more... (she smiles).

NEXT SCENE: MIRACULOUS HEALING

C: There is a boat. There are people screaming "that man in the sand!" He's not breathing. He tried to get from the water.

M: What are you doing there?

C: I was walking with Yeshua. He runs over and starts to pray...his hands...he starts using his hands. He's praying. I watched him. I saw. This man's face is blue (body shaking and arching). He's praying. There's so much light. (Body still shaking.

Her hands are up off the bed, fingers outstretched.) The man starts to cough. (She coughs also.) He's not blue. (Still moving her arms and hands and fingers.) And he's fine.

M: A miracle.

C: All the people, they are grabbing him. "Stop grabbing." (Moving her arms and hands rapidly on the bed.) Grabbing his shirt...they're grabbing. They say he can bring back the dead. "Help me, help me." They want help. "How do you do that? I want that. Give me that. Help my mom. Help me! Help my mom!" I'm knocking people down. Everybody is following us. I'm holding his hand. Everybody is following us.

M: What does it feel like?

C: Strange. Powerful. Everybody wants to know who he is. Everybody wants to have him at their house. Everybody wants him. I don't want them to see where we go. Go to the village. Go to the village. I see two horses are racing; we're galloping.

M: Where are you galloping to?

C: Somewhere across the field. We're moving. We're leaving. They want us to go. We want to go. They want us to go.

M: Where will you go?

C: I don't know. They don't understand us. They don't understand us.

WORKING WITH THE HIGHER SELF

M: Thank you very much for sharing what you shared with us today. I was wondering if there is anything you'd like to share about why you shared these scenes. Why did you share these scenes?

C: There is a path to love that creates. I can create, bring life. The universe is so much bigger than we've ever imagined. People want what they don't have. Sometimes they want to take it instead of work for it. They want to stay powerless and broken, and they don't even know how powerful they are.

M: In one of the scenes, Yeshua was explaining that his father is the Creator. I was wondering how that relates to the time that Nikki is speaking of Source, there is also God and also the term Goddess. Can you explain how all of that works together in reference to Yeshua describing his father?

C: The Light co-exists in the level of divine masculine and feminine, equal balance of earth and sky. So, within the Light, there is a masculine and feminine principle.

M: Can you share some more thoughts about that because I think often people think gods are male, a father. May you share more about the feminine principle of Light, the goddess, the mother?

C: *The Mother is the purity that gives birth to the physical and holds the Light of all creatures and beings.*

M: You are saying that the Mother is the purity that gives birth to the physical? So, what is the Father within that?

C: *The protector.*

NEXT SCENE: LIFE IN EGYPT

C: *Pyramids. Two big pyramids, just lots of sand. A man on a camel who's with us. He's our guide, guiding us. He's dark-skinned, white turban, gown — blue and white. His face is covered, and I can only see his eyes.*

M: What are you wearing there?

C: *It's like a blue dress, long cloak, and some sort of thing on my head. It's windy, really windy.*

M: What's Yeshua wearing?

C: *White pants and white shirt. We're traveling through. People are growing food. There's civilizations, towns. Something about the towers. These pyramids are towers. There's energy coming from them. It's like this light source; it's really strong. It's a conductor. He's telling us about the water; there's water underneath. It makes electricity, some sort of power. Everybody feels good when these are on. We're here to experience it. It's like the light that comes from the hands, that comes from Yeshua's hands. The healing energy that we use is the same energy. It's a huge, huge resource of healing energy. There are farms; there are lots of different types of farms there. There are aqueducts. Just working on the land. This water goes under the pyramids too. It's creating the energy that's in the pyramids through the tide in the ocean. The river, the rivers, there's rivers moving water, moving energy. Conductor. Conducting.*

NEXT SCENE: PRIESTESSES OF EGYPT

C: *I see lots of women. I see a crowd. Crowds. I see crowns and hooded cloaks. Yeah, there's a lot of women, a council. They're in council. I see a chalice. I see swords. High priestess.*

M: What about the high priestess?

C: *Mary. Mary's the teacher. Mary's teaching. Blood mysteries, magic. Sensitivities. Psychic. Getting our moon blood to the earth, earth offerings.*

M: What happens when you give your blood to the earth?

C: *She receives our blessings. Blessings are received.*

M: What happens when she receives those blessings?

C: *Peace, healing. Sight. Seeing. (Mumbles) Six stars, six stars, six stars... (Says this about six or seven times.) Six-pointed stars, chalice, six-point stars, moon, sun moon, earth sky, sun moon earth sky, energy, up down, down up, two-directional energy. Ascension, manifestation, Anahata [heart] chakra, divine masculine moving with the feminine. It's multidimensional. When you hold it, you hold it. It connects to the sky. Connects to the earth and it's pulling energy from both directions.*

M: How does this six-pointed star become manifest?

C: *Through the heart. Focus, we focus on prayer, and it materializes.*

M: So, you go into prayer, and it begins to generate from your hands from the Anahata chakra? Then what do you do with it?

C: *It's like clear sight. Visions come through it. It's like a crystal. It's so clear.*

M: Wonderful. You said you were there with Mary. Tell me more about her. You said she's a high priestess.

C: *Mmhmm, she's so beautiful. Light skin, it's like porcelain. Piercing green/blue eyes. So calm. So peaceful. Love, so much love.*

M: Wonderful. Are we talking about the mother of Yeshua?

C: *Yes. She's teaching all the women. There are thirteen. There are thirteen circles of thirteen. They make the grid. The grid of Light.*

M: What happens when these groups of thirteen women meet?

C: *We're connecting with the stars. Sirius. Venus. So much Light energy. Clear vision. Clear vision and what to do.*

M: So, you know what to do when you get the energy?

C: *Organize what to do. How to create things. Plans. Connecting to the stars, the starlight. Helping the people use the earth, the power of the earth. Ascend...ascend; the Earth is ascending. The chakras. Energy, energy centers.*

M: Are you talking about the earth centers or the human centers?

C: *The human centers and the earth centers. They're both ascending.*

M: What does Yeshua do when you're meeting with the women like this?

C: *(Giggles) He supports it. He knows. He's gathering the men. The men protect the land. There are people who are not awake who want to take this land, this sacred land. Men are there to teach and support our plans.*

M: **That's nice. So, Yeshua helps to gather the men around to protect and to teach? What kind of things does he teach?**

C: *Love, compassion, trying not to fight. Everything is a fight. Teach the feminine. The heart. And to be kind to the land.*

Mary and Jesus are traveling with three boats in what she calls Turkey. They are traveling with three friends named Mark, Anthony, and Simon. They are traveling around trading fish. She describes women on the shore in red gowns and different colored fabrics on display. People recognize Mary, Jesus, and the group and begin to gather and bring their friends to listen. She described a man with armor, who she calls the Prince of Greece, who has come to warn them and tell them to leave the area.

NEXT SCENE: TRAVELING TO TURKEY

M: **Why does the prince want you to leave?**

C: *Blasphemous, it's blasphemous.*

M: **What are you doing that's blasphemous?**

C: *Speaking truth: "God is within you." That we have the power inside of us to heal ourselves and to bring peace and love to the people. People have power. People have the power! Power's not in the hands of the few; power's in the hands of many. In everybody's hands. The truth. We teach people. We're trying to teach people. We teach and trade our fish, and we sit and talk. And we tell people of the stars, and we talk about ascension and moving our bodies and healing energy, opening our vision, clear knowing.*

Some hear and some don't listen. Some are so scared; they don't believe it; they don't have anything. They don't have the power to do anything. No rights. We want them to come to our land where there is peace. It's idyllic. There's peace, everyone's fed, and there's lots of love.

M: **Where's your land?**

C: *Strip of land near the pyramids. So lush. So beautiful. So much abundance. Endless energy. Everybody's needs. They have what they need. We decide to leave. We will return another time.*

NEXT SCENE: STUDENT OF MOTHER MARY

In the next scene, Mary is in a vineyard surrounded by grapevines, red apple trees, and mountains. She referred to the place as Burgundy. She is writing down some of Mother Mary's teachings and plans for creating caring spaces for women to gather. She writes about tantric teachings of divine union between masculine and divine feminine energies which meet together at the heart. She describes notes from her meetings where they would use breath and meditation to create an arc of light through the body similar to the shape of the Egyptian ankh. Later when I brought the client to wakefulness, she was excited because she had never heard of Mary Magdalene doing tantra practices. I encouraged her not to do any research so that we could keep our findings pure.

NEXT SCENE: ANKH OF LIFE

M: How do you use that arc of Light?

C: It regenerates energy through the bodies. Through the orgasm. You go into sacred soul contact, and you open up your energetic field, and as you breathe together you bring the energy from the root all the way up to the crown and circulate it, bringing it back to into the earth. It activates, it activates sight. The pineal gland. Visions, clear visions. Using it for ascension to understand how to use this human organism to heal the planet.

M: How else would you use the organism to heal the planet?

C: Brings down information from the star systems, like an antenna.

M: How does that work? Tell me what you're seeing there.

C: It's the Merkaba, the six-pointed star keeps coming up again. (Whispers) Six-pointed star. Torus energy. Spinning, a spinning energy field. The six-pointed star is rotating. It's in the body and around the body, up and down, like a figure eight. It's like a generator. There's limitless energy. It's Creation energy.

NEXT SCENE: INNER EARTH

The next scene was of Mary descending a staircase inside a crystal cave. It was clear to me that we were visiting a high-frequency space because the client's eyes were fluttering rapidly behind her lids, almost rolled completely back. Her body shuddered as waves of electricity moved through her. It was hard to get much information from her because she mostly spoke in Light language when responding to my questions. I did manage to get her to share that the cavern had white crystalline walls and purple amethyst spikes, shining prisms, and a geode doorway. She was invited down a staircase by tall, pure, white-light energy beings who introduced themselves as Lemurian. She described the environment as pure, loving energy with no suffering at all. I decided to move from the scene once the client descended down the stairs because she would only answer my questions in Light language!

NEXT SCENE: JESUS AND MARY IN JAIL

In the next scene, Mary is inside a prison cell. She and Yeshua had been arrested by a bunch of men and separated into different cells. When I asked her what they did to get arrested, she described them standing amongst many, many people and Yeshua delivering a teaching.

M: What's he talking about?

C: *He's talking about love, love and kindness. People are so fascinated by him. He speaks and everybody listens. There's so many people who just follow him around. I see sheep and horses and so many people. It seems like we're always running. We are always running away. We're always hiding and running and hiding and running. I'm so tired.*

M: Does it put any stress on your relationship?

C: *Yeah. It's hard to find time to be alone, to be intimate. We know that we have plans, but we can never stop. We can't. There's nowhere to stop.*

M: Yeah, you just have to keep going, huh? Do you ever fight or bicker?

C: *Sometimes, but not that much. Not that much. We understand.*

M: Yeah. What do you feel like your biggest challenges are when you're relating, like when you're getting triggered?

C: *Just ease, why, why is it hard? It feels like we have to convince people. We feel so much love and they don't feel so much love. Why do we have to convince them of what they have already inside of them? Sometimes it feels lonely.*

NEXT SCENE: MOONBLOOD RITUAL

C: I feel walls, stone walls. There's light. It's a tunnel. It's winding around. I'm going to meet the other ladies, the other women. It's a full moon. Rituals.

M: What's the purpose and intention of the rituals?

C: We meet with our blood moon. Blood moons. (moon blood, menstrual blood)

M: You meet with your moon blood? Yes? Why do you do that?

C: It's an offering, offering for the earth. There are thirteen women.

M: What do you do in the ritual?

C: There's six, six women; we stand in a star. We hold our, our blood and a bowl and we pray. We're around an altar. I see a light in the ceiling; it's a hole. It's like moonlight is trying to come through the hole.

M: So, six of you stand around this altar? What do the other women do?

C: They're standing around us. Mother Mary's in the middle. She's the pillar, the center pillar. Pure energy. Every woman has a woman behind her, she's in the center. Each woman holds her blood, and the light comes through from the Moon, and all the women hold their hands up towards the light and the light shines through her crown and she turns into like an angel. She's luminous. So much Light!

M: What are your prayers for in this ritual?

C: Healing, healing the planet. Healing the people.

M: Why do the people on the planet need healing?

C: There's so much greed. So much darkness.

M: So, you're doing this ceremony to help to clear it? How does that work? As you know it you can share. You can see it and describe it to me. What do the ceremonies do?

C: I see triangles of light. It's like a Merkaba. It's like it's three-dimensional. Light emanating everywhere.

M: That's so beautiful. Where are these women from?

C: Different star systems.

M: Different star systems and they're incarnated as a human? Why are they here from other star systems?

C: Yeah. Because the Earth is transcending. The Earth's moving into Light. There are other systems that are, they wanna be on this planet. There's so much life on the planet.

M: So, you've all come to help prepare the planet?

C: *There are other beings that are on the planet already. There are beings that come and go from the planet.*

M: **What do they do when they're coming and going from the planet?**

C: *The information. There's information here. It's hidden but there are people that are here to access it. Yeshua's here to access it. Nobody wants him here.*

M: **What do you mean nobody? Who's nobody?**

C: *The people on the planet. There are forces on the planet that don't want him to be here because he knows how to access it. It opens up the energy fields. It wakes up the people. We're here to protect it. It's underground. There are crystals under the earth. They hold these keys, this information. It's encoded energy. It's under the earth. Crystals. Crystal cities. Just other planets that have encoded it. Stars. Starseeds.*

NEXT SCENE: GOING HOME TO THE PLEIADES

The final scenes that I had with Nikki were of her traveling with her daughter Sarah to meet a man from Mt. Carmel who she wished to marry. At this point, Yeshua had already made his Lightbody transformation and would only visit from time to time in Lightbody form or dreamtime to check in on the two of them. There was no mention of other children. When Mary transitioned out of her physical life, she traveled through a tunnel of light to her home planet in the Pleiades. From there she met with her council of guides and described looking out over the multiverse which she described as many "universities" to choose where she was going to incarnate next.

Transcript: Another Perspective of Mary Magdalene

Here is a session with another client who regressed back to the lifetime of Mary Magdalene. Without the clients knowing one another or having any understanding of what material I had, this other Mary Magdalene transmission filled in the blanks where the other client was not able to "see." We can thank the Higher Realms for coordinating that!

SCENE: WITH JESUS ON THE HILL

C: *He speaks to the people on the hill. People are sitting and standing and wondering who this man is. Intrigued with his message — some are spies; some are innocents. What does he want with them? How can he change their lives? They are simple people, and they are under the rule of the Romans, so how can he bring them freedom, and yet they gravitate towards his magnetism. What they hear is profound and strange and foreign to them because the rabbis do not speak to them in this way.*

M: What does he say to them?

C: *He encourages them to be of their own mind and heart. Not to be subservient to any ruling power of the day. That their greatest empowerment is from inside of themselves. They are not lost, yet they keep themselves in that place of being lost, which is why they draw to themselves overlords — because they make themselves out to be victims, and yet they are far from that. He is a rabble-rouser. He is a true rabble-rouser.*

M: A true what?

C: *Rabble-rouser. He wishes to overturn their hearts and minds as he did the tables in the temple. See the Light. See the Light he implores them. They question because they see one reality and yet they know not of their Creator-given abilities to become more than they are. They...they talk amongst themselves. They question. They question him. They question themselves. Some are quiet and pensive. They realize what he says with his stories and his words, it makes sense — yet, what are they to make of this? They hear stories; they have seen his miracles, and so there is a part of them that wants to believe, and they feel his magnetism which is...and his love, genuine love.*

And so, this is why they, they follow in a way, they want to hear more. It's like putting one toe in the water, and then another, and then the foot, then the ankle — slowly, slowly dipping in to find out more because they are curious even though this is strange. And even though, they wonder about him and who he is. He implores them to search their hearts and minds for meaning and purpose — greater than the reality they are existing in now. Something greater. Something more magical. Something more empowering.

M: Well, what do you do as he gives his message? What are you doing there?

C: *I am listening. I follow. Some women — some people — mostly the women, the men do not really engage. The women — they have questions, and I do my best to respond in the way that I can from what I have understood of his teachings.*

NEXT SCENE: THE LAST SUPPER

C: It's the Last Supper. Passover. And the disciples and some women around the table. There is wine; there are flatbreads. There is a lot of talk and a lot of jovialities.

M: What happens next?

C: Yeshua looks across at Judas. Judas looks at Yeshua. They stare into each other's eyes. Judas almost shakes his head as he can't do this. He cannot do this (whispers), and Yeshua looks into his...directly at him, and it is like they are transfixed. "You can do this," he says to him. "And you will. You will follow the will that has been declared in Heaven. Will you not?" They are locked into some invisible transmission. He stands up — Judas — and he is angry. He is very angry and afraid at the same time. He pushes his chair so violently that suddenly there is silence. Everyone looks around. "What is the meaning of this? What is the meaning of this," they ask? He looks at Yeshua one last time, and Yeshua is resolute and calm at the same time. He has a great knowing in his presence — a sadness, a knowing. And Judas leaves the room.

Everyone is quiet, quiet. What is going on? They start to ask Yeshua, "What is going on? What is happening?" He is silent for a few minutes. It seems like an eternity. "I will not be with you for long," he says. "Not in the way that you have known me to be." Suddenly there is shouting. "What, what, what do you mean? What is this? What is happening?" He raises his hands. "Stop. Bring your peace, bring your hearts to a place of peace and trust in the will of the Heavens. Trust in the name of Hashem. This is not what I have taught you. This is not what I have taught you."

I am feeling a little shocked and dismayed, and I observe the men. They are confused, reactionary. They look over at me, some of them, and I have nothing to offer them but just my silence. They think of themselves. "What are we to do? What's to become of us?" they ask. "Greater things you will be and do than I have," he says. "I have taught you well. You will spread the message. You will go out and teach amongst those who have ears to hear and eyes to see who you are and what you are about. Do not despair. I am with you always. I am in your heart of hearts. I will always be with you. And so, you will carry out that which you have been ordained to, and fear not, I am with you always. Your steps will be guided. Your thoughts will be directed. And you will journey amongst mankind and spread the message of love, and this is all I can say right now. Follow your hearts and believe in your message of love — all that you have seen and heard and learned. Remember these words, and we will go now. It is time to let what needs to unfold. Let it happen."

SCENE: THE CRUCIFIXION DECISION

C: *Chaos in the streets. There is chaos in the streets. He has been taken. He has gone in front of Pontius Pilate, and we know not where he is exactly. And the disciples are in chaos. "How could this be? Such a great man. How can this be?" They are in denial. Many times, they are in denial. Some flee. They hide for their lives. Some are standing in the shadows observing. There is commotion amongst the people in the neighborhood. They don't like to have the presence of more soldiers than is necessary — especially this night of Passover. Consternation. Fear. Deep fear. Everyone is unsettled, and most stay awake through the night. Incredulous. In deep denial. Confused.*

And Judas is kneeling. There are no words to describe his sense of...on the one hand, it's betrayal, and yet, on the other hand, he was gifted with a vision from Yeshua for this higher purpose. But how can he live with himself? The physical wounding is too deep. He goes away. He dares not show himself in front of the others, for he knows they will kill him. So intense is their anger and sense of betrayal. So much commotion. Questioning. I have hope, and yet, my heart pounds. I cannot leave this place until I know what it is to be.

The darkness turns to light. The sun is coming up, and we are still waiting for news of him. Still hours away. My gut aches. My heart aches. I need to be with the children, but I need to be here to know where he is and what will be. I run to them to comfort them. There is someone to look after them until I find out what is going on. My heart races. I race back. Together with Mother Mary, we are holding each other. We support each other.

M: **What happens next?**

C: *There are rumors that he is to be held for a little while the courts decide. My head is hurting. It's...I am filled with fatigue, and the hours are long, but eventually, they have decided that he will be crucified. There is great shock and disbelief. "How can this be? How can we, how can we save him?" The women cloister around Mother Mary and me (deep breath). They offer love. They offer support. My knees are weak, and I feel like buckling down to the earth. Weak. I have to see him. I have to see him. But still long hours before (pauses) anything* happens. This is excruciating pain, and my body is numb. I cannot eat. The women force us to drink water. Stay hydrated. But I cannot eat anything. The men have fled. Although I hear some are hiding close by.

And then there is news they will bring him out. It is to happen that day. And it will happen in a hurry because of Shabbat, and the Sanhedrin have declared it needs to happen before Shabbat. Who are these people who are so blind to the truth and what he has tried to do? His message of love goes above their heads. They have the power, and they fear him. They fear the crowds and the miracles he has drawn and performed. Want him gone. They want him out of the way. He is interfering with their relationship with the Romans — the status quo. Who are the traitors here? Who are the traitors here? Then the gates open and there is a great uproar. People running and calling out, and I see him. Finally, I see him! Oh, my Lord. Hold on!

M: What is it like to see him?

C: *They have pushed the thorns into his crown into his forehead. He is bleeding over his face. Mary and I and the other women...we...they are supporting us to stand. It is so hard for me. I cannot endure this vision of him. I cannot be...one of the soldiers walks behind him with a whip (gasps)...and they position him to a cross. They tie his wrists to the poles. He buckles, but they pull him up, and they command him to walk. And people...so cruel. Some are jeering; some are crying; some are just watching. The Roman soldiers are pushing them aside as he walks through. "Raboni, Raboni — look at me. Look at me. Please look at me." But his eyes are...he walks and yet his eyes are...I feel he does not see us. He does not see me. The wood makes a trail in the sand. As it goes over the stones, it makes that noise of being dragged along. It's too much to bear. I cannot...I cannot. (Big breath.) It's too much for me. We follow. Just crying in disbelief. How can this be? How can he endure this? How can this be? We see Joseph of Arimathea. He comes running over. He is speaking to Jesus, Yeshua. He is saying prayers in Aramaic. Walking...it is too long out to that place. They have prepared two others on either side. They are already there; it is agonizing to see them up. I have never wanted to see this, and now I am faced with it with my beloved.*

I say prayers for him. I implore Hashem to give grace to somehow change this all — somehow stop this madness — this insanity. I feel my pleas and cries are not being heard because everything is going as they wish it to. They are nailing him — his palms — and tying his feet to the bottom. I cannot bear this. I cannot. My head feels like it is going to explode. We are weeping and weeping and weeping. We are being held by the other women — Elizabeth, Joanna, Ruth. They torture him so. He is bleeding. His body is filled with blood. And we sit at his feet below him. Weeping, crying for each other, for him, for his torture — for this pain, for this agony. They want to hurry this up because Shabbat is coming. The Roman pierces his side — ahhh. His body writhes in pain, and the blood spurts. It is too much. It is too much.

He telepathically says to me, "My love for you is...is eternal. We are always together. We will always be together." The people start leaving to go home for Shabbat. I want to stay. I cannot leave him. They have taken him for dead, but I feel there is still life there. I feel there is still breath in him. He is not gone. He has been trained. He has been trained in the East. He knows how to hold that energy force despite everything that is going on in his body; he's holding on. He was trained for this. He was trained to hold his soul despite the condition of the body. I know he can do it, and he will. Just holding on. They have decided to bring him down. Joseph helps to unbind his wrists and feet. Oh...the nails. I can't bear it. I cannot bear to look as they release him from the...cross. Joseph is crying. He loves Yeshua as his son. He weeps as he cleans him. I hear "All is not lost. He is here. He is still with us." My body is weak from the trauma. Mother Mary and I, we hold each other. And before I go, I want to clean his body too. I want to wipe his body, so he is clean. So, I help Joseph. They wrap him up in the liniments and place him on a cloth that they can carry. They take him away to the tomb. I have to go home. It's Shabbat. I have to see my children. My love, I will see you. We will be together. I know. I know we will. I will see you. I will see you, and we will be together. (Deep breath and sigh.) We have to go.

M: Tell me what happens next.

C: We are up all night. I cannot sleep. I am just rocking and rocking and rocking. Just Mary and me and some of the other women. I need to find faith and trust that this is what the Divine Spirit wants. What he agreed to. What he came for...and perhaps it could have been different.

M: What did he come for?

C: To wake people up. To overturn their consciousness. To bring them to love — back to love.

M: So, what happens next?

C: Shabbat is long. I want to go back to the tomb.

M: Go back to the tomb.

C: It's empty. The tomb is empty. Where is he? Where is he? Where are you? Where are you? I am standing outside. I don't know where he is.

NEXT SCENE: PARTING WORDS

C: He is there with the disciples, and he keeps his distance from them. He has to tell them what their mission is. He has to inform them that he cannot be with them in the physical as he will go away. It is not safe for them to be together. And it is their choice — those that wish to travel to spread the message as far and wide as they can and to leave as quickly as they can because it is not safe; they will be hunted down. It is a dangerous time. They have everything they need. They will always be provided for. They must go forth. His energy, his illumination, is inside of them, and that divine spark will be the words that come from their mouths — be the thoughts that they think — that guides them to be where they need to be, to journey in the directions they need to go. They are always guided and protected when they listen to that inner guidance.

Some will not escape the wrath of the overarching powers of the day, and it will be their destiny to fulfill this further will of their soul contract. Everything in life is as it is meant to be. Have faith, trust, be strong. This is why they came to Earth at this time with him. They have the energy and the love in their hearts to be that guiding light, to be that teacher, to be that healer for others who are ready to hear the message. He must go. I must go. I will be taken with the children and my maidservant, and we will go with Joseph of Arimathea. We must leave in a hurry. There is no delay. There is no time to tarry. We need to leave. Some of the men cry like children. They weep for their master. And yet they know this is the hour for them to step out into the world and be strong and be brave. So, they disperse.

Yeshua and I stand in front of each other. Our eyes are locked in that now, that knowingness, love. "Everything will be fine," he says to me. "Joseph will take care of you. You will all be fine, and I will be fine. I need to go away. We all need to go away. What has transpired is...is what is meant to be. You will, in your own right, be that love in the world. You will bring the children up with that love as only you know how. And you will find community, and you will find solace in the love that you receive as much as you share."

M: Does he share with you where he's going to go?

C: He will return to the East to his teachers there. He will return to the monastery that he stayed in when he was younger. Perhaps he will live out his life there. Perhaps he will return. He does not know. For now, he needs to journey east, and I will go west. To "fly on the wings of Spirit," he says to me. "Fly over the water; be safe. Be sure. Know my love is with you always. I am inside your heart as

you are in mine. And not a day will go by that I do not think of you and bless
you and send you my love, as I know you will for me."

SPEAKING WITH THE HIGHER SELF

M: And in the lifetime with Mary, why did you show the scenes that
you showed?

HS: Her presence, her presence as a grounded, holding energy — she could hold
the space for Yeshua. She could match the complementary energies in a receptive
way — the magnetic, empowered, receiving, holding, sharing a balanced way.
And she did this for him. It has taken many lifetimes to build her vessel to be
that, and she did. She was his grounding while he traveled and spent most time
in Spirit. She was grounded in holding that space for him.

M: We were wondering — Jesus the ministry was brought to the
collective at that time, and the collective was in a certain
vibration in a certain way — we were wondering how that
message translates to this time? What is needed in this time for
the collective?

HS: The codes — the love, the energy, the consciousness was implanted and
imprinted into a deeper matrix on the planet at that time to be unearthed as
such, revealed in this time for the collective — for humankind. And so, it has
lain dormant, overlaid by the false matrix that was input through control and
narrative on the planet. It was and is emerging now more and more as the
collective awakens. The message of love, beauty, truth, joy, play, empowerment
— the ability to create this new reality, this new creation, and birth this new
light on the earth. It was an imprint into the collective unconscious at that time,
and that imprint in the unconscious is being triggered as and when each of the
seven-plus billion souls are ready to awaken to it.

M: When I share this type of information publicly — there are
people that consider themselves devout Christians who say
things to me like I am being led astray by the darkness or by Satan
because I don't stick to the narrative that they learned in church.
What's your perspective on that and how to respond to it?

HS: Well, we know those projections are projections from people's own shadow self,
their insecurities, their inability to transcend the boxes they have put into their
minds. They will point fingers because they do not know anything else, and it
is safe to do that; it gives them power over their insecurities. They do not wish

to rock their own worlds, their little bubbles, because they would not know how to experience anything different at this time. So, therefore, they project at you. They do not know how to handle your truth, your knowing, your innate wisdom. There is no response to people until they do their own shadow work, until they drop their consciousness into their heart. It is only when they live from their heart that they can access the truth — see it, feel it, sense it, know it, hear it.

The only way is to love them and leave them. Send them love. That love, that light, into their hearts and into their energy field is what will impulse them to go deep and deeper into their unconscious. They will open access for the light to heal the shadow — to bring the shadow into the light. They have been trained in something that was falsified for greater purposes of another agenda, and so one can only feel compassion for them at this time.

M: Yeah. So, what is the next stage of that work that the ministry started at that time? What is our next stage of that?

HS: As more of the collective wake, and as the valuable work that you do supports people to understand and clear their core issues, more and more people will come to that place of deeper inner knowing and trusting of the truth that is unfolding on the planet at this time. It happens one person at a time. On a quantum level, it is expeditiously ramping up —mMore so than we can even imagine. And so, that inner truth that has been with us always and is innate to us all — every single soul on this planet — will be birthed with each soul opening in its appointed time, for its appointed reason. And they will, we will, humankind will collectively be transported into the matching vibration of that energy — the ascension of consciousness.

M: Thank you. If Jesus were alive today, what would he share with us to inspire our awakening?

HS: It is very simple. Know that ye are love. He would teach. He would lead by example to be love. It is all energy; it's all vibration; and he would be in the marketplaces; he would be in the fields; he would be in the cities; and he would just be — that love that is highly magnetic. His presence would open hearts, and people would be inspired to seek the truth, and he would encourage them to go inside and find the truth inside of themselves and to themselves live their presence, which is the highest form of love they can be. And they, in turn, would spread that energy and so it would go around the entire planet. And that way...very simple yet we have overcomplicated our lives. And he would overturn much of the teachings of the church. He would invite people to discard all they would deem as the higher ruling authority. He would empower people to be their own leader in love and truth. You do not need emissaries. They are their own emissary to their true light and creative source.

M: I learned growing up, the quote that was used often was from Jesus saying I am the Light and the Way and the Truth. What does that mean? What did that mean from him?

HS: The energies, the codes of love, the sacred geometry, the light that is, and at that time was his energy field — the DNA. It's all energy. This is the energy that will open up. This is the connecting bridge for people to connect into their own hearts to find that consciousness, that super consciousness — unify all that is inside. He was carrying...he was the consciousness that is emerging on the planet today. That consciousness is the build, the bridge builder; it is the wayshower, so therefore he is the wayshower. His consciousness is the wayshower to each person's empowerment, to each person's revelation of their own personal light and ability to transcend and ascend into the highest realms that they are ready for. I am the Way. He is the bridge. His energy field is the bridge. His consciousness is the bridge. It is not about the physical avatar per se as it is the recording of the DNA that he in-filled and imprinted into the subconscious, and that's what needs to be revealed and aligned with the superconscious and conscious aspects of self. Yes.

M: Aha. What was the greater purpose and intention of his life at that time, and what did he leave behind for us?

HS: The culture at the time and society was lost and in decay. It was losing itself in circumstances that were drawing people away from their greater sense of self and purpose and community and sharing. There was an indulgence in material, the material world, and so, there was a split between the spirit and the material. He came as that bridge builder to draw people back into their hearts, connect to their spirit to take back the sovereignty of their essence — soul essence. The soul is sovereign and was being buried deeper and deeper into the psyche and the unconscious. It was his mission to bring the revelation of the soul back to the conscious heart-minds of the people to find balance, to find personal freedom. And finding their empowerment at that time, they would have overcome the need for the oppressors as the mirror to their victim mentality. And in this time, he will say the same thing again. To overthrow that victim mentality, and in doing so, you eliminate the need for the oppressors to weigh down on humankind.

We are no longer slaves. We never were. It is time to shed the shackles. It is time to free the mind and the heart. It is time to find the soul buried deep in the unconscious and bring her up to her former glory — to seat her in her throne of love in the heart and to relegate the ego to be seated behind the throne as the humble servant. The ego, whilst needed in some way, shape, or form, usurped the beauty of the soul, and now she will regain her rightful place. And the ego will be the servant and do the bidding of the soul as was always meant to be. And this is part of the transition, part of the emergence, part of the ascension, part of the revelation.

M: Some people say that his flipping of the tables was a justification of anger in some ways. Why did he flip those tables?

HS: Righteous indignation. Spiritual righteousness. In overturning the tables and causing the money to fall to the ground, it was a symbolic, metaphoric gesture to place the material on the earth. To turn the table upside down was to reveal the vessel — an empty vessel — meaning the vessels of the people were empty, devoid of any connection to soul and Spirit. The vessel being the empty table overturned, sat on top of the money — meaning — build the vessel, infill it with light and love as the true meaning of life. And that the earth and whatever the earth can provide comes secondary, or comes naturally, abundantly, automatically, and with grace through the love of that vessel, filled with light and joy and creativity, and putting that intention into life.

The legs of the table turned upwards are symbolic of the arms of the human raising up, reaching up to the heavens, the Light, to Source, to Spirit to infill and build the vessel with Light and Love. The flat surface of the table like the avatar — when upright blocking the infusing light, but when turned over and lying flat on the ground, covering the money — the material being secondary to the Light; the arms are reaching up to the Light to receive the Light into the empty vessel.

MESSAGE TO HUMANKIND FROM HIGHER SELF

We have shifted to a new realm as more of the collective wakes up. The healing is starting to infiltrate deep into the unconscious psyche to release the fear that was placed upon humanity around this particular event. The debris is being cleansed and cleared and will continue for some time throughout the collective as that old matrix is falling away, that old paradigm of control.

The message is to record, re-envision the new reality that is being birthed. Live it, feel it, sense it, taste it, smell it. It is to be your ongoing experience in the new lives being birthed. A new you is emerging, and we speak to the collective. You can put away those old stories. They no longer have any — should no longer have any emotional charge. They are being cleansed out of your emotional subconscious, unconscious energy fields. You are being cleared of all of that drama that was perpetrated to keep humans enslaved. Do you know this now? Will you awaken to this truth and believe it and then release it without any judgment — only love in your hearts — for the storyline that kept you enslaved just as long as you needed. And as you give up your victim role, so more and more truth will be disclosed, and more and more of the perpetrators of that lie and deceit will come to reveal themselves or be revealed.

And we ask that you see the bigger picture for both the Light and the Dark on the planet and find forgiveness in your heart as every single person in the collective has had some part to play in the dance between the light and the dark. So, therefore, we can release this polarity and the game of the polarity and the story of the polarities through the love that we share in our hearts. Release any emotional charge; release any anger; release any fear that no longer serves the collective or any individual. The story, the narration is now passed, and we ask you to recognize this. It is no longer relevant in this new reality and the birthing of this new Earth. There is no place for any of this in Heaven on Earth. Enjoy your freedom. Enjoy your freedom; enjoy your empowerment. Enjoy the All That Is. Enjoy the moment of your creative expression and how you can infill this beautiful planet, bring her back into harmony and stasis through all the elements and all the four directions.

As we all work together now to heal and clear, release and transform, and enjoy the beauty, the reality that is — the Earth that she was meant to be and will be soon.

Dropping the Veils, Rising in Love

Let us move beyond the illusions of separation and come into deep unity with our own Inner Christ. Let us use the redemptive power of forgiveness and compassion to stand in our divine-human expression and be ambassadors of eternal grace and eternal love.

Let us be visionaries of Paradise upon the Earth and walk forward into this new light spectrum reality and build a New Earth.

TWENTY-FOUR

Jeremiah: Disciple of Jesus

When Dina came into the scene, she described big cumulus clouds and a jade-colored sea. The landscape was dry, and she stood on a pier or dock. When she looked at her body in the scene, she described a bald man wearing a red and blue tunic with sandals. He is carrying a satchel of sacred texts containing the teachings of Jesus and a shepherd's stick, a crook. The man has a wife and a son and lives in a simple home.

SCENE: HEALING MIRACLE

C: *I'm at a fountain. There's a gathering. There's a teaching today. Everyone's really excited. I think...Jesus and his disciples are coming. He's going to be performing a healing. There's a blind girl, and she's going to see again...or see...or see for the first... Well, there are people there that believe and lots of people who don't. It's a dangerous time to be doing healing.*

M: **What makes it so dangerous?**

C: *People are unhappy about his teaching and the people who are following him...who know the truth of his words. I'm there because there's something wrong with my son. He can't walk. Yeah. My son and I are sitting by the fountain. Hopeful.*

M: **Do you have a name for your son?** (C: *Daniel*) **What do you call yourself?** (C: *Jeremiah*) **What's happening now, Jeremiah?**

C: *I'm taking my son through the crowds to Jesus and asking for help, for healing. I'm nervous. I'm elated and happy. He's wearing creamy white...creamy clothes...long robes. Dark hair. Dark skin. He's beautiful. He's welcoming me, asking me what it is I've come for. He knows that I believe and that I've been passing along his teachings to my friends and family. I've met him before. We're watching him heal the little girl. It's powerful. He has his hands over her eyes, and he's speaking in Hebrew. It's like the light in the courtyard has gotten brighter. Everything feels electrified. There are people crying in joy and awe. And...now he's done, and she's laying there, and he asks her to open her eyes. She's crying. She can see. And he's looking at me...and I'm bringing my son to him... I'm asking for healing, but it's difficult. It feels like a burden to ask when he's already given me so much, so much wisdom...but it's not for me, it's for Daniel. And he smiles and laughs. He has a good laugh. And he holds my boy in his arms. (Deep exhalation)*

M: So, he's holding Daniel in his arms now? What's happening?

C: Well, Daniel looks happy...but he's supposed to be this way. He's not going to walk. And I feel sad and...that there's a different path for Daniel. Not one that he needs his legs. That he needs his mind so he can be a great channel...a wealth of information. He's here to observe, and he is very...he's to use his craft.

M: So, he has a different path. How does that feel?

C: Conflicting. But I know that...in my soul that it's true, and I feel at peace with that. I want to...I ask if I can follow him...if I can travel with him. He leaves it up to me. He says, "If you would like. Yes." I decide to go. Even though I feel sadness because I want to be with my family and provide for them, I feel a calling to walk.

M: Does he deliver a teaching that day?

C: Yes. He's teaching about love and what separates us from love and from being connected and how...no matter who we are or where we come from or what journey led us to this place now, we're all the same. We're all one. Your beliefs don't necessarily have to all be the same as long as you're living in your highest self and sharing the joy in your heart with others. You forgive. (Deep exhalation) In a lot of ways...teaching that it's not about religion and the rules and asking us to lay down our swords against each other and to join hands in harmony. Teaching us that each of us is divine. And...talking to the people who are gathered in the back who are angry that he is there and telling them that he loves them and that it isn't magic or heresy or...it's God's Light and Love that moves through him.

M: And how do they respond?

C: Some of them are scared because the girl can see. And some are angry, and some are crying because they witnessed a miracle, and they can't explain it.

M: And how does he handle it?

C: He's smiling. He's just loving them.

M: Is it just him, or did others come with him?

C: No. Others are there. There's a woman.

M: A woman? What is she doing?

C: She's standing...a little to his left, a little bit farther back, behind some of the men, but she's important.

M: **How can you tell she's important?**

C: *There's just a presence. There's a connection. It's like she's standing behind out of respect, out of tradition, but she is close to Jesus. Yeshua. Not Jesus...it's the wrong name.*

M: **What else do you notice about the group that came with him?**

C: *They're all so peaceful...except...one of them is still learning...still...I can see him clearly. He has a beard and a gruff, harder face. He had a different name. His...name was Saul. Now it's Paul.*

M: **Mmhmm. What else do you notice about Paul?**

C: *He's still at the point where miracles of Yeshua are overwhelming in a way. It's a lot for him. It's awe-inspiring. It's letting go of past beliefs and stepping forward into true understanding.*

M: **Mmhmm. What else do you notice as you look around at the group?**

C: *Everyone is hard traveled. They've been traveling a long way. They're tired, but also there's a light about them. It's comforting to be in their presence, but they've come a long way to be here.*

SCENE: RESURRECTION TEACHINGS

C: *(Deep exhalation) We're inside. It's dark. It's a tunnel. And torches light the way. It's a very sacred place. My body feels very hot right now.*

M: **What's happening in the sacred place? What are you doing there?**

C: *We're...learning ancient alchemies of life and death, and there's a blue fire.*

M: **A blue fire? Tell me about this blue fire and what you're learning there.**

C: *(Deep exhalation) I want to say we're learning how to raise the dead...to bring someone back to life...something...I don't know.*

M: **Well, relax into it. Allow more information to emerge. You're going to be raising something from the dead?**

C: *Yes. This is...we're learning. We don't know how yet, and so today is the day we move from smaller to a larger animal. And Yeshua's not here; he's in the flames. You see his face in the flames, and it's like he's whispering through the fire to us.*

M: **What is he whispering to you?**

C: *He is saying that only God...the true power of God can bring someone, something back and only in very certain circumstances...this is a sacred place where only very few people will go in order to learn. The fire is getting bigger because we are bringing back this little calf, and it's making my head hurt.*

M: So, you're bringing back a small calf? How do you all do it?

C: It's a laying of hands and words from a book...a book lost to us now.

M: If it's appropriate, you can share the words with me.

C: (Deep breath) From ashes, we come and ashes we rise, as you lay dying, you lay ascending... (long pause).

M: What's happening now?

C: We're all joining hands around the fire, and the calf is on an altar and starting to twitch and move. Energy...that energy is so strong in the room. It's very powerful and very...it's almost frightening, but not in a scary way...but in a scary, powerful way. The calf is walking around (chuckles).

M: That's wonderful. Who are the other beings that are with you? Look around and describe who's with you.

C: There's a woman. There are actually three women. And...two men. One of them...I think...well, she has a headdress on... You can see her face. Black-brown hair. A plain dress. The other one is older. Very old and very wise. She seems to be the teacher of the younger one I just described. I think they're related.

M: What about the other woman?

C: Um...she has blue eyes and blonde...no...light brown hair. She's different. She's not from here.

M: What do you mean she's not from here?

C: I don't know. She's not like everyone else. She's very like...she has more...she has lighter skin...and fair. Not from this part of the world or...maybe not even of this world.

M: Mmhmm. What about the men? What do you notice about the men?

C: They're very holy men. They're quiet. Tall. Funny hats on. Um...but expensive, very expensive robes. They're like high up in the church...I don't know if it's called that...but important figures.

NEXT SCENE: GROWING UNREST

C: We're riding. Hmm. There are palms. People have palms. Following...um...a procession...on our way to a council on something...I don't know.

M: What will you be meeting with them about?

C: There's great unrest. The people in power don't like the teachings of Yeshua and the things we have been learning and sharing with...with the public and with...with each other and...it's...but the people, the people are so thrilled and happy to see him. So, it's very conflicting sides and voices.

M: What's happening now?

C: We're entering into a tent, and I'm in the back. I'm not important...not that I'm not important, but I'm not in the main circle.

M: What's being discussed there? What's happening?

C: People are asking Yeshua to...to just take a break for a minute and let things settle down. They're worried. They are advising...they're advising him to...I think to go into hiding. But he doesn't want to. He's very determined to push forward...to continue with his work...and...

M: What happens next?

C: I don't know. I'm scared. I'm scared for him. I don't... He's my friend, and I don't want anything to happen to him. I think it's more...it's beyond my...my human understanding of what's happening. He's...he says it's time to do the washing of the feet, and so...because we've been traveling a long way. So, we're washing each other's feet, and there's great joy in this. It's a very intimate connection between everyone in the room. And, um, a woman is washing Yeshua's feet, and they know each other. He seems to have a great connection to her.

M: What do you notice about their connection?

C: I want to say it's Mary Magdalene.

NEXT SCENE: TAKING JESUS AWAY

C: I'm so sad (emotional). They're taking him away, and we're in hiding...or I am. They're...I'm devastated. I'm...my teacher and my friend is going to die, and I'm scared because I put down everything to follow him and I don't know...what I will do or [how to] move forward...it's confusing. It's like I know that everything is okay, but at the same time, I have a great fear of what's to come. I'm not hiding. I've come out of hiding, and I'm in the crowd, and I'm watching. It's horrible.

M: What's happening now?

C: They beat him. And he's bleeding, and they're walking him over...(emotional). They're walking him over to a cross and making him carry it. I want to yell out, and I want...(emotional) to tell him that I'm there, but it doesn't matter.

My heart aches. We're watching him walk up the hill...and...there are many of us gathered. There are many that have hate in their hearts for him, and those of us who don't are quiet. Trying to support from afar and...(exhales). Then... They're nailing him to the cross. He's screaming (emotional). It's so painful to watch, and some people are laughing. I want to leave, but I stay...and...I'm trying to force my way through the crowd (exhales). I make it to the front and I'm trying to fight the guards and...I did what he didn't want me to do. I let my emotions take over. This is...I'm getting arrested and beaten and...I'm so angry that this is happening to... It's like all the lessons I learned and the teachings, they went away, and I let my love and my fear take over (deep exhale). I think they kill me. I think...I don't see anything else.

Transcript: Resurrecting a Dead Calf

Here is a transcript from a client named Tyra. I worked with Tyra several months before the client above. I never know where my clients are going to go or what they are going to run into during the session. The energies during this session were so powerful that my client was shaking back and forth as her system was being upgraded. You can imagine my surprise as she seemingly described the previous resurrection process as mentioned before.

C: *It's a temple. It looks like a temple from India maybe. It's a temple. A place of worship and study. The floors. They look like marble. Wow... it's very expansive inside the temple. The floors are white marble with black veins, and I have sandals on my feet. I think I'm female. I'm stunning! I'm otherworldly beautiful.*

M: What are you wearing?

C: *It's like a gown. It's funny because it seems Egyptian, even though the temple seems kind of like India, but I feel Egyptian in the way that I look. It's white shimmery with an inch-wide gold edging. It looks very Egyptian. I think I have a staff. Just a staff, I don't know why...it implies leadership. It implies this sort of status. It feels powerful in a way. I don't know if it's literal, but I feel like I could clap it onto the marble and command things — attention, change, something to materialize even. But I'm not entirely sure if that's metaphorical or true, but that's the feeling of the staff. I'm going to set it down, okay? So, I can pay more attention to myself for a moment. I have a headdress on too. It's very Egyptian...maybe I've traveled.*

M: What does the headdress look like?

C: It's gold. It's simple but has a stone at the center of it. It sits above my head. Wow!

M: What's the headdress for?

C: It's again like status.

M: Do you live in this place?

C: I think I'm teaching here.

M: What are you teaching?

C: Oh! How to move matter. Yes. You have to command the matter. You can command the matter to change, to move, to use your will. To use your will joined with Creator's will. I see many things moving around in the air, around me. Mmm. I am very serious in a way, although things keep striking me funny, too. I'm a good teacher.

NEXT SCENE: BLUE FIRE AND THE BREATH OF GOD

C: We're in a room that's dark. It is dark on purpose. There are no windows; it's an inner sanctum. It has a blue fire. There are others. Yeshua is here. This is a very sacred gathering. It's very holy. We're in the holy of holies.

M: What's happening in this gathering?

C: It's like learning to raise the dead, animate life. We are learning to breathe this holy fire...we are breathing the breath of God. And we are joined as one mind and one heart and one purpose. We're like a sacred gem, like a sacred sapphire. We're animating life.

M: What are you animating now? What do you see?

C: I see a calf. The calf had died and we're bringing it back to life. It's a joining. It's a oneness of our energy. We became one, fused, with intent, and we've pulled down the Breath of God.

M: How do you pull down the Breath of God?

C: You will it to be so. You come together in pure intent. We're there for one reason. One reason only — that is to understand the Will of God. Operate as one with the will of All That Is. We join in the Fire of Light. It's blue. It's the first sign that you've joined as One. Sapphire blue. Now you know that your energies have joined in pure and perfect intent. (Gasp, breathes heavily) Power...life.

Tyra was shaking and shuddering as energy coursed through her body. This same energy moved through me and filled the space we were in. I began to use Light language and suggested we ask the energies to assimilate easily.

C: I'm better now. The calf has woken up. The energy got very intense as we brought in the animated Breath of God that woke up the...(laughs). The calf is alive now and there is a celebration. I see Yeshua in the firelight. He's very jovial. We're all celebrating.

M: What does he look like? Describe him to me.

C: It's a little hard to see him in this light...any of us really; we're kind of shadowed. His hair is brown, kind of curly, or wavy. It's hard to see him in this light. I feel him more than see him.

NEXT SCENE: YESHUA AND THE ROUNDTABLE COUNCIL

C: We're at a great table. It's big. It's large with a shiny surface. There's a council there. Yeshua is speaking. He's speaking of what's ahead for his life. We're gathered as a council of supporters for him.

M: What's he sharing?

C: He's sharing about a time of unrest. There will be a time of sowing and reaping...the power and the potency of what's been learned. He'll go out and do the miracles, you know? He says that it's short-lived, but also eternal...something about a stone. Setting something in stone. He's talking about putting something in motion, and it's set in stone. It can't be undone or changed.

M: What is it that's being set in stone? That's being set into motion?

C: Energy. Christed Energy. A potential for all beings to be Christed. It's like from the stone through time things spiral outward and upward, building generation upon generation. He talks about the many changes throughout humanity. He sees what's coming and we're the council. We consider all that's being said with wisdom and sobriety.

M: Look around the table. What do you notice about this council? Describe them to me.

C: I don't feel like they're all human. I don't even feel all human necessarily. I feel star heritage, which feels Arcturian or something. Anyway...let's see. Who is at the table? Many masters. There's a lot of us here. It's many members of the Galactic Federation — ambassadors, many of them in human form holding the collective energy.

Transcript: Worlds within Worlds

This next scene is a portion of another client's session describing a teaching that happened around a fire with Yeshua. There was so much in this session that may be released at a later date. For now, let us sit around the fire for a little more time with Jesus.

C: *I'm in a closed place, there's a fire in the middle. We're in a meeting. Yeshua is there. There's Anasha, Sheniha, there are these women and men, and there are also people in the background that are not in human form. They're like part of the council that is hiding. They're invisible, but I can see them. This is a big meeting, yet it is concealed in front of a fire.*

M: **Who are those first two, that you said were with you?**

C: *Anasha is like a wise woman. She's just like Magdalene, but she's not Magdalene. She's very sacred. She's very imbued with beauty. There is also Nichema who is like the brother. So, there's this, these are next to Yeshua. They're guardians, they are like guardians. They're guarding him, yeah, they keep his energy intact, so that he can do his work. So, they guard him against any disruptions in his timeline. They're also time jumpers.*

M: **So, there are other beings, you said, that have come in for this meeting as well? There are others there present?**

C: *Yeah, there are people from Orion and Sirius. They are very toned, very big in energy, and ancient. We're looking at the fire. The fire is not a fire, it's like a hologram. They're looking at all these planets and systems. They are doing a plan. From the outside, it looks like a normal fire, but when you look closely it's a window to a universe. It's like a night fire that contains many systems and stars, and it's like a window. It's like a hologram.*

M: **What are you all looking into as you look into this hologram? What are you observing?**

C: *Observing planet Earth, just observing it as it's spinning, and it's part of a bigger picture.*

M: **What is this bigger picture describing?**

C: *It's flat. There are rings. The planet, the sphere of what we know of Earth is not Earth. It is Earth, it's not as we know it. There are rings around Earth. Each ring is a world beyond Earth. The Earth is just a sphere in the middle of this, but it's part of one thing that's bigger. Earth is bigger than we think, WAY bigger. We are just inside a sphere but outside the sphere, there's more. There are rings of different nature worlds. It's really interesting.*

M: **So, these rings or are they like different versions of Earth? Or different dimensions of Earth? Are they completely different realities?**

C: *They're like Earth. They're physical. They're very real. We just don't know them. We can't see them. From the point of view of Earth, we're just floating in space but it's an illusion. Outside there are rings and each ring is a part of Earth. It's like a mountain world, a garden world, and an ice world... Yes, it's like worlds, within worlds. It's like we expand into different spheres, Earth has 13 spheres. It's like those Russian dolls, like that of Earth. Each sphere or ring will turn on for us as we progress. It's like Earth is going to be able to see the next ring and then the next ring, and then the next ring. It's like Earth is suddenly realizing its within many realities at the same time. It's that we just don't know. We don't see them but they're there. It's like we need to turn them on or like we need to be able to see them. So, there's no outer space really. It's like outer space as we see it is just a hologram. It's like a firmament. It's just a show. It's like a light show so that we can think that we are in a universe but we're not. We're contained within another sphere, within another sphere, within another sphere, 13 times.*

M: That makes sense. So, what is this group doing with this information as they watch them, what is the intention?

C: We're learning. We're learning how it works. I mean it's unveiling the truth. Like we need to know where we are. What we are really needing to do. It's like we're shut down. In the middle. It's like we're trapped in the middle like the human race is trapped in the middle.

M: So, what is Yeshua doing in the scene or these other members?

C: He's the one showing this to others in the fire. Everybody's looking at the fire. He's kind of showing them. He has the power to unveil the fire and show the others. So, they all marveled at this meeting. There are humans, and there are also nonhumans. The humans don't know that there are nonhumans. Yeah, he's just showing, he's just teaching them the reality, like the truth.

Collective Ministry Team

Jesus did not act alone in his mission. His incarnation was part of a much larger Redemption Plan involving many beings over a timespan of several generations. Many beings incarnated on the Earth to support his life's mission, and many supported from beyond the Earth. Here we stand at the culmination point of so many efforts to restore humanity and this Earth. Bless us all as we complete the restoration and manifest New Earth!

TWENTY-FIVE

Through the Eyes of Jesus

This next client often goes into a somnambulistic trance when we work together. It was mentioned in a previous session that she would have some information about the life of Jesus to share with me. This session was remarkably unique in that the client was taken INTO the body of Jesus and Mary Magdalene at times and was able to tell me what he was thinking and feeling at different stages of his life.

I will also mention that this client knew nothing of Jesus besides from a few years of occasional church visits as a child. Everything that she shared in this transmission was brand new ideas about the life of Jesus and Mary.

C: I see sand and water that looks like a lake, but it's not a lake, it's a sea. It's very dark, the color of the water, and the sand is also very dark; it's not like sand that you find normally on the beach. Hmm... Seems like there is a...somebody doing a ceremony there, in this water, looks like...wearing white like a priest. I think they are baptizing some kids in the sea.

M: What does this person in white look like?

C: He looks like a reminder of what happened there. He's not real. He's...he's just the...a spirit there. It's not...it's not an actual body. I just see them not touching the ground and they're just in the air and they're just white. Umm...white energy or something. And around I can see there is a priest and he's holding a baby and he told me it's a memory of what happened here. So...yeah.

M: What happened there?

C: They were doing the baptism of the kids there, in this kind of black sea that looks like a lake. It seems that this is an important place because Jesus was there. The waters are holy waters, and they used it for years for this purpose, of cleansing the impurities of the people that they would put their bodies in these waters. Like cleansing their souls, like cleansing the karma when you go into this water.

DESCRIBES HER BODY

C: I am...I'm flying above the lake. I don't have a body. I am...I am one with the...with Jesus's consciousness, somehow. Like I'm...I'm just spinning around observing and sometimes I see him as a vision. Comes in and out, and I'm just nowhere, but at the same time I'm all of it. I'm part of all of it, yeah.

M: What else do you see there? What else is happening?

C: He's..he's um...I see Jesus praying there, wearing white and putting his hands on the water, like giving healing to the waters. Then a woman comes to him, she's wearing black and red. She's very beautiful and she has long dark hair. She looks like a gypsy a little bit. Dark skin, darker skin, and she's like "We have to go now, we have to go somewhere." Like, like...feels like...they're in danger. Somebody wants to...to take them somewhere, and he's like "Oh, let me finish that and we...we can go somewhere else to hide."

M: So, he's going to finish up his work with the water and then they're going to go?

C: Yeah, yeah, he's making the water holy or something.

M: How is he doing that?

C: He's just putting his hands on top of the water without even touching it. Just sending energy to the water. He is putting the christ consciousness into the water. That's why it's cleansing. He's making the... the...how to say... something that has no substance, something [that] has no... no form and puts that into the form so that it becomes that. Yeah.

M: So, he puts this new energy into the...into the water.

C: He connects the...he connects what is on the physical realm with the spiritual realm let's say. He connects the two worlds. That's what he does. He brings this energy from up there down to Earth, and he puts his energy in some sacred places so the energy can be there when he will be gone, because he knows he's going to be gone. So, this space can hold his energy still and do the work. Yeah, that's what he's doing.

M: What else do you see happening?

C: It's... I see them hugging, um...the gypsy woman and him. They're sad, but not, at the same time. They know that sadness is something very human and is...they...they feel it, but they know what is beyond all this sadness and what's the purpose and they're very serious about their purpose, and they know kind of who they are and what they came to do, and they're hiding because...actually they want to kill the woman.

M: Tell me about that.

C: So, they're hiding because she's in danger. So... she was... I don't know what she was doing but a...maybe he's not allowed to be with her for some reason.

M: I wonder why he's not allowed to be with her.

C: Hmm...I don't know, maybe...I don't know why they're not allowed to be together, because they seem...they seem...they're...they're in love with each other and they have a good relationship, but umm...I don't know why they're not... They cannot be together somehow and there are people following, like a military to...or villagers, whatever they are, to...that's why they're hiding. He's...he's protecting her. He's taking her away from...some reason but she knows that he's going to die, and she has to stay. And that's why they're sad and they're hiding. But this sadness is not...it's...how to say it...they know...they're above their sadness. They're fine and at the same time, they're sad. They have a lot of faith. They have a lot of faith, yeah.

NEXT SCENE: JESUS IN PRAYER

C: This is...it comes to me in Greek, Oros Sina. This is a mountain. It's Jesus there, praying. And he seems, he lost his faith. He lost his faith; he's done with all of this. He's tired. He can't be with his love, because if he's with her they're going to kill her, so they can't be in public together very much. He lost his...his student kind of...he knows that some people will betray him and his fame about him is spreading out that he's a...it's true in what he says and he's just desperate and he's asking for help. He's asking the angels, the archangels to help him. He says, "My father denies to give me guidance." so he's calling the archangels for guidance. So, to help him, and...Gabriel comes to him. It's Gabriel above him to give him a message. He's really, really desperate; he's crying and he's losing the...it's this moment of crisis for him, where nothing works, and Gabriel tells him to trust, trust, trust. To trust who he is and what he came for on Earth and trust what he is doing and all this and...and love is something eternal; everything is love. He's falling into the human desire with the love a little bit, so it's giving him pain as well.

M: So, he's starting to be weighed down by the human experience of being in love and...

C: Yeah, yeah, exactly, exactly.

M: How does he respond to Gabriel's message?

C: He says, "That's the last time."

M: The last time for what?

C: I think the last time he does that or something. He's...he probably knows he's going to die soon so... He's...he's kind of done at the same time with his life, but also, he's attached to...to what others think of him and to love and to others...other emotions. He's confused now; that's why he lost the faith.

M: How does he know that his life is coming to an end?

C: So...he heard it. He told him that.

M: Who told him?

C: I think...I think his...his...his guides...or his ancestors or...other...the ones...his family from the stars, actually, the Sirians.

M: Tell me about that.

C: He says the Sirians are involved with that.

M: How are the Sirians involved? Go see it now.

C: I think they...they say that he's one of them. He's connected with the Sirians, and he came to bring the golden light to Earth, the same you are doing here. So, he was...he kind of knew he's going to have a short life, because that was...that was the purpose, and he just did it and nothing else...sometimes when he was speaking with angels or other stuff, they say they were speaking to him as well. So, it's a...

M: So, when the angelic beings were speaking with him also these Sirian extraterrestrials were?

C: Yeah, that's what they say, that it is all connected to that, and it just comes in the form of angels sometimes but actually, also for us, as the way we can take it because we are trained to...to be...to not be afraid of them. So that's why sometimes they come in form of angels, but they are actually our brothers and sisters from Sirius or from other galaxies sometimes also, that they're here to help and you know that already — that we're helping you so...so we do the same, and we are bringing this Christ Consciousness, but the name comes from Jesus and..because he had this mission, coming to Earth, and that's how it became...but this is something very old. This is something that is part of the whole and it's always been. It's nothing new. It's just a new story to humanity but it's not new. So yeah.

M: So, tell me what's happening next with Jesus.

C: So, he's...he's going down, down from this mountain; he's walking down. He's wearing some sandals and a long white...looks like a sheet from the bed actually, like a weird white thing with some gold strap here. Like ancient Greek a little bit also, looks like. He's covered his head; his head is covered with this white, like this, like the women do, the Eastern women and he seems like he got some power from this mountain. He seems like...determined to just go and do it, so he's going to find his students and prepare a special ceremony and talk to them about something, so he's going to do this now...ahhh...he's going to tell the students that he's going to die.

M: Tell me about it. What do you see happening there?

C: But he's going to come back afterward, so he's...he has to tell the students what he received at the mountain, the message kind of. Yeah, he will die, and they'll have to continue the work after he leaves. So, what...that's what he is going to do and the girl, the girlfriend or whatever...she is there as well, in the dinner, they're all there, all there, the students and her and...

M: Describe the room to me. What else is going on?

C: Maybe she's...maybe she's also a student of his, maybe she's also a student somehow, um...

M: What's happening in that room? Describe it to me. Is there a dinner?

C: It's...it seems like a very basic place, very poor. Seems like everybody is spread out; they're not all sitting at a table. They're spread out in this room, and they have a little table between two or three people and everybody seems worried. Mary Magdalene [first time she is called by her name] is touching the feet of Jesus and feeling very sad and then I see somebody eating an apple; there's...there are some animals also at the back there. Looks like a farmhouse or something. Looks very much...very basic...I don't know if it's wood, but it looks like destroyed wooden walls, and it's not really food; it's not like the dinners we have. They just have bread and olives I see. It's just very basic, and wine, red wine. And some fruit, they have fruits.

M: So, he's sharing the news with them?

C: Yes, so they're all...all spread out in the room, and they have a little food, and he's like "Come together, sit down." They are all sitting down, like in a circle, not on a table, on the floor, and he's like "You have to know, you have to know who you are, you have to know what you came here to do and nobody... nobody's superior to you. We're all one, and we are doing the same, and now I have to leave, and one of you will betray me for...for divine order, because it has to happen this way." without putting any shame or guilt to this person that will do it, because he has to do it for some higher purpose. And they're like, um...they're just freaking out with this information, and they're crying and Mary Magda...Mary Magdalene I said?

This woman... Maybe they became really furious, and she's...she's very cool about it. She's not reactive. She's sitting there, like she knows already these things; she's not reactive, and she's actually trying to understand who is going to do it, who is going to do the betrayal and she's very strong in her intuition, and she's looking to understand and it's...it's a man that looks very...a little bit ugly actually. Short, very...looks like he works in nature; he has a very strong body and also destroyed a little bit, from the sun, from scratches. He has curly black hair; his eyes are black, and he's...his face is kind of ugly... like... she recognized him, that it's him, he...he's going to do it. And he's angry, but he seems...you know they just look at their eyes kind of and he got it that she knows that it's going to be him and he's just behaving like weird...kind of, but the other ones, they don't understand that it's him, just like...being next to Jesus and trying to touch him and say "No, this is...maybe you got it wrong; this is not happening." So that's what's happening and..and they're just, um...trying to find a solution and he is saying that "This is nothing to find a solution for. This is the way it has to be; it's divine order; it's the law of the universe; it's the law of God."

M: How is this the law of God and law of the universe? Does he explain that?

C: Yeah, it's more like, it's all one and it has to...when something is not balanced some people have to come and bring the balance. The same with you guys, so it's like it's not balanced and it's a lot of war, a lot of killing, a lot of bad things happening back then, so he had to come to show love, that nobody else would talk about that before. So when the unbalance comes, somebody has to do...somebody or something has to come and do the work with the balance and he's...he's very much connected with...with the Sirius planet and it's very high intelligence beings that come and take on human forms through reincarnations and sometimes it's not just reincarnations, sometimes they just go in and out of human bodies just to be in certain missions [walk-ins], so they also do that.

M: So sometimes they just walk in?

C: Yeah, yeah, they do. They do. They can't really interfere. They can't really do much, but if you are sensitive you can feel them sometimes around and...it's hard for them also to show the way they look, because they don't want to scare you but when you see blue auras around they probably are them, even if you think that they're angels, it's just Sirians most of the times, yeah, not all of them...blue aura, yeah.

NEXT SCENE: ANGRY JESUS

C: I see...Jesus is very angry and he's going inside a temple and destroying the temple. He's doing that. He's very angry. It's a lot of cages with birds and stuff, and...ahh...they're doing, sacrificing animals there in this temple...probably... And he's like "What are you doing, why are you doing these things?" and he doesn't understand why they're doing these things and like they're killing these animals; they have these temples but they're still idiots, kind of, you know? So, he's...he's...he got super angry, very angry, and he's saying, "In the name of God I'm taking this down." and he's kicking, screaming, trying to...to destroy the temple and he's kind of done with the humans (laughs), seems like he's really like "These guys are really...they don't get it." Yeah, yeah, yeah.

M: And how does everyone respond as he has his temper tantrum?

C: Yeah, they're...they are looking like, freaked out, like what is he doing, you know? And some of them, they're saying, "He must be the Messiah, because he behaves this way, nobody ever did this way." Some of them really follow him afterward when he leaves and [they] say, "Tell us, what should we pray to, what should we do, because these gods didn't help; help us, look what is happening here." And he says "Ok, follow me and I'll show you." And some others, they stayed at the back and they're just like freaked out by what he did to the temple, you know? And they're going to call the militaries, militaries or whatever they are, ones from the village to search for him and see what's going on, why he...how he can do that to them.

NEXT SCENE: A WALK-IN EXPERIENCE

C: He's doing energy healing work. It's a woman that is not feeling well and they're desperate. They call him to help her and he's doing energy healing; he's not touching the body, he's just sending energy with his hands. Seems she's getting awake, she's alive now. She was dead...so she was dead or something or she was...she seems...she seems pretty good, like he just gave her the Light again, the light of life.

M: How does that work?

C: Yeah, this is weird what he does. He's reactivating the light inside the heart. So everybody has a light in the heart or this is closed, is blocked, and his role was to really light that flame from in the heart and so white light...white-golden light in the heart, and some people had to die because they were very closed in the heart and they couldn't stay and they were also um...creating more trouble for the other ones to find the light. So, it was like a big pandemic back then and a lot of people died from...from disease, because of that, because it had to clear up all the souls.

M: So, people were dying because their heart was closed?

C: I mean...kind of what's happening now, similar thing with the virus. Like some people had to...some souls have to leave because their heart is very closed and they're not helping the others to rise, also they're really putting the energy down, so they just have to leave. That's what happened back then as well, the same thing.

M: So, it's similar to what's happening now?

C: Yeah, it's very similar; it's very similar.

M: So, tell me what you're seeing...yeah, what you're seeing there?

C: And the Sirians are helping now as well, very much. That's why they're bringing so many um...let's say souls or intelligence from there.

M: So, Jesus was bringing this woman back to life? What do you see happening now?

C: Yeah, yeah. He's um...he's doing what I'm doing (moving hands in the air in mudras), but I don't know what I'm doing but he's doing this (laughs). He's doing this... and he's bringing back the Light. He's activating the Light in the heart. It's a...and this woman is like (coughs)...she's coughing and she's coming back to life, and her face looks young and beautiful and...she was very old before and now she's... she's still old, but she seems like the Light made her so beautiful, so different like a new soul came inside of her or something like that. So, what he says to me is that what he did, he let the old soul go to reincarnate somewhere else and he brought a new soul straight into the body. So, this woman will continue for a purpose to share the story but is another soul that came in. The other one actually died and a new one came, and this is a very common thing that you guys experienced already; it's happened also to you — where a different part of your consciousness came in.

M: What do you mean that we understand because it happened to us?

C: Like in terms of the person you were like ten years ago and the person you are now. It's a completely different consciousness and you can see that. That's exactly the same. You couldn't operate now with your old consciousness, so it had to recede and it had to die, and it had to die through a very strong depression, or that's how it dies usually or something that really hurts you or in...in the life, some events that put you really down and it allows this old thing to die and a...it's a different process for you guys because you have a different path than others but briefly it was like that. That's what Jesus was doing, and he was...he was working on the chakras that are the energy centers of the human body; he will open them one by one and connect them to the heart and open the heart. And this woman can spread this Light now, she has it already.

M: **That's wonderful.**

C: *That's the...that's the plan. The mission.*

M: **Very good.**

C: *He is putting three crosses on the heart, to seal it.*

M: **And what is this symbolism of the three crosses? How does that work?**

C: *This is the beginning of everything. This is like um...how all this got manifested. 'Because everything started from being nothing, it manifested like a little dot in the center and the first manifestation was like the cross, like the feminine and masculine energies then created the rest. This is the beginning of everything. This is a symbol also you can use for sealing your energy when you need to make a cross on your body. That will seal your energy field and keep it inside, keep it protected.*

NEXT SCENE: SHIFTING INTO MARY

C: *I feel and...I'm not Jesus anymore. I am...I feel I'm shifting between being him and the woman, because I'm...I'm feeling now anxious and I'm going to die then I'm going back into...I'm going in and out in different bodies I feel. So, I'm once the woman and once him and um...now I'm feeling very anxious because I feel I'm in the body of Jesus and he is walking barefoot and holding his cross going to the mountain to die, and then the woman... The woman behind is following the crowd, but he's...she's keeping a distance, so they don't recognize her somehow. Yeah.*

M: **How does it feel to be Jesus as he's on this walk? What does his inner guide feel like?**

C: *He's a...feeling a ha...a hand...on his head, giving him trust and support and saying this is an illusion and don't worry about the death because there's no death and you know about it in the first place, and he's telling him that he's one with Maria; he's never going to lose her because they're one and even when he dies he can be with her because he will see it from a higher perspective and he will understand that. Now he is in his human desires. He can't really have clarity because of that, but this is going to end soon, and he has to see it as a liberation, not as something that is a punishment to him because he's only done good, so he doesn't have to feel guilty. He has to release this...the guilt and see it as a liberation process and really just have fun with...because he knows the truth and he's...he's crying.*

M: And how is this for Mary? What is she going through as she follows?

C: She...she's very intuitive as I said, and she knows...she kind of knows already everything. She...she knows...she has this deeper knowing; she understands why this is happening and it's something beyond her desire to be with him, and she's...she has a lot of compassion and he's used her kind of strength in the same time like she's experiencing the deep sadness indeed, but some part of it knows that this is not real anyway; it's an illusion. She's fighting between two worlds.

M: And how does it feel in the crowd as he moves through? What does it feel like as he moves through this place?

C: The crowds are horrible. They're very angry. They're throwing things at him and screaming at him. They...it seems like they hate him.

M: Why do they hate him?

C: Because, um...they don't understand him. First, they think he's crazy, but then they think he's arrogant crazy, and then they think he's spiritually arrogant crazy. So, at these times this was not permitted, and he was speaking badly about their religion and beliefs and that was not permitted to happen back then, so...people...the human life didn't have so much...it was not precious so much these years. So, it was...it's not like now, they can kill like...for nothing. So, when somebody was different, they would kill him. Yeah, something like that.

NEXT SCENE: GOING TO THE CRYPT

C: I hear Mary Magdalene saying, "Let's go to the crypt." She's going... He's...he's already out of the body and she wants to go to the place his body is or something, because she wants to see what happened. She's sure that something is going to happen there. She's very happy actually. She's super happy and she says, "He told me, he's going to be there, let's go." and she's talking with another woman, older than her. She seems also very spiritual, like really into it, and they're going there; they're wearing black and it's a...illumination of...it's the body of Jesus is...it's...how to say...energy body, it is white energy, you can still see that it's him and he's changing faces to me now, he's like... I can see different...like Osiris; I can see Shiva; I can see different ones right...changing constantly like shuuu! They're very happy, they're just blind from the Light and he's saying, "There is no death. It's an illusion; you are the first to witness it and you are women, that's why you are the first to witness it."

M: Why are the women the first?

C: Because the women are more receptive, they're more connected, more understanding to spirituality than men, especially at these periods and because one was his love and the other was...I don't know, looks like a mother or something, or something from the family, so it was the dearest women of his life.

M: What happened to the physical body in the process once he was put into the crypt?

C: It's...I hear in Greek...the answer. It's called...it's...I don't know what to...how to translate it. Aya...ayase? It's like when somebody becomes a saint and the body becomes holy and kind of dissolves, because it has to show that is...when the body is holy it just dissolves somehow, that's what I hear. It just disappears somehow, dissolves, I see, disappears...and then...I don't know why it does that, that is what I hear, and he's... He's a...he's um...he's, he's showed himself on his kind of energy body, Lightbody, and he's very big as well, very big; he's very big, like...they're...they're blind from that...from the Light; it's big. It's like apocalyptic... It's like...whoa!

M: What was happening while his physical body was going through its dissolving process? What was his Lightbody doing?

C: He's...I see he is laying on the back; the physical body just starts (makes crumbling sounds) disappearing like this, eating...eating itself, and then the white soul body, it's a white body, just comes out of the tomb and rises up, and it's just in the air now. And he says, "I can be anywhere now." He doesn't have to walk; he can just be anywhere now. Like...seems like he's...tele...telekinesis. He's going very fast to different places, yeah.

M: So, he's able to travel anywhere very quickly?

C: Yeah, yeah, yeah, yeah.

M: So, when he appears to the women what happens next?

C: So, they...they're very happy. It confirms their faith and everything they were receiving. All the information they were also receiving from the angels, confirms what happened, and um...they're just very happy and very like...wow, it's true what he was saying. Like...they start believing... I mean, they believed even but now it's like whoa... "We have to give this... they ha... We have to tell the other students." And they had to tell the other students also and this has to be in books, in...it has to spread, this information. Slowly, because they will kill them as well, they have to be careful in the beginning, especially Mary has to be very careful.

M: So, what do they do?

C: Um... She decides to spend some time in isolation, so she will just process whatever happened and try to get guidance and hide to protect herself. Seems she's having a kid or something.

M: So, she's pregnant?

C: Hmm...seems like. She's...she's going into a cave to give birth to this baby that nobody has to know.

M: So, she's going to give birth to this child?

C: So, she's in the cave. She's pregnant. She's very happy. She's trusting as never before. She knows that she has to protect this kid, and she knows that she's going to die very soon as well. She knows she's not going to live very long for some reason. They know everything (laughs), and then what I see is they're sitting there and seems like some students are taking care of her. Like, she's in an isolated place, but they're going to bring her food. She's there with some animals. She's meditating all days; she's a refugee, like...protected there. And the baby is...needs to like...nobody needs to know about it and...

M: And why should nobody know about the baby?

C: Because they were not supposed to be together. Because he was a teacher, she was like...a woman from a...bad neighborhood or something I hear. Like not a very great background. Like she was from a place where very poor people live, they had no good behavior towards each other, a lot of violence...and they mistreated women there very much, so...

M: Has she given birth to the child yet?

C: She's um...she's having the pain now. And Jesus is there; he's there...like well...white (in his Lightbody form) He's supporting the process and talking to her. She's just freaking out (laughs) that she sees that.

M: How is he supporting the process?

C: He's...he's there for her, standing in front of her and he's...seems like he's taking out the baby and holding it with his hands somehow, and he also says nobody has to know about that. Because if they knew, they would kill the baby, that's the thing. They would kill the baby if they knew about the baby.

M: So, tell me about this baby. What do you notice about it?

C: It's like um...it's blond, with curly hair and blue eyes. It doesn't look like her at all. She's more dark-skinned and brown, you know. They spend a lot of time there in isolation with animals and support of students bringing food and support there. It seems that she's sick now. The baby is like five or something.

M: And what is the sex of this baby?

C: He's a boy. Yeah, I see a boy, yeah. She knows she's going to die and what it's going to do...she's worried about the baby. She's doing some channeling and asking what to do. One of the students, he's going to have to take care of the baby. I hear Yacov, in Greek, I don't know what it is. So probably him, he's going to take care of the baby. She has to leave the body for some reason and the baby is going to learn with the student of him and be now undercover and continue the work for him. That's what he says.

Christ-Magdalene Bloodline

The bloodline of Yeshua and Mary had to be protected to secure the ascension of humanity. I imagine that part of the reason why information regarding the precise number of children is blurry has to do with the information being enshrouded to protect the lineage.

It is similar to how some psychic information is being blocked or limited when looking at the future ascension timelines. Many beings would do harmful actions if they had the exact information, so I believe the information is being "fragmented" to protect the work that has been done thus far with the genetic enhancements. More will come out over these next years!

TWENTY-SIX

Esther the Essene

I had the pleasure of working with Neomi several times over a few years both in-person and remotely via video conferencing software. When I work with clients repeatedly, I use a keyword to induce them quickly into a trance state. As I say the agreed-upon phrase, the client immediately begins to drop into a hypnosis trance. I can tell because the face and body posture soften, their eyes begin to flutter, and the energy of the room begins to shift. At this point, I can either suggest that we move to a specific time and place, or I can ask that we be taken to the most appropriate time for us to learn. Typically, I like to use the second option so that the higher realms can show me what is most important to be shown. After researching what "spontaneously" shows up, I guide the client to specific times that I want to research. Most of the times that I did this with Neomi, she most often went back to the same lifetime as Esther.

Esther lived in a small, private community that seemed to be a spiritual community. Her mother and teachers taught her to work with herbs for healing. As she grew up, she was taught more advanced skills of meditation and telekinesis, moving objects with her mind. There was a powerful storyline including a deep bond with her sister and best friend, Rae. As a young girl, Esther was abused and raped and ended up producing a child, a young boy named Josiah who she gave to another healer in the area who would raise the boy and train him in advanced psychic and esoteric arts. She described the woman as a powerful medicine woman who wore raven feathers in her hair. In the middle of the second session, she gave me the name of her community and the story of her relationship with Jesus began to be told.

What you will read here is a reduced summary of all of the sessions I did with Esther. Esther deserves her own book and maybe someday I will get to it. For now, I share with you some of the lost stories of Jesus through the eyes of his dear friend and student, Esther.

Esther shared that the human collective at the time was extremely polarized and fear-based. The Romans and the rabbis spread messages of fear throughout the region. Jesus had been traveling through the region sharing teachings of love, faith, and community, and people were beginning to come together as Jesus seeded these new ideas into the collective consciousness.

The first scene was when she was a young girl, maybe four or five years old, and Jesus has come to visit her community, which she calls Qumran. Jesus meets with each family and marks certain members of each family, children included, with a cross on their forehead by gesturing with his hands. He explains to young Esther as he marks her that she will be working with him in the future to do healing work.

When I move her forward to the next scene, she is a bit older and is working for a "king" in the kitchen of what she calls a palace close to the temple. She secretly works with different people by doing hands-on healing work and sharing spiritual guidance. While working in the kitchen, there is a lot of excitement about an important visitor who is coming to meet with one of the rabbis for a Passover dinner. The rabbi shares that "The Nazarene is coming!" Esther is confused because she had never heard of a man with this title and the rabbi was acting like a king is coming over.

When Jesus arrives, she comments on how bright his energy is. Jesus recognizes her energy signature that she holds and remembers her from Qumran. He requests that she gather a few women together to meet privately later that evening in the kitchen.

NEXT SCENE: MEETING WITH THE WOMEN

C: *We were able to gather nine women, so there are eleven of us together, and we have drinks for all of them, water, and some bread. He comes in, and he's just so glad to see us all. He has us stand together in a giant circle and hold hands. The kitchen is very...it's generously large here, so we are able to do that. He has us bow our heads and breathe in and center ourselves and just feel how united we are together, and to feel our hearts combine together as one.*

So, we breathe into this meditation, and as we do you can just feel...just a warm, warm energy ripple through everyone — through our hands and through our hearts, and it just feels like we're on a different plane. It's just so amazing. So, he has us breathe into this for quite a while, and we just all sit down together in a large circle, and he asks us if anyone has any questions...if anything has come up that they have any specific questions on.

One woman raises her hand and says that it's so hard to believe in anything when the soldiers come around so often and then the rabbis ask for things. So, she feels she has so little, that it is so difficult to keep going some days knowing that she's just working so hard, long hours, just to have everything taken.

He says, "Well, did you have adequate food today and shelter?" And she says, "Yes." He says, "How are your neighbors? Did you speak with them today?" She says, "Yes." And he says, "Do you have a loving family around you?" And she says, "Yes. I do." And he says, "You have all of these things. You have love. You are so rich." He said there are others who don't even have a fraction of that and to possibly consider every morning upon waking, just pause...pause and maybe kneel down and go inward. Think of the things that are surrounding her and be grateful for just a little while before starting her day. Just that small amount of gratefulness and love and appreciation for everything will spread throughout the day.

If you don't find...if you just find it difficult to keep going...just turn to your neighbor or to your family and just speak to them...and ask them for some uplifting words. So many people keep the fear inside and if you would just speak up and ask. Just tell your neighbor how you feel; they'll be more than happy to give an uplifting word, or maybe invite you over for a moment and just listen. If we can all stay together as one and unite in love, every day will be easier to go on. Have faith. When you don't have faith, just maybe kneel down and go inward. Just go inward and feel that light that's within you.

You, as women, have the most amount of intuition and you can feel the subtle differences in energies and people's feelings. So, when you go out, if you see in someone's eyes that their light is slightly dim, then approach them and ask them if they can use a hug or would they like to talk. Just reach out to them. I think that will help everyone to stay together.

If you hear any new information, speak with each other and spread that energy information, and just sit with each other. Don't isolate yourself. If the soldiers come by, that is difficult, but just know...don't lament in it. Just know that tomorrow is another day, and you are loved, and you have light inside you, and you can spread that light. In each day you can choose to do so, or you can choose to live in fear. When you choose to spread that light, that light will grow, and it will touch one person to the next person to the next and create this grand light, this loving light, and the kindness will spread. And eventually, the soldiers' grip will weaken on everyone. They won't be able to keep up a stronghold for very long. The kingdom will crumble. So, keep faith within each other so you can rise up and live in peace and ease one day. Know that it is coming.

He's saying that he must leave. If we have any questions...but everyone seems satisfied with the lessons he has talked to them about. He did go on to say that everyone is capable of healing with their hands — that their hands are another chakra, and so he encouraged us women to get together regularly and speak to each other and possibly, just work with our hands. I know how to do the healing, so I think I'll try to lead up the women's group and show them the general steps of how to work with healing energy.

I'm very intimidated by this because we're supposed to be...we have to be discreet. We have to be very discreet. There are nine other women here besides my sister and me, but I believe if we meet a few times, we can gain trust within the group, and I can show them the healing so that they can go out and spread the healing, even if they start with their families and move outward. But if they can heal and work with the children especially, so that the children have this knowledge and then they can go out and just change how things are when they're older. That maybe they can go against the grain and understand that there doesn't need to be separation, even though there will be for a long, long, long, long time, but just putting the idea in their heads of the equality and the healing — that they're able to heal themselves and have faith. So, the women are disbursing and they're leaving.

NEXT SCENE: WALKING THROUGH JERUSALEM

C: *We're in Jerusalem. On my way home though, I see a man speaking with some of the council for the temple...and then I realize, it's Jesus. He notices me...you know...I have to walk past them. So, I'm walking up and he looks at me and says, "I'll talk to you later on this afternoon." But he doesn't say it out loud. It's telepathic. So, I acknowledge that, and I walk past, and I go to my living quarters...*

So later on in the evening Rae and I go into the temple to eat. So, she comes back, and we go in to do that and we're...We got there late so we missed the supper with everyone, so we just grab some of the leftover food and we're just eating. And he [Jesus] enters in the kitchen and he just talks to us briefly. He acknowledges us because he knew us from when we lived with our parents in Qumran. So, we're just chatting with him nonchalantly. So, he's going to be staying at the temple for three days, and he just asked if we'd like to sit in on the women's meeting. So, we'd love to do that, so we'll meet up tomorrow. So, we'll see him then.

NEXT SCENE: A CLASS ON SELF HEALING FROM JESUS

C: *Well, there's a handful of women and we're in someone's home. He's saying thank you so much for coming because I know that...this sort of set-up for women in the city is frowned upon. He thanks us for coming and for being discreet. He's just so happy to see us. So, he just wants to talk to us about some updated teachings that he has. He said he was traveling in the far, far East. He said he wanted to talk to us about energy work and channeling the divine into yourself to heal yourself. So, he wanted to show us some basic things and go over them to help us with stuff to use.*

M: What did he share with you?

C: *He started talking about going into meditation. He has his hands at heart center and he's just looking down. His gaze is towards his fingertips and he's just breathing in, starting to relax. He's sitting upright. Then he starts going into a chant. He's saying, "Om Shanti." So, he's chanting that a few times, and then he picks his head up and he puts his hands down on his knees and he just starts breathing. And he explains to us to breathe in and breathe in all the air around you and pull your energy inward. So, he's showing us how to breathe in, inhaling in, and pulling your energy inward, and exhaling that just around you so that your energy is concentrated inward towards you.*

Then he's saying, if we could lie back, if there's enough room, and start by placing your hands on your heart. Then he's showing us to breathe in there and feel any changes and to fully, fully relax and to release any fears that we may have and just understand that everything is God's will and divine plan and it's set up. So, we mustn't worry about things that don't make sense to worry about because it's out of our control.

(This next part seems more comfortable sitting upright.) Then he's having us put our hands upon our shoulders and he's saying to breathe in here and to open your elbows outward...so don't crunch over, so be open to the energy and breathing in here. He's inviting us to feel the energy flowing down our hands, down our fingertips, and back into us. And he's explaining its divine energy.

Then he's putting his hands on the back of his neck, down by your spine and he's breathing in there. And then he has his hands go up behind his head. So, putting his thumbs in the little notch in the base of the skull and all of his fingers...so all four fingers pointing upward towards the crown. So, he's like pressing into the zeal and then he's directing the energy upwards towards the crown and having it stay there.

And then putting the hands on the head...so your fingertips are pointing up towards the back of your head and your thumbs are outward...and breathing in there. Then over your face, touching right above your eyebrows and cupping your hands over your eyes. Then at the jaw...and then down at your solar plexus, sacral chakra, and root chakra and then out to your hips. And then bending one leg at a time and holding each foot...and staying a really long time at your feet.

And then bringing your knees to your chest and running your hands from your feet all the way up to your knees and then extending your legs and running your hands up your whole entire body, all the way up, past your crown and extending your hands and breathing in the divine energy all through you. So, he's showing us how to do that.

And then afterwards, when we're feeling energetic...if people are ill or things of that nature, working with them. So that's what he went over and then he said he'd follow up and teach us more the next time he comes...because he's supposed to be going and learning more information soon. So, he'll have more to share with us...and keep us up to date.

Then some people are asking about his journey, if he will, in fact, be coming through because it seems like there is pressure on him by the soldiers and government and people in charge. But he said he'll be able to still come through, nonchalantly...and keep teaching us so we can work behind the scenes to heal people.

M: Does he share where he will be traveling to?

C: *He said it's far, far off into the East. So, he said it would be months before he was back, but he was already there for a few months, so he learned the beginnings of this energy work. So, he wanted to share it with everybody and then he'll go for further training soon when he was ready. So, this is wonderful, because you can definitely feel the energy pulsing through you and such a connection, so this will be wonderful to share with people and I think they'll be very receptive to it.*

M: Wonderful. You said he was working with other people and

helping them with their illnesses. How's he doing that? Tell me what happened.

C: *He's going by each person and speaking with them, and it's typically...if someone has an illness, it's usually because they have an imbalance that's manifested into their body. So, he'll usually speak to them and find out what spiritual dis-ease they have and speak with each person to reassure them of Spirit and then by holding their hands and using this energy that he is channeling, he's able to work to heal the person. But it's usually never of the body, it's of the spirit.*

NEXT SCENE: LEARNING WITH JESUS

C: *He [Jesus] comes to my women's meetings when he comes into town. He always speaks at them. He has just come back from the Far East, and this has been his fourth time there. So, he has shown us different mudras with your hands and just a few basics that he has learned the last time. He was telling us some mantras, but he was really explaining last time about meditation and how that was the most important way to connect with Source and the universal energy and the Light. The pure, pure loving Light.*

So, everyone is sitting on blankets and he's getting comfortable on a blanket in front of the room and I'm sitting beside him. He asks if anyone has had any experiences with their meditations where they have had visions other than their surroundings.

A woman raises her hand and says that yes, she's experienced seeing different beings and was confused on what that was because it wasn't anything that she's seen and it was slightly alarming, but they meant no harm. He said as you get into your meditations you may start to travel. He explained to us that though we were "fresher" so-to-speak to the Earth that we had had other lifetimes and so many times you'll travel to those lifetimes. He made us aware that you could ask questions. You could explore in the lifetime when you're in your meditation, and if anything alarming comes up, then just slowly come out or just observe it with love.

So, he was explaining this to us, and he was saying that we had...with using our energy work so much...and doing the work, meditating, and having a regular discipline that we would see more and more but then also, on occasion, see less in others. Not seeing them as lesser but seeing less in their eyes. That as we brightened and became more awake, we would notice when someone was not awake yet and there would be a dullness within them. What was most important was that it was our job to be friends with those people and be kind and just glowing and radiating this oozing, positive light so that they would be intrigued by it. Then, possibly, down the road being able to offer them a healing or praying with them...offering to pray with them to help bring this awareness and awakening to them.

So now that we were at that point where we were experiencing visions, it was now time to share it with others in a friendly manner that they would understand, to be nonchalant. That was most important. That's what he was learning in the Far East is to interact with others, naturally, but yet weaving in the Light so that it was slowly resonating with them and bringing them to a conscious awareness. He invited us to go out and subtly work with others and interact with them. He said it will be difficult and just be as nonchalant as possible, slowly weaving it in.

So, a lot of us, you know, the people there being women, we're hustling through our work throughout the day and feeding people and this and that. So, he said it will take the utmost patience, so we need to step back and just be patient and just keep weaving it in and keep weaving it in and just like a weaver weaves, we will have beautiful, beautiful cloth full of light and just the most radiant, beautiful light by the end of our lifetimes and that's why we're here. That's the point, our purpose here this lifetime. It sounded simple enough but very difficult to undertake. Especially in the area where we were living in because we just had to be nonchalant about our work as it is.

NEXT SCENE: MEETING WITH JESUS AND MARY

C: All the women, and it's a huge group — much bigger than when we first started. There are maybe forty women just crammed into our kitchen area and we are waiting for Jesus to come and talk to us and let us know the new information he received from the East. And we're talking amongst ourselves. Our focus, mainly, is the exploration of the energy work. There is a handful of women, the ones I usually go talk to, that are masters in different aspects. And we're trying to teach everybody how to get back to those original abilities. So, I am excited to see what Jesus will say about any new modalities we are able to incorporate or add, maybe that I could learn.

Finally, he's arrived. We allow him to come in and have some water and rest a moment from his travels. I go over to him and embrace and express...wait a minute...entering in with him is Mary! She has never come to one of our meetings before!

M: Describe her to me. What does she look like?

C: *She has this radiant energy. She has this kind of olive-ish skin, long, dark hair and is slender. You can tell she radiates this indescribable mystic energy. Just really...she's very indescribable. She comes in and smiles, and she's wearing a cloak. She slides down the hood and all the ladies are in awe because we didn't know she was going to come as well.*

She has large gold hoop earrings. There's an Egyptian look to her as she has on her face lining around her eyes and some green mineral on her eyelids, but not heavily, just really lightly. She just looks really regal and beautiful, and yet, very humble and just like one of us.

So, Jesus starts laughing because I am so surprised she is there. And he's like, yes, he just wanted to wait a moment until she came in. He knew I would be excited to meet her. So, I go over and embrace her, and you can just feel this radiant energy pulse through you when you touch her.

And she just wanted to come tonight to talk. The palace has a huge staff, so she wanted to slide in as one of the staff so that she could work with us for the next three or four days so that we could learn the energy work that she and Jesus use to assist people in healing, but also to shift their perspective so that they understand that they're not needing to be held down by the rules of the palace and the city. That they can transcend the mundane and they can rise above them, and it doesn't need to be in a violent or way of an upheaval, just in their regular, everyday lives. We are just elated.

Jesus starts to talk about how he went east and worked with the monks but there were also people visiting from the Far East visiting the monks that he worked with as well. So, it was kind of a culmination of Chinese and new energy. A lot of the women know a little bit about energy work, so he just goes over breathing and a meditation practice to connect to the energy as usual and things that we already know to do with the hands and that.

He said that he had a new energetic overlay that allowed him to increase his frequency and vibration, so he wanted to pass that to each of us so that our energy would be enhanced, and he was going to show us how to do that energetic overlay. He uses me as his model for this.

He puts one hand on my chin and one hand on my crown, well a little bit more towards the back than that, and he starts there and then he covers both ears. Then he has one hand on the back of my head, on my occipital ridge, and then one on my third eye.

And then he places his left hand over my heart in front. The feminine he said. And then the backside of you, being the will, his right hand — the male aspect. And so, he places his left hand on my heart and his right hand on the back of my heart chakra, on my back.

And here in the work, he does the overlay. He is just breathing, and you can feel the energy going through him and right into my body. And so, I feel this most like, what nowadays it would look like, a digital overlay of a person laying on this radiant gold, yet there's an intertwining of a blue, like a light teal — a beautiful, radiant blue, with it as well.

So, I feel such a huge difference after this. And just with those hand motions, the opening up of the pineal gland to help bring this energy into the heart is the purpose of touching the head so I can work with all of the glands to help inform the aura and all of the energetic layers...about guiding them, about letting the energy guide the person.

This energy is just radiating through me so much I can barely speak to the group or anyone. It's as if my skin is shaking...vibrating, and I can feel my bones become warm. I can feel it in my heart, just this radiant opening. I can physically feel it, and I can feel the energy rise up my spine, all the way to the crown of my head. And it fuses each chakra as it goes up with the radiant new energy. It's really almost overwhelming, and yet it feels so good.

He's laughing and putting his hand on my shoulder and asking if I am okay. I tell him I just need a minute. The ladies give me some water. He said it's a very moving practice. After engaging with someone you should probably let them rest for a while, to assist with the energy.

For the sake of the meeting, I attempt to re-ground myself. He tells us that Mary is going to stay with us for a few days so that she can work with people individually. And as we learn how to do that, spread it amongst our group and do it to each other and infuse each person with this...this new overlay of energy, to raise the vibration in the city because there are so many ladies here, and then we're encouraged to work with others.

There are many people that the ladies work with, but we can't have everyone come to the meeting as we don't have enough space. But my skin is still buzzing. My bones feel so warm, they are almost hot. I feel like I am levitating.

In this next scene, Esther is reunited with her son Josiah whom Esther had previously sent to be raised by another woman who wore black raven feathers in her hair who was to teach Josiah advanced healing and psychic skills.

NEXT SCENE: TRAVELING WITH JESUS AND MARY

C: I have gone back from the meeting to the Essenes' community with Jesus and Mary. We worked with everybody and they're going to do these overlays. He brought me back because he and Mary wanted to talk to me about something. They wanted to ask if I would travel with them south, towards Egypt.

I ask what the purpose of this trip was, and he said he wanted to work with the energy of the pyramids and gain insight from a contact that he had there. He thought the ladies had their meetings and that handled, but it was time for me to do some other things now and to travel around to teach.

I tell him I will return back the next day with my answer. He will be there for a few more days so there is no rush. I enjoy looking into the other rooms of the community and see the younger people get training on things that I know.

And then I ask Josiah...he coordinates, or matches, the children with the masters. There are so many masters there that know different things; they are experts in different modalities. And so, Josiah can intuitively tell what strength each child has, or young person, and then he matches them with the master.

And Josiah is much older now...and so I wonder what happened to him after he left the woman with the raven feathers. So, he is managing that. So, I talk with him at length 'cause that's my son and I ask him how he is doing and it's wonderful to see him.

And he invites me, instead of going back, if I would just write a letter to my sister to make arrangements so I can stay in his quarters so we can refresh our connection. So, I tell him yes, that would be wonderful, so I compose a letter to my sister, and they send a courier. The courier has to travel at night because the Roman soldiers are still out there. They are hanging out amongst the rocks now. They are not stirring up or doing anything.

So, I ask him what new things the masters are teaching since I have last been there. It's been quite a while. And he was delighted to show me. And we go into different rooms, and in the first room, he told me well before we were at the doorway, on approaching, to be extremely quiet. One master was working with this young child, and he was levitating an orb above the table. Scrying into it.

So, the master was showing him what his lesson was for today — how to move the orb — to move it to the left, to the right, to try to control it with his mind. So, I watched that for quite a while; it was wonderful.

And then the next room, he said that this is new and slightly controversial within the community. The master was working with the child to move air. Well, they're not in a room, they are in a courtyard. And in the courtyard, this master was working with this child to control the weather, so if they needed a cloud to come by for shade, or something of that nature, is what they were working on in the sky.

And it wasn't seen upon as evil, it was just very...obviously because they were teaching it, there were just some questions attached to that. But there was only one child that was able to work with it, so it would never be in a negative way obviously. But in conversation people debate and ask questions about it.

So, it's getting to be supper time and he says he'll show me more in the morning, and we just go to eat with everyone, and we just catch up, and I stay. And in the morning my sister was waiting for the courier, and she sent a letter straight back encouraging me to travel and she would take care of everything and why would I even worry about it, but I am so close to her it is almost like we are one sometimes and it is hard to separate.

So, after we break our fast in the morning, I am drinking water and some small amount of cheese and vegetables; I talk with Mary and Jesus and tell them I will be embarking with them on their trip. And so, I enjoy some time to relax with Josiah before I need to get ready to go.

They have extra clothing and all sorts of things and so I don't need to go back to the palace to get my things. And since I've come along in this life, I used to carry talismans with me, and I just see no need for that anymore. I just like to do the work directly.

I accept the clothing they have in the community and enjoy an evening with Josiah, and we are to head out in the morning. And there is some talk about whether the soldiers are going to disrupt anything, and so we decided last minute to go ahead and leave at night. And it will be much cooler then anyway. I hug my son and we head out onto this journey.

The journey is so long. I know we will get there, but it just seems that it's taking so long. But what breaks up the monotony is that we are able to stop and visit different people in different cities, so that's been wonderful. I spend more time talking with Mary at length. We know all the same energy work and healing techniques already, but she radiates this different, purer vibration and it's so wonderful to be in her presence.

She has such a pleasant disposition. Everywhere she goes people can feel her radiate and she brings joy to everyone without even really having to do anything. I ask her how her children are, and she says they are doing very well, and they are going to be coming to the Essene community within the year to begin their training. Right now, they are having to be discreetly held.

M: How many children did she have?

C: *Three. Two boys that are older. Not old. Maybe, at this time, twelve and thirteen. And a daughter who is nine. The daughter will continue the energetic lineage. So will the boys but they will end up being masters in the Essene community, and the girl will travel and teach. So, I am very excited that her children will be coming soon, and she is too because she does miss them terribly. She knows she will see them soon.*

So, it's a long journey. Discreetly stopping in cities and towns. It tickles me. I love traveling and adventure. It is amazing how many people they know — that we arrive in different towns along the way, and we can immediately make our connection and can have places to stay and have an enjoyable evening or daytime until we travel again. But we generally travel at night so that we can be most discrete.

We finally arrive in Egypt and a big market. So, we travel at night and now it's morning. So, this is a huge market, and we go in to get something to eat and then we're to find our friend there. The market is so beautiful. It's like nothing I have ever seen before. The fabrics. The food comes from all over. It's so exotic and beautiful. I want to stay here. I want to just stay in this city.

We go and find our friend who happens to work and oversee what happens inside of the pyramid — the specific rituals that take place and also ritualistic practices that are more spiritual. So, we meet him. We are at his home where he resides. He gives us all beds and we rest for the day because it has been such a long journey. He will feed us and let us rest for a few days before we explore the pyramids.

M: Does he share his name with you?

C: *It starts with an A. Arul? Yes, Arul. And he is such a kind man. He is our age. Jesus and Mary. It seems that we are in our early thirties. I feel like I am thirty-*

six, but I don't think so. I think I am younger than that.

He is so kind and he takes us back to the market and shows us all the new and exotic things that have come in. And he says that tomorrow we are going to go into the pyramid, and he is going to show us what he has been receiving.

And so, the next morning, before dawn even, we discreetly go to the pyramid with him, and we go down in. I thought you would just walk into the pyramid, but you don't. You go down, down, down, down, and there's all these different corridors.

We go into a special chamber that has a beautiful marble altar in it, in the middle of the room. It's a table for you to lay on, an altar for you to lay on so you can receive the energy. He asks if Jesus wants to go first, and he says yes. So, he gets up onto this slab and Arul holds his ankles. And he is just standing there holding his ankles, and he says that all of the work will be done automatically because where we're at in the pyramid is directly under the center. So, he says just relax and wait and the energy is going to beam down into him, into his heart, and radiate through his heart.

And so, after a moment of breathing, you can see this bluish light coming down from the center. You can't see it physically, but you can sense that it is there. But you can see it going into his body, and it creates this ruby-red energy that permeates him. At first, it's uncomfortable for him. He curls up slightly onto his side, but Arul grounds him with his energy and says to just lie back and relax.

And he says that this energy is going to allow him to upgrade the energy of others, and we will be able to do so as well. All of a sudden there's a flash...like a camera flash, and Arul has to take Jesus off the table. He looks exhausted.

So, in the early morning, before we were doing this, Arul had said there is a specific astrological configuration where energy is the strongest. So, it may take a few days for us to recover. Jesus is literally just like lying on the ground limp, but he's smiling and nodding his head. So, he's okay. I just think that the energy is so strong and concentrated he's just taking some time before he's alright.

Arul says he needs to get someone else on quickly. Mary goes ahead and goes on. The same thing with her. Arul holds onto her ankles and this beam of light comes down, and she starts to shake. She doesn't keel over with the energy. Her whole body is shaking and convulsing, so it seems to know what everybody needs. So, her session is shorter, but it's just as powerful.

Arul lifts her off the table and places her next to Jesus, who's starting to come back. And then it's my turn. After seeing this, I am a bit nervous. He holds onto my ankles, and I feel like my body starts to spin. My head is in one place, but my body is rotating. My head is the focal point. My body is starting to dial round in a circle like the hands on a clock.

I can sense this essence coming. It's like starting to be a tornado, and then the light hits directly into my heart space and it hurts. Through my whole body, it's painful. It's so strong. All the way down to my bones. It flushes everything out of my body and creates this pure radiance. My body starts to shake. not convulsing like Mary's. Like a vibrational hum, small shaking, and then it goes away.

So, I understand how the others felt because you can't move. So, Arul takes me off the table, puts me down next to Jesus and Mary. They've almost come back online. We just lay there. I am not shaking like on the table, but I am still shaking.

A few minutes go by. We start to come back and feel more grounded. And Arul said that this energy for him opened up the chakras in his hands so brilliantly that he said everything and everyone he touches can feel it, and his energy work is so much more powerful now.

So, we thank him, and he invites us back to the place where he resides so we can rest for the next few days.

Our bodies hurt and our energy bodies are aching, but we feel good just the same. Arul said for him it was three days, but for us, it is four to five days to assimilate the energy. We are just laying around, eating minimal but drinking a lot of tea and water. The water is infused with different flowers that Arul gets from the market, to create a high vibration, to help infuse us with that.

Finally, on the fifth day, we are able to leave Arul's place and just go to the market so we can go out and get some fresh air. And we feel radiant but in such a way that when you're coming upon someone, I have telepathic and visionary talents and skills, but almost you can't look at one person and not but know their entire life and know why they are there and what they need assistance with and know all about them just by connecting with their energy.

It's very interesting, and it's almost a little overwhelming to be at the market. And Mary asked, "What are you experiencing?" And I told her, and she is experiencing the same thing. She said it's almost like instantly you know that person's entire life and what they need.

Sorry, I thought that Jesus came to the market too, but Jesus stayed back with Arul to speak with him.

Mary and I are practicing, so to speak, so we pick the same person and then we report to each other about what we saw and about their life and about what they need right now. And we're exactly experiencing the same thing with each person, so this new ability is fascinating. It will be so helpful in healing others and getting to the root of the problem they thought they had but seeing what actually is causing the problem, and so being the most efficient healers we can be.

It's like everything is very bright, almost like looking at life through this white tunnel of light. Almost like we can look upon the Earth in this otherworldly sense. Almost like we are watching ourselves in our human bodies from afar. We are knowledgeably speaking and interacting, but yet we are sitting in the heavens watching — watching it play out like we're watching TV. But we are aware of what we are feeling and what we are experiencing. It's just this connection to Source and divine energy that's really phenomenal because we can toggle our view from that aspect or come into our human body.

M: Makes sense to me. What happens next?

C: We are going to head back. We are going to stay for just a little bit. And Arul says everything that we are experiencing is what he experienced as well. He asked what we thought about bringing people there. We said it's just such a long journey for people to travel there but we would definitely spread the word about it and maybe those that could travel easily would go. And Jesus said he knows that the monks would be interested in coming and their journey would take a very long time but maybe they could stop and stay in the community for a week or so and carry on. He was excited to show them.

He asked Arul if there was a way to take the energy with you or experience that elsewhere, and Arul says that no, it's only in the pyramid, you have to come. And Mary asked what if you replicate a pyramid? And Arul said you may receive the energy, but it would not be in such a heavily concentrated way. We thank him so much for showing the information to us. We are getting ready to depart and we're going to head back to the community.

NEXT SCENE: WORKING WITH THE ESSENE CHILDREN

C: All these kids having fun. They're having fun because we're working with them with the beautiful mystical powers that they have, and they are just elated to be able to put their talents into action. And they're so happy that they're accepted and that there are adults around them to support them, and it makes me happy to see that they can be here — that the world's not so heavy — that they can have fun and they're in a supportive environment. There are all these teachers around them to love them.

M: Sounds very special. What do you see as you look around? What kind of place are you in?

C: I'm in the community — that Essene community. I'm in a courtyard, like an open area; it's not big. So, it's not really a courtyard, but it's an open area. And each child is working individually with teachers on all kinds of different things. So, I'm with one girl, and we're working on the weather and the movement and control of the clouds, and I'm also explaining the proper ways to do that. Where you're not interfering with nature, where it's just helpful if we need a little bit of water or something of that nature.

M: How do you discern whether it's helpful or not helpful?

C: Just get a feeling from the energies around, just an intuitive feeling that if things are really dry, I can ask if it's appropriate to...if we can have some rain, and then I just can feel. I can feel that's appropriate. So, it's not from a person. It's just from the energy that surrounds us.

M: Tell me what is happening as it happens as you let the scene continue.

C: I'm working with her, and I asked already earlier in the day if we can work with her about the rain. They said yes. So, I'm showing her how, by sending energy through her gaze in her hands, to manipulate the cloud, and maybe put a few together to condense it smaller so that it'll rain in a specific place. She's able to hover it close to the garden, and then I help her reel it in over the garden. Then we concentrate the energy even more and it rains a little bit on the garden, just as much as we need it and maybe to fill up some vessels that we have there, so we have some water saved.

There's another boy working with a man, and he's actually creating visible energy between his hands, not a glowing energy, like in electricity, like fibers, like lightning, electricity between his hands. And it's not hurting or burning him, but he's just working with that. And they've got these small boxes, it's like a box with... I'm too far away to see but there's a piece of metal in it and a wire and he can send the actual electricity to this little lamp-type box and then it illuminates. So, from the energy, they have a lamp. Some teachers have these in their places where they stay, their rooms, not many. So, he also wants to work with the boy and tells the boy that part of his duty is to...they're going to learn to build more of these lights so that we can have evening light in that community.

Another woman is working with this little girl on medical, healing ailments, but this is different. She's working specifically through the heart space to then heal the body. We do energy work all the time, but this is a little bit different because it's not science, it's through the heart specifically. She's getting into the person that they're working with, another teacher.

She's focusing her energy so strongly, almost like in a meditation, on the teacher's heart space. The teacher has part of his hand blackened. I'm not familiar with what that is, but she's getting into his heart with her energy healing but also power. There's a power behind that, not just the regular energy healing we do. It's deeper than that and more intensified, and she's able to almost place her essence or her being into his heart to then correct and talk to him about the emotions and what happened that caused his hand to go black. It's almost like she's in a trance when she's doing it, then the black starts to go away and she comes out of the trance. It's almost right before your eyes; it just fades back to flesh. And she comes out of the trance and she's exhausted.

There's one more teacher working with a few kids on telepathy, so he's having them talk to us at random for practice. So, I hear one of them ask me what my favorite color is, so I answer back purple via telepathy. I'm comfortable with it. Some of the other teachers, you can notice, I can see as I look around, that they perk up because they're hearing the question, but they don't feel confident that they can answer back but they just have to think of the answer, and he'll know. The child will know what it is. So, most of the teachers have certain things that are their forte. Some teachers think they can't do everything, but everybody can. It's just a matter of what you're going to work on. Then someone comes out in some robes like we wear and announces that it's time for afternoon meditation, for break, and so we're done with school for the day. Everyone retires back to where they stay. Some people stay in this open area. It's just a free time for everyone to either meditate or pray or whatever they like to do, visit with others before dinner.

M: Let's learn some more. Let's close that scene and move to the next scene that has information. Be there now. Where are you?

C: We're still there but at a different time. There's a big uproar in the community because the child that works with the electricity accidentally killed another child with it by accident. Now there's a big uproar about using the special powers and the other special talents in the community and a handful of coordinators are trying to figure out what to do there because this is really awful. The healers are trying to work with the child that was affected, but they're not able to bring them back. So, this is very upsetting, and the child is extremely distraught because it was his friend. He didn't mean to do it.

M: So, this is something you all are able to do, is to bring people back?

C: *Sometimes, yes, but in this case, his power was so strong that I don't know that the healers will be able to bring them back.*

M: How do people bring souls back? How do they bring people back to life?

C: *They just communicate with the soul and ask it to come back to the body. So, if it sees fit, if Council tells it can come back, it can, but if Council says that that lifetime is complete, then it cannot. So, it's not so much we're doing it, we're kind of just helping facilitate its introduction back into the body.*

The healers that are most comfortable with the soul retrieval are working with him. The teacher that teaches the boy is one of them. He flags the boy over, so the boy comes over and he's crying and so distraught. And he calms him down and stands up and takes him by the shoulders, and he tells him that he's to help. So, the boy said, no, I can't do that or do anything else. And he said, but you're so powerful that you'll be able to. You're going to be able to do this. We're not powerful enough because he's so young and has this amplified energy.

So, the boy kneels down amongst maybe six or eight people that are surrounding this young boy. When he puts his hands on his heart and his teacher tells him to just lightly pulse the energy within his friend, he's so scared to do it. He says look, he's already...we can't do anything, either that will work or not. So, he pauses first, the teacher, and asks a higher energy that if it is meant for this boy's soul to come back then it will happen now, and then he nods to the boy to pulse the energy. He does and he has his eyes closed and he just freezes there after he pulses the energy. And just like an electric shock through the little boy's body, his eyes shoot open, and he takes a huge gulp of air and sits up. And the little boy just, they both are crying and hugging each other.

The little boy tells the teacher that he doesn't want to do it anymore. And he said, "Oh, no." He said, "Look at what you've done." He's like, this is a miracle. He said, "No, we'll work with it more, so you understand it. It's okay. It's all right." So, everyone is so relieved and just amazed by what just happened. So, they take the boy back to where he stays so he can just kind of rest, but he says really, he doesn't want to rest he's so hungry. So, it's almost time for supper with everyone, so they take them to the eating area. And everybody's milling, talking about the miracle that they just saw. How amazing that happened.

WORKING WITH JESUS AND MARY'S CHILDREN

C: We're going to release the first group of children. I'll stay in the small abodes, on the mountainside. Then it's time to start with the next wave of children, which is much smaller. In the first wave, maybe there were twenty children, and in this group, there will just be seven. So, Yeshua and Mary's children are there out of the seven. So, they are already comfortable with the abilities that they have, but we're going to dive in because they especially know the little girl has strong, energetic talents that we can dive into more deeply. Yeshua works with her but doesn't have... He wanted someone else to work with her further, to deepen that so that she can connect deeply into their essence and work with them on that level.

So, we get started. She's very quiet. I'm asking her questions to see what she knows so that we can get started. She says she has a concern. Her concern is what if her essence attaches to another essence and can't let go. So, I tell her about separating. "You're done with your energy work." She was relieved; she didn't know that. She expressed doubts about her abilities. She wasn't sure that she wanted to do this sort of work. I told her let's just explore it and see how you feel when you know a little bit more.

This girl is so powerful. She could gaze upon you, or barely touch your arm, and you could feel the wave of electricity pass through you. It was also an energy straight from the universal life force energy, the Source energy. It was so pure and full of love and compassion. I have never experienced an energy like this before from anyone. It's truly amazing. I'm not going to have one of Yeshua's sons. He's with the raven woman working with telepathy and he's very clear with it so he's going stay with her the entire time. I will work with his oldest son.

He seems like maybe fourteen or fifteen. He's really tall though. We will do energy work as well. So, I'm completed working with his daughter for the day. The son comes over; I think his name is Benjamin. He works in a different way *with energy. His is very graceful and is the opposite of his sister's; hers is very powerful and intense. So, I'm working with her on how to control that and make it more smooth. His son already has that ability so that when he engages it's like honey, just very beautiful, golden, warm. Very delicate. So, we work with directing it, so I can tell him more about it, so he has a deeper understanding. We complete our time together. He greatly appreciates the lessons that I've taught him, and he said he's looking forward to coming back tomorrow.*

M: So sweet. Did you ever get his other brother's name?

C: Let me see if I can find it? Elijah. His daughter, Seraphina? An absolutely beautiful, little girl.

NEXT SCENE: ANIMAL MAGIC

C: I'm walking down a small corridor to meet with this daughter. And out of her room comes a long serpent — long, thin serpent, like, I don't know, five-feet long. I see her appear in the frame of the room. She's smiling and giggling, and I asked her "What are you doing?" I step aside and the serpent is so beautiful, but it naturally just knows where it's going. She slowly walks behind it and practically escorts it right out. It goes into our side passage and leaves, disappearing into the rocks on the mountainside. I ask her, it is Seraphina, what caused that to happen? Did you bring the serpent in? She's laughing wildly and she said, no, it was in the corner of the room, but she was able to connect with his essence and tell it how to exit safely and it answered back to her. She had never experienced that before. It thanked her because it was frightened and just really wanted to leave back to the mountains.

So, she was laughing and so empowered that she was able to communicate energetically and telepathically with this animal and talk to it as if it was human. Escorting it out as if they were old friends. Yes, so I thought that was amusing as well. I said, well, that's something we'll work on some more then. She's such an exuberant soul. So, we decide to track outside of the community to see if we can find other animals for her to connect with. So, there's a bird. There are not very many animals because it's so dry. They are all in hiding. So, we did find a bird that was looking for water. She could pick it up and I could pick it up as well. So, I said go ahead and instruct the bird how to find the water, which we have water in the inside of our community, which birds can fly over into.

So, she looked at the bird, engaged with it. We both watched as it flew over the wall of our community and came back out, its thirst quenched and very grateful for her assistance. At that, she squealed and laughed wildly again because she was so easily able to connect and talk. So, we end our lesson and Yeshua comes to check and see how she's doing. I tell him about the animals. He says she's always been drawn to them, but she's never communicated with them like this before. So that was wonderful! Then he asks how the meetings in the city are going. I said they're well attended and will continue on even though I'm here training. He said very good. So, then he had expressed that Mary had wanted to talk with me at length and discuss a few things with me. So, I said that would be fine, we can meet, or we can talk at supper. He said that'd be wonderful. So, I say farewell to him and that I'll see him later at dinner.

We seem to have made such a close relationship over the past so many years, so when he talks to me, he almost acts like I'm his sister. Like he will touch the side of my head or hold my shoulder and it's always comforting to see him. He expresses that he's always comforted by my presence as well. So, we head to the area where we eat, and Mary is there waiting, so I go over and sit next to her and ask her what she would like to talk about. She just asked what my experience in the community was growing up, if I enjoyed it. I was away from my parents a lot even though they were in the mountainside close by. I was in intensive training for so long. I said I really enjoyed it and she said she was thinking of traveling on her own, to assist in empowering women more. She would need to leave the children behind, maybe six months, maybe even a year, if I thought they'd be okay with it. I told her yes, there are so many people here that would care and love them.

So, she seemed relieved. I could tell she already had her mind made up to leave. She just needed reassurance that the children would be cared for. She also felt that she was expecting again. She would go on her travels and see what happens. She offered some written tablets, some practices that she does with the women that she would like me to start teaching women that I work with, so I was very open to knowing what that would be. She said it was about how they're teaching in the religious temples about the sacred union. How they're expressing it to be for reproduction purposes only almost, and that's not the case. So, she had practiced for years and still practices with Yeshua, connecting, not running the energy out of your body, and bringing it back into your body, to connect up your spine, to connect with the Source, to connect the circuitry between them.

I thought it sounded wonderful and I could break that out for more women that come and was very intrigued to know where she learned. She said she learned from some of the servants that worked in a monastery in the Far East as they follow that tradition, and they started experimenting with it.

M: When you say the Far East, what would that be in Neomi's modern life?

C: India. Indian mountains. It will take them forever to get there. A long time to travel that far.

M: Thank you. Is this the fourth child that is going to be born from Mary?

C: She believes so.

M: And all of the children are biological and belong to Yeshua?

C: Yes.

M: Wonderful. Tell me what happens next.

C: I assist her in packing and though she's had the other children she's always had midwives help her, so I'm well versed with that. So, I packed her satchels of herbs and things that she may need in the event that her pregnancy comes to fruition. She thanks me immensely and I reassure her that I will continue to work with the children. I will come back to the community and check on them often. I also let her know that if they express that they wanted to stay with me or anything, that I can keep them busy around the palace. They're welcome to do so until she sends for them.

Yeshua comes over and they have such a close connection. They know they can connect (psychically) all the time but there is a sadness in his eyes that he may not see her (physically) for many months. She reassures him it will be just fine. Meanwhile, she expresses that she's so surrounded and encompassed by the Divine that she says that she knows no harm can come to her and laughs, but it's true. It's almost as if she's so divine she can't be touched. So, he knows this but still, they part, and she has all of her things that she needs. I can tell she's holding love for him and sending it to him so as to uplift him because he's just a little sad to see her go. She doesn't want to express her sadness as well. She just wants to express her love. So, she leaves in the evening and Yeshua talks to the children and lets them know that he will be traveling for just a few weeks and then he'll come back and check on them and then we'll see what to do from there.

So, the children are okay with this because they have traveled so much. They enjoy new things and experiencing new places. Seraphina is a little sad to see her parents go, but I reassure her that she can come to the city and stay with me. I will be with them for another few weeks anyway, and she seems comforted by that because we have bonded and have a deep love for each other.

NEXT SCENE: THE FOURTH CHILD

C: *So, I am in the kitchen back in the palace. On the edge of the kitchen, there are ornate tables and Seraphina is sitting around, swinging her legs, and she's helping me cut some sort of root vegetable. I have really taken her under my wing. She stays with me. She works on her talents, and she helps me with the meetings with the women. I debated if it was inappropriate for her or not, but it's not. We have been talking about and working with a small group of women about the sacred union. So, we've been practicing that and experiencing such positivity and so much energy and vitality and divine connection. Someone asked me about it and the women come back in and we talk about the experiences and if anyone has anything to share.*

Seraphina is extremely curious about this, so she moves closer to the group and slides down the wall. So, we talk, the women and me. The first woman has had great success with it and maybe the emotions that are clarified through you when you're engaging. I ask if anybody had known or figured anything in advance and to share other ways. One of them wants to talk but doesn't. I assure them it's a small group to talk about [this] with so all that's shared is confidential, but she won't come forward. She finally speaks up and she says that the energy rushed up the spine to the skull and she left the body, and was that appropriate, up into the cosmos. And I ask her what alarmed her about that, and she said it was difficult to get back into her body after that. It took her maybe two hours for her to consciously put herself back in her physical body and all along her lungs kept pumping to keep her physical body alive.

M: So, what happens next?

C: *One of the people from the community comes by, very urgently and super excited. I am to get my work covered and come back to the community with Seraphina. Seraphina already knows. She knows that her mother came back with a new baby, so she's running. I can barely keep up with her. It's a long trip back. We've already been working all day. And we get back to the community and she runs in, and she embraces her mother and then swoops in to pick up the baby from her mother's arms. She looks to see if she has a brother or a sister. She* *can't tell, but she wants to figure it out herself. So, I notice she's connecting with the baby to see what kind of energy it has.*

She has a puzzled look on her face and her mother says, I know. She can't decipher what the baby is, so she says give it time. She asks what the baby's name is, and Mary says she hasn't decided yet; she just had the baby on the way back and she needs more time to think about it. Seraphina seems a bit disappointed. I say just because the baby doesn't have a name it doesn't mean you can't connect with it. She kind of brings that to her awareness; she is more mindful. She gently helps to take care of her mother, so I let them have their time together. I go and sup with the others and catch up with them. Yeshua is on his way back.

M: Did Mary share where she was traveling when she had the child?

C: She said she was traveling south, down towards Egypt, towards the pyramids. She wanted more information from the people there about how to move the circuitry of the energy when engaged in the sacred unions so that she can teach it more adequately with others. She found someone who she became very close with that she was able to learn how she needs to engage her energy so that she can explore it more, and she says in time she will practice this with Yeshua so she can be clear in what she is teaching. So, when the baby is a bit older, she will travel back to further her knowledge.

Yeshua returns and he is elated to see her. Seraphina runs to him. The boys were in the city, and they were called for. Two of the teachers had jobs they could do while they were waiting. He is excited about the baby too. He [told] Mary quietly that he thought the baby was born of two sexes. Mary says that intuitively she thought what happened with the baby, as it got older, it may just be perfect because it blended the masculine and feminine energies — the divine energies together, encompassing that energy in one being, transcending duality. And he is thinking upon this but not yet sure what to make of it, so he spends time with them.

I take Seraphina back to the city, just for a few days until the end of the week. So, she is very excited about going back to the city. She likes it there. As the time has gone by, she seems almost eight. And she asks if she can live with me when her parents travel. I say yes. She expresses her concern about maybe the baby having both sexes. I say we will learn more as the baby gets older. We don't know why it was supposed to be like that. She seems reassured by that.

M: Very good. Let's move forward to the very next scene. The last scene for the day. Be there now. Tell me what you see.

C: I am back at the community. The whole family is going to travel and depart. They are all going to travel together down towards the pyramids. The man...woman that Mary was apprenticing with has found a small home for them to reside in so that she can continue the training. A few months have passed so Yeshua is interested in moving more with her as meeting with others in Egypt. Seraphina is very sad to leave me, but I reassure her we will see each other often. The children have had the opportunity to fine-tune their abilities and their talents so they can share them with others. So, we all say our farewells and they leave, and they head back to the city. I tell Seraphina to bring me back some beautiful fabric and I can't wait to hear about all of their adventures.

NEXT SCENE: BASIC TANTRA

C: Everyone's talking and are excited because...and the kids, his kids, and her kids, that Mary and Jesus are returning from separate journeys. Some of the teachers have been watching their other kids while they left.

So, Mary arrives first, and she brings the baby. It's much bigger now, maybe eight months old or something. Her kids are so happy to see her; they run up and they've missed each other so much. They just start talking over each other, all the new things they've learned while they've been gone. Then they want to see the baby. So, they're just fawning over their sibling. Then she asks if Jesus has gotten back yet, and she knows he'll return by sunset, so they tell her not yet. She knows he's on his way because he's to meet her there that day. So, she's just so happy to see the kids.

The children all perk up because Jesus has come back, and he came in. So, Mary stands up and they embrace, and then the children start telling their father all the same stories they already told their mother and then when they're done, the children go to eat. A teacher comes to get them and take them. Mary and Jesus start to talk about what she learned in Egypt. It was a fascinating union of energy that you engage with another to combine your energy together so that you can illuminate the energy between the two people so that it is more concentrated and powerful. So, she said, she has learned of these different practices. So, he said that he was fascinated by what she had learned. He had learned a practice where you could leave your body, leave your human body, and you could travel through time with your soul to different places and even leave the Earth and then come back. So, she was very fascinated by this and would like to express wanting to learn how to do that. He said they would probably stay there in the community for probably about a month so that they could rest from their travels and the children could continue to learn. So, he said, after they rest, because they were so weary from traveling for so long, that they'll start to teach each other the practices.

M: Where did Jesus learn these practices? Did he share?

C: *From the East, he traveled far east, but very far this time, past the monks he usually works with. I cannot know the name...now was to like China, way past...he doesn't have a name for the teachers. He just calls them teachers. That's how he says the monks.*

M: Very good. Let the scene continue to play and tell me what happens next.

C: *They decide to go eat with the children. Jesus just wants to be with the baby because he hasn't seen it for so long. And then after they eat everyone's talking to them and asking them about their travels. Then they go to rest and just get the family together and start to rest. But Mary is asking him if he wants to, if she can start to show him some of what she had learned. So, they sit together facing each other. She said we will just start with our telepathy and communicating through our eyes, so that's what they do. They just sit knee to knee, and they just gaze into each other's eyes and start with the telepathy and just talk without talking. They do this for seems like an hour and then she said, that's a perfect start to the practice that they will continue more the next day. He's very fascinated by this practice. He said tomorrow evening because it is most easy to start when you're sleeping at night. He will show her how to leave her body. So, they lie down to rest for the night.*

It's the next afternoon, at break time you'd say. The kids are just taking a break. I talk with Mary because she asked how long I'll be there teaching. They said another month before I go back into town to gather the women and teach them some things. She said she wanted to show me the practice that she learned as well so that I can teach the women. So, she asked me to...it's funny because I tell her that I don't know that I'll be able to practice it because I've never been with a man before in my life, even though I'm older. She said that's okay. She said you can do this with a girlfriend or a female friend you have or someone that you're close with. There's some kind of relief because I thought I was going to learn something about something sexual and I wouldn't be able to do it because I was by myself and not really interested so much in that.

So, she has me find my close friend in the community. She and I and my friend and Jesus, we go into where they stay. So, she shows us the gazing. You sit with your partner, just sit in their lap and you keep gazing. Then you can connect by your thoughts, by your energy or touching, whatever that you see fit. Then she explains about starting to run the energy up your spine, through your crown, and into the other person; start to cycle a circle between you. After just breathing and the eye contact and the running of energies, there's this heightened, light-static feeling that runs through you. It just only lasts like a split second. This is almost like a flash of white light, like you're taken somewhere else, just for a split second. She said that's perfect. That's exactly what it is, but then if you practice more, you'll experience that white light and that surge of energy up your spine to your crown for longer periods of time. So, to practice. I asked her what is this for? She says that it helps open your connection to spirit so that you can connect directly and be engulfed in the creative energy, the energy that created us. She said it will open up your mind to many realizations and just inner knowings and wisdom and also remembering.

I personally just feel so elated and energized, just very revitalized, and so does my friend. It's really amazing. So, we agree to engage in the practice every few days so that we can elongate our feeling of connection to that creative energy to see what happens. Mary says as we're practicing, they'll be there about a month too. If I have questions to let her know, so she can guide me to any answers that I need. She would very much like me to teach the other women, the women that come to the spiritual meetings in town so that they can start to engage in the practice with their friends or with their partners.

NEXT SCENE: CRUCIFIXION

C: *I can see...I see a...the crucifixion with the other two men. And I'm very saddened by it but I knew, and all of the followers knew, that this was going to be occurring soon, though it's very saddening. I can just see this gigantic, this blinding white, light-blue glow around Jesus and it's so beautiful. It just keeps intensifying and intensifying, then suddenly, you see a blinding flash of light, and the light's gone and his head slumps forward. I know then that his soul has departed back home, but to see this actual light manifest around him, this blinding white light — the edges were beautiful, crystal blue. It was...wow! Very amazing. Then all of us knew, all of his followers knew that it was true — that he went back to Source.*

422 | THE ILLUMINATION CODEX

I go back to the temple, and everyone is very saddened by what happened.

We just can't believe that a divine person like that, that he wouldn't find some way to go on because they tortured him so much and so many times. We all knew he was able to heal himself, so he was never...it just didn't dampen his spirit, so we're somewhat dumbfounded why he would choose to go on when he could do so much work. But he has so many teachers and followers now. Maybe he felt that it was his time to move on to the next assignment.

NEXT SCENE: RUMORS OF ASCENSION

C: My sister and I are working frantically in the kitchen because some of the...someone I work for...so their family came in. So, there are fifteen extra people, so my sister and I are frantically working to cook for them. And one of the other servants comes in and asks if anyone has come to update us on what had happened, and we said, no. And she just kept saying, "He wasn't there. He wasn't there. They didn't find him when his uncle came to get him."

We all thought maybe he was able to...and Source was able to manifest his body, to just dissipate into dust. So anyway, we were fascinated by it and thought that that was... Wow! Just almost unbelievable. I mean almost unbelievable. We believed it ...but it was just amazing! But it was just a brief talking because, oh, my gosh...just us two having to cook for all these people so we... Hopefully, we'll be able to get together in our women's group and discuss it.

NEXT SCENE: BELIEF IN THE LIGHT

C: A couple of us ladies were able to get together. There are just three of us. We know the story that the body wasn't there, so we're just talking about different speculations. We mostly all agreed that he just went back to Divine Source and just showed us, really physically, because of the blinding bright, white light with the blue surrounding it...and then the flash and disappearance. There were just so many things that people could see, visibly see, that it was just undeniable.

How phenomenal, that everyone could actually see what happened and know that that was his soul and energy that left, and we could visibly see it. That was just phenomenal. So, hopefully, we were talking, that it will be easier to spread the word, more, because for something to happen...you couldn't...maybe more people will be interested to see what he had to teach.

TWENTY-SEVEN

Melchizedek, David, Jesus

This session has several timelines giving information regarding the Melchizedek priesthood, the bloodline of David, and events surrounding Jesus's ministry.

C: There are, there's sand beneath my feet. My hands are human. I have sort of a robe on. It seems to be purple with a rope to tie it around the waist. I feel female. I have long flowing dark hair. I'm carrying some sort of pot. There's water or some liquid in it. There seems to be something on the mind. My face and my brows are furrowed. I am in deep thought and thinking about the person I'm going home to.

M: Take me with you on that journey, and it'll get clearer as you walk and journey home.

C: I'm approaching a town. There's still sand on the ground around this town. The walls match the ground, made of dirt or something, dirt or mud. Very square buildings. Looks like a scene out of Aladdin.

M: What makes it look like that? Tell me about it.

C: The style of the houses. The people's dress as they walk by. People don't wave just keep walking.

M: When you arrive in front of your home, tell me what it looks like.

C: It's very small, can see the kitchen immediately when you walk through the door. There's a small, small room that you walk into right away, where you take off your sandals. I see a place to boil water and fire. I see a table in between the kitchen and the entry room. There's a room to the right, closed off by blankets. I move the blankets and go into this room. There's a mat on the floor for sleeping, seems to be a table in the center next to the bed, it's a kind of altar.

M: What kind of things do you have on the altar?

C: Seems some sort of figurine, which I can't make out, a small piece of art.

NEXT SCENE: EATING A MEAL

C: I'm sitting at a table between the kitchen and entry room, and the man is very large, sort of hunched over his food eating ravenously. I'm watching. He must be my partner. It doesn't seem that we're well connected. Like, like we don't understand each other, rather like he doesn't understand who I am or that I understand him.

NEXT SCENE: BAPTIZED BY THE LIGHT

C: *I'm standing on the shore of the sea. I'm looking at its vastness, there's sort of a mountain on the bank furthest from me. I'm barefoot. I am appreciating the stillness. There are people here, but I'm away from them. There are some people wading out into the water, about knee deep. We are all wearing white. There's a man guiding people into the water, and he dips them under it in baptism. He puts his hand on their head, on their forehead, says a prayer, dips them down under the water and when they emerge, he gives them a hug. There's a line of people and he's doing this over and over.*

M: **Will you be receiving it today?**

C: *It feels like I want to, but I'm not going to. I'm just watching. I'm scared and sad. (crying) I don't know why I won't do it. Everyone looks so happy when they come out.*

M: **And you just don't feel up to it. What's the sadness about?**

C: *It has something to do with my partner. He doesn't know what they're doing, he doesn't approve of it. I feel like I'm one of them, but it doesn't look like there are any women going under the water. (Crying) It seems like people have finished being baptized, and they stay there knee-deep in the water, and the man who is dipping who was baptizing them has his arms in the air. (Crying) He seems to be saying something about God. (crying) He's saying the people are clean now. I just continue watching, I want to be clean too. (Crying.)*

M: **You want to be clean? What feels dirty? What do you want to be cleaned? You can confess it now.**

C: *(Crying) I don't love my husband. We don't pray properly. (crying) We should pray like the people in the water. (crying) We don't need an altar. (crying) We don't need a figure.*

M: **You don't need an altar, and they don't need a figure. What do they need?**

C: *Themselves. I begin walking into the water. (crying) Maybe I can get some approval. (crying) The man giving baptisms has me. His arms are still open. And he puts his palm over my forehead.*

M: He puts his palm over your forehead and what happens?

C: He just looks really deep into my eyes, and he doesn't say anything. And then he invites me to dip myself into the water. (crying) I come out of the water even more brightly. They come out of the water. He gives me a huge hug. He whispers something to me I don't understand. I don't know the language. He says that I'm ready. (crying) I feel that I'm ready to be a part of these people like I've always been.

M: Like you've always been what?

C: Part of them. As I move into the group, the faces of disapproval are still there, but they approve more.

M: They're approving of you more now? What happens?

C: The man doing the baptism puts his hands together in prayer over his heart, and I look around, and all the men in the water are doing the same. So, I do it. The sun comes through the clouds over all of us. There is a feeling of purity within myself and in the air.

M: So wonderful, so what will you do next?

C: Feels like I have to go home. I'm exiting the water, turning around, and I see the man who baptized me. He's just watching me, and we hold eye contact for a moment before I turn around and walk home, and there's fear with me as I walk home.

M: What is the fear about?

C: About what I was supposed to do about the man in my house, who does not understand? I come home, he is there at the table where he was eating the night before, but he sees me dressed in white. Like I can't feel how he feels, it's just a look of disbelief.

M: Yeah, so what do you do?

C: I just stand there we're just looking at each other. He doesn't know what to make of my dress and the look on my face which doesn't seem angry with him anymore, which doesn't fear him. Then we're just still looking at each other as if seeing each other for the first time.

NEXT SCENE: MEETING JESUS

C: There is a large gate, with tall walls around it surrounding some other building. People are sort of assembling in front of the gate. I am watching from the outskirts as they gather. I'm unsure what they're there for. The people seem like they are the way I was before I went in the water. They want to but they are scared.

M: So, what happens next?

C: So, I approached the gate and there's somebody sitting on the steps, and people, a small group are gathered around. (crying) He's teaching them. He looks at me as I peek my head in and invites me to come to sit on the steps. There is a small group of people that don't acknowledge me. So, I come closer. The people from outside the gate reject that I should be there.

M: Why is it that you shouldn't be there?

C: It's because I'm a woman. The teacher is not saying anything. He's saying so much. It's so loud, but he's not using any words. I feel the energy growing in my solar plexus. The teacher's arms are spread open embracing all the people sitting on the steps and all the people outside watching. It's like a field of light is surrounding all of us.

M: Describe what this teacher looks like. What does he look like?

C: This one is different from the one who was baptizing people, but the energy is the same. This one doesn't have the same eyes, the one who did the baptism had bright blue eyes. This one is also powerful but is not the same, and the group is different. And he's saying that we can do it. We should do it, to share. Share the light, the light in the presence that we're sitting in is ours, it's everyone's. My hands are now, energy is concentrating in my hands, vibrating, and they feel that they're strong.

M: What else does the teacher say?

C: Our hands are healing hands. We need to go heal the people.

M: Does he share anything else about his guidance for the group?

C: Now, the group is moving away from him now.

M: And what do you do?

C: I never fully joined the group I sort of watched from inside the gate, but on the outskirts of the group. I just stand there looking at him and he's looking at me as if he's feeling me from the steps like he's assessing me. He seems to approve and starts descending from the steps. He's looking at me the whole time, walks right past me, and does not touch me or say anything to me, just walks out the gate, and I'm left there in the courtyard by myself.

M: How do you feel about this exchange?

C: I don't know what to make of it because there's no difference between myself and the teacher. He approved of me, but he did not say anything. I don't know why, but I don't, I don't feel like I need to be part of the group. I don't need to be. I feel like I don't need to learn from him. Feels like I know what I'm supposed to do.

NEXT SCENE: CRUCIFIXION

C: There are two scenes happening at the same time. On one side I can see the place where I was baptized. Now, on the other I can see is the scene of the crucifixion. It feels like it's a foreshadowing, and I'm not actually there. It's like I can see it, but I'm not there, and I'm standing before the lake or the sea, and I can feel this crucifixion occurring before it happens. I understand that things are changing. Big changes are occurring.

M: What's changing there?

C: The world, and the person that, the people who, the people who I'm a part of are facilitating this change, and that the people who are resistant to them, like the soldiers, government, teachers of the law, they're scared.

M: What are they scared of?

C: Scared of this change. They don't want it. They've never wanted it.

M: What's happening there around you? What do you see there?

C: People are kneeling before the cross, it's like there's a phantom of the person on it, but there's not a person really on the cross. People are kneeling before it, and the people who are kneeling before it are chosen. Men who disapproved before welcomed me. First of all, I feel like I'm allowed to be there, and people are so sad. I'm sad too because I understand the great teacher has passed, but I'm not sad like the others because I didn't know him.

M: Tell me more about that.

C: They all were very close with him and learned from him, and I didn't, but I'm still part of them and they don't understand that I understand, but I know that I am, and they know that I am. We're still just kneeling. The energy is very strong.

M: Describe the energy of this place.

C: It's almost as though there is a force field of light all around us. There's a sort of web which forms and arcs out of my crown into the crown of all the other people and we're all interconnected by this sort of light grid between us as we kneel before the cross. This light grid is fueled by, it's blue coming from our crown into the crowd surrounding the cross, being fueled by the yellow golden forcefield energy around the cross, which surrounds us.

M: Tell me what's happening as it happens.

C: Standing up now, seems we're all going our separate ways. As the distance between each of us grows, as we each go our separate ways, the light grid, the blue light grid, which we can access, stays the same, just as strong. Seems like we were in a circle around the cross, and now we're all going in different directions away from it. But despite that, the cross is in us.

M: So where will you go?

C: It's like I'm going south. South, I don't know from where this is. The climate is changing. I'm moving away from the desert. Seeming as if the people are surrounding me like I'm teaching this time.

M: What do you share?

C: There are children and women around me. I am telling them that they have power. That the world is no longer the same place it was, even years ago. I tell them not to be scared and that God is within us, and they all believe me. I tell them that they are the same as me as their husbands don't pray in the same way, but I'm activating these women. I explain to them that they have power. That they are the Earth, they are the earth that they walk on. That the Creator is within them and to know they are creators. In the same way, God brings life, and so do we.

M: And how do they respond?

C: I can see that they want to believe me, but they don't. They don't because of the way of the world, but they want to help me. It seems like some of them do. As they walk away, some of them follow at a distance, and others go home. I continue to walk. I go through more towns, and I continue to do the same thing by myself at all times. I am being followed.

NEXT LIFETIME: MELCHIZEDEK PRIESTESS

C: I'm in a sort of palace. there are long flags hanging down from the wall, which is maybe 30 feet high, a grand entrance, and large steps. I'm walking into the palace. My robes are nice, they're long and they're purple, and I'm walking into this palace as though I belong. I'm walking into a throne room. It feels appropriate to sit on the throne, but I don't do it. I wait.

M: What happens next?

C: A man enters from a room behind the throne, and he has the heir of a warrior. His furs are over his shoulders, large. This seems to be a different time period from that I was describing previously. There's no throne next to him like there's no queen. This man is light and handsome, very strange looking despite his handsomeness. He doesn't say anything. He just sits on the throne. I'm several steps beneath in my purple gown looking up at him. It seems that I'm giving him counsel. It's occurring to me that I'm telling him about his dreams. I'm explaining to him the steps that must be taken to protect the people.

M: What do you share with him?

C: I'm saying, the plants will wither to trust in God and not man. The living water is within us and water from the sky will not bring the plants to life.

NEXT SCENE: GUIDING THE KING

C: My third center is activated. I'm here in this palace. It seems like people are congregating outside of the palace. The King is watching from the balcony, and the moment I step into his field he feels me. There's a distance between us as we look out at people from the balcony. He seems to have a lot on his mind. The people seem to fully trust this man. He has nothing to say to them and nothing to give them, but he wants to give them everything.

M: So, what do you do?

C: I'm just holding space for him right now. I can feel his doubt growing. He does not, his faith in God is wavering. He wants to have faith, but he doesn't know what it means to be a man, to be mortal. He doesn't understand why he should be placed in charge of all of these people, to be given this false sense of power that he can provide, when only God can provide, and then even still, God is not providing. I am standing near him as he processes this doubt and watches over his people.

NEXT LIFE: MELCHIZEDEK PRIESTHOOD

C: I see some sort of giant turtle. On the side of it, they're giant statues on either side of the turtle. They're guarding the turtle and the turtle is guarding something else. This is very, very old. I can sense multiple priests. They're unlike priests I've ever seen or felt before, and they are aware of my presence. I don't know how many there are. They don't necessarily feel light. They don't feel dark either. They're just powerful.

M: Become aware of your form and tell me what you see.

C: I'm a man. I'm strong with intelligence. Very, very keen set faith in God, the Creator. These men and statues, if they are statues, they seem foreign to me. Like they're from some distant land, but they don't reject me. They don't welcome me. And yet I'm there. As it's like this area's like protected, It's secret and yet I'm there. I can feel these people, but they don't even wonder why I'm there.

M: And why have you come? What is your purpose there?

C: I came to learn. I want to know; I want to know the secrets.

M: What kinds of secrets?

C: About what's really going on on the planet, in this in this ground that we walk because it feels extra-terrestrial. I'm on the Earth, my home, but I know there's more. There are more presences and I need to know.

NEXT SCENE: INNER SANCTUM OF THE PRIESTHOOD

C: I'm in a circular room. It's a dome, but the middle of the dome is open. There are columns around the inside. So, the sun is shining directly through the circle on the top of the dome. It's beautiful. There's grass growing there in the center. Seems to be a kind of altar, and I can't decide if these people are... the term Melchizedek keeps recurring in my head. I can't decide if they are light or not.

M: Tell me what you see and what's happening there in that scene. What do these priests do?

C: It's like they are, it's like I'm in the light and they're all against the closed-off walls, like around the pillars, it's dark. They're sort of in the shadows as I take the scene in, just watching me. I approached the grass in the center, and I sit, and three of them come out in long dark robes. They just look at me. They approve of me. They're willing to teach me, but they don't, I don't know why I came. So, they're unwilling to teach me until I know.

M: So, they've accepted you into this path of learning.

C: Yes, they would not have led me into this space if I was not accepted. It seems as if they were expecting me.

NEXT SCENE: INITIATION

C: There's an altar there in the center now. It seems I'm bringing, being brought to the altar. I'm having visions of being stabbed, but it's as though I'm willing to do this, so I'm not being forced into this ritual. I'm handling it with bravery. I gasp and cry out, but no blood falls. They stab me right in my third center beneath the sternum and blood comes onto the knife, but it doesn't fall from me. A rounded red dagger. They pull it out, there's blood on the end. My skin mends.

They place it on the altar.

M: What does this mean there? What happens?

C: I've been given information to carry. Information that I will never forget, like I will always be a student of these priests, but I will never be a priest. It's not who I am. These people are not people. They remain priests throughout their lifetimes. I'm not supposed to be a priest.

M: When you say they're not people, what do you mean by that?

C: They're not from this planet. They may look like they're humans but they're not humans. They know they're not humans. They are here to watch and help humanity. They are the Gatekeepers of Dark and Light, that's why I can't tell if they're dark or light because they're both. This seems to be why they watch humanity because humanity is the same dichotomy.

M: So, these beings, you said Gatekeepers of the Dark and the Light, how does that work?

C: They have rituals. They stand in some sort of circle, perform chants and dances, sort of swaying in a circle which turns into other shapes. The people dance backward and forward, rotating. High, high energies, benevolent energies come. They're welcomed to the center of the circle. They're strange looking. It's not a starship, but just some sort of angelic agent which guides the priests who guide humanity.

M: Is this one being or multiple beings you are speaking of, this agent?

C: It's one thing, but there are many in it. It doesn't have a form. It's showing us some sort of like light form that sort of swirls and moves, but it doesn't need this, it isn't this.

M: So, this energy guides the priests that are upon the Earth?

C: Yes, and the priests guide people whose souls are connected to this agent. These are the indigo children. These are the people whose souls come from other places. This is a light being, and it's assisting the priests and assisting the light beings who are on this Earth. So now, this spirit, a string of light is coming through it, coming away from it and through all the priests. Their hands are together. The light is passing around the circle through all of them. I'm sort of watching this from above. Then, once it's concluded there's like a circle of light and a single beam of light. The Light Being just turned into a huge, it's like lightning from the heavens, and goes all the way up the outer space and then vanishes. It's nighttime, but it's still bright, as the sun is still shining there into the center of the dome.

M: So, what is this light that passes to the priests? What does it do? What's it useful for?

C: This seems to be some information about how humanity will be guided, about how they're to do it. It's about the role that the priesthood will play.

NEXT LIFE: KING DAVID

C: There's a war at the base of the mountain.

M: War at the base of the mountain?

C: People fighting with spears and swords. There's a light at the top of the mountain, and they're so busy fighting that they don't even realize they can both have the light at the top of the mountain. I'm sort of walking through the battle. People are fighting all around me, but I'm just going unnoticed and untouched. Just watching these people. Now, I'm ascending the mountain. I turn around and I see one young man on the outskirts of the battle looking up at the light. He seems to be the only one who understands they all can have it.

M: So, what happens next?

C: The battle is over. There are many dead people there, and the young man who saw the light at the top is part of the side that won. And it seems like people who fought the battle just want to stay at the base of the mountain, they don't want to go up to the light. They're the side won that won the battle.

M: So, what do you do?

C: I'm still watching from the outskirts of the mountain, halfway up the mountain, and just watching and waiting. My eyes are on this young man. Now he's climbing the mountain. He goes to the top and almost as if I'm like a spirit, like no one is recognizing me or ever saw me the whole time he climbed, very strong and handsome. And there's like, it's like a little sun here at the top of the mountain. There's a small plateau, and he sees the light, closes his eyes, and continues walking towards it. Then sits underneath it, just sits, sits, until eventually, the light fills him. In his heart center, and from his heart is a beaming angelic white light, and it's as though angel wings come from around him, huge wings. And it seems that I, I entered this young man, I am him, he is me. He is David. I am clearly human, but I don't look human for some reason. My ears are slightly pointed, my eyes are big, my cheekbones are defined, and still young. Just sitting in this light, I enjoy it. I thank God for helping me to win the battle and helping my people to survive and I for the first time realized that I'm different.

M: How are you different?

C: Others believe in the God in the heavens, and I believe in the God in myself. At the same time, I believe in the God of the heavens.

M: And tell me what happens next.

C: The light which filled me becomes less and less intense to my senses, and I descend the mountain back into the camp. There are men drinking, laughing, eating, and celebrating victory. There's a tent at the end of this camp filled with adornments. It's clearly a regal tent and I enter it, and there is the king in the tent. And I'm realizing for the first time that I'm still a boy, yes, a young man. To the right of this king who, I don't trust him, and he seems to love me and fear me at the same time. Although, I'm just a boy, and to the right of him there's a harp.

M: So, what do you do?

C: I smile at him because I love him, and I go next to him, and he puts his hand on my shoulder, and I begin to play, and the room becomes lighter, becomes lighter.

WORKING WITH HIGHER SELF

HS: He needs to remember who he follows. Where he has learned, who he's been so that he can bring this information into this lifetime. He has strong faith in the power within us all and the memory of the teachings of the priests. He is to lead by example to share with others the truth by his own light. Show them their light within. The priestess had knowledge of the teachings of Melchizedek. She helped the descendants of David remember David's way. He will help to remember forgotten teachings, and he will remind people who, in their past lives, have learned this information.

M: He had said he had some questions about what it means to be from the line of David. What can you share with us about what that means for him?

HS: The house of David is one of the chosen lines, lineages of people who have been divinely guided toward bettering humanity. David was chosen. His DNA was special, therefore, of all the wives that he had, he had so many children, and all of their DNA was special. He is supposed to help activate this DNA in the people who are related.

M: And how can he do this?

HS: Just continue on this path.

Closing Statement

I hope you have enjoyed this journey through the Cosmic Christ Transmissions. I hope that it has inspired deep inquiry and rapid multidimensional healing and awakening, propelling you forward on the path of realizing your own Christhood. Much more is to come as we venture into the NEW EARTH TRANSMISSIONS!

GATEWAY TWO PART THREE: NEW EARTH TRANSMISSIONS

Future Timelines of Gaia

TWENTY-EIGHT

Starseed Phenomenon

Since the fall of Atlantis, many benevolent star beings and high beings of Light have volunteered to come to aid in the freeing of Earth and humanity from endless cycles of suffering created by negative polarity consciousness and karma. All throughout history, there have been secret orders that have carried the pure teachings of Light. These wisdom-carrying communities studied the ancient teachings of science and spirituality passed down from divine prophets and messengers. They mastered the human body on all levels — physical, etheric, emotional, mental, and psychic. These priests, priestesses, sages, shamans, monks, nuns, seers, philosophers, physicians, alchemists, musicians, healers, and scientists protected this knowledge with their lives. They often studied and did their advanced work in secret underground tunnels, remote areas, and cave systems to avoid persecution from controlling powers.

Highly advanced orders such as the Druids, the Essenes, the Melchizedek priesthood, Kabbalists, Rosicrucian, Cathars, Priests and Priestesses of Isis, Indigenous medicine people, master yogis, and so on have carried these teachings throughout time. These wisdom traditions teach of the hidden Mysteries and the secrets of Earth and the Universe. Highly advanced celestial and galactic beings have been incarnating as humans into these communities on the Earth at the darkest times of Earth history to hold the Light and protect the sacred artifacts and teachings so that we do not lose the ancient knowledge from our ancestors and our extraterrestrial and celestial families of Light. Each incarnation, those "on mission" are guided back to the sacred materials to activate DNA coding and remember their higher purpose so that we can continue to support the expansion of consciousness upon the Earth.

With the support of benevolent extraterrestrial beings and the Hierarchy of Light, humanity has been slowly ascending in consciousness. This is still a free-will planet, and direct interference is not permitted. Humanity has to choose peace and unity on our own. Time and time again, humanity has chosen war, domination, and separation. Each moment we have a choice to follow the path of love or the path of fear. That being said, this is the last battle, and the restoration process is underway as many starseeds, and highly evolved souls have incarnated en masse all across the planet at every level of government and cultural influence to deconstruct the shadow structures of the Earth and liberate this world from darkness. It has been said that "It is done." and what we are now watching is the replay of what we have already done and the trickle-down effect from the higher dimensions.

After the Fall of Humanity, the cataclysm of Atlantis, many efforts have been made to resurrect humanity from consciousness decay so that we could remember our divine identity as spiritual beings. We, as individuals and collectively, make our own choices and are responsible for our own destiny pathway. It is not that God has abandoned us; it is that we as humans have abandoned our divine light and have chosen war and destruction repeatedly. The power of our destiny is in our own hands in this free-will universe.

Countless wars have happened all over the planet since The Fall. The teachings of Jesus and the Ministry were distorted and used to torture and kill millions of people for over two thousand years. During the Spanish Inquisition and the Crusades, many people lost their lives "in the name of God," a distorted version of the Divine created by the human ego. Countless libraries of sacred literature were destroyed. During this time, many highly advanced souls incarnated around the world to protect the sacred texts and artifacts left from previous generations that hold keys to our remembrance. Many innocent healers and wisdom keepers were burned, tortured, and slain. All of this happened within our free-will creation. At any point, humanity could have decided to follow a different path.

After two world wars and the development and use of the atomic bomb, Gaia and the spiritual beings who watch over the evolution of Earth and humanity sent out a distress call for help. It was obvious that if something were not done, humanity would destroy itself and the planet. This planet holds vast amounts of significant data stored within its DNA and the Akashic Records (spiritual records). If Earth were to be destroyed, the negative implications would ripple out and affect many other planets and star systems beyond the Earth. A plan was devised to assist Gaia and humanity in their Ascension to avoid the destruction of the planet.

In my sessions, clients describe many ways that the higher realms and benevolent star races developed and activated plans to support Gaia and humanity. Along with Jesus, countless souls volunteered to incarnate as humans to influence Earth from the inside and support humanity and Gaia in this Grand Shift. Dolores Cannon writes about this mission in her book *The Three Waves of Volunteers and the New Earth*, which describes three generations of souls who incarnated to raise the planet's vibration and humanity's consciousness so that we may all ascend.

Common Traits of Volunteers

Volunteers, also called starseeds, blue rays, indigos, and lightworkers, often have a few common traits. Volunteers often feel that they have a big "mission" or something significant to accomplish in their life even if they cannot remember the specifics. They feel a deep connection to the Earth and the natural world. They are disturbed by what is happening to the planet's ecosystems and animal life. Volunteers often prefer isolation over crowds and animal companionship over human friends and feel uninterested in mainstream activities and culture.

Many volunteers report that they feel that they do not "fit in" or they feel "different" than most people, the odd one in the group. This does not mean that they feel "better" than others but feel out of place even with, and often, especially with their family members. It can be quite a lonely experience. Many feel homesick and have spent much of their lives wondering if others have similar "vibes" and perspectives.

Many are highly empathic and intuitive and feel the suffering of the world. Often, they feel abandoned or left on the Earth and want to go "back home" to God or the stars. Many develop heavy addictive patterns to numb the pain of human life and to drown out their hypersensitivity. Some decided to leave early and have committed suicide to exit the Earth realm.

Many souls heard the call to volunteer, and only the best and most suited for the job were selected to incarnate as a human to play out this Grand Mission. Earth life is dense, and nothing can prepare you for all the experiences one can have as a human on Earth. Many volunteers chose to incarnate into the densest and darkest parts of humanity to experience human suffering and transmute it through their light. Even with extensive training and preparations in the spiritual realms and past lives, many were

440 | THE ILLUMINATION CODEX

still unprepared for Earth's density and have experienced much suffering at the expense of their service.

Some of the Volunteers have been to Earth before and have traveled great distances to support this global awakening. Most commonly are souls who are starseeds from Sirius, the Pleiades, Orion, Arcturus, and Andromeda. Each of these regions of space has its own planets and schools. To "come" from a certain star lineage means that your soul spent time incarnating and learning in that experimental zone. We all truly come from Source.

The added challenge was that once incarnated, Volunteers would forget where they came from and why they came, but most know that their life has a BIG purpose and may spend a lot of life unsure what that means. While some people have specific directives in their mission and particular things to accomplish, in general, we came here to awaken fully in our consciousness, share unconditional love, and assist in bringing humanity back into union with the Divine and one another. We also assist Gaia in her Ascension by being lightning rods that anchor higher dimensional energy through our bodies and intention.

These brave souls have dedicated their awakened life to "midwifing" this grand birth of higher consciousness. Volunteers agreed to stay relatively unconscious to the mission for some time and begin awakening and remembering the mission at a certain point in their lives. Now, all across the planet, thousands upon thousands of awakened volunteer starseeds are well into their awakening and embodiment process. Many of us have remembered why we are here and are actively working together to raise the Earth's vibration. You will find us teaching classes, performing healings, creating art, writing music, working the Earth, teaching children, and many other activities to raise the vibrations of the planet. Some starseeds have more background roles like bus drivers and janitors/custodians who encounter many people and share their lovelight with all they meet. Many of these jobs are similar to what they have done in other lifetimes, like driving spacecraft or cleaning up experimental zones of space.

Along with the embodied star-seeded volunteers, lightships with higher dimensional beings and extraterrestrial craft are cloaked around the planet, sending powerful waves of energy and love to Earth. They are directing, focusing, and guiding the solar wind radiation from our Sun that carries

DNA upgrades and codes from the Great Central Sun to transform every level of life on the planet. Many star systems and civilizations are involved directly or indirectly with this operation. When the time is right, the disclosure will begin, and humanity will be told about these other advanced beings and their involvement with humanity's evolution. In truth, these beings are other aspects of our Oneself, helping us to remember our Oneness and Divinity.

Many clients are surprised to find that while they have an aspect of their oversoul on Earth (their own incarnation), they have higher dimensional aspects on spaceships and lightcraft outside the Earth's atmosphere. Some even have other aspects of their oversoul incarnated on Earth in different bodies simultaneously, and some even discover that an aspect of them is already in the New Earth reality, preparing to welcome humanity after the shift. We are not just one being. We are One and Many.

This massive multidimensional, intergalactic armada is made of highly skilled and accomplished ascension leaders, master healers, and great cosmic scientists. These beings have achieved high spiritual maturity levels and work together in many star systems to mature consciousness and the various biological experiments throughout Creation. Many of these beings have experienced ascension in multiple lifetimes. They have assisted planetary species by incarnating at key moments to boost consciousness and lead the species through pivotal transformation processes at nexus points in the ascension and descension phases. We move from planet to planet, assisting each realm in its ascension. I once heard an Indigenous elder speak of the changing times and how he was taught by his elders that it is the same souls incarnating again and again to help during grand transitions. In his words, "We have done this before, and we will do it again!"

There are many levels to this process beyond individual ascension. For example, there are spaceships with medical treatment centers to help assist species through transformation. They restore DNA, work with radiation toxicity, clear stagnant emotional energy, and upgrade information stored in the species' consciousness. I have clients describe massive ships, arks, filled with ecosystems teeming with life. Massive holding tanks carry whales that are recalibrated and healed so that they can be readministered to Earth's oceans to energetically clean the waters with their songs. Samples are taken of myriad life forms to be taken to other "Earths" to seed life.

Even physical human beings are being taken onto ships for healing and upgrades, which is especially common for major ascension leaders on the ground. This is not to be confused with abductions and experiments from our past from beings like the "Greys" from the star region of Zeta Reticuli, but friendly interactions with the star family that has been pre-approved from the higher realms before incarnation.

Some ground crew starseeds consciously and unconsciously act as a feedback loop for the Galactic Federation and higher realms. Their bodies subconsciously scan the environment for information which is then sent to ships where information is processed to measure progress and plan for the next steps in assistance. Some starseeds have higher aspects on spacecraft in charge of transmitting positive vibrations to the Earth through advanced crystal technology.

Some starseeds are utilized to activate and restore ancient technology at sacred sites and various points across the planetary grid through their energetic field. Most starseeds can relate to the experience of receiving internal messages or some type of sign to travel to certain places on the Earth or to attend certain events. While they may not seem like anything out of the ordinary, they are guided to move about the Earth to transmute energy, anchor in Light, and meet others on the Mission to exchange coding which is mostly unconscious.

I have had many clients describe being in the higher realms preparing for their next incarnation on Earth. They speak of their excitement to incarnate and bring the power of Love to the Earth. There is much training that happens before they enter their physical Earth life. In fact, many lives are lived in preparation for this Grand Event. Clients speak of higher dimensional training groups where people practice telepathy, telekinesis, and energy healing for when their abilities "turn on" in their physical lives. Everything has been rehearsed so that the proficiency of skill is stored within the subconscious. When the time is right and the veil is lifted, we will have tremendous knowledge and powerful abilities to reform this world into a shining Light Kingdom (Queendom if you prefer).

Some clients describe lives on other planets where the entire species received a telepathic call for help because Earth was in distress. I have had clients describe massive ceremonies where communities celebrated their relatives and comrades who were disembarking to travel across space to help humanity and Earth. Earth has been home to many, many souls over these last 13+ billion years. Countless beings have contributed to this evolutionary garden and to the life force of Gaia. There is much love for Gaia and humanity all across Creation.

Young Masters

The new souls coming into the Earth School are advanced beings of Light here to build a New Earth. These are our future architects, leaders, doctors, healers, engineers, and pioneers of consciousness. They are coming in with higher levels of consciousness and a different perspective of the world. Many do not conform to mainstream society already from a young age. Gender is mutable for many as they are free to explore the full spectrum of gender and sexual fluidity. Many have zero interest in mainstream culture and look at the world in disgust and horror as they watch a seemingly dying world that they will inherit from us.

Encoded in the DNA of our young masters are the star technologies, philosophies, and plans for the building of New Earth. We will teach them to levitate, communicate through telethought, move objects with their mind, and other abilities. They will use advanced quantum physics and the metaphysical arts to build a new civilization of Light. The family structure will change into a more communal support system as humanity reactivates the template of a happy, thriving, diverse village.

It is up to us to forge a future worth living for these young masters. We need to create educational programs and high-frequency environments that guide young people into their mastery and activate their intuitive skills. Meditation practices, guided visualization, and energy healing practices teach them how to self-regulate and tune into their Inner Being. Many of these children have powerful extrasensory perception and vivid dreamtime where higher learning and spiritual communication happen. We need to encourage creativity, imagination, and intuition in these young beings so that they can be the visionaries and revolutionaries that they came to be.

TWENTY-NINE

Starseed Transmissions

This next segment comes from a client named Ariella who had a fascinating regression that I hope to share in full in the future. She was part of a cosmic team of human-like beings from Venus who traveled the cosmos as defenders of Light and Truth. Her team came with Lady Venus and ascended master Sunat Kumara to create a higher dimensional reality upon the Earth called Shambala. This armada of illumined beings brought great love power to the Earth to begin reclaiming the planet from a group they called the "Fallen Ones." The session included several battles between forces of Darkness and forces of Light. At the end of her life, I asked that she be moved to when she was meeting with her guides.

C: *I am reporting to a council of Light...what is happening on Earth and my great concern that there need to be many, many more volunteers to go and help...and to be trained to bring its vibration up...to bring the Love up. And they agree that they will send out a call for that for those who are strong enough to do that. And they said they want me to train those who were going to go down to Earth...to get ready.*

M: **So, tell me what happens next.**

C: *I'm back on my beloved planet Venus and we are training thousands...along with others...I am only one of many. We are training thousands through various initiations and classrooms of highly sacred teachings and abilities. Only those with the most pure intentions can learn how to bend time like I do.*

M: **What kind of training do you put them through?**

C: *The trainings are...they're filled with love, camaraderie, highest respect for each other. It's very, very important that they love others as themselves. They must have a strong connection to Source. This is paramount. They learn the ways of protecting themselves with energy...using energy...the highest vibrational energies...how to stave off and notice when an energy is coming to distort theirs...with this pure shield, with a pure shield. Abilities to see through dimensional walls...see clairvoyantly. Intuitively. Clairaudiently. Being in tune with the person that you are next to. Not taking on their power but knowing their power. Not taking their power or weakness and using it against them, but actually empowering them so they overcome their weakness. It's a very high initiate who is learning these things through the love of others and respect of others and not looking down or overlording or being better.*

It's learning how to teleport...to be able to be anywhere at any time, through thought alone. Through thought. To influence...positively influence...this is a very big one...to positively influence the outcome of the situation through intention and thought. But this must only be for the good of mankind. Not in a negative way. So, also taught: the law of causality and how strict it is...to follow it and see the direct correlation of cause and effect happening simultaneously. It's almost like a martial arts kind of a class, where what you put out is automatically coming back to you. It's very interesting how this particular class is like a mirror game. Whatever energy you are putting out immediately comes back. So, you are seeing everything in the form of that energy and how it materializes very quickly and how it can move against you...and not to use it to move against somebody, so that you are getting immediate effects from good or bad causes. You can see it simultaneously as if it is...as if you are doing martial arts or you are doing swordplay and whatever you have inflicted on anybody else is immediately coming back to you. So that you are learning the law of cause and effect, physically. Very, very acutely. So, it is ingrained in your DNA. So, whatever you are putting out, you are immediately getting the effect. And that you must adhere to this law of the universe. It's very, very paramount. That's one of the classes. It's a very thought-provoking, interesting class to teach the young people.

Transcript: Simulated Training for Earth Mission

Neomi, the client who brought forward the life of Esther, found herself on a monochromatic grey planet. The entire landscape was made of jagged grey rocks and no vegetation. She described her body as grey and blue with the texture of turtle skin. Her home was a simple grey cubicle with a stone bed that she rested on without needing to sleep. Her home had a device that she could insert her head into and be projected into an Earth simulation where she practices being a young human girl playing in a field. When she pulled herself out of the projection device, she looked out of her dwelling to see a large crater where the town was located about seven miles from her home. She followed a jagged path into town and described what she saw there.

C: Then we get into town, and it almost seems like this is training. I feel like I'm in training. So, you go into the town and it's like an older town like in ancient times, like a bazaar. There are wooden carts and people selling things...and like material and food but I know I don't use these things, so this is training. So, I guess if I want to, I can go experience this to learn more. It seems like there are some humans there, but it's an illusion. They're just part of the training.

M: What's the training about?

C: You go to the bazaar, and you interact with the humans, and you can buy things and get food, but we don't eat the food because we don't need it. They have things so you can touch the food. I can pick up an apple and it's super red, but it's not really...this is not an apple like here on Earth. It's like an illusion. It's super bright, neon red. It's like they're trying to recreate it for training, but it's okay. I can hold it. It's smooth. I know that I eat it and that I can look at it and see the stem on it and look underneath and then I hand it back.

M: What's the purpose of this training?

C: So, I can be more comfortable and natural. So, let me walk further into town. So, on the outskirts there are these peddlers I can pretend to buy things from. It's like play. It's like here on Earth I play with my kids, and they make me food with their playset. So, I walk into town and there are little buildings set up, little wooden buildings that you can go into. Very simple. So, there are women wearing long skirts...like Little House on the Prairie. It's like that. So, I went into this building, and it was the general store, and they had all kinds of fun things, candies and such.

Then you go into the next store...and...Oh! It's like a modern-day supermarket! They have all the things, organic stuff, or you can buy the stuff, yucky pesticides...and you have to make a decision of what you are going to buy. So, you have to know to get the organic things, and then there are so many cereals...and not to buy those...and meats and don't buy those. So, there's...it's really hard to buy the food that you need in this store. It's really difficult to look around and find what you should get.

M: A lot to choose from, but nothing you want.

C: Yeah. There are lots of vegetables and fruits you can get organic, but the rest of the store...and people are buying LOTS of things, but they shouldn't be buying that. Hmm...so, that's kind of challenging. Well, I feel like I found... there are nuts, like almonds and cashews on the middle aisle I can eat, and some dried berries and things are okay. And there are the fruits, but I'm trying to find...I can't... there are not very many things in the boxes that I should be...I know I shouldn't be getting those things. So, maybe there is some water, but...let me see... Yeahhh (sighs). There's only one jug of water that is okay to get...so I'll get that.

M: Why aren't there other good waters?

C: There are all these other waters, but they all have things in them you shouldn't get. Oh, gosh! And people are getting them, but they should not...they should not be having that water! There's only the one, these square jugs of water...that are like two...they are bigger than the other gallons of water...and bottles. So, this is really hard because...to pick...to feed yourself...so if you had a family or something it would be hard to feed them...the right things. There are a few choices though, so I think you can make it. So, okay. So that's hard. So let me see what's in the next building.

M: Yeah. Well, you said you were on your way to the crater.

C: Yeah. Well, all this is in the crater. It's a training area. You get to go into these different places, and you know what you should do but then you have to...it gives you an opportunity to challenge yourself and try to make the right decisions.

M: Why are people making the wrong decisions?

C: Because all of it's available...and easy. It's just there so I think they don't know. The other people, they're walking around like zombies. There's no life in their eyes. They're walking around and they're getting these things. They're interacting with each other...but there's a glaze over them.

M: Why do they have this glaze?

C: They can't...there's...they're missing a light. They don't know...they don't know what they should be doing. It's like they're walking around in their sleep. They're sleeping.

M: How come they don't they have their light?

C: I think they just need someone to show them, but no one has touched them yet. I don't know.

M: What do you mean by touch them?

C: If I walk up to this one guy...there's this one guy he's got...he's a middle-aged man in a plaid, blue shirt and he has grey pants on and brown shoes...and he has bright, blue eyes but they're just looking forward, glazed. But I can touch his arm and then he turned and looked at me and he smiled. And now he's okay! Now he sees. Well, that seems so easy...but there are so many people...but I don't know...I don't know if I should touch everybody. But this is training...so...but he came right to life. He just looked at me and he smiled and he... It's like their soul's not...their soul's in there maybe, but it's really trapped. It can't interact.

M: And so, when you touch them, what happens?

C: Their soul came into their body and expanded into their, I'll say, meat suit, and then they're alive. But prior, their meat suit...it felt like their soul was in there, but it was withered...like it was withered inside. If you just touch their arm, then they're okay. They can interact and they have love and emotion, and they look at you. And he is so happy. He's got tears of joy and he's looking at his hands. He's okay. Well, that seems so easy. So, okay.

NEXT SCENE: PREPARING FOR EARTH

C: (There is a light pulsing from over the horizon.) It's sending my...it's sending my fellow beings elsewhere. People are leaving where they stay and so am I. And now we're next! So, I'm supposed to go to beyond the training area in the crater. There's a path that goes beyond there. So, it's kind of a while.

And we're sitting in seats, but we don't have arms on our chairs. It's just a plain, ninety-degree-angle chair carved out of the earthen surface and it's just hard, grey, and they're in lines and we're sitting. So, we're next and I see in front of everyone is...there's a gentleman there and he has a flat circular orb, and it has in it... It's metal on top and bottom and in the middle is this light that's going to pulse...and we're going! So, he's standing there, and he has his hand on the light...it's like a metal, flat lamp and in it is sandwiched the light. He puts his hands on it.

And he's talking to us and he's telling us "Be the love and the light." And he's saying, "Save them and wake them." He's just telling us to go do it. He's just saying, "Save them. Don't let the planet die." He's saying, "Don't let it turn black." He said, "Let it be the Light. It must shine like a star soon. So go and use your training and interact and help them."

And he's saying to just sit back and put our arms by our sides and take a deep breath and he's saying it will not hurt. The light will pulse two times and then you will be there on Earth in your human form. So, we're going to be born.

So, the light... So now I can see myself, the light must be so fast. So, I can see myself being born from my mother. Oh, my gosh! I'm just like coming...I'm just being born, and the nurse picks me up and I'm covered in goo. They cut the cord and I'm screaming. It is so bright, and I'm just being manhandled! All over the place! So, it's not really pleasant. And then my mom left. She went to go have a cigarette (laughter). So...

Then I'm just in this box and I'm thinking it's kind of funny because I just came from like a box, waiting in the side of a mountain, and now I'm in this box! I can't do anything. I'm just waiting for someone to come back. But I'm in a white blanket and I'm cozy and I'm okay, but I really wish someone would just come pick me up and love me, but I'm just separated in this box. They're not doing this right. This is not very loving.

So...my mom just came back, and she smells like cigarettes (laughs loudly). I can't say this to her, but I'm thinking in my brain, "Oh, my gosh! This is going to be quite a ride!" (Laughing) And I feel like I'm really going to have my work cut out for me in this life because this was not in the training, this infant part. But it's okay because I can just get used to this human body because it's really mushy. I'm used to my turtle-like skin. I'm all held together there. This is just...I'm like very floppy. So...I'm...this should be okay because I need to get used to this.

So, I'm okay with the infant stage. So...I didn't think I would have these feelings, but I feel upset, and we'll have to change things from the ground up. So...starting here at birth, this has to change. I feel like I'm being really too picky about the whole thing, but I'm not because I think when I got here, I should have more love. They told us about this interaction and emotions but I'm not getting any. Nobody's doing that to me. I feel like someone should be showing me that and it's not happening, so this should change now...so that's something I'll do.

Transcript: Galactic Council Sends Energy to Earth

I met Manu in Costa Rica through a mutual friend. He had read *The Three Waves of Volunteers and the New Earth* by Dolores Cannon, and we had a lot of fun talking about the material. A few months later, he and I scheduled a time to meet online for a session. Here is a segment from what we discovered!

C: *There's sort of a council of beings. It's sort of a metal floor, metal walls...like a spaceship. And they're small, blue beings. Large circular heads. And bigger soldiers that look kind of like dinosaurs. They're planning some kind of operation. They're sending...they're sending a few beings to Earth. There was a training of some kind. It feels very serious.*

M: What kind of training was this? What was done?

C: It was to blend in. Language. Body language. Tactical movements. Communication.

M: So, they had to practice being human. What else is happening there?

C: There's a window. I see other stars. Some are close by. Suns. White suns.

M: You said there is a mission. What's the mission?

C: Light-encoded DNA filaments. There's an activation process. In the right environment and circumstances, certain beings can unlock certain abilities through light-encoded filaments. We're sending certain technologies through certain beings in order to contribute to this... But the people are not entirely connected with everyone else there. It just feels like they're...they're outsiders a little bit...outside the ship.

M: So, it's almost like they don't fit in, even when they go?

C: Right.

NEXT SCENE: BEAMING ENERGY

C: There's a silver pyramid. There's a bunch of beings in robes standing around it. There's like a ceremony of some kind happening. People are from all different planets now. Different kinds of beings but wearing similar...similar outfits. The top of this pyramid is somehow going to have light emanating from it. It's going to go up off of this planet. There's a real camaraderie among the beings...a collective purpose. There's just compassion and humbleness and a wanting to serve.

Somehow this light is going to help ease the energy...or ease the transition at this time. Seems like the energy is somehow going to go back in time. I think it's something for Earth. Earth is going to go through a portal, but...so it's like...it's going to help with that transition. So, it's sending a certain kind of light resonance. It's going to help raise the collective frequency. Once it reaches that correct time period.

M: So, you're all there together to start this energy?

C: Yeah. There's a representative from each system. Each star system that has intelligent life.

M: **What makes Earth so important?**

C: *Earth...Earth's transition can help trigger the transition of other planetoid beings...can reformat the way the galaxy works. It's a cell in the body of this particular strand of light. If the resonance of that cell is out of correlation with the rest of the cellular structure light strands, it's going to create a dissonant resonance, and having the resonance be harmonic is important for all the frequencies to line up in a row harmonically. It will ripple out. It will affect everything.*

NEXT SCENE: ON THE SHIP

C: *I'm back and now I'm on a ship. And I'm...this was the original...now. I guess this is the future of where I live.*

M: **What's happening there?**

C: *There's an urgency to send a message...to send certain kinds of energy patterns out...which is what we're doing in the physical realm...but a certain frequency alignment that can help with the mission. I guess we're doing our...we're doing a certain part of the larger work on this ship, but we're broadcasting certain light.*

M: **What's the urgency?**

C: *It's not a panic...but there's a sense of purpose in terms of accomplishing it in a timely manner. Certain kinds of Light symbols. Certain kinds of symbols that are made of light and energy that can help...if broadcasted properly, can help lubricate. We all communicate telepathically, so we're moving some things around the ship, but mostly we're synthesizing each other. We can connect deeply with each other's minds so it's less about doing, it's more about consciousness.*

There is a recommendation to not eat certain foods and to go where there's a lot of stones. The more stones that are nearby, the better...is what they say.

M: **So, when they say don't eat certain kinds of food, what kinds of foods are they describing?**

C: *Like red meats. Things like that. No cream...things that are creamy. No tomatoes. I'm just...things that are red, I guess, aren't healthy right now... Apparently, there's so many species of tomatoes here [Earth]. Many of them were not indigenous to Earth except the small cherry tomatoes. They grew here naturally but the other tomatoes have a high acidic level.*

M: Will you be going to Earth?

C: *They will send a piece of Light to Earth. They'll imprint the blood of this being with this race. They're going to send these light...these shapes made of light...and they're going to broadcast them at a certain time. And at that time, they'll have a certain kind of imprint...like a sonic imprint on this being so that they can send energy to and from.*

M: What's going on with the humans? Why are there so many issues there...that they need so much support?

C: *They can't really see what they are and so...like young children, they don't understand what they're becoming. They don't understand the consequences. They don't know how to behave in a way that provides them with access to other frequencies, other experiences, and they need to be looked after the same way that children need to be looked after.*

M: Has it always been like this?

C: *No. No, no. There are beings that...that like...this particular area of the galaxy would be a good...what you would call "good real estate." So, the purpose is to change the resonance here so that it's not against the rest of the network. If this particular cell can be turned backward in the resonance, then that can spread into other cells. There's a...they've tried to...tried to change the flow in a different direction.*

M: Where do these beings come from?

C: *Alpha Centauri.*

M: And how are they affecting the humans?

C: *There's a certain frequency that they send via the Moon and what you would call "cell towers" that can create frequency locks that limit the DNA's lighting code filament and for...they're like consciousness caps. But obviously, there are many here that are not affected by that.*

M: What can the humans do to deflect this?

C: *It depends on the human. Each one...well...there's a small number that are truly aligned with us, the purpose of moving through Earth's portal, and they are flowing with that energy and are assisting that shift. But the humans at large can all change and grow, wherever they are now, they must evolve...even just a little bit more...grow a little bit more. Develop. Soften. Develop virtue. Center themselves. Every little drop counts. Every little drop matters. There is no waste in this universe.*

Open to Your Star Lineages

There has been much fear programmed into human consciousness about extraterrestrial life. Not one of us humans on the planet is "from here." Our species was brought here by extraterrestrials. Our souls come from higher dimensions and have experienced life in many forms and experimental worlds. The negative ET invasion already happened, and they are part of the driving force behind the media and institutions. The craft we see in the sky, disarming military weapons and nuclear power plants and such, are POSITIVE beings here to assist humanity.

We can release our fears and negative stigmas about extraterrestrial life. There are countless species of organic life spread throughout this universe, let alone the other universes and all their experimental zones of creation. There are many intelligent and unity-focused species in our multiverse who are beaming love and encouragement onto the Earth and into the hearts of humanity as we approach our graduation from 3D and move into the multidimensional unity consciousness of 5D and beyond. These are our family members and truly our Oneself in many forms.

THIRTY

Making the Transition

This next client, Rachel, was taken to a lifetime where she was working in a greenhouse growing plants to be planted on different planets throughout the cosmos.

C: It's a blue plane, and I can see the surface of the planet, so it is blue, and I can see the curve to the planet. I can see the night sky as the backdrop of the planet. I am just on the planet. There are like craters to it but not so much as the moon. But I can see when I focus that there are structures that fade in and out of existence, so they are not solid. It's like when you put your focus on them, they become a little more solid, but they are not completely solid.

M: That's interesting. What do they look like?

C: Geometric shapes. Like I am getting a rhombus.

M: Very interesting. Is there any plant life or any other life on this planet?

C: No, but I'm getting that if you move into one of these structures, it's a lot more abundant — like plush inside the structures, not on the surface, not that you can see.

M: Well, before we go on that journey, I would like you to look down at the ground and tell me if you can see your feet.

C: It's just a blue energy. It comes more into form as I move up the body so it becomes like you can see in a jellyfish as you move away from the sides. So, in the middle, there's more structure to the body.

M: Are you carrying anything or holding anything.

C: It is like a scepter. It's got a blue beacon — like a round, cylindrical shape on the top, and I think it sends energy. Yeah, it sends energy. It can help the plants grow. So, it revitalizes, and yeah, it expedites their growth.

M: That's nice. Do you have anything else on your body? Any other components?

C: It's like a utility belt. It has seeds in it, different compartments with different seeds.

M: And you plant those around somewhere?

C: In the structures.

M: Well, let's go visit one of those structures. Take me on the journey and tell me what's happening as it happens.

C: So, it has a door that can open, but it's like an energetic see-through door. As you pass through the door and shut the door behind you, everything changes. Like you cannot see the outside. You can't see the planet anywhere once you step in. It's like an atrium of life, of different plant life. There are ferns, and it's mainly green, and it's like the plants are moving on their own — like they can move and communicate with us.

M: That's nice. You said, "us." Are there others like you there?

C: Yeah. In the distance, there are a few others working, tending to the plants. I think I grow them for other planets. So, we cultivate them and grow them, but like they're special in the way that you can plant them on other planets, and they will communicate back to the plants on this planet. And they can talk to these plants and get the information from the planets that we have planted these plants on.

M: So, what do you do with that information once that feedback information has been sent?

C: We collate it and send it up to the motherships and they analyze it. It's to do with the oxygen and the atmosphere of the planet that they get sent to.

M: What about the oxygen? What's so important about the oxygen?

C: It needs to be kept at certain optimal levels.

M: And so, the plants help that happen?

C: Yes. They send the information back up to these plants, and they tell them if more is needed on the planet.

M: Wonderful. That's very valuable information. Do you enjoy your job?

C: Yes, but I want to go where the plants go. I want to visit where they are — to go on adventures.

NEXT SCENE: ON A MOTHERSHIP

C: Now, I am up on the ship. It's like a donut. It's huge. It's like a donut-shaped vessel, and it's got a number of different beings on it from all over the galaxy. There's a lot of humanoid-type beings. Yeah, insectoids — so the mantis beings. Everyone has their own jobs. So, one where I am standing at the moment is the leisure viewing platform. I can see Earth.

M: What's happening on the Earth right now that you all are observing it?

C: The starseeds are bouncing back information about the ascension, the ascension process. They are like beacons of light that beam, then they are collating the information like the most minute detail is recorded and analyzed.

M: And what are you all learning from the starseeds?

C: How to help them balance their own energy. How to help them in their own process. How we put positive intentions down to them without interfering.

M: How do you send the information and help without interfering?

C: Through intentions, our positive and loving intentions.

M: And why is it that you don't interfere?

C: That was a decree.

M: So, there was a decree not to interfere?

C: Yeah. They've got to do it themselves. They can feel us. They can feel us. Yeah. They are connected to us. We are their higher applications.

M: Well, what's happening now? What are you doing?

C: I am just observing people on the observing platform. They are observing themselves. There are people playing music. There are beings specifically there to heighten the vibration to bring joy and love so that everyone on the ship is in the highest vibration possible. So, the serious work it is very joyful and yeah — people — beings connecting with each other and telepathically swapping stories of their journeys. People are talking about the tipping point. It's the buzz in the air about that. They are really excited.

M: What are they saying about the tipping point?

C: That it is so close. People are feeling the energy waves as they are coming in and embracing them and it's making them all over-excited.

M: That's wonderful. What does the tipping point mean to everybody? How do they know they are at the tipping point?

C: Some feel it. It is like an energetic wave of rainbow light that will just be apparent.

NEXT SCENE: BRINGING HUMANS ON THE SHIP

C: We are in the sleeping pods. So, we have our own quarters — our own white rooms that are like large pods that we connect one on one there.

M: What do you mean one on one?

C: Each one of the beings comes in and speaks to each other telepathically, one to one, and shares stories. I am connecting with another being.

M: What are you connecting about? What's being shared?

C: Our lifetimes on other planets. So, this story about children playing on the grass and just being free spirits. And the more that we can share this positive white energy — the more that we can build it and harness it, and then send our intentions to Earth, and help with the energy of pure joy and love.

M: That's so nice. It sounds like you all really love this planet and love your work. Why do you love this planet so much? Why are you so connected to its process?

C: Because part of us is down there. It's an aspect of us on the planet. It is us.

M: What are you seeing happen next?

C: Next, we start bringing people up one by one to acclimate them to the higher frequencies. So, it's only small numbers at the moment that are coming up.

M: How do you bring them up? How is it that you bring them up?

C: I am not sure. I just see them in the pods. They are like jellybean white pods. They spend a few days up in the pod, and we observe them, and some of them come out and join us on the viewing platform, so they understand what's happening to Earth. Some of them didn't understand, so they needed to be brought up and shown.

M: And how do they respond?

C: They think it's amazing. They had a hunch. They kind of knew.

M: Yeah. It's exciting to have the humans starting to come up on the ship. What happens next?

C: They go back and start sharing it energetically. They have this now innate knowing that it is real, and it is happening, and they can share it with others that they have this found faith now that is true. And even if they don't talk about it, they share the vibration with everyone they come in contact with.

M: That's wonderful. What does that do for the people on the planet who might not be aware? How does this vibration help them?

C: It opens their perception — so you see their crown chakra starting to tingle and sparkle when this awareness — the energy touches them. It just opens it up.

M: That's so wonderful. What's happening now?

C: Right now, I have got an overview of the ship, and I am not on the ship anymore. I am sort of floating around it.

M: Do you see any other ships around?

C: I can't see them, but I feel them coming closer. I feel that more of the ships are huge, but they won't take everyone.

M: **What do you mean? Tell me about that?**

C: *Well, at the moment, there are only pods for maybe half a dozen people, but there's much, much more needed. So, I feel the other ships are coming closer.*

M: **And why are they going to be taking more humans onto the ships?**

C: *The same purpose. They just have to try it first. They just have to observe what would happen if humans came up and then went back again.*

NEXT SCENE: GOLDEN EARTH AND GOLDEN HUMANITY

C: *Now there's a cylindrical dome with all these donuts in the sky surrounding the Earth completely. It's like they are all holding energetic hands with each other touching in a circle formation, all the donut-shaped ships.*

M: **So, they are all surrounding the planet? Why is that?**

C: *So that all the loving intentions are concentrated on Earth. Well, there's a golden light that's shone upon the Earth...yes, and the Earth is transformed. It's a mixture of all the positive intentions on the ships along with the human intention that kind of join forces, and this golden light just beams from the planet and the planet transforms. It's like the golden light sheds the layer of the outer surface of the Earth and what's inside the Earth comes forward to the new surface. So, the inner Earth becomes the outer Earth. It is like a snake sheds its skin — the inner, renewed part comes to the surface, so it's fresh.*

M: **That's so nice. Does it change things on the planet? How does it look when it's renewed? How does it...what's the process look like as it happens?**

C: *Everything looks fresh...the trees are just a new color, like glowing. Everything is more vibrant.*

M: **That's nice. And what are you doing now? What's happening?**

C: *I am still observing from afar — the ships and the donut shape and the Earth sort of just coming forth into this new reality. It's quite a sight. It's like you just can't take your eyes off it — so beautiful.*

M: **I bet. So stunning. What's happening with the people on the planet?**

C: *It's like the people were just under the surface of the old skin, and they are coming up with the new planet. So, I can see them like rubbing their eyes and seeing the light because they have been down further in some darkness. And they are taking their first breaths and filling their lungs with a new type of oxygen*

— like it feels different to them — their lungs. (Takes a deep breath and sighs.) Feels easier to breathe. They have got to relearn a lot of stuff. They have forgotten how to share and how to live in harmony. They've got to relearn communities and to work together — and help one another.

M: How did they relearn?

C: They just feel it. They feel now that they need to work together. It's just their knowing that they are one, and to help each other benefits all. So, I can see them having different methods now working in fields and with agriculture. They have different technologies to grow, so like the scepter; they use energetic...it's like funneled energy to grow the crops rather than relying on GMO or anything to boost the growth...they can just use pure energy now.

M: How do they access that energy and use it?

C: They can bring it up from the center of the Earth, or from Source energy they can channel it down, bring it down through their bodies. Bring down and through their hearts, or they can use tools...there are scepters that are receptors.

M: And where do they get these scepters from?

C: There are now visitors from off-planet that are welcome.

M: So now the space families are now coming back onto the planet?

C: Yeah. There's no fear anymore. The humans don't perceive as they used to. It diminished. It dissolved with their renewal.

M: Wonderful. Has anything happened to the human body now that the shift has happened?

C: They can absorb more light and they breathe in the oxygen. It is a lot freer. So, when they breathe in more light, it just fills them up so more efficiently with light than it ever has before. So, you don't need to concentrate on filling yourself up with light anymore. It just happens automatically with each breath. So, the energetic body is renewed with the light, and each cell is a lot more light-filled. The humans can choose whether they want to be in their solid form or move into the golden light form.

M: Tell me about those two forms.

C: So, the human form's a lot like we have now, but just more golden and light-filled, but they can with intention completely move into this golden light form. It allows them to move to different planets...they can move wherever they want. They can move to the other side of the planet.

M: Wonderful. So, they just shift into this golden light form and just travel?

C: It takes a lot of practice. It doesn't happen straight away but the ones that are already on their ascension path, they can master it a lot more quickly because it is like when you meditate and you go out of the body — it's that feeling; that feeling signature that you lose, you lose contact with your body. The body dissolves and moves into this golden-white form and then you can reanimate however you choose.

M: Wonderful. So, when humans travel off the planet or around the planet, what do they do when they are doing this traveling?

C: So, it depends on what their interests are. So, for example, the planet that I was first on and was shown — they will go to those planets to learn agriculture and learn the new ways of doing things and take it back and apply it there.

M: That's wonderful. What do you see happening now?

C: I see the Earth is less densely populated because of this. So, because they can move freely once they have mastered the movement and it becomes much less densely populated, which gives space for new growth and for the Earth to really regenerate itself to its former glory — to its heaven on Earth. She becomes the true oasis.

M: That's wonderful. So, it just starts to get regenerated because fewer people are there, more information is coming in, more knowledge?

C: Yeah. It's like self-perpetuation, regeneration. It's been slow going to begin with — like it's still happening now. It is very dense and slow, but once this intentional shift from the star beings and the healings — once that is a collective concentration, it happens more quickly.

NEXT SCENE: GREAT CENTRAL SUN RAINBOW BRIDGE

C: It's like a pure, rainbow-white-stream column coming down to Earth. It's like a waterfall column that's going straight into the Earth.

M: Where's it coming from?

C: The Great Central Sun.

M: And what is this light doing? What is this rainbow light stream doing?

C: It's bringing in the even higher density energies that have never been possible before, like six density, twelve density — like a huge portal. The Earth couldn't sustain those higher energies before.

M: What are these energies doing?

C: I am not sure. I am just watching the energy go back and forth. It's like a stream.

M: It sounds very beautiful.

C: Yeah, it's directly from Source. Before it's been filtered, and it couldn't come so seamlessly through. I am not sure of the higher purpose of it.

Transcript: The Rainbow Bridge

Another client shares a bit more about the "rainbow bridge" concept.

M: Why is it important to keep singing?

C: The powers that are trying to repress the people do not want you making sounds, noise. They know... They don't want you gathering to sing together. After three minutes of singing together, everyone's heartbeat syncs up to the same rhythm. They don't want us synced up. What they are trying to block ultimately is the ascension, and so when you sing together it helps the group ascend together.

We are all going on a journey together; we're walking each other home. We're climbing a giant mountain and it's a long steep path. You can only go one at a time on this journey but when you look in front of you there is a line of people in front of you, and when you look behind you there is a line of people behind you, and the people in front of you are not better than you, the people behind you are not below you, they're just two minutes...it's just a timing thing. They're just two minutes behind you on the road. It's not a good, better, or worse but we're all going together.

Where we go one, we're all going, and we have to go together (crying). It's sad to see the fear and to know that...even as I stand on the trail, I see those standing in the woods that need to get on the trail and they're afraid, but we're not...like nobody gets left behind.

M: What does that mean, "No one gets left behind?"

C: It means that this will take as long as it takes until everyone that got promised ascension to, at this time the promise was made, and so the population on this planet is very specific to the ascension. People who tell you that the planet is overpopulated don't understand the spiritual significance of what's going on right now.

We're not having this giant population to like damage and rape the Earth or anything like that. It's to do...it was to bring down as many experts...like all the ascension experts are here now, in body, whether they know it or not, they're the ascension experts and they're all down here now to get us to twenty...you know, to get us through the next two decades as we work through this process. I don't know the timelines specifically of how long it's going to take, but I know it takes to get everyone across the rainbow bridge, to get everybody over the bridge, to get everybody up to the peak.

THIRTY-ONE

Main Wave Event

This client came to see me to facilitate a surrogate session for her husband who has had difficulty accessing the information he wanted in previous sessions. One of the ways I do surrogate work is first to do a full IQH session for the new client and then ask if it is appropriate to receive healing and information for the person requesting the surrogate session. This works best when the people know one another but it is not necessary. All is connected through the unified field of Consciousness.

The surrogate client is named Mona who did a session for her husband Ian. In the session, her Higher Self uses the analogy of "clean air" which symbolized "clean emotional and psychic energy" earlier in the session. Although, I have a feeling this could also mean literal clean air as major smoke and pollution have been talked about in other clients' sessions. The time period given for this energy event pulse is estimated around 2024.

M: Question about, she does not feel the urge or the excitement to travel. Is there anything behind that?

C: *Something is coming, a strong wave of energy. It's coming. And when it comes the house will fall. It will shatter everything they believe in. Their family will need their guidance then, so they cannot be absent. That is why they can't leave, not now. They need to be present for this wave, so they can lead the house into the new phase. It's going to be a new movement. The air will be clear then. Once it's clear, their lungs will not know how to breathe in the clean air. They have been plagued with. The family will need them then. They'll need guidance.*

M: What is causing this wave? Where is it coming from?

C: *It is coming from all around the Earth. It is going to push out all bad energy. It will be extraordinary. The movement will cleanse everything. And those who have lived in darkness will not know how to breathe in the clean air. They may not be able to adapt. Ian does not want to leave them behind in the darkness. Neither does Mona. That's why they don't want to leave. They want to guide them, The people they love, they want to guide them into the light when this happens. So that they're not left behind. Their hearts have a strong light, but their lungs are full of dark energy that they have been breathing in collectively.*

Mona and Ian have been adapting. They have been cycling through this dark air, through their lungs, and cleansing it with the clear air that they have created in their space. They know how to remove it from their systems and how to accept the light. They need to lead both their families. They need to teach them how to adapt to what's coming.

M: When you say it's coming, how, how soon? You can use Mona's understanding of time.

C: There's vibration in her hands now. It's very strong. She senses it's close. The vibration is very strong in her hands. She could sense that it is very, very close. It will be in your lifetime. You will experience this on Earth. It's coming within the next few years. Before they leave this home, they will experience this new Earth. It's coming. It will be two years. That's when the wave will come. It's already started to build up.

M: What will it be like here on Earth From now until then? What's this time about? Globally? Personally?

C: There will be great darkness that spreads around the Earth, leaking into everyone's lungs. Trying to stop them from being able to adapt to the light that will come. As it will be very heavy. Will fall into a depression. And all of the senses; financial, emotional, mental, everything. They'll fall into a dark depression and their lungs will be filled with darkness. They will need to remember how to breathe in the light. Only those will be able to pass through the new wave. They need to remember that after the darkness comes the light. They need to be patient and not forget what they are. What they can be and the light inside them. They can overcome the darkness that will come to pass. There will be light on the other side and fresh air to fill their lungs. All the darkness will disappear if they just learn how to breathe it in and accept it in their heart.

M: Is there any other guidance about this passage between now and the big wave of light?

C: The vibration will cause pain. It will cause physical pains. It will lead them to believe their health is deteriorating but it isn't. This is only the body's adjustment to the new wave, the new vibration of the new Earth. Once the wave comes the pain will subside. They need only to endure. It has been coming for the past few years. That's why all this pain is arising. All these strong emotions are arising. It's heightened now. We're at the peak. You need only endure this time as you have been enduring in past years. It's slowly been building your strength. That we are at the peak. You need to build your strength further so that you can endure what is to come. If you endure it, you will be ready to accept what's happening on the other side of the wave.

M: What about planetary changes? Earth changes? Do those begin before or after the wave?

C: There will be drastic changes after the wave. I cannot share them now. They will be severe. New Earth cannot survive as we are now. These changes must occur. There's no need to be afraid. I feel that many fear this new Earth. There's no need to be afraid. We all need to endure these two years. Everything will be okay.

M: And how can people endure this? Or assist others in enduring?

C: Do not give in to the darkness that will fill your lungs. It will come from all directions. To make you believe that humanity is hopeless, but it is not. This is only an illusion. It is only an illusion to fool you all into believing that there is only darkness but there is light. You just need to keep the hope. Keep believing in the light for it will come to those who are patient. Those whose hearts are strong. Those whose hearts are strong need to lead those who are weak. Lead them out of the depression, out of the darkness. You need to share what little light we have. Shine it on those who are drowning in the darkness. That is their role. That is our role.

M: Yeah, thank you. I know for many that there are concerns about... I'm going to be careful with my words, um the things that were injected, put into people's arms over this last time. And how it might negatively affect people or the process of this awakening. Can you share anything about that?

C: It will make their process more difficult. The thing they injected is part of the darkness. It's part of the larger cloud that has trickled down. It has been put into millions of people. This will make their process more difficult. It will make it much harder for them to remove the darkness in their lungs because now it is in their bloodstream as well. It was part of a ploy to pull mankind darker and deeper into despair. It will cause many health problems. It will make it feel like there is no hope. They had to endure only a small amount of pain. Now, those who accepted this into their bloodstream will endure severe pain. Their journey will not be easy. They have been fooled by the darkness into accepting this into their bloodstream. but it's not hopeless. They can persevere.

M: How can they persevere? How can they be supported?

C: *They need leaders. They need to be led by those who can breathe the light. Mona feels a great sense of responsibility. Her body is being crushed by the weight. She knows she's one of the leaders. Her body is not ready to accept this fate yet. It is creating a crushing weight, vibrations in her body are shaking her very core. She needs time to accept this fate. She will be ready but not now. This realization is causing the vibrations to intensify in the palm of her hands and her knees. She needs time to accept her destiny, but she will be ready. All those who are meant to lead will be ready when the time comes. No need to fret. We will not put any weight upon you that you cannot do.*

M: Very good. Thank you so much for that. I had one more question about this wave of light when it comes through. When it moves through, how will it change our experience of reality?

C: *The waves will push what humans call "the soul" out of the body and the physical and the spiritual bodies will become separated. Once it's pushed out of the physical body, the cleansing would happen. The spirit [subtle bodies], as they call it, will be cleansed from the darkness but those who keep the darkness within them will stay tethered to the physical body, and they will not be able to be separated.*

You will still be able to communicate with those who are still tethered to the physical. But the chances to guide them to the light will be few. The chances to guide them will be much more difficult. There will be few if not none. The guidance should happen before the wave. This is very, very important. Those with the light need not doubt themselves. They need to rebel against the ideologies of humanity. They need not worry even if they're not accepted. No harm will befall them. They need only spread the light and those who will accept will accept and those who will not will also continue on their journey, but no harm will befall the leaders, the spreaders of light. They need to start acting. The time is now.

M: So, question regarding, so it sounds like this soul or this spiritual energy will separate from the physical body for those that are making this transformation but they'll still be able to interact with the people in the physical body that didn't make the transition?

C: *Yes. The people in the physical body will doubt the movement. They will not believe that it has occurred. They will see those who are on a higher vibration as though they are their old selves, but they will not be so. Their eyes will view them as they always had but those who are on a higher vibration will know the difference between the two. Doubt will blind them from what has happened. People in the physical body will blind themselves with doubt. They will make themselves believe that the movement was not real. So, when we try to guide them through the spiritual body the doubt will greatly tether them down to the Earth and the physical world. It will be very hard to guide them once you are on a different plane.*

M: And those that are in the physical bodies what will they be experiencing, sensing once the shift has happened?

C: They will feel nothing. They will live senseless lives continuing on and feel nothing. No happiness, no sadness, no purpose, no fulfillment. It will continue on like robots completing daily tasks that have no meaning and no purpose. But they will not understand this. They will only continue on this path until the time when on this Earth has ceased. After that beings that are physical will no longer be created. The entire Earth will shift to a new vibration once all the physical bodies have deceased and moved on.

M: Those that have made the shift in, let's say to the New Earth energy, when the wave comes through will they be on a different planet, will they be in a different plane, will they be seeing everything and just standing right next to those people who are still in the darkness? How does that experience happen?

C: The Earth will change. They will still be here, but they will be able to travel and experience the Earth in very different ways. They can travel in the blink of an eye to wherever their hearts desire. They will not experience the Earth the same as they did in their physical bodies. Nothing will be the same as they know, everything will be new and beautiful. They may still communicate with the physical humans, but this is only to ease the separation of the connections they have created while they were here. That is its only purpose. To ease whatever regrets they might hold with this separation, to not pull them back down into the physical world. To reconnect with those they have loved. The only reason they can connect and speak with those who are in the physical bodies. So that they can be free of it, free of doubt, and free of the question 'what if?'

M: Can you give an example of what the ones that shifted to the new Earth, let's say, within the... once it shifts what are the activities that they'll be involved in right after that shift has happened? For the next days and weeks after that wave has come through.

C: In the beginning, there will be a very slow shift. They will, it will allow time for them to shift their minds from the physical to the next plane. To shift their hearts from what they loved here and to understand that it's okay to move into the next plane. That is why we allow their connection, and communication into the physical world. So that this shift will become easy. Once they have completed this phase.

M: That makes sense.

C: Once they have completed this phase, they will leave the Earth. Into the abyss of the universe. And then they will know their real purpose. I cannot share more than this.

M: When you say they will go into the abyss, these are the ones that have shifted? The ones that have ascended.

C: Yes. Once they have detached all of their connections from the physical world then, and only then, will they be able to move to the next plane.

M: Okay. I understand that. And you were saying the ones that were stuck in the darkness, stuck in the physical, like they stayed there and that there would be a point where they wouldn't be able to make new life, new children coming in...will there be great deaths that happened rapidly?

C: They will not seek to reproduce. The emotions that they have now, that lead their lives, will no longer plague them. They will only continue on until they decease.

M: And that decease will it still happen gradually over time, or will there be other experiences that create more rapid exits?

C: Many people will pass on, as they say, quickly after the wave, They will accept that they did not move on to the next phase and they will pass on. Many people have already passed on and have started to do so. But there will be a rapid amount of death after the wave. But some people will hold on much longer and will take much longer to accept that it is time for them to move. They will grow to old age and then die naturally. Because of the doubt of the movement that is blocking them from believing.

Transcript: Restoring Earth with the Children

I had the pleasure of working with this client, Dina, around five times including the one where the story of Jeremiah, a disciple of Jesus, was brought forward. In many of her lifetimes, she was a protector of a holy blue flame that emanated evolutionary higher consciousness coding to the Earth plane. The theme of the "blue flame" has come up in several sessions with clients in different time periods. It seems to play a big part in the balance and harmonic evolution of the Earth.

C: *Rolling hills. A river. And a large, very white light pouring out of me. Hands on the ground. It's like my shape is shifting between human form and something not so human. Angelic light being. There's blue light flowing into the ground and connecting different energetic points in the ground. My hands are really hot.*

It's helping fortify and raise the vibration of Mother...of giving the Earth the power to shift on a cosmic level. This shift will cause huge vibrations on Earth's surfaces. Volcanic eruptions and earthquakes...large waves. It's like resetting the clock. There are many of us all over, not just where I am, but all over the planet. It's like every corner of this grid has a key that needs to be placed in it and turned so that the door can open, so the Light can shine through. I guess in a visual sense, if you can picture the chakras of a human body and each chakra...as you open it, it needs a key to be twisted in a clockwise rotation to make the vortex of the chakra start spinning faster and faster.

M: **And so, when you lay your hands on the ground, how does the key work?**

C: *At first, it's pouring energy in, and then it's finding the electromagnetic fields, pulling and spinning it out with one hand on the Earth and the other moving in a clockwise position outward and then upwards, towards the sky. It's like just as bodies have to unwind, so does this grid. We're continuing the work of creating one river and merging all the bodies of water energetically to flow as one. This takes many people. It's like...the four elemental bodies: fire, earth, water, and air will be coming back to their purity, merging as one, and we as lightworkers, we as healers of humans and of Earth will be connecting these bodies of water, these energetic bodies of water together again to purify. It's like cleaning the water. Making it drinkable again. It's like the water is changing from a muddy color to a blue jade, clear water all the way down to the bottom. The trees and the leaves and nature are so green. It's overgrowing. Some of the cities...so fresh and vibrant. It's like the leaves are singing.*

M: **So, everything is being restored. What else is happening?**

C: *A much simpler lifestyle. People are dancing and singing. We see lots of children's faces as they laugh. And the children are huge helpers in this process as they are showing us...what true joy there is in our childlike nature. Helping us hear the plants talk and which rocks need to be collected from the rivers to be placed into other rivers. Some of the elders know, but really the children are the ones that are tasked with going and picking the rocks.*

M: What's so unique about the rocks that they need to be moved from one river to another?

C: The rocks are the densest form of energy. Slowest moving. Longest to change over time. So as these rocks are placed in rivers, these old energies can move in with the moving water and flow and spread downstream. It's learning how to combine light energy with the denseness of the Earth and converting the denseness into light.

WORKING WITH THE HIGHER SELF AND THOTH

M: What about the restoration of Gaia?

Thoth: *Most will see it as the world on fire, but it is from the ashes that the beginning will rise. It is from the dust that we will form a new earth. Pure waters will flow, and waves will crash down, and Mother will shudder and shake, and new life will come from it. As the restoration comes forth and unfolds, you pillars of Light need to stand strong, expand your arms, share the message, and the love. So much love is needed.*

M: What about the human changes?

Thoth: *It's a slow progression. Many years until humans are shapeshifting back and forth between angelic bodies and human bodies, which is why the groundwork is so important right now...in order to prepare the vessel for the energy coming out of your hands...may not be blue yet, but the light will come soon.*

Like a Thief in the Night

In the Bible, it is written that no one knows the hour or the day of when this shift will occur and that it will come as a "thief in the night" surprising many with a quickening of energy and a PULSE of LIGHT. Projected dates come and go which take all who are focused on them on an emotional roller coaster ride. To avoid unnecessary suffering, it has been recommended to stay present in the NOW and allow the process to unfold. Surrender to the process and align yourself with joy and peace as you walk your path towards the New Earth!

THIRTY-TWO

City of Light

This client came to me with some questions regarding her dreams where she was astral traveling to training courses to prepare herself for the shift. She also frequently visited an astral healing center that she felt would eventually be on the Earth. Her inner messaging said that she was going to play a part in that sanctuary space and that it would be in her hometown area in the Pacific Northwest.

C: *I'm talking to Spirit. Or something.*

M: About what?

C: *I'm not done. I'm not done with what I was doing to help. Going back, going down on Earth. To be human, I think. To help. I'm excited. I know I can help people. I know I can wake them up. I have to wake myself up because I have to forget. When I wake up, others wake up.*

Going to be in the United States. It's very important to be in the United States. They need help. There's help all over the world. The United States needs a lot of help. I'm going over. I can see cities. I can see cars. Roads. The West Coast is very important. Bringing light like a beacon.

M: What are some of the plans for that life?

C: *To heal. To bring awareness. Bring spirit. Can make people's focus shift. They're not focused on anything. There are a lot of distractions that need to be simplified. People's work needs to be simplified. Their thoughts need to be simplified. The way they live. There needs to be more spirit. More light. I keep seeing the Northwest.*

M: Let's focus there, what's important in the Northwest?

C: *Something starts there. I feel like it starts. I chose to be in the Northwest because it starts in the Northwest.*

M: What starts there?

C: *The shift. People want more peace in their lives. They want to be less stressed. They start wanting to be at peace. (M: Yeah.) I feel a lot of energy. There's going to be a lot of energy.*

M: What's going to bring that energy.

C: *I think it's the center. Like a star. A light. Shimmery. That's where it's coming from. It pulses kind of, but there are different energies. The star is familiar. I feel like I've seen it before. The energies cause things to happen, causes people to think differently. I'm questioning a lot of things. It feels like there's going to be movement, but I don't know. I feel like people are going to start grouping together. They're going to start reaching out more. They want to know what's happening. A lot of chaos there too. A lot of people look confused and think it's scary. Very chaotic. Panic. Fear. I feel like there is some natural... There's something natural happening too, with the weather. The weather is scaring people. They're scared by what it's doing. I feel like there are storms. A lot of water. Rain. People driving. They want to leave, and they want to leave quickly. They're scared. I feel like areas are going to flood. There's going to be flooding. A lot of rain. Wind. Cold. People are getting angry with each other. The ones who are scared are getting angry with each other. They're snapping at each other a lot. Nobody knows what to do. Nobody knows where to go, but they can't stay. Not there.*

M: Where do people go to be safe there?

C: I feel like they're driving away from the cities. A lot of people are going into the trees. There's something there that can help them. Like they feel safe in the trees, but they don't know why they're going to the trees. I feel like some are being drawn to the trees; they feel drawn to the trees, some feel like they're trying to hide.

M: When you said people were starting to get together, where are people getting together there?

C: I feel like there are groups that start before the chaos starts, before things get really chaotic. Before the weather does that. I feel like they group together. They start asking questions and understanding, kind of, that things are changing. I feel like they group together in the trees, and they help each other. Like they're starting a community. Some people get there, and they're scared, and they're confused. Some people look very comfortable and they're helping the ones who look confused. There is a machine that they put people into. They can put people into. It looks like energy. Energetic, healing. It's a white machine. You lay down and something arcs above your body. It feels like it heals you, helps heal you.

M: Where did they get this machine?

C: I feel like the blue people gave it to them. People are healing. Some people are sitting down. There's a man crying. Very scared and he's confused. There's something that's happened. Looks like something major has happened with the world. A lot of weather. It seems bad to people, but it's not really. Very soon.

It looks like there are people who heal the ones who are distraught, and when they're healed, you can physically see light from their hands to the people's hearts. Their foreheads. Their hands are directly on them. I still see the light.

M: So, they're healing them with light? Hands-on healing?

C: Some people are being sent off. There's a woman there. I don't know her nationality. She kind of seems to be in charge a little bit.

M: What's her name?

C: I don't know her name. I don't feel like I know her, but she's expecting people. A lot more people. Healers who can heal people. Then there are people who she's talking to, and they walk away like she sent them somewhere. Maybe to help bring more people.

M: How are people brought?

C: I see people walking into a clearing. They're coming through the trees. Some trickle in, just a few, and sometimes there's a lot more people that come in crowds and when the crowds come, the healers move very quickly. Very swiftly. People when they're healed, they want to know what's happening. And you tell them it's not for them to worry about right now but to just feel the way they feel because when you heal them, they feel better.

M: How did the healers get this ability to heal so rapidly?

C: I think the machine does something. The machine looks like it goes through the pores; it goes through the bodies. Everything. It looks like a lot of them did work on their own too.

M: What's happening now?

C: Some people are sitting underneath the trees. It's very pretty, very pretty where we are. It's easy to forget about what's going on out there. People are still in states of distress. People, healers it looks like, are running out. They move very smoothly. Something about the way they hold themselves that's different. They hold themselves very confidently, very peacefully. Very fluid. Their motions are very fluid. And they go straight up to people, and they'll kneel and they place their hands on them. Seems like on the forehead and the heart. Seems to be the main ones. And we put our attention for healing and peace. You can tell that they feel it when it's happening. When they're being healed, they can feel it. I think it surprises some people. They didn't realize they were in pain.

M: What do they call this place?

C: I want to say Eden, but that was my feeling. It feels like an Eden. Very peaceful.

M: I wonder if you can find the leaders of this place?

C: I feel like some have communication with the blue people. I feel like some have better telepathy. Some can communicate with them. Others I don't think are too interested. They leave it up to the others who can. I see some who've been healed, maybe this is later, some who have been healed. And they're playing with each other in the trees. It looks like we stayed, but where does everybody sleep? I don't know. It feels like we've stayed though. I see people talking. It seems like there are more people.

M: More people that are coming?

C: More people that are already there now. That's why it feels like we stayed. (M: Yeah.) Some feel or look like they're feeling lighter, but there's still self-work, I think. They're still healing.

M: What ways do they heal themselves?

C: They play and talk to each other. There are arguments at times. When they argue, there are groups, there are groups that help them like talk about what came up with them to cause an argument. What were they holding on to?

M: You said there are groups that are doing this work together?

C: Yeah. There's talking. When there is an interaction with someone that's not good, they work through it right there.

Transcript: Building New Earth Temples

David was introduced to me by another friend at brunch when David was traveling through our town from Egypt. I shared about my work, and he immediately wanted to have a session. During his session, we met his Andromedan soul aspect and found out more about the City of Light in the Pacific Northwest.

C: A star being on a golden throne. Looking at the Earth and emanating Light, like a ray.

M: What does this ray do?

C: Activate and heal.

M: What do you call yourself? What do they call you there?

C: Arius. I'm approaching the Earth. My ship is like a golden eagle. As it enters the atmosphere, it becomes transparent. I become transparent. I go down and meet my allies. We hug and greet and celebrate the joyful union.

M: Are these human allies?

C: *They're mixed beings. They appear human; they're not. There is something supernatural about them and royal. They're telepathic and their eyes are glowing. There is so much love, and we're holding each other and creating this grid. Building a grid of Light that protects this planet, cities of Light, temples, pyramids, crystal altars.*

It's the art that we're trained to do. Build civilizations and train them and hold grids of Light built on free energy and resonating with star frequencies and creating a unity of what is above below. It becomes a sacred mirror and miniature cosmos on the planet basically. It reflects the microcosm. The structures are harmonic, and they have the sacred ratios and geometries and material that we use that can help hold those frequencies.

M: Who trained you to do this?

C: *The Creator. It's part of my lineage. It's just our art. It's our gift. I've studied it; it's in my DNA. My DNA trained me.*

M: Why are you doing this on the planet now? On the Earth?

C: *Because there has been a lot of destruction and we are building harmonics, and the Earth is ascending. New life emerging, like springtime. All the timelines and the multidimensional aspects of myself are coming together. Celebrating this moment and the union. Feeling accomplished, the big job on the higher planes and watching it manifest on the earthly planes. So much heart.*

M: Who else is involved in this building?

C: *Elohim. They are igniting the sacred fire that powers the grid.*

M: Beautiful. Tell me what's happening now. What do you see here?

C: *Sacred fire surrounding the Earth, spreading crystal light flames. Transmuting negativity. Shifting the tones, the frequency of the planet. More crystalline structures are emerging from the surface, from the Inner Earth out, and more of the mythical beings coming back to the surface. The children are really happy, and they're playing. Their parents look very much awakened. It is like our Elven DNA is coming back into full operation.*

It's the closing of a cycle. Our job is done. It's time to move onto other planets and see them. And so, we say goodbye (deep exhale) and leave.

WORKING WITH THE HIGHER SELF

M: Can you share more with us about his mission? What is he here to do?

C: Build new Cities of Light.

M: Can you share with us that process? What is it like? What will he do?

C: Yes, it starts with one phase, one healing center, one temple. He'll create a template, and he'll go with a team to replicate, recreate according to the energetic structures of the land, and adapt to them. It will be places of high frequencies that attract people to come and thrive and create and move from one spot to the next and rebuild these temples with these templates.

M: Where is this first temple space?

C: Here [Ashland, OR]. It's near some water and forest and mountains. It's very sacred, mystical.

M: Beautiful. Is there anything else that wants to be shared about that center?

C: It's a sun gate. It's a gate to the Sun. A gate to Source. A higher dimensional portal grounded in the physical where the magic happens.

Sanctuary Communities

There will be multiple "Cities of Light," multiple sanctuary communities around the Earth. Everything will align for these communities to manifest in accordance with the Divine Plan. Let us continue our inner work and work within our local communities to raise the collective vibration. Let us follow our inner guidance to lead us swiftly and easily towards our Higher Destiny.

THIRTY-THREE

After the Shift

A lina came into her first scene and described a big theater room that was being used for a council meeting. There were many important people gathered to hear her give a report. Some were human and some were non-humanoid intelligent beings. When she looked down at her body, she described it as her body but upgraded and enhanced. Everyone is in celebration mode and is excited to hear what she says in her mission report.

C: Mission completed!

M: What were you completing?

C: Good question, good question. Transportation has been completed with great success. They are in remission, and everything went according to plan, but then again, we knew this wouldn't be easy. So, me and my crew are the ones that have been working with this and seriously need some healing and R&R. [rest and relaxation] (laughs). But we are all very happy that this work has been done. I have a feeling that this was transporting the, shall we say, lower frequency souls off from Earth into quarantine or wherever. Different locations for different categories, but we've moved the ones that needed to go first. Yeah. Some were resisting, of course, but they all went in the end.

M: Where did you send them to?

C: Colonies, but they were in different locations. Some back to Source, some to colonies, some to healing chambers of some sort...rehabilitation of some sort.

M: What is being shared by the group now? How do they handle it?

C: They are relieved and happy, and the feeling is, "We knew we would do this, but thank god it's done." (Laughs). Though it's not complete, this part is completed.

M: Are there other parts that you know about?

C: Similar, but these were the lowest-frequency entities. So, we took the toughest, roughest, first — the worst, if you will, first. Yeah, because they now have to go through the cycle of, shall we call it, karma — cause and effect of what they chose to experience in this experiment. And we are grateful that they did because we needed them to do that for us, but as we are now shifting, they were given the option to shift but chose not to. So, these are the ones that chose not to shift. They have now been relocated.

M: What was the process of relocating them? How did you take them?

C: They were grouped. So basically, I, the people on the ground did that and I was steering the fleets. I was in command of all the ships and fleets and making sure that everyone got on the right ship, that everyone was there basically. But I was in the highest command of this, so I had my crew, or people, report to me. But I am very hands-on, so I am always there also with everyone. We are doing this together.

M: Was this obvious to the humans on Earth? Did they feel it?

C: No, not to all, no.

M: How was it taken without people noticing?

C: I can't speak to that.

M: What's happening now?

C: We are discussing more about everything. Everyone in the room knew the plan, and so we're just going through and confirming what happened and what we did was successful in the end. Yeah, just basically going through it. Some are asking some questions about the details, but that's not important. Everyone is really focused and happy and relieved because this was a huge task, and it was important that we get it done in time. We were on a very tight schedule, apparently.

M: What made it so tight?

C: We were standing by to execute when the command came, and when it came, it had to be done right away; the timing was very precise from Source or whomever. So, when we got the command, it was go, go, go, go, go! We were able to beautifully coordinate, so really, it went smoothly for that type of job.

M: Very good, what will the council do now?

C: Celebrate.

NEXT SCENE: WHERE SHE LIVES IN THAT LIFE

C: Oh, it's down here. It's here, literally here [current house], but I have other places as well. I travel a lot. I have many bases. I go everywhere. Ships, other planets, different places on Earth, different star systems, different galaxies.

M: What do you do when you're in these places?

C: Work (laughs).

M: Tell me about your work. See yourself doing it and tell me about it.

C: I am laughing because I get paid to talk. I am organizing; I am structuring; I am commanding — not from the human perspective of commanding — delegating maybe is a better word. I am, shall we say, the spider in the web connecting all the different works being done and going wherever needed in any given now moment to assist in any operation...in any specific location. And then I go, and I report back to this room. I have different briefings as well, of course.

NEXT SCENE: FLYING AROUND THE WORLD

C: I am flying.

M: What are you flying through?

C: Good question. I am in my body, so I am flying down here on Earth. I am not really doing anything, just flying. I am pretty high up, so I am sort of in the clouds. I don't really see much. I think I am flying over the ocean. I think I am crossing the Atlantic. I feel like I am going back to New York, or something like that. It looks like the streets of New York.

M: What do you notice about the streets of New York?

C: I'd say they're glowing a bit more than I would imagine they are not, but I feel it looks pretty similar. I haven't actually been so...

M: So, what are you doing visiting the city?

C: Yeah, I think it's like a business trip. I'm really all about business, aren't I? (Laughs) It's consulting. It's the same. I am doing consulting in anything, everything, new versus old. Transitioning. I guess I am going into another type of those meetings that we were just in.

It's the same thing as before in how things work. Ah, this is the transition work. These are very sensitive times because we are reshuffling so much. People are going to be shifting out of their old roles; the ones who aren't already in the positions of their passion are going to leave, and they will be redirected by their higher aspects to their proper positions. But this transition is, of course, sensitive from the human perspective because many people are going to be leaving and starting new. And so, there are a lot of fears involved in this, though everyone is handling it without...it's just sensitive. We need to have compassion for everyone doing this transition because even though they are mentally aware that they are going somewhere better, it's still an experience for them to make this transition.

Transcript: Treehouse Communities and the Rainbow Bridge

This client came to me just as she was starting to awaken and was making her way out of the Mormon community. She knew that she was meant for the New Earth and had concerns about whether her partner would be shifting too. She had been trying to have a baby and wasn't sure if she was meant to bring in a new child at this stage of the Ascension.

The client came into the scene and described herself as a light being above the Earth in space observing the planet. When I moved her forward, she saw herself now on the Earth resting by a beautiful waterfall. The client tells me that her heart is pounding as energy surges through her body.

C: *The water is glowing like the stars, or like when you go to the ocean, and it has that glowy stuff when you walk. That's what it looks like, but it's coming down in a waterfall. And I'm just on the banks watching it, but it smells clean. And the stars are up; it is very beautiful. It's so beautiful.*

M: **Are you alone there, or are others with you?**

C: *Well, I am alone here, but I know there are people close. I'm just sitting there on a rock.*

M: **Do you sleep or eat?**

C: *I don't think so.*

M: **Feel into it. Tell me, how do you get your nourishment? How do you stay charged? Trust what comes to mind.**

C: *I feel like what I'm doing right now. Just sitting there. Oh yeah, there's an energetic exchange between the trees there and myself. It's basically like we are feeding each other kind of. It's just light...just energy, so just is.*

M: **So, there is some type of exchange? A relationship between the life force of the tree and yours?**

C: *Yeah, because it's the same thing. It's like a blue energy that I am feeling and seeing. It's also the same with the stars; it's the same with the water; it's the same thing that I look like.*

M: **What do you do with most of your time?**

C: *Right now, it feels like I would probably just want to play in the water. It feels like I am a keeper of the forest. I am. I know the trees and flowers and they know me. So, right now, I am walking in the forest. It's daytime now. It's so green! I am visiting with the plants. I'm touching them, talking to them. I can feel like I am more in a body now. I am female, yeah. I am just walking barefoot.*

NEXT SCENE: EARTH COUNCIL MEETING

The client saw herself in a meadow next to an ocean. She was meeting a group of different intelligent beings in a council. She described two of the council members. One was blue with white-grey robes. Another was an insectoid, praying mantis-like being.

C: *I am in a long, white robe-y dress. This is like a council of some sort. We're gathering around now. It seems like very wise people, quiet people. There's not a lot of talking, just gathering around a table, but we're outside.*

M: **Look around at these other beings around the table. Do you notice anything? What sticks out?**

C: *Lots of non-human looking people, and some human-looking people as well. Somebody next to me looks like an elf with long, blonde hair, blue eyes, and white robes. We're sitting in these tall, straight-backed chairs. It seems very Lord of the Rings-esque (laughs). We are gathering a council.*

M: **What is the purpose of this council?**

C: *It's discussing Earth it seems like.*

M: **What about Earth?**

C: *What happens next. These people seem to be interested in a good part…let me think of how to say this. There seems to be a concern. Most have positive energy of wanting good. I'm sorry my heart is pounding so much. It's so strange because I feel like I am myself here.*

M: **So, tell me what else you are learning at this council. What else is being talked about?**

C: *So, I can only tap into a feeling. I am an advocate for humans. That is why I feel that I am there. I am holding space. I am very compassionate. I am still a female. I am feeling we're looking at planet Earth. It's like we're up in the sky looking at it. Let me see if I can feel these other people.*

M: **What is happening where humans need an advocate? What's happening on the Earth?**

C: So much sadness. There is a lot of pain (emotional). Some of these beings don't feel what humans can feel, but I can. And so, I am advocating for them, or speaking for them, that we can't abandon them. That is not right. It doesn't sit with my vibration, and the laws of the universe don't allow us to do that to them.

M: Why would they be talking about leaving humans alone? What happened?

C: Some feel that it's a lost experiment. To just let it be, let them destroy themselves. Other people know that cannot happen — that the planet cannot be destroyed. Some people would like to take away the veil, or the shield that leaves the humans in the dark.

Some are feeling that it's too soon and that humans couldn't handle that. I agree with them. It has to be incremental; it can't happen all at once. It seems unsafe; the chaos would intensify that they are not ready yet. I seem to want to advocate for the waking up of the human race. That keeping them shielded is not necessarily working like we hoped it would work.

M: Why did you shield the humans?

C: Well, we chose it. Humans chose it. We wanted it. It seems apparent to me that I am human.

M: Why would the human race choose to be shielded? Blocked off?

C: We wanted that lesson. Just like we learn as we become conscious and awake, we realize we chose it as a lesson. We needed that so we could wake up to it on our own. We needed to learn that internal shift, but what's happening is not many humans are finding that way back. They have gotten so lost. A lot of humans are really lost. We're discussing how we can have an awakening. How do we do this without removing the shield completely? Is it possible? It is what we are doing already; [it's] working because people are waking up, but not enough.

M: So, what will you do to help?

C: Oh, yes...oh, it's so interesting. Some don't want the experiment to end. That praying mantis insect doesn't see it as a negative, as a problem. The experiment, that's what it started out to be. It always was an experiment. Why would we deter from what is just naturally happening?

M: So, some are for the support of humans, and some don't see any reason for it.

C: Right, and it doesn't necessarily feel negative. It feels detached. I feel like this praying mantis does not understand emotion and cannot see why this is painful. Pain doesn't make sense. It's like watching bacteria grow sort of, he views it as just natural and interfering because of our emotions doesn't make sense. Emotions are very interesting. A lot of these people here don't understand emotions. And I am advocating for it, that is why we went to Earth. It created something for us.

M: What's happening now?

C: I just stood up. I am trying to explain something. Okay. They respect me. I look different. I am tall. I am standing at this table. I am not really talking. Basically, my heart chakra is just exploding out. I think I am trying to share with these beings why I chose to be a human, and this heart lesson, this chakra opening, I am pulsing out, and they are feeling the vibration of it.

M: How do they respond to the vibration?

C: A lot of them resonate. A lot of them understand already. It's interesting. Not all of these beings have the same chakras, maybe. It's different. And so, it doesn't necessarily resonate.

We're looking back on the Earth now. It seems the general, the majority of these people feel the same way I do. We want to help. Help is an interesting word, it's maybe not the right word. It's assistance.

M: How will you assist?

C: They already are. That's what is becoming very apparent to me. There is a lot of love that is being directed at that planet right now. Yeah, oh my goodness. It's...

M: It's strong, isn't it?

C: There is no worry anymore. They already decided. I am sort of seeing this Earth; it's very interesting.

M: What's so interesting, tell me.

C: It looks like a puzzle falling apart, sort of. Like it's blowing open and inside is just light. Ooh. But we're watching it. It's already happening. It's happening. We're kind of celebrating. There's a relief. I feel really drawn to it.

M: What's happening now?

C: Well, I see light, a lot of light coming from this core booming out. The old Earth looks like a puzzle piece that's floating away sort of. This is interesting; there is a light from the Sun. A huge sun, though.

M: What's happening with this light?

C: There's a beam; it's coming from the center of the Earth. It's matching up to this huge sun. It's like a welcoming; it's like part of the Sun. It's just becoming one with this light. It's just beaming. Being born. I'm sorry I don't have the words; it's just all really bright.

I'm zooming down to this light; I want to be in it. Bright blue-ish, white light. I have an image stuck in my head, and I can't really move forward. I think because I am actually observing it. I want to zoom into it, but I'm not.

M: What is the image?

C: It's an image of that huge sun and this planet just bright. It almost looks like a star. I'm observing it like I am in space.

M: Is this bright star the Earth?

C: Yes.

M: What's so interesting about this connection between the Earth and the Sun?

C: Ok, let me zoom out, actually. The Sun is just so huge. I can't see the whole, only a small part, but if I zoom out, I can see better...okay, yes, I can. There is a bridge, a connection between... Woah, I ...

M: Tell me about this bridge. What is it doing?

C: So, it looks like an electric current sort of, to me. There's an energy field around the Earth and the Sun, but they are connecting. Again, it's vague. It's like a tunnel kind of. It keeps trying to zoom from place to place. This is something that I've dreamt about already. It's this blue, the only way I can describe it is a wormhole like you would see in Star Trek. When they get in a wormhole and they're flying through this energy in blue light.

M: Where are you? Are you in the wormhole?

C: Yes, but I can choose it. It's so strange. I can zoom out and observe it in a different way. I can zoom in and be inside of it. My heart. In my dreams I always wake up before I get to the other side. It's getting brighter and brighter, so I just burst into this meadow.

M: What do you see there in the meadow?

C: Trees and it's so bright.

M: What else do you see there?

C: So, I am running and jumping really high, and I'm flying up in the sky. Amazing! I'm up in the sky, and I see mountains, then I just come back down to the meadow.

M: Is there anyone else there with you?

C: Not close, well, maybe. I kind of sense, again, I don't know if I am doing this right or if I am just making it up, but I definitely sense me. Just now me. And I am just jumping around and playing. I'm wearing this loose white dress, but it's short, so I can run. It's very flowy. But I sense my kids with me (laughing). I'm showing them. I am running and jumping into the sky and laughing and flipping around, and then they are doing it too.

M: Oh, wonderful, you're teaching them how to fly. What a joy. What else is happening?

C: I am observing my body. Oh, it's really beautiful (emotional). My skin is different. I am looking down and my stomach is healed. Strong. I can touch my skin; it's firm and browner. It's glowy.

NEXT SCENE: TREEHOUSE LIVING

C: Where I zoom to is a tree. A home in a tree. And I've heard this before, so I don't want to make it up; it's just what naturally happened when you said to change. It's a home in a tree. It's like stucco, or I want to say wood. Yeah, maybe wood. Oh, there are windows all around, and I can look out. There's an ocean out there, but there are trees all around me. There's a fireplace, which doesn't make sense to me at all (laughs). But I'm sitting there playing. There's a little girl (emotional). She has blonde, curly hair. She's wearing a white dressy-thing, rompy-thing. Oh, she has bright blue eyes! She's my little girl.

M: Look down at your body and tell me what you see about your body.

C: It's the same body that I was in at the meadow. Strong, healthy — very healthy — I have really long hair. Oh, this is so weird. I can sense that she's my baby, but I don't look like I've had a baby (laughs). I feel young, very healthy. Oh, I think...again, I don't know if I am making this up, I just looked in the kitchen and I saw my husband. Yes. It's our little girl.

M: So, you both made it to the New Earth.

C: Yes. Oh, it is so wonderful. I feel so happy. And my kids, they're outside. I have all my kids, and they're in the trees, swinging on vines and climbing up ladders, being crazy hooligans. But they're flying around, and I am not worried about them at all. They just are. They're with a bunch of other kids. If I look out my window, there are all these houses in trees, and there are just lights in the trees. And I feel completely whole because they are my family. It's all my family.

M: Why do you all build your homes in the trees?

C: It is just our natural place to be. That's just what came to mind. I don't understand it fully, because we just fly up there; we don't have to climb a ladder. The trees love us so much. They are holding us in their arms basically, and so it's our happiest place to be. That's where we want to be.

M: What are some other things about this new home for you? What's life like there?

C: My first observation is how I feel. I feel so complete. I don't feel scared for my kids. That's the first thing I am noticing — I don't feel scared for my children. They are completely safe and whole. I just get to enjoy them. Oh, now we're on the beach with a whole community — all people. We're dancing, playing music. Kids are so happy.

NEXT SCENE: NEW EARTH BABY

C: I am definitely pregnant. I have a baby inside of me growing. I am by a river. It's different than having a baby here; it's not riddled with pain, but, oh, it's different. It's still human. I'm still a human, and I'm still giving birth like a human. I'm surrounded by all sorts of beautiful things. Okay. Because we've recognized nature as technology almost, its intelligence; there's nature spirits and trees and animals. And we don't need hospitals and things like that because we understand nature so much, so it's completely safe and beautiful. It's technology. That blue light that I always see in the water and in the trees, it's some form of really advanced technology, but it's what we would call "nature" (laughs). I know that doesn't make any sense, really...

So, nature is technology. It's coming and holding the baby as I birth it, and I am breathing in this blue energy from the water and the air and the trees, which immediately heals my body, and the baby is immediately just healthy.

M: So, if you don't get sick there, if you're healed so easily, how long will you live?

C: Oh, my goodness. I feel like I could live forever. I would choose, probably, if I wanted to live that forever, I don't think I would age unless I chose it. Oh! Just, I was observing that scene from such a kind of scientific observation, watching this energy exchange, and then, all of a sudden, I realized that is my baby (emotional). That's my baby.

M: How wonderful to receive this gift.

WORKING WITH THE HIGHER SELF

HS: There is energy right now coming from the Sun to the Earth. Some are calling it "The Event." This is what we were showing her.

M: Can you tell us more about this process and how it's going to happen?

HS: It is already happening. More and more feel it. It's coming in waves. This bridge is...it looks like a bridge between the Sun and the Earth; it's a bridge between New Earth and Old Earth. The energy from the Sun is what is creating that bridge.

M: How can we work with these waves in a way that supports our evolution?

HS: Just by choosing to incarnate at this time, you chose to work with it. You don't really need to do anything at this point. It's happening. If you are here on the planet now, then you already made your choice, and you will feel this. There is no way to escape. If you want to enhance it, continue your personal raising of vibration. But even with that, even without that, everyone will feel it.

M: Can you tell us more about the experiment with the humans?

HS: I think that to humans, sometimes it can feel cold, detached. It is a form of experiment, but humans actually chose it. People here right now chose to be a part of the experiment. The experiment, it's not as horrible as it sounds. It's actually very beautiful. It's an experiment of consciousness, of vibration. That is all any of this is. An experiment, all an experience, which is an experiment. You can feel the human as a piece of the experiment, of experience, a piece of consciousness. If you can pull out of feeling like this is all there is, then you can view yourself, your Higher Self, the completion of you not as a human experience. It's just a piece of it. So, if you can do that, if you can pull out of that, you understand that an aspect of yourself wanted to learn lessons that could only be experienced in coming to planet Earth.

M: What was happening in Earth or human history that made us choose this way of being? This disconnect? Was it always like this?

HS: It has not always been like this. If you take yourself back in human history, way, way, way back to some of the lost cities when humans chose to descend into the third dimension, they did not understand the consequences. They did not know what it would feel like. They didn't know the disconnect from Source.

*That's why it's called an experiment. It was unknown. They chose it for lessons to be learned, and as some of these humans are waking up — as you call it — do you not feel excited about the lessons you are learning? (**M: Yeah.**) That's why you did it (smiles). Reconnecting with Source — you've always been connected to Source but remembering your connection to Source is one of the reasons you came.*

M: What are some of the other reasons?

HS: Third density, the third dimension, is the lowest frequency. This planet is the lowest vibration planet. We wanted to know what the third density felt like. It was not and isn't associated with something negative. It's not that. It's something new in the universe that some of us wanted to feel. Brave souls.

M: So now that she has this information, how does this apply to her life?

HS: What we want her to do is to grasp her power of conscious creation. Playing with it right now in her life. We want her to become a master manifester, a manipulator of energy; we want her to know that she has the power fully — and always has — we want her to remember. Wake up!

Transcript: New Earth Treehouse

This client is the same who brought forward the Master Alchemist life scenes. It is interesting how some of the same themes show up multiple lifetimes. Let us travel to New Earth and learn more about the civilization.

C: It's very futuristic. There's flying vehicles. Buildings are shaped uniquely. It's beautiful. There's activity but not too much activity. There's something about it that looks like wonderland. There's a theme park here that has rollercoasters. I don't know, there's something about it that makes me feel like it's fun, like wonderland. It's colorful. Buildings aren't just clean and boring. Some are just like clean color, like off-white, but then there's bits of colors and tubes and things.

M: Look down at your body and tell me what you notice.

C: Woman's feet. And again, in a thong shoe sort of. [I'm wearing] somewhat like a sari, because it has beautiful silk and colors, and sort of the way it's wrapped, but it's loose too. It feels so good to wear it. I love the way it moves around my body, very flowing, like I'm flowing.

M: Are you holding anything?

C: *It's a silver rod, like a sparkling silver rod in my right hand. It's not a torch...there's something about the top of it that reminds me of the torch on the Statue of Liberty, but it's smaller, like a wand more. Cadu...caduceus?*

M: **What do you use it for?**

C: *My magic! (giggles)*

M: **What kind of magic do you do with it?**

C: *I make beautiful things, everywhere. Beautiful. People like the spaces I make for them to live in. I can make anything, but I like to make art out of clothing. It funnels my energy and abilities, just like in the pyramid that I showed previously. And it funnels through, except I'm sort of the crystal. There is a crystal in it, in the top. That's why it has that top to it, okay. Like, the top of the pyramid is like what I hold in my hand, and I am like a receiver. Yeah, like I'm like the top and it goes through me, yes, and then I can distribute it in smaller measures, and use control with it to create things. Like a paintbrush.*

NEXT SCENE: HER TREEHOUSE

C: *(Giggles) Oh, I love it. It's a giant tree, but I have built it. You walk up to the giant tree and there are flowers everywhere. It's like the shell of a snail, that material, so it doesn't hurt the tree, right? And it wraps around the tree, going up, not tightly like the snail, but like you would walk around a circular staircase. And it's all beautiful colors, so the light, when you first go it's like the darker shell, but as you go up it becomes like a lighter seashell color, and the sunlight and everything can go through it. The light can go right through it and illuminates. Oh, and there are holes, like windows, but you don't need glass or anything.*

So, as you walk up the spiraling staircase you have the holes and you can see down over the community because I'm on top of a hill, on a big tree. Because I do live off of my own, I come and go. I go into the village and in the town and create things for people and work with other artists, but I always go back to my own space. And it goes up and I can see the town and I can see the water, like the beach. We all like to go to the beach.

The vines and all the flowers, they droop and hang inside and outside, and then I go up and...I can make it really high because there's no rush and I don't get tired going up stairs (laughs). I enjoy every step and I enjoy the view every single step, and so it's great that it's high up. I could just fly up, and I do sometimes. I don't have to take the stairs (laughs), but sometimes I like to take the stairs.

And then, yeah, it just opens up and oh, it's just so open. And the view, it's like the shell kind of just expands out around the tree and through the different branches that form off. I can travel around, and the monks don't even like...it's open so that the birds and animals can just come and go.

NEXT SCENE: EATING IN HER HOME

C: Flowers! (laughs) They just grow right in my kitchen. I have these big windows all around. It reminds me of the starship Voyager, where they have these big, oval windows where you can look out to space, well, it's like that but they're just open. So, it's just like these big, beautiful flowers that are just so voluptuous and big, and they grow right in there, just for the pleasure of me eating them. I don't really need anything else, like vegetables and berries and things, you know, but some things just grow right to me. They just grow right to my room, and I can just take them and pick them and eat them, or I can make things with them like salads that you might want to share with people.

I don't really cook food anymore, but there's like a preparation area because we like to prepare food together sometimes. If I'm just eating myself, then I just eat my things, but when other people come, they will bring things like the flowers that grow for them in their space, or vegetables. They bring the things that grow for them because it's a reciprocal energy process that they exchange with the plants so, you know, in essence it's like part of their consciousness and their energy goes into these plants and it's like this sharing thing and so when they bring them over, that's why we would make a salad, because everyone brings their own energy in with the food that we bring, and then we share it together and it's just even more wonderful. Yes.

M: Wow, nice. Does anybody eat meat?

C: No. (Giggling) No. (Strongly)

M: Well, when you have food coming to you like that, I can see why.

C: Oh, no. You wouldn't hurt anything or anything like that. If you want a flower that tastes like steak, you can have a flower that tastes like steak. You don't need to eat a rabbit! (Laughing) Leave the poor thing alone! No. They sleep with me! They're all around everything. Even animals that I wouldn't have around me here now, I enjoy their company — we communicate, we laugh together.

I'm not going to eat one of my friends! (Laughing) And I'm not going to let anyone else eat my friends. Nobody does that.

M: Friends don't let friends eat friends.

C: Friends don't let friends eat friends. No, silly. We're all laughing at that right now around the table. It's like you're there, too, like you're there on the TV, and we're all sitting and having this conversation with you; we're sitting and laughing at the joke of it.

M: What was it like for everyone there at the table to make the transition to this place?

C: Blink of an eye. Poof! It's magic (laughing). One of them even went poof, like a cartoon, just like poof! It's magic, and one of them just made sparkles (giggles).

M: Does anyone there have a story about what the transition was like? What was happening before the magic came in?

C: John says that he will share his story. So he was in the city, on the pavement, in the street, and everyone is just going about their business, talking on their cellphones, and then he feels a prickle in the air...but it's like, because the trickling and intensity is building, and he's going "Is this it? Is this it?" It keeps getting stronger and when he starts to feel the prickling, he's like "Is this it?" But then it just keeps getting stronger. He's like "Ok, I'm definitely not dreaming now." He stomps his foot on the pavement; he had a newspaper in his hand.

M: And so, what was it like after his skin started to prickle up?

C: Like a bright flash, just whoosh, flash! And everyone was like 'woah!' and dropped to the ground like stones. Nothing is working. Nothing is working. Nothing is working. John says he's still with me, still sitting at the table.

M: Ok, what does John want to say?

C: Well, so, it's a bright flash. Like you can see, just like in the animations, like a ring flash around so bright that everyone's blinded, but as they get up and start blinking their eyes they realize okay, the phones aren't working, cars aren't working, traffic lights aren't working. The lights are all off. So, they're all so focused on the technology that they're not noticing the cloud, but as soon as the technology is off, I'm like okay, that's pointless. I know it's not going to work; there's no point, so I look up. Everyone is looking down and around. They only start to look up when the sky starts to get dark. At first it seems like when a thunderstorm starts to come in, like when everything gets dark because the clouds are dark, but it's touching down on the atmosphere, and that's when they start to run.

M: Where do they run?

C: *Everywhere (laughs). Amok! But John just sat there. He was like okay, there's no point in going anywhere. Anywhere. He was sitting down already, and he considered that a blessing. He was ready to go, and he knew what to do. So, he just went in. He went in, in preparation, and tuned out all of the people running around, but he's not the only one. There's someone by a fountain that sits, in a green shirt. Somebody gets out of the car and sits down on the ground. Someone else just lies down on the ground, away from the people running around. So, he's not the only one. And there's an awareness of each other too, so it's time, and there's a unified energy. As it comes closer, it's purple, and as it breaks through it's like rainbow electricity breaking through the sphere almost as if rainbow lightning were to go across the top of a sky. But the purple clouds, okay, waving up and that's what it is, so it is...there's a joining of when the light hits; it did touch down and activate something at the center of the Earth. It did. So, it's not just that it's coming; it's the meeting of the two energies that causes the wave. Pulse in, zap, activate, pulse out, out from the center of the Earth out to the atmosphere, and when those touch each other, that's when the wave spills over, and that's why it's so massive. All the way it's so massive that the city buildings that I was around even seem puny. Like if it was a thunderstorm, the buildings would block out some of those dark clouds, but it minimizes everything.*

M: **So, what happens next?**

C: *It comes, like a wall. So, as he sees it, he's sitting in a cemented area, there are some stairs going down, there's like a large building with stairs going down, and the wave comes and reaches the faces of the buildings that are closest to him, like a wall of the ocean, like when Moses parted the seas, it approaches. And as it approaches, he just closes his eyes. He just lets it come.*

M: **And so, what happens after it comes?**

C: *A wall of energy that you just almost dissolve into color and sound...truth... remembrance, and... the bliss of love.*

M: **What happens to the physical body?**

C: *It disintegrates. Like sand...but not lost. It's like if I were to look at cells of the 3D body, they turn to sand in this reality, but in that, they become like clear bubbles, crystal-clear bubbles of light and energy. So, once they were a dry thing, now it is like fluid, like water, crystalline and pure. The great alchemy of turning sand into water, sort of. It's a transfiguration. So, what falls away and disintegrates is like the outer shell of this 3D form, but it transmutes and comes alive in essence. It sheds the old, dead idea.*

M: What about the other people? What happens to them, the ones that were running?

C: Taken. They were taken away. They were taken on the ships.

M: Where to?

C: Healing. Preparation. They will be returned to the Earth. So, they are taken somewhere unconsciously. They are not all consciously aware. Not all are returned. Some are returned. Some are kept, healed, and helped, and able to transfer on. Some not as yet and are returned to carry on with their story. They cannot unplug from the concepts of 3D. Their ego is fighting way too hard, so it's not their time yet. There are those of us that are just able to... that's what we came here to do, so we are able and prepared to transmute instantly. So, with that comes the great knowing, with the great knowing comes access to any information needed in that moment of now, so you just know where to go.

M: Do you stay on that version of Earth?

C: No. We go to where we are now; we go to the New Earth now. Yes. Done with that now. We did our grid holding up until the moment that the wave arrived, we plugged in, like we talked about before, the tent pegs were held in, we held it in, put the stakes down, that was our job. We can go back and forth if we want to, to teach and carry missions but we don't have to go back in that form, and that's what will help others because they need their miracles.

All Roads Lead Home

There are as many pathways to New Earth as there are people. Once "the shift" happens, everyone will move to where their next evolutionary phase will play out. Stay in your heart. Stay with your breath and trust your footing as you walk towards this new reality.

THIRTY-FOUR

New Earth Civilization

When I worked with Neomi, I always cued for her to go to the most appropriate place for our learning. Most often, Neomi would often go to the same lifetime of Esther, the Essene. On a few occasions, we would get a surprise. Let us journey with her to the New Earth

M: What do you see as you look around? What comes to mind?

C: Like a rocky cliffside with trees and I'm way, way, way high up on the cliffside. Below me, down below in the distance, is a town. I don't feel...not really in a human form. I'm like a bird. I'm feathered and a bluish coloring. I'm the size of a human and I'm male. I feel like it's my job to observe over this small...well, it's a medium-size village. It seems that humans are living down below. So, my job is to watch over them and make sure nothing comes into sight or discovers their location. It's somewhat like a desert there. It's really rocky and sandy, but there are trees here and there. Down in the village area where the people are, there's grass and bushes and things, but I just live in this sliced-out side of the cliff. I don't have anything in this space where I live. It's just my duty to sit there and watch over them.

M: How long have you been doing this?

C: I feel like I've been doing this a long time, like maybe twenty years or thirty years. I'm to look out for things coming in via the sky, so just like anything from up in the heavens or anything. What will happen on occasion is that an aircraft will come in, and it's cylindrical like a disc. I'm to alert the people. I'm to fly down, and there's a designated person in the village that I'm to inform. That's my duty. It doesn't come very often, but as soon as it's in the air, I'm to alert them. It doesn't seem to be dangerous. It's as if I'm informing them so that they can then coordinate with the aircraft.

M: What does the aircraft do once it's here? Why are they coordinating with them?

C: It comes down, and it will pick up the human beings on occasion and it just comes in broad daylight, in the middle of the afternoon. I'll go ahead and let them know they're here. It's a valley they are in, so the spaceship has to land on

the other side of this...kind of like a foothill of a mountain. So then just a handful of people will travel over to the spacecraft and then they will leave. Then after some time, it's usually a long duration, usually seven or eight months, they bring them back, and they return. It's different people that go at different times. It's as if they are supposed to be going for a training. They go to train and then come back.

I believe they're training the beings that are coming in on the aircraft. They're going back to where they reside, and then the humans train them in what they do...like as to be human and about emotions, and they explain to them how they live. But it's odd they don't stay here... They take the humans with them and then bring them back. It seems it would be much more efficient training if they stayed here to train, but they don't.

M: Do the humans also get trained?

C: *When they leave, they are attuned to different energy systems. When they come back, they have more skills as far as telepathy and energetic skills...so that they can elevate objects using energy from their mind. So, there is an exchange. I feel like this isn't too radically off into the future from the present time. I feel like this is just like maybe 200 or 300 years in the future.*

There's one other person...I'm not sure what to call myself...that is like a...like a bird person that lives in a cutout opposite me across this valley. So, the both of us do this, but there are no other beings like us that are around. I don't feel like there are any other humans anywhere near us. I'm not quite sure if there are any other humans on Earth besides this settlement.

M: What kind of structures are in this settlement?

C: *It's just small houses. So, it's set up like a village. They're built with a lot of silver material, and it just seems like there's...it's slightly futuristic... So, it's like silver roofs and the walls are white, but it's not like siding or anything. It's almost like a plastic white exterior. There are paths in between the people's houses. They come out and they interact throughout the day.*

They do have gardens and things. I don't see any animals around. There are no birds or anything. It's just the humans living here. So, it looks like they're able to provide for themselves with the gardens that they have. They're just wearing very simple clothes, just like robes or whatnot. They just have a tie at the waist, so they're dressed very simply. They have sandals and that. They gather regularly to eat. They eat in their homes, but sometimes they'll gather outside. But they're very, very peaceful people. They do seem to keep records a lot. There is one building that serves as a library, and so they're always going in, and they're scribing different information. So, I'm not sure if they're recording information from their own knowledge or...I'm not clear what they're recording. So, they go in and out, and sometimes they have groups that come in and talk amongst themselves, just kind of learning and having meetings.

But I don't know exactly what they're talking about because I'm not involved. I can see in when they open the doors and that, but I really don't get a break or anything like that. I'm really to watch out and protect them as well.

M: When do you get to Earth? Or how?

C: I was brought in on the ship by the beings that are bringing them in. I was from another planet. Our planets communicate with each other. So, there are more like me on my planet. We can talk telepathically...all of us...and it was deemed by the Council that just the two of us bird men [would] come in and watch over and then be a contact point between the humans and the beings that come in.

We have many agreements in the planets that are outside of this galaxy...the Earth galaxy and the Milky Way. There are many others, so we communicate amongst ourselves. The different planets...there's the Council so they set up information...it's not as far-fetched as it seems to be in the human's mind to go to other planets and travel because we have modes of transportation that...I can't fly to other planets. We can go into vehicles and get to other planets to have meetings or collaborate on things that we need to do. And I had volunteered for this position. They had asked, and I accepted.

M: How did you first get in contact with Earth?

C: Well, the Council makes decisions sometimes, so sometimes things need to be done, or the humans have needed assistance over the years, and so the council will...they're not to interfere, they can only send and assist and honestly, hope for the best sometimes. So, I was approached this time, other times you have your resting period, and you can go to Source and re-energize yourself. Some people that come to Earth, they're just so exhausted, it really takes everything out of them, and they need a long time to rejuvenate and re-energize. But others, it doesn't take very long, just a mini vacation or something and then beings are ready to come back. So, then you're just able to submit that request to council and then decide what your journey will be. Or, if it needs to be...if they need anything done. They need volunteers a lot.

So, I usually always volunteer. I love serving so I ask them what their needs are and then we incorporate that into my lifetimes. It kind of makes...it's more *fun that way. I get to have...so I'll serve a purpose that they deem necessary, but then also sprinkle in, sometimes, say like in my human lifetimes...you know...just regular human problems. Kind of mixes it up.*

But there's been some things happening over the years...so the Earth was very sick for a long time, so a lot of destruction happened. So now we've arrived at this small village...this small group of people... It's not a small group, there's...I would say there's a few hundred people down there. So, they are re-establishing themselves, and they're going to go ahead and grow again. So, it's going to be a slow process, but I think everything has been weeded out so that there isn't the destruction and the heavy darkness and the violence. All of those just heavy, heavy low energies spread all over the Earth. That...with these people...it will be able to grow and flourish again as a healthy planet.

M: You said, "weeded out." What happened to the rest of the humans?

C: They just weren't ready for the transition. Some just didn't accept...just have faith and truly accept the information that they were given. I don't really mean weeded out in a bad way. There were many, many beings that were just on a self-destructive path...so they were...those lives were terminated. But there were others that...they had faith, but they just weren't strong. They didn't have a true faith, and so they had to be relieved of their lifetime and go back to Source, for now. So slowly...hopefully...those souls will re-energize and reset, and with this slow growth of the planet, then they'll be reintroduced to the planet, or possibly other planets.

But everything went spiraling out of control, so it just had to end. There were many, many, many people that survived. It's just that with the destruction, some people didn't end up surviving, per se...as far as being able to survive from a survival standpoint. They lived through it, but they weren't able to collaborate and thrive. So now it's...the people that were able to, have collaborated into this village. There were people that thrived for quite a while, but just...then they just didn't collaborate in groups. So then, as they passed, their smaller groups died out.

M: What made this group so successful at surviving?

C: They just collaborated together. They realized that they needed to come together and set up a peaceful place to live and start up their gardens...rally all of their resources and knowledge to thrive in a healthy manner. So, nothing that will be in a...like pollute the Earth or anything like that. With all the destruction and what happened, the Earth was wiped clean. So, it was...it was made rid of all of the pollution that the humans had built up over hundreds of years. So that was able to be removed, and so now this group is starting...and the smaller groups did too...with a clean new Earth.

So, with this new Earth, they need to respect it, and they're aware of that. So, they're very careful to put their resources...to gather water, grow with the gardens...store things in a very responsible manner because they're understanding of what happened in the past. That may be part of what they're scribing, so it doesn't happen again in the future.

NEXT SCENE: INCOMING CRAFT

C: *Ok, now there are numerous...numerous aircraft coming in, and they are landing along the outside of this valley where the humans are living. They've brought, each craft has brought maybe eight or ten people, so they're bringing them back and bringing new people in adult form. So...I'm not...I don't have the information of how that's happening, but they're bringing in new people to integrate but they're already adults. So, people who were not here previously. They're just re-integrating them into this group. The group seems very receptive. It seems like they know these people. They're embracing and hugging them like they were expecting them, but it's just interesting because they're already coming in adult form as if they're being adopted. So, the people who have already lived here have built new houses for these newcomers to reside in. So, it looks like they're expanding the population, but I don't have the information on how they're, you know, mysteriously bringing these adult humans back here. So that's fascinating. But they're embracing them and very peaceful.*

It seems like the alien, well, the extraterrestrial beings are coming in, and prior...years and years back, they were not able to leave the aircraft, but now they can come out of the aircraft and walk around and speak with the humans as well. And they can speak to them as if...nobody's alarmed to see them. So, I don't know if, over time, they developed the skills to be able to withstand the surface of the Earth and the atmosphere. It seems prior to this they were not able to.

M: Why weren't they able to?

C: *The Sun was just way too harsh and radiant and just the air alone would burn their skin. So, they just couldn't...it's almost like they couldn't stand the light as* *well. Well, they came from…it's a rocky, craggy planet and it's really dark. It's very dark and grey. They talk telepathically and that, but it's very…if a human went there, they'd say it's depressing. It's all monochrome. It's just one grey color kind of, just shades of grey. And the beings themselves are a blue-grey color themselves as well. And it's dim. And the air there is very dry and there's no humidity. So, I think when they came to Earth the humidity was irritating to them and like I said…the Sun, they just couldn't stand the rays.*

Now the extraterrestrial beings…they're talking with the humans, and they're greeting them and everyone's happy that this is happening. I think, possibly, this is the first time this has happened and they're really happy that this is a successful venture, and I'm starting to get the feeling that the humans they brought in are the extraterrestrial beings and they were able to morph into a human form so they could live on the planet and integrate in. But you can't tell the difference between the native Earth person and the extraterrestrial Earth person, so I'm not sure. I'm not getting a read on why they are doing this because it seems like the village has grown in the past few years and everything is thriving and healthy.

Neomi finishes her mission as the bluebird being and returns to Source and the council where she enthusiastically volunteers to reincarnate on the Earth as a human in the new colony. She mentioned that there was less to prepare for because Earth did not have the low-vibrational experiences anymore and that it was simply about building up the new society. In that new life, she was trained by a Christ Conscious Avatar, a very high, divine being who was also living in the community. She commented on how successful the new civilization was growing and that many new babies were being born on the Earth in pristine, high-frequency birthing temples to ensure the happiness and health of the future generations. Mission complete!

Transcript: Culmination of the Divine Mission

When Laura came into the scene, she described a crystal pyramid which refracted rainbow light. Other pyramids and crystalline structures spread out around her. All of the life forms were etheric and radiant. She described herself being a Lightbody form of a feline humanoid wearing a gossamer fabric gown and carrying a crystal tablet filled with information from her soul's Akashic records. I asked for her to tune into the data and tell me what she was reading from the tablet.

C: It is referring to this time in the present moment. It speaks of the leonine energies embodying in this timeline on this planet, in this new creation for the evolution of the planet, the overturning of the old ways — the birthing of the new. It's a very exciting time. It's a very noble time. It's a very expansive time for humanity to awaken out of their slumber, to come to full consciousness of the radiance of the divinity of who we are as a collective. It seems there are thousands or many hundreds of thousands of beings from different star seeds, different planets working together — for this momentous time. And, apparently, it is drawing nearer.

M: When you say it's drawing nearer, what do you mean by that? What do you see there?

C: I hear the word culmination — the culmination of a great many efforts and plans and meetings and battles, and victories ongoing in the cleanup of the old ways — the old consciousness. A step up — it's a step up for all of creation. Yeah...it's, it's on its way.

NEXT SCENE: MEETING WITH COUNCIL OF ELDERS

C: I am in a meeting with the Council of Elders. There is a discussion on what is progressing and how things have progressed, and they are very pleased with how things are moving forward and relieved. It's been a hard, intricate strategy to awaken mankind and to deliver mankind from the clutches of dark entities — the shadow consciousness. They were uncertain at some point in the timelines, but victory is the Light's. Victory is the Light's.

M: When you look around at this Council, tell me about them.

C: Babaji. Yogananda. Mother Mary. Sananda [Jesus]. There are some of the Kumaras there. St. Germain and other beings from other star systems that I don't know.

M: Well, what else is the Council sharing? Tell me what's happening now.

C: Making ready to advance humanity in the recognition of and welcoming of other advanced civilizations to promote humanity finally into the galactic community. Humanity needed to recognize the great play and deceit and turn away their attention from the attempted dramas, and over time they have done this in a noble way — opening their intuitive reckonings in their hearts and reaching in to remembering that we are not alone, and as...and when they have reached this tipping point in the collective, they have lost or released their fear of the star beings.

And there is a part of them that remembers that they, too, are star beings, and they too have lived in many realms and dimensions and planets and cultures and civilizations. They have come to a place of being open to living amongst and with the star brethren as equals — not as lost children, but as equals in the eyes of all our galactic brothers and sisters. And this is part of the work the Council and many, many other councils have engaged in over the decades to prepare mankind for this evolutionary outcome and shift towards the galactic ingathering.

M: It sounds like we've been working a long time to get to this place — to be right at the tipping point.

C: It started 2,000 years ago — the seeds were planted in the Age of Pisces for the dawning of the Age of Aquarius. And in the late 18th century, people were impulsed, having come out of the Dark Ages, to bring the Light forward — upwards, the knowledge of spirituality, the knowledge of esoteric traditions — to start impulsing, planting seeds, and awakening mankind and we are right in the cusp.

M: So, what needs to happen before we move into that shift point? How close are we?

C: It's like a great cosmic computer is set. The program is set. The program is running, and we are in the process — we have been, but that process is speeding up infinitely now with the Earth and her creatures and inhabitants. She is moving; she is readying herself for the full mass ejection of Light from the Cosmic Center. It's like the image of a racehorse at the starting gate waiting for the bell to go — waiting for the boom to lift. There's a great sense of anticipation, excitement to have more and more of the collective wake up, to have that quantum energy excel and expand — quantum consciousness. So, the energies coming in keep impulsing more and more people. The whole of the planet is being impulsed — it's like electrodes just pulsing and pulsing and pulsing, and people's awareness is shifting rapidly towards this culmination of the Light.

M: Very good. Is there anything else that the Council would like to share? What would they like to talk with us about?

C: They say we are...we are well pleased. We are well pleased. Everything is flowing according to the great galactic ascension. All eyes are on the Earth for she is the pearl of the universe, and that pearl will become the diamond — the radiant diamond — the radiant sun in her own right. As she ascends, they watch with eagerness and an excited tension, rapt attention to monitor everything that is transpiring for things to stay the course. And for those starseeds to step forward and radiate — continue to radiate their magnificent Light and Love, to be the beams of Light as they have been and more of them to come out of their hiding to grab their courage and their will and come forward, and to be themselves in their true divinity — whether they are to be themselves, and also to exhibit and attend to their life plan and purpose amongst mankind.

M: What makes the difference between the average human and the starseeds? What's the difference between them?

C: The starseeds have remembered who they are. They have come in more awake and with the remembrance of their life plans and their purpose, and the regular humans have taken much longer in their evolutionary process to awaken in the sense that they, in the same way, have volunteered to only awaken at certain times in order for this drama to perpetuate. A much deeper will and desire for the Light in its perfect place and perfect time. Everyone has had their divine purpose planned as such, and their awakenings planned according to the Grand Design. The Light and the Dark needed to play off each other.

NEXT SCENE: EARTH IN THE FUTURE

C: I am in some sort of community building. It's like a school. And I am training to lead and teach young children. And we go out on nature excursions, and we do many things with learning to manifest at will, to use our minds to create, to project, and receive messages — telepathy. To learn to be in tune with all species on the planet, to communicate and receive direction and healing from everyone and everything. It's very beautiful.

M: That sounds very beautiful. What do you call this planet that you are on now?

C: This is Earth. This is Earth in the future. Two hundred years from now. We can teleport. We can avail ourselves of great healing...technologies. We can be anywhere we choose at any time.

M: And how are you able to travel to any place at any time? What is the experience like?

C: Well, there have been antigravity machines for some time now so we can travel in those, and when we learn to teleport, we can transport our bodies from one place to the next.

M: That's very nice. What else is happening there that you can do now?

C: Communities come together. There is a great deal of sharing. There's a great deal of building together. There's a great deal of support and sharing and creative endeavors that belong to everyone, as everyone shares in its creation — whatever that means, whatever that looks like that smaller communities need. Everyone works together. There's a great deal of cooperation and sharing.

M: What did it take to get to that point on the planet?

C: As every portal came opened, more light — higher frequencies — the resonance and magnetic gauss on the planet — shifting and changing — there were many timelines collapsing into a more unified field where people's hearts, wills, intentions, and desires are aligning into one collective consciousness and unconditional love and unconditional vision. And then there was the wave that came from the Galactic Center to harmonize, to shift — to transport the Earth into the higher timeline and density. And it has taken some years for certain people to be impulsed to bring through technologies, a new way of building homes, new ways of utilizing energy, a new way of healing, a new way of eating, and technologies were brought forward from the star brothers and sisters to cleanse the earth, to cleanse the waters, to cleanse the air, and to re-impregnate the earth with vital minerals that the topsoil was totally stripped of.

So, it has taken decades to pull this all through everyone working together for the highest good of the planet and the collective. And each generation and each decade has moved through in a purposeful way and purposeful consciousness and direction, vision — to open up this new civilization, and working together with star brothers and sisters. in cooperation with them, to accept their technologies, and to learn from each other, and to work and play with each other, and grow with each other and harmonize with each other. It's taken many decades, and it is flowing, and it has flowed and will continue to flow beautifully, peacefully, harmoniously, productively. And everyone experiences a great deal of prosperity, happiness, creativity, and joy, and play.

M: And speaking of play, tell me more about the educational systems. You said you were working with children and learning telepathy and things like this. What else is sticking out about the educational systems?

C: Children begin to learn about technologies that are being used, enhancements with technologies for the highest and greatest good of all. It starts out simply with very simple dynamics of say antigravity machines — the coils, the metals, minerals that are used as the conductive materials, their qualities. Crystals — the healing power of crystals — pulling through all of the elements of Earth and the universe. Bring them all together so the children can learn to...how to use these, to understand them and to grow with them so that technology is a commonplace. Learning to access the Akashic fields so that they remember who they are...they remember their lifelines, timelines. They know who they are in Spirit...they can connect with that part of themselves very easily, education.

M: How do you help these kids tune in to the Akashic fields? What's an exercise that you do with them? See it now.

C: They ask a question in their minds, and they learn to drop their conscious awareness down into their heart space, and they look for symbols, colors, and messages. They learn — they are trained to learn to listen. They are trained to learn to go into the still, quiet space — a very deep, deep space in the heart to hear the answers quite naturally, to see the answers, to feel them, hear them. Use all their inner senses — inner taste, inner smell. They ask the question, and they go down into a very deep place like a zero point where all things are known. All things are revealed to heighten their intuition. They have to go into these meditative places. The more they do this, the more they are able to access the Akash. It becomes second nature for them because they are young, and they are open — this is why they are trained at a young age.

NEXT SCENE: COMMUNITY COUNCILS

C: For each community, there is a group of people who monitor and supervise and watch the communities, watch their particular community. And so, I see in a room a group of people evaluating processes, evaluating how the community is doing — if there are any queries or questions if anything comes up. These people are elected to work through these and to find solutions for the best and highest good of all concerned. And these change periodically so that there is a — so there is equal opportunity for everyone to sit in the committee to lead the community, to have their say to work on different issues or any issues that come up, to resolve them and to learn and grow from them as a teaching method for all. And in this way, everyone participates; there's no hierarchy; there is equal participation with everyone in the community.

M: And how is it that people are selected? How is it decided by the people?

C: *It is circular in the sense that it's a round table. Everyone has an opportunity to be at the table. Everyone has an opportunity to have voted in the first ten to twenty people. And it's like there is a roster where everyone has their chance. As soon as that table has completed their term, the next table comes up.*

NEXT SCENE: COMMUNITY FIRE GATHERINGS

C: *I see this huge fire. There is a massive fire pit, and there's this huge fire that is built in this large temple. There are many people. Many people coming from many communities in the area, and they…it's an ingathering, a harvesting of fruits and vegetables and produce that people bring as an honoring in the old ways to Mother Earth. It's the sacred time of the year where many communities come together to share what they have, to offer what they have, to respect Mother Earth, to respect the elements — the elementals. In a way even though we are in the future — we as humans remember how important it is to appreciate Mother Earth; and this is a very beautiful, sacred ceremony by the elders, by the children, by the young people to glorify, to deify, to appreciate, and to honor the bounty of Mother Earth throughout all the eons, throughout all the civilizations — the culmination of all the ages.*

It is very beautiful, and everyone is laughing and singing and dancing and sharing the light of the fire — the energy of the fire. Singing to Mother Earth and really celebrating this culture — this new age, and our ancient roots and connection to Mother Earth.

M: What do you see there as you look around the celebration? What's it like there?

C: *The feeling is of deep, deep gratitude, deep reverence — a holiness. People hold the gratitude and appreciation in their hearts. People gravitate towards each other and mingle and mix, and exchange gifts and things they have created as a gesture of goodwill and humanity that just knows no boundaries; just unconditionally loves and shares — coming together — circles of light, of love, of joy; time away from the regular day-to-day life — just a holiday. There's singing and music, and the children play.*

M: Sounds perfect there.

C: *Yes, it is. It's beautiful. The love is palpable.*

HIGHER SELF CONVERSATION

M: When we were talking about disclosure and us returning to our connection with our star families and being able to travel across time and space, do you have anything else you would like to share with us about those subjects?

C: (Laughs) It's such an amazing time for all of humanity to realize our destiny amongst the star beings — our homes, all the homes we have come from — and that there is the opportunity for beings to travel wherever and whenever they wish. That opportunity is coming, and that is so exciting for mankind. This is such a great turning — such a great time, and that excitement is what needs to propel both this one and many others to excel in their work, in their light, in their beingness, and their sharing with the rest of humanity.

M: Do you have suggestions to help us get through these times?

C: We say find quiet times. Set your intention to receive with each portal with each new astrological event, with each new waking day. The new Light codes that come through are bringing through all of those abilities, which need to be integrated, which is why there is a repeated call for rest, lots of water, lots of fresh food and meditation, exercise, yoga. To really prepare the body, the mind, the heart for all these abilities that are coming through to each individual as and when they are ready to receive them. Their vessels need to be ready to receive these gifts, and this is why the call for care of the physical bodies is so vitally important. Just to take care of ourselves in the sweetest way as we grow and expand, and like we can nourish ourselves all the way through this.

And appreciation of the body. The body is the temple. The body is the vessel. The body is the housing to integrate, align all that is physically, emotionally, mentally, spiritually — so aligning all those aspects and keeping...keep calling into alignment those aspects into the body, into the incarnation, into this timeline, into this presence. As a daily, perhaps hourly practice — and cleansing, smudging, cleansing — calling in the I AM Presence to cleanse the bodies, because there are still energies out there that are untoward. And so, calling for Spirit to ensure the energy bodies and the energy field is clear, strong — any openings or any aberrations to be healed, cleared, and strengthened and transformed.

THIRTY-FIVE

Family of Light Blessing

Another client named Neli was taken to meet several groups of intelligent beings who are supporting this grand transition.

C: I feel more like a spirit. Like an energy spirit, like a round energy. Yeah, I travel all over. It feels like that. I travel all over if I want to. There are no colors, more transparent. A bright light. Feel safe but still, there is a concern about Earth. Like I am picking up information from Mother Earth. That's the concern. I am receiving information that all is not well. Something has shifted. This energy is coming in, this dark energy. It was not there before. It's like it's moving in from the sky. Like a big storm coming in, but it's not a storm; it's energy. It's dark, and it feels like sticky energy.

NEXT SCENE: JESUS BRINGS THE LIGHT

C: I feel that I am standing on the Earth right now, and I can see all of the rainbow colors. I see Jesus. He's telling me that all is well. That he has come to lift the darkness. And I see him walking the Earth like his footsteps are prints on the Earth. There are some birds flying in the sky. It's showing he takes long walks alone. He can change everything in an instant. It may seem like a long walk, but it can change immediately.

M: When you say it changes, what do you mean?

C: I don't know. I see him dividing the sea. He caught the fish. Miracles.

M: What kind of miracles?

C: Like dividing the fish and dividing the sea and changing the scenery. He's telling us now that we can all do this in this lifetime. We can do this ourselves. That we can welcome this right now, we can welcome change. We have to believe in it. We have to believe that we can. He walked the Earth to show us. He is giving it to us now. It's up to us now.

M: Like he's passing a torch?

C: Yeah. It's time to change gears. It's time.

M: I wonder what he means by it's time to change gears.

C: We have all the answers inside of us. We need to believe it. We need to believe that all is possible; there are so many still going on in our old beliefs. We have new paths to walk now; we have new dimensions to walk. He will walk with us. He wants to walk with us. He has come to do so now with all the humans that are ready to walk with him. He is walking with everyone ready to do so. He's with us. So much, so much. He's here because it's time to take the next step.

M: I wonder what the next step is.

C: It's to act in PURPOSE. To ACT at the next level. To let go of the physicality in the way we believe in it. To understand that everything is energy. It's not what it seems like. The lightworkers are ready now. We have this deep, deep, deep information inside of all of us that is available. It wants to come through us, but we have to go inside. We will never find it on the outside. We find it on the inside out. The deep information it's like soul-level type of information. We have discernment of what we are to give. We have to stay true to ourselves, to our path, to our truth. Nothing but the truth. We all have a flame in our hearts. It has a lot of information; it will show us the way. We need to go inside. When it opens, we go through a new passage. To know ourselves. The grand awakening. We are ready now. We are so ready.

M: How does one go into their heart? How do they unlock it?

C: There are different ways. Every person is to find their way. What makes them feel good. To be romanced. To turn down the volume of the outside and unlock the inside. The best way to do that for yourself is to sit in meditation. For some, it's to take a walk in nature. It takes you into the space where you feel expanded. It's easier now because every step we take, where we are right now, it's going to be easier. I get a picture of the darkness moving into Earth, inside of Earth to the middle part within the Earth; it's also the same picture for us. The darkness has moved further inside.

M: What does that mean?

C: It means it's ready to be released. It needs to be released from the inside, from the inner Light, from the inner realms of Light — where we have lots of lots of lots of Light helping. The darkness can come to light.

M: So, these light beings are helping to clear this dark energy?

C: Yeah, if we turn inward. If we don't turn inward, it will have to play out in the outer.

M: So, the more of us that go inward, the more the energy gets cleared?

C: *Wow, yes. It will affect the whole Earth. The whole consciousness of Earth.*

M: **What happens if we don't go inward. What happens?**

C: *It will continue to play out the way it used to. We will see a lot of darkness playing out because it's the only way it can be seen. When it's seen, there is a chance for it to transmute into awareness. The faster way is to go inside and ask for the help. I see it's complex; it's like thousands and thousands and thousands of light beings and angels inside. They're just waiting for us to cross over. They're like, "Come on, let's go through this portal so we can receive you, so we can welcome you home." They are so ready to welcome us home. They have waited so long for this.*

M: **So, this going inward is the way to them?**

C: *It's the only way.*

M: **I wonder if they can give us a process of going in so we can connect with them and make the change.**

C: *It's about being still, not letting your world deceive you or lead you outside to yourself. To practice stillness and to almost see like a lantern inside that grows bigger and bigger. It's like a feeling. The feel of soft alignment. It's not difficult; we are not looking for big things.*

SCENE: MESSAGE FROM MARY

C: *Mary. I see her. She is so beautiful, giving the divine spark of the divine feminine. She is giving it to us. To humanity. To us all. She is surrounding the Earth with it. She is also in each individual heart. She's holding this soft light like she's showing the way into the heart — the path of softening yourself. To not have expectations. It's like walking through the door, and Mary is on the other side. So close, to be kind to yourself. To be at peace with yourself. To not make life so difficult. To feel like you can always turn inward to the softness because she is waiting there with her soft light taking you through. They are all there taking us through. They are all helping, but Jesus and Mary are coming through because we know them so well.*

M: **So, because we have more of a collective relationship with them, they are more at the forefront?**

C: *Yeah. It makes it easier for us.*

M: **But there is help coming from many?**

C: *Oh, there are so many.*

NEXT SCENE: MESSAGES FROM INNER EARTH

C: *Showing a lot of people under the Earth. There are many under the crust of the Earth. They are blue beings. They are here to help us love. They are coming, more and more, to the surface, but we are not quite ready.*

M: Do they have anything to share?

C: *They will when the time is ready. It's not right now. We need to go through this portal. When we do, they will be available but also help us pass through. It's not time now to be heard. They want us to know they are there.*

M: I am wondering, what needs to happen for people to go through this portal? I know many are doing heart-based practices and connecting with their heart. What needs to happen for someone to make the transition?

C: *It's on a collective scale. We know about the frustration you must feel that you are working hard to make the passage, but it's more like a tipping point. And it's very, very close to that tipping point right now and that's why we say it has become easier to go inside this portal because when many people do it at the same time, when we practice this all together, it will take over. It will be easier and easier. The tipping point is like being in a new place. Everything will change from the inside out. That's what we are waiting for right now.*

M: What are some ways we can accelerate this process?

C: *It's this softness. More feminine space. Softness. To allow. Not to run after things, not to try to make it happen, it's more like a process of leaning inwards softly like a soft, warm embrace of ourselves. We don't have to work as much as we used to do. We don't have to work as much on clearing, on clearing our bodies, because it's happening all the time. So, we can drop these exercises more and more and just be. Be the feeling. Be in the center. Take your place in the center of your being. Practice alignment. And then, at the same time, it's a waiting process until the tipping point is reached. The tipping point will happen. It may feel like you are doing too little, but sometimes that is better than doing a lot or doing in general. Everyone can come into a softer focus, and when we allow, things will come to us.*

NEXT SCENE: MESSAGES FROM STAR FAMILY

C: *(Laughs) Hmm. Oh. I see (laughs) extraterrestrials. They look like small beings, but they have such fun energy. They are stamping and clapping. I see them as a group consciousness.*

M: Do they have anything they want to share?

C: They want to share joy! Joy, joy, joy! Lots of joy! They want to lift us into the new with joy. They are sending us the joy — upliftment. It's uplifting energy. Ah, what they are doing — clapping and stamping — they are doing it to raise the vibration. It's actually time to celebrate. It's right around the corner. They are already celebrating. It's so close, and we have come through the darkness, even with what we see play out — it's in the past. It just shows because people are holding it in their perception. It's really in the past.

M: What about when things...I'll give an example that is coming from American culture right now. It's being presented to the whole world how women were hurt in the past and so this is bringing up a strong charge from all the other women who have been hurt by men, by different situations, and I am seeing people grab onto it, attached to that story. How can we individually and collectively work with things like that? That have a charge to it? That have a history of being hurt?

C: It's meant to play out. It's part of the collective. It's part of Earth's memories. Earth is releasing these memories, and of course, every human being is connected to Earth, so it's like an earthquake inside of these human beings. The best way to go about it is to be in love, connectedness, awareness, to embrace and help each other to embrace it. To move in from a high vibration, if possible, to create a high vibration in order to caress it. To envelop it. It needs to be freed; it needs to have its outpouring. It's needed. A deep cry, a deep sense of hurt, it needs to come through, but see it only as the past and not to hang onto it too much. Not have too many stories around it, don't give it too much attention. It's guided to come through.

M: Beautiful. What else are you seeing now?

C: I see the Earth is opening up.

M: What do you see?

C: I see two Earths. And then I see many, many Earths. There are as many Earths as humans. It means that every human has its own individual Earth experience.

M: Beautiful, what happens next?

C: It's the same energy coming through for us; it's the same for us. Our heart energy is the same. The One is returning to us.

M: The same flame in our hearts is in the center of the Earth?

C: Yeah, but also the humans. Every heart is the same material, the same energy, the same One. The same Creator.

M: The energy of the One is in all of us.

C: Yes, and in the center of the Earth as well. In all the Earths. It's time to come together as One.

Closing Statement

I hope that this material has activated multidimensional awakening and expansion for you. I hope that it brings you comfort and joy as we make our way through this transitionary corridor between old Earth and the New Earth. May you count your blessings and walk your path with increasing faith and luminous devotion. The best is yet to come!

Now, let us make our way into the PATH OF AWAKENING: KEYS FOR TRANSFIGURATION material!

GATEWAY THREE: PATH OF AWAKENING

Keys for Transfiguration

This transmission is a library of information to help you on your path of awakening, healing, and Lightbody ascension. I will describe the ascending pathway out the shadowy depths of suffering and distortion so that you may emerge into the blissful and joyful unification with your True Nature. May these pages help illuminate the path of your exodus from bondage and suffering into the promised land of liberation, abundance, and lasting peace!

THIRTY-SIX

Path of Illumination

OM Lead us from the unreal to the Real
From darkness unto Light
From the illusion of death to the truth of immortality
OM Peace! Peace! Peace!
—English translation of the Pavamana Mantra

Everyone has their own unique definition of what spirituality is and what spiritual awakening means and entails. For me, spiritual awakening is about moving from spiritual ignorance into higher truths and higher consciousness. It is about doing shadow work to illuminate and integrate subconscious patterning that obscures my access to joy or causes suffering for myself or anything else. It is about learning the truth of who I am as an eternal, infinite being of divine light and facing all of life with increasing faith and consciousness. Spiritual living involves growing in devotion, seeking divine knowledge, living a life of higher altruistic service, and repeatedly bringing my mind to focus on and contemplate the Divine.

Humanity awakens in stages and groups so that those who have experience in the ascension process can share support and wisdom with those who are moving through an earlier stage of the process. With each wave of Light that ripples across our planet, another group of souls begins their awakening process, and another layer of distortion and trauma rises to the surface of our individual and collective awareness to finally be released. Most people will have no idea what is happening to them as they begin to go through their purging and healing phases and begin to activate spiritually. As they tune into their Inner Being and intuitive intelligence guidance system, they will be led to information sources to help them.

There is a saying "you cannot serve mammon and God," meaning you cannot serve the selfishness and greed of this world and simultaneously serve the higher will of your Divine Nature. Spiritual awakening is a radical act of rebellion because you are inherently detaching from the mainstream culture and walking on a less traveled path. This does not mean that you cannot have and enjoy riches or luxurious experiences. We can use the goals of our life, our desires, possessions, careers, relationships, and all of the other activities to serve our higher dharmic path and live a life of spiritual ethics.

Four *Purusharthas*: Four Goals of Human Life

Before awakening, our life is driven by the conditioning of The World and by our selfish desires. As we awaken, we begin to convert our mentality from "the ways of the world" and turn our focus, will, and intention towards a higher path. It is said in the ancient scriptures that there are four main goals of human life; the four *purusharthas* are:

1. Pursuit of Higher Purpose (*dharma*) — Virtuous path of living one's higher purpose and performing the duties and responsibilities of one's life in accordance with spiritual ethics.
2. Pursuit of Material Prosperity (*artha*) — Acquiring the means and material comforts of life such as a nice home, a good career, and financial security.
3. Pursuit of Happiness and Pleasure (*kama*) — The desire for love, intimacy, pleasure, and affection.
4. Pursuit of Liberation (*moksha*) — God-realization, the highest purpose of human life, said to be achieved when *dharma*, *artha*, and *kama* are achieved and balanced.

Activation of the Mystical Path of Liberation

Before awakening, we are fully invested in the life of the material world, our physical body, and our egoic identity. We are seemingly cut off from everything else and often tormented by cycles of suffering, fear-based lack-consciousness, and victimhood. We are indoctrinated by "The World" through institutions, familial conditioning, and societal conditioning, having taken on their respective limitations, distortions, and control programming.

At some point, a person may look beyond their physicality and limited human identity and become curious and aware of their own essence, their own soul, and how it relates to a Higher Power. A curiosity stirs within their being and the honest seeker sets off on the sacred journey to discover the truth of who they are. It may start with a prayer. It may start with a crisis. It might start with a serendipitous encounter or something else. Whatever it might be, an activation occurs, and the spiritual potential of the initiate begins to stir and rise within their consciousness.

When we start to awaken, we start to move out of the stage of endarkenment where our intellectual understanding of who we are as a limited egoic identity starts to fall apart. Some call this the "dark night of the soul" where the things that used to give us meaning and enjoyment now seem frivolous, unfulfilling, and superficial. People may turn to distractions, substances, and other numbing experiences to avoid confronting this existential crisis. For others, they begin to seek out answers to the questions that are stirring within them. They may even have mystical and synchronistic experiences that start them on a journey of seeking higher philosophical and spiritual truth.

After the endarkenment phase, we begin the self-inquiry process and the quest for higher truth. For some, spiritual awakening is focused on a system of religion where the individual is seen as imperfect and corrupted and union with God can only happen in a heavenly realm. This is the path of blind faith where communication with the Transcendental Divine is done through reading institutionally approved scriptures and enacting prescribed methods of prayer. Devotees must work hard to overcome sin and imperfection to earn their place in the Promised Land. For some, this path is sufficient and brings much joy and relief. Others may find this path heavy and limiting and yearn for something more.

Each religion on the planet is a different school for studying the soul and the Divine. Souls are likely to have been students or devotees in various traditions throughout their many incarnations. There is no one better than another. Even an atheistic life is still serving a higher purpose for a soul. All paths eventually lead to the same Source, and God-realization is available for everyone regardless of their religious affiliation, traditions, and customs.

Another path is the path of spiritual knowledge, investigation, and introspection fueled by psychological and philosophical studies, alchemical spiritual practices, and self-inquiry. This path illuminates what you are and what you are not, what is real and absolute, and what is an illusion, temporal, and untrue. In the pre-awakening and religious path, our mind is externalized, and we look for the keys to salvation outside of us. In the path of knowledge, we detach from the ways of The World and direct our mind inward towards the Light that We Are. We increasingly perform our actions from a place of selfless service, devotion, and altruism as we strive to serve the Divine in All. On this path, we do not have to wait until we die to hopefully get into Heaven. We do not have to live countless lives paying back negative karma. On this path, a dedicated aspirant can achieve union with the Divine in this very life!

As we awaken, we begin to turn our focus inward to our inner realm, to explore the energies of our beingness. Often what we find is a huge mess! Layers upon layers of trauma, limiting beliefs, and a sick body full of density and chemicals. As we begin to clear out the density, we make space for the Pure Light of the Divine to dwell and expand within us.

Spiritual growth is the ingathering of Light within our beingness and body. As we welcome the Light and Wisdom of Source to come into our being and follow the call of our inner Source, every cell begins to transform as everything begins to be renewed by the Light. This desire to "Know Thy Self" moves the consciousness of the person beyond biological evolution and into the Higher Evolution, the alchemy of the soul. Belief in a Higher Power of Love and the willingness to follow Divine Truth has begun to set them free, and a new life begins. This can be called "gnosis" as one begins to directly experience the Mysteries of the Divine in life and one's own being.

When a soul chooses the journey of awakening beyond the mundane and into the mystical, an inner voice of higher reasoning awakens (*ruach*). This voice of reason counsels the consciousness of the seeker through the compassion of the heart. Sometimes it is subtle, and sometimes it is powerful. Nonetheless, the soul is "born again" as it moves from generic human consciousness and begins its Higher Studies of Light, Unconditional Love, and spiritual Wisdom.

Spiritual evolution takes time and space to flourish. Time allows us to feel the experience of growth. Space allows us to reflect on our success and opportunities for refinement. With time and space, you can honor your past experiences and see the value in them. You are no longer a victim of the past and you can begin to see your future as a choice. You begin to notice that your inner world is creating your outer world, and you begin to take authority over your experience. The Fourth Dimension (early awakening) is all about growing in compassion, sovereignty, and cultivating the presence of Inner Light. It is about freeing ourselves from the indoctrination of "The World" and allowing the deeper divine truths to emerge and be embodied.

Holding Space for Self

So rarely do people give themselves time to tune into their inner experience and process the complexity of their emotions, thoughts, and desires. Humanity jumps from one activity to the next, one trauma to the next situation, without deeply observing the energy information from the experience. Our bodies and subconscious mind store it all. Over time we develop aches, pains, illness, and disease as the unprocessed information crystallizes and becomes physical.

Holding space is a term used in spiritual growth and self-development circles that means "to hold suffering in an alchemical container of loving awareness so that it may heal." When we tune into our inner experience, we can observe and transform the stagnant energies and open ourselves to more flow, ease, and joy. We can acknowledge that something from the past hurt us more than we were initially aware of and transform it through loving awareness.

The Four Immeasurables: Virtues of a Divine Heart

The *Four Immeasurables* are sublime states that one can achieve through spiritual practices. Cultivating these qualities brings the initiate out of negatively polarized separation consciousness into heart-centered connection, presence, and expression. These virtues of the heart are essential when holding space for yourself, another being, and The World.

1. *Metta* — Loving-kindness

Translated as unconditional friendship, benevolence, and kind-heartedness, the quality of *metta* is embodied as wishing well for all beings. To grow in *metta* requires us to transform our bitterness into wisdom and all our harshness into gentleness. As we grow in loving-kindness and unconditional friendship with all beings, we become a safe and healing presence for the world's suffering. The quality of *metta* gives us the ability to hold the highest outcome for all beings because we can see beyond the separate self and victim patterns and genuinely express care about the well-being of another.

2. *Karuna* — Compassion

Compassion can be translated to "to suffer with." Meaning, through the empathetic capacity of the heart and psyche, we can feel and relate to another's suffering. Since we know the experience of suffering from our own life experiences, we can relate to another's suffering. Our suffering is their suffering. It takes an open heart to feel and have compassion for the suffering of another.

Compassion creates a bridge between you and another. When we soften into compassion, we come into a deeper understanding of another's suffering because we, too, know the experience of pain. We can relate to the ways we behaved when we were tormented by our emotions and have a deeper understanding of the experience of the other. When we are compassionate, we see beyond the separate self and see our being's interconnectedness with all other beings. When we acknowledge that we are truly One, we become concerned with the suffering of the world and do everything we can to relieve the suffering of others because we know that truly there is no "other."

3. *Mudita* — Empathetic Joy

Mudita is embodied when we find joy in the joy of others. Empathetic joy amplifies the joy and liberated light in another. It starts a chain reaction that is infectious and can spread to the hearts of others. When we cultivate an inner state of compassion (*karuna*) and loving-kindness (*metta*), we can even celebrate the good fortune of those who we see as villains because we can see beyond the victim story and into the deeper truth that we all want to experience joy and liberation. When we celebrate the joy of another, we share in one heart.

4. *Upekkha* — Equanimity

Clear-minded, unshakable awareness that is not affected by the changing conditions of life. As the polarities of perceived loss and gain, praise and criticism, sorrow and happiness, and the need to maintain public reputation dissolve we rest in the perfection of pure awareness.

Equanimity is a quality of consciousness that sees beyond polarity and into the sacredness and higher meaning of all expressions of life. In the cultivation of equanimity, we release the game of valuing any person over another, any race over another, any nation over another. This intention generates a mental calmness as the mind releases the habit and polarity of judgment to truly be an ambassador of peace and restoration.

It is important to emphasize that the purpose of awakening is to liberate yourself and all beings. These sublime qualities are easily practiced towards the ones we have little to no conflict with. These sublime qualities of consciousness are harder to evoke when we succumb to the mind's conditioning and the illusion of a separate self. The villains, tricksters, and tormenters of our life show us where we give power to our conditioned minds.

Holding Space for Others

The intention of communication and relating in the highest form is to assist in relieving the suffering of another. When you hold space for someone else, you create an alchemical container of loving nonjudgmental awareness to witness and validate their experience and support them in transforming their suffering.

For this to happen effectively, the witness must be anchored in compassionate, nondual awareness so that they are not triggered by the emotions and potential projections of the other who is suffering. This requires deep listening within and connection to the innate quality of intuitive knowing emanated from the Self. From this place, the Listener can hear the subtle nuance in the sound and emotions of the Speaker and gain insight. To be able to effectively listen to the Speaker, one must become aware of fear, judgement, and desire to interject or rescue the other person and return their awareness back to loving awareness and deep meditative listening. Through the witness's alignment with their Higher Self, the sharer can borrow strength, bravery, and compassion for their own process, where they may not have been able to access these qualities on their own.

I first read the term "spiritual partnership" in the book *Seat of the Soul* by Gary Zukav. Spiritual Partnership means that we support one another through the stages of life as equals. It means that we hold the highest and best vision of our community members. Each of us has what it takes to hold space for another. All we need is to enjoy deep, conscious breathing and rest in our hearts and allow unconditional love to do the rest.

Holding Space for the World

During this grand transition, we are invited to hold space for the human collective and life on planet Earth as layers of shadow and trauma come to the surface for healing. Many will be in various experiences of distress and chaos. Every moment that we choose to live from our heart, we become a living prayer for a higher destiny outcome for all of the world. We are invited to establish ourselves in Divine Neutrality and be "in The World but not of it." From this middle path, we can participate in the transformation of this planet without getting swept away by sensationalism and polarity. It's OK if you dip into the polarity. When you do, notice what hooks you into the wheel of suffering and do the work to reconcile that part and return to center.

Growing in Compassion

You are not a failure if you cannot hold these qualities for all beings. Therefore, spiritual growth is made of "practices." We use the practices to reclaim our Light. Start simply. Acknowledge the beings and circumstances in your life that are easy to radiate these qualities towards. Notice how it feels to find that illuminated, joyful appreciation towards their beingness and these pleasant living conditions. Then move to someone or something that irritates your inner realm occasionally. Practice transforming the mental attitudes that you hold towards that being or those conditions until you can be rooted firmly in loving-kindness, compassion, empathetic joy, and equanimity.

As you "build it up," you will find confidence and momentum towards your goal of liberation. When you can emulate these qualities towards a person, a group of beings, or some other life conditions that you hold a mild negative charge towards, you can build up towards emulating these qualities towards even the worst of the worst. This does not mean that the other's actions are justified. It just means that you can remove your own judgments and rise above the lower consciousness of victimhood and the conditioned mind. From this place, you become an ambassador of True Peace and a servant towards the liberation of all beings. If someone has harmed you in any way, transform your suffering and pray for their liberation, even to the point of praying they achieve enlightenment faster than you.

As we create more beauty around us and our personal interactions, we hold the space for higher outcomes for us all. We can detach from the mainstream drama and hold space for peace and reconciliation. We can use the power of compassionate listening to become an agent of harmonic transformation in the world. When we hold that prayer and shine with this light, it inspires others. When enough people are aligned with the Source of Light within them, the world will reflect this, and we will create a New Earth.

THIRTY-SEVEN

Taking Refuge in the Ideal

As spiritual beings on the path of Ascension, we need sources of nourishment to feed our spiritual appetite for Knowledge and Wisdom. Knowledge and Wisdom are the living waters that quench the thirst of the soul. The path of Buddhism describes "The Three Jewels" which I have expanded to encompass an interfaith path.

1. The Enlightened Masters and Ascended Beings (*Buddha*)

There have been souls who have achieved high levels of embodied Truth and Wisdom through their enlightened minds and open hearts in all cultures. Great Masters have incarnated all across the world, and throughout their life, they studied and taught the mysteries of Wisdom and Knowledge. These are the forerunners of consciousness, our spiritual role models. We can look at their examples and emulate the wisdom they embodied.

2. The Teachings of the Masters (*Dharma*)

Sacred texts and enlightened teachings of Oneness and Unconditional Love clearly lay out pathways of remembering the Absolute Reality and the power awakening the limited ego-self to the transcendental infinite Self. Studying the sacred texts helps us to unravel our conditioned mind and reprogram our consciousness to align with Higher Truth.

3. Spiritual Community (*Sangha*)

Spiritual friendships and spiritual partnerships are made of like-minded individuals who empower and support one another on the path of awakening. Everyone is at different stages with their growth. We can glean valuable insight and wisdom gained through experience from our elders, peers, mentors, and teachers. Furthermore, a community that prays together stays together. As we strengthen our bonds through shared spiritual focus, our communities become a liberation force for all beings.

Three Marks of Existence

In Buddhism, there are three pervasive qualities or "marks" of existence: *suffering, impermanence, non-self*. These three marks of existence are a description of inherent qualities of reality and the knower of these principles can use them to transform their reality.

The First Mark of Existence is *dukkha*, suffering. The Buddhists recognize that suffering is inherent in life and that we cannot avoid suffering. Some beings will not incarnate on Earth because of the density of emotional suffering experienced through physical form. You can either get caught up in the illusion and create *karma* here which binds you to the Earth, or you can use suffering for growing into mastery and ascend beyond the need for incarnation. In pre-awakening suffering is seen as a punishment and a prison. In the process of spiritual awakening and high alchemy, suffering is fuel for spiritual transformation and holds the keys to one's liberation when held in the transformative container of loving awareness.

The Second Mark of Existence is *annica*, impermanence. Impermanence means that life is constantly shifting and changing. The whole experience of life and its components and our bodymind complex, our psychophysical self, can be broken into five aggregates or five *skandhas*: material form, sensation, perception, mental formations, and consciousness/awareness that perceives the other *skandhas*.

Each of these components works together to create our mental being. Each of these manifestations has a birth, an existence, and an eventual dissolution. When we become attached to these manifestations, we get swept up in the *maya*, the illusion, and we get lost in *samsara*, the ungraspable world, believing it is real. Remember that spiritual awakening is about learning to discern between what is permanent and what is impermanent, what is real and what is unreal. In the world we live in, the forms, sensations, perceptions, mental formations, and mental awareness are not the true reality. It is but a dream, a temporary appearance, and our task is to awaken and remain conscious while in the dream.

Vairagya, non-attachment, is an inner state where we are disconnected from the pull of the mind, senses, and emotions. First, we can make a mental effort to move the mind away from sensory pleasures. From this place of intentional abstinence, we can see how frequently the mind is drawn towards attaining habitual sensual pleasure (*vyatireka*). From there, we can quiet the senses as we become more aware of the mental attachments and aversions (*ekendriya*). Eventually, this leads us to a neutral state where temptation no longer manifests, and aversion does not exist (*vasirara*).

Para vairagya is a state of supreme detachment, the realization that true happiness comes from within. We are unbound from conditions of the mind and the draw of seeking sensory fulfillment in the world. We can be "in the world but not of it," residing in our Buddha Nature, Christ Nature, Krishna Nature, and our True Self.

Most people spend their lifetimes searching endlessly for the magical component that finally creates a sense of complete fulfillment and lasting happiness. This experience is available for you at this very moment. Take a few moments to breathe long, slow, and deep breaths and release the need to search for something outside of yourself to complete you. Call off the search, even for a moment, and see what is already available for you in fullness.

The Third Mark of Existence is *anatta*, or non-self. When most people think of their "self," they are probably speaking of their physical form, their sensations, their perceptions, their beliefs, or their awareness. Simply, their bodymind complex. All of these have birth, existence, and death so they cannot be the Eternal Self. Even the soul or oversoul are forms and names within the realm of Creation that evolve from one state to another. Our True Self is beyond all names, concepts, and forms. When we look at how the Vedic teachings define *Brahman* as vastness, the Kabbalists speak of *Ain Soph* as Limitless or No-thing, I believe that they are using different perspectives and language to talk of the same thing and each point to the core of our being as this emptiness and vastness.

To understand *annica*, non-self, Buddhism speaks of interbeing, that everything is made up of components of the All. If the sun was not shining, then I could not exist. If rain did not exist, the crops would not exist and therefore, I could not exist. I am part sun. I am part rain. I am a mixture of the All! Everything is interconnected and interrelated, and all components are the by-product of infinite fractals of causality.

To summarize, suffering is inherent in life. We suffer because we cling to the world of form thinking that it is real. We suffer because we forget our True Nature and believe ourselves to be the character we play out in our life. When we accept these three basic concepts, we can begin to unravel our story of suffering and embrace the limitlessness that we truly are!

Three Types of Suffering (Buddhism)

When we begin to awaken, we notice how we have created our own suffering. We begin to detach from stories of victimhood and begin to study the deeper mysteries of our suffering. The Buddhist tradition acknowledges that suffering is inherent in life, and it is up to the seeker to understand the deeper causes of suffering. From the Buddhist perspective, suffering can be separated into three different categories of everyday suffering, the suffering that comes when the conditions of life change, and the background suffering of this world.

One: Everyday Suffering (dukkha-dukkha)

There is the inherent suffering of life's difficult moments and stages. This includes physical and mental pain from birth, aging, death, illness, and general distress when life is not going the way we desire.

Two: Suffering of Change (viparinama-dukkha)

The suffering that occurs as pleasurable moments and stages shift towards unpleasant experiences. Everything is always changing. Life is impermanent. We suffer when we believe that our experience of the world of names and forms is what brings us joy and wholeness.

Three: Pervasive Suffering (sankhara-dukkha)

The suffering that arises from the conditioned mind, the background suffering of existence. This type of suffering arises from unfulfilled desires of the bodymind.

In summary, life inherently has experiences that are not comfortable and cause suffering. "From the womb to the tomb," we all experience dis-ease and discomfort as we go through our life. Life's pleasurable moments will inherently give way to less pleasurable experiences. We suffer when we do not surrender to the changing of time. We suffer because of our uninitiated, conditioned minds. Spiritual knowledge and spiritual practice elevate our minds to become in sync with the perfection of All That Is.

The Four Noble Truths (Buddhism)

The Four Noble Truths of Buddhism are the foundation of the teachings of the Buddha. Understanding the Four Noble Truths helps to liberate one's being from endless cycles of suffering. Simply put, the Four Noble Truths are:

1. Suffering exists.
2. There is a path that leads to suffering.
3. Liberation is possible.
4. There is a pathway that leads to liberation.

1. Truth of Suffering and the Three Marks of Existence

Suffering is inherent in life. 1. From the most subtle discomfort to the most extreme and excruciating pain, life contains a full spectrum of experiences that cause suffering. 2. Impermanence (*anicca*) is inherent in life. Life circumstances are always shifting and changing. It is our attachments to the world of form that causes suffering. 3. We also suffer because there is suffering in the world and our conditioned mind creates suffering because of ignorance. Grasping at and chasing after sensory experiences eventually brings us to the truth that true fulfillment comes from internal, spiritual growth.

2. Truth of the Cause of Suffering

The cause and origin of suffering, *samudaya*, is attachment, craving, and desire. When we chase sensory experiences for their temporary fulfillment, we suffer. When we desire to be something other than who we are in the present moment, we put ourselves in a prison of suffering. When we try to stop life experiences from happening, our fear and resistance create suffering. The three poisons of greed, hatred, and ignorance limit our light and keep us in cycles of suffering.

When we believe something outside of our self will complete us, we believe in the illusion, and we endlessly search outside of ourselves for the magical component that will end our suffering. Our senses drag us through our lives as if we are being pulled by wild horses in every direction. Therefore, many wisdom traditions value sensory deprivation (*pratyahara* in Sanskrit). When we retract our senses and turn inward, we detach from the eternal shifting of the physical universe and begin to empty ourselves of all the thoughts that create suffering so that we can discover the treasure that lives within our very being.

3. Truth of the End of Suffering

Redemption is available for all souls who wish to awaken. If we want to end our suffering, we can continuously acknowledge our power to awaken to higher consciousness. As we release the misperception that happiness and wholeness are found outside of us, we begin to discover the keys to our liberation found within our own being. As we hold to the truth that liberation is possible, we begin to discern what is resonant with our higher path and what is not. We begin to detach ourselves from the Wheel of Karma (*samsara*) and the endless cycle of reincarnation and death.

It should be reiterated that "stepping off the wheel" of endless reincarnations is the birthright for those who choose to follow the path of Ascension all the way through in this life. It may be hard for some to envision this world without suffering of any kind. It may even seem impossible. Yet, for those who are willing to completely release all of their misidentifications and misperceptions, full liberation is theirs to claim, and it shall be theirs!

4. Truth of the Path that Leads to the End of Suffering

The Buddhist's path of liberating one's consciousness from suffering is through "Right Understanding." Right understanding is knowing that there is no fixed self (*anatta*), suffering is inherent in life (*dukkha*), and life's conditions are impermanent (*anicca*). The sacred scriptures of India, Tibet, Egypt, and the mystic traditions like the Gnostics and Kabbalists contain detailed instructions for freeing one's consciousness from the mind's conditioning. There are as many paths to salvation as there are humans upon the planet. There is no "one path fits all" formula. The one principle found at the core of all the wisdom traditions is the redemptive power of unconditional love.

In the teachings of Vedanta, they say, "The knower of Brahman attains the highest." Meaning that nothing of this illusory world will give you the richness that God-realization can give you. You could add up all the riches of the universe and it will still not add up to the immense treasure that is your divine inheritance. The ingathering of spiritual Light is attained through ritualized connection with Source, with the Absolute, through routine spiritual practices aiming to dissolve the negative influences of the ego and merge consciously with the Oneness of All That Is. This leads us to true liberation from cycles of suffering. Practice! Practice! Practice! Source-realization can be yours!

THIRTY-EIGHT

Path of Nondual Knowledge

Patanjali's *Yoga Sutras*, a treatise on classical yoga, describes eight limbs of the yogic practices that aid the practitioner on their path of awakening and God-Self Realization. This path was expanded on in the work of the great Indian philosopher Shankaracharya such as in the text *Aparokshanabhuti*. In this text he describes his fifteen-fold path which merges *raja yoga*, the path of meditation, *with jnana yoga*, the path of knowledge, using the non-dual teachings of *Advaita Vedanta*. Pitanjali's eight limbs are noted with *.

Central to Advaita Vedanta is the concept that only Brahman, the Divine Consciousness is real and that all of Creation and its many manifestations arise, exist, and dissolve within that One Consciousness. That Atman, the inner Source Consciousness, our true Self, is seen as the same as Brahman. We are that One Light of Consciousness, and we only perceive ourselves as separate limited beings with a bodymind stuck in cycles of suffering and reincarnation because we have forgotten our True Nature as the pure Light of Source.

The fifteen-fold path is summarized as follows:

1. *Yama* (ethical observances for all is Source/Self) *
2. *Niyama* (self-conduct for all is Source/Self) *
3. *Tyaga (renunciation of the world, fullness comes from Source/Self)*
4. *Mauna (silence for revealing Source/Self)*
5. *Desha (auspicious place, no distractions from Source/Self)*
6. *Kala (auspicious time, Source/Self is now.)*
7. *Asana* (comfortable posture to think about Source/Self) *
8. *Mulabandha (restraining root lock, rooting awareness in Source/Self.)*
9. *Dehasmya (straightening body, merging body with Source/Self)*
10. *Druk Stiti (fixing of the gaze to see Source/Self everywhere)*
11. *Pranayama* (control pranic force by maintaining Source/Self connection) *
12. *Pratyahara* (sense withdrawal, withdrawal of the mind from sense experiences, immersing the mind in Source) *

13. *Dharana* (concentration, focus on the object of meditation, keeping mind on Source/Self) *
14. *Dhyana* (single-pointed focus/meditation on Source/Self) *
15. *Samadhi* (absorption into Oneness of Source/Self) *

ONE: The Yamas

The Yamas are a set of inner observances, restraints (the "don'ts") and universal ethics that lead towards the balance of Life. From the knowing that all is Source and Source is your True Self from a non-dual perspective, we can use the Yamas to control the senses to bring about non-dual focus and Self-realization.

Ahimsa: Non-harming, Non-violence

Kindness and compassion are the core of spiritual growth and the root of all spiritual virtues. All beings have the right to life, liberty, and the pursuit of higher consciousness. Practicing *ahimsa* soothes old suffering and keeps us from creating more suffering in the world.

Satya: Benevolent Truthfulness

Benevolent truthfulness means that we do not speak falsely and mislead others. When sharing truth, we do it gently. It also means that we do not divulge information when we know that it will harm someone. Practicing *satya* exercises your right to dignity. People learn that they can rely on you to be honest and dependable when sharing your truth.

Asteya: Non-stealing

Non-stealing means not taking anything that is not rightfully yours. Everyone has the right to property, yet we should live within balance. Renunciation of materialistic conditioning and sharing from a generous heart are expressions of *asteya*.

Brahmacharya: Right use of Energy, Sexual Harmony

This observance means that we use our life force energy towards the freedom of suffering of ourselves and all beings. This includes using our sexual life force in a way that honors the divinity and heart of another.

Aparigraha: Non-greed or Non-hoarding

Greed and hoarding stem from separation consciousness and the belief that we will not have enough of what we need to survive. *Aparigraha* is rooted in the belief that we are always being provided with what we need to sustain our path.

Refrain from intoxication (Buddhism)

Mindfulness and responsibility, the ability to respond with maturity and compassion, grow when the mind and senses are not dulled and degraded by adulterants and powerful sensory experiences. Abstaining from addictive patterns and intoxication helps us remain clear and heart-centered so that we can make appropriate observations and compassionate actions.

TWO: The Niyamas

The *Niyamas* are a set of observances in self-conduct (the "do's") that increase a sense of commonality and a sense of oneness, harmony, and bliss that leads towards knowledge of one's True Nature and Higher Self.

Saucha: **Cleanliness**

Purifying the mind, body, and spirit with spiritual practices and higher wisdom harmonizes our thoughts, intentions, actions, and habits. This means not only taking care of our inner realm but also tending to our physical experience and the environment we inhabit.

Santosha: **Contentment**

Growing in acceptance and gratitude for current life circumstances, creating a sense of optimism. Even if life is challenging, we can appreciate what we have and the opportunity to grow.

Tapas: **Discipline, Austerity, Burning Enthusiasm**

Honoring the inner fire that drives us to evolve and do what is noble and good for our path. This often means going against the grain of our deeply imprinted patterns and beliefs. Discipline in our pursuit of true liberation is the fire that burns away our karma, moving us out of cycles of repeated suffering and into higher states of freedom.

Svadhyaya: Study of Self and Sacred Texts

To truly "know thyself," we practice reflection and self-inquiry. We source wisdom through the examples of the enlightened masters, the knowledge from sacred texts, and use our spiritual community as sacred mirrors, reflecting back to us our current state of consciousness.

Isvara Pranidhana: Surrender to Supreme Contemplation of the Higher Power

We express this quality when we dedicate our lives to the Service of All. We continuously surrender our will to the Divine Will of Source and the Higher Evolution. Our life becomes a moving prayer, an act of reverence for and devotion towards the Love of the Universe.

THREE: Tyaga (renunciation)

In this observance, we are constantly disengaging our mind from the pull of the world, identification with the bodymind, and the illusion that true happiness comes from any finite experience. As we renounce those notions we can source our wholeness from the Source within us, our true Self. From here we can dissolve our inner distortions and see the divinity within all of Creation while also recognizing that all of our experiences are arising within the consciousness of the Self. In this awareness we understand that the material reality and our possessions are not what bring us lasting fulfillment. Practicing minimizing our material possessions is an expression of this observance.

FOUR: Mauna (silence)

Ultimate reality is beyond speech and language so we must find inner silence and outer silence to meditate on the Self and the divine deeply. Many spiritual traditions have practices of verbal silence and quiet isolation so that one can focus on the deepest Self and divine consciousness reality. Having one day a week of silence and contemplation is a powerful practice with many benefits. Practicing silence in community can reveal a lot about the dynamics of how we relate to one another.

FIVE: Desha (auspicious place)

Our spiritual practice (*sadhana*) is amplified in potency when we are in an environment conducive to focus, having as little distractions as possible. Our personal practice is best done in solitude within a harmonic space to train the mind to expand into the all-pervasive space of the Divine found within and without. Practicing in the same space repeatedly creates a positive field that supports and regenerates the practitioner with each continuous session.

SIX: Kala (auspicious time)

Our personal practice is amplified in potency when we align the timing of our practice with natural rhythms and auspicious astrological events such as sunrises, sunsets, new and full moons, equinoxes and solstices and other auspicious times. Doing your practice at the same time each day is another way of working with this observation. Ultimately, training the mind to be established in the eternal unfolding of the now moment, trains us to use each sacred moment as a time of spiritual practice. Source is right here, right now.

SEVEN: Asana (posture)

Many are familiar with the *hatha yoga* postures known in Sanskrit as *asanas*. As one settles into a posture, one moves the center of one's consciousness deeper and deeper to the vantage point of pure non-dual awareness, from the comfortable seat of pure awareness. This helps to train the mind to continuously focus on the Supreme Reality, the Kingdom of God that exists within us and all around us.

EIGHT: Mulabandha (restraining root lock)

In meditation and asana practice, one is guided to use the root lock, a lifting of the pelvic floor, to stabilize the physical body, focus the mind, and direct pranic force up through pranic tube along the spinal column. With intention, the dedicated practitioner uses this practice to establish their consciousness on the Divine, the root of one's existence, with increasing consistency.

NINE: Dehasmya (straightening the body)

Conscious embodiment practices train the entirety of the body and mind to work with alignment, precision, and symbiotic harmony. Similarly, we can train the entirety of our bodymind complex to work in symbiosis with the Divine as we practice merging our consciousness with the higher consciousness reality. In this way we walk straight on our path of righteousness and nobility as conscious embodiments of divine will in action.

TEN: Druk Stiti (fixing the gaze)

This speaks to not only how one holds one's gaze during meditation practice but also how we train awareness to see the divine in all. While our physical eyes look upon this world, our inner eye of knowledge can be focused on the divine consciousness reality.

ELEVEN: Pranayama (control of pranic force)

In many traditions there are practices of breathing to increase life force and purify the bodymind. One can elevate the practice by using the four stages of the breath to focus on the Source of Eternal Life and shed attachment to the material universe. An example of this is:

Breathing in: I am Divine Consciousness (*aham brahmasmi*)
Exhalation: releasing attachment to external reality and thought

TWELVE: Pratyahara (withdrawal of the senses)

In some yogic practices, one may limit sensory experiences such as by covering the eyes or ears to assist with inward focus of the mind towards the divine Self. When moving about one's life, a dedicated practitioner uses all experiences to see the Self, the divine consciousness, operating in the background of all experiences.

THIRTEEN: Dharana (focus on the object of meditation)

In meditative practices, a focus point is used to steady the fluctuations of the mind. Beyond typical concentration and holding the gaze on a particular physical location, one can train the activities of the mind to focus on the Divine Reality wherever the mind journeys.

FOURTEEN: Dhyana (meditation)

Various practices of meditation are found throughout the many wisdom traditions of the Earth. The highest intention and practice of meditation is *Atma Dhyana*, meditation on the Supreme Self. As we train the mind to continuously focus on the divine reality, within and without, we establish and stabilize our mental activity on the truth that we are that infinite existence consciousness bliss. The essence and power of this high spiritual truth is felt and declared in the mantras of *aham brahmasmi*, I am Brahman, or I am that I AM.

FIFTEEN: Samadhi (Oneness)

Spiritual practice transforms our mind from a carnal, animalistic nature to that of divine consciousness. In the initial stages of awakening, we experience dullness, agitation, breaks in attention, attachments to sensory experiences, suffering, distraction, attachment to bliss, and even blankness of mind. When one is able to continuously maintain the awareness that "I am Divine Consciousness" one is absorbed into the reality of the highest truth, the supreme reality of existence consciousness bliss resulting in the state that goes by many names in many traditions including *samadhi*, *nirvana*, and salvation.

THIRTY-NINE

Spiritual Ethics

The Eightfold Path of Buddhism offers us a set of ethical observances to help us grow in nobility. The practice of these observances is an ongoing reflection fueled by personal revelations. They help us to live a peaceful and orderly existence in the community. Practicing these values and virtues keeps us from creating more negative karma or from adding to the suffering of the world. These values meet the practitioner where they are on their path of awakening. Every life experience is valuable as we learn to discern what is essential for life and what distracts us from and distorts our vision of our True Nature.

The Eightfold Path of Buddhism is a guide to spiritual awakening and liberation from cycles of suffering. This path consists of moral conduct, mental discipline, and the attainment of divine wisdom. The word "samma," a Pali word, is often translated as "right." When used in this context, right is not describing a system of "right" and "wrong," but quality of expression rooted in compassion and illuminated by Higher Wisdom. As we learn to walk the path of righteous nobility guided by a loving heart, we embody the potential of the liberation of all beings from the cycles of suffering.

The root quality of these morals is *ahimsa*, nonviolence, and non-harming. We can look at our life or our consciousness as a garden. In our garden, we have many varieties of seeds planted. Some seeds are seeds of suffering. Some of these seeds are of compassion and love. In every moment, we have a choice to water our seeds of suffering or water our seeds of love and compassion. Living a righteous and noble life is a practice of watering the seeds of compassion and love. Make your garden beautiful by watering seeds of patience, tenderness, kindness, gentleness, and other qualities of love and compassion.

One: Right Understanding, Right View (Samma Ditthi)

The Four Noble Truths and the Three Characteristics of Existence can help us to better understand the nature of reality. We understand that how we see our self is always shifting and changing and that life is impermanent. We understand that suffering is inherent in life and that pleasurable moments eventually shift to less pleasurable moments. We understand we suffer because we hold conditioning from this world. We understand that not only does suffering occur but there is also a path to suffering. We understand liberation is possible and that there is a pathway to liberation.

Two: Right Intent, Right Resolve (Samma Sankappa)

This is our commitment to the path of awakening and dedication towards the liberation of all beings from suffering. This happens by guiding one's thoughts and intentions back to Unconditional Love and Oneness and dedicating our beingness to Service to All.

Three: Right Speech (Samma Vaca)

We can use our communication to relieve suffering and create harmonic agreements. This includes refraining from lying, using divisive or abusive speech, slander, and even idle gossip. Often people use communication to distract themselves from fully experiencing their Inner Being. Gandhi said, "Speak only if it improves upon the silence." Before communicating, ask yourself, "Is it kind? Is it true? Is it necessary? Is it helpful?"

Four: Right Action (Samma Kammanta)

With right action, we dedicate all actions of the body towards compassionate living and to relieving the suffering of all sentient beings. This includes nonviolence, non-stealing, and sacred sexuality.

Five: Right Livelihood (Samma Ajiva)

Our livelihood, our way of generating income, gathering resources, and creating a career path should be done honestly and in a way that promotes equality among all sentient life. This means that our work does not harm other beings or nature and that our participation in society reflects our Service to the Greater Good of Life.

Six: Right Effort (Samma Vayama)

We strive to train the mind towards wholesome, positive thoughts that create positive, life-affirming action. We grow in an "attitude of gratitude," shedding negative thoughts and making a conscious effort to move towards joyful determination.

Seven: Right Mindfulness (Samma Sati)

We practice training the mind and our conscious awareness to be fully focused on the present moment. This includes growing in our awareness of the body, feelings, mind, thoughts, breath, and the ever-shifting phenomenon that we call reality.

Eight: Right Concentration (Samma Samadhi)

This is the practice of joining the mind with the Absolute. Seeing Heaven on Earth through single-pointed meditation, which results in unbroken attentiveness and a deep feeling of tranquility and bliss.

Creating Pathways of Transformation

While each of us has different karma, different mental patterning, and different soul contracts, there are simple key principles that can be applied to any negative condition to transform it into a higher state. If we wish to purify our bodymind complex, we need to follow fours steps:

1. Cease to deny the presence of patterns within our mind that cause suffering for ourselves and others.
2. Cease justification of those patterns.
3. Release guilt around the patterns of distortion and limitation that we carry.
4. Actively seek out and practice methods of purification and God/Self-realization.

Mental Alchemy: Evolving to Higher Thought

The mind is constantly generating thoughts. Some are pleasant and empowering, and others are generated from the shadows of our unprocessed trauma and ignorance. When one becomes aware of negative thoughts that keep us in cycles of suffering, we have three options to make change.

1. Discard the thought, jerk it out of the mind.
2. Discard the thought for a higher vibrational thought. ("I bind this thought pattern of anger. I call forth and set loose the power of serenity.)
3. Intensify the thought/emotion and direct it towards Source such as in the tantric traditions. This option should be done with caution as intensifying powerful negative emotion/desire/thought can cause more chaos and suffering.

Seven Pillars of Personal Transformation)

Below are seven keys for personal transformation to guide you through your awakening and ascension processes. Use each key to fine-tune your actions to create lasting positive change.

One: Sankalpa — Intention

Intention is everything on the path of awakening. *Sankalpa* is an intention that comes from the heart and serves your Higher Path. Sometimes we have unconscious intentions of avoiding suffering or discomfort, which keep us from going through the experiences that give valuable insight into the nature of our suffering. This concept is reflected in Newton's First Law of Motion which states that an object will remain at rest or motion until acted upon by another force. Your intention is the force that creates the architecture and trajectory of your future.

Attention and *intention* are qualities of consciousness. *Attention* energizes consciousness. Wherever the mind goes, the energy follows, and we become increasingly aware of what we focus upon. *Intention* transforms whatever we hold within the container of our awareness.

Intention shapes our destiny. Unconscious intentions are those of our subconscious and often operate in the background. Most of humanity operates with the unconscious intention to survive and protect their body and future. They haphazardly fumble through life from one event to another, from one emotional reaction to another, asleep in their own dream.

As we awaken and begin to become deliberate conscious creators of our reality, we begin to focus our intention and attention in a way that sustains us on our path of spiritual growth and personal mastery.

Two: Tapas — Intensity and Dedication

This is related to Newton's Second Law of Motion, which states, "The rate of change of momentum of a body with respect to time is directly proportional to the net external force acting on the body." Spiritual growth is dependent on the intensity and duration of our practice. Our commitment can be seen as low, medium, or high intensity.

Three: Shani — Slowing

Becoming aware of our subconscious drives requires us to slow down our physical, mental, and emotional actions to understand the subtle and nuanced shifts in our consciousness. While high-intensity practices may result in faster spiritual growth, it is important to discern when rest and a gentler pace are what is most needed.

Four: Vidya — Deep Awareness, Clear Sight

Self-inquiry and mindfulness help us see and understand our habits and self-limiting, self-sabotaging patterns to transform them into higher states. Mindfulness of any condition immediately begins to transform the condition into a higher state through loving awareness.

Five: Abhaya — Fearlessness, Bravery

Change takes courage. Lasting change requires us to acknowledge our fear but not let it dictate our actions or inaction. Pushing our edge requires us to be comfortable within the discomfort and release our need for external validation, anchoring us to our own internal compass of truth.

Six: Darshana — Inspired Vision

Having a vision of what the higher outcome looks and feels like is essential to our path of spiritual growth. When we want to create new patterns, we can create an inner image of our ideal life when we are free of the limiting patterns and beliefs of the ego and subconscious patterns.

Seven: Abhyasa — Persistent Practice

Spiritual growth is not linear. It winds, curves, backslides, and stagnates at times. There are no "failures" or wrong ways on the spiritual path. There are only opportunities to reflect, gain insight, and practice again.

Moving Beyond Limitation

To create lasting change, one needs to cultivate *discipline*, an attitude and actions that are of *service* to others, and consistent *practice* towards one's higher goals. *Discipline* is the fire that drives and is needed to build momentum in a new direction. *Service* to others helps us step out of the limitations of the false ego and into universal connection. Through spiritual *practice*, the unconscious becomes conscious, and we can choose to step out of the patterns that cause suffering in our lives and move into higher states of freedom. It is said that over ninety percent of our cognitive processes are subconscious, operating mostly in the background undetected. Deeply ingrained unconscious beliefs are like ghosts that haunt our consciousness, driving us towards frustration and limiting patterns. Spiritual growth is dependent on awareness and action taken in a positive direction to mature our consciousness and heal the echoes of past trauma that call out from our subconscious and unconscious minds.

Growth takes time and comes in stages. We can look at the progression of the evolution of personal transformation in four stages:

1. **Unconsciously Incompetent:** Before we become aware of limiting beliefs and self-destructive patterns, we are unaware that we lack the skills needed to move out of cycles of suffering.

2. **Consciously Incompetent:** When the pattern is revealed through the light of our awareness, we become aware of the pattern and our

lack of the skills and knowledge required to move into a higher state of living. At this stage, we can seek information and guidance to lead us onto a higher path and a higher perspective. We likely cycle back through the old patterns as we refine our intentions and actions and gather more data to support our new path. Compassion, forgiveness, and grace help us understand that we are not our past behaviors, and we are on a path of learning and discovery.

3. **Consciously Competent:** Once we start to implement our newfound insights, we move out of a pattern of limitation and into a higher state. There is still an awareness of the impulses and momentum of our old habits, but the persistent practice has laid a new path for us to journey on and we become increasingly more confident on our new trajectory.

4. **Unconsciously Competent:** After consistent practice, we fully integrate the new way of being and become completely rooted in our new path. Since we have transformed our subconscious beliefs through spiritual practice, the old ways fade completely into the past and we enjoy our new way of being.

Now you should have a foundational understanding of spirituality, spiritual awakening, and the path out of suffering and bondage. Now we will explore how to apply the practices of spiritual alchemy to catalyze multidimensional awakening and true liberation. Set your intentions and diligently dedicate yourself to your path. Slow yourself down and deepen your awareness. Face the challenges of life with bravery while keeping your inner focus on your inspired vision of Heaven on Earth. There is much love and support for you. Practice! Practice! Practice! All is coming!

FORTY

Meditation

The main tool for spiritual alchemy is the practice of concentration and meditation. Meditation is the experience of single-pointed focus which occurs through practices of mindfulness and concentration. There are countless benefits of practicing meditation including stress relief, liberation from fear of death, development of magnetism in your personality, reduction of heart rate and blood pressure, reduction of inflammation, lowering of cortisol in the body, and elevating spiritual connection. Simply put, meditation helps us create the conditions for the mind to be as useful as possible. When the mind is calm, it translates into the other layers of our being.

In modern society, it is common knowledge that meditation is an excellent tool for personal transformation. The challenge for individuals is twofold. One issue is developing confidence and skill. The other is dedication and commitment to do the practice. My suggestion for those new to meditation is to find a teacher to walk you through the basics of meditation so that you do not get discouraged in the early stages. Then commit to doing the practices for at least 10-20 minutes a day. New Earth Ascending has instructional videos to get you started!

Many different types of meditation exist. Some are passive practices like seated or supine (laying on the back) meditation practices. Some are active movement practices that develop mindful awareness like hatha yoga and qi gong. Try a variety of practices until you find one that feels right and then repeatedly perform that method to unlock its benefits. I highly recommend finding an experienced guide to instruct you with new meditation techniques so that you can quickly develop confidence and skill in the art of meditation. If you find that you have a hard time quieting the mind, combine active practices to regulate and focus the bodymind and then move into stillness practices to go deeper within.

Meditation practices most often involve conscious breathing to unite the physical body and subtle bodies in your awareness. Tuning in to the breath at the beginning of meditation practice is like saddling up on a horse for a journey. Focusing on the breath trains the mind for the journey inward and helps to regulate the autonomic nervous system so that you are relaxed and calm but focused and alert for the journey.

As we progress in meditation practice and throughout our day, we move through five stages of the mind:

1. *Mudham*: dull, forgetful, delusion, and lethargic.
2. *Kshiptam*: raving, wandering, restless, distracted, disturbed state of mind.
3. *Vikshiptam*: oscillating, occasionally steady, easily distracted, thought in process of purification.
4. *Ekaagram*: one-pointed, tranquil, focused, concentrated.
5. *Niruddham*: restrained, cessation of the waves of the mind, controlled, regulated, highly mastered.

Many people give up on meditation because they erroneously believe that they should be able to immediately quiet the mind. When beginning to work with meditative practices, it is expected that a person will naturally be in stages one and two as one develops the awareness and skill needed to move into quieter, more focused states of the mind. Awareness is the first step to creating positive change. The process of developing meditative skill is accelerated when guided by an experienced teacher or when meditating with others. Drop all expectations of what meditation is supposed to look like or feel like and keep practicing stillness and awareness. All is coming!

Meditation Guidelines

Posture

Some practices ask that you are seated with your spine erect. This is not always easy and comfortable for people. I suggest using pillows and blankets to prop yourself into a comfortable position, sitting in a chair, sitting with your back against a wall, or laying down flat if seated positioning is not easy for you. What is important is that the spine is long and that you are comfortable. Seated meditation practice allows the spine to act as an antennae system with the Earth and has many benefits such as strengthening or elongating certain muscle groups, and you are less likely to fall asleep in a seated meditation posture.

Breathe through the Nose

Most breathing practices focus on nasal breathing. Breathing through the nose filters and adjusts the temperature of the air to prepare it to pass through the body. Breathing through the mouth releases life force energy through the moisture that is exhaled in the breath. If you are congested or inhibited in any way, it is perfectly fine to breathe through the mouth.

Diaphragmatic Breathing

The diaphragm is our bridge between the higher spiritual chakras and our lower earthly chakras. When we breathe primarily from our chest, we are ungrounded and floating off the ground. When we focus on initiating breath with the diaphragm and allow the lower abdomen to expand and contract with each breath, this creates a sense of being grounded and connected to the Earth. It also massages our internal organs. To get the most from our breath, we should use "yogic breathing" or three-part breathing to use the full range of movement of breath in the lungs. This is explained more in the *pranamaya kosha* section.

Focus the Mind

Notice all four stages of the breath, including inhalation, retention, exhalation, and suspension. Equalize and extend each stage to create an effortless rhythm. If the mind wanders, bring it back to feeling the sensations of breathing. You can also use affirmations and counting to keep the mind focused on the experience of breathing.

Watching the Breath

The foundation of meditation practice is breath awareness. It is like the horse that you saddle onto for the journey of meditation. As you breathe in and out, deepen your awareness on the experience of breathing. This alone can create powerful energy and clarity. You can use numbers to train the mind into the present moment. For example, breathing in for a count of four, holding for four, exhaling for four, and pausing for four. This trains the mind to be solely focused on the act of breathing. Using a mental mantra or affirmation helps to train the thought patterns to focus on the intention of the meditation. For example, as you breathe in, focus fully on all the sensations of breathing in and mentally say to yourself, "I am aware that I am breathing in." As you exhale, focus fully on all the qualities of breathing out and say to yourself, "I am aware that I am breathing out." This can be simplified to "breathing in" and "breathing out." This practice is my first recommendation for new meditators.

Be Gentle on Yourself

If breathwork or meditative practices add stress to the body or mind, stop immediately, and return to normal breathing. Breathing patterns can be difficult to break. No one is expecting you to master this right away. When you are calm, you can try again.

Emotional Release

It is not uncommon for people to experience a myriad of thoughts, sensations, and emotions as they begin to practice conscious breathing and meditation. Sometimes, powerful emotions can surface that are remnants of unprocessed trauma and past experiences. If this happens, continue to breathe deep and calm breaths and allow the emotional energy to be felt and released.

Energy Movement and Sensations

When we breathe consciously and deeply, we oxygenate the blood and tissues much more than they are used to. This can create tingling sensations, involuntary muscle contractions, heat, and other sensations. Stay calm and continue breathing slowly and deeply to continue moving the energy. If it startles you too much, you can slow down or take a rest.

Basic Meditation Procedure

1. Find a comfortable seated position.
2. Adjust your posture to ensure that you can sit easily for a while with a long, vertical spine. Use props like a wall, meditation pillow, blankets, or a chair to support the body's positioning.
3. Aim for body stillness (*kaya sthairyam*) and progressive relaxation. (Scan the body to soften tension and align the bone structure.)
4. Practice breath awareness (*anapanasati*).
5. Observe the inner planes from a place of witnessing and non-attachment.

6. Add additional practices like *mantra*, breathwork, and visualization to enhance the practice.
7. Experience thoughtless state (move in and out of 6 and 7).
8. Return to waking state of consciousness.

Various Methods of Meditation

Mindfulness Meditation

One type of meditation is mindfulness/witnessing practices. All meditation methods have this quality of paying attention to what arises in one's experience with increasing mental awareness of subtlety and nuance. Mindfulness can be cultivated while breathing, walking, dancing, talking, yoga asana, tai chi, or any other normal day-to-day activities like riding a bike or washing dishes. Every moment holds an opportunity to cultivate mindfulness.

Sublime State Meditation

There is a lot of benefit in simply meditating on the sublime states or virtues such as Peace, Equanimity, Kindness, Compassion, and Joy. Simply evoke the state and supporting imagery in your mind and breathe into it as you allow yourself to bask in the Love and Light of the Sublime.

Antar Mouna: Inner Silence

This meditative practice was made famous by Swami Satyananda, and I discovered additional steps in an article written by yoga teacher trainer Christian Möllenhoff. "*Antar*" means inner and "*mouna*" means stillness. This practice helps you understand the complex functions of the mind so that you can develop a tranquil state of inner silence. The stages of the practice are as follows:

1. Setting up body sturdiness (posture and breath awareness).
2. Externalizing awareness of the senses.
3. Awareness of spontaneous thought processes.
4. Creating thought sequences and willfully stopping them.
5. Awareness and discarding spontaneous thoughts.
6. Awareness of Inner Space (chidakasha) and Emptiness.
7. Alternating between Step 2 and Step 6.
8. Resting in Universal Beingness, Atman.

Mantra Meditation

Another type of meditation is mantra meditation. A person recites, out loud or internally, repetitive thoughts or spoken words that bring the practitioner into loving awareness, unity, and personal empowerment. Many traditions use mantras to create alchemical changes in consciousness, especially in the Tibetan, Vedic, and Jewish traditions. The use of the holy names of the Divine and holy mantras connects the practitioner with the momentum of all the other practitioners who have used these same vibrations throughout all of time and space, including the higher dimensions. These mantras focus the practitioner on higher thoughtforms outside of the mind's conditioning and begin a process of transmutation that happens on all levels of one's being including the DNA. Mantra meditations are also preventative medicine for the consciousness as they protect the mind from absorbing lower thoughtforms.

Mantras or devotional songs in your native language that come from the heart are often the most powerful. If you have any hesitation about reciting mantras in another language, stick with your own language. Here are some mantras from non-English traditions that I have learned that have been helpful in my own healing and transformation. I recommend learning a variety of mantras and devotional songs to infuse many varieties of higher consciousness thoughtforms into your system.

Om/Aum (Sanskrit)

Translates as the primordial sound of Creation, the sound that began all vibrations in Creation. Reciting OM opens the body-mind-Source connection and works at bringing all systems into the original harmonic resonance. Chanting OM alchemically leads us through the four states of consciousness of waking, dreaming, deep sleep, and supreme equilibrium within the sounds of A-U-M and the silence that follows.

Gate Gate Para Gate Parasam Gate Bodhi Svaha (Sanskrit)

"Going, going, going on beyond, always going on beyond, always becoming enlightened"

This mantra connects us to the Higher Evolution of consciousness, moving us from what is currently known and experienced in limitation towards our own Buddhahood and liberated mastery. An extra layer of intention is that recitation of this mantra not only supports your ascension but also extends to assist the ascension of all of life.

Kadoish Kadoish Kadoish Adonai Tsabayoth (Hebrew)

"Holy! Holy! Holy! Lord God of Hosts"

This mantra connects us to the many higher consciousness light beings that serve the Living Light, activating multidimensional transformation for the practitioner.

Lokah Samastah Sukhino Bhavantu (Sanskrit)

"May all beings be free of suffering. May all my words, thoughts, and actions contribute towards that liberation." or *"May all beings be filled with joy, love, and light!"*

Mindful Breathing with Mental Mantra (Ajapa Japa)

Another way to practice is to shift from verbal mantra recitation to mental recitation. Start with a few rounds of your favorite mantra articulating each sound and feeling the meaning and wisdom of the mantra. Then silently repeat the mantra to yourself in your mind while also feeling the meaning and wisdom shining throughout your inner being. In this way, the mantra continues to play in the subconscious throughout the day to elevate the brain patterning.

Trataka Meditation

Another type of meditation is Trataka meditation, which includes focusing one's mind on a single object to induce a trance and inner focus. This is commonly done with a candle, sun gazing, and *yantras* (sacred geometric designs with psychic healing effects). As the practitioner concentrates on the object, they simultaneously remain unattached to any intruding thoughts to develop a state of clarity. Trataka can also be done by imagining that the sacred images or symbols are superimposed on the screen of the mind or in the heart field to bring the qualities of the object of meditation into the inner realm.

When working with a candle, be sure the flame is at eye level, motionless, and that the room is as dark as possible. Stare into the candle while holding meditative awareness. Resist the urge to blink for as long as possible while holding single-pointed focus on the flame. Allow the tears to emerge. When you can no longer hold the gaze, close the eyes and allow the tears to wash through the eyes while holding an inner image of the candle flame. When the image fades, you can begin another round of Trataka. Additionally, you may add mental mantra recitation.

Focusing on an object for even less than a minute cultivates a relaxed mind and a relaxed body. This is commonly experienced in "road hypnosis" when someone loses a chunk of time while driving because of their mind's focus on the road. This also happens when someone is listening to another person speak. We have about twenty to thirty seconds to make a point when we are communicating with others before they start to slip into a hypnotic trance.

I suggest practicing mindfulness if you are watching a TV screen or scrolling through smart devices as these technologies quickly move us into a hypnotic trance with a high level of suggestibility where other thoughts and attitudes can be implanted into our subconscious. When we use these technologies with mindfulness, we know when content is not good for our mind, and we can avoid being programmed subconsciously by changing the content or turning off the device.

Guided Visualization Meditation

Another type of meditation is guided visualization or imaginative meditation using the inner technology of the *chidakasha,* the screen of the mind. In guided visualization, the practitioner visualizes imagery through their imagination to evoke certain emotional experiences such as imagining peaceful scenery like flowing water or sunny fields of flowers to evoke a sense of peace and tranquility. Practitioners can imagine light formations to raise their vibration, like being within a bubble of white light. This practice can be expanded into advanced psychic practices like remote viewing and astral projection as the practitioner learns to project their nonlocal consciousness to other places and times. We do this every night when we sleep as our astral body travels to learn and heal in other realms.

Yoga Nidra

Yoga Nidra is a practice of "yogic sleep" where the practitioner is led through waking consciousness into a deep relaxation that mimics the experience of deep sleep and then intentionally guided back into waking consciousness. This is a great practice to do if you have trouble sleeping or need to take a quick yogic nap to rejuvenate yourself during the day. It is best to have this pre-recorded or have someone lead you through the stages of the process.

Repeated Practice Leads to Mastery

Find a practice or two that you feel resonant with and practice it every day to get used to it. The longer and more consistently you practice, the more benefit and mastery you will experience. After you understand the basics of these practices, you will likely find yourself using them throughout your day. It is perfectly normal to be challenged at first or to have practice sessions that are more challenging with the "monkey mind" jumping from thought to thought. Compassionately accept where you are in your process and keep practicing!

FORTY-ONE

Koshas: Layers of Being

The human body is a multilayered system of subtle energy fields of various vibrational frequencies that are in a constant state of transformation. What people typically call their "body" is actually several different bodies overlapping one another. *Kosha* is a Sanskrit word for "sheaths" as it describes the different bodies fitting into one another like a sword into its scabbard. Each one fits inside the other like Russian nesting dolls or a hand fitting into a glove. Each layer is inserted into, pervades, and extends beyond the previous. Each exists in its own bandwidth, its own density, from the most physical to the ultradimensional part of us that exists beyond this illusory world. We are truly multidimensional holographic beings of Light!

The term 'holarchy' is a word created by fusing together 'whole' and 'hierarchy' to describe individual components which have their own wholeness but contribute to a greater wholeness and unification. The human body is a mirror reflection of the greater cosmological order. Just as Source is the greater sphere which all other spheres of creation exist within, the Source within us lays the foundation for the other layers of our being to emerge.

While each layer is whole and has its own functions and properties, each layer contributes to the greater wholeness of our being. We separate each layer to understand its components, functions, and purpose, yet we should keep in mind that each layer contributes to the entire hologram of our being and all layers interpenetrate, occupy the same space, and work in symbiotic relationship so that our soul can have the experience of physicality and evolution.

Different traditions have different classifications and numbers of layers of the *koshas*. Most traditions have between four to seven distinctly different layers of the aura of our consciousness vehicle. They mostly describe them as the same but separate some layers into sublayers.

After looking at several philosophies, I have come to find great value in the Advaita Vedanta model of consciousness, as well as the contemporary models presented in Theosophy, the work of Meher Baba, and other lineages. The following theoretical model is a fusion combining the wisdom from my research.

Three-Body System

The human form can be separated into three different major bodies which can be separated into different planes of consciousness. The base for these layers is the Source Self which projects other layers to experience Creation. Note that I categorize these slightly differently than Vedanta. The three major layers are:

1. *Physical Body:* Physical, Material layer
2. *Subtle Body:* Etheric layer, conscious mind, subconscious
3. *Causal Body:* superconscious mind, buddhi, auric film

Some occult traditions break this into the categories of body, soul, and Spirit. The soul is the lightbody which is the combination of the subtle bodies and causal body from my model. This soul is what moves from life to life. The Spirit is the Atman/Self/Source, which is Absolute, omnipresent, omnipotent, and ever free. This is your True Nature.

The Causal Consciousness Body, the most subtle body is the first layer that manifests and is the seed layer from which the other layers emerge. It holds the karmic imprints and mental patterns from past lives which lie dormant until triggered by life experiences. The causal body gives birth to the subtle body, which create the template matrix for the physical body, which is the medium through which the soul experiences the Material Realm. In the model I use, the causal consciousness body includes the superconscious mind functions, the higher mind that is cultivated in spiritual awakening.

The Subtle Consciousness Body gives us the capacity to feel and sense our experience. This grouping of layers is made of the etheric structuring of the physical body as well as the functions of the conscious and subconscious mind. The subtle body gives us access to the subtle realms and bridges us with the higher consciousness planes. It is the layer in which universal *prana* enters our body and is converted for life processes. In some traditions, the life force layer (*pranamaya kosha*) is combined with the physical layer to create one "body of action." In other traditions, the pranic layer is considered part of the Subtle Body. I find understanding in both. For the sake of the ease of this transmission, I will link the vital layer with the Subtle Body.

According to Vedanta, the subtle body is said to have nineteen or seventeen main components, depending on the lineage of the teaching. In this system the higher and lower mind functions belong to the subtle body. The components include:

- five organs of knowledge (eyes, ears, nose, tongue, skin)
- five organs of action (mouth, hands, legs, genitals, anus),
- five pranas (*prana, apana, vyana, udana, samana).* I will also note the chakras and nadis here.
- four internal organs (mind/*manas*, memory/*chitta*, *intellect/*buddhi*, *ego/*ahamkara*).

The Physical Body exists in the physical plane. It is the densest layer and is made of all the physical organs, tissues, and their processes. It is the physical vehicle for soul, our subtle bodies, to experience physical life through. The transcendental Self, the Atman, pervades each layer, conducting the orchestration of all systems at once. Our True Nature, our True Self, is that One Light of Consciousness, the Awareness and Witness of all objects of experience including the bodymind and the world.

Within the three major bodies are the subplanes of each plane of existence with different functions that contribute to the whole. If there is curiosity, I recommend researching the lineages that I have sourced this wisdom from.

- **Physical Consciousness Body**
  - *Annamaya Kosha*: Physical Layer: Material Sheath
- **Subtle Consciousness Body**
  - *Pranamaya Kosha*: Vital Layer: Pranic Sheath
  - *Kamamaya Kosha*: Conscious Mind: Desire Sheath
  - *Manomaya Kosha*: Subconscious Mind: Mental Sheath
- **Causal Consciousness Body**
  - *Atimanasa Kosha*: Supramental Mind: Intuitive Sheath
  - *Vijnanamaya Kosha*: Subliminal Mind: Intellectual Sheath
  - *Anandamaya Kosha*: Subtle Causal Mind: Bliss Sheath
  - *Atman*: Pure Consciousness, Source within, Spirit

It is a common belief that we are a physical body that can have spiritual experiences, but the truth is we are a spiritual being that experiences ourselves in form. We originate beyond form and develop a causal body, subtle body, and physical body. In this way, we can think of these sheaths as layers of ignorance that distract us from perceiving the Atman/Source/Self, but they do not cover the Self because our True Nature is all-pervasive, vast, limitless, and unblockable. We just need to quiet the noise of the mind and senses to notice what is always there in the background of our awareness. We are Source right here, right now, and forever.

These coverings inhibit us from experiencing the knowledge of the Source Self. Our Source Self "sits" in the background witnessing the different bandwidths of density overlaying our Divine Nature. We are not the body that walks about this world of solid form. We are not the "breathing body" of vital energy and its vital processes. We are not the thinking consciousness, the egoic identity, or our memories and desires. We are not the intellectual processes of our higher mind. We are not even the blankness of the bliss consciousness. We are the Seer of all experiences. We are the pure Consciousness that observes them all. We are the Witness of these illusory phenomena, pure unbridled beingness. Through the process of Ascension, we are not rejecting the body or mind but elevating it to the highest capacity and functioning so that the full Light of our Being can shine through each kosha.

These sheaths are symbiotic, working together to create the vessel that you experience life through. These systems are always working toward harmony and vitality to create a resonant, unified field of pure light. This state of balance is called homeostasis, made through the harmonic organization and coherence of each sheath. As you come into deeper awareness of each layer and reconcile its distortions, the healing benefits spread to the other bodies so that the whole system benefits from improvements. This next section will take you through each of the koshas and provide thorough instructions on how to purify and strengthen each of these bodies in preparation for Ascension.

Moving from the Unreal to the Real

The koshas are the robes that Jesus spoke about when he taught of cleaning the robes to prepare for the next garment of Light. What we eat, what we give our life force to, and the thoughts we think affect our ability to tune into the brilliance of our Divine Nature.

Why do we not know our True Nature? We are confused and ignorant of our true beingness because of our misperceptions, misidentifications, and the roles connected to each of the koshas. Our awareness is focused on and distracted by our own *samsara*, our own suffering mind-body complex. We have become enamored and intoxicated by the dream spell of *maya*.

To understand our True Nature, to know what we ARE, we can negate or remove the layers of what we are NOT. As we peel back the layers of our *koshas* like we peel the layers of an onion, we arrive at the true knowledge of who we are as pure Consciousness.

In Advaita Vedanta there is an understanding that the True Nature is the Atman, the transcendental Self, which is Brahman (Source) having an experience in form as the individual self. The Atman is the Seer of Creation, so it can never be seen as an object or reduced to a form. It is the Atman, the Source within us, which gives us sentience, the awareness to witness the ever-shifting forms and names within one's experience. The pure Consciousness is stable, changeless, and ever-present. If your True Self is the subjective consciousness, sentient (aware), and changeless, we can test each of the *koshas* to see that they do not match these criteria. The physical body cannot be aware of the Source. The Etheric Body is constantly changing. The higher and lower mind faculties disappear in deep sleep and our experiences of bliss and unity come and go. Yet it is our self-luminous Self that shines the Light of awareness on all of these ever-shifting experiences.

The words we speak are like spells that can either move us into higher states of expansion or they can anchor us into the illusion even more. Every time we say the words "I am..." the words that follow have an immediate effect and can show us which layer of our personality we are identifying with. When we say, "I am ugly," we are identifying with the physical body. When we say, "I am exhausted," we are identifying with our vital energy system. When we say, "I am mad," we are identifying with the emotional body. "I am confused," we are identifying with the mental body. Yet, all the while, the soul still shines as Pure Consciousness. A more accurate statement would be "I am pure consciousness experiencing this body, vitality, and the manifestations of thought and insight." You are ever the witness and never the witnessed. You are pure consciousness itself!

When we get our awareness overly involved in the different layers of our personality, their roles, and the manifestations in those layers, we overlook our Divine Self. It is a paradox in that the spiritual journey is one of seeking and looking for the "Truth of Who I Am," yet Source is always there. Our True Self is always present, yet most of humanity consciously or unconsciously decides to "look the other way" and gets caught up in associating with the distractions of the different layers of density that make up the koshas. Yet, at some point we "hear the call" of our divine nature saying "Come, find me." and the spiritual journey begins. We begin to remember the mission of ascension that we planned for ourselves before we entered this physical world. We begin to turn away from the "ways of the world" and begin to seek fulfillment from living a spiritualized life focused on awakening to the True Nature of reality.

How do we free ourselves from our limited egoic identity, spiritual ignorance, and karmic prison? There are infinite ways! Every spiritual wisdom tradition has ways of focusing one's life towards the Higher Consciousness. The yogic sciences encourage us to fine-tune our awareness and action towards altruistic actions that serve the good of all (*karma yoga*). We can balance the polarities of our bodymind complex (*hatha yoga*). We can grow in devotion to and our love of God (*bhakti yoga*). We can meditate on our Divine Nature and the Divine Reality (*raja yoga*). We can infuse our minds with Divine Knowledge (*jnana yoga*). While these names are Sanskrit terms, similar concepts can be found in all wisdom and faith traditions.

From the perspective of linear time, our many incarnations evolved our individual consciousness by progressing from the simplest to most complex consciousness forms to the point of taking human form. In human form, we can begin the process of liberating our consciousness in what is called God-realization, Self-realization, or Ascension. Even though the divine presence of our True Being is always there, yet it requires seeking, searching, and spiritual practice to fully establish ourselves in that pure Consciousness state. For most, it takes many lifetimes to fully realize what we have always been.

It is said at the highest state of realization, we live in the knowing that we were never caught in karma, we were never born and never died. All was just an appearance, a game of Light and shadow we played with our Oneself. We have always been free, we are free, and we will always be free we just have not yet noticed it through direct experience and embodied knowledge.

The next portion of the book takes you deeper into each layer so that you can uncover the treasure that lies within the core of your being and permeates every atom of your physical form. As we journey through these layers of our personality, we find that the Kingdom of Heaven lives within our very being! Take a moment to still the body and quiet the mind and listen to your inner dimension and see what is already there. What you seek is closer than you think.

FORTY-TWO

Annamaya Kosha: Physical Body

When most people think of who they are, they think of the physical body. This is the matter, muscles, skin, bones, connective tissues, organs, blood, cells, DNA, etc. The physical vessel is transient and passes through the stages of birth, growth, degeneration, and physical death. The *annamaya kosha* is related to the Root Chakra, your physical DNA, and your maternal and paternal ancestral lines. This dense energy envelope is made of the food you eat and is the vehicle for our Source Self to experience physicality. At the base level of the physical body, you find the five elemental energies of earth, water, fire, air, and space/ether which organize in countless ways to create things like bone structure, bodily fluids, digestive power, movement of breath, and the space that surrounds and separates the many parts and systems of the body. This body is not who we truly are. From ashes to ashes, dust to dust, five elements to five elements it will go. Yet, we are eternal.

Experiencing the Matrix of Existence

Our movement through the activities of our life is powered through a multidimensional exchange of energy information. Energy information passes through the physical sense organs of our eyes, skin, ears, tongue, nose and brain which give us the perceptual power to experience the subtle elements of form, touch, sound, taste, and smell. As this energy information is processed from the physical body into the subtle body via the etheric structuring of the *pranamaya kosha*. It is then directed into the mind where it is experienced, processed, and stored. Almost immediately impulses of desire and willpower ripple out through the mind into the vital energy structures and our physical brain and body to direct physical processes and the organs of action which include the mouth, hands, feet, excretory organs, and reproductive organs.

The physical vessel is constantly receiving energy information and transforming it into useful data for the body systems. The systems of the physical body include the skeletal, muscular, nervous, endocrine, respiratory, reproductive, immune, urinary, digestive, circulatory, cardiovascular, lymphatic, and integumentary systems. This complex network of systems is always working towards harmony and balance called homeostasis.

Illness and Disease

Physical illness is a manifestation of dense, toxic energy eliminated through the symptoms of the illness. The root of all illness, disorder, and disease can be found in the subtle bodies as manifestation is always energetic before it becomes physical. We think a certain way, which energizes our body into speech and action which move us into situations of balance or imbalance, health or disease. Even hereditary illness is an echo of thoughts and karmic actions passed down through our genetic lineages and humanity's collective unconscious. Latent mental patterning stored in the Causal Body can also be reactivated by our environment causing us to recreate injuries and illness from past lives.

Our health is affected by the things we see, the quality of the air we breathe, the things we eat, the sounds we hear, and the things we put on our skin. We are inundated with toxins from our environment and distorted programming from the mainstream industries. Many people live in areas of pollution and eat poisonous food. Finding natural solutions and detoxifying our bodies is essential for Ascension to ensure a clean and clear Ascension vessel, the physical body.

Understanding Stress

One of the major causes of physical body imbalance is stress. Stress is a feeling of mental, emotional, or physical tension that occurs as we face the challenges of living. In some cases, stress can be healthy and drive us to accomplish our goals. Stress can also be detrimental to our health, such as enduring traumatic conditions or unhealthy mental pressure from the conditioning of the mind.

Stress and anxiety wreak havoc on the systems of our body and consciousness. Erratic emotions, body tension, fearful thinking, and unhealthy behavioral patterns are symptoms of us being out of balance.

Mindfulness and wellness practices move our bodymind systems out of stagnation and decay into regenerative states of cohesion, balance, and flow.

Stress, real or imagined, has an immediate effect on all body systems, including the nervous system, digestive system, reproductive system, respiratory system, mental cognition, and so on. One of the keys to understanding stress and stress management is through the autonomic nervous system. Following is a summary of the components and functions of our autonomic nervous system and how we create stress or harmony through our physiology.

Autonomic Nervous System

The autonomic nervous system (ANS) regulates bodily functions such as breathing rate, heart rate, digestion, urination, and pupillary response. This system helps us adjust to daily living demands from a place of stress and anxiety or a place of flow and balance. The ANS acts mostly unconsciously and has two subsystems that create the "fight, flight, or freeze" responses of the body (sympathetic nervous system) or the "rest and digest" response (parasympathetic nervous system).

Sympathetic Nervous System

The sympathetic nervous system (SNS) is activated when the body and mind are under stress. This could be from actual stressors in our environment like toxins, loud noises, or stressful situations. This can also happen when the mind drifts into memories of past stress or projects stressful outcomes in the future.

When our sympathetic nervous system is activated, our digestive system stops working, and the blood is redirected to the arms and legs so that we can fight our stress or run from it. In this stage of ANS response, our heart rate elevates and becomes erratic. When our body and mind are in various stress states, we switch from deeper diaphragmatic breathing to shallow upper chest breathing as the sympathetic nervous system activates.

With the diaphragm frozen in movement, the upper chest and neck muscles pull on the rib cage to make space for the lungs to expand. This results in shorter, shallow breathing that leaves our neck and chest muscles tight and agitated. Our autonomic nervous system often stays in fight or flight response way after the initial stressful experience partly because the respiratory system stays locked in defense mode while our subconscious stores the unprocessed energy information. This creates trapped emotions that continue to oscillate in one's mental field creating tremors of reactivation within the bodymind complex.

Modern Western society is a product of the SNS where everyone is fighting to survive or climb an invisible social ladder. We are inundated with blatant and subliminal messages that we are not enough, and our future is bleak. This constant stress manifests as chronic illness, emotional disorders, and beyond. One of the most radical things you can do to unplug from this machine's momentum is to develop mindful breathing and presence.

Parasympathetic Nervous System

When our parasympathetic nervous system (PNS) is activated, our heart rate slows down, our breathing deepens, our digestive system runs smoothly, and our overall mood and mind are balanced. When our body and mind are calm and relaxed, we naturally use our diaphragm for breathing, allowing our lower abdomen to expand and contract. This movement and type of breathing are easily seen by observing an infant or sleeping dog.

Diaphragmatic breathing is natural and effortless for the body. The diaphragm, like the heart, can continue contracting and releasing without tiring or needing rest. When we practice diaphragmatic breathing, our respiratory organs and digestive organs are massaged, cleansed, and toned by the rhythmic movement caused by the expansion of the diaphragm and lungs.

Vagus Nerve

The vagus nerve system of neural pathways originates in the brain stem and weaves a serpentine pathway through the body, touching upon various vital organs and neural networks before it fractals out into the intestines. This family of neural pathways interacts with the *hara line/sushumna and* chakras to send information to the brain to modulate emotions, translate intuitive "gut" instincts, create bodily sensations, inform relationship responses, and activate processes for environmental adaptation.

The Dance of the Autonomic Nervous System

The vagus nerve plays a significant part in transferring from the SNS (sympathetic nervous system) to the PNS (parasympathetic nervous system). "Vagal tone" is our ability to respond to stressors in our life. When the vagal tone is low and unhealthy, we are quickly agitated and stressed out by life. When the vagal tone is high and healthy, we can quickly and easily manage life stressors and return to the states of homeostasis and flow.

Activities for increasing vagal tone: dancing, yoga, meditation, massage, singing, chanting, prayer, cold exposure (cold shower), positive social connections, and other relaxing and inspiring activities.

We are constantly shifting in and out of PNS and SNS responses. Both the SNS and PNS are activated within a single breath cycle. As we inhale, the SNS activates, causing our heart rate to increase. We feel alert, active, and inspired during the inhalation phase. As we exhale, the PNS activates, causing our heart rate to lower and the vagal response to increase. As we exhale, we soften, relax, and settle into ourselves. There is nothing wrong or bad about the SNS, we just should not live there out of habit, or we will likely fry our systems.

Conscious breathing directs our mental awareness to our experience of breathing, where we can become conscious influencers of our autonomic nervous system. When we link our awareness with our breath, we almost automatically switch to calmer, deeper breathing, and a more balanced state of being. As our parasympathetic nervous system activates through conscious, diaphragmatic breathing, all our body systems begin to balance and restore.

When someone takes a "sigh of relief," this is the bodymind complex releasing the physical, vital, and mental responses to the stressful experience. Deep sighs of relief are signs that the ANS is switching from SNS to a PNS response. Walking in nature, meditation, physical exercise, and spending quiet time alone all help the PNS activate and restore our body systems to homeostasis, coherence, and flow.

One of the best ways to increase vagal tone and increase our vital energy is through conscious embodiment practices like meditation and yoga. Conscious breathing practices are simple tools we can use to regulate subtle energy in our body systems and establish states of rejuvenation and calm presence. These are spoken of more in the *pranamaya kosha* section, and the mental component of stress is discussed more deeply in the section on the *manomaya kosha*.

Physical Body Focuses for Ascension

The physical layer of our personality will be transforming with us as we transmigrate from this dimensional reality to the next. The biological and subtle energy processes of ascension need nourishment to ensure an easy transition. Below are a few keys regarding the physical layer maintenance through the ascension process.

Physical Body Training

Physical training and self-care should incorporate a balance of active and passive activities to regulate the autonomic nervous system, develop overall strength and flexibility, and reduce stress and neuromuscular tension.

For those who tend to have higher levels of stress and body tension, passive practices such as restorative yoga, self-massage, sound healing, journaling, and long baths can be added to activate the parasympathetic nervous response to calm the bodymind. Long, gentle stretching helps to loosen the connective tissues of the body to create harmonic flow in the physical and subtle body systems.

For those who need to develop strength and willpower, active practices such as working out at the gym, martial arts, hatha yoga, and brisk walking help to energize and strengthen the body. Active practices help to develop muscle tone, increase coordination and create movement in the organs and tissues of the body for healthy elimination and detoxification.

Overall, each individual's practices and life activities should be a balance between movement and stillness, active and passive, fast and slow to bring the bodymind systems into harmony and cohesion.

Self-Massage Practice

There are a variety of ways to do self-massage. Here is a short description of a self-massage practice to improve circulation, balance overall skin health, reduce stress, and so much more. Go slow. Enjoy the sensuality and use it as a practice of devotion towards yourself, your body, and beyond.

1. Use warmed organic oils like coconut oil, sesame, or something similar. You may wish to use organic essential oils as well.
2. Start at the scalp and work your way down to the collarbone. Use the fingertips to make tiny circles. Pay special attention to Crown, Brow, Zeal, and Throat Chakras.
3. Progress from fingertips to shoulder with long strokes on the limbs and short, circular strokes at the joints. Repeat on the other arm.
4. Employ the same concept from feet to hips.
5. Massage the abdomen with clockwise strokes.
6. Massage across the low back/sacral.
7. Rub center of the chest outward.
8. Pause for 5-10 minutes. Bonus if you use Reiki on yourself or meditate during that time.
9. Rinse with a cold/cool shower.

Diet and Water Intake

Every human body is different in what it needs to sustain itself through this process. Whatever you ingest, try your best to have organic foods that are grown locally and ethically. It has been suggested that we eliminate dairy because it creates a distortion in the energy layers that makes energy upgrades difficult. Plant-based diets are most recommended but if you must eat meat, make sure the animal was raised humanely and organically. Be sure to give thanks to the life expression of that being for its sacrifice.

Foods should be living and fresh, not processed or from cans. Supplements are recommended to ensure that you are getting all the nutrients that you need. Superfoods that have high nutritional value help keep everything vibrant and healthy.

Water is super important for the alchemical transformation of Ascension. Spring water or from other pure natural water sources is the best, and it is recommended to add hydration salts and trace minerals if using purified water. Municipal water sources should be avoided as the water is most likely highly contaminated with chemicals that negatively affect the body and mind.

It is recommended to perform intermittent fasting and periodic detoxification protocols to rid the body of toxic waste. These are excellent to start around the full moon as the waning movement helps with the release of physical, energetic, and mental patterns that are not of the highest benefit to your well-being.

Take time to pray over your food. Hold your hands above the food and envision Light shining from your hands and/or your brow chakra to enhance and purify the food. Send gratitude to all the forces and beings that played a part in bringing you your meal. Eat mindfully, slowly, and allow yourself to have a multidimensional experience as you eat.

Proper Rest and Sleep

Proper rest is important for optimal physical, vital, and mental well-being. Everyone is different with how many hours are needed for rest. Find ways to increase the length of time in the blankness of deep sleep. This includes limiting screen time before bed and reducing the amount of stimulants and caffeine taken into the body. Have a self-reflection and winding down practice to get the body ready for rest. This will help to clear the mind so that you are not too active in dream states and can spend more time in the state of dreamless sleep.

Progressive Relaxation Body Scan

Progressive relaxation practices help develop body consciousness and an overall feeling of deep relaxation. The fascial grid is a network of connective tissue that surrounds all the muscles, organs, tendons, and even the bones. Our bodies have many habitual holding patterns which limit the free flow of subtle energy throughout our system. The fascial grid acts as a passageway for vital energy. Holding patterns in any area of the grid limit the free flow of vital energy and cause disruption and imbalance. As you practice this body scan, imagine the whole fascial network softening to allow the free flow of subtle energy.

Progressive Relaxation Body Scan Procedure

- Lay down or recline in a comfortable position.
- Breathe into the naval center, diaphragmatic breathing, for a few rounds to settle into your body.

- Feel the breath in the throat for a few rounds and set intention to relax the bodymind.
- Breath into the nostrils and allow yourself to settle into even deeper subtle consciousness. Take this profound feeling of relaxation and focus throughout the body scan. Take your time and enjoy the process.
- Relax the scalp and crown of your head.
- Relax the muscles of your face.
- Relax the forehead, eyebrows, and eyes.
- Relax your cheeks, tongue, mouth, jaw, chin, throat, and neck.
- Relax your shoulders, upper arms, elbows, lower arms, wrists, hands, and fingers (rest for five breaths).
- Relax your heart center and sides of chest
- Relax your solar plexus and stomach.
- Relax your lower abdomen, pelvis, pubic bone, pelvic floor, and lower back.
- Relax your upper legs, lower legs, ankles, feet, and toes (waiting here for five breaths).
- Reverse the process back up to the crown without pausing. Relax for several breaths and slowly return to waking consciousness by deepening the breath and moving the fingertips and toes tips.

Bless Your Body

Before incarnation, you chose the perfect genetics to experience this life through. Love this physical body and treat it well as it is the temple of your Divine Light. Celebrate the body and dedicate it towards your higher purpose, using it as an instrument for your liberation. Enjoy your senses; enjoy your path; and dedicate your physical vessel's life expressions towards the liberation of all beings from cycles of suffering!

FORTY-THREE

Pranamaya Kosha: Pranic Body

In the beginning stages of spiritual awakening, we begin to realize that there is something more to physical life than what can be experienced with the physical senses and mainstream reality structure. We begin to sense something mystical to life and begin to turn inward to listen to our inner realm and tune into the interconnectedness of life.

As we awaken, we begin to discover that we exist within a unified field of light and vibration, a continuum of energy that is constantly shifting and changing through an infinite latticework of geometric grid patterns which mesh together to create the holographic matrix of the universe. When I use the word 'energy' throughout this book, subtle energy is what I speak of. Subtle energies are the substratum of all manifestations in Creation and act as the organizing principle, providing the pathways and movements of Consciousness as it evolves within the Unified Field of Creation. Subtle energy is interactive with our own consciousness. As we focus on it, it begins to transform immediately as it links with our consciousness giving us the ability to transfer will and intent across time and space such as in prayer and psychic phenomena.

It should be mentioned that not all energy is "good energy." There are seemingly negative, entropic energies that take away life force, and there are positive, centropic energies that sustain and revitalize life. These energies aren't "good" or "bad" as each frequency serves a purpose or function. The "problem" with energy comes when things are out of sync with Natural Order and are not able to balance and integrate back into wholeness.

In Samkhya, dualistic Vedic philosophy, there is the pure Self, *purusha*, and matter and form, *prakriti*. Prakriti, *maya* consists of three fundamental forces: *sattva*, *rajas*, and *tamas*. These forces called *gunas*, translated as "strand" or "fiber," are the threads that weave the web of the manifestation of the cosmos. All phenomena that can be experienced, seen and unseen, is a manifestation of the weaving of the matrix with the force of the *gunas in conjunction with the subtle and gross elements of earth, air, fire, water, and ether (space).*

These forces can be described as follows:

- *sattva*: harmony, purity, light, beauty, balance, consciousness revelation, balance, inspiration
- *rajas*: change, activity, active energy, unsteadiness, movement, agitation, transitions us to sattvic or tamasic
- *tamas*: darkness, conceals consciousness, ignorance, depression, dullness, stagnation, inertia, stability, mindless, intoxicating, inaction

All of these forces can be positive when in balance with the other forces. Ultimately, we should be guiding our experience into sattvic states of balance and inspiration versus the downward spirals that leads to ignorance, decay, and stagnation.

Most ancient cultures have various ways of accessing, manipulating, and understanding the many subtle energy categories and their qualities. There are many names in many cultures for subtle energy. *Ki* (Japanese), *prana* (Sanskrit), *chi* (Chinese), *ruach* (Hebrew), and *life force energy* (English) are just a few.

Prana is the animating life force of the physical body and the active power behind all vital phenomena in the universe. We receive this "breath of life" from the food and water we ingest, our environment, our inhalations of breath, and from our soul and higher consciousness connection. While *prana* is necessary for biological life to exist, too much of it causes nervousness and psychosis and in the most extreme case death. Having too little of it causes exhaustion, and our physical life is over when there is no longer *prana* in the physical body.

Alchemical practices like tantra, yoga, qi gong, and the laying of hands work with subtle energy to restore balance and harmony to a person's physical, vital, and mental bodies to create homeostasis and alignment with one's True Nature. Group prayer and ceremonies create a powerful energy field that amplifies prayers and intentions, and many people experience spontaneous healing and emotional healing through the group prayer field.

Many people who have not had a subtle energy experience of their own find it hard to believe that subtle energy exists, believing in only what they see with their physical eyes. Many reject the idea of a subtle energy reality. Scientific communities are beginning to develop instruments that can measure subtle energy. Many hospitals and clinics in the West are now beginning to allow practitioners of acupuncture and hands-on healing methods like Reiki into the hospital system to support patients' recovery.

Simple Energy Exercise

One of the best tools to sense and interact with subtle energy is with the hands. The awareness is amplified when you apply conscious breathing to the task.

Bring your palms together and begin to rub them vigorously while you consciously breathe in and out of your belly. Close your eyes and feel the sensations. Intend to generate powerful energy and heat. Use your breath and intention to amplify the vibrations, intending for the energy field to grow stronger and brighter. After a few moments, begin to open your hands slowly. Tune into the sensations between your hands. What do you feel? What do you sense? Trust your feelings. Can you feel both the electric and magnetic qualities? Warm or cold sensations? Tingling? This is a form of subtle energy. You can take your hands and lightly move them across your face and body and sense the energy there. When finished, keep the awareness, and open the eyes.

The Human Energy System

Inserted in the physical body and extending slightly beyond is the vital body, also called the etheric body or pranic body. The human body is a multidimensional bio-transducer, meaning it constantly receives, transforms, and emits various levels of subtle energy. The vital energy system translates energy information into the physical systems to create physical body functions like heart rate, hormone release, breathing rate, and beyond. This sheath bridges our physical body with our mental body by translating subtle energy information for physical and mental processes.

In Theosophy, this layer is called the Etheric Body Double because it is similar in shape and size to the physical body. Every cell of the body, every particle of bodily fluids, bodily gas, and organic material is surrounded by an etheric energy envelope that weaves a matrix of pathways to unify all systems. As information streams in through the physical sense experiences, information is passed from the cells into the etheric double of the cells and is translated through subtle information pathways to the etheric brain and mental body. Higher consciousness information and mental patterning experienced in the mental body are transmitted through the etheric pathways and etheric brain into the physical brain and nervous system to direct the body's actions and functions.

Aura: Your Personal Space

All living organisms have an auric field which is called a biofield in science. The human biofield is a toroidal field of electromagnetic light that emanates from the core of your being and creates the matrix framework for your physical body. The aura includes the etheric structuring of the *pranamaya kosha* as well as the oscillation and activities of the mental and causal bodies. Our aura is multilayered and is in constant evolution and transformation based on our mood, thoughts, the food we eat, location, etc. Our auric field is the instrument we use to interact with the subtle energy world around us. It receives energy information from outside of our physical body and radiates energy information into the Unified Field of Creation. Our overall light quotient in our auric field is dependent on the health of all our koshas. Our auric field becomes unstable and distorted when we are in states of aggression, sadness, or other lower emotions. Our auric field is harmoniously organized and coherent when we are in higher vibrational states like joy, creativity, and devotion.

Aura Experience

Close your eyes and begin to focus on your breath and the subtle sensations of your experience. Call the Light to be with you and feel your vibration begin to rise. Imagine that within your heart center, in the core of your being, is a sacred fire, a beautiful bright Light of Source Energy. Use your intention, focus, and breathing to expand this source of energy until it surrounds you. Make your space feel beautiful and loving and filled with light. Deep, full breathing amplifies the radiance and love from this Light. Allow your thoughts to be purified and your mind relaxed by this Light. Feel your intention to merge with the Light and evoke feelings of peace and tranquility. Amplify these positive sensations with your breathing. Notice how far your personal energy field goes. Is it a bubble or does it fade out into the space around you? Feel the energy within you. Notice any stagnant areas, and breathe light and awareness into them, inviting movement and flow.

As you inhale, pull your field back into the core of your being. As you exhale, pulse your light back out. Keep repeating this pattern as if you are flexing your etheric muscles. With each exhale, your aura is brighter, cleaner, and more pronounced. Enjoy this for as long as you desire. When you are complete, feel your aura strong and illuminated. Feel blessed by the experience and open your eyes.

Boundaries

It is important to do frequent aura clearing and restructuring throughout the day, especially if you live a hectic life. Having healthy, energetic boundaries ensures that we do not take on the energy of other people and places. Having a clear aura helps you to have clear thoughts and a joyful mood. Practices like smudging or spraying "aura mists" over the body help to clear and recharge the energy field. It is especially important to intentionally restructure and strengthen your energy field when you go into public so that you remain sovereign and clear of others' energy.

Five Movements of the Breath of Life

We access and regulate the *pranamaya kosha* through the act of breathing, our main source of *prana,* and intentionally through the power of our mind. As this universal life force enters our body it is separated into five "winds" with different movement patterns and functions. These five pranic winds stimulate all bodily processes and govern our health and vitality. Any disruptions or imbalances in the flow of these life force patterns manifest on both the physical and mental planes of our personality. The five major movements of *prana* in the body are as follows:

One: Incoming Energy

Prana vayu, located in the region of the head and chest, moves inward and upward and deals with inspiration, intake, receptivity, and forward momentum and is associated with the heart chakra and brow chakra and the air element. Prana enters through the organs of perception from the food we eat, the air we breathe, the sights we see, the sounds we hear, and through the skin. Imbalances may present as dysfunction in the lungs, heart, brain, and circulatory system.

Two: Outgoing Energy

Apana vayu, located in the pelvic region and lower abdomen, expels downward and outward, deals with elimination movements like perspiration, defecation, and urination. It directs the reproductive processes of ejaculation, menstruation, and childbirth and is associated with the organs below the naval. It is associated with the *muladhara chakra*, the Root Center, and the earth element. Imbalances manifest as dysfunction in organs of elimination and reproduction.

Three: Digestive Energy

Samana vayu, located between the navel and heart, is the balancing energy of the body which deals with multidimensional digestion and assimilation processes and is associated with the *manipura chakra*, the solar plexus, and the element of fire. *Samana vayu* draws energy into the solar plexus center for processing our food, subtle energy, thoughts, and energy from the physical holographic reality. Imbalances can manifest as over or underactive digestive patterns, abdominal discomfort, and gas.

Four: Upward Energy

Udana vayu, located in the throat, has an upward movement and deals with speech, expression, growth, and the upward ascension of prana and kundalini. Associated with the *vishuddha chakra, udana vayu* emanates from the throat center in a circular motion around the neck and head, thus assisting with mental clarity and focus. It directs the self-transformation process and the recalibration of willpower to a higher purpose and vision. Imbalances manifest as dysfunction in the throat, neck, and head.

Five: Circulation Energy

Vyana vayu, located in and around the whole body, has an outward from center movement pattern and deals with circulation, expansiveness, and pervasiveness as it directs subtle energy throughout the 72,000 pathways of subtle energy called *nadis* which physicalize as communication networks like the nerves and fascial grid. This movement provides a connection between the senses, nerves, tissues, cells, and the mind creating a feeling of wholeness and containment. This circulatory movement is associated with the *svadhisthana chakra*, the sacral center, and the element of water. Imbalances manifest as feeling unstable, containerless, and clumsy. Overall, the imbalance manifests as systemic dysfunctions of the body

There is an ancient saying that says something like, "If you can extend the length of your breath, you can extend the length of your life." Our quality of breathing, from day to day, determines our quality of living. As we train the breath, we become more radiant and vital. Many spiritual and mystical traditions revere the transformative power of the breath. Life can be thought of as one long breath cycle starting from the first inhalation as a newborn to the last breath of life. Breathing transforms our experience of time. Fast, shallow breathing is parallel to the experience of rush or not enough time. Slow and steady breathing brings us to the present moment where time endlessly unfolds in the eternal NOW.

Hara Line: Bridging Heaven and Earth

You are connected to universal life force and the regenerative consciousness field of Gaia by a pillar of Light that passes through the center of the body, which I call the hara line or pranic tube, or the sushumna nadi when speaking about the physical body. This pranic tube is the axis of the toroidal field of your auric field.

This subtle energy tube tethers us to the subtle planes and the electromagnetic fields of planet Earth. This is our lifeline and our connection to our battery. When we are in the states of love and trust, this pathway is open and clear. When we are in the states of fear and separation consciousness, we are severed from our battery, and we lose life force.

Our hara line, our pranic tube, is the main intake and outtake pathway of our subtle energy body and supplies our chakras with energy from Source and Gaia. When we have a healthy hara line, we feel centered in our being, connected to Source and Gaia, and alive and aligned with our Divine Purpose and the Divine Will of the Universe. We feel energized, alert, and connected to Higher Love.

When our hara line is distorted and blocked, we can feel a myriad of physical, mental, emotional, and spiritual issues. In my opinion, most, if not all, issues stem from hara line distortions and misalignment since the chakras also lay on this major pathway.

Pranic Tube Meditation

Sit or stand so that your spine is erect, and you feel comfortable. Begin to breathe into your hara line and heart until you feel calm and present. Imagine that there is a shining, golden-white star far above your head. This will symbolize your Source, God/Goddess/All That Is.

Invite and imagine that a flowing stream of energy flows down from Source and passes through your crown, all the way through the body, and down into the Earth. Breath this Source Light into your Hara, into your womb, filling it with pure, clear, golden-white energy. Exhale and send the energy down into the Earth. Repeat this breathing pattern a few times and allow this pure Source Energy to sweep away any stagnant or dense energy and release it down into the Earth to be composted. This will not harm the planet. She lovingly takes all our sorrows and struggles and transforms them for us.

Bring your hands onto your heart and feel your own heart's energy. Breathe into it and help it shine. Intend to sense Gaia's heart. Intend to connect to her pulsating rhythm of love. Begin to breathe her love and evolutionary coding up through your hara line into your own heart. Fill your heart with this love and as you exhale, send this love back to Source. Continue a few more times, breathing all this love up into the body and feel Gaia's heart, your heart, and the heart of Creation flowing together and synchronizing.

Bring your hands down to your lap and breathe normally. Sense what has shifted and enjoy your moment. When you are finished, feel blessed to have this connection and open your eyes.

Pranic Tube Tune-Up and Boundaries

Throughout the day, you can clear out your hara line and realign with your Divine Purpose. Simply use conscious breathing, intention, and imagination. As you inhale, bring the energy down from Source into your hara channeling down the Divine Presence, then exhale, grounding the energy into Gaia. Inhale drawing earth energy up from the core of Gaia into your heart. Exhale, send the energy back to Source fully establishing the bridge. Inhale from Gaia and Source, then exhale, radiating light outward, re-establishing your field's boundaries. Make your entire "breathing space" illuminated with compassionate presence. Repeat the pattern until you reach the desired state of stability, peace, and wholeness. In just three breath cycles, you can completely refresh and revitalize your entire energy system and your consciousness and avoid unnecessary suffering.

Nadis

Nadis, Sanskrit for "river channel," are pathways for our subtle energy to move throughout our bioelectric system. The physical manifestation of the nadis include the nerves and fascial grid. Some ancient texts say that there are over 72,000 nadis that weave a matrix of light around and within your body that lead to every cell of your physicality. The three major nadis as called *ida, pingala,* and *sushumna.*

Ida and Pingala

Ida and *pingala nadis,* related to the vagus nerves, represent the feminine and masculine polarities of our personality. These two serpent energies weave through our chakra system to create conduits of consciousness that meet in the Brow Center. These two energy pathways play such an important role in health and wellness that the symbol of the *caduceus* has been used by the medical/healing world for a long time. This symbol is depicted as the wand that Hermes or Mercury carries in Greek and Roman mythology.

Ida nadi, the feminine pathway, starts in the root chakra on the left and weaves its way up through the chakras finishing at our left nostril at the brow center. Often associated with the moon, this feminine energy is considered reflective, intuitive, cooling, and nurturing and is described as the mental force, *manas shakti.* This current is active when the left nostril is flowing, and the right hemisphere of the brain is active.

Pingala nadi, the masculine pathway, begins at the root chakra on the right and weaves its way up through the chakras finishing at the right nostril at the brow center. Often associated with solar qualities, this masculine power directs life force energy, *prana shakti,* to energize all essential life processes and is related to heat, logic, assertiveness, and action. This current is active when the right nostril is flowing, and the left-brain hemisphere is activated.

As we breathe in and out through our nose, air carries subtle energy through these two pathways to clear and revitalize the chakra system. As we switch between our consciousness's masculine and feminine qualities, one or the other pathways become dominant. Although without balance and awareness, we can either overstress our energy systems or become lethargic.

The most direct and transformative way I know to balance the masculine and feminine qualities of our consciousness is through the alternate nostril breathing technique, *nadi shodhanam,* and the system of hatha yoga. That being said, all effective healing and personal transformational processes inherently involve the balancing of these polarities.

Sushumna Nadi and Kundalini Shakti

The *sushumna* is the part of our hara line related to our physical body and the seven-chakra system. This tube of light charges and energizes the chakra system. It runs from the base of the spine at the perineum up to the crown of the head. At the base of the *sushumna,* wrapped around the base of the spine, lies the *kundalini shakti,* the ecstatic expression and spiritual potential of your spiritual being.

The *kundalini* energy is said to sit coiled at the base of the spine in *muladhara chakra,* the Root Center. As a soul progresses through incarnations, certain interactions begin to activate this dormant energy and it begins to rise up through *sushumna* balancing the polarities of each chakra as it makes its upward ascension. These two polarities eventually join at the Brow Center to create an experience that some call *Hieros Gamos,* which refers to this alchemical unification of the twin flame polarities within which is the goal of *hatha yoga* practices. Once this has occurred, *kundalini* can make its full ascension to the Crown Center to create the experience called *moksha, nirvana,* salvation, or any of the other names which describe fully realized Godself Consciousness.

Kundalini awakening can be felt like a surge of electrical current from the root of the spine into the higher energy centers of the brow and crown chakras. This can be experienced with body tremors, waves of wisdom and insight, waves of ecstasy, spontaneous mudras and positionings of the body, big emotional shifts, visionary experiences, sensory overload, and more.

Kundalini shakti, the ecstatic, spiritual potential within one's consciousness, begins to rise up the spine and activate each chakra and balance the consciousness at each center on its ascension towards the crown. For most people, *kundalini* rises and then goes back to rest in the Root Center while the practitioner reconciles their consciousness. Progress in one life carries over to the next life. Many "spiritual people" or those on the awakening path have had *kundalini* activation in previous lives and will continue this lifetime working in the chakra that they left off with in the "previous" incarnation. It is said that most of those on the "spiritual path" have at least activated the first three chakras and are beginning to work towards the heart chakra.

As humanity ascends, the awakening of the serpent energies can be quite powerful and intoxicating. As we heal and integrate our consciousness's masculine and feminine qualities, we awaken and stir our creative, sexual-spiritual energies. It is important to learn practices of grounding to work with these energies effectively and safely.

Ascension alchemy practices like Ancient Egyptian sex magic, true tantra, and kundalini and hatha yoga are designed to awaken these energy systems, purify them, and unify our consciousness with the Absolute. While it can be intoxicating and exhilarating to stay in states of kundalini activation, it is also important to ingest foods and participate in activities that nourish and soothe our nervous systems so that we do not "burn out" or overstress them. I recommend seeking out a teacher or a guide who can safely guide you through kundalini awakening if you are feeling unstable through your awakening process.

Chakras: Lenses to See the World

Emerging from *sushumna* channel, we have the blooming of seven main energy vortexes commonly known as the "*chakras*." The chakra system goes by different names in different traditions. These seals/wheels/lamps/vortices tether our physical body with our subtle body processes. They are toroidal in shape and always in states of movement and evolution. They contain life force energy as well as mental energy. Like individual minds, each contains our programmed beliefs about the seven major areas of our life, such as community and physical life, self-identity and relationships, willpower, compassion, communication, vision, and universality. Besides the seven main chakras, there are many sub-chakras and micro-chakras throughout the body with some existing outside of the body. However, these seven are the most important when cultivating consciousness liberation and holistic wellness.

Each of the seven main chakras relates to certain glands in the endocrine system, nerve plexi, and particular organs and bodily systems. As energy information passes through the aura, it is processed through the chakra system and creates emotional/mental/physical experiences based on our beliefs and previous experiences with similar dynamics. This energy ripples out across the subtle energy pathways (nadis/meridians) into the nervous system and endocrine system to create sensations, bodily functions, and events.

Chakra Locations

Here are the locations of the seven main chakras, the two minor chakras, and the three newly emerging ascension chakras:

- **Soul Star Center:** Felt 6-12 inches above the head
- **Crown Center:** Crown of the head
- **Brow Center:** Between the forehead and occiput
- **Zeal Center:** Emanating from the medulla oblongata, attachment point of the spine to the skull
- **Throat Center:** Center of the throat
- **Heart Center:** Felt between and behind the manubrium and xiphoid process of the sternum
- **Solar Plexus Center:** Just below the diaphragm
- **Sacral Center:** Low abdomen behind the naval
- **Root Center:** Base of the spine at the pelvic floor
- **Earth Star Center:** Below the feet when standing, below the pelvis when seated
- **Palm Chakras:** Center of the palms
- **Foot Chakras:** Soles of the feet

Chakra Filaments: How We Feel Our Environment

Chakras radiate filaments of light, just like the rays and filaments of the sun. The number of filaments on a chakra relates to the frequency of the chakra. The higher the frequency, the higher the number of petals opening from the electromagnetic flower.

These filaments reach out to interact with a specific layer of our auric field. Picture a plasma ball from science class with the violet plasma whipping across the inside of the glass globe. Each filament reaches through its environment to absorb the energy information in the world around us while simultaneously broadcasting our essence into the field. The chakras respond to our attention. As we focus our energy on an object, they begin to drink in the energy of the object of our attention.

Attachments and Cords

When we develop an attachment to an object, our energy forms a habit of focusing on the object of our attention. Unhealthy relationships are a result of unhealthy beliefs and a habit of attaching our energy to the object. They are habits of where we direct our life force. Cords develop between people that relate in unhealthy ways, thus creating codependent patterns.

To reconcile this once you become aware of an unhealthy relationship, practice the Hara Line Aura Meditation and return to sovereign alignment with the Source Within You. To create permanent change, you can work on identifying and shifting your belief systems that caused the unhealthy patterns, or they will return later until you fully see and heal this part of your subconscious.

Distortion in Our Subtle Bodies

Even before we are born, we begin to absorb the mental patterning of the world beyond our mother's womb. Some people experience trauma within the womb and carry it throughout their life. Additionally, our DNA is filled with energy information from the lifetimes of those who came before us who passed down the genetic coding through our lineages. As mentioned before, life experiences also reactivate stored information in our causal body that brings forth patterns created in past lives.

Traumatic life experiences, memories, and energies often get trapped in all layers of the bodymind complex. Slowly over time, they release so that we do not feel the full brunt of the psychophysical trauma at the moment of the event. When energy is not reconciled, the bodymind tries to release the energy in some way. This can look like crying, sighing, shaking, screaming, sleeping, illness, dreams, and so on. If we practice meditation and self-healing, we can speed up our recovery process significantly.

If we suppress or ignore our emotions and trapped energy, the negative effects begin to show up in our physical bodies. Over time patterns begin to crystallize and become more physical as the bodymind tries to eliminate the distorted energy information. From the most subtle inflammation to the most aggressive cancer, it all has its roots in the subtle energy system. We can use our conscious awareness to reconcile traumatic injuries in our bodies and return to wholeness and vitality.

The *chakras* are constantly broadcasting our internal world and magnetizing events to them that reflect the stored subconscious beliefs. The distortions and trauma stored within our subconscious show up in our life as manifestations of similar circumstances that trigger the trauma patterning. This "clashing" brings our unconscious patterns to the surface so that we can exhaust and potentially integrate the energy information from the past experience and grow in consciousness maturity. From this perspective, we can understand how we create our reality and how everything truly begins within our very own consciousness. As within, so without.

With conscious awareness and subtle energy healing techniques, you can unpack the information stored within the emotions, thought patterns, and physical body events and reconcile the energy. This naturally brings a deeper understanding, and wisdom is revealed through the healing process. This frees up the pathways so that energy can flow freely, and we experience a more joyful, conscious life.

Illness and disease are the body's intelligence giving us a massive wake-up call to tune into our inner being and create a rich, inner life that is luminous and vital. As we tune into subtle energy, we unlock the mysteries of the bodymind's intelligence and begin to accelerate in consciousness growth and authentic empowerment.

Pranayama: Entering the Dimension of Prana

Breathing is one of the main ways that we regulate the movement of the life force in the body. Each inhalation brings in fresh, new life force energy to be used by the body's cells and systems. Each exhalation expels old stagnant energy that is no longer needed by the body. One of the secrets to living a long and vibrant life is the power of conscious breathing.

Breath cycles are made of four stages. *Puraka*, a deep, rich inhalation, focuses the mind and energizes the cells and systems of the body. Inner breath retention, *antar kumbhaka*, equally distributes, calms, and clarifies prana. Conscious exhalation, *rechaka*, releases toxins and calms the bodymind. External breath retention, *bahya kumbhaka*, moves *prana* up the spine to the brain and creates a sense of non-attachment, peace, and inner silence. Women who are pregnant and people with high blood pressure, lung, heart, eye, or ear problems should not hold either phase of breath retention. Instead, they should focus only on the inhalation and exhalations.

Below is a descriptive list of breathing practices, called *pranayama* by the ancient yogis, to get you started with the basics. When you first begin practicing *pranayama*, start with learning to equalize the duration of the inhalation and exhalations in a 1:1 ratio (using a count of four or five seconds) with a slight pause in between inhalation and exhalation. Then increase exhalation duration by doubling the number in a 1:2 ratio. Once this is mastered, add in inhalation breath retention for a ratio of 1:2:2. For more advanced practices, I recommend checking out the *Hatha Yoga Pradipika*.

As you do these practices, keep an easy mind and relaxed body while sitting in a tall, meditative posture. If at any point you feel frustration or tension, stop the practice, return to neutral, and start again when you are ready.

Another practice that I highly recommend is the use of a *neti* pot which looks somewhat like a tea pot and is used for a sinus washing process that clears obstructions out of the nasal passageway. This practice called *jala neti* will increase the body's absorption of prana during breathing and help to awaken subtle consciousness in the brow center.

Three-Part Breathing or Yogic Breathing (Dirga Pranayam)

This breathing style incorporates the full range of breathing capacity utilizing abdominal, thoracic, and clavicular breathing awareness. This practice oxygenates and nourishes the whole body and is great for reducing anxiety and stress.

First, exhale completely until you feel the lower abdomen contract and the pelvic floor lift. Softly release the lower abdomen and allow it to expand with your inhale. After the abdomen expands, allow the chest to expand, feel the energy of the inhale rise up through your spine and into the crown of your head. Softly exhale and reverse the process and allow the air and energy to drain down from the head, softening the chest, exhaling completely until the lower abdomen contracts and the pelvic floor lifts. Repeat, softly extending each segment of the cycle of breath. As you do this, you can imagine that you are surrounded by brilliant, clear, white light. With each breath, you can breathe this fresh light into all the cells of the body.

Samma Vritti: Equal Flow Box Breath

This breathing practice is called "box breath" as the patterning can be thought of as the equal dimensions of a square with inhalation, breath retention after inhalation, exhalation, and breath retention after exhalation. Start simply with a count of four during each stage. Then you can increase the number as you develop control and calmness of the bodymind within each stage. This can be done with regular yogic breathing as well as in alternate nostril breathing.

Kapalbhati: Skull-Cleansing Breath

This breathing practice gets its name because of its revitalizing and healing properties. *Kapalbhati* clears the mind, burns away stagnant energy, clears the respiratory system, and brightens the face and higher chakras. In this practice, inhalations are relaxed, and deep and rapid force is applied to the exhale.

Pregnant or menstruating women should not do this practice nor should people with spinal injuries. If you have high blood pressure, stomach ulcers, or any other health issues, be gentle (one pump per second) until you see how the body works with the practice.

Using the three-part breathing, inhale fully and allow the belly and chest to fill with air. On the exhale, contract the abdomen strongly back towards the spine, feeling a strong pulse of air exit the nose. Softly relax the abdomen and allow the lungs to fill with air. Repeat this pattern, slowly increasing the cycles' speed, creating a rapid breathing pattern that is also relaxed in mind and emotions.

Repeat for around twenty to thirty rounds. On the last exhale, gently push out all the excess air until you feel the pelvic floor and abdomen contract. Drop the chin towards the chest and gently lift the heart towards the chin to make an energetic lock. Hold for a few moments, then release the head and soften the throat, abdomen, and pelvic floor. Find a neutral position of the spine and return to normal conscious breathing and observe your internal experience. If it feels right, you can add consecutive rounds of practice.

Bhastrika: Bellows Breath

Bellows Breath energizes the mind and body, tones the abdominal muscles, and builds the digestive fire. This is a great practice to do if you are feeling tired, confused, or sluggish. It focuses on equal force of inhales and exhales. The practice is often done with arm movement to help with the expansion and contraction of the lungs.

Sit comfortably and find your natural, three-part breathing. After a complete exhale, bring your arms up above your head, spreading the fingers wide as you reach for the sky, and inhale deeply with gentle force. Exhale by strongly contracting the abdomen towards the spine while simultaneously closing the fingers into fists and pulling the elbow down towards the ribs, contracting the muscles of your arms and abdomen fully as you exhale. Inhale deeply to raise the arms back up above the head and repeat the cycle for twenty to thirty rounds. After you exhale, bring the arms down, rest the hands on the legs or ground, and observe your inner experience. If desired, you can repeat the practice.

Bhramari Breath: Bee Breath

Bhramari Breath uses breath and toning of the vocal cords to send vibrations through the throat and skull. The long exhalations assist the autonomic nervous system by inducing a relaxation response through the lengthened exhales. This practice is excellent for anyone who needs to calm the mind and focus their intention.

Sit comfortably in your meditation posture and do several rounds of full yogic breathing. Raise both hands in front of the face with your elbows pointing outwards, in line with the shoulders, with the palms facing you. Close your eyes, gently press the index fingers to the inner corners of the eyes, place the middle fingers on either side of the nose, the ring fingers above the lips, and the little fingers below the mouth. Use the thumbs to gently close the ears.

Another option is to take your hands and rub them together, activating them with light and energy. Bring the hands up to each side of the head, blocking the ears by pressing lightly on the tragus of each ear to close the ear canal. Take the other fingers and lightly touch the brow with the pads of the fingers. Fingers should be spread across the forehead and hairline.

Once your hand position is set you can begin the "bee's breath." At the top of the inhale, begin to make a humming sound with the lips closed. Draw out the sound and play with the pitch of the tones. Feel the vibrations moving throughout your nostrils, sinuses, throat, and brain. Imagine that your hands' vibrations and energy pulsations are breaking apart unhealthy thought patterns and upgrading the neural pathways. Fill the skull and throat with vibrations. Do this for about six rounds. Then drop the mudra and sound and feel the subtle shifts happening along the pathways of energy.

Nadi Shodhanam: Alternate Nostril Breathing

Alternate nostril breathing balances the right and left hemispheres of the brain and the masculine and feminine principles of consciousness, creating a state of calm focus. This practice is especially useful when you feel anxiety or stress. It is a wonderful practice to do before you start anything that needs your full attention and awareness. There are a variety of methods to do alternate nostril breathing. Here is a basic practice:

Take the index and middle fingers of the right hand and lightly touch the center of the brow. You will be using the inside of the ring finger and the pad of the thumb to block and alternate the passage of air through the nostrils. The other hand can be resting on your lap, in jnana mudra, resting on your heart, or in any other comfortable position.

Using the thumb, gently press against the outside of the nose to close the right nostril and exhale completely through the left nostril, gently contracting the lower abdomen and pelvic floor at the bottom of the exhale. Then breathe in through the left nostril as you release the abdominal contraction. Feel the air and energy circulating in the center of the brow under the fingertips. Gently pause at the top without adding tension to the face or upper torso.

Switch nostrils, block the left nostril with the inside of the ring finger, release the thumb off the right nostril, and exhale through the right nostril until you feel the abdomen and pelvic floor contract. Pause for a moment. Then breathe in through the right nostril feeling the air circulate at the brow. Pause again.

Close the right nostril, open the left nostril, and exhale through the left until you feel the abdominal and pelvic floor contractions.

Repeat for at least two to three minutes or longer. Meditate on smoothing out and evening each segment of the breath. A suggestion of ratio would be to start first with a 1:1 ratio, building up to 1:2.

Combined Practice Suggestion:

- 3 rounds kapalbhati (30-50 pulses per round)
- 2 rounds of Bhastrika (30-50 pulses per round)
- 3 complete breaths (natural breathing)
- 3 rounds of nadi shodhanam (2-3 minutes per round)
- 2-3 minutes of bhramari
- Breath awareness
- Meditation

For a shorter practice, you can skip the *bhastrika* breath and keep the cleansing benefits of *kapalbhati*.

Circular Breathing

This breathing practice goes by many names, some of which are trademarked. This type of breathwork involves deep, continuous breathing cycles that highly oxygenate the body and reduce carbon dioxide. This circular breathing pattern is known to help reduce depression, process and integrate trauma, eliminate fears and phobias, and much more. It is known to induce altered states of consciousness and awaken unconscious memory for processing and integration. Many people report having psychedelic-like experiences. It is not recommended to do this practice if you have cardiac or respiratory health issues. Go gentle at first and see how you respond, then you can decide whether to increase or reduce the intensity or duration of the practice. It is recommended to do these practices with a trained facilitator who can guide you through emotional experiences, involuntary muscle spasms, or other powerful experiences. If you are doing this practice alone, go gently and feel it out.

1. Lay down on a flat and comfortable surface. You may wish to cover yourself with a blanket. Keep the head flat on the ground, no pillow, so that the spine stays long and even.

2. Start with a progressive relaxation body scan.

3. Begin the circular breathing pattern with deep inhalations and deep exhalations, no pausing in between. Try to make it seamless.

4. Be careful not to push or strain the body. Back off the edge a bit.

5. Pick up the speed. Do it a little faster than normal but not so fast that the body tenses.

6. It is perfectly normal and common for the face muscles or the hands or feet to contract. Keep breathing through it, nice and gently.

7. If fear or other powerful emotions arise, breathe through them. You can back off the intensity a bit if you wish.

8. Do the practice for about 10-20 minutes. Then relax completely and feel the effects for another 10 minutes or so.

The Microcosmic Orbit

The microcosmic orbit circulates life force throughout the entire system of the body. Sit mindfully and quiet the mind by bringing your awareness to your breath. Bring the tongue to touch the back of the teeth and roof of the mouth to close the "heavenly gate" and gently lift the pelvic floor to close the "earthly gate." This creates an energetic loop that connects the front and back of the body. Breathe mindfully into the pelvis and imagine that the pelvic bowl is filling with white light. As you inhale, sweep the white light towards your sacrum and up your spine, cresting at the top of the head. As you exhale, sweep the white light down the front of your face and body and back to your pelvis. Continue circulating your awareness, breath, and the white light through this orbit until you feel clear, clean, and balanced in your energy. When you are finished, simply return to regular conscious breathing, and observe your Inner Being's sensations.

Pranic Body Summary

We are a bridge between the higher consciousness realms and Earth, existing in an ever-changing matrix of subtle energy. We access this connection through our hara line and personal energy field. As energy information passes through our energy field, it is dispersed to energy vortexes called chakras, transforming the data through our belief center programming, creating emotions. Emotions pulse out a charge of energy that fractals out along the nadis/meridians to create physical body processes and our perception of ourselves and the world around us. We can use the power of our breathing and breath awareness to reconcile our consciousness and return all systems to health and balance. As we raise our vibration and awareness, we move beyond the need for illness and disease as a teacher of karma and move into the perfection of our Divine Blueprint as conscious embodiments of the Breath of Life.

FORTY-FOUR

Postures for Channeling Light

Mudra is a Sanskrit word for energy locks. They are different ways to posture the body to affect the flow of subtle energy. Different traditions have different ways of holding hands to shift subtle energy. If you know any of them and their effects, you can use those when channeling Light. Otherwise, use your intuition. You may have already noticed that the body subconsciously moves the fingers into certain placements at different times throughout the day. This is especially true for those who have studied healing and the Mysteries in other lifetimes. The subconscious remembers the training and guides the body into postures to open the flow of energy and healing.

When we use the power of mudras, we open our body temple instrument to be an oracle for Divine Consciousness. Mudras are keys to unlocking pathways to meet the energy that is being evoked to channel. When we create a mudra and intend to connect with the Light, our biofield and etheric structures rearrange to allow the Divine Frequency Transmission. This sends waves of Light emanating from the entire body temple out into the field.

As we move about the Earth, we can consciously transmit divine frequencies into the field around us. Our bodies are bio-transducers, constantly absorbing energy from the environment and transmuting it through our body systems. As conscious beings, we can support the collective ascension process by channeling divine love into the Earth Reality.

When you consciously tune into Source Energy and the life force of Gaia, you naturally stand tall with an open chest. You beam loving energy through your entire being, bridging Heaven and Earth. You can beam Truth and Oneness out into the world through your gaze and broadcast light from your hands as you breathe consciously.

I will describe some hand *mudras* and their possible psychospiritual effects. Although each person will experience the power of these hand positions in their own way, I describe specific hand gestures for different mudras. Experiment with the opposite hand as well and discover your own experience with the hand's placements.

Take a few minutes to try each of these hand placements and postures to feel their subtle energy and consciousness effects. If any of them feel uncomfortable or if you notice unpleasant shifts or changes happening after practicing the mudra, stop working with that mudra. A full list of contraindications for each mudra can be found online or in texts dedicated to the various effects of mudras.

Anjali-Gassho: Prayer Hands Mudra

This mudra is made with both palms together in a prayer position with the thumbs touching the Heart Center. This mudra is used by many spiritual and religious cultures around the world and back through antiquity. This mudra unites the right and left sides of the brain and closes our auric field. It connects us with our divinity and to the power of the heart-mind.

Gyan/Jnana Mudra: Knowledge Mudra

This mudra is made by connecting the index and thumb fingertips and extending the middle, ring, and pinky fingers creating the hand symbol of OK. It is also commonly accepted to do it with the tip of the index finger touching the base of the top knuckle of the thumb. This seal is considered the mudra of Knowledge. It focuses the mind on peace, higher intelligence, and wisdom. When the same mudra is made with the palms facing down it is called *chin mudra* (consciousness mudra) and evokes a feeling of groundedness and concentration. Both are excellent for meditation.

Dhyana Mudra: Meditation Mudra

This mudra is made with the right hand holding the left hand. Allow the thumbs to connect to create a triangular circuit of energy. This mudra connects and unifies the body, mind, and soul through the heart field. It charges our central channel and connects us with the prayerful beings and enlightened masters of the Earth and beyond.

Bhairava Mudra: Fierce Mudra

This mudra is made with the left hand resting in the lap while the right hand rests on top. This symbolizes the masculine (right side) resting into the feminine (left side), creating a harmonious feeling (enhances *pingala*). When reversed with the right holding the left, the masculine energy supports the divine feminine energy for awakening and manifestation (enhancing *ida nadi*). It is said to eliminate negative effects of ego and illness.

Varada Mudra: Bestower of Boons Mudra

Associated with the sharing of blessings, mercy, and love, this mudra is made with the right or left hand with the palm facing forward and the fingers pointing down. I typically place this mudra along the right side of my body below the level of my naval. For me, this mudra generates a peaceful, grounding energy that blesses the field around me.

Abhaya Mudra: Courage/Fearlessness Mudra

This mudra is made with the right hand to the side of the body level with the heart. The palm is facing forward with the fingertips pointing toward the heavens. This mudra evokes peace, dispels fear, and welcomes the protection and presence of the Divine.

Abhaya & Varada Mudras: Blessings & Courage

Combine both mudras using the right (upward) and left (downward) hands to bridge the blessed energies of Earth and Sky. Feel the combined energies of grounded peace and the higher frequencies of the higher realms.

Prana Mudra: Life Force Mudra

This mudra is made with the right hand with the pinky, ring finger, and thumb touching. The peace fingers and index and middle fingers are extended upwards and connected. This mudra activates the flow of prana and the root chakra's grounding power, creating a powerful energy transmission.

Prithvi Mudra: Assimilation Mudra

This mudra is made with the right thumb and ring finger touching, with the peace fingers and pinky extended. This "Seal of Life" creates stability by strengthening and healing the physical body. This balances the earth and fire elements of the body and is powerful for healing many ailments.

Ardhapataka Mudra: Half-Flag Mudra

This mudra is made with the thumb, index, and middle fingers extended while the ring and pinky fingers are bent towards the palm. This "sign of benediction" bestows blessings and frees the consciousness of nuisance and disturbance.

Karana Mudra: Purification Mudra

The mudra is made by pressing the pad of the thumb over the nail of the middle finger with the other fingers extended. The ring finger will likely be bent a bit. This mudra "dispels darkness" by clearing obstacles and challenges on the path of awakening and Ascension.

Intent Mudra

This mudra is made by bringing the palms together in a prayer position in front of the solar plexus with wrists touching the solar plexus and the fingers pointing out away from the body. Right thumb crosses over the left to make a circuit. Space between the palms with fingertips touching. This is a wonderful mudra to do whenever you want to cultivate willpower and strength.

Whole Body Transmission

Bring soft tension into your arms and hands and intend for healing energy to flow through them. Tune into your hara line and your loving connection to Source and Gaia. Turn the palms in the direction that you wish to direct the energy.

While you do this, broadcast Love and Light through your Brow Center in the direction of the person, place, or object you hope to illuminate. Feel radiant and filled with Unconditional Love and Unity. Beam undulating waves of love from your heart. Beam dazzling rainbow light from your entire being and completely fill the space with light. Finish with a blessing and dedication, said out loud or internally, "May all beings be free. May all beings know love."

Heart Beacon

Bring your nondominant hand to your heart and intend to connect with your inner Light. Form the other hand in *abhaya mudra* to hold light and shine it into the world around you. If you want the energy to be a higher frequency, have the palm facing outward, in line with the heart or higher, with the fingers pointing upward. For more subtle and grounded heart energy, have the palm down by the side, fingers pointing down towards the Earth in *varada mudra*.

Creative Beacon

Bring your nondominant hand to touch upon your sacral center/lower abdomen/womb space. Feel your connection to Source and Gaia. With the palm pointing outward and fingertips pointing downward or to the side, beam creative and grounding energies into the space. As you create the energies within yourself, they flow out of your field and into the space.

High Calling

Bring the arms up to the heavens to call in Divine Light from Source. Feel your hara line and breathe into it. This is a powerful pose that will generate a powerful feeling.

Earth Field Awakening

Bow down and place your hands upon the Earth to connect to the planetary grid. Slowly begin to stand and use your intention and movement of your arms to raise up frequencies of Light from within the Earth. I often use the imagery of calling up cities of light and illumined beings from Earth's Light realms. Use this connection to make a dance that awakens the radiant energies of Gaia in your awareness.

Spinning Vortex of Light

Imagine that you are connected to Source and Gaia through a bright pillar of clear light. Spin the body in a clockwise rotation with the arms raised out and imagine that you are spreading light in infinite directions. This will naturally clear your auric field and send beautiful light all around you. Come to stillness slowly. Ground down through your legs. Bring one hand to your heart and one hand to your hara and feel the powerful vortex you have created.

If you would like to learn more about the power of the hands for healing, I suggest studying the sections dedicated to the art of the Laying of Hands.

FORTY-FIVE

Planes of Human Consciousness

Inserted into and extending slightly beyond the etheric structuring and life force processes are the layers of "the mind." The human mind is an ever-shifting kaleidoscope of thought patterns involving reception of sensory impressions from the five senses, creation of mental associations of data input, storage and access of memory, intuitive sensory abilities, discriminatory functioning, universal connection, and pure awareness. As sensory information enters through the physical and etheric body, this information is processed through the mind which then stores sensory data and directs the body of action in its engagement with life.

The mind is the link between body and spirit. When the mind is clouded by limiting beliefs, unresolved trauma, and various forms of toxicity that erode our consciousness and vitality, we perceive life in distortion and limitation, disconnecting our physical self from our spiritual self.

Four States of Mind

The ancient yogis described the mind in three states of waking, dreaming, and dreamless consciousness. When we are the Waker, we experience our physical life and its activities. In this state, all the koshas are active and present even if we are not aware of them at all times. When we go about our day-to-day life, we shift through the awareness of our physical body, breathing and vitality, thoughts and sense of I/me, intellectual knowing and insight, and moments of bliss and unity.

When we are the Dreamer in the dreaming state, we lose awareness of our physical body, but the mind continues to modify the breath, process thoughts and emotions, experience intellectual understanding, and sometimes even experience flashes of joy and bliss from our Bliss Sheath. This is a realm of illusion where objects from our waking life are rearranged into dreams. Much learning happens in dreams as subconscious impressions play out to be exhausted and released. Intuitive dreams offer clues and premonitions of what is yet to manifest in waking life. Many people can have lucid, conscious dreams in which they travel to other dimensions within the Subtle Planes, visit with spiritual guides and soul family, and even travel to friendly spacecraft to be updated for their Earth missions.

When we are the Deep Sleeper in deep sleep, the physical, etheric, mental, and higher mind faculties disappear, and we find deep rest in the undisturbed blankness of the Bliss Body. Even though we do not remember what happened, we know something occurred there because when we awaken, we feel rested and refreshed. We did not fade out of existence temporarily. Our True Self enjoyed the untroubled rest of the blankness and bliss of the *anandamaya kosha* with no objects to experience, just pure Consciousness. This is similar to looking at deep space thinking it is darkness. Yet, when a meteor passes through, we see the light bouncing back off the meteor. Light was there, yet we could not see it until there was an object of experience. Pure consciousness always remains. The Light that you are shines eternally.

As we begin to stir awake, we emerge through the layers of the density of our koshas and take on the issues and identifications associated with each layer. We begin to identify with the bodymind and all its roles and functions becoming the Dreamer once more and then the Waker.

There is yet another state of the mind called *turiya*, which is the pure superconsciousness of the True Self. This "supreme equilibrium" is the conscious experience of salvation, liberation, and Godself-Realization. Once a person achieves and continues to maintain this state of enlightenment, they can exist in the Waking State but are aware that it is a superimposition over the True Nature of Reality. There are no more delusions or limiting mental impressions. Even as they walk through this world, their inner focus is completely established upon the Source of their Being, pure Consciousness itself.

Swami Sarvapriyananda gives a great, real-life example of this using the experience of going to a movie theater. As the Observer watches the projected light images of different names and forms upon the screen, the scenes may change but the Observer remains constant. Even if the screen goes black, the Observer, the Witness of the experience, remains. Pure Consciousness is eternally present; we just get caught up in the projected illusion and the changing forms of our perceived reality.

Brainwave States

(Beta, Alpha, Theta, Delta, Gamma)

The activity of the brain can be looked at in terms of vibrational frequency. When the vibrational frequency is high, mental activity is higher. When the brain is in states of rest or deep sleep, the brain's vibrational output is lower.

Beta brainwave states occur when we are awake and alert. This level of brainwave activity is used when we are active in our day and using analytical thinking and problem-solving. These brainwaves are mostly stimulated by our external environment to keep us safe and engaged.

Alpha brainwaves occur when we are relaxed and focused. This is the first level of trance that hypnotists and meditators use to access their subconscious and higher intellect. This state happens when we are physically and mentally relaxed. We begin to enter this brainwave state as soon as we close our eyes. This brainwave state creates the "glossy-eyed stare" of daydreaming and highway hypnosis when we forget driving segments.

Theta brainwave states are created when we are in deep relaxation and have cultivated inner peace. We are in this state when we are in REM sleep and deep hypnotic trance and meditation. This brainwave state gives us access to non-ordinary reality and shamanic experiences.

Delta brainwaves are the slowest brainwaves and are associated with deep, dreamless sleep. In this state, our physical and subtle bodies are in rest, and we enjoy the blankness of deep sleep.

Gamma brainwaves are the highest frequency brainwaves and are associated with high levels of cognitive functioning as all senses work cohesively at this state. Operating with gamma brainwaves gives the perceiver a higher level of unity consciousness, and loving-kindness. Tibetan monks and proficient meditators have higher levels of gamma brainwave activity. This is related to *turiya*, supreme equilibrium, and the blissful, mystical, transcendental states of superconsciousness including *kundalini* awakening, creative genius, flow states, and *samadhi*. These high-consciousness vibrations are generated by inner experiences and spiritual practices that focus awareness on the Self and unification with the Supreme.

Antahkarana: Source of the Mind: Inner Instrument of Being

Antahkarana is the source of the mind, the internal organ, and the cause of thought. The mind can be broken into four functions that work together to create our mental and emotional realm.

Transactional Mind: Manas

This is our everyday thinking mind. It coordinates sensory information before it enters our awareness. The senses include taste, touch, smell, hearing, sight, and our ability to sense subtle information. It is our connection to the external world of physical manifestation and subtle energy. A lot of this data enters our mind without our awareness and is stored in the subconscious. We then take sensory information and data from our subconscious which play out on the screen of our mind. This is where indecisiveness lives as conflicting desires and thoughts are bounced back and forth in the duality of the lower mind.

Subconscious Mind: Chitta

The subconscious mind is our heart-mind that creates our emotional state as energy information is processed through the lenses of past experiences and deeply ingrained impressions and beliefs, *samskaras*, which seem to emerge from the background of our mind. This includes the memory of events from this lifetime and other lifetimes buried in our unconscious mind. This is the data center of our dream state as images from our past are reorganized in dream sequences to exhaust subconscious patterning. Within the storehouse of *chitta* are the root causes of biases, proclivities, illnesses, fears, and other impulses that drive our thoughts and actions.

Ego: Ahamkara: The "I" Maker

This is the egoic faculty of the mind and what most people mean when they say "me" or "I." This faculty gives us the awareness of a sense of "I" and is concerned with self-preservation and keeping the body alive. This faculty is the center of all physical, emotional, mental, and intellectual functioning. The ego is not "bad;" it is only dysfunctional when it is clouded by the distortions in the koshas. As one awakens, one disentangles egoic identity from the physical and subtle bodies' associations, moving the sense of "I-ness" into the higher consciousness planes to realize one's true identity beyond individuality. When one meditates on the phrase "I am that I AM" They turn their lower egoic identity and mind towards their higher consciousness identity.

Intellect: Buddhi

Buddhi is the intuitive, enlightened intelligence, the voice of reason, the intellect. It understands, analyzes, discerns, and decides what is most beneficial for our path. If *manas* is the realm of confusion and indecisiveness, *buddhi* is the realm of clarity and insight. This power of the mind can be experienced as flashes of insight, abstract thoughts, intuitive messaging, and knowledge from beyond this physical life. We will get more into this part of our higher mind capacity when we look at the layers of the Causal Mind and buddhic consciousness.

To understand this internal organ, the *antahkarana*, let us visualize an angry lion coming in our direction. *Manas*, the transactional power of the mind, uses the sensory organs to notice something large is quickly approaching. *Buddhi*, our intellectual mind, understands that it is a lion, and it is angry and is coming to attack something. We may have a flash of a memory from our subconscious memory bank, *chitta*, of someone telling us that lions are dangerous. *Ahamkara*, our ego, adds in that the lion is coming towards "me."

Planes of the Mind

Beyond the physical brain in the *annamaya kosha*, the physical body, the mind can be separated into five subtle planes. All six planes are as follows:

- *Annamaya Kosha*: Physical Brain

Subtle Mind: Lower Mind

- *Kamamaya Kosha*: Conscious Mind: Desire Body
- *Manomaya Kosha*: Subconscious Mind: Mental Body

<u>Superconscious Mind: Causal Mind: Higher Mind</u>

- *Atimanasa Kosha*: Supramental Mind: Intuitive Body
- *Vijnanamaya Kosha*: Subliminal Mind: Intellectual Body
- *Anandamaya Kosha*: Subtle Causal Mind: Bliss Body

The first two layers of the subtle mind, *kamamaya kosha* and *manomaya kosha*, are the standard layers of human mental activity and are developed through the struggles and experiences of physical life. This layer of mind deals with our feelings, emotions, and concrete thought.

The deeper three subplanes can be called the superconscious mind, causal mind, or higher mind. The superconscious mind perceives beyond the material reality into the subtle planes and higher consciousness. These layers begin coming "online" once the involution or spiritual awakening process begins. These layers are more rapidly evolved through spiritual practices, being around others of higher consciousness, and through intense desire for unification with the Supreme. As a human being starts the awakening process, it purifies each kosha and untangles itself from the misidentification with the bodymind, moving the center of awareness progressively deeper and deeper towards the knowledge of the transcendental Self, the Source within.

Kamamaya Kosha: Desire Body: Conscious Mind

At the most superficial level of the mind, we have the layer called the *kamamaya kosha*, the body of desire. Some call this the "emotional body," but not all emotions come from this layer. This layer is called "the crude mind" as it deals with our likes and dislikes, our attractions and repulsions, called *raga* and *dvesha* in Sanskrit. This animalistic level of mind deals with the primitive desires of eating, sleeping, procreating, and action in response to our environment. This plane is where our struggles of morality play out and is the birthplace of physical and psychological addictions. This level is developed by life's struggles and is recalibrated and matured through embodied observance of spiritual ethics.

This is the plane of the human personality which is the coloring of the mind from experiences of one's life. This includes collective conditioning, familial conditioning, social conditioning, past deeds, and impressions from past lives which have been reactivated by current life experiences and environments. As we experience life, we begin to reflect on information as it streams through our senses into the mind and take action based on the information and the conditioning and coloring of past experiences. Since we are ignorant of our True Nature as wholeness, desires arise. When we take action from those desires born from ignorance the consequences can be good or bad. True fulfillment comes from directing our desires towards the Divine and service towards all of Life.

Kamamaya kosha is how we sense and give action through the physical body. As subtle energy information streams in from the external reality, the layer receives the data, generates desires based off the sensory input, and propels the organs of action to materialize those desires. When you feel hesitation to go down a dark alley or rush into the arms of your dear friend you have not seen in a while, it is this layer that holds you back or propels you forward. Before awakening, this layer is run by our false ego and the momentum from past experiences. This layer is purified by focusing your mind and actions towards altruistic actions and higher ethical values such as the *Yamas*, *Niyamas*, and Eight-Fold Noble Path described in Buddhism.

What we feed our conscious mind through perception is stored in the subconscious and eventually overrides our conscious mind creating our external personality. As one begins to correct misidentification with the body and false ego, the next step is to control the conscious mind through purification and awareness. A dedicated aspirant will grow in discernment of what sense experiences they wish to engage in. Does a certain activity support liberation and purification, or does it feed the limited ego, dependency, and cycles of suffering? Do sensory experiences feed the six afflictions of passion, anger, greed, delusion, and attachment, or do the activities nourish and inspire your path of liberation?

Four Instinctual Drives

The desire for the mind to experience physicality gave way to the evolution of sensory organs and a physical form, and this layer governs the four primal desires of the body such as self-preservation, hunger, sleep, and procreation. It is said that all other desires "spring up" from these four sources.

While there is nothing inherently "wrong" with these desires, we can either use them from an animalistic, survival mindset and continue on the path of *samsara*, or we can use each of these four instinctual drives to fuel our awakening and the liberation of ourselves and others from suffering. We can use our drive to eat to acquire food from ethical food sources that are organic to contribute to maintaining the health of our body and the health of Gaia. We can use our sexuality to create deeper bonds and unite with our True Nature. We can dedicate our sleep to continued healing and awakening. We can discern when we are acting from egoic self-preservation, or we can follow our Inner Light to do what is harmonic and serve the good of All.

We are constantly streaming information through the sense organs which tends to be intoxicating for the senses and mind, distracting us from our inner world and True Nature. Anyone can relate to an experience of being distracted by some outer experience that derails us from attaining a goal. Most people habitually focus their awareness on the four instinctual drives and the attainment of sensory pleasure with the error in the perception that happiness comes from something outside of us. This is a never-ending cycle as we are constantly shifting and changing from one experience to the next. Happiness comes from union with our Divine Self. In the fleeting moments where we attain some sensory pleasure, we temporarily relax our mind and endless searching which allows a flash of the joy from our Divine Self to be experienced. Soon after however, that experience fades away and we are back on the hunt for more happiness.

To master the instinctual drives, the spiritual seeker needs to learn to detach from the endless seeking for sensory fulfillment and tune into the fullness of the True Nature. This does not mean that one should never eat or never engage in sexual expression, but that one can use those actions to connect deeply with one's True Self, the true source of joy and fulfillment.

As the practitioner grows in increasing awareness of their True Nature, they become discriminative over what desires to follow to bring higher states of union with their True Nature and clearer focus to achieve their goals. Whatever you do, take your inner Source awareness with you and allow this union to bring joy and satisfaction to every area of your life!

Manomaya Kosha: Mind Processing Center: Subconscious Mind

Inserted deeper into the mind, we have the manomaya kosha, the processing center of our mental functions including information management, philosophical ponderings, computation, and memory. This transactional layer uses the organizing power of *manas* and the storehouse of memory from *chitta* to direct our various processes. This layer of the mind deals with instinctual functions, motor sensory functions, perceptual activities, rational decision making, emotional experiences of pleasure or pain from the conditionings of our past deeds, and regular dreaming. This layer controls the conscious mind and is developed through thinking, remembering, and reacting. It is reconciled with *pranayama* practices, proper diet, development of concentration, sacred mantra repetition, meditation practices, and contemplation on divine knowledge.

What Is Yoga?

"Yogas chitta vritti nirodhah" — Divine Union is achieved by calming the mind's fluctuations. This happens as we train our awareness to stay focused on the Absolute Reality, our indwelling Divine Presence. Spiritual growth involves growing awareness of the shifts and changes happening in the subtle realms of our experience. As we transform our deeply ingrained beliefs of duality and separation consciousness with compassion and align with the Absolute Oneness of Life, we ascend from our animal nature to merge with the divine.

The tendencies and habits of the mind (*vasanas*) create ripples and fluctuations (*vrittis*) across our mind. These movements of the mind generate our *karmas* (actions), which generate other habits and tendencies (*vasanas*). Continued habits of action create grooves within our mind and create deeply ingrained habits (*samskaras*).

Samskaras are the reactive momenta stored within our mental body from highly charged past experiences that left tracks across our mind. Negative *samskaras* keep us in repetitive cycles of suffering and the need for death and rebirth to continue working out our unhealthy patterns. While some *samskaras* can be pleasureful and intoxicating, it is often the negative *samskaras* that we are most aware of because of the suffering that arises from them. These subconscious mind patterns sit in the background undetectable until activated by some trigger in our experience or when receiving healing.

Samskaras are carried over from one life to another. Whatever work we do not complete in one life is transferred to the next. Mostly, these energies operate in the unconscious parts of our being, casting a spell on our mind and limiting our perception of reality, thus reducing our perceptions of freedom and sovereignty.

Negative *samskaras* can be developed through one intense trauma like experiencing a great cataclysm, being attacked, or from endured suffering such as living in an abusive home. Either way, the patterning is established in the mental field and is reactivated by some stimulus. All negative emotion is the product of reactivated momentum from unprocessed trauma.

We are constantly absorbing information into this data processing body. We should be vigilant in monitoring what we take into our mind. To mature and fortify this body, we should use the alchemical power of mantra to transform our thought waves, pranayama practices to reconcile distortion, take action in life from a place of higher morality, and read sacred scriptures to feed the *manomaya kosha* with higher thought patterning.

When we begin to awaken, we begin to infuse our conditioned mind with Higher Truth and Wisdom. We begin to see our life through the lens of enlightened consciousness (*bodhicitta*). We begin to clear our stagnant energies and limiting belief systems to pursue true liberation (*moksha/nirvana*). You can step out of the Wheel of Karma (*samsara*) and achieve liberation by eliminating the self-defeating tendencies and habits of the mind and adopting higher thoughtform patterning through your connection to your Higher Self and Source.

Emotions: Your Guidance System

Most people are experiencing an average of three emotions at any given time. Emotions are indicators of where we are in our path of creation. Take a moment to scan your emotional realm and notice what unique combination of emotional energies you are experiencing right now. Some have a stronger, more dominant charge, while some emotional energy has a weaker charge in the background.

Emotions are energy information created by thought patterns in the mental planes. When most people speak of their emotions, they are speaking about a set of actions initiated as eruptions in the subconscious mind which emerge in the conscious mind to then be rippled out through etheric pathways into the physical body creating changes in heart rate, breathing, muscular tension, and hormonal fluctuations in the endocrine system (*chakras*).

Emotions want to be felt, integrated, and released. Negative emotions like sadness and grief, when repressed and avoided, can stay with a person for lifetimes if not reconciled and cared for with compassion. Any emotion in excess is out of balance. Even positive emotions like joy, pleasure, and creativity can become ungrounded, chaotic, and intoxicating.

Emotional freedom happens when we learn to release any habits and distractions that keep us from experiencing our emotions fully or block us from the insight that the emotion is pointing us towards. No matter how terrible it feels, each emotion can be experienced directly within the loving presence of conscious awareness.

You are not your thoughts and emotions. You are the awareness that observes the rise and fall of each of these experiences. When we still the mind and integrate the information from our emotions, we settle into the framework that supports all experiences, pure loving awareness.

If you find yourself seeking something outside of yourself that will heal you, fix you, bring you love, success, or anything else that you believe will complete you, I invite you to call off the hunt! What you seek is already within you. Bring your awareness to your breath, calm your mind, focus on your heart center, and see what is already present and alive in the very core of your being.

Five Kleshas: Warring of the Mind

Kleshas, translated as "stains" or "pains," are the veils coloring the mind which keep us from seeing reality and our True Nature clearly. They are wave patterns in our mind that make up our blocks, prejudices, addictive cycles, and limitations that keep us from embracing each moment and living life to the fullest.

One: Ignorance — Avidya

When we know better, we do better. When we become aware of a part of ourselves or life that is not understood correctly or we do not have enough information about, we can seek knowledge and learn. This also includes the "veil of forgetfulness/amnesia" from incarnating on Earth.

Two: Overidentifying with Ego — Asmita

The ego is useful in helping us stay out of danger and make certain choices in our life. The ego "goes with what it knows," and resists change. Our soul desires spiritual growth and expansion. Our ego and our soul can work together to create harmony in our lives and make choices that serve our growth. In this way, our higher nature helps our conditioned mind to untangle itself and perceive clearly.

Three: Desire or Attachment to Pleasure — Raga

Suffering arises from our attempts to control or cling to life circumstances or endlessly fulfill our sensory desires. True fulfillment, true pleasure, happens naturally through alignment with our inner Source.

Four: Avoidance, Aversion — Dvesha

Knee-jerk reactions of rejecting new ideas or experiences come from painful experiences of the past stored within the subconscious. We can bring awareness to our aversion to uncover parts of ourselves that need healing so that we can make choices from a clear mind and fresh vision.

Five: Attachment to Life, Fear of Death — Abhinivesha

The root of fear comes from our fear of physical death and the mortality of our human body. When we root our identity in our soul's eternal nature, we can bravely face life and its circumstances in the pursuit of spiritual growth.

Death

Everyone has a different view of what happens after the death of a human body. Much of our beliefs about death come from religious programming that is based on fear and judgment. Most people fear death, consciously or unconsciously, and spend a lot of energy on the fear of death or aging. Much trauma is carried by people because they do not process the death of loved ones healthily. Religious dogma leaves many questions unanswered, and judgment is placed upon people who seek the truth that is missing from their religious institutions. Part of humanity's healing involves reorienting our relationship with death. To know death, we know the deeper value of life. This is the freedom that comes from knowing of and aligning with the truth of Eternal Life.

Three Dantiens: Centers for Meditation

In the meditative and alchemical practices of ancient Asia, three major subtle energy centers are used for meditation and higher consciousness embodiment called the *dantiens*. These three energy centers relate to the chakra system and can be focused upon, purified, and regenerated to create a clear mind and high level of spiritualized embodiment. Here is a brief description of the *dantiens* and how they relate to cognition and intuition.

Brow Dantien

The brain is made of the right and left hemispheres of the brain which are associated with the conscious mind and the subconscious mind.

The conscious mind is made of everything in our awareness at any given moment. The conscious mind is the part of our mind that is analytical and linear. It is useful for helping us make decisions and plan. It operates on what it can see and measure at the moment. It pulls information from past experiences and projects future outcomes and probabilities based on current and past information. It holds our biases and is in control of keeping the body safe. The conscious mind is the part of us that doubts and connects us to our fears. The conscious mind is associated with our personality because it uses the memories and patterns of the past and the projected future outcomes to create a "now" expression and activity. It is self-preserving and "goes with what it knows."

The subconscious mind can be subdivided into two layers. The top layer of the subconscious deals with recent memories and background thought processes, while the unconscious layer of the mind deals with long forgotten or repressed memories including those of other lifetimes.

This dual-layered subconscious mind records all the sensory input from our life experiences with incredible detail. The subconscious is connected, not only to the records of this life, but it is also etherically connected to the memory bank of our other lifetimes and the ancestral memories stored in our DNA. This side is used for reflection and contemplation and is useful for observation and creativity. Both sides of the brain, the reflective and administrative, the spiritual and human, can learn to work together to create cohesion and flow within the mental patterning.

Heart Dantien

The heart-mind is the compassionate processing region. The heart feels out what is best for all and what choices will usher in our desired spiritual growth. Many cultures point towards the power of the heart as being the seat of the soul. Christ taught that the Kingdom of Heaven, the access gateway that connects us with Higher Light Realms of Creation, is within our very own hearts.

Hara/Lower Dantien

This *dantien* is the most known and can also be called the *hara*, the womb, the soft belly, or the sacral chakra, and is our intuitive processing center, a synthesis of vital, emotional, and mental energy. The hara holds the vital life force energy that we received through our connection to our mother. It expands and contracts in three dimensions as we breathe through our belly. It is said that when we extend the length of our breath, we extend the length of our life. When we breathe through our *hara*, we are grounded in our being. We are connected to our emotions and our creative and sexual vitality when we breathe and feel into our hara.

If we truly desire to be grounded, present, and open to life, we can grow in our awareness of these processing centers. Cultivating dynamic symbiotic awareness in each of these areas simultaneously helps us feel more grounded, present, and open. We can easily make choices that align us with our Higher Path and the Greater Good.

When we are in the states of fear and anxiety, we stop breathing from the hara and the heart, and all our energy rushes into our mind. Our digestive system stops, and all our blood rushes to our arms and legs, ready to fight, freeze, or flee. Since our diaphragm is frozen, our neck muscles begin to lift our ribcage up to make way for air. People who do not breathe with their hara habitually tend to have more anxiety-ridden lives and fear the future. They often have chest, shoulder, and neck tension, as well as headaches. To restore a sense of balance and repose, we can practice belly and heart breathing to restore our physical, mental, and emotional bodies.

Exercise for the Three Dantiens

Hara/Lower Dantien

Close your eyes and bring your hands to your hara with the intention to connect and heal. Lightly touch your womb space (men, you have one too) and gently begin to sense and expand your belly breathing. Notice the four parts of the breath. Inhale, pause, exhale, pause. Smooth out the edges of each stage. Imagine that there is a spark of light in your abdomen. With each

breath, this light expands and fills your entire womb/pelvic space.
- On the inhale, think "I am grounded."
- On the exhale, think "Here and now."
- Do this for a few moments until you achieve a calm emotional state.

Heart/Middle Dantien

Bring your hands to your heart center and begin to breathe in and out of your heart and upper chest. Relax the shoulders as you gently breathe in and out of your heart. Imagine a spark of light within the core of your heart and help it grow with each breath.
- On the inhale, think "I am the Love."
- On the exhale, think "I am the Light."

Brow/Upper Dantien

Bring your hands so that one hand cups the back of the head in the occiput and the other hand rests on the forehead. Begin to breathe into the brain and skull. Let it pulsate with life force energy. Imagine a flame in the center of the brain and use your breath to expand the light until you feel it pulsing further than your skin.
- On the inhale, think "I am clarity and peace."
- On the exhale, think "I am present and free."

Bring your hands down to rest on your lap and bring your awareness to all three centers. Breathe in and out of all three until you feel radiant and whole.

Identity Beyond Bodymind

In summary, we are not our desires, thoughts, memories intellectual understanding, or the limited egoic self. We are the pure Consciousness that observes all these experiences of the bodymind. As we continue to align ourselves with our higher purpose and walk our dharmic path, we begin to ascend from the animal nature of our primal instinct and egoic nature and begin to see the events and experiences of our life from a higher perspective. No matter where you are in your life, no matter what you have done in your past, you are worthy of stepping off the wheel of the suffering mind and stepping onto the solid ground of your True Nature and being elevated to a whole new reality of being.

FORTY-SIX

Superconscious Mind

Going deeper within the mind and permeating the previous layers, we find the layers and functions of the superconscious mind. The superconscious mind is also called the causal mind as it is the consciousness vehicle which causes the string of incarnations and movement of our divine will through the bodymind complex. This layer gives us access to wisdom and knowledge from beyond our everyday thinking minds such as wisdom from our past lives, information from the universal hologram, inner promptings from our higher consciousness identity (oversoul), and wisdom from our spiritual guides and masters. When one hears the "voice of God/Spirit" it is because of this higher mind capacity.

The Superconsciousness itself is the Atman, the pure Consciousness which lends existence to our individual consciousness. When I speak of the superconscious mind, I am speak of the higher mind capacity that is illumined by the Superconsciousness.

According to the occult mystery schools, the causal body contains the blueprint seed forms for our subtle and physical bodies. It is the storehouse of past life impressions, holding the Akashic records of the individual soul and memory from past lives.

As Source comes into individuated form as a singular soul/lightbody to begin a string of incarnations, it first takes on a base layer, sometimes called the auric film. The auric film is made of the purest, subtlest matter and is the storehouse which holds the seed forms for the lower consciousness vehicles, *koshas*. As one progresses through incarnations the virtues, wisdom, and memory from other incarnations is consolidated and stored in this layer.

As the soul-lightbody moves into the next incarnation, latent patterning from previous lives is reactivated by life experiences and is then expressed through the personality of that incarnation. This includes the suppressed and unprocessed reactions, *samskaras*, which must be reactivated, expressed, and converted into virtue and wisdom in the following incarnations until full reconciliation and ultimate liberation is achieved.

Causal consciousness, the mind illuminated by enlightened consciousness and soul memory and soul knowledge, deals with abstract, holographic thought and is accessed by refining intellectual capacity, spiritualizing one's mind, and reaching for the divine. This layer is slowly activated through one's incarnation. While the lower activities of *kamamaya kosha* and *manomaya kosha* deal with details and concrete linear thinking, causal consciousness deals with essence and holographic intelligence, giving rise to higher intellectual capacity. When one receives "downloads" it is experienced as a flash of holographic information that is slowly unpacked and integrated.

This higher mind structuring is the arena for rapid spiritual evolution. A person who uses the superconscious mind makes a habit of withdrawing their senses through meditative awareness and contemplation to feed an inner philosophical discussion in an attempt to understand the cause behind all things. The superconscious mind gives us the ability to witness life as an observer, a witness to the mind, energy, and material world. It is a higher mental body that is not directly engaged in moment-to-moment life but is rather acutely aware and quietly infuses the lower mind processes with higher knowledge, flashes of insight (aha moments), and wisdom. Beyond the superconscious mind is the pure Awareness shining from the Divine Self, which illumines all experiences of the bodymind and external reality.

The superconscious mind is where we begin to experience awakened intelligence, *buddhi*, and the ability to discern and grow spiritually through meditation, reflection, and self-study. *Buddhi* is the vehicle for our Inner Source and the conduit for divine knowledge to reach our mind and give action through the physical form.

The causal mind or superconscious mind is the seat of our spiritual morality that moves us out of animal nature and into ethical, spiritually informed thoughts and actions. It satiates the hunger for sensory intoxication and replaces it with the ability to surrender to higher willpower and grow spiritually. This is the place in our being that fuels our growing capacity to be in Service to All of Life. The superconscious mind gives us the power of divine conscience, discernment, discretion, deep knowing, and intuitive feeling. Establishing our awareness of this level of our being moves us out of the darkness of ignorance into the ascension of consciousness.

When we have purified the physical, etheric, and lower mental layers, we begin to establish ourselves in the Higher Mind and our awakened buddhic intelligence. We access this *kosha* through mindfulness, meditation, intelligent self-care that is heart/self-love focused, reading sacred texts, traveling to new places, being around others of higher consciousness, and direct self-inquiry into the true nature of our being.

In Advaita Vedanta, they call these layers the *vijnanamaya kosha and the anandamaya kosha*. In another philosophy, these *koshas* are separated into a three-layered system with each layer having distinct functions that contribute to the qualities of that sheath. The layers of the superconscious mind are as follows:

- Intuitive Layer: *atimanasa kosha*
- Intellectual Layer: *vijnanamaya kosha*
- Bliss Layer: *anandamaya kosha or hyranyamaya kosha*

As we start to turn our focus inward to the subtle parts of our mind, we begin to discover a "still small voice", spiritual consciousness, that begins to lead our lives into higher expressions of nobility, devotion, and intuitive genius. As our higher psychic sensitivities activate, we begin to work with the powers of the universe to manifest higher outcomes for our life and move out of linear, finite consciousness into quantum cosmic consciousness. We begin to cultivate laser-sharp focus and the ability to discern what is right and good for the highest benefit of All and act from a place of selfless service and compassion. We begin to move from standard evolution to a higher order of spiritual involution to realize ourselves as Source in Form, moving from mundane human life into multidimensional superconsciousness. Now we will go through each kosha of the superconscious mind to understand how it is developed and the qualities of consciousness it provides.

Atimanasa Kosha: Supramental Mind: Intuitive Layer

The most superficial layer of the superconscious mind is what is called the intuitive layer or the *atimanasa kosha*. In the Vedic systems, this layer's functions are considered to be the *vijnanamaya kosha*. This supramental mind is beyond the comprehensibility of the average human mind. This is the level of the mind which begins to shine with the desire for spiritual awakening as our mundane human mind begins to contact the Cosmic Mind and ascend towards superconsciousness. Accessing this layer moves us out of the experience of linear time and into nonlinear time giving us access to information from past, present, and future.

This is said to be the layer where *samskaras* are stored and reactivated to be experienced through the *manomaya kosha* acted upon though the *kamamaya kosha* and physical form. As the mind clashes with itself, a process starts that awakens higher understanding and perception and begins to move the processes of the mind beyond normal human experience. We access this layer when we are in states of contemplation or in our creative "flow state." This layer gives birth to the creative genius, flashes of insight, and serendipitous discovery. When the lower mind is confused and hindered, this layer disseminates flashes of insight birthed from an understanding of past, present, and future events.

This is the arena for all paranormal and psychic phenomena of the mind. This psychic layer gives us access to extrasensory perception and psychic gifts such as telekinesis, telethought communication, precognition, intuitive message dreams, inner prompting through synchronicity, and the "*clairs.*" Activation of this supramental capacity is stimulated and enhanced by being around others who are psychically activated and of higher spiritualized embodiment. Supramental activation happens when we travel to new environments and through spiritual education.

The Clairs: Intuitive Psychic Senses

The descent of *buddhi* from the higher planes into our consciousness is described by the Christians as the white dove of the Holy Spirit descending upon the believer to activate spiritual awakening and the Gifts of the Holy Spirit. The Gifts of the Holy Spirit include our extrasensory perception capacities, our spiritual gifts, and the ways the Divine Will moves through us to inspire enlightenment in the world.

The development of psychic gifts, or *siddhis,* is a natural occurrence that happens as we go through the involution and activation process of Ascension. As the samskaras are exhausted, our extrasensory perception increases, and we are able to access our spiritual gifts and receive intuitive messages from our Higher Self and spiritual guidance team with greater precision and clarity. Our vessel needs to be cleared of distortions in the physical, etheric, and lower mental bodies to give us the ability to discern what comes from the conditionings of the mind and lower egoic identity structure and what impressions come from enlightened and divinely influenced sources.

When we begin to awaken, we become increasingly more energy-sensitive as we tune into the subtle parts of our experience through our Inner Being. We move beyond the typical five senses and begin to expand and incorporate our intuitive and empathetic senses.

While most people are aware of the standard five senses, many have developed extrasensory perception and have become multisensory as described in *The Seat of the Soul* by Gary Zukav. Everyone on the planet is evolving to multisensory perception as an expanded empathetic nervous system comes online as the superconscious mind capacity activates in humanity.

Highly sensitive people, sometimes called empaths, have developed a range of senses that exceeds the standard sensory perception. These people have an acute ability to notice, sense, and feel shifts in energetic frequency, sound, and other people's emotions, thoughts, and intentions. Due to their sensitivity to stimulation, many "empaths" isolate and develop phobias around social situations. Energetic hygiene practices and learning to work with one's own light power can build resiliency so that highly sensitive empaths can stay grounded, centered, and clear in their own energetic boundaries.

In the early years of life, we may have been "more open" and in tune with our empathetic and intuitive senses but over time learned to dull our perceptive abilities because of conditioned belief systems and toxins in our food and environment (e.g., fluoride), or we may have "dimmed our light" for emotional safety and to blend in with our family and mainstream culture.

These extrasensory abilities give us access to the unified quantum field, allowing us to "download" information from the information matrix. This allows us to receive information telepathically from other people and beings that are local and nonlocal. Our third eye allows us to project our awareness into other times, places, and dimensions. We can also use this natural psychic intelligence to receive information about future events so that we can navigate timeline probabilities and adjust our intentions and actions to manifest the desired outcome. While someone is talking to us, we can also be aware of what emotional and mental projections they are broadcasting simultaneously, so that we can interact from a place of deeper understanding.

We can use this system as an "upload" technology to project our highest visions and intentions to allow the hologram of reality to materialize our inner dream into reality. This naturally happens when someone prays for truth and healing. This communication system will connect ascending humanity through heart-resonant telepathic communication as we move into New Earth. Many are already experiencing an increase in psychic communication and extrasensory perception.

Psychic intuitive abilities are our natural birthright. As we awaken spiritually and detoxify all of our systems, these senses become sharper and more pronounced. Everyone has these abilities. Soon, everyone on the Earth will have them activated and online fully at a level that we cannot even imagine from our current level of understanding. These intuitive abilities are often referred to as the "*clairs*," which derives from French and means "clear." As a prefix to one of the senses, it conveys a super-sensory extension or the ability to gain insight beyond the range of ordinary, physical perception.

Below is a list of the basic intuitive senses and a general connection to the individual learning styles: visual, auditory, verbal, physical, logical, social, and solitary. Your primary and secondary learning styles are most likely your primary and secondary intuitive senses.

Commonly Known Intuitive Senses

1. **Clairsentience:** Clear physical feeling is the ability to receive subtle information from the world around you. This includes sensing the past, present, and future energies of people, places, and objects. Can be connected to kinesthetic learning

2. **Clairempathy:** Clear emotional feeling is the ability to sense and feel the emotions, thoughts, and physical sensations of another being in your own body. Can be connected to social learning and kinesthetic learning.

3. **Claircognizance:** Clear knowing is the ability to know information intuitively without having it physically manifested. This information is downloaded from our Higher Self, who has a higher, broader perspective. Can be connected to self-enquiry and solitary learning.

4. **Clairaudience:** Clear hearing is the ability to hear messages from

your Higher Self or spirit beings. This includes hearing the thoughts of other people. Can be connected to aural/auditory learning.

5. **Clairvoyance:** Clear sight is the ability to perceive information through internal imagery. Can be connected to visual learning.

6. **Clairesalience:** Clear smelling is the ability to intuit information through the sense of smell.

7. **Clairgustance:** Clear tasting is the ability to receive intuitive information through the sense of taste.

8. **Clear Channeling:** Mediumship, or spirit channeling, is the ability to communicate with nonphysical beings and consciousness structures. This can include souls who have passed beyond the veil of physical life or beings that exist in other dimensions. Can be connected to verbal learning.

Astral Realm Precautions

When we use our intuitive abilities, it is important to process the information through the light of our heart and higher consciousness. Information from high sources is always loving and patient. The Astral Plane is a parallel plane to our physical universe consisting of subtle energy, desire, emotions, and nonphysical beings. We explore this plane each night in our astral body, the consciousness body of our mind. There are many wonderful astral beings of light but there are also nefarious beings and pervasive energies on the lower parts of the Astral Plane.

Some people who say they channel higher consciousness beings are channeling lower astral beings who feed off low vibrational emotions such as fear and confusion. If someone claims to channel ascended beings or some collective star nation, be sure to check and feel their energy and vibration to see if they are truly a pure conduit. Information coming from high consciousness beings will always be empowering and uplifting.

Use your heart and body to discern what information inspires love and what information causes contraction and fear. Many empaths are tortured by psychic attacks because they have not developed a powerful light quotient in their field, do not practice proper energetic hygiene, and have not learned how to discern energy through their heart and higher consciousness. While everyone has a "teacher that lives within," I always suggest that people find a professional guide and quality education as they explore new frontiers of their psychic capacity.

Everyone who is awakening is beginning to open these spiritual senses. Eventually, everyone on the Earth will be masters at these abilities and much more! They are the natural birthright of any human being, and everyone will develop them at their own pace and at the appropriate time.

Try not to compare yourself with others. For some, they are "scheduled" to open their gifts later than others so that they can stay focused on the task at hand. If we were all highly empathic psychic channels, we would likely be distracted from doing some of the more mundane daily tasks that are important for our missions.

We should also be careful of the spiritual ego that tries to attain these gifts for power or to make us feel valuable. Continue cleaning the body, working with prana and breath, and feeding and training the mind with divine knowledge. Practice! Practice! Practice! All is coming!

Vijnanamaya Kosha: Subliminal Mind: Intellectual Layer

Going a bit deeper, we have the Intellectual Layer, the *vijnanamaya kosha*. This "special knowledge" sheath gives us the feeling of sentience and the ability to discern what is truth and what is an illusion. This is the layer that helps us be "in the world but not of it". It gives us the power to be unattached to sensory experiences and see life events from the perspective of the Observer, keeping us from being entangled in the psycho-emotional polarities.

This is the layer of the reflected consciousness of Source in each human. This reflected consciousness creates the sense of an individual self by capturing the Light of Pure Consciousness and reflecting it upon the ego, the sense of "I". The "I sense" then illumines the rest of the mind. From this the body and sense organs get consciousness and start functioning. The body borrows awareness from the sense organs. The sense organs borrow awareness from the mind. The mind borrows awareness from the reflected consciousness. The reflected consciousness borrows awareness from the Witness Consciousness, the Pure Light of Consciousness. We mistakenly think the body or mind is conscious, yet all borrows existence and sentience from the Light of the True Self.

618 | THE ILLUMINATION CODEX

To understand this, we can think of when a person looks into a mirror and sees their reflection. The person is the True Self, the mirror is the reflected consciousness, and the reflection is the ego, the limited self. This is how the Intellect and Ego, the mirror and reflected image, merge to create the individual self via the power of the Witness, the pure Consciousness which you are.

Imagine a garden filled with different shaped buckets of water all around the garden. The one sun shines and is reflected in each bucket creating individual reflections. The conditions of the water in each bucket are different. Some are pure water, some are muddy, some are disturbed and rippling. Yet the one sun shines in all. From this example, the buckets are our unique bodies, the conditions of the water symbolize the conditions and contents of our mind. Yet one Light of Consciousness shines through all.

We use the reflected consciousness to observe and experience the conditions of the world and our bodymind. The problem is that ego gets entangled with the bodymind and not the true Source of the reflection, the pure Consciousness which we truly are. In meditation, we use this reflected consciousness to turn inward towards the True Self, the One Light which illumines all.

The "wisdom" or "special knowledge" from this layer is not typical worldly knowledge but wisdom that comes from our True Self giving the individual direct cognition, clear knowing, pure intelligence, and higher understanding.

Access to this layer gives us the ability to be nondual in this world of duality. This layer gives us the power of *viveka*, the power of discrimination and discernment of what is right or wrong for our being and what is illusion versus what is of the Absolute. This is the seat of *vairagya*, or non-attachment to and dispassion for worldly pleasures and sense gratification. This layer gives us the higher consciousness qualities of patience, one-pointedness, serenity, humility, grace, and intrinsic nobility.

This sheath is developed through psychic clashing, practices of concentration and meditation, as well as the study of sacred texts and philosophies. These practices activate one's inner wisdom and develop the powers of discernment and dispassion for worldly pleasures so that one can source joy and fulfillment from one's True Nature. Tune in. Turn on. All you seek is found within!

FORTY-SEVEN

Bliss Body and Unity Consciousness

Going a bit deeper in the superconscious mind we discover the *anandamaya kosha*, the Bliss Body. I have read of this layer being called the *hyranyamaya* kosha, the Golden Sheath because of the golden radiance that shines from one who accesses this layer. It can also be called the Buddhic Body or Spiritual Body as it is the layer that shines with awakened spiritualized intelligence.

The function of this layer is to fuel the desire for limitlessness and catalyze devotion towards the Divine in All and to inspire yearning for unification with the Supreme. This layer expresses itself through buddhic consciousness or what many call unity consciousness giving us access to the highest levels of love, unity, charity, and sympathy.

This layer is considered *avidya*, ignorance, because it is the veil of *maya* that is first projected from pure Consciousness to begin creating the experience of a limited being. Yet ignorance is bliss as some of the Light from our True Nature shines through this veil to create the other layers of our bodymind. We transcend this layer as we gain knowledge of the transcendental Self.

This is the most evolved layer of the mind giving us the highest experiences of joy, serenity, contentment, love, and peace. This layer gives us access to the spaciousness and emptiness of mind and pure bliss. If the Intellectual Layer witnesses the experience of bliss, this layer gives us the experience that we ARE the bliss.

This part of our being is felt as completeness, wholeness, and fullness and is anchored into our awareness after long practices of concentration and meditation on the luminous bliss of our True Nature. When we experience flashes of bliss, unity, and joy in our waking life, it is because we have tapped into this layer of our consciousness.

When we access these states of being, we bridge ourselves with the unity of Creation and become active, organic extensions of the grace and benevolence of Source. When we are in these states, we are deeply nourished, our cup runneth over, and we emanate the redemptive power of Source Consciousness.

As an awakening individual progresses step-by-step through the subplanes of this level, incrementally realizing higher and higher levels of unity consciousness, a point is reached where the individual no longer sees other people as separate but experiences the "other" as himself or herself in another form. This is beyond understanding this concept as "theory" but truly being aware that all individuals are our True Self looking out through different forms. As one's conscious awareness grows wider and wider, this love extends out to all of humanity and all levels of Life, whether good or evil, as they are all reflections of the Oneself.

At this level of the superconscious mind, we are accessing divine knowledge, divine wisdom, and divine intuition as we begin to push the upper limits of our awareness to perceive the transcendental Self. In the intellectual intuition of the *atimanasa kosha* and *vijnanamaya kosha*, we perceive information about external events through psychic impressions and direct knowing. In buddhic intuition, we can empathetically FEEL the information within our own conscious awareness as if we were that being or circumstance.

When this level is developed, the aspirant has established their mind in the awareness that there is no separate self, yet one's individuality is one with All. The aspirant has thus released all doubts and uncertainties regarding the spiritual impermanence of existence because of dedicated self-study and through an embodied understanding of Universal Law. At this level, the aspirant has dissolved all superstitious beliefs and egoic desires for sensory fulfillment so that one's will is clear and determined and is engrossed in higher wisdom and higher love. At this stage, the aspirant knows that there is no path above any other and that all paths lead to the same realization of Unification.

This part of our being is undiscovered and underdeveloped in most of humanity. Most do not know this state of beingness is possible because they have not quieted and purified their mind enough to listen to the deeper part of themselves. Maybe they are distracted by physicality and endlessly look for happiness "out there." Maybe they believe themselves to be impure and would never dare think that such divine bliss lives within them. Yet those who are brave enough to face their shadow and take the inward journey are most blessed to discover complete liberation, freedom, and the truth of their immortality.

Samadhi and the Development of Liberated Consciousness

We access our Bliss Body when we are in acts of selfless service (*seva*), acts of devotion (*bhakti*), and the joyful calmness of mind focused on the Divine (*samadhi*). We access this state in deep sleep or states of untroubled rest. In this state, we are completely absorbed in the eternal unfolding of perfection of the NOW.

In *samadhi*, we rest in blissfulness with no attachments, no desires. We are untethered from the pull of "the world" and are absorbed in the luminosity of our True Nature, shining our golden radiance into the world. We naturally enter this state at night when we rest in the blankness of sleep and awaken feeling refreshed and rejuvenated. Yet the true practice is to enter this place of unification and revitalization while in the waking state.

The general concept of *samadhi* is that the practitioner begins to be able to unify their mind with the higher consciousness reality more and more consistently until full and lasting liberation and unification are attained. There are different steps and stages of *samadhi* described in different philosophical traditions. Some are states of unification with objects outside of one's individual self, and conversely, there are states of *samadhi* achieved by turning one's awareness inward towards the *Atman*, the Source Consciousness within.

The experience of divine bliss of the Buddhic Body comes from dissolving concepts of separateness and surrendering the limits of intellectual understanding. From this place, all that is left is the desire for unification with the Supreme. This reaching of one's awareness towards the Divine then begins to open a level of liberation that is only found by transcending even the bliss consciousness to the nirvanic consciousness of your True Self.

The Bliss Layer gives us the brilliant radiance of our unhindered I AM presence. When one establishes their center of consciousness from this plane, the lower ego has completely dissolved at this final stage before complete unification with the Supreme. This merging with the Light while maintaining the "I AM Consciousness" presence is the last station before full realization.

As the Initiate continues to amplify this desire and devotion, the I AM experience fades away and all that is left to experience is the continual experience of Light. A being with this level of consciousness could be called a *jivanmukta*, a liberated being who shines with the brilliant light of true joy and true bliss. These liberated beings walk through life's day-to-day activities while maintaining this golden radiance of higher consciousness. This level of enlightenment is called an *asekha* in Buddhism, a "non-learner" who has realized and maintains nirvanic consciousness while being in physical form to bring the higher dimensional plane to the physical plane to assist others in their evolution.

Beyond this phase exists the state of consciousness that goes by many names in many traditions. This highest state of unification and absorption can be called *kaivalya*, or *nirvana* as it is called in Buddhism, *moksha* in the Vedic traditions, and the "salvation" that the gnostic Christian teachings speak of. In this state, there is complete absorption in the Absolute as the individual mind has completely dissolved, merging Subject and Object as One in radiant nondual consciousness.

As one progresses through this final station all desires are dissolved including the desire for unification with the Supreme as one progressively realizes they have always been that One Light of Consciousness. At this level of enlightenment, the Seeker has released all egoic identity, all samskaras, all distorted limiting belief structures, all efforts of the mind, and crosses permanently into the liberated nondual consciousness of the True Self. Once one pierces into this plane, they have moved into a level of consciousness that is inconceivable to the average human mind that only knows life through the experience of the senses and limited egoic identity structure.

When one achieves this state of liberated consciousness, they have achieved the state of Ascended Masters, beings who have perfected their consciousness with divine bliss, divine wisdom, and divine power and live as immortal intelligence. These beings have no need to take on a physical form for developing consciousness and only come to Earth on "mission-related" incarnations to assist collective human awakening.

You Hold the Keys to Heaven

Most people spend their entire life slaving away and wasting their life force to build an empire to enjoy during retirement. They then spend all of their retirement using their acquired resources to repair their body and mind that they damaged by trying to build external wealth and external power. True happiness cannot be bought, hoarded, or acquired through the physical world. Even if we have immeasurable talent, youthfulness, wealth, health, and intelligence, there is still a greater state of fulfillment and joy that can be experienced here and now through union with your True Nature.

You do not have to wait until you die to receive salvation or liberation from cycles of suffering. The doorway to the Kingdom of Heaven is within your very heart right now and you hold the keys to unlock your blissful inheritance. If you can detach from the drives of the body and the desires of the mind that obscure your bliss, you can awaken to the God Force that lives within you. You can detach from the endless seeking of sensory attainment, walk the path of devotion, and claim the benefits of Heaven in this very life.

You do not have to be a renunciate to do this, you can align with your inner teacher, your inner monk, and make Ascension and God-realization your sole purpose in life. In each moment you can choose to release intentions that protect your egoic identity and align with Unconditional Love and Service to All.

Every act in your life can be of reverence and devotion which moves you from seeking worldliness to spiritual seeking, to the attainment of true and lasting peace and liberation. This is the blessing promised to the God/Higher Love-seeking souls of this generation, to finally step off this wheel of suffering and claim our divine inheritance as Children of God. Let us fully awaken as Source itself, right here, right now, forever and ever!

FORTY-EIGHT

5D New Earth Consciousness

Some believe that *samadhi* is the final stage of awakening. There are other levels of ascension beyond what is currently experienced on the planet. Yeshua ben Joseph, Jesus of Nazareth, demonstrated this after the resurrection when he appeared to his closest disciples in his Fourth Density Lightbody form. This is the same form we all will be developing into as we transition into New Earth with renewed bodies with 5D+ consciousness or what has been coined as christ consciousness.

Jesus exemplified and publicly demonstrated what the sages and mystics have practiced in secret caves, monasteries, and hidden orders throughout time. He followed his spiritual path, his *dharma*, to the end and beyond. Even while nailed to the cross, he KNEW that the truth of who he is exists beyond the physical, etheric, mental, intellectual, and bliss bodies.

Our True Nature as God can be described as "*Satchitananda*:"

- *Sat:* Eternal Existence or Eternal Truth
- *Chit:* Eternal Light of Consciousness
- *Ananda:* Eternal Bliss

Or in the words of Christ, "I am the Way, the Truth, and the Life!" This means he realized himself as that One Light of Consciousness, the nondual Source of Creation. We are all that One Light of Consciousness. Part of his mission was to publicly demonstrate the path we all can take and the level of ascendency we all can attain.

I have had a somnambulistic client who channels all the consciousness levels in her legacy with perfect clarity. When we are working together, her oversoul completely merges with her body and shares profound information about all the client's many lifetimes and has access to many higher consciousness beings. When her oversoul does not have an answer, her oversoul says "Let me shift up to the monadic level to see if there is information there." Then I speak with that part. She has shifted even higher to a 16th-dimensional archangelic aspect of her that is harder for her body to channel because the frequency is so high and the information is abstract, more like light geometry than actual decipherable messaging. In The Book of Knowledge: The Keys of Enoch J.J. Hurtak describes the higher aspects as the oversoul, christed oversoul, and elohistic oversoul. Even further beyond that is the pure Source Consciousness, our true point of origin, our True Self.

We are eternal, existing beyond time and space. We are the pure Light of Consciousness that illuminates the Cosmos. We are the Absolute Bliss of Source experiencing itself in myriad forms in an eternal dance of Ascension and Descension, forgetting and remembering the Truth of Eternal Life and Eternal Love and Oneness.

When we are in the dance of life, we are not the physical body, the skin, the muscles, the bones, and the blood in motion. We are not the breath and life force that power the rhythmic flow of our body's movement. We are not the thought process that guides the body into rhythm and flow. We are not the sense of feeling that "I am dancing." We are not even the joy of being lost in the dance. We are the nondual Consciousness that experiences all of these names and forms arising, abiding, and dissolving in the light of our awareness.

As we travel through our different *koshas* in search of our True Self, we discover that there is no object of Self to be found and that our true identity is paradoxically transcendental and imminent. What has seemed hidden from us has in actuality always been present. We are all-pervading, everexistent, and eternally free! This illuminates the power of the Hebrew mantra *"Ehyeh Asher Ehyeh."* — "I AM THAT I AM." The use of this powerful statement acknowledges the ability for the individual identity to be absorbed into the divine identity. It immediately connects us to the Higher Consciousness Reality and the power of Ascension.

Bring your hands to prayer position at the heart and sing the mantra repeatedly, in Hebrew or English, with focus, devotion, and praise. Let the reverberations echo through your being to dissolve all that no longer serves you. Keep singing it until you are absorbed in the vibrations of Eternal Existence, Eternal Consciousness, and Eternal Bliss!

You are the Ocean of Consciousness. Pure infinite existence itself. Let the waves rise and fall. Entire universes arise, exist, and dissolve within you, the One Light of Consciousness. Let karma do as it may. Let old age come, let disease come, let poverty come, let death come, let ill fame come. You lose nothing by it. All exists within you, the One Light of Consciousness. What has been, what will come, is nothing compared to the fullness you are here and now!

Test Run of the New Human Template

On February 24, 2017, I experienced a rapturous, transformational experience that completely shifted my perception of reality. I was downloaded with a higher coding and was blessed to experience a "test run" of humanity's next embodiment. I was transported psychically to a higher dimension, where I met with a council of radiant Elders who began to place a new holographic overlay on top of my current subtle operating system. My sacral center was updated and expanded (possibly to a fifty-foot radius or more), and I was told that I would use this energy field to attract others. Two golden chakras formed above my shoulders, and codes of Light from foreign languages flowed all around me. The codes were strange letters and symbols, Light language "fire letters," that I assume are from a higher vibratory alphabet.

Not only were they illuminated as I watched them sparkle and shine around me, but I could tell they each had sentience. I had a distinct feeling that I was in a "*merkaba*" even though I did not know what that was at the time. A *merkaba* is a Divine Light Vehicle used by higher dimensional Beings of Light and Ascended Masters to travel throughout Creation. We all will have access to our own individual *merkaba* field as we shift into the New Human Template and 5D consciousness.

When I was brought back into my body and became aware of where I was on the Earth again, I felt merged with all of Creation. I felt one with the air around my body. I felt that not only did I experience the breath and movement of the Universe, but I had a clear knowing and feeling that I WAS the Universe breathing and moving. Powerful feelings of life force and magnetism pulsed from the core of my being. The stars throbbed love and sentience. It was as if I was seeing stars for the first time. It was as if each star was a unique being witnessing my transformation with great joy and compassion.

As I walked around the forest, I felt that I was intimately intertwined with the consciousness of Nature and all of her kingdoms and that I could control the elemental forces at will. This was a bit concerning for me as I realized the immense responsibility that comes with such power. I felt that I was not limited to one time and space and that, if I wanted to, I could project myself where I willed myself to be.

As I was walking, different Elders and higher consciousness forms moved in and out of my psychic awareness sharing information and perspective with me about my future and role on the planet. A fearful thought rippled through my energy field as I feared that I was insane or arrogant for believing this experience. This caused me to noticeably drop in confidence and life force. I immediately heard that I was "just not used to this level of embodiment in this life. Get used to it!" and was immediately recharged with energy. I was psychically aware of a large, cloaked spacecraft docking close to where I was. I felt I had a deeply personal relationship with that ship, and that the beings on the ship were witnessing and conducting this rapid, evolutionary embodiment process.

I found a place to lay down on the ground as "They" performed multidimensional psychic surgery on all my layers and bodies, completely recalibrating my cellular structure. I had a feeling that "old me" was leaving and that a newer, wiser aspect of my consciousness "walked in" and was being downloaded and integrated into my body.

This went on for several hours. Eventually, I went to bed and woke up twenty hours later. I was extremely dehydrated and quickly chugged about a gallon of water. At this point, the effects of the upgrade had integrated and receded into the background to be reactivated in the future at the appropriate time.

This experience catapulted me forward on my path of awakening. Since that experience, I have a much higher spiritual station that is my default consciousness mode. I have had a few other situations similar to this one that I have mentioned previously in this book where further updating has been done on my body's organic technology and my consciousness.

One of the reasons I had this experience is so I could share it with humanity to let them know that major cellular and consciousness transformation is coming that is beyond having a more positive approach to life (regular awakening). Many people acknowledge spiritual awakening but do not fully grasp or accept the truth of the rapid planetary and human biological transformation happening NOW.

Many people think that the "New Earth" is simply humanity learning how to get along where everyone is polite, vegan, and recycles trash. There is MUCH MORE! The New Earth is a completely new light spectrum reality where we exist in perfected, restructured, and upgraded bodies of Light with a fifth-dimensional and above consciousness anchored in multidimensional unity consciousness. This will be true for every single person left on the planet as she shifts. This is available to all people regardless of sex, gender expression, genetic lineage, socioeconomic status, political affiliation, and so on. This is for ALL SOULS — every member of our human family who has opened their heart to Higher Love.

We cannot even comprehend the world we are about to inherit. Miraculous reality will be our moment-to-moment experience. Our bodies will no longer have diseases because we will be in a vibration beyond disease. We will have multidimensional communication abilities with the higher realms. We will be physically present on the Earth while simultaneously projecting our conscious awareness into the higher light dimensions. Our bodies will be avatars for the Overself meaning we will be more of a collective of souls than one individual identity. Supersonic human life is coming, and it is ours for the claiming!

Charge to the People of Light

So, this is it. This is our opportunity to shed every single whisper of shadow and rise up into our greatness and Light. While grieving is inherently intertwined in this global transformation process, it is also time for celebration for making it to this Grand Transformation of Life. Every step is part of our victory march as we finalize what all of us have been working towards for many, many lifetimes. There is no stopping the avalanche of Light that is coming!

This is the last temper tantrum of humanity. These are the last wars, the last of illness and disease, the last of oppression, the last of murder and human trafficking, the last of the crimes against children and the Earth, the last of all of the muck that humanity has been slinging back and forth for thousands of years! This is the completion of an eternity's worth of karma for all who are ascending!

We are the generation that finally puts an end to this madness. We are the builders of a New Earth awakening to our own Christhood, Buddhahood, and Krishna Consciousness. Doesn't it feel GREAT TO CLAIM THIS IN OUR KNOWING?!!

- Let us release fear and lack consciousness so that we may receive the full bounty of our divine birthright as beloved Children of Earth and Heaven.
- Let us release our egoic identity and come into the right relationship and connection with all of Life as Divine Creators in form.
- Let us put aside our service-to-self compulsions and rest in the Divine Will as pioneers of consciousness and leaders of the New Earth!
- Let us use the redemptive power of forgiveness and open our hearts with loving-kindness, compassion, equanimity, and empathetic joy as reflections of the Love of Source.
- Let us use our voice as a beacon of benevolent truthfulness to create beauty and a heavenly reality as we sing the songs of Remembrance.
- Let us hold a clear vision of harmony and peace and open ourselves to divine guidance as we project our inspired visions of Heaven on Earth.
- Let us open our minds to the Divine Light and Divine Intelligence and become a People of Light!
- We ARE the unification of Life! We are the Lovelight of Source Creator! We are infinity consciousness bliss. Right now! Right here! Forever!

Blessed be!
Aho! Amen! Jai!
Hallelujah!
We are here. We are awake. We are One.
And so, it is!
OM

GATEWAY FOUR: CHAKRA YOGA DISCOURSE

Keys for Higher Consciousness

This section initiates the reader into the deeper psycho-emotional components of the chakra system to reconcile and balance the polarities of each chakra to create coherence and the unification needed for Ascension.

FORTY-NINE

Wheels of Light

"Behold, I stand at the door and knock: if any person hears my voice and opens the door, I will come into their being and will sup with them, and they with me." Revelation 3:20

To sup is to drink liquid or liquid food. Yeshua ben Joseph often talked about water and the quenching of thirst. To truly quench your soul's thirst, one needs to discover what desire is at the core of thirst. What is at the core of hunger? What truly nourishes and satiates hunger? What truly quenches thirst?

True nourishment comes from union with the Divine. We, as humanity, have had the Light of Source knock on our own Crown Chakra. It is up to us to acknowledge and welcome the Higher Consciousness Reality into our being, to bring Heaven to Earth through our bodies. We can invite the "dove" of the Holy Spirit to descend through our Crown Chakra and begin to transform us from within.

We, as a species, are being invited to step out of mundane, biological evolution and cycles of karmic suffering into a higher spiritual evolution called Ascension. We are being invited to lay down our weapons of ignorance and receive the Light of Truth in our very hands, hearts, and minds.

Let us accept the Higher Realms and the truth of the pathway of Ascension and welcome the Higher Light into our being. Let us eat and be satiated. Let us drink from the eternal waters of Higher Wisdom and Compassion and let the depths of our thirst be quenched. The door is open and available for all souls to release their attachment to the conditioning of the world and open to the pure Light and Love of our Source.

To receive our Divine Inheritance, it is essential that we learn to see beyond the illusion of duality-based polarized mindsets and unite our awareness with our True Nature and the Divine Presence. This process involves activating our lightbody and purifying the physical, etheric, and mental bodies of any contamination and distortions. As we "wash our robes," we begin to connect with deeper spiritual truth and liberate ourselves from our own karmic creations and their repercussions. As we do this, we naturally become agents of cosmic spiritual transformation through every atom of our being.

Chakra Yoga is the process of recalibrating our subtle energy body and fortifying our energy centers through spiritual practice. Each chakra is a lens of perception that can be cleansed and cleared of distortions that keep us in cycles of karmic entanglement and suffering. To step off the Wheel of Karma, *samsara*, it is essential that we liberate each chakra and its associated mental patterning from the conditionings of the world and update each of these processing centers with Higher Wisdom and Truth. This is how we can be "in the world but not of it." We can train our mind to see beyond the 3D duality-based matrix into a higher perspective of Unity and Divinity.

The ancient spiritual teachings of *Advaita Vedanta* give four qualifications (*sadhana chatustaya*) for an aspirant who wishes to unify their consciousness with the Divine and achieve full self-realization. If you are reading this book, you likely have some level of all of these. Our work is to continue to continue to develop these skills:

Viveka — Discrimination: Discrimination is the quality of mind to discern between what is transient and what is constant in past, present, and future (Brahman/Absolute Reality). This ability to distinguish what is real versus what is an illusion, what is permanent, and what is impermanent withdraws one's mind from the snares of *samsara*, the cycles of suffering, so that one can focus their mind on Higher Truth and their True Nature.

Vairagya — Dispassion or Non-Attachment: Dispassion is the quality of having an absence of desire for enjoying the fruits of one's labor. Since true fulfillment comes from alignment with our True Self, the aspirant becomes increasingly aware of when they believe their source of fulfillment is from outside of themself. Spiritual growth and the attainment of true, lasting happiness is truly an inside job.

Shadsampathi — Six-Fold Inner Wealth: A spiritual aspirant needs the discipline to focus their efforts to achieve all the fruits of ascension. As we learn to *master the mind (sama)* and *master the senses (dama)* by focusing them on our path of awakening, we repattern our mind to *automatically meditate on the Divine Presence (uparati)*. Spiritual growth is not linear; it has ups and downs, so we need to cultivate *endurance and perseverance towards our goal of awakening (titiksha)*. We do this through *faith in the sacred texts and the teachings of the enlightened masters* which guide us on the path of awakening to the Divine *(shraddha)*. All these qualities merge so that we can have a *single-pointed mind focused on the Divine (samadhana)*.

Mumukshatavam — Desire for Moksha or Liberation: This is the desire above all desires. It is born from the clear knowing that "the world" is illusion and that true happiness and fulfillment is an inside job. The desire for true and lasting liberation fuels the process of awakening and secures your footing on the dharmic path. Whatever you do in your moment-to-moment living, use it for the purpose of unifying with the God-force within you. Use every activity of your life as a spiritual practice for unification with your True Self.

In summary, as we grow in the capacity to discriminate between what is permanent and what is impermanent, we learn to detach from the ways of the world to focus our life on the Divine. As we learn to master our mind and senses, our focus on the Divine becomes automatic. Through perseverance and faith in the sacred teachings, we develop cohesive focus and deliberate action to fulfill our desire of true liberation from cycles of suffering and union with the true source of our happiness and wholeness.

Yeshua ben Joseph, Jesus the Christ, exemplified the discipline needed to walk the dharmic path fully. To accomplish his soul's mission, he had to completely clear his mind of all distortion so that he could maintain a single-minded focus on the Divine. No matter how much pain was inflicted, no matter what was promised to him by "the world," he followed his dharmic path all the way through.

A christ-conscious being is an ambassador of the radiant Wisdom and Knowledge of the Divine in full Service to the Greater Good of All. Whether one calls it Krishnahood, Buddhahood, or Christhood does not matter. The path is still the same. Once we no longer need anything from the world to bring us happiness, we stand as fully illumined beings in Service to All!

This next section of *The Illumination Codex* material is a deep dive discourse into the seven-chakra system commonly known through the practices of Hatha Yoga. I also include additional chakras that are beginning to activate as we shift into the recalibrated, restructured, and updated Fourth Density Adamic Form.

Throughout my years of seeking, I have studied the subtle body through a variety of lenses. I have been most impacted by the literary work of Dr. Synthia Andrews, ND and the video transmissions of Neeta Singal. These two subtle body visionaries have impressive bodies of work. Be sure to check them out!

FIFTY

Root Chakra: Grounded in Being

The Root Chakra is located at the base of the spine and is associated with the color red. It has a horizontal spin with the vortex opening down towards the legs and up towards the crown. This chakra connects us to the physical world, to our body, food, basic resources, family, and community. It is our connection to our primal instincts and animal nature. It helps us create structure and plans and helps us ground into and expand time while connecting us to the foundations of the physical world, physical body, and the Earth element.

When our Root Chakra is balanced, we feel secure in our environment. We feel stable in our life because we easily tend to the basic structures and systems that support a healthy flow. We feel supported in our life process and easily create a wide network of community bonds with varying degrees of depth. We feel a sense of security in our being and find solitude to be healing and rejuvenating. When our Root Chakra is open and flowing, we feel grounded and supported, and we rest in knowing that all our basic needs are met. This creates a feeling of safety, and we can face any challenges that come our way.

The Root Center connects us with the Earth. While we incarnate on the Earth, we are lovingly and unconditionally supported by Gaia, the soul of the Earth, the Mother of Life on this planet. She does not give for greed, only for need, and provides us with all necessities to keep us healthy and strong.

For example, when walking in the wilderness we may feel inspired to pick some berries from the bushes to eat. As we approach the bush, we can tune into our intention to harvest and tune into Mother Earth and the bush. If we listen closely, we can sense through our inner being if harvesting is appropriate. If we get a sense that it is permitted, we may begin harvesting. At a certain point, we may get an inner impulse that we have harvested enough from that area. We have a choice to give in to our own desires or to honor the communication from the Earth and the bush. We can be grateful for what we have been given and carry on along our path trusting that Mother Nature will continue to provide, or we can succumb to lack-consciousness and steal more from her without her consent. Mother is quite forgiving, and you could take more but it will have an immediate energetic effect. Now multiply that same action of greed across the whole human species and we see why we are in the predicament we are in now with the imbalance and environmental damage rampant across the Earth. If we would have been taught this basic skill of communication with our Earth mother as children, our civilization would be much different. The Indigenous peoples have much to share about living in balance with our Earth Mother.

We will never be without as long as we are open to this connection with the Earth Mother. Like any loving mother, she gives all that she can to support her children so that they can be happy and free. We can lay upon her like a baby lays upon its mother and receive supportive energy. We can explore the world with a sense of safety knowing that Mother is nearby. We can confide in her and release all the density of our soul into the loving arms of our Earth Mother. She is open to receiving all the negativity that we hold onto and happily transmutes it for us.

Imagine that the body is a tree with a wide root system that runs deep into the Earth. You can receive all of the nutrients you need to grow towards the sky and Father/Mother/God. Those connected with the Love of Mother Gaia are like a system of trees, a community that other beings can take refuge in and borrow strength from.

Root Chakra Imbalance

When our root chakra is imbalanced, we are cut off from our connection to the Earth, and survival and lack-consciousness are activated. This can manifest as fears related to resources, time, community bonds, and so on. Overall, a sense of lack creeps in, and we feel isolated, singular, and cut off from the abundance of the world. We may perceive that there just does not seem to be enough to go around. The world seems unsafe, and we begin to seek power outside of ourselves by controlling the external world to survive. Fear, anxiety, and loneliness are symptoms of an imbalanced root chakra.

When the root chakra is overactive, we may find ourselves overcompensating as if we have not done enough or are somehow missing the mark. We may feel struggle as we are cut off from a co-creative relationship with physical reality and feel that everything rests upon our shoulders. We may overemphasize our needs out of fear that we were not heard or understood or that we might miss out on what we desire. Because of this, we may collect things and hoard things because we have a deep-seated fear that there may not be any in the future. We envision a future of lack because we are creating from the belief that there is not enough and that we are not safe.

We may become rigid and over-rooted, making it hard for us to grow and evolve because we are trying so hard to control our external reality to feel safe. We may try to force others to be like us because we do not trust beyond what we know. This fear can keep us stuck in unhealthy situations and relationships because we fear the unknown. We could become like an obedient dog and be loyal no matter how unfulfilling our relationships, jobs, or environments are. If we feel that life is out of control, we could develop unhealthy relationships with food and use food to control our emotions.

If our root chakra is underactive, we may feel unrooted in our life, floating around and unable to commit to anything. We can change jobs and relationships at the first sign of conflict. We become like a little mouse and scurry away, unable to face our fears and challenges. When fear is activated, all the blood leaves our torso and rushes to our legs and arms so that we can fight or flee. Sometimes the fear is so strong that we are frozen in one place, unable to move in any direction emotionally or physically.

The physical manifestation of root chakra imbalances could manifest in the feet, legs, and bones. One may develop knee issues because they are subconsciously afraid to move on their path. One may develop foot issues because they have not fully committed to their dharma and path of growth through incarnating. One may develop excess tension in the body because they are in constant stress and fear. Nervous system issues may develop because of habitual states of nervousness, anxiety, and agitation. These are just a few examples of how Root Center imbalances manifest in the physical body.

What Blocks the Root Chakra?

False Evidence Appearing Real

Fear arises when we feel threatened, overpowered, and undermined. Fear happens when taking information from our past and projecting it into our future. We take limited information and create a story from it. Fear can arise because of an external circumstance like a dangerous situation. It can also originate from subtle subconscious thoughts that mostly operate in the background of our mind unnoticed. Fear is insidious. It eats away at our freedom and keeps us from feeling free. It blocks us from having a higher perspective and seeing the bigger picture.

Many fears originate from unresolved trauma in this lifetime. Fear can also be from other lifetimes, where we experienced past trauma. For instance, someone may have died in a car accident when crossing a bridge and flew out into the water and drowned. Subconsciously, when that person drives across a bridge or near water in this lifetime, fear may begin to creep in and create havoc in their emotions for a seemingly unknown reason. This is the power of the samskaras, the reactive momenta from the past, over our bodymind's expression.

The Root Center and Crown Center work in a symbiotic relationship. When we are afraid, we instantly close our root and crown chakras. We become identified with our "separate self" and feel disconnected from the world. We cut ourselves off from the stability and safety given to us through a clear connection to the Earth field and from the limitlessness of the Universe.

Fear is an invitation to grow in alignment and trust. Even in the most chaotic and dangerous situations, we can still maintain clear trust and presence.

This type of clarity and groundedness can be seen with medical staff who work in the emergency room in hospitals. Fear or anxiety may arise in them, but their job is to ignore the projections of people in pain and focus on making clear and calculated choices to keep their patients alive.

Parents/Caregivers, Family of Origin

Our family of origin sets up the foundation of our beliefs. This includes the root chakra qualities of stability, structure, support, and solitude. This is where we learn how to be a community and how we relate to the world around us. Much of our wounding in this life comes from our childhood and our relationship with our parents and family. These relationships are continuing to play out in our extended community and in our adult relationships. When we complete the emotional healing from our childhood wounding, we can have flourishing relationships with our community and a healthy relationship with life.

The Deification of Parents, Familial Domestication

When we are born, our parents provide us with our initial education about life. From our human perspective, we believe that they are our source of food, resources, shelter, and love. They become the god and goddess of our universe. We deify them and see them as all-knowing and all-powerful beings. They give us a name and begin to transfer to us their knowledge about the world. They begin to transfer their language and definitions to us and teach us their values and perspectives. They tell us who we are and who we are not. They tell us what we are capable of and what we are not capable of. Since we are so small and they hold so much power, we believe them and adopt their laws and beliefs as our own.

Parents need to teach a child how to be in the world to grow up and be happy and successful. Parents can only teach what they have learned from life and their parents. To train young children to be like them, parents establish a system of reward and punishment. When we are a good boy or girl, we get human love and resources. When we do not please them, they can withhold love or resources from us. Since we are dependent on them, we begin to adapt our behavior to please them. This way, we receive love from them and get what we want from them. At a certain point, we learn their system well enough to no longer need them to reward or punish us because we do it for ourselves.

Later in our development, we often begin to question our parents' knowledge and authority as we start to see the flaws in their systems. Sometimes parents encourage their children to go beyond what they have learned, but this is often met with resistance, which can lead to a battle between the child and their parents.

If we experienced or witnessed violence or abuse, we will have fears related to this. If our homes had yelling or fighting, we learned that the world is not safe, people are dangerous, and we can get hurt. We may have learned that we need to watch out because people are violent, the world is a violent place, and we cannot trust people. Because we hold these emotions and energies from our trauma, we attract the same situations into our life so that we can learn deeper truth and return to wholeness.

To fully heal the root chakra, we need to make peace with our parents and our siblings. This does not mean that our parents need to change, but we can evolve and do the internal work necessary to heal our wounds from childhood so that we feel safe and secure in our life. This does not mean that we have to condone the actions of our abusers, but we can acknowledge that they behaved in the way they did because they were suffering. Compassion and forgiveness are the way out of the karmic bonds created through abuse.

Ancestral Lineage Imprinting

Many of our family beliefs and emotional patterns started long ago in our family histories. We are a collection of our maternal and paternal lines of knowledge and experience. What was not healed and integrated from previous generations is passed along to the next generations. This information is stored in the DNA of our bodies as micro-packets of information and mental fields. While some of the emotional, mental, and biological patterns skip generations, certain patterns reactivate in later generations. This is seen in hereditary diseases, where the echoes of ancestral trauma continue to wreak havoc on the biology, mental attitudes, and emotional patterns of modern generations. Epigenetics studies the ability to alter the DNA to create harmonic gene expression. We can abandon the fate of heredity and choose health and vitality by evolving beyond our ancestors' inherited mental and emotional patterns. Here are some questions you can use as part of your own ancestral wound healing process:

- How attached are you to your family identity?
- What role do you have in your family? Was it self-proclaimed or projected onto you?
- How did you respond to your parents' authority as a child? How did you cope?
- Were there instances or patterns of neglect? Physical abuse? Sexual abuse? Mental abuse? Emotional abuse?
- Have you forgiven your parents for what they did in states of ignorance?
- Are you able to fully send love to your parents and siblings?

- What mental attitudes have you adopted from your family?
- How has your parents' relationship with one another been reflected in your own intimate relationships?
- What was your childhood relationship with your Mother? With your Father? How do those dynamics play out in your adult relationships?
- Where do you still give power away to your parents? What causes you to become critical or return to the "child seat?"
- Tracing back through your family lineages, where did the traumas begin? What hereditary illnesses sprang from those traumas?

Money

Parents pass along their beliefs about money and resources such as "You have to work hard to make money." or "There is never enough to go around." We may have distortions in the root chakra if one of our parents lost their jobs or if money was a concern and our parents talked about it or fought about it in front of us. Since we are so devoted to our parents and see them as all-knowing beings (deifying), we believe them and take on their beliefs consciously and subconsciously.

Whatever work we do in the world, let it be done as an act of devotion by bringing our full spirit into the work and acting from a place of selfless service (karma yoga). If we are doing our work primarily for money or external reasons, we quickly drain the joy out of our experience since money and success are temporarily satisfying. This does not mean we should not receive compensation for our efforts but that we should instead find the richness and security that lives within, and then everything else is a bonus.

If we look back over our lifetime, we will see that we always had the basic resources to get us by. We were always able to find what we needed eventually. We may have had to ask a friend or borrow something from someone, but we were always provided for in the end. Solutions are always available. If we can release beliefs around lack and trust that all is being provided for us, we open the gates for more abundance to flow in.

- What are your beliefs around money? Positive and negative?
- What are your parents' beliefs about money, finances, and work?

- How did you hear your parents talking about finances and wealth?
- Where do you think money comes from? How does that relate to the laws of the universe?
- Do you have any fears about your basic needs being met or the future of your finances and stability?

Community

The way we experience our community and relationships is a collection of many facets, including the initial patterns we learned from our family of origin, cultural attitudes, and subconscious patterning from other lifetimes. We see these subconscious patterns out picturing in our relationships. We can use our community members as divine mirrors to reflect where we are in our current state of consciousness development.

We do not need to stay in any toxic relationship any longer. Once we become aware of the subconscious fears that keep us in isolation and loneliness patterns, we can release those patterns and form a new path for ourselves. Find a community of people that love and accept you. There is much love out there for you. Be brave and build bridges wherever you go. Say hello to strangers and open the door for people. Connect with your Inner Light and smile at people with your whole being as you pass. Look into the clerk's eyes at the store with radiant love and allow yourself to be seen. Build a network of connection and love.

- Do you feel safe in your home? In your community? Workplace? Nation?
- What are your general beliefs about people?
- How do your beliefs affect how you walk in the world?
- Do you feel like you belong? Do you think others do not belong?
- Do you find yourself trusting others?

Fear of Instability

If we experience unstable conditions in this life or other lifetimes, we can hold that fear of instability in our energy signature. When we project our fears into the future, we create them.

We are not helpless victims, enslaved by the patterns of our past. We are powerful, Divine Creators, and we are always being provided with what we need to sustain and raise our quality of life. The tighter we grip life and attempt to control it from a state of fear, the more things go awry. Trust that you are being provided with everything that you need and envision a future of opulence and ease.

- Do you have fears about not having enough to make ends meet?
- Do you have a positive or fearful perspective of the future?
- How do you feel your life is going to progress?
- Do you find yourself saving up for when things go bad?
- Are you often waiting for the "other shoe to drop?"
- Do you feel guided by the Divine? Supported by the Earth?

Physical and Mental Attachments

Attachments are a way for us to distract ourselves from our true source of pleasure and life force. Our alignment is what truly feeds us and brings us joy. It may seem like our body, our car, our lover, or our XYZ brings us joy and pleasure. The truth is it always comes from our experience of allowing our alignment with the Source Within Us and our ability to trust in the Universe.

Where does your safety come from? Where does abundance come from? Where does your joy come from? Do you fear losing XYZ and the suffering that it would bring?

Fear of Change and Impermanence

Everything is constantly changing and evolving. When we fear change, we try to control our environment's external circumstances, and we keep ourselves from growing and evolving. We need to become comfortable with the unknown and trust that we are being supported through the process. Many stay in cycles of suffering and limited perception because they fear the Mystery. They go with what they know because the Void of the Unknown scares them. We can make peace with the Void and allow ourselves to navigate the uncharted waters of our consciousness.

- Where do you resist change? What do you cling to?
- Do you trust in your ability to navigate uncharted waters and new experiences?

- Do you actively seek paradigm shifts and growth?

Struggle

The belief that we need to struggle to succeed generates patterns of struggle in our lives. The struggle is resistance, and when we are experiencing resistance to what is currently manifested, we cut ourselves off from the loving guidance and intelligence of our inner Source.

When we believe that life is hard or that life or God is against us, we keep ourselves from being able to access the part of our being that is connected to divine guidance, and we create from a sense of lack. Be solution-oriented, forgiving, easy, and gentle. Be optimistic, open, patient, and present. Do not take life so seriously. Nothing is so serious. When we are met with challenges, we can take a deep breath and open ourselves to receive the solution.

- Do you feel working hard makes you more valuable?
- Do you find yourself constantly busy?
- Do you have a "no pain, no gain" attitude?

Laziness and Sloth: Physical Effort, Training the Body

The root chakra also governs our beliefs about the use of our body and how we show up physically in our lives. The body enjoys being strengthened, toned, and developed. The more we use our body, the more grounded and stable we feel in our body. The body is like a horse that you need to train. Make it sweat; feed it healthy foods; make it strong; test its abilities.

The more we give in to feelings of laziness and sluggishness, the weaker we feel, and we begin to wither away. If we procrastinate and delay doing what our life is asking us to do, our body takes a toll. If we have an aversion to physical effort, we can tune into what beliefs create the resistance. Was it something from our past? Are we afraid of being tired? Why are we unmotivated? When we are willing to show up and do the work, we grow in confidence and stamina.

At the same time, if we are not listening to our body's requests, we can become overworked and drained. This is usually happening because we are working from a place of fear.

Quiet your mind and tune into your impulses. What is driving you? What are you running from? The work is never done, and the list will never be completed. Take a rest. Self-care is an art form that is radical in a world where achievements are valued more than balance.

- How often do you exercise your body? How often do you push its capacity to grow in strength and flexibility?
- Do you avoid daily tasks or life choices to avoid putting in the effort?

Structural Awareness and Systems of Support

Tending to our physical environment and needs also helps us to feel organized mentally and emotionally. Eating regularly, keeping a routine, cleaning your spaces, and organizing areas of your life all help to create a sense of internal balance.

Many people pass up opportunities because they are afraid of or feel overwhelmed. When an opportunity presents itself that calls to your heart, realize that these opportunities are meant for us and our growth. We do not need to miss out on anything. We can create systems to support our dreams and desires. We can call upon our community, adjust our schedules, be creative, and find solutions to participate in all that life brings to us.

Many people believe that there is no support for them, and that the world is pushing against them. If we believe the world is scary and unfriendly, we will create that reality. If we think the world is unforgiving and terrible, it will be. If we think that people will rip us off and danger is around the corner, we will experience that. The emotional charge of fear is a powerful attractor. What we send out, we get back. When we are open to seeing people and the universe as supportive, help comes from all directions.

- What is your relationship with organization and delegation?
- Are you able to ask for support easily?
- Do you have an active support system and community?

Standing Your Ground in the Face of Adversity

There will be times when you will have to face situations that feel like a confrontation. These situations activate a response to fight, run away, or freeze in your tracks. No one else is going to fight our battles for us. We must be ready to stand our ground. When we trust ourselves, we can face challenges and fight for what we want. It is common for spiritually-minded people to think it is more spiritual to be passive. While choosing your battles is wise, we must also be prepared to stand up as an ambassador of Truth and Justice.

- Are you comfortable with asserting boundaries and standing up for yourself?
- What is your relationship with conflict? What are your habitual and historical responses to conflict?

Presence, Faith, and Trust: Everything in Divine Timing

Know that everything is coming at the right time. We are never late. We are always where we need to be in life to get to where we want to go. Trust in the unfolding of your path. If you miss an opportunity and it was truly meant for you, it will come around again.

- Do you feel you have enough time to accomplish your life goals?
- Do you feel patient while also maintaining focus and determination towards your goals?

Belonging: You Belong, So Does Everyone Else

Go out into the world and know that you belong, and so does everybody else. We are all family, distant relatives with varied pasts. We all want the same things, such as love, acceptance, and freedom. These qualities are already available to us if we would only allow them into our experience. Just like a tree, spread your roots far and deep. Be rooted in many places and cultivate many relationships, many levels of connection and support. You matter and should be shared with the world.

- Do you feel you belong? In your family? In your workplace? In your community? On the Earth? How do those beliefs affect how you move in the world?

Illuminated Tree Trunk Meditation

Close your eyes and imagine yourself as a tall and sturdy tree. Feel your roots grow deep and wide into Gaia. Imagine nutrients absorbing up through your roots helping you to feel strong and nourished. If there is any density in your being, allow it to dissolve into the ground through your roots.

Feel your branches growing wide and far towards the heavens. Imagine life force from the universe pouring in through your branches and revitalizing your whole system. You can even allow your tree to flow gently in the wind.

Feel that you are a loving tree that many sweet animals love to come and take refuge in. Imagine that your love is so strong that magical creatures like to come and play around the tree. Radiate this love out into the world.

Feel the other loving trees across the world that are connected to your root system. Feel them pulsing love and strength out into the world. Take a deep, long breath and feel the power of this connection.

Amplify this intention by chanting the sounds of LAM or OM over and over, sending waves of vibration out through your being.

When you are finished, return to normal breathing, and open your eyes.

FIFTY-ONE

Sacral Chakra: Divine Creatorship

I t is said that all our suffering is from a root ignorance of not knowing who we are as divine beings of Pure Consciousness. We falsely believe that we are this body and our limited egoic self. Since we erroneously think we are only this limited self made of flesh and bone, we endlessly chase sensory experiences thinking our happiness will somehow be found in the world. We have created an entire civilization built from this ignorance and suffer greatly because of it.

We are each Source Consciousness reflected as an individual soul appearing to have a temporary physical experience as a human. Once we incarnate, we forget our spiritual legacy and are born into a world of limitations. We become entangled in our identification with our body and mind. We are told our names and given a family identity and history. We live in a community that has a communal identity. We live in a nation that has a certain national identity and ways of behaving. We are told we are human, and even this has certain rules and regulations on behavior and certain limitations. We even extend our identity out into a galactic and universal identity. All these identities are temporary and change with each incarnation. We are not a finite being existing in only one place and time. We are the One Light of Consciousness in which all of Creation appears within.

When we identify as our body, egoic identity, memories, family, emotions, circumstances, our careers, mistakes, and so on, we lose focus on our eternal nature and identify with some passing experience. We cut ourselves off from our Source-ness. Spiritual growth is about aligning with our Divine Nature and remembering the truth of who we are. As we continually refocus ourselves on our Divine Nature and the Light of Source, we transform into an embodiment of Source Energy.

The Sacral Chakra, located in the lower abdomen in line with the sacrum, is all about identity and how we relate to the world around us. Everything is in a relationship. This center is related to creativity and sexuality. It is represented by the water element and connects us to the flow of our vital body, our subtle energy system. It inspires movement and connects with our desires. It shows us what we feel drawn to, what we have aversions to, and if we value ourselves enough to attain our desires.

When we are in a flow state, we are aligned with the energy of creation and are absorbed in the experience of creation. When we are in our knowledge of who we truly are and not wrapped up in our egoic identity, our sexual connections become a technology to experience Source in another through sacred sexual union.

This center gives us the ability to sense our emotions and connects us with the emotional projections of those around us, especially concerning intimacy, sexuality, and desire. We can sense if others are drawn to us or if they are not interested. When people's Sacral Centers are imbalanced, they have difficulty processing emotions and relating to others. This center manifests our ability to move and create in the world. Are we open and free? Do we have limitations and rigid rules of relating?

When this center is balanced, we feel artistic and creative. We are inspired to follow our visions and dreams. We have a charismatic and engaging expression that inspires and uplifts others. We have healthy sexual relationships. We have clear emotional, energetic, and sexual boundaries in our relations. We see ourselves as equal to others and can connect deeply with others and create intimate (sexual and non-sexual) bonds. We enjoy spontaneity and freethinking and are creative problem solvers.

When this center is imbalanced, we may experience a lack of creativity. We may have trouble connecting authentically or creating deep bonds with others. We may sell out on our dreams because we do not feel we can achieve them and instead, follow the money, convenience, and prestige. This may keep us in a state of perpetual longing and an unfulfilled desire for a more purposeful life. We may blame others because we cannot see that our emotional/mental patterns are creating our reality. We may have unhealthy sexual relationships, sexual addictions, and poor emotional, relational, and sexual boundaries. We may blame others and project our emotions onto them. We may be critical and judgmental of others' creativity. We may experience moodiness, pessimism, and apathy. We may be deceitful and manipulative to get our needs met by others.

This could manifest physically as reproductive system issues, sexually transmitted infections, painful or irregular menstrual cycles, erectile dysfunction, lower back pain, bladder problems, and more.

What Imbalances the Sacral Chakra?

Not Meeting Our Own Expectations

Life is full of challenges, and when we experience emotional trauma from perceived failures, we may lose sight of who we are and identify with our mistakes or shortcomings. This causes us to give up on ourselves, and we feel like a failure.

The truth is that life is about learning. Sometimes we hit the mark, and sometimes we fall short. We are not our bodies, thoughts, behaviors, or past actions. Each challenge brings us opportunities to grow, and when we do not meet our expectations for ourselves, we can use the experience to learn. You do not have to change YOU. You simply need to develop new habits and practices.

- Do you have positive or negative self-dialogue with yourself?
- What are your knee-jerk judgments about yourself when you do not meet your own or others' expectations?
- Do you expect failure or success?
- Do you compare yourself with others?
- Do you feel accepted by others?

Self-doubt and low self-worth are common effects of the process of domestication used by our family and our culture. Maybe we were criticized or compared to others growing up. Maybe we were rejected or insulted by others. This also happens when pressure is put on young children to perform a certain way, such as achieving high grades or excelling in sports. Simply, the belief is, "I am not enough."

What people think about you has more to say about them than it has to do with you. You are a unique being with your own set of qualities that make you one of a kind. What really matters is if you accept and unconditionally love yourself. Source loves you. Your Higher Self loves you. Your guides love you just as you are. When you shift your identity to your Divine Nature, self-love is natural because that is what you are. When you love and appreciate yourself, you surround yourself with others who honor and respect you.

- Do you celebrate your uniqueness or feel out of place, not able to fit in?

- When you walk into a room, do you find yourself trying to brace yourself for unpleasant interactions?
- Are you afraid of engaging in conversation with new crowds or people?
- Do you assume that people are judging you?
- Do you feel yourself overcompensating to get attention and love?
- Do you feel like a sinner? Less than worthy?

Unable to Protect Identity or Enforce Boundaries

This happens when we experience abuse of any kind. We may have been overpowered by someone who asserted their will over ours and we experienced defeat. We may have been bullied or singled out, or even cast out from our social circles.

The Sacral Center and the Throat Center are very connected. When you are connected to your Divine Nature, you can easily communicate your boundaries and desires. We need to be able to compassionately establish boundaries and enforce a boundary when it is crossed. You must learn to stand up for yourself and defend your identity, your unique essence. Some people believe that if you genuinely love someone, you will accept any behavior. When we communicate and enforce our boundaries, this allows people to learn how to love us in a way that feels good to us. We do not need to be a doormat for people.

Your parents teach you this lesson the most. When you can express yourself truthfully and transparently to your parents, it will be much easier to accomplish this challenge with others. If you find yourself constantly standing up to others and it falls on deaf ears, honor your soul and find others who are supportive. This is especially true for your family. You can create a new family that loves and honors you completely. The choice is yours, and it always has been.

- Do you find yourself constantly adjusting your behavior to avoid conflict?
- Do you feel you are authentic in your relationships? Are you able to communicate honestly? If not, what are you afraid will happen if you are transparent and honest?

- Do you find yourself staying in relationships that are painful, hoping that eventually they will change their ways and finally love you the way you want?
- Do you communicate and enforce your boundaries swiftly and easily?

Codependency

Codependency is an unhealthy relationship pattern where one person sacrifices their own personal needs for the needs of others. This pattern is often created in childhood when children learn to overlook their own physical, mental, and emotional needs to survive through unhealthy relationships involving addiction, neglect, and abuse.

People with codependency patterns have a distorted perspective of love because they learned that receiving love meant they had to behave in a certain way to receive positive attention. This belief manifests as an unhealthy reliance on people for approval and a sense of value and identity. This expresses as anything "overly," such as being overly apologetic or overly giving as an attempt to manipulate others to feel safe and loved.

Codependency manifests as low self-esteem, people-pleasing, poor boundaries, reactivity, caretaking, control issues, manipulation, dysfunctional communication, perfectionism, external referencing, feelings of emptiness, intense and unstable relationships, obsession, dependency, denial, problems with intimacy, and other characteristics.

When we are dependent emotionally, financially, and physically on others, we cannot feel equal to them, and separation occurs. The same happens if we feel that others are dependent on us.

If we believe that others are dependent on us or we are dependent on others, we are not free to relate to them authentically and often manipulation occurs. Because of this dependency, we may compromise our dreams and beliefs to sustain this ego dynamic.

Interdependence is a healthy relationship pattern where two people are aware of and value the emotional bond between each other and can maintain a strong, clear perspective of individuality while in the dynamics of the relationship. These types of relationships are built on transparency, vulnerability, and trust. Each person takes full responsibility for their own emotional and mental well-being. Each person's autonomy is supported, and everyone can maintain their own values and unique perspectives.

Healing codependency involves becoming aware of the beliefs and patterns that distort our perspective of who we are and all the ways we limit ourselves to manipulate other people into seeing us as loveable or valuable. This involves reorienting how we relate to others, especially the ones closest to us. It is a moment-to-moment process and practice of compassion and self-love.

Realize that everyone is in a partnership, and everyone is equal. Release others from feeling dependent on you and transform dynamics where you feel dependent on others. Empower yourself and others to follow their highest joy. When everyone follows their joy, everyone benefits, and there is an equal exchange between everyone.

- Do you feel overly responsible for other people's lives and well-being?
- Do you make excuses for other people's behavior?
- Do you try to control or manipulate others to get your needs met?
- Do you find yourself seeking revenge for the wrongdoings of others?
- Do you find yourself seeking the approval of others?
- Do you find yourself limiting yourself or holding back out of fear of causing waves?
- Does the thought of ending unhealthy relationships frighten you?
- Do you take on the guilt or embarrassment of others when they behave inappropriately?
- Is it hard for you to say "no" when someone asks for help?

Sexual Trauma

Sexual trauma affects people long after the initial trauma. It can limit how we show up in intimate relationships. Many of my clients experienced sexual trauma as children, causing their sexual expressions to be distorted. Many of these wounds have been caused by men, which causes people to have fears of men and relationships with men. Often these wounds started long ago in other lifetimes and are now being re-experienced so that the person can heal.

We can heal our sexual trauma and develop a healthy relationship with our sexuality. Maybe it happens slowly over time, or maybe it is something that we can accelerate by finding a professional to guide us through the process. Healing is possible, and we can learn how to open the flow of creative sexual energy in a way that helps us feel compassionately connected to our sexuality.

- What is your sexual history from childhood until now?
- What were your first experiences with your sexuality? Did this involve other people? Was it an enjoyable experience?
- What were your parents' beliefs about sexuality? Masturbation? Did those beliefs get passed on to you?
- Do you have religious beliefs around sexuality that consider sex shameful or immoral?
- What are your beliefs around monogamy, polyamory, homosexuality, and bisexuality?
- Do you feel comfortable with your sexuality? How often do you self-pleasure? What are your beliefs about masturbation?
- What are your thoughts and feelings after orgasm?

Rejecting Womanhood or Manhood

A lot of pressure is put on women to look and behave in certain ways. Some women end up subconsciously hating their womanhood and repressing their feminine qualities. A lot of men are insecure about the size of their penis or body structure and feel that they are not "manly" enough. Some people do not feel that they fit into a binary gender system. All these issues can distort how we express ourselves in the world.

Everyone can feel sexy. Everyone can feel attractive. Everyone has what it takes to be a good lover. Sexiness and beauty are feelings that we can generate in ourselves. We can learn to be connected and confident lovers. Accept that you have masculine and feminine qualities that contribute to your own unique balance. Neither needs to be repressed, and both can be celebrated.

What are your beliefs around your womanhood/manhood or about your masculinity or femininity (regardless of biological sex)? What does it mean to be a man or a woman? What qualities and responsibilities do men and women have in society? When is it acceptable to show emotion? Do you fit into that model? How can you celebrate your masculine and feminine qualities? Do you find yourself repressing one or the other or both? How do you compare yourself to others of the same sex? Opposite sex? Do you hold judgment about transgenders?

What If You Don't Believe in Relationships?

We may have become closed to intimacy and closeness if we experienced our parents fighting growing up or if they are separated or divorced. We may have experienced the tragic loss or death of a loved one at some point in our life. We may not have had good examples of the sweetness that is possible in close relationships. Maybe we were hurt by others and closed ourselves to love.

In each moment, we have an opportunity to open ourselves to love and align with our Divine Essence. As we learn to trust connection and affection from others, we begin to move more freely in the world. When we learn to be vulnerable and connect with others, we open to the abundance of the universe.

- Are you open to intimate bonds, or do you find yourself hiding your true desires and soul expression?
- Are you open to sexual connections, either with your partner or others? What do you do when your sexual energy activates? Do you repress it? Feel shame? Deny it?
- What thoughts or beliefs drive your aversions or desires?
- What are your beliefs about dating and marriage? Who were your models for relationships growing up?

Fear of Impending Doom

If we are afraid that danger lurks around every corner or that the world is a scary place, this affects how we show up in the world and limits our creative expression. When we focus on the darkness of humanity and the darkness of the world, we miss out on the sweetness that life has to offer. As we learn to trust and build open and honest relationships, we blossom and start to feel safe and secure. Everything is in a relationship, and in every moment, we can choose to be in acceptance and expect goodness, or we can choose resistance and expect to suffer.

- Do you expect your future to be positive or negative?
- Do you find yourself "waiting for the other shoe to drop?"

Sacral Center Meditation

Close your eyes and begin to breathe consciously and deeply. Bring your awareness to your pelvis. If you would like, you can make a triangle with your thumbs and index fingers touching. Bring the triangle to rest so that your index fingers rest on your pubic bone and your thumbs touch close to the belly button. Your palms will gently rest on your lower abdomen. Breathe into this place and imagine that it is filling with light. Fill every part of your pelvic bowl with the light of your awareness. If there is any stagnant or distorted energy in your pelvic bowl, imagine that you can clear it with the light of your loving awareness. Feel your sexual organs. Imagine that you are filling your sexual organs with Divine Light and Love.

Let any negative energy or thoughts fall away as you bring light into your sexual organs. Continue breathing like this for a few minutes. You can chant the words VAM or OM to amplify the healing. When you're finished, return to normal breathing, and open your eyes.

FIFTY-TWO

Conscious Relating & Sacred Sexuality

From the moment we are born, we absorb our family and culture's thought forms and belief systems. Many of us are taught that the body is shameful, and that sexuality is dirty and disgraceful. We project those values out into the world and pass them along to the next generations. These limiting beliefs are like a wet blanket put over the light of our soul, restricting the free-flowing brilliance of creative pleasure.

Sexual wounding and dysfunction are held by all of us. We deny and repress our innate drives for connection and pleasure, which fractal out into a myriad of dysfunctional and self-serving behaviors that can harm ourselves and others. Over the coming years, we will be invited to hold space for all the collective healing regarding sexuality and how we connect intimately.

Intimacy and sexuality are two different qualities bodymind experience. In modern society, they are often confused as the same. I wrote this section to bring deeper awareness to what intimacy is and what sexuality is, and how we can grow and mature in both areas.

Intimate Relationships

Intimate relationships can be measured by how many areas of life we are open to sharing with someone and how deep into those areas we are comfortable growing in that relationship. Some relationships are superficial and practical, like an exchange between people in a grocery store, and some relationships involve sharing a wide variety of experiences and going deep into one's heart like with a parent or a life partner.

A lot of people experience their sexuality from an animalistic and service-to-self impulse. Some use sexuality to control, manipulate, or dominate others to fulfill their own desires and fantasies. Some repress and deny their sexual desires to fit into societal structures of "purity" to cover up their own shame and guilt.

Sexuality in its highest form is for the cultivation of Divine Light and Union with the Divine. In the highest form, sexuality uses our body temple, senses, and creative power to connect with and channel our divine nature's pleasure.

Divine Partnership and Twin Flame Relationships

As we grow spiritually, we release the control and manipulation patterns of the old and open to true partnership. In Spiritual Partnership, each person is seen as an equal, and the bond is used as a technology for spiritual growth. Any relationship can be a spiritual partnership. In spiritual partnership, both people take responsibility for their own emotional and mental well-being.

Twin Flame relationships are a major phenomenon on the planet right now. As many are finishing their soul's karmic contracts, they are now ready to meet their Divine Mirror. In Twin Flame relationships, each partner is committed to serving the other on their path of healing and feels that their relationship is meant to serve the collective of humanity.

Twin Flame relationships are examples of true Divine Union and create a new model for relationships on the planet based on transparency, unconditional love, and planetary service. These "power couples" work through the last of their conditionings together, the last of their unprocessed emotional trauma, and exemplify cooperative collaboration in its highest human form. Many Twin Flames are now finishing up their purging and activation phases and embodying Divine Androgyny, also called *Heiros Gamos* by some in the ascension community.

I felt it was important to note the "spiritual trap" of the term "Twin Flame" in the ascension community. In many ways, the old models of relating have been superimposed on the pathway of divine partnership where people are "on the hunt" for their Twin Flame. People use the word "Twin Flame" as a control and manipulation tactic just like some who use the term "I love you" to guilt others into playing a role for them. Some feel like they aren't ascending or somehow have less value if they do not have a Twin Flame relationship. I must say, I am in a Twin Flame relationship, and we hardly ever call each other that. We do not label ourselves in that way because it can create control structures. We do not use the term to say, "Now that we are Twin Flames, we cannot do this, and we have to do that." True divine partnership is finding union within one's deepest self which is supported by and reflected by the other but is never dependent on the other person. That power is in the individual.

Divine Androgyny: Balancing Masculine & Feminine

The fabric of nature is woven by feminine and masculine principles engaged in an eternal dance of creation and evolution. We experience this Law of Gender through the two sexes of our species and the expression of gender. We depart from the classroom of polarized gender and move into an exalted state of androgyny when we embody more of a balanced embodiment of masculine and feminine qualities. We see this outpictured as women come into places of power and men come into the softness of their hearts.

Pre-Life Contracts on Sexuality

Before incarnating on the Earth, we choose how we are going to explore sexuality in our life. Some choose to be attracted to bodies of the same sex; some choose to be attracted to members of the opposite sex; and some choose to be attracted to both. The truth is everyone falls somewhere on the spectrum of attracted-to-same or attracted-to-opposite, and the placement on that spectrum fluctuates over time.

Non-Traditional Gender Expression

Many young people do not feel connected to a binary gender system and feel that their gender expression and sexuality are much more fluid compared to the mainstream model. These forerunners of consciousness not only bring in a new embodiment to the Earth School, but they also help us to evolve the old belief systems of judgment and bigotry into a higher unity of the heart.

I believe that as we clear limiting beliefs and trauma, we will all become more gender-fluid and open to more levels of intimacy, touch, and sexual expression. It is up to each of us to do the inner work to heal the wounds of our past regarding sexuality and learn to embody our unique expression of sexual truth.

These times are challenging for those who are bringing in this new energy and new embodiment. Many of these beings have never been in a physical body, let alone a body that has a specific sex. Some of these souls come from star systems where they have only lived in androgynous forms. Some have lived in opposite expressions many times and wanted to try the opposite in this incarnation to learn balance. Some needed the experience of being "different" so they would awaken quicker to their starseed origins.

The challenge and invitation are for these unique souls to make a home within their bodies and make peace with themselves in the world. It is a noble challenge that bears much fruit. These beings, especially the new children, cannot be defined by labels of any kind in terms of gender and sexuality. Each being is unique and beautiful! Imagine how powerful their souls must be to come at such a time and face such judgment and ridicule only to use it to awaken in their consciousness. They are truly changemakers!

The prototype for this new energy was a child of Yeshua ben Joseph and Mary Magdalene. A high-vibration androgynous being was born into the new crystalline bloodline created by Jesus and Mary to test out the biology's capacity to hold such a powerful soul. This intersexed child, having both male and female reproductive organs, was trained in the esoteric arts and on the path of mastery and awakening. I cannot even begin to imagine how empowered this being was considering his parents were cosmic tantric illuminated masters!

We are invited to grow in compassion and understanding and support those of the two-spirited, transgendered expression to embody the magic that they already are and assist them on their path of discovery who they are beyond their bodymind. They are divine and perfect as they are! Having this beautiful, rainbow expression of gender and sexuality marks a renaissance of love across this planet.

Everyone is being invited into their sexual truth to explore their deepest, most soulful erotic expression. Each person is invited to expand their concepts regarding relationships and sexuality. We have so much love to give and receive! Let us help one another come into profound, intimate union with our deepest selves and celebrate our creative spirit! May all wounds around sexuality and our body be healed now and forever!

Sacred Touch

Many people are starved for true, loving affection in their life. Sacred touch is experienced as a loving, conscious physical interaction between two or more people where there is an honoring of each person's divinity. When we hold hands, we can invite the Divine to be with us. When we hug one another, we can invite the presence of the Light to move through us and wrap us in a loving embrace. We can invite the Divine into all our connections and relationships to lift us up into a higher experience of Love and Unity.

We, as a collective, confuse intimacy and touch as sexuality. This confusion keeps us from experiencing a deep, loving connection with one another. There are even different cultural rules and limitations depending on people's sex and gender. We have so many rules and regulations of how we should interact with one another that it leaves many feeling alone and disconnected from their community.

I see this strongly in male relationships. Men have been programmed to believe that sharing a loving touch or an embrace shows weakness or somehow reflects their sexuality or status in a negative way. Many men are completely deprived of non-sexual physical intimacy. On a deep level, men are deprived of a true sense of brotherhood and intimate connection because of this. Distorted programs around sexuality, touch, and intimacy are so deeply embedded in male-embodied beings that we see a huge amount of suffering created in the world by men. Many men turn to drugs, alcohol, closeted sexuality, sexual abuse, and even suicide as a symptom of this distortion and deficiency.

As we normalize loving touch and consensual embraces across sexes and genders, we will see less and less perversion in human sexuality as a collective. As we embody higher sexual honesty and celebrate our sensuality and sexuality, we clear the past generations' distortions and protect future generations from sexual trauma and repression.

Relationship Models

Old relationship models passed on from previous generations and religious institutions are often experienced as systems of control based on fear and dogma. Some traditions view women as the property of men. Jealousy is seen by some as a sign of "true love," and women are taught to be servants to their husbands, relinquishing their own sovereignty to fulfill the needs and desires of their husbands. Some cultures force the younger generations to secure public image and familial financial legacy. In many ways, marriage has become a hunting act, where people are chasing the person they think will complete them or make them happy. People copy the manipulation tactics from television to coerce people into staying in relationships much longer than is healthy because of public image, fear of the unknown, guilt, and low self-worth.

I know for myself, as a gay male, I had to come to terms with the fact that I would not be following the traditional model. I had to do much inner work to deconstruct the belief systems passed on of what it means to be a man, a son, and a lover. There was so much trauma, conditioning, and secrecy to work through. I had to learn how to live an authentic and joyful life publicly as a male who is only attracted to men. It was extremely painful but was the only way for me to truly live a happy life and have honest relationships with others. We all have sexual and relating karma to clear and as we heal ourselves, we heal the future generations as well.

These old models limit authentic behavior and expression of humanity and keep people trapped within their relationships. New Earth relationship models honor the free-will sovereignty of each individual. Instead of controlling our partners, we empower them to follow their intuition and path to grow. Instead of making assumptions and placing expectations on one another and the relationship, we choose to grow in the ability to communicate our needs, desires, and limitations honestly and with full transparency. Instead of blaming others for our experience, we take emotional responsibility and use conflict to learn and grow into maturity and compassion.

Monogamy is the choice to explore sexual energy cultivation and deep intimate emotional bonds with a single partner. Non-monogamy is when someone chooses to practice relating beyond the dyadic relationship structure of monogamy. Within non-monogamy are a few different categories of relationship styles. Some people identify as polyamorous and feel open to multiple romantic and/or sexual relationships or may practice polyfidelity where they are committed to multiple partners. Some people choose to have a primary relationship where they have consensually agreed-upon commitments and secondary partners that they engage with on certain levels which could be sexual, romantic, or both. Open relationships are becoming more of a trend in the younger generations who wish to create new relating structures; this is especially true amongst the gay male population. Couples may engage sexually with other couples, "swinging," or be mostly monogamous with certain degrees of outside sexual or romantic engagement at certain times in their life. Some call this being "monogamish." These diverse relationship styles require conscious communication, transparency, and honesty to work and are not for everyone. They require one to be willing to work on themselves and grow in sovereignty or else things can get dramatic quickly!

Inherently, life is polyamorous, but we may choose to focus our time and emotional/energetic investment on one single partnership for any duration of time. This does not mean that once in a relationship, either of the partners should deny or repress their natural human attraction to other humans. The energy of attraction and arousal is natural, and we should work with it in healthy ways within whatever relationship styles and structures we currently practice.

Everyone is free to create relationship structures that support their spiritual growth, joy, and freedom. While non-monogamy and polyamorous relationship styles are growing in popularity, it is important to intend that all of our relationships be focused on mutual growth and love. No one should be forced into being monogamous out of fear and control. No one should be polyamorous or in a non-monogamous relationship if that does not support their higher vision for their life and their level of comfort. Monogamy is beautiful and should be respected just as much as the non-monogamy styles. What matters is that love, compassion, integrity, honesty, and the willingness to refine one's inner world are present in all relationship styles.

Conscious Communication

Conscious relationships involve clear and honest communication. When we utilize our relationships for spiritual growth, we acknowledge when we are afraid, insecure, or jealous. Instead of controlling our partners so that we feel comfortable and perpetuate patterns of limitation, we can communicate our fears and doubts and transform our fearful parts into true and authentic empowerment and freedom. The highest form of communication is to set the other free. Deep listening and nonviolent communication pave the way to freedom and joy for all.

Compassionate Listening: Setting Intention

Compassionate listening means that we have emptied our mind and simply rest in the intention of relieving the suffering of another through deep listening. As we listen to the other person and practice compassionate listening, we do not plan what we will say next. We notice when we want to jump into the conversation and choose to stay in simple, mindful awareness of the one who is sharing while being deeply anchored in inner presence and breath.

Triggered Reactive Emotion

As someone shares the story of their suffering, their body re-experiences the traumatic energy so that it can be released. You may start to feel the same feelings and sensations that they do, or it may trigger your own trauma stored in the body. When you are aware of this, take a deep breath, connect with your Pillar of Light, the hara line, and re-establish your alignment with your Higher Self. As you exhale, release the energy that is triggered and unsettled within you. This also helps the other person become aware of and release their triggered energy. As you clear, they clear, and both of you feel the support of your shared conscious awareness. This light structure meditation is talked about in *pranamaya kosha* section of this book.

Body Language & Guiding Self-Inquiry

For some, moving from irrational thoughts and painful emotions takes a little more time. Notice the posture, micro-muscle movement in the face, dilation of the pupils, and breathing patterns of the person sharing. Body language tells a lot about what a person is going through internally. Asking questions helps them go deeper into their feelings, thoughts, and sensations so that they can get to the core of the issue and understand the deeper nature of the conflict. You may notice them tensing up as they share their perspective as their body and mind re-experiences the pain. Ask them what they feel as they share their story. Contractions or activating energy in the body point to the chakra where the limiting belief and stored trauma are held. When we tune into that part of the body and practice compassionate listening with our Inner Being, we can uncover valuable information for transformation and healing.

Internal Imagery Mindfulness

We are constantly broadcasting mental imagery out into the Unified Field. Every fluctuation of thought sends packets of data into the field that can be picked up by others. For most people, this happens unconsciously. As we awaken and become aware of our internal processes and intentions, we become deliberate creators. We begin to choose our thoughts and create our future from an inspired vision versus creating from our past memories, trauma, and conditioned thinking.

When we are thinking of or talking with someone, we are broadcasting imagery in their direction that they are filtering through their energy system through their subconscious. When we are listening to another, we are receiving imagery and energy from them as they share.

Notice your internal messaging and images you receive while listening and be mindful of the images you project. While the other is sharing, you can hold an internal image of what it would be like when they are transformed by love. As you hold this internal image, your subconscious begins to pick up on this broadcast. Depending on the amount of internal resistance occurring, their subconscious picks up the data and begins to signal to the conscious mind to match the higher frequency and ease.

Refocusing and Regrounding

If you notice that a person is getting unfocused or holding a lot of tension, you can guide them through your own ability to stay connected to your higher consciousness and grounded beingness. Sometimes people unconsciously disassociate and drift away to avoid feeling the pain of what they are going through. Helping them come back into their body with deep, conscious breathing empowers them to face the issue with mindfulness and confidence. Sometimes people drift off because they have lost interest in their own stories. If you start to feel unsettled in yourself, you are likely absorbing their energy and mental imagery. Breathe consciously, connect with your hara line, strengthen your field, and settle into your heart.

As you ground your energy, the other person unconsciously receives the messaging from your broadcast, which can activate grounding and presence in them.

Triggering and Venting

If the person sharing vents in your direction, it is important not to take it personally. What you are witnessing is them tapping into the original wound that happened way before your conversation, sometimes lifetimes ago. Get curious, not furious. Take a deep breath and clear the energy that may have been triggered in you from their projected suffering. Breathe into your whole spine and heart. Do your absolute best to clear any energy within you that may come from a place of needing to defend yourself. Let them know that you see that they are suffering and care for them. Practice mirroring and asking questions that lead to deeper answers.

Validation, Feedback, and Mirroring

For many, being heard is enough for them to release deeply embedded suffering. Repeating back what you heard in your own words helps the person sharing feel heard and understood. What was at "the heart" of what they shared? Once you have repeated back what you understood and heard, you can ask if you missed anything. If you have missed an important detail, let them share what you missed and repeat it back to them to make sure you have touched on every part of their perspective. It does not matter if what they are saying is accurate. What matters is that they feel heard and validated.

If you have insight into the nature of their suffering, try asking questions to help them come up with the answer themselves. Ask questions that help them feel and see clearly. This empowers them to be their own healer, their own redeemer.

When someone shares from a vulnerable place, it is important to validate their experience so that they can feel safe enough to release the energy completely. You can say something like, "I see how painful that was and still is for you. Would you like to take a deep breath together and let some of that energy go?" This willingness to feel the pain instead of running from it is often enough to make a significant shift in their perspective and health as well as builds a deeper bond between the sharer and the compassionate listener.

Advice

I find it is most beneficial to help others discover deeper levels of truth within themselves before offering advice. Many people have walls of resistance that come up when they feel like they are "being told what to do" or when someone seems to think they are "better than them." Using mirroring and compassionate inquiry can help avoid running into this wall.

Before giving anything that may sound like advice, ask if you can share your perspective. Honor their "yes" or their "no." If they say yes, let them know they can take what is helpful and disregard the rest. When sharing, use "I" statements. "When I went through _____, I discovered that _____. Do you feel this relates to your experience? Is that helpful at all? If so, how could you apply this to your life?"

Reframing

We often frame the experience of a traumatic experience through the lens of victimhood and limited perception. "Reframing" helps us understand the traumatic event from a higher perspective, which opens the pathways to healing and redemption. Reframing moves us out of the experience of victim mentality into a higher understanding of how the situation served our soul's evolution.

Envisioning the Ideal Circumstances

So often, people create their NOW and future based on their past experiences and traumas. We can climb out of that lower trajectory by creating an inspired vision of what we would like to manifest in the most ideal ways. We can help our community members to do the same so that we all collectively envision a higher trajectory for ourselves, our community, and our planetary civilization.

Agreements in Conscious Relationships

Within the structure of any pairing, monogamous or non-monogamous, agreements are made consciously and unconsciously about what actions and behaviors are acceptable while in the container of the relationship. Conscious relating evolves us out of assumed gender roles and societal norms and into unique connections that honor each individual's sovereign creation. Agreements can be made on sharing resources, sexual intimacy, household duties, responsibilities, when time is spent together, when time is spent with other people, when time is spent alone, and so on.

High Sexuality: High Alchemy

The highest form of sexual activity is for the attainment of higher consciousness and union with the Divine. Old systems of sexuality are control systems that describe when, how, if, and with whom a person can participate in a sexual act. These systems will fall away as more and more people become aware of the ascension technology that is activated by sexual pleasure.

I would like to propose that sex falls in the spectrum between service-to-self and service-to-all where the lowest forms involve violence and domination, and the highest forms involve heartfelt service, pleasure, connection, and devotion.

When someone is aroused sexually, creative life force energy begins to move through the body's electric and magnetic fields as it prepares to create new energy and, ultimately, new life. All the best energy of one's being is offered up from the cells and endocrine system as the body prepares to create a new life. This process happens much faster and more powerfully when two or more people are engaged in sexual touch and play.

At the core of sacred sexuality is self-love. This is not an egoic worshipping of yourself but a compassionate and caring attitude towards your being. Loving another as you love yourself requires you to love your own body, mind, and Spirit first. When we deeply love ourselves, we naturally and effortlessly radiate that love out into the world.

Cultivation

Cultivating sexual energy charges the body with powerful healing and transformative energy. When circulated and anchored properly, sexual energy cultivation improves creativity, focus, mood, and our relationship to the world around us. In ancient times, the priests and priestesses would cultivate sexual energies and anchor them into the collective field of their community to raise the collective's creative potential. Everyone benefits when individuals are trained in the high alchemy of heart-based, sexual energy cultivation.

Self-Pleasure and Self-Cultivation

When you activate your own sexual, creative energies, you can circulate the energies to heal the body with self-love and pleasure. Stroke and caress the skin of your body to activate the electromagnetic fields. Explore the sensitive erogenous areas of the body like nipples, perineum, and genitals. Use deep, conscious breathing to amplify the electric and magnetic waves of energy that begin to flow through you as you begin to charge the body. Circulate the energies by doing the microcosmic orbit, alternate nostril breathing, or other conscious breathing patterns to bring the energies up the spine and spread them throughout your whole body. Imagine that all your cells are illuminating and being healed as you spread this light through your systems.

Multi-orgasmic Men

Many men around the world are lost in the shadows of sexual addiction and porn industry programming that focuses on assertiveness and ejaculation. Many men are beginning to tune into the sexual arts to heal these toxic patterns and distortions in their sexuality. I highly recommend the work of Mantak Chia.

A male orgasm is made of two physical responses. One is the explosion of orgasmic power, and the second is ejaculation. Ejaculation uses a considerable amount of life force energy. While it may be exciting and pleasurable to experience, ejaculating immediately creates a depletion in energy. Using different tantric practices, men can learn how to control their sexual energy to have multiple orgasms without ejaculating.

Another level of sexual growth for the majority of men is the feminine quality of lovemaking. The Divine Feminine in a male form is what makes them a good lover. The softness, receptivity, gentleness, and care are what moves men out of porn sex and into the higher arts of sexual alchemical wizardry and noble kingship!

Womb Magic

Within the female womb is a powerful energy portal that allows the passage of a soul from the Higher Realms to the Earth matrix. Priestesses would use this vortex to channel energies into the Earth plane for healing and rejuvenation. Ancient priestesses would use the power of stem cells in their menstrual blood to heal and strengthen food crops and regenerate the Earth.

Womb-en all around the world are healing their sexual trauma and celebrating the power of their sexuality. Lifetimes and generations of trauma are stored in the womb and are ready to be transformed and healed. Sister Circles, Goddess Temples, and Red Tent spaces create healthy containers for *womb-en* to tune into the power and wisdom of their wombs.

The following is a short transcription from an IQH session with a somnambulistic client named Emma's Higher Self.

M: I am wondering if you have any final messages for Ron and me?

HS: There is a new movement — you are talking about it quietly. You are not sure how to bring it out into the open because of certain taboos, but it is going to be a great part of empowering others. Once you release certain boundaries, you don't notice the programming of sexuality is heavy. These practices help you to listen fully and walk through the door.

M: What's the movement that you speak about?

HS: Bodies. Many pleasuring together. Shameless. Love. Trust. Vulnerability is power. Everything at once. Pure.

M: So, are you speaking about sexual liberation?

HS: Sexual truth.

M: And how is sexual truth important in our lives or on our path?

HS: The barriers are always made up of small denials. We deny our powerlessness. We deny our power. We deny our now. We call shame to our impulses, and we cry havoc to our words. We stuff them down — all of it tied in a ball — weighted down — keep it earthbound.

M: So, what role do we have in this movement? What do our souls have to do in these bodies regarding this movement?

HS: Once you find the right words, you will feel more comfortable about broadening, but you are going to collect more souls that agree. It has already begun. Just remember, they are not your shape (energy signature), and so you cannot relate to them in the same way that you have been related to. You must speak and leave it for others to own in their own way. And in that way, even though it will be a great and easy thing to do, you will continue to stay humble and not fall into an ego trip because this is going to be intoxicating.

M: Intoxicating in what way?

HS: To power centers.

Introductory Tantric Practices

Tantric practices use the mind and intention to move subtle energy through the body for healing and awakening. Here are some basic skills that one can use to deepen their relationship to their sexuality or connect more deeply with another.

Breath Awareness

When we are aroused, our heart rate and breathing become erratic as the pleasure rises in our being. Learning to be mindful of the stages of breathing and expanding each phase of a breath cycle helps to control sexual energy. For example, as men approach orgasmic climax, their breathing becomes shorter and faster. Extending and equalizing the breath stages helps to control ejaculation so that orgasms can be extended, multiplied, and amplified without needing to ejaculate.

Visualization

Learning how to visualize the movement of energy in your own body helps to direct the energy to where it is needed. Sexual life force can be directed into various organs, tissues, chakras, energy pathways, and so on to promote healing and expansion. You can also use visualization and intention to direct energy through your partner's body and energetic field to develop a deeper connection and provide healing energy to your partner.

Spinal Awareness

When we activate sexual energy, it is important to direct the energy out of the genitals, up the spine, and into the rest of the body. This will help awaken the pleasure centers in the body, unblock pathways of energy, and prolong and amplify orgasmic power. The most commonly used technique is the Microcosmic Orbit from Traditional Chinese Medicine. Various meditation and breathing practices are found in the chapters to help circulate and cultivate vital, subtle energy.

Guidance for Connecting with Another

Sexual Attraction

When we connect our sexuality with our sacred hearts, we desire an intimate connection with those we are sexually attracted to. There is nothing shameful about sexual attraction to other people. What we do with the energy and the intention behind our actions is what is important. Sacred sexuality puts love, compassion, and free-will choice at the forefront of any sexual interaction.

Voice Your Attraction

Talking with someone about your attraction to them can be uncomfortable, and it can also open the door for deeper intimacy and transparency. If you feel chemistry with someone, you can voice your attraction if it feels appropriate. Once you voice your attraction, you can listen to their response and see if the other person feels the same. Much suffering happens for people due to unrequited love and unrecognized longing.

Consent is Sexy

With consent, there are no grey areas. "Yes" means yes. "No" means no, and "maybe" means NO.

Often people engage in sex with partners they do not want to connect with. Notice body language, yours and theirs, and honor your perceptions. If you notice discomfort or resistance in yourself or another, honor that. Be vocal and communicate what you are noticing. This may start a transformative conversation for both of you that results in a deeper intimate bond.

Setting a Container

If someone is interested in exploring a deeper way of relating with you, you can set a container together for how you will proceed. This may look like talking more, scheduling a date, cuddling, or sharing deeper levels of affection. If the connection moves towards sexual energy cultivation, talk about what you like in advance so that everyone knows each other's boundaries. This is especially important if you will be exploring parts of sexuality that one or either of you has never explored before, such as someone who has never been with someone of the same sex or has not been sexual with someone in a long time or never at all.

Stages of Sexual Play

Cultivating sexual energy alone or with a partner(s) can be broken into three sections. Foreplay, building to a climax, and what can be called cocooning.

Conscious Multidimensional Foreplay

Before we begin to activate sexual energies, each individual can take a moment to connect with their own heart and breath. Conscious and complete breathing that utilizes the lower and upper abdomen creates a container of awareness to observe and utilize subtle energy. If you are connecting with another, take a moment to synchronize breathing, and look into each other's eyes. Use foreplay to open the senses and activate the subtle energies of yourself and your partner. Stroking the skin with a light touch and gentle kisses activate pleasure sensations in the body and open the body for more powerful energy experiences and awareness.

Building the Orgasmic Waves

As the energy builds, allow it to ebb and flow in several ranges and arcs of pleasure. Tune into the sexual energies of yourself and your partner. Communicate what your partner can do to increase your pleasure and feel more connected. Let your partner know when something is uncomfortable or when you feel disconnected.

Allow yourself to enjoy the experience fully. Use your mind to visualize the movement of energy up the spine and throughout the whole body while staying in conscious connection with your partner and your own breathing. You can use your eyes, body, and breath to direct your partners' energy as well, healing them as you generate love and pleasure. Continue to deepen and elongate the breath to keep from rushing over the edge of pleasure.

As you climax, direct the energy up the back of the spine, arching the energy over the crown and back down the front of the body into the heart. Circulate this energy using the microcosmic orbit to ankh the energy in an infinite loop of pleasure sensations up the back of the spine and down the front of the body.

Cocooning in Radiance

After the climax phase(s), spend time cocooning in the energy cultivated with yourself and your partner(s). Breathe this potent energy into the cells of the body, recharging them with vital energy. Guide the energies back to a grounded place with light kisses and loving touch and rest in the radiance you have created.

Take time to talk about what you liked and what could have made the experience more enjoyable. This helps both of you become more connected and conscious lovers. It may also get the energies flowing again for more play.

However you choose to explore your sexuality, do it with Divine Love. Sex was meant to bring us closer to our True Self, closer to our partners, and closer to Source. Having positive sexual perspectives and experiences is a sign of spiritual maturity. Release all shame connected to your body and your sexuality and embrace the powerful, sexual, creative being that you are.

By healing your own layers of shame and sexual trauma, you help heal our ancestors and future generations, which is an honorable and noble act of service.

My Wedding Vows

I have decided to share my wedding vows that I wrote when Ron and I made our sacred agreement to unite our paths in front of friends, family, and the presence of the Divine. I made these agreements in a way that empowered both of us to live an interdependent and loving relationship. We wanted our marriage to be used as an ascension technology to liberate our consciousness and the consciousness of our beloved. Feel free to use these vows for your own sacred ceremony or create your own.

Ron, my beloved partner,

My heart has been searching for its true love for many years, possibly even many lifetimes. I know that this longing search has truly been a search to find myself. I am the one that I search for. You are my mirror, map, and compass, always reflecting back to me and directing me to the Truth of Who I Am.

I vow to remind you that you are also an extension of Source Energy and that your existence on this planet is far more important than any of us could ever imagine. I encourage you to boldly follow your excitement, filling all that you do with your Light.

I vow to take full responsibility for my own emotional well-being. I will not be dependent on you for happiness and will instead work vigilantly on transforming my own seeds of anger, jealousy, pride, and so forth into a garden of compassion and bliss.

I vow to use my gift of language and speech in the most conscious way, being a poet of honesty and loving-kindness. I do this so that you know the depth of my love for you and this life we are creating together.

I vow to practice non-violence in thought and action and to honor the body as the sacred temple of your soul and divine nature. I promise never to touch you in a way that does not benefit our independent and mutual spiritual development.

I vow to take care of this planet and all its intricate and beautiful forms of life. I vow to be in constant service to the Greater Good, for I know that I am of Source Energy just as much as the trees and stars. If we are blessed to have the gift of children, I want them to experience the beauty that this world has to offer, just as we have.

I love you as I love myself. I vow to align myself with my highest vibration, following my soul's true excitement. It is my hope that as I continue to radiate my love for myself that you will always be inspired to align yourself with all that excites and nourishes your soul. I vow to give you the fullest me that I can.

FIFTY-THREE

Solar Plexus Chakra: Divine Willpower

True power comes when we are aligned with our Divine Self. Our Divine Self is like the Sun of our Solar System. It is bright, powerful, and independent. It remains shining even if clouds cover our perception of it. It continues shining even if someone curses at it and says that it is too bright. Even if we are in emotional turmoil, our True Nature is there shining eternally. We are each the center of our own universe. If we truly want to feel powerful, we must be like the Sun and align with our True Nature and shine out into the world.

Our Solar Plexus Chakra, our Power Center, is the home of our willpower and personal strength, is located in the upper abdomen, and is associated with the color orange. It is connected to the element of fire and to the mental body which we access through self-inquiry and mindfulness.

The Solar Plexus gives us the ability to act independently. When this center is balanced, we can face any challenging circumstance without a sense of perfectionism. We take a role of leadership without overpowering, forcing, or dominating others. When we are asked to go out of our comfort zone, we are confident and able to accept the challenge and grow through the experience. In fact, we are likely excited about the opportunity to expand into greater mastery! We can digest the beliefs and opinions of others without needing to make them wrong. We can process our own beliefs and opinions with ownership. We feel calm and collected, residing in our purpose and clear intention.

When this center is imbalanced, we may associate personal power as being bad or unholy. We may become doormats and let others do as they wish, giving our power over to them to make them happy. We may magnetize people to us that confirm our powerlessness and seek the approval of others. We may feel victimized, complaining about how life is never working out for us. We may feel unstable and unable to take control of the circumstances of our life. We may feel reactive, pushy, passive, defeated, frozen, trapped, lethargic, make excuses, or be demanding, controlling, manipulative, and so on.

Imbalances in the Solar Center manifest as digestive system imbalances. We may not be able to process foods and toxins easily. We may find our digestive system is overactive and too hot or underactive and stagnant. We may develop ulcers and cancers as anger eats away at our tissues and cells as well as have other issues in our liver, kidneys, and other digestive organs.

This center is connected to the mind and processes our own thoughts as well as the thoughts and projections of others. This is where we get the phrase, "I can't stomach to even think about it!"

What Imbalances the Solar Plexus?

Dependency, Real or Imagined

If we feel that we are dependent on anyone or anything, we give our power to it. This includes physical, financial, emotional, and mental dependency. While dependency in the Sacral Chakra is about how we feel and emotionally relate, dependency in the Solar Plexus Chakra manifests as our actions, will, and intentions. These two centers are intrinsically related and connected.

Dependency can manifest as manipulative patterns where we behave a certain way to get what we want, or we allow other people to do as they wish out of fear that they will take something from us. It can also manifest as an excessive force when we try to overpower another's will to get them to follow our will. We can feel dependent on our spouse, our career, community, substances, and more.

Dependency causes us to lose track of our own inspired vision and become pessimistic. We may feel that we are always asking for favors and giving our power away in the process. We can also feel and manifest circumstances where others are dependent on us. This gives us a false sense of importance and can keep us from being honest with ourselves and others. It also disempowers the others who feel dependent on us.

Remember that everything is a partnership and that everyone is equal. There is a natural give and take in healthy relationships, an interdependence. We do not need to take responsibility for others' experiences and well-being. We can trust our ability to manifest what we want and empower others to create their own path and to own their creations.

- Where do you believe you are dependent on your parents? Spouse? Government? Parents? Job? Employer? Children? God? This can be financial, situational, emotional, and so on.
- Is that true? How can you adjust your perspective or behavior to exercise and affirm your sovereignty? Your ability to be self-regulated and self-sufficient?

True Consent

Yes means yes. No Means no. Maybe means no! When someone asks something of you, take personal inventory and feel if it aligns with your path and is resonant with your Inner Being. Everyone is familiar with the confusing feeling when your internal realm is in a conflict between your own personal decision of what is best for you and taking care of others' needs. When we feel rushed or pressured, we give our power away. If you are unsure, wait and gather more data to make a sure and clear decision.

- On a scale from 1-10, to what degree are you honoring your internal compass?
- Why might you give in to someone else's needs or requests when they are not a match to the truth of your Inner Being? What beliefs support that behavior?

Empower Others to Be Independent

Empowering others to exercise their free will releases them from patterns of dependency. Release them to follow their highest joy. When we empower others to follow their own intuition and inner knowing, they will blossom, and everyone will benefit. Encourage others to be who they are and to form their own opinions and beliefs.

Drama Triangle: Perpetrator, Rescuer, Victim

Stephen Karpman, MD created a simple tool to understand the patterns of social conflict in relationships. The triangle includes three entry points: Rescuer, Perpetrator, and Victim. These roles have roots in our family of origin, and everyone has a habitual entry position. While people may jump from seat to seat in a conversation, eventually everyone ends up in the

Victim position unless they are able to return to their sovereign self and take full ownership of their creation.

- Where does drama play out in your relationships?
- How do you create the conditions consciously and unconsciously?
- Do you find yourself giving people unsolicited advice?
- Do you take responsibility for other people's duties? Are you the one always giving?
- Do you feel you need to be forceful to be heard or understood?
- How can you empower others to take responsibility for their own path?

Processing or Adopting Opinions of Others

When we worry about what others are doing, saying, thinking, and feeling, we drain ourselves of power. We step out of alignment with our Divine Self's wisdom and put our faith into the external environment. From this place, we are unable to make decisions for ourselves. We lose concentration because of our worry and doubt. We become stuck in the past and project our fears into the future. We cannot say no to others and are unable to confront situations with our full power.

Realize that everyone's opinions are situational and based on their own beliefs formed from their own experiences in life. Their beliefs and opinions have nothing to do with us and everything to do with them. Their interpretation of us is based on limited information and passed through the filter of their own belief system.

If we avoid confrontation because we do not want things to get worse, they probably will. If we are afraid of losing the relationship by acting and speaking authentically, we create our own prison. If others have opinions that aren't aligned with love and compassion, we can let their words pass by us. They are simply air and vibration. They cannot hurt us unless we give power to them to do so.

We are each incredibly valuable, and if a person leaves because of our honesty, we can release them and trust that more supportive friends and allies will come into our experience. Be honest about who you are and what you believe. Let it be seen. If we experience self-doubt, we can check to see if we have given away our power and formed an unhealthy dependency. We have the right to form our own opinions and believe in what is best for us.

- Are you afraid to behave or act in a certain way because of what people may think or do?
- Do you find yourself limiting yourself or holding back in any way because of what others may think, even fearing judgment from God? How does that affect you emotionally and physically?

Fear of Responsibility, Leadership, and True Empowerment

We can experience an imbalance in our Power Center if we have a fear of responsibility. We may believe that we are not able to be a leader and are afraid of taking charge. We may have judgments of power because we have seen people do harm with power and authority. We may associate wealth and power with greediness because we saw wealthy people and businesses take advantage of others. We may be afraid to stick out because of our role as a leader. We may fear power and leadership because we are afraid of failure.

Responsibility is the ability to follow our Inner Being's guidance and do what is best for us and the Greater Good of All. Accountability is the ability to take transparent ownership of our actions. What we decide to take on, we are accountable for. This means that we are ready to face situations without blaming others. These qualities give us the ability to lead and guide others on their path.

We have a responsibility to follow the desires of our souls to grow and expand through experience. When we hold ourself back from following our higher goals and aspirations, we may experience shame and guilt. When we are afraid of risk because we fear failure, we limit our growth and keep ourselves from experiencing the pleasure of success. If we desire to take action in the direction of our higher goals, we must take it or face the discomfort that comes from limiting our path.

- In what areas of your life do you procrastinate?
- Where can you show up more in your life?
- Where do you avoid people? Interactions? Places?

Discipline, Integrity, and Self-Respect

Integrity is a state of being whole and undivided by being honest and having strong moral principles and uprightness. When we are aligned with our Divine Self, we are whole and complete. When we align with our fears and doubt, we fracture ourselves into incomplete pieces.

When we act from a sense of morality and goodness, we harness our personal power. This is especially true when others are not aware of our actions or are present to witness them. Our Divine Self is always present, and when we act against our moral code or commit crimes, we shrink our personal power.

When we live a life of integrity and truth, we are prepared to express our authentic selves no matter what. We develop self-respect by living a life of righteousness and nobility. Living a noble life often means choosing courage over comfort and doing what is right versus doing what is popular, easy, and fast. When we live a noble life, we attract others who respect us because they see us as honorable.

- What gets in the way of accomplishing your goals in terms of fitness, finances, relationships, education, and spiritual growth?
- What practices and actions can you start today towards those goals?
- What support systems do you have in place to ensure that you are staying on your path? Do you have a mentor or an accountability partner?
- What rituals can you do to ensure positive momentum towards your goals and aspirations?

Solar Plexus Meditation

Close your eyes and begin to breathe consciously and deeply. If you would like, bring your hands to rest on your upper abdomen, your solar plexus. Imagine that within your solar plexus is your own personal sun. Using your breath and your imagination, make your sun grow brighter and stronger. Imagine and feel yourself as a divine, solar being. Feel your power and strength as a Divine Being of Light. If you feel any cords or attachments to your solar plexus, allow the light of your personal sun to burn them away. Feel your freedom. Feel your sovereignty.

Allow this Light and feeling to expand until it totally surrounds you. You can chant the sounds of RAM or OM to amplify this intention.

When you are finished, release the visualization. Open your eyes and continue your day with this feeling of empowerment and radiance.

FIFTY-FOUR

Heart Chakra: Divine Love

The Heart Chakra is located in the center of the chest and is associated with the color green, the wind element, and the breath of life. Universally, the heart is the symbol of our ability to love. The heart is where we express our devotion and connection to Source. The Heart Chakra bridges Spirit and the physical world, brings love-based spiritual insight to be used for heart-centered creation, and brings our human motivations up from the lower chakras to be transformed in the heart with spiritual wisdom. We broadcast this light out through our hearts to illuminate the world. Our heart sends waves of energy down through the arms and out through the hands to bless all that we touch. The heart is truly the gateway for ascension, the door to the Kingdom of Heaven. As we clear the heart of distortion, we see the Love of God shining back at us in all that we see.

The HeartMath Institute is a nonprofit organization that has researched and developed reliable, scientifically based tools to help people bridge the connection between their hearts and minds. Its research has discovered some impressive facts about the heart. When in utero, the heart develops before the brain and syncs with the heartbeat of our mother. The electromagnetic field of the heart, measuring five to eight feet away from our body, is the body's largest field and is constantly pulsing with information. More signals are sent from the heart to the brain than vice versa. The field of the heart has been measured to be 5,000 times stronger than the field of the brain.

Living "in the heart" gives you access to this powerful processing center. Living in the heart means processing our life events through the compassionate energy that is the heart center. When we focus on the pure energy at the core of our heart, we naturally emote loving-kindness, compassion, empathetic joy, equanimity, patience, and understanding.

When our Heart Center is balanced, we know that love is the most powerful force in the universe, and we see the goodness in people and the world. Our actions come from compassion, and we see and encourage goodness in others. When the Heart Chakra is balanced, we can accept the differences between ourselves and others easily. We live with a sense of unbridled joy and work to better the world around us. We are naturally generous and give from the heart without expectations. We use the heart to make decisions in our lives and receive intuitive information from our environment through the Unified Field. We understand the suffering of the world and are concerned with inequality and the harmful actions of others.

When this chakra is imbalanced, we may feel "hard-hearted" or "cold-hearted." We may build walls around our hearts to protect ourselves from getting hurt. We may see the world as a dark place, void of color and full of trickery and deceit. We may feel bitterness and be closed to the emotions of others and even be apathetic, unable to connect. We may judge ourselves and others by a harsh set of rules, regulations, and limitations. We may feel deeply hurt by others like a knife is lodged in our hearts. We may be ungiving, unloving, and grief-stricken. We may have a hard time forgiving ourselves or others and feel contempt and disdain for those who have wronged us.

When the heart is closed, we are closed to the unified field of Creation, so we are closed to our intuition and sense of the field we exist in. We may be dependent on others' love and attention because we have a gaping hole in our own love center. We may experience self-loathing and hold bitterness for others. The heart is truly where deep suffering is experienced.

We may experience health problems related to the heart and lungs. We may develop issues in the arms and hands. We may cave our chest, round the back, and feel armored and bound in the upper torso and neck. It could even be said that all illnesses and diseases stem from Heart Chakra imbalance because we have not been able to tune into the full redemptive powers of forgiveness, compassion, and unity.

What Imbalances the Heart Chakra?

Creating with the Heart vs. Creating with the Mind

The heart processes energy and emotional information. The heart can feel and sense into energy that is present and use it creatively for the greater good. It can feel into the past and into the future. It is intuitive in how it deciphers memory from the mind and information gained from the field. It leads to love and focuses on the positive of every situation. When we process experiences through the wisdom of the heart, we can never "get it wrong" because everything is processed from the perspective of growth and love.

The mind is the home of the egoic sense of "I" and "me," the limited self. The mind can create linearly. It can plan and strategize. It qualifies and values one experience over another. The mind, contaminated by the world's conditioned thought programs, distorts our reality through its biases and limited perspective.

If the mind is the realm where the battle between "good and evil" plays out, the heart is where we find true and lasting peace. The heart is the gateway to the Kingdom of Heaven. It is our access pathway to our Inner Being and the power that creates worlds. We can use our heart to process the energy of the mind so that we can move through life, making choices that align with our highest destiny pathway and the greater good of the All.

- Do you believe there is a right way or a wrong way to be or act?
- In what areas of your life do you hold polarized judgment?
- Where do you believe in good and bad, holy and sinful, safe and unsafe, worthy and unworthy? How do those beliefs feel in the body? How do they affect your mood and relationships with other people?

Expectations: Moving from the Heart to the Mind

When we have expectations of people and the world to be a certain way, we set ourselves up for disappointment. When we expect something, we move out of the heart's present awareness and into the duality of the mind and ego. The ego wants to control and possess reality. The mind wants to understand it. The heart has no expectations and loves what is.

Self-hatred and self-loathing develop when we place unreasonable expectations on ourselves and do not process life events with loving compassion. This may happen because we identify as our behaviors and actions, resulting in feeling guilt and regret. We are allowed to make mistakes and grow from them. When we punish ourselves from a perfectionist mindset, we close the heart and dampen our light.

The reconciliation process of the Ho'oponopono prayer "*I am sorry, I love you, please forgive me, I thank you.*" opens the heart to love and makes peace possible. You can say these phrases, sing them, write them, or even paint them. Use the process found in these words to reconcile your relationship with yourself, with another, with Source, with Gaia, or with anything or anyone else in your life that needs forgiveness.

We can forgive others even though they have not forgiven us. We can release the hurt. We can release the anger. If we genuinely want to be free from suffering, reconciliation and forgiveness are the way. If you forgive others and forgive yourself, half of the work is done, and peace is more possible for everyone involved. We do not have to condone the harmful actions of others, but we can forgive.

- What small things can you forgive today?
- Can you forgive someone who did something that caused you suffering that has a medium charge?
- Can you forgive someone who did a terrible thing to you?
- Can you forgive people who have done the worst things to the planet, animal life, and humanity? Where can you do your part in healing resentment?

Egoic Love versus Universal Unconditional Love

Unconditional Love is the animating force and foundation of the universe. The Source of Love is always flowing to us, and there is nothing we can do to stop this outpouring of Love and Grace. We can, however, block this love from coming into our experience. When the heart is closed, we inhibit the flow of Universal Love that wants to express itself through us.

The ego can create an idea of love that is based on possession and control. Much of what mainstream culture considers to be love has truly little to do with the heart chakra. It focuses on the concept of love created by the personality. This type of love is generated in the lower chakras and is not the same as the Divine Love found within the heart.

When we are in egoic love, we see love as a sense of ownership and contractual agreement. Egoic love uses the attention, presence, and affection of another person to fulfill sensory desires. Egoic love has rules and regulations for how love and affection can be expressed. Ego says that we can only love one person, and they are required to fulfill us on all levels.

When we love without conditions, we set our relations free to follow their own path. We allow them to be and explore as they wish. Loving a person does not mean we control them. Being loved does not mean we are being controlled. All are free to follow their highest joy from moment to moment. We accept them as they are and take responsibility for our own joy and well-being.

Egoic trust is a concept based on control and manipulation. Egoic love says, "I trust you to do what I want to satisfy my needs." while Universal Love says, "I release you to do what you need to support yourself. I love you as you are." True trust is placing our faith in Source and knowing that all is happening as it should and that we are eternally provided for.

Everyone is behaving in a way that reflects their own beliefs and attitudes towards life. Another person's hurtful actions reflect their own mindset and have nothing to do with us. We can look at someone's behavior and intuitively know what actions to take. Maybe that means not being around them. Maybe that means using our voice to communicate that we are experiencing hurt. We can make adjustments in our relationships without any love being lost.

- When do you withhold affection towards others?
- When do you close your heart to others?
- When do you feel hurt by others?
- When do you want to punish others?
- When do you feel your judgments and rage are justified?

Blind Love and Blind Faith

Blind love and blind faith happen when our expression and experience of love are based on illusion and fantasy. This happens when we run with our emotions, sensations, and fantasies and do not see ourselves and the other in truth. This type of love is full of dependency and impulses to maintain the illusion and naive story we tell ourselves. When we live like this, we ignore what is right in front of our noses and make a habit of overlooking or denying the reality of other people's hurtful actions and behaviors.

True love is willing to look at deeper truth and accept the deeper meanings of what we find. We can love and keep boundaries. We can love and keep our intelligence, clarity, and groundedness.

- Are there people in your life that are behaving in a way that does not honor you?

- Are there any relationships where you can be more honest with yourself about certain dynamics or red flags?
- What spells do you cast on yourself to habitually overlook these issues?

Feelings of Betrayal: A Broken Heart

Everyone is always following what they feel is best for them from moment to moment. They are doing their best, even if they may be guided by selfishness, greed, anger, or fear. They are doing what they think is best, and it has little to do with "you." In this way, there is no such thing as a betrayal. People are following their Inner Being and mind.

If you feel as though someone has taken something from you or betrayed you in any way, they have given you something much more valuable. They teach you where your dependencies are. They teach you where you are conditional with love. They teach you where you have put your faith in something outside of yourself to bring you joy and completion. We can take full responsibility for our emotions and mental health and understand that everything is happening for a higher purpose. Everyone is free to do what they need to do to allow joy and love into their lives. When everyone is free to choose, love abounds. This does not mean that you condone negative behavior or spiritually bypass it, but you can come to a deeper understanding of the cause of your suffering.

- Where do you blame others for your suffering?
- Do you believe someone or some group has betrayed you or your family?
- Can you grow in compassion and a higher understanding of the nature of your suffering?

Honor Thy Body as Thy Temple

Self-soothing and self-care honor the union of the body, mind, and spirit. Dedicate your life to learning to love yourself more. When you love yourself, you experience love with others easily. Take long baths. Go into nature. Dress yourself up. Sing to yourself. Marry your essence and promise to cherish it forever and ever. Fall endlessly in love with the light that you are.

- Do you take enough "time off" and have enough alone time?

- Do you treat yourself to luxuries or gifts from time to time? Do you feel guilty or feel you need to justify this?
- How can you treat your body better?
- How can you treat your heart better?

Desires of the Bodymind

We have many layers of desire, manifesting, and evolving. We have desires of the body to walk, run, and eat. We have desires of the mind to grow, learn, and plan. Our senses desire to touch, taste, smell, hear, and experience. All are temporary experiences and beautiful.

True and lasting nourishment comes from spiritual growth and our alignment with the Love of the Universe. When we tend to the desire of the heart and soul to evolve and expand with love, we are filled with the deepest sense of satisfaction and wholeness. When we follow the desires of the senses, we follow the maya, the illusion.

The heart desires recognition. It desires purification. It desires to love with no bounds. When we do the work to dissolve our limiting beliefs and heal from our past traumas, we allow the Love of the Universe to flow through us, as us, and we embody the Light of the Divine.

- Where are your addictions? How do they affect your life?
- What needs are you not taking care of?
- Do you have a strong and consistent spiritual practice?
- How can you expand or deepen it?

Creating Coherence in Your Life

"Coherence is the state when the heart, mind, and emotions are in energetic alignment and cooperation," HeartMath Institute Research Director Dr. Rollin McCraty says. "It is a state that builds resiliency — personal energy is accumulated, not wasted — leaving more energy to manifest intentions and harmonious outcomes."

Personal Coherence

When we are coherent, our heart and mind work together to find optimal experiences and creative solutions. We are living in connection with the wisdom of our inner Source and have more intuitive access and flow. We can tap into our inner technology and multidimensional being to uplevel communication with the world around us. This slows down the mind and opens our higher perceptual centers of the brain (cortical facilitation). It is said "a change of the heart changes everything," for when we live through the heart's wisdom, we are open to experiences beyond our current cognitive understanding.

Social Coherence

When we are in a state of personal coherence, everything and everyone around us benefits. We raise the vibrational frequency of the field around us and create the potential for higher outcomes for all. Our mere presence is a blessing and a catalyst for healing and spiritual growth. This can also inspire others to drop into their own state of personal coherence.

When this happens, we sync up energetically, connected heart to heart, and communicate on unseen levels. We feel each other on a deep level and hold each other in the best light.

Global Coherence

When we are in a state of personal coherence, we are connected to universal and planetary energies. We stand as a bridge between physical and nonphysical reality and feel a deep connection to All That Is. When we are in a state of coherence, we are connected to the Earth's holographic field and the collective mind of humanity. Like a moving, living prayer, we are broadcasting an invitation for global peace and unity. When we take the time to anchor ourselves in loving awareness, we create the potential for Heaven on Earth. On the New Earth, all of humanity will be united in global coherence.

Coherence Meditation: Inspired by HeartMath Institute

Close your eyes and begin to breathe deep and satisfying breaths. Feel the length of your spine and allow your shoulders to fall away from the ears. Deepen and elongate the breath and completely focus on the act of breathing for a few moments. Bring your hands to rest on your heart center and imagine that you can breathe in and out of your heart center. Imagine that in the center of your heart is a spark of divine white light. As you breathe in and out, allow that light to grow and shine brighter. Allow this light to extend beyond your body until it totally surrounds you with beautiful white light. Make it sparkle and shine. Imagine that you can breathe this Light into your being and allow it to fill your entire body.

Think of something that brings you joy. Maybe it is a loved one. Maybe it is a sunny day. Bring into your mind images, sensations, and feelings connected to this object or experience that brings you joy. Continue to breathe in and out as you imagine all of the blessings and appreciations of your life. Feel this joy spreading throughout your entire field.

You can chant the sounds of YAM, OM, HU, or AH to amplify these vibrations.

Stay with this feeling for a few moments. Then, be silent and listen to your Inner Being and return to normal breathing. When you are finished, open your eyes feeling deeply blessed by this experience.

FIFTY-FIVE

Throat Chakra: Conscious Communication

Our Throat Center radiates out from the center of our vocal instrument and is associated with the color blue and with the element of ether. It governs our ability to communicate, and I also associate this chakra with vibration and sound.

We use our voice to share our thoughts, desires, and intentions with the world. This center also gives us the ability to hear and sense what is being communicated by others. The power of the word has the potential to create or destroy. When we speak from our fear or pain, our words are like poison that can rob us and others of life force. Our words can create walls of separation that keep us from having relationships built on love and trust.

When we align our voice and communication with our divine nature, we cultivate intimate connections based on transparency and honesty. We can listen to the deeper meaning of what is being communicated by others. When we communicate from a pure center, we can turn mishaps into miracles and speak our dreams into creation.

We communicate to change our environment and modify our relationships. We use language and communication to interact with others, exchange ideas, and express ourselves. When we cannot communicate clearly, we miss out on opportunities and confuse ourselves and others.

When our Throat Center is balanced, we communicate our thoughts, desires, and intentions clearly. We are articulate and deliberate with our use of language and expression, using our voice as a powerful tool for manifestation. We are persuasive and charismatic and easily manifest our ideas into reality. We comfortably speak in front of groups and may actually enjoy the act of speaking publicly. We are succinct and compassionate with our words and value the honesty and straightforwardness of others. We can hear the deeper truth in what is being communicated by others and speak directly to the soul of another person. We value quietness and use our awareness to listen to the communication of our Inner Being.

When our Throat Center is imbalanced, we may easily follow other people's will because we cannot communicate our own desires and vision. We may have trouble finding the right words to express our own perspective. We may lie, tell partial truths, exaggerate the truth, and play with words to get what we want. We may say what we think others want to hear. We may feel like something is blocked in our throats as we suppress our voice out of fear and self-doubt. We may drop our own plans at the first perceived sign of conflict and opposition. We may speak harshly and use nasty words that are bitter and riddled with resentment.

If the energy of our throat center is overactive, we may try extra hard to convince others. We may be overly talkative with the belief that no one is listening. We may cut people off, talk over them, or interrupt other people's sentences. We may hold our breath in our chest, waiting for the moment to jump in, unable to deeply listen to what others are communicating. If the throat center is underactive, we may have an underlying belief that it is best if we are silent and act timid or shy. We may withhold information out of fear of what people may think or do. We may say things we do not really mean and feel guilty later.

Imbalances of the throat chakra can manifest as throat, ear, and thyroid issues. Often people will start to lose their hearing because they need to listen to their Inner Being more attentively. Those with hyperactive thyroids most likely have subconscious beliefs that propel them to be overactive talkers while hypoactive means someone's belief system is keeping them from speaking their truth or else tells them that they should be quiet.

What Imbalances the Throat Chakra?

Imbalances in the Throat Center have roots in the first four chakras because we need to feel safe, connected to our inherent value, empowered, and connected to our heart's deepest truth to communicate honestly and transparently. We may be afraid of damaging or losing relationships. We may be afraid of sounding harsh and filter what we are communicating. We may feel and fear that others may think we are unintelligent. We may fear being wrong and remain silent. We may be afraid of causing conflict or debate. Maybe we are uncertain what could happen if we express ourselves fully and authentically. If we feel inferior or even superior to others, we may adapt our communication and expression to match that belief. We could fear being abandoned, shamed, ridiculed, or rejected for communicating or expressing authentically. We may fear to express ourselves on any level simply because we are afraid of being vulnerable.

This is a massive wound for the human collective as we emerge from the Dark Ages. Females and the Divine Feminine have been repressed and oppressed for thousands of years. Many of us carry lifetimes of trauma related to our throat center. A big part of our awakening is healing the wounds of the past and finding our voice. We also have a responsibility to use our voice for the voiceless, including the women, children, Indigenous peoples, Gaia, animals, trees, and others who have been silenced and oppressed.

What Balances the Throat Center?

Take Responsibility for Your Reality

Everything is happening because on some level, consciously or unconsciously, we have willed it into being. Our fears, thoughts, actions, intentions, and vibrational offerings create our reality. No one else is to blame for our experience of reality. When we take authority over our experience, we use our voice to create the life we want.

Every time we say the words "I will" and "I am," the following words have an effect on the body and mind. These are spells we put on ourselves. Be very deliberate and care-FULL of how you use your words.

- What thoughts and communication patterns cause you suffering?
- Do you speak in ways that belittle or disempower yourself or others?
- Do you speak in a way that paints a negative picture or victim perspective of your life or future?

Honesty and Integrity: Tell the Truth

Telling mistruths and lies blocks our Throat Center. It depletes us of life force energy immediately. This lowers our vibration and changes our point of attraction. Instead of saying mistruth, we can say, "I don't know," when we do not. Instead of speaking on someone else's behalf, we can say, "This is not my place. It is better to ask them." Gossip and character assassination hurt us way before it hurts another.

- Where do you tell white lies?
- Do you exaggerate or withhold information out of fear of what the outcome might be or out of fear of judgment?
- Where do you speak on behalf of others?

Be Impeccable With & Honor Your Words

When we say we are going to do something, we should be sure that we can follow through. When we honor our words, our yes means "yes," and our no means "no." If we are uncertain, we can communicate that we need more time or that we are not certain that we can commit at this time. We can feel into our body and sense our Inner Being to feel our truth. If something is even a little wobbly, honor that. If we make a decision, we are allowed to change our mind. Communicate it as soon as you are aware of the change.

- Do you follow your own agreements?
- How likely are you to follow through with verbal agreements?
- How do you notify people when you become aware of changes?
- Do you have any hesitation? How does it feel in the body?

Lost in Translation

Try your best to communicate important matters face to face, or at the very least make a phone call. Too often, important matters are discussed via text or social media. So much is lost in translation. Most of what is communicated is nonverbal anyway. We are empathetic and observant beings. We need body language, energy, and the presence of the other beings we are communicating with to experience all that is being expressed and communicated fully.

- Have you called the people you love lately?
- Are there any communications that you should address more personally rather than through text or email?

Check connections to Solar Plexus, Sacral, and Root Center beliefs to clarify the Throat Center distortions.

Release Guilt

Guilt happens when we have not met our own expectations. If we do not settle our guilt, the situation, circumstances, or feeling comes around repeatedly. We can get caught in a cycle of behavior-guilt-justification, behavior-guilt-justification, etc.

Our guilt is there as a teacher. It shows us where we are off in our beliefs and helps us to adjust our behavior to achieve optimal and pleasurable experiences. We can realize that the guilt is self-created, strive to understand its origins, release it, and find a solution that reflects expanded awareness.

A lot of religions teach that God judges and punishes us based on our actions. Source/God/All-That-Is loves you completely and wants your success and liberation. There is infinite grace for all our stumbles. Guilt is the creation of the ego. Each ego has a different definition of what behaviors are unworthy or punishable. These are all illusions. Divine Love and Grace are available at all times for ALL people, regardless of past behavior. Release guilt and allow your voice to express freely.

- Where can you forgive yourself for past deeds?
- What lifestyle and ethical changes can you implement today to create a more authentic life?

Release Jealousy & Realize Equality

We experience jealousy when comparing a limited aspect of someone else with limited aspects of ourselves. Experiencing ourselves as inferior or superior in comparison creates division and separation. Everyone and everything are equal. Everyone has a unique purpose and unique expression to accomplish within the continuum of evolution.

- What criteria have you used to evaluate who is above and who is below you?
- Do you think you are better than others? Inferior?
- Do you envy what others have?
- Do you compare yourself to others?

Release Beliefs of Dependency

When we feel that we are dependent on others or that others are dependent on us, we can say what we think they want to hear or use our words to manipulate them. When we have healthy interdependence in our relationships, each person honors and values the other's honesty, transparency, and vulnerability. When we release beliefs of unhealthy dependency, everyone is responsible for their own well-being and experience.

- Where are you afraid to take action or assert boundaries because of beliefs of dependency?

Notice Argument Patterns

"Never argue with a fool." —Albert Einstein

As people argue, they get more and more specific about what they do not like, which creates a stronger and stronger negative charge, attracting more instability and hostility. We have become a culture of "debate" versus a society of mature, transparent dialogue. The ego says these are "my" beliefs and has a hard time accepting differences. The Self can hold perspective and be open to seeing from another's perspective without fear of the loss of power or identity.

When a conversation gets heated, go general and light. If the person you are communicating with wants to get deeper and deeper into the details and suffering and you follow along, a professional arguer who is unmovable in their perception and intention to dominate will eventually wear you down to their emotional and vibrational level and overpower you. You know what is true in your heart. Speak your truth simply, then let it go. You are not responsible for changing someone's mind. They are. Walk away and find something better to do.

- Do you have people that you regularly argue with?
- Do you expect people should see things how you do because your way is right or better?
- How open are you to changing your own perceptions and beliefs when presented with new data? Is there room for all perspectives and opinions?

- Do you try to "win" in conversations? If so, the relationship loses.
- What happens to your physical body when you argue?

Heart-Centered Communication: Identifying with Your Soul

Speak from your loving heart. If you cannot speak from a loving place, it is best to find another time to communicate and express what is rising within you. Identifying with your suffering — "I am angry." versus "I am the awareness that experiences anger." are two very different perspectives. Spend some quiet time in reflection and self-soothing to raise your vibration. Spend time with your Inner Being to find the message from your Higher Self.

Illusion of Good & Bad

Good and bad are judgments and definitions made up by the dualistic nature of the human ego. Each person has their own definition of good and bad. Judging something or someone as bad lowers our vibration and causes us to suffer.

When we look at our experiences and relationships with compassion, when we look deeply into the cause of the behavior or experience, we can find compassion and a higher spiritual meaning. Everything simply IS, but we place meaning and judgments on Creation. When we accept things as they are and release our definitions, we can see the bigger picture.

- Where do you project meaning onto events and people?

Frustration: Things Left Unsaid

When you are in a state of frustration, your intelligence stops working. Stop. Take a breath. If you are frustrated and others are involved, remember that you are frustrated with the experience and not the souls of the beings involved. People are not their behaviors. Learn to work with their shortcomings. Set a boundary if necessary.

- What are some healthy ways to deal with conflict to keep your cool so you can speak from your center?
- What is the core cause of your frustration? Check your dependencies.

The Magic of Words

Words can be like white magic or black magic. They can be in Service to the Greater Good or service to our ego. As we become more and more deliberate with our words, intonation, and delivery, we begin to become powerful masters of manifestation.

Using our words for dark magic happens when we use words with the vibration of fear and judgment. Using our words for white magic means that we use our words to intentionally elevate our experience with love. Realize that it is not WHAT you speak but HOW you communicate that matters. Are you speaking from fear and suffering? Are you speaking from love and compassion? Coming from love means that there is love within you and that you create from that compassionate perspective. This type of love is not superficial. It is unconditional and regenerative.

- How can you use your words, spoken internally and externally, to create more of what you want?
- When do you use your words to give power to the shadow creation?

Throat Chakra Meditation

Close your eyes and begin to breathe consciously and deeply for a few breaths. Bring your hands to lightly touch or hold them slightly away from your throat while you tune into the subtle vibrations of the hands and Throat Center. Imagine that the center of your throat has a beautiful, dazzling flame of blue-white light. Softly begin to make long tones. Make them feel soothing and imagine that the sounds are originating from your Inner Being. You may use a sound like HAM, OM, or any other sound that feels good for you. If any judgmental thoughts arise, let them dissolve into the healing tones and bring your awareness back to your Inner Being.

Allow yourself to be playful and create your own angelic tones, your own language of Light.

Connect with a sense of beauty and orchestrate a tonal symphony with many ranges of tones. Let the tones move throughout your body. Send the healing vibrations into all of your tissues and cells. Imagine that each cell begins to reverberate with these healing tones. Fill your body with light and vibration. Do this for at least a minute or two.

Once you are complete, return to silence, and feel the vibrations and sensations in your throat center. When you are finished, open your eyes.

FIFTY-SIX

Brow Chakra: Divine Vision

The Brow Center, located within the forehead and associated with the color indigo, gives us spiritual sight and the ability to perceive our inner and outer world. This inner eye gives us the ability to see beyond physicality and perceive through foresight and intuition. There are differing elemental associations with this chakra, but I connect it to Light.

Often called the "third eye," this center senses the blueprint and matrix of the Unified Field and what is needed to manifest an idea into reality. Like an internal movie screen, the Brow Center allows us to receive internal imagery from other people, our Higher Self, guides, and Source. It allows us to project imagery and thoughtforms into the matrix to draw forth our manifested desires and outcomes like a broadcasting device and homing beacon. It connects us to the essence of life, giving us the ability to make clear decisions that resonate with the Light of our Inner Being. Physical manifestations of dysfunction in the Brow Center include issues with the eyes and brain.

When this center is balanced, we can quickly see the inner workings of things and what is needed to maintain balance and harmonic evolution. We enjoy the challenge of finding creative solutions and can lead with a clear vision, mental focus, and intuition. We are able to create goals and envision the pathway to successfully achieving them. We can ride the waves of life with ease and make quick decisions sourced from profound understanding and insight. We can understand the deeper intention of people's motives through a telepathic connection and exchange. We can self-reflect and receive guidance from psychic perceptions. We can understand complex issues while also having the openness to see life from a different perspective.

When this center is imbalanced, we are easily confused and have trouble focusing and grounding. Our uncertainty and lack of consistent and clear focus on our vision create issues with manifesting what we truly wish to cultivate. Decision-making is slow because we overthink the possibilities. We may force our ideas and perceptions on others because we cannot think beyond our current paradigm. We may be stubborn, skeptical, and have unwavering tunnel vision regarding our beliefs. We may resent others for their achievements because we cannot see our own potential or feel blocked when turning our dreams into reality. We may be skeptical of new systems and new concepts because we do not understand them and cannot think outside our own paradigm. We may avoid the reality of our life circumstances, seeing only what we want to see.

Health problems associated with this energy center include all cognitive and brain health-related issues such as memory loss and difficulty with concentration and also include issues with the eyes, ears, and nose.

What Imbalances the Brow Chakra?

Confusion: Trouble Making Decisions

This center becomes imbalanced when we are afraid of making the wrong decisions or afraid of a future failure. This creates a struggle in our mind as we bounce back and forth between potential outcomes and risks. When we are in alignment, we make decisions that honor our Inner Being and our environment. We make decisions based on our NOW moment. What feels good now? What honors my soul now? Be careful with this as the ego/mind often masquerades as enlightened consciousness and many avoid spiritual growth by creating comfort for the mind. When we take care of our own energy and Inner Being first, everything else falls into place.

- When making a decision, do you feel pressure to make "the right decision?"
- What concerns do you habitually have when making day-to-day decisions and bigger decisions when more is at stake?
- How do you respond to inner imagery, inner guidance, and intuition?
- Do you follow your guidance or doubt and suppress it?

Living in the Past

We are only supposed to know the past happened. We are not supposed to live there. Our awareness of our past experiences gives us an idea of what we enjoy and what we do not enjoy. Our future is made of our choices and our vibration of the present moment. So often, people project their fears and traumas from the past into their vision of the future. When you hold a vision and vibration of what you do not want, you create it. To manifest what we truly desire, we can hold an inspired vision and emotional vibration that matches our desired outcome.

To make a decision, connect with your Inner Being and your Inner Light, then ask your body, mind, and senses what decision is best for you NOW. Asking others blocks your own intelligence and may confuse you even more. What decision inspires YOU? What decision honors YOUR Inner Being and Divine Self?

- Do you project fearful outcomes into your future when planning and making decisions? If so, what happened in your past that makes you feel that way?
- What is your general outlook on the future?

Physical & Mental Attachments

Clinging to or grasping at people, places, things, and ideas keeps us from seeing the bigger picture. We may begin to believe that we NEED something and that our happiness would be lost without our object of desire. Attachments cause suffering and limit our ability to see the bigger picture.

Shedding attachments does not mean neglecting ourselves or keeping ourselves from having experiences that we enjoy. It does not mean we should leave our beloved, sell our house, or not have nice things. It is, however, inaccurate to believe that our happiness comes from having those things. Our partner may decide to leave, or our house may burn down, and now the same object that once was associated with joy is associated with suffering. We easily allow joy to move through us when our manifestations match our desires. Even in the absence of them, we can still allow joy into our experience. Everything outside of ourselves just simply exists, and we project meaning onto it. When we release our attachments, we can experience life in pure loving awareness without the need to cling to any circumstance or manifestation to experience joy and wholeness.

- Where are your attachments? What outside of yourself do you give power to?
- How do you behave when you feel attached and dependent?

Desires & Aversions

Strong feelings of distaste, resentment, and resistance inhibit our perception of the divine perfection in all things. When we have deep-seated hatred or detestation, we lower our vibration and poison our own self. If we condemn something outside of ourselves, we are the ones who experience the suffering connected to the judgment. When we learn to release judgment and the resistance it generates, we can see life without the lens of duality.

- Where are your aversions? Where do you have automatic responses of rejection and denial?

Egoic Identity Structure

The ego, the personality, is our sense of "me" or "I." The ego is not our True Nature because it changes and evolves. Sometimes it is present and sometimes it is not such as in deep sleep. It is a projection of the mind that veils our True Nature.

Ego identification creates an illusion that we are separate from others. It takes limited pieces of information and creates definitions and judgments based on that limited information. The ego filters our present and future through past experiences and trauma. When we release our ego's definitions and positions, we can perceive the world clearly. To perceive clearly, it is essential that we connect with the power of our Inner Being that sees beyond concept, duality, definition, and judgment.

- Where do you have attachments and emotional investments in the belief of a separate self?
- What instinctual drives do you act upon that do not serve your highest and best growth?

Ignorance

Ignorance, misconceptions, misunderstandings, and incorrect knowledge block people from making clear decisions that support their highest development. To be born on Earth is to be born into ignorance. Our body could not sustain the full brilliance of our True Nature; it would burn out!

It is okay to be uneducated and ignorant about things. You can always learn more. Education empowers the individual to make better decisions. We can strive to dissolve our ignorance by actively learning and growing. We can read, study, and become wiser on any subject and choose an informed position.

- Are there topics or areas of life that you feel drawn to learn more about?
- How often do you read sacred texts?
- What practices of self-study do you implement regularly?
- How do you expand your internal library?

Will to Live: Fear of Death and Change

The desire to keep living and the fear of change are buried deep within our subconscious. The fear of death can keep us from seeing life clearly and from doing things that we may truly enjoy. If we cling to physical life, we cling to impermanence and we inherently suffer. We may subconsciously protect ourselves and "keep it safe" to avoid the real or imagined danger that keeps us from the spiritual growth available in new situations. We can develop trust in the support of the Divine and rest in knowing that we are always guided.

- What are your beliefs around death and what happens to you when you die?
- Do you have any fears of what the repercussions of your death may bring?
- How do you deal with the death of other people or the truth that we all go through the death experience?

Brow Center Meditation

Close your eyes and breathe consciously and deeply. You can bring one hand to the front of your brow and one hand to the back of your skull, cupping the bony ridge of the occiput. Sense the space between your hands. Imagine a spark of light within your brow center that grows bigger and brighter as you breathe in and out. If your mind is busy, imagine that your thoughts are like clouds in the sky and allow them to drift by until you see only a beautiful, clear blue sky.

Take a few moments to envision yourself as clear and confident. Allow your mind to generate images, feelings, and sensations of what it would be like if everything you desire to create was already here. Where would you live? What kind of activities would you be involved in? How would your relationships look if everything were ideal? What would you create with your time? What would the world look like? How would it feel to be your ideal future self? How would you move in the world? Have fun envisioning the images and evoking the feelings of your ideal future reality.

Envision your neural pathways weaving new circuitry to prepare to "dock" with that future reality. Feel your cells beginning to light up, transform, and prepare to experience this ideal reality. Feel the universe restructuring to bring you all that you desire. Feel your deservedness of perfection in all ways. Charge yourself up with pure creative potential.

When you are finished, you can chant the sounds of OM to amplify these healing intentions. When you are finished, drop the visualization, return to normal breathing, and open your eyes.

FIFTY-SEVEN

Crown Chakra: Divine Limitlessness

The Crown Center, blooming from the crown of the head, is the entryway of universal consciousness into our physical body. Different traditions have different elemental associations. I think of it as the unity of all elements, sounds, and vibrations or the pure thoughtform transmission of the divine energy.

This chakra is called the "thousand-petaled lotus" and is associated with brilliant white or radiant violet. It is our connection to the greater Universal Hologram of Unity and Oneness. We use this center when we are in experiences of wonder and connection to All That Is such as when we walk through the magic of a forest or look at a beautiful sunset. As we open this center, we allow the Light of the Divine to fill our being with grace and openness.

Through this center, we trust in Divine Timing and our higher understanding and know that all is in Divine Perfection. We know that everything is happening for the greater good. It is our connection to our battery (Source) and the limitless energy of the Divine. This center is activated through acts of service and devotion. We see the image of the Crown Chakra around paintings of Jesus, the Holy Mother, Quan Yin, and Buddha to show the power of their enlightenment made possible through their Crown Center. Physical dysfunction of Crown Chakra imbalances involves issues with the brain.

When the Crown Center is balanced, we may feel like we are wearing a shining crown of Light. We radiate presence and patience and are in collaboration with Divine Timing. We experience synchronicities and feel connected to the magic and miracles of Life. We are deeply satisfied as we are nourished through our connection to All That Is, and we ARE that! We are connected to our soul purpose and have deliberate intent in our interactions with Life. We see mishaps and mistakes as learning opportunities and use them to grow consciously. We easily guide and support others because we are tapped into our Divine Essence. We experience bliss, gratitude, and a deep connection with Life and take personal responsibility for our alignment. We experience the miraculous unfolding of life seen through direct perception, openness, and bliss.

When this center is imbalanced, we are disconnected from our battery and divine guidance. We may place our faith in external authority figures, government systems, and religious figures. We may be easily discouraged and feel spiritually disconnected, blaming our misfortunes on destiny, genetics, our culture, ethnicity, luck, God, or the universe. This can cause depression, hopelessness, worthlessness, and despair. We may feel that life is meaningless and without purpose. We may be critical of other people's beliefs about politics and world affairs. This is the center of religious fanaticism, grandeur, and the God/Messiah complex. We may desire spiritual dominance over others, even to the point of being worshipped by them. The opposite is also true. We may deny spiritual reality or be critical of others' spiritual practices and beliefs.

What Imbalances the Crown Center?

Dissatisfaction

In each moment, we are currently receiving everything that we are a vibrational match to. We do not get more for being a "good person." We do not receive less for being a "bad person." Look at society, and you will see this is true. If we desire more and it is not manifesting, we can grow and change. The universe is energy and vibration. We can raise our vibration and become a match to our desires.

When we hold the energy of dissatisfaction, we hold the vibration of lack of manifested desire, and what we want cannot come to us. We are blocking our own desires from manifesting. We can find gratitude for what we have and do the work to grow spiritually to achieve our higher aspirations.

- Where can you grow in appreciation for yourself and the blessings of your life?
- In what areas of your life do you experience dissatisfaction?

Perceived Limitations

The Crown Center connects us to our infinite potential. It is our connection to the Oneness, and it connects us to the truth of our limitlessness.

Our beliefs of limitation, whether self-created or indoctrinated from the world, keep us from experiencing the fullness of who and what we are. If we have beliefs of limitation, we will experience them. We can release our beliefs of limitation and allow our intelligence to guide us through each moment of discovery and expansion.

When we project our beliefs of limitation onto others, we cannot see them in their full potential. We see them in limitation. When we empower others to be more, do more, and follow their own guidance, we watch them blossom into their fullness. This is true love.

To reach our full potential, we can dream bigger and allow our imagination to dream up a new reality and paradigm. We are here to develop spiritualized consciousness. We are here to push the edges of what we think is real. We are pioneers on the leading edge of consciousness with the blessed gift of this life to pioneer new frontiers of perception and embodiment.

- Where do you believe you are limited?

Fear of Death

Fear of any kind immediately distorts our crown and root chakras, cutting us off from our connection to the Earth and our connection to Source. When we leave this body, we live on in other forms. Most of what we are is outside of this body. We are eternal beings. When we fear death, we keep ourselves from receiving all the wonderful energy of the universe that wants to flow through us. To truly live, we need to make peace with the fact that we will leave this body one day.

This is apparent when observing who in the population is stepping into sovereignty and ascension and who is hiding away in fear and buying the media and government narratives. Fear closes the Crown chakra and keeps people from receiving the higher evolutionary coding. Truly, these next few years will "separate the wheat from the chaff" as we are presented with opportunities to reconcile all fear and come into Trust and Unity with our True Nature.

- Have you made peace with the idea that you will experience physical death?
- Have you made peace with the idea that those you love will experience physical death?

The Illusion of Luck

Luck is a superstitious belief that blocks us from our full potential as masterful creators. Believing in luck places our power outside of ourselves. We are always manifesting what matches our vibration or what is best for our path. If we feel that we have bad luck, we can practice self-inquiry to understand what limiting beliefs or energies we hold to manifest the "bad luck."

- Where do you believe in luck or superstition? Where do you place power outside of your own divine ability to manifest?

Traumatic Experiences

Emotional and physical trauma can keep us locked in our past experiences. It can keep us focused on the transient parts of our smaller self (i.e., mind, emotions, body) so that we lose awareness of our Divine Self. We could think, "Why me?" or even blame God, "Why have you forsaken me?" Healing our trauma allows us to open to our Higher Self and our limitlessness.

- Do you blame God for anything? Do you feel cursed or limited by your past actions?

Distorted Ideas about Money, Wealth, and Power

We are powerful beings of Creation. To embody that potential, we can investigate our ideas about wealth, money, and power. We are currently getting everything we deserve, and we are worth SO MUCH MORE. The universe is abundant in nature. There is plenty to go around, and there is always more. Maybe we learned that we don't deserve richness or have accepted that people with money are bad. Maybe we hoard our money out of fear that there won't be any tomorrow. When we hold the vibration of lack, that is what we create.

Money is an energy exchange that likes to flow. When we need to pay money, we can allow it to leave our possession graciously, knowing that more is always coming. When someone offers us a gift from the heart of any kind, we can receive it with gratitude. This sends a message out to the universe that we are open to receiving. This also allows the circuit of goodwill and abundance to continue flowing throughout the world. If you have a habit of evading gifts or blessings from others, notice how it feels in your body the next time an opportunity to receive arises.

- What are your beliefs about money, wealth, and power?
- How does that get outpictured in your life or keep you from taking steps that would benefit your relationships, career, and finances?

Denial of the Divine

To complete our ascension, it is essential to open to the Living Light of God, the Limitless Light of Source accessed through our own reaching towards Higher Love. This often means that we move beyond our mental constructs of the Godhead and learn to have an experiential relationship with the Divine through our crown and heart chakras. The Living God is beyond all religious concepts and beyond the duality of human consciousness. We must invite the presence of the Divine, the Holy Spirit, to make a home within us. We cannot make the quantum leap of Ascension without that relationship and harmonic connection.

The Divine Presence is always there; our True Nature always exists. When we are in our joy, the Light of Awareness is there with us. When we are doing something out of integrity, the Light of Awareness is still there as we act it out and follow the mind or the impulses of the body. It is up to each of us to commit to moment-to-moment living to perceive that unwavering, ever-present, changeless presence that pervades All!

This is especially true in these times as people have a limited perspective and understanding of what the Divine Plan is. Everything is Source. Everything is God. Nothing can ever be separate from it. When we judge something as wrong or evil, we deny the presence of the Divine within the manifestation and follow the duality. All is Source Consciousness projecting a transactional reality in evolution. As we learn to step out of the shrunken, distorted perceptions of duality, we can learn to live in fascination and awe of the many faces of the Divine. Even the battle between "good and evil" arises, abides, and dissolves within the pure brilliance of Source.

This does not mean that we should not try to improve the quality of life upon the planet or that we should spiritually bypass the suffering of others.

It means that we can face the challenges of life with this higher understanding and use our spiritual understanding to guide the world into greater states of harmony and balance.

- Is there anything that you judge as outside of or separate from God? If so, where does that belief come from?

Crown Chakra Meditation

Close your eyes and breathe consciously and deeply. Bring your attention to the crown of your head and imagine that it is opening up like a thousand-petaled lotus flower. Imagine that each petal is shining with pure white light with rainbow sparkles. Use your hands to "fluff up" the emanations of the Crown Chakra. Make it shine and make it beautiful. Imagine that universal energy is flowing into this luminous lotus, filling it with cosmic knowledge of the Divine. See this radiant energy flowing into the crown of your head. You can chant the sound of OM repeatedly and feel the vibration of this mantra radiating from the crown of your head. Give gratitude for the opportunity to awaken and unite with the Divine.

Play with this visualization for a few minutes. When you are finished, return to normal breathing, and feel the vibrations you have generated. Open your eyes and enjoy the rest of your day!

FIFTY-EIGHT

Ascension Chakras

D escribed below are some of the less commonly known chakras that are now resurfacing in human awareness. Each of them gives access to unique energies and sources of information. I have included a basic practice for each chakra to help you connect with it. In the back of the book, I have written an entire manual to guide you through the art of laying hands. Included in the "Laying Hands: Reiki and Beyond" section, you will find instructions on how to heal yourself and assist others in healing by learning to channel Source Light. There are also instructions on hand and body mudras to help your body channel and transmit spiritual light. Be sure to check it out!

Soul Star Chakra

Located approximately six inches above the head is the Soul Star Chakra. Although, I feel a more appropriate name would be the Oversoul Chakra. The Soul Star Chakra is our connection to our Higher Consciousness Identity (Higher Self) and the data bank of all knowledge and wisdom gained through our many lifetimes. When this chakra awakens, we begin to establish a bridge between our physical body and our Higher Self. This bridging prepares us for the next stage of consciousness evolution for humanity.

This part of our consciousness is connected to the Hierarchy of Light, the Star Nations, and all the Ascended Beings. Through this chakra, we begin to establish communication with these evolutionary allies. It is our connection to our Greater Divine Purpose and Cosmic Consciousness. The energy is potent, pure, and infinite.

As we begin to interact with this reservoir of Light consciously, every chakra begins to shine brighter as the codes of the Higher Consciousness begin to pour into our body and subtle energy system. The Soul Star updates our entire system from the DNA to the finest particles of light and respatializes the physical and subtle energy architecture into higher geometric harmony and vitality.

Soul Star Activation

Bring your hands to your knees, palms down, and close your eyes, practicing conscious breathing as you tune into your subtle energy and inner realm. Connect with your hara line. As you inhale, lengthen your spine. As you exhale, ground your energy and soften any tension in your body.

Gassho: Bring your hands to prayer position at the heart. Call upon the presence of the Light and feel your vibration begin to rise. Intend to activate the light of your heart, breathe into it, and expand this light. Feel the energy flow into your arms and activate the hands' chakras with the light of your heart.

Reiji-ho: Bring your prayer hands up to touch your thumbs on your forehead. Tune into the center of your skull and activate the Brow Center by intending for it to illuminate. Breathe and expand this light. Intend to activate your inner sight and your connection to the Higher Mind, your Higher Self, star lineages, and guides. Welcome their presence to be with you and ask for their loving consciousness to communicate to your Inner Being.

Bring your hands to the top of your head, palms down, fingertips touching at the center of the head, wrists lightly resting on the side of the head. Tune into the crown chakra and invite it to activate. Tune in to the sensations of your hands as they lightly float just above your head. Breathe into your sensations and invite the energy to flow powerfully as you feel the exchange of light and sensation between your crown and palm chakras. You may sweep and clean the head energetically if you feel called to. Always fill in what you clear with Light.

Begin to peel open the fingers so that the wrists rest on the sides of the head, fingers pointing up like a crown. Slide the hands up so the wrists are at the top of the head. Keep reaching the hands up until you sense that you are holding your Soul Star Chakra. You may feel it light up or even see it in your inner eye. Radiate your love from your hands into the Soul Star Chakra and feel the love there. Make it beautiful and shining bright with the brilliant, golden-white diamond light. Breathe deeply as you connect with the Soul Star and imagine its brilliance and beauty.

Invite the Great Illuminated Ones, the Hierarchy of Light, to work with you. Invite the Star Families of Light to work with you. Welcome your cosmic oversoul consciousness to activate. Breathe into this intention and notice your internal realm.

Begin to bring your hands down to rest on your head, motioning the flow of your Soul Star to connect with your crown chakra. Breathe the energy down through your crown and let it wash through every cell in your body. See each cell and strand of DNA activating with this diamond light.

Open your eyes when you are ready. Know that something deeply transformative has happened. Take this Light out into the World!

Earth Star Chakra: The Super Root

Located six to twelve inches below the feet is the Earth Star Chakra. This is our Super Root connecting us to the Earth's electromagnetic field, grounding our chakras and subtle body. It is a composting system, as we allow any dense energies to be offered to the Earth to be transmuted and cleared from our system. When this center is balanced, we feel connected to our inner power, and we dynamically interact with Gaia in a mutual energy exchange. When it is imbalanced, we may feel dizzy, disconnected, ungrounded, or lightheaded.

The Earth Star Chakra connects us to the life force of Gaia, bringing with it the codes of Inner Earth and the wisdom of the plant, animal, and mineral realms. It is said to contain our karmic imprints, DNA legacy, and information from our past lives on this planet and beyond. It unites us with wisdom from ancient times and our ancestors. It connects us to the evolutionary codes pulsing through the ley lines connecting sacred sites on and off-planet. By establishing a connection to this energy center, we are committed to our life purpose, fully embodied in the NOW moment.

Earth Star Activation

Ground, center, and tune in using Gassho and Reiji-Ho.

Start sitting to get familiar with the chakras of the feet. Bring your hands to the soles of your feet and intend to activate the foot chakras in the soles. Breathe consciously as the chakras in your hands begin to interact with the chakras in your feet. Intend them to connect and trust your sensations. Use your breath and imagination to grow the light and sensitivity in your foot chakras.

Come to standing in mountain pose, *tadasana*, with your feet under your hips. Bring your hands together in prayer at the heart center. Lightly bend the knees and press the edges of the feet into the ground to feel soft length in the legs. Breathe up and down your hara line and sense about six to twelve inches below your feet to your Earth Star Chakra. Intend to connect and know that you are. Trust your sensations.

Breath Light from Source through your hara line and ground it into the Earth Star with each exhale. Let it fractal out like the roots of a tree and spread far and deep into the planet, immersing in her energy. Make it beautiful and powerful. As you do this, imagine that the light is washing all of the dense and stagnant energies you carry down into the roots with gratitude.

Breathing in, drink up the nourishing life force of Gaia and the Earth Kingdoms of Life. Feel the knowledge and wisdom of the Golden Ages of Gaia beginning to fuse with your energy system. Feel your connection to the sacred sites of Earth and beyond. As you exhale, send the energy into the Soul Star Chakra as your entire field blooms like a cosmic fountain pulsating with rainbow light. Let the energy fractal out and create limbs of light that reach out to the higher realms and distant stars.

Breathing in and out, enjoy this exchange of information and light. When you are finished, bring your radiant field closer to you, condensing the light to a comfortable bubble around you. Ground your energy with gratitude, open your eyes, and move throughout your day as a conscious bridge between Heaven and Earth.

Zeal Chakra

The Zeal Chakra, also called the Golden Chalice, Mouth of God, or Well of Dreams, is located at the base of the skull in the occipital ridge region, radiating from the medulla oblongata.

In my research, I found varying information about chakras at the back of the head. In the ancient texts, they speak of the Bindu Chakra and place this energy center at the upper part of the back of the skull. Tradition Chinese Medicine describes the Governing Meridian that runs through this region with several energy points. Maybe the Zeal and Bindu are the same? At the time of this writing, I experience both places activated. Other writings found on the internet describe another structure called the Alta Major

Chakra. I believe all these structures are part of a complex system. Use these descriptions to guide you in your own research. Meditation on this area will reveal what is true and active within you.

The medulla oblongata oversees autonomic nervous system functions like heart and blood vessel function, heartbeat, breathing, and other mostly unconscious functions of our body. The Zeal Chakra connects with the heart's energetic systems, the third eye, crown, and spinal system, including the kundalini. Cosmic Intelligence comes in through the Zeal Chakra to flow through the entire physical and luminous system. We see this idea demonstrated in the movie *The Matrix* when the characters download programs of consciousness from the mainframe computer system into their brains and into the mind of their avatar within the matrix simulation.

As this center activates and regulates, we may begin to experience sensations in this region, including tingling, congestion, headaches, heat, and more. We can do energy work to open the pathway to make room for easier downloading and integration.

Zeal Chakra Activation

Close your eyes and begin to focus on your Inner Being. Bring the hands to the back of the skull, fingertips pointing up towards the crown of the head, wrists resting directly on or lightly over the curve of the occipital ridge.

Take a few moments to tune into the electric and magnetic qualities there. Notice your sensations and inner messaging as you breathe consciously.

Gently use your thumbs to begin to unfurl the petals, the emanations, of the Zeal Chakra. Move the thumbs from the center and outward as if spreading out the energy.

You may have to do some clearing to move out the density. Do this gently with your thumbs. Imagine pure crystalline energy and coding feeding into the emanations of the Zeal Chakra. Imagine that you are receiving evolutionary coding and healing energies from the Divine through the Zeal Chakra. Use your breath and mind to amplify the regenerative feeling.

When you are finished, bring your hands to your lap or heart center. Consciously breathe and notice your sensations. When you are complete, you can open your eyes and enjoy your new connection.

High Heart Chakra

The High Heart Chakra is slightly above the heart center, originating from the thymus gland under a bony protrusion below the center of the clavicle.

This is the Sacred Heart connected to Divine Love. Awakening this High Heart Center brings us out of the old model of conditional love and into the ever-extending grace of unconditional love. Having a healthy High Heart Chakra gives us a healthy immune system as the thymus regulates immune system function. Connecting from this center before we speak ensures compassionate communication and deeper understanding. It brings us into the energy of reconciliation and trust. Connecting with the center before healing sessions opens the pathways of selfless service so that the love of Source can flow through us.

High Heart Activation

Bring your fingers and palpate this region until you find the little bump in the high center of the sternum and begin to lightly tap the bony area with the pad of your fingers. Allow the vibration to echo deep and far into your sternum with the intention of awakening your Sacred Heart. Allow your breath and mind to penetrate deeply into this energy field to invigorate and illuminate this center. Begin to tone or hum, directing the vibrations into this region. With your intention, connect with Divine Love as if the Sun is beginning to rise within your Sacred Heart. Do any clearing that you feel is necessary here. Connect to a sense of gratitude and appreciation for the blessings of your life.

Bring your hands to your lap and feel your sensations. Notice your mood and thoughts. Enjoy your renewed vibration.

GATEWAY FIVE: LAYING OF HANDS

Reiki & Beyond

This section instructs the reader in the healing art of the laying of hands. Instruction is given for personal healing, sharing healing energy with others, and working together in a group to channel spiritual Light.

FIFTY-NINE

Reiki: Laying of Hands

Reiki Precepts:
Just for today, I will give thanks for my many blessings.
Just for today, I will not worry.
Just for today, I will not be angry.
Just for today, I will do my work honestly.
Just for today, I will be kind to my neighbor and every living thing.
—Dr. Mikao Usui

Many ancient cultures around the world have systems of healing that involve the laying of hands to clarify, heal, and balance body systems. As a child, I was fascinated by the stories of Jesus and the disciples healing people from illness and even resurrecting the dead. When I heard or read these stories, something moved within me as I fantasized about what it might be like to do something like this.

During my awakening process, I was introduced to the Usui System of Natural Healing, more commonly referred to as *Reiki*. This system gave me the foundational teachings of the laying of hands and channeling Divine Energy for healing. The dogma and limitations of how the method was taught by some teachers inspired me to continue searching for a Higher Truth regarding channeling and casting light (laying of hands). Contemporary use of the word "Reiki" has become synonymous with the laying of hands and spiritual light casting.

Since learning *Reiki*, I have studied other philosophies of hands-on healing from different perspectives. My ideas of what Reiki is have evolved beyond what is usually taught in traditional Western practices of Reiki. I have also learned much about hands-on healing through my clients during hypnosis sessions. I have merged all this information into a practice that I call Embodied Light, although these practices are inherently interwoven throughout all my teachings and offerings.

Embodied Light is a system of practices you can use to raise your personal vibration and guide you into your most radiant embodied expression. These practices are easy to learn, and anyone can use them. Embodied Light's system uses meditation techniques, breathing practices, healing touch, movement, and energy attunements to support you in feeling grounded, centered, and joyously free.

These practices, many of which are in this book, focus the intention of one's being on compassionate, heart-based living. All ancient traditions speak of the power of the heart and the importance of beliefs based on unconditional love and reverence for life. As we learn to concentrate on spiritual principles like forgiveness, gratitude, bravery, honesty, and unconditional love, we can manifest a world that reflects those same values.

Embodied Light training encourages the cultivation of individual spirituality and a personal relationship with the Divine Source. We honor the Light and Wisdom of all traditions and faith practices. These practices can create a new spiritual path for yourself or enhance the religious and spiritual practices you already study.

What is Reiki?

Reiki is made of two Japanese words *Rei* and *Ki*. *Rei* means "spiritual wisdom," and *ki* means energy.

The laying of hands works with what Dr. J.J. Hurtak, the writer of *The Keys of Enoch*, calls the Shekinah Universe, the inner universe that transforms Creation. The power of the laying of hands comes from the Shekinah, the Divine Presence/Holy Spirit which activates the spiritual gifts in humanity. It is what people call Reiki — the nurturing, regenerative Light force of the Divine.

When a practitioner lays hands on a client, or when a person "runs energy" for self-healing, I teach my students to intentionally connect to Source/God/Goddess and invite the Divine Energies to flow through them to use for healing. As the energy passes through the channel of the practitioner, it raises their vibration to match the higher frequency of energy that begins to flow through them from the Source.

This should put anyone's religious fears to sleep as the number one thing I hear from Christians is that they are forbidden to work with healers because it goes against Christ and God. This is understandable since the true teachings and life of Jesus have been heavily distorted. As you can see, practitioners of Reiki and the sacred teachings of the Judeo-Christian lineages are speaking of the same healing power.

Reiki is active prayer that brings the power of heaven into this world. Any religious figures that shame or condemn the use of these healing practices are heavily programmed and working within a control system that is not reflective of the Grace of God. I suggest for anyone in such a dogmatic religious group to discover the Truth of the Living Christ Within You who is beaming encouragement for you to use these tools for healing and awakening to your own Christhood.

Embodied Light Reiki Principles

Reiki is Non-Religious

Learning to cast light and be a lightworker will enhance any spiritual or religious practices. For many, learning to work with Divine Light is the first time they feel a true connection to God or Spirit. Learning to channel reiki is available to all people regardless of religious background.

Anyone Can Learn

Learning to work with Light and transmit Source-sent energy is simple to do, and anyone can learn it. It is our birthright. We are extensions of Source energy and extensions of Source's plan for creating harmony within the Universe.

Do All Healers Use Source Energy?

There are many forms of energy healing being practiced all around the world. Some people are taught to use their own energy for healing. Some pull energy from the world around them. Some use the energy of the Earth. There are limitless sources of subtle energy. I always teach my students to connect with Source and invite the highest, clearest, and brightest light available and appropriate for the client.

It is important to use your heart and Inner Being for discernment when choosing an energy healer or energy teacher. You want to choose someone who embodies unconditional love and health. Many people use spirituality

724 | THE ILLUMINATION CODEX

as a cover for negatively polarized agendas. Trust your intuition and choose a healer or teacher that uplifts and honors you as an individual.

Divinely Guided Healing

Reiki channeled through a person with the intention of healing is intelligent in that a practitioner simply needs to empty the mind and allow the energy to flow through them. The energy goes where it is most needed in the body. While someone may lay their hands on a specific area of the body, the energy begins to flow throughout the recipient's entire energy field, treating the whole system.

Holistic Healing Method

This is a holistic healing system that works on the physical, mental, emotional, psychic, and spiritual aspects of one's being because Reiki works with the fundamental building blocks of Creation. The laying of hands draws forth the radiant wholeness on all layers of one's being.

Reiki heals the superficial manifestation of disease and works to balance the root cause of whatever is causing the suffering by encouraging the natural ability of the body to self-regulate and heal itself.

Clear the Channel

Those working on others' energy should have a clear mind, body, and energy field. While being in a heart-based focus, a person should also be clean of chemicals and intoxicants so that the energy is not contaminated as it passes through the body.

Sharing Divine Energies

Once one has dedicated their vessel and life to working for the Light and has received an activation through an attunement ceremony, self-attunement through prayer and intention, or spontaneous divine activation, all that is needed to run the energies is to lay the hands with the intention of healing. When this is done, a bridge is established consciously or unconsciously, and the energy begins to flow from Source through the practitioner's heart and overall energy field. All one needs to do is call on the

Light for healing and allow it to flow through you. This is your birthright!

Reiki/Source Energy Is Non-Harming

Reiki is non-harming and life-supporting. You can never give too much or too little. Although, recipients of the healing energy may not ever want you to stop! Source Intelligence is Love, and it restores everything it touches.

Channeling Source Energy Never Depletes Your Energy

It is important to understand that we are not using our personal energy to create healing when we work with reiki. Energy medicine practitioners who do this often feel depleted, and many develop illnesses or at the very least, burnout because they use their own energy for healing others. When we use reiki, we become a channel for the endless supply of Source energy. As reiki passes through us, it heals us. While it may be tiring at first to focus or stand for the duration of a healing session, most of the time, a practitioner feels charged and buzzed by the high energies they channel during a healing session.

Levels of Embodied Light Reiki

Level 1: Personal Healing and Lightbody Ascension

This level focuses on self-healing and the ascension process. We explore subtle energy basics and subtle energy anatomy. We focus on developing personal self-healing practices and setting a foundation for living a spiritually focused life.

Level 2: Reiki Practitioner

This level is about sharing reiki and energy medicine with others, in-person or remotely. Business training is offered for those who wish to use this work as part of their professional services.

Level 3: Reiki Master Teacher

During this level of training, initiates are taught how to initiate and teach others Reiki and energy medicine.

Attunement and Initiation

Divine Light is available to all people simply by having the intention to connect with the loving redemptive energy of Source and allowing the connection to flow. Through this intention, you connect to the truth of what you are, a conduit for Source energy.

Many souls have been doing this healing work in other lifetimes and find the process of channeling Light simple and natural. For others, working with a teacher is essential to activate or enhance this ability in through a powerful process called an attunement.

An attunement is an alchemical ceremony to connect a person to higher frequencies of Source energy to use for healing. The process enhances the recipient's natural ability to connect to divine Light and "opens the pipes" for more energy to stream through. While self-attunements are certainly possible and valid, being attuned and trained by a teacher proficient at working with these healing energies is often a life-changing experience that brings deep insight and healing to the recipient. Multiple attunement/initiation ceremonies can be done depending on the teacher's lineages or the needs of the student.

Self-Healing Tool: What Are You Ready to Understand and Heal?

The attunement ceremony is a powerful statement for the recipient. It is a declaration that they are dedicating their vessel to light for personal and global healing. As they welcome these healing energies into their being, a powerful process begins as lower energies and blockages begin to be cleared from the body of the initiate. The entire cellular structure begins to shift as Source energy begins to transform the DNA to hold a higher frequency of Source light. Over the next few weeks, many people experience physical, emotional, and spiritual changes as the system begins to heal and raise in frequency. It is recommended to practice daily self-healing to support the integration process.

Manifestation Tool: What Are You Calling into Your Life?

The attunement process is also a powerful technology for manifestation. I ask my students to set an intention of what they want to call into their life experience. During the attunement and the weeks following, their frequency rises to meet their desired outcome and draws it to them.

In-Person or Distance Attunements

There is a great benefit in receiving multiple attunements throughout one's lifetime. Each attunement helps to clear out stagnant energy and blockages so that one can become a more powerful and clear channel for reiki. These transformative ceremonies can be done in person or guided from a long distance as we are all connected through the Unified Field of Creation.

Once I "uploaded" an attunement for a friend with the intention for her to receive the attunement at a specific time. My friend could not "tune in" during that time, and it took her a few days to do so. As she laid down to connect, her heart rate began to increase as healing energies began to course through her body. She was wearing a device that measured her heart rate throughout the day. When she checked the measurements to see what her heart rate was during the meditation where she received the attunement, she noticed it was higher than when she had been on a rigorous hike earlier that day. At the time, I was still struggling with the dogma taught by the Usui Reiki system I had been trained in that insisted attunements are only valid and effective in person. This experience was all I needed to shatter that belief and align with the higher truth of limitless Source energy.

Various Experiences

Each initiation ceremony is unique to each person. Like my own first attunement, some people hardly experience anything significant but have a feeling that they participated in something deeply meaningful as they committed themselves to healing and working with light.

Other times, people may experience flowing energies and various sensations as their body systems restructure to become a clearer vessel and channel for Source energy. People may see colors in their meditative state or are reconnected with spirit guides, star families, or loved ones who have passed on. Some people experience spontaneous healing as they shed old energies no longer needing manifested symptoms to teach them a lesson. Every experience, subtle or profound, is exactly what the recipient needs on their individual path of awakening and healing.

Integration after Attunement

Over the next few weeks, some people may experience healing symptoms like headaches, tiredness, and other indications that the body is releasing toxins and old energies as it moves through a process of healing. Doing self-treatments can reduce discomfort and speed up the healing process as the body aligns with the new energies.

Power of Three: A Holy Trinity for Healing

A channel needs to understand that they are not solely responsible for creating a healing experience. For healing to happen, the channel, recipient, and Source need to be in equal agreement with what level of healing is appropriate and possible. If there is resistance within any member of the trinity, the healing will only go so far. Let's look at this from the perspective of each part of the triad.

One: Source and the Soul of a Client

A client may have agreed to experience these conditions to balance karma or create conditions for others' learning on a soul level. If complete healing is not aligned with their soul path, in agreement with the Divine Plan for that soul, it will not happen no matter how many sessions they have. In instances like this, it is important that the practitioner does not take this as a personal reflection of their abilities but instead, surrenders to the Higher Will and Divine Plan. The client can continue to meditate and adapt their perspectives and behaviors to truly discover the true source of their suffering. Many times in my sessions, the Higher Self will not do complete healing because the client needs to work on themself for it to create the transformation they desire.

Two: Client/Recipient

To heal completely, a recipient needs to be willing to release the old energies, identifications, and belief systems that keep them in a cycle of dis-ease/disease and discomfort. This requires self-reflection, honesty, and a commitment to embodying higher truth. Illness and stress are invitations for self-awareness and deeper understanding. Some people are not ready to take those steps. People often create an identity for themselves through their suffering. Therefore, a good intake conversation is crucial to see where a client is open to change.

Three: Practitioner

It is our noble responsibility to hold the highest vision for our clients. An effective practitioner of any transformative therapy puts aside judgments and embodies their Higher Self, who only wants the best for the client. We surrender our will to the Divine's will and trust that whatever happens during the session was for the highest and best of all involved.

Intention, Attention, Compassion

All powerful energy healing sessions are conducted through the compassion of a heart of service guided by the Will and Love of Source. We become a channel for and presence of divine healing energies when we intend to connect and shine this healing energy. As we focus on the object we are wishing to transform, we bring the perfection that already exists forward into reality.

During the healing session, the channel is to remain focused on the intention of healing and service. If the practitioner is not able to hold the intention of running healing energy, the bridge disintegrates. Conscious breathing, visualization, and heart-centered focus are key elements to running Source energy for healing.

Consent

In honor of everyone's free will and power of Divine Creatorship, we need to ask permission to touch or send healing energies to others. When a person agrees to receive, their energy field opens to make way for the transmission. If a person is closed to receiving, it will likely cause more discomfort and suffering to attempt to lay hands. There are many stories, often of men, who use the disguise of a healing session to inappropriately touch another person. If something does not feel right about a healing session or the practitioner's vibe, you have every right to say something and reject the healing session.

Everyone has different parts of their body that they consider private. It is important to describe to a recipient where and how you will be applying light touch to their body and confirm that you have permission to do so. This is especially important for people who have never had hands-on healing work. This helps them relax their nervous system and open their bodies to receive healing.

If you are doing distant healing work, ask the recipient if they are open to receiving healing from afar. This agreement creates an energetic link for the exchange of energy. You may even want to synchronize times for them to tune in with you in some way, although this is not necessary.

If you cannot communicate with the person, you can intend to connect with the receiver's Higher Self through your own heart and see if the client is open to receiving. Trust the intuitive messages you receive in response. If you get a "no" or feel your own energy close, use your time for something else. If you get a "yes" or your energy "lights up," have fun connecting with this person for healing. If you get a "no" and feel that they may be open to this energy later, you can create a "bank" of healing energy that is available for them to receive when they *are* ready.

Using Symbols in a Healing Session

Symbols are a powerful way to activate and amplify intentions. Like the Usui Reiki symbols, many symbols are purely charged with the love of countless beings who have used them for healing. Using symbols that generate loving energy like rose petals, luminous hearts, and angels brings those symbols' energies into the sessions. Some people use Light language codes (divinely imbued symbols) that they receive through their Higher Self and guides to adjust the frequency of the Light they channel to create a variety of healing effects.

Symbols are a wonderful tool to train our ability to "turn the dial" on the energies. I always had resistance to the idea that a symbol "gives you power." If anything, your focus on the intention behind the symbol brings those qualities and intentions into your experience from your Inner Being. For some, learning the symbols is crucial to help them focus their intention and attention. For others, the symbols are a distraction and seem to limit. Follow your heart. It always knows best.

In the Usui System of Natural Healing, there are three symbols used for conducting healing sessions for people initiated into the second level of Reiki. Other symbols are used in the Master Level training and other forms of Reiki.

The first two symbols of the Usui System of Natural Healing are ancient Tibetan healing symbols. The third symbol is a Japanese *kanji*. These symbols are activated when you intend to use them. You can also draw them with the palm of your hand, visualize them, or chant their names to focus your intention and attention on the symbols' qualities. Reiki is limitless, and so are the uses for the symbols.

Out of respect for the lineages of Reiki, I have decided not to include the actual symbols in the book to protect and honor the sacredness of the lineages. They are shared in the Embodied Light course, or any Reiki master can share them with you after an attunement.

The Power Symbol: Cho Ku Rei — CKR

The Power Symbol amplifies the power of reiki. It can be used anywhere where you want to increase the healing energies. It can also be used to seal energy work. This is a wonderful symbol to use when charging objects like crystals or pendulums. Different people draw the symbol with different directions of the spiral. The way I was taught, start drawing the symbol from right to left with a clockwise spiral.

The Emotional/Mental Healing Symbol: Sei Hei Ki — SHK

The Emotional/Mental Healing symbol is used to transform emotional and mental patterns. This is a wonderful symbol to use when working with trauma and addictive patterns and to bring deeper clarity. Both CKR and SHK can be used to create healing spaces by placing the symbols on the walls of the space through visualization and intention.

Remote Viewing and the Distance Symbol: Hon Sha Ze Sho Nen — HSZSN

Remote viewing allows our mind to connect with the unified field of Creation to tune our conscious awareness into other aspects of Creation. We have local and nonlocal consciousness, meaning, we can be present and focused on our body, *and* we can also project our consciousness across space and time to remote view other people, places, realms, and time periods. We are not limited to one place and time. We simply need to calm our mind, set the intention to connect with the object of our focus, and listen to what is being communicated. From that shared connection, we can transmit and receive imagery, intentions, and healing energies.

The Distance Symbol is used for remote healing or when we want to beam Reiki over longer distances. It is also used to send healing energy into the past or into the future to be accessed later. To use this symbol for remote healing, simply draw, visualize, or chant the name of the symbol and dedicate the session to the recipient by stating their name or visualizing the person to which you are sending the healing energies. The same process is used if you were to send healing to another location on the planet.

In the Usui lineages, there are a few versions of this symbol since Hawayo Takata, protégé of Mikao Usui, shared different versions of the symbol with different students. It intends to connect to the timeless space of the unified field to transmit healing to the most appropriate place that is important here. That is the power of this symbol.

There is no limit to how we can work with the Light. We are only limited by our conditioned thinking. Be playful and allow your imagination and the power of your Inner Being to guide you into new and exciting ways to work with Light and Consciousness.

SIXTY

Pillars of Embodied Light Reiki

The process of conducting a hands-on healing session for yourself or another person is a simple structure that can create profound effects. The structure of a healing session can be organized into five pillars or sections.

Pillar One: Gassho Activation — Grounding, Centering, and Tuning In

From a seated position, bring your hands to your knees, palms down, and close your eyes, practicing conscious breathing as you tune into your subtle energy and inner realm. Connect with your hara line. As you inhale, lengthen your spine; as you exhale, ground your energy and soften any tension in your body. The same process can also be adapted to a standing posture with the hands gently touching the hara and the heart or any position that feels grounding.

Bring your hands to prayer at the heart center. In Japanese, this is called *Gassho*. In the Sanskrit traditions, this is called *Anjali Mudra*. In English, we simply call this Prayer Hands. Call upon the presence of the Light and feel your vibration begin to rise. Intend to activate the light of your heart, breathe into it, and expand this light. Feel the energy flow into your arms and activate the hands' minor chakras, the center of the palms, with the light of your heart. You may even want to rub the palms of the hands together to activate the electromagnetic fields of the hands.

We create a sacred temple of Light during this phase by bringing the Light into the healing space. Use your intention and attention to expand and clear your auric field to totally envelop the space you are working in. Invite your heart field to shine brightly!

Pillar Two: Reiji-ho Connection — Higher Mind, Guides, Client

This is the invitation where we invite the co-creators for the healing into our quantum healing space. You may feel the vibration raise or have other psychic experiences as higher beings' consciousness emerge within the quantum healing field. Trust your sensations.

Bring your prayer hands up to touch your thumbs on your forehead. Tune into the center of your skull and activate the Brow Center by intending for it to light up. Breathe into and expand this Light. Intend to activate your inner sight and your connection to the Higher Mind of Source and your Higher Self and guides. If you are working on another person, you can invite their higher consciousness and guides to work with your consciousness to guide you throughout the session.

Pillar Three: Chiryo Laying of Hands — Intuitive Session

The third pillar is the transmission of the healing energies. This is done through the laying of hands or psychically for remote sessions. Different traditions teach these steps differently. What is important is that you find a way that feels comfortable for you.

Hand Placements

When we work with our hands, we can learn a set pattern of hand positions to use or else allow the hand placements to be guided intuitively. While learning, set hand placements create a nice structure to ensure that the whole system is treated. Most practitioners find that a hands-on-healing session is an intuitive dance. I recommend practicing many different approaches to find your own unique way of feeling authentically connected and confident.

Sacred Touch: Listen, Feel, Trust

The electromagnetic field of the body extends many feet beyond the physical body. There are times that you may find your hands resting completely on the body, and other times, you may be guided to work with parts of the field that are further away from the surface. Trust your internal messages and sensations.

Let the hands hover close enough or far enough away from the physical body that you can sense the electric and magnetic qualities of the subtle energies being exchanged between your palms and the field that you are working on.

A lot of information is being exchanged the moment we intend to make the connection. Trust your sensations and inner messages. It takes a good minute or two to truly establish a deep connection. Some new students move around a lot when they first begin doing sessions. "Park it" for a little bit at each place you are guided to and simply listen to understand what is needed. Most of the time, a simple presence is enough to heal.

As we lay hands, we hold a high vibration within our entire field that "invites" the lower energies that we treat to raise in vibration. All kinds of events may happen as the energy shifts, including tingling sensations, hot/cold feelings, bodily noises, deep sighs of relief, shaking, and even strong emotional releases that include crying or screaming.

Whatever emerges, let it. Hold space for the energy to rise up to the surface to be felt and released. If someone is crying, do not stop them from crying. Allow it to continue for as long as needed. For many, fear of being alone has subconsciously blocked them from facing certain aspects of their life fully, and it is our job to hold a loving presence so that the energy can be integrated and released completely. If it continues for a few minutes, ask the client if they are okay. Most of the time, they will nod yes. I allow the crying to continue and direct more Light to the heart of the recipient.

Receiving Images and Intuitive Messages

While laying your hands on a client, pay attention to internal sensations, images, and messages. Nonphysical guidance comes in various forms and is different for everyone. Many start to rapidly develop psychic gifts and extrasensory abilities when they begin facilitating healing sessions. This may include mediumship, channeling, timeline work, and more. Trust what you receive. Release doubts that may arise after receiving intuitive guidance and stay in the flow.

Pillar Four: Closing and Sealing Sealing with Gratitude

Thank the Guides and Families of Light using *Reiji-Ho*. Bring your hands to *Reiji-ho*, hands in prayer position with thumbs touching the Brow Center. Take a moment to send gratitude to Source for this experience. Thank your spiritual allies for guiding and supporting the work. If you are working with another client, thank their guides and Higher Self as well. Tune in and listen if there are any final messages for you or the client. Messages from the Light will always be loving. Trust what you receive.

Dedicating Your Practice (Gassho)

Dedicate the fruits and efforts of your practice towards anything that you choose. A simple, yet powerful gesture is dedicating the practice towards the liberation of all beings from cycles of suffering.

Pillar Five: Disconnecting Energy Dry Bathing (Kenyo-ku)

This practice is helpful anytime you feel that you have "picked up" unwanted or extra energy from other people or places. There are many ways to do this, all of them have to deal with the intention of clearing any unwanted energy you may have picked up and returning to your own sovereign alignment, fully disconnected from the client/recipient.

Set the intention to stop the flow of energy from the hands to keep them from "running hot" all day, which is uncomfortable for some people and may create a "spacey" quality if left running all day. If you find your hands filling with energy throughout the day, use the energy for personal healing, healing the Earth, or even a pet. The energy is charging in the hands because something in the environment is in need. Go ahead and share!

I generally use *Kenyo-ku*, followed by washing my hands in cold water and splashing cool water on my face to reset the energy.

Kenyo-ku Dry Bathing

Set the intention to clear your energy and sever connections that no longer serve you.

Bring the right hand to the left shoulder, sweep the palm down and across your torso, brushing the end of the energy behind the right side of your hip. Repeat with the left hand. Repeat with the right.

Bring the right hand to the top of the left shoulder. Extend the left arm, palm facing upward. Swipe down the left arm with the left hand, brushing the energy off the left hand's fingertips. Repeat with the left hand sweeping the right arm. Repeat with the right hand sweeping the left arm.

Slide and clap your hands together as if you were brushing off dust. Do this three times with the intention of stopping the flow of energy from the hands.

Bring the hands to Gassho/Prayer Hands. Close your eyes to tune into your own energy field. Ground and center yourself. Bring your field in closer to your body and seal it with gratitude.

Distance and Self-Healing Time

After you facilitate a healing session for someone else, you are primed and ready to do self-healing or remote healing for others or the planet.

Take advantage of the "extra charge" and use it for something else if you have the time to do so. More instruction on Distance/Nonlocal healing is given in the Embodied Light appendix in the back of the book.

SIXTY-ONE

Hand Placements: Self-Healing

There are various schools of thought that set hand placements for healing sessions. Some start from the crown and work towards the feet, and some do the opposite. Some methods use the chakra locations, and some include the major joints of the body. Every session is unique. All of the variety of hand placements are valid and useful. Here is a set that I use and teach to my students.

Intuitive Treatment for Self

1. *Gassho*: Ground, center, and tune into the Unified Field. Feel the subtle vibrations and amplify the sensations and connection with your breath. Feel your connection to Source and Gaia through your hara line. Evoke the emotions of Higher Love and Compassion. Feel your heart field expanding and strengthen your energetic field with Light and Love.
2. *Reiji-ho*: Connect with Universal Mind, divine guides, and your higher aspects. Welcome the infusion of your consciousness with the Wisdom and Presence of the Family of Light.
3. With hands in Reiji-ho, ask your Higher Awareness where you need healing.
4. Trust your internal messaging and allow your hands to be led to where they are needed.
5. Hover your hands above this target area, listen, feel, and trust what you receive through your Inner Being.
6. Transmit Love and Light from Source into the area you are treating. Invite wholeness and vitality and hold internal imagery of pure Light and Love. Use your breath to release excess energy that accumulates in your internal realm.
7. You may practice extraction or clearing practices or any other work you are guided to do here until the energy shifts to a balanced state. Often the hands will stop running energy as much when the target

area has taken as much energy as it needs. When you feel you have finished working with a target area, seal and bless the area with your intention.

8. Return to Reiji-ho and ask to be guided to the next area or immediately go to the next area if you are already receiving the following location in your awareness. Continue the process, keeping the mind focused on the intention of healing and compassion.

9. When finished, close with Reiji-ho to send gratitude for the assistance and connection to the higher realms. Use Gassho to ground, center, and strengthen your field. Be sure to bring your aura close to the body so that you feel contained and clear. Use Kenyo-ku to clear the body and finalize the transmission.

Scanning Method (Byosen Scanning)

In this method, I describe using your dominant and non-dominant hands for different steps. This is not a concrete rule. Try both and see which method works for you. It may even change over time. We are using the hands and senses to find distortions in the field.

1. Perform Gassho and Reiji-ho.

2. Hold your dominant hand off to the side and imagine, sense, and feel that it is holding a shiny ball of Source energy.

3. Using the non-dominant hand and starting with the palm facing the front of the Soul Star chakra, slowly bring the hand down the hara line, passing over each energy center.

4. Notice the sensations and listen to your internal messaging. Feel for any distortions or bumps in the field. Trust your intuition.

5. When you find distortion in the field, move the hand closer to the energy center and away until you feel the strongest, most noticeable layer of the distortion. Bring the other hands to meet side-by-side and channel fresh Source energy into the target area. Use your imagination to make it beautiful and radiant. Sweep and extract. Comb and fluff out the emanations of each center. Fill and seal with loving intentions.

6. When you feel the energy is balanced or the energy slows or stops

running from your hands, bring your dominant hand back up to hold the ball of Light and continue the hara line scan with your non-dominant hand, repeating the process wherever necessary.

7. Finish with Reiji-ho, Gassho, and Kenyo-ku.

Full Hand Placement Series

1. *Gassho*: Ground, center, call in, and activate the Light.
2. *Reiji-ho*: Connect with Universal Mind/Source, guides, higher aspects.

Soul Star Chakra

Bring the hands six to twelve inches above the head to connect with the Soul Star chakra. Trust your internal messages. You may feel the field of the Soul Star connect with the chakras in the palms of the hands as if "clicking" into place. Beam energy from your palms into the Soul Star while practicing deep, conscious breathing. Make it dazzle and sparkle with the brightest and clearest light. As you breathe in and out, imagine that fresh, Source Light is saturating the Soul Star chakra.

Crown Center

Bring the hands down to touch the crown of the head lightly. Move the hands closer and further away from the skin until you feel the edges of the Crown Center. Beam energy into the crown and use your imagination to clear, balance, and illuminate the Crown chakra. You may even want to use your fingers to comb and fluff the chakras to refresh them. Scrape and extract any energy that is stuck or stagnant, always filling and sealing with Light.

Brow Center and Face

Bring the palms down in front of the face, fingers pointing upward, and beam energy into the Brow chakra and upper face. Use your imagination to make the Brow chakra beautiful and radiant. Sweep and Extract. Comb and Fluff. Fill and Seal.

Zeal Center

Bring the hands to the back of the skull, fingers pointing up towards the crown, beaming Light into the occipital ridge/connection point between the spine and skull. This center is newly opening in many. You can use the thumbs to gently spread the energy open from the center of the chakra and outward to encourage the center to open. Sweep and Extract. Comb and Fluff. Fill and Seal.

Throat Center

Bring the hands to the side of the neck, close to the jawline and region of the thyroid gland, and beam Light into the Throat chakra. Use your imagination to make the Throat chakra beautiful and radiant. Sweep and Extract. Comb and Fluff. Fill and Seal.

Heart Center

Bring the right hand to lightly touch the High Heart chakra, right below the collarbone. Bring the left hand underneath of it at the Heart chakra center and beam Light into both of these centers. Use your imagination to make them beautiful and radiant. Sweep and Extract. Comb and Fluff. Fill and Seal.

Power Center

Face the palms towards the upper abdomen and lay them just below the diaphragm with the middle fingers touching and beam Light into the Power chakra. Breathe into your digestive organs. Use your imagination to make everything beautiful and radiant. Sweep and Extract. Comb and Fluff. Fill and Seal.

Back of Power Center (Optional)

Bring the palms to the back of the body and do the same process on the back of the upper rib area. Breathe into the back of the ribs as you beam Light into the Solar Plexus chakra. Use your imagination to make it beautiful and radiant. Sweep and Extract. Comb and Fluff. Fill and Seal.

Sacral Center

Front: Bring your palms to touch the lower abdomen or womb space lightly. Fingers may even make a triangle with the fingers meeting at the pubic bone, and the thumbs point towards or touching one another just below the naval. Beam Light into the Sacral chakra and organs. Use your imagination to make it beautiful and radiant. Sweep and Extract. Comb and Fluff. Fill and Seal.

Back: Bring your hands to the back of the pelvis/lower back, fingers meeting at the sacrum. Breathe into the organs and beam Light into the Sacral chakra. Use your imagination to make it beautiful and radiant. Sweep and Extract. Comb and Fluff. Fill and Seal.

Root Center

Option A: Bring the palms to the outside of the hips in alignment with where the femur head attaches to the hip socket (acetabulum) and beam energy to the Root chakra.

Option B: Bring the hands under the pelvis, cupping the hands over the perineum and beam Light into the Root Center.

Use your imagination to make it beautiful and radiant. Sweep and Extract. Comb and Fluff. Fill and Seal.

Feet and Earth Star Center

Bend your knee and adjust your posture in a way that you can cup one foot in your hand. Holding the hand approximately six to twelve inches away from the foot, beam Light from one of your hands to the entire foot, especially the sole of the foot. Use your imagination to make it beautiful and radiant. Soften your gaze and use your eyes to beam Light into the area you are working on. Sweep and Extract. Comb and Fluff. Fill and Seal. Repeat with the other foot. When finished, place both feet on the ground and tune into their magnetic connection to the Earth.

Beaming

If you cannot reach your feet, you can transmit the energy from your hands towards the area you are treating. Use your mind to visualize a powerful and healing stream of energy flowing from your hands to the area you are treating.

Full System Flush and Blossom

Bring the hands to rest on your knees or lap, perform Gassho or place your hands in prayer or any other position that helps you feel deeply connected with yourself. As you inhale, intend and imagine that you are breathing Light from Source down through your entire energy system, Soul Star to Earth Star. As you exhale, imagine that your whole system BLOSSOMS with Light. Continue breathing in and blossoming out until you feel radiant and bright.

After you have finished self-healing, this is a wonderful time to do distant healing or communicate with your higher aspects and guides. Your channel is now significantly brighter and open for higher communication. Use this time to visualize the highest potential outcomes for your day, week, or projects. When finished, seal your practice with Reiji-ho, Gassho, and Kenyo-ku:

Reiji-ho: Thank your higher aspects, guides, and Source. Dedicate your practice towards the benefit of all beings everywhere.

Gassho: Ground, center, and adjust the boundaries of your aura.

Use *Kenyo-ku* to clear off any stagnant energy and to stop the flow of Reiki consciously.

Additional Reiki Skills

Gyoshi-Ho: Transmitting Reiki with the Eyes

Eye contact plays a huge part in the transference of Light from one person to another object. As you look towards the object you wish to transform, soften your gaze, and consciously connect with Source, Gaia, and your breath. Imagine that loving, regenerative Source energy is shining from your eyes. Beam this Love from your eyes into everything that you see. Through your inner focus on Light, everything outside of you begins to transform into Heaven on Earth. There are unlimited ways to use this ability for self-healing and beyond. Everywhere you look, you can send healing energy!

If you find yourself around dense and/or chaotic energy, use your skills to ground, center, and broadcast Light into the field around you. Use conscious breathing to transmute the energy as it arises within and around you. Focus on Source as you anchor Light and watch as the dense or chaotic energies begin to shift. Use your inner sight to visualize the resolution, peace, and harmony, and broadcast this inner imaging into the field for others to source from. You will likely notice the circumstances in your outer experience shifting instantly as you anchor in a new potential into the timeline for everyone and everything to align with.

Koki-ho: Healing with the Breath

There may be times where you feel an area needs a strong dose of Light to clear and revitalize it. You can use the breath as a vehicle to transport healing energy and intentions for healing.

- Ground, center, and intend to connect with Source.
- On your inhale, breathe Source energy down through your hara line, filling your hara and entire being with Light from Source.
- You may also visualize a symbol or draw CKR or SHK on the roof of the mouth before you exhale. Exhale by contracting the abdomen strongly until you feel the pelvic floor contract. Direct the breath into the area that needs healing energy. Cover the area with your hands to seal in the healing energy with intention. You may also use CKR to seal the energy.

Clearing, Dedicating, and Charging Healing Objects

Many practitioners use various tools to support a healing session, including crystals, wands, singing bowls, pendulums, chimes, and so on. I believe it is important to clear the object of dense energies, dedicate it to the Light, and charge the object with Divine Energy before using it for healing or divination purposes.

- Ground, center, and establish a connection to the Light of Source.
- Hold the object or visualize the object in your mind.
- Using your dominant hand, chop above the object three times while synchronizing with sharp exhales as you intend to clear the object from dense or pervasive energies.
- Hold the object in your hands or in the light of your awareness and, using your intention or voice, dedicate the object to the Light for healing.
- Invite Source energy to flow through you powerfully into the object to charge it with light and healing vibrations. You may also visualize CKR, SHK, or any other healing symbol within the object's field.
- Intend that this energy will continue to renew and clear itself until you do it again.

Additional Energy Healing Skills

Drumming, Tapping, Padding

There may be times when you are called to drum lightly upon your body to direct vibrations into the muscles, connective tissues, and bones. Using the soft pads of your fingers and palms, lightly pat on the areas that are needing revitalization. Less is often more in the case of force. As you do this, use your imagination and breath to direct the vibrations into the dense parts and feel the energy breaking apart and disintegrating. After thirty seconds or so, stop drumming or tapping and cover the area with your palms, sealing the vibration and directing Light into the area. Use your breath to pull the healing energies deep into the target area.

Shaking

Shaking is a natural action performed by many species when they want to release energy. Imagine a dog shaking its whole body and the happiness they feel right after. You can use this technique to re-energize and clear stagnant energy.

1. Bring the feet under your pelvis or widen your stance a bit more. Stand tall and practice deep, conscious belly breathing.
2. Raise up onto the balls of your feet, lifting the heels. Begin to gently and rhythmically drop the heels to the ground and feel the vibrations traveling up your skeletal system. Feel the vibrations traveling through your muscles and tissues.
3. Imagine that old, stagnant energy simply falls away as the vibrations travel throughout the body. Use your breath and imagination to scan through the body and bring some extra shaking to those areas. Keep your face soft and allow the muscles of the face to shake as well. Especially shake the arms and hands to fling off any energies that are stuck there.
4. Imagine that Source is showering down clear, bright light that washes over you and recharges your system. Be playful, like a bird in a birdbath kissed by the Sun.

Toning/Sounding/Light Language

Using your ability to tone and sound is a powerful technology for clearing and activating energy. Different tones originate in different parts of the body. When linked with your mind and intention, you can direct the vibrations from the tones of your voice into various areas of your body and begin to heal.

1. Ground, center, and connect with Source, practicing deep and conscious breathing.

2. Take a long, deep inhale and begin to make a tone or humming sound. Play with it and find higher and lower tones that feel healing. Trust yourself and go for it, even if it feels silly at first. Generally, lower tones work with the lower chakras, and higher tones work with the higher chakras.

3. Using your hands and inner vision, lightly touch areas that need healing and begin to experiment with creating healing tones and direct them into the areas.

4. Play with different syllables using various consonant letter and vowel combinations and begin to create different combinations while holding the intention to heal and transmit Love and Light. Allow your heart to guide you as you transform the sounds into a Language of Light, harmonic tones that carry healing energies. Trust yourself and experiment with different sounds with a sense of joyful playfulness. Let your Inner Child come out to play!

5. When you have finished, bring your hands to a resting position, ground, center, and seal your field.

Cocooning with Light

When completing a session for yourself or someone else, you may choose to fill and seal the entire auric field. Intend that the cocoon will hold a healing container for the transformation to continue over the next few days and nights until the healing is complete.

Hold the hands wide out in front of you and imagine, sense, and feel that you are beaming bright, beautiful Source Light into your entire field. See it swirl and wrap around your entire being, filling and sealing up every part of you with healing, loving energy.

SIXTY-TWO

Facilitating Healing for Others

As you practice channeling Source energy, you become a healing presence for everyone and everything around you. People will begin to comment on how calm they feel around you and will likely begin to share deep parts of themselves with you because of the healing presence you emanate. Learning to facilitate a healing session for others is a skill that will come in handy as you and the world awaken to the Divinity that We Are. Energy medicine is the medicine of our ancient past and our future.

I suggest that people who desire to facilitate healing for others commit to self-healing for some time until they are comfortable with all the steps that I introduced in the previous sections for self-healing. Practicing self-healing gives you the experience of your own energy field to become aware of what is YOUR energy and what is not. It helps you trust your intuition and proficiency in the foundational skills for conducting a healing session. When you feel confident in your ability to connect with Source and channel Divine Energy for healing, you are ready to conduct a healing session for someone else.

Healing Presence

As you practice connecting with the Source and channeling divine energy, your energy field begins to transmute dense energies. It becomes saturated with high-frequency energy that raises the vibration of everything in your environment. This may look like people "lighting up" when you are around, and it may also trigger the lower energies and beliefs in some people. Many people learned to reduce their light because of trauma from the past, including childhood and even other lifetimes. I encourage everyone to push their edges more and more and learn how to stand tall and confident as they reclaim their sovereignty and embody the Light of their divinity.

Facilitating a Healing Session

Sharing reiki with others is natural and effortless as we learn to align with our True Nature. Conducting a healing session creates a deeply personal and heartfelt connection between the people who are involved.

When I was teaching energy healing under Usui Reiki's traditions, I found that people did not take a Level Two course because they did not want to be a practitioner who sees clients. While someone can certainly create a profession from energy healing sessions and counseling, I believe that facilitation is a skill for anyone to learn and share with those whom they love and want to support on their path of healing and awakening.

Imagine what a world we would live in where everyone had the foundational understandings of subtle energy medicine. Imagine what our cultures would be like if people practiced channeling Light from the Divine. Imagine what our world would look like if we all took responsibility to heal our own energy and support others through practices of healing and awakening. There would be no illness and disease. Our relationships would flourish. Every atom of life on the Earth would entrain to match the Light power of awakened humanity.

I will share the formal steps of conducting a healing session as if someone were seeing a client in a clinical setting. I will use the terms "practitioner" to refer to the one who facilitates the session and "client" for the one who receives the healing session. An informal session follows the same structure but may not necessarily contain all the same components because it is less formal. If you follow these simple steps and observances, you will know how to conduct a powerful healing session for a client or loved one.

While there are many benefits in learning how to facilitate a healing session for other people, including more skills, higher confidence, and the rejuvenating effects of facilitating a session, not everyone will find this information important for where they are NOW in their process. If this feels like you, please move forward to the next section of the book that speaks to you. You can always circle back when you are ready to explore further!

Divine Coordination of a Healing Rendezvous

I believe that these healing sessions are coordinated on higher planes before the session happens physically. This means that the Higher Self of the client and practitioner have agreed that meeting for a healing session would benefit both the practitioner and the client. Clients are drawn to a practitioner who has the skills they need to facilitate an appropriate healing session for that client. New practitioners can trust that whoever comes to them for healing is drawn to them because of what they can offer.

Clients may also be healing something similar to an aspect that needs to be healed in the practitioner. In this way, everyone benefits from the healing experience. Sometimes a client is brought to a practitioner because something about the healing session will teach the practitioner a new skill through higher guidance. Trust that whoever comes to you for healing is coming because you have everything needed to conduct an appropriate session for everyone involved.

All that is needed is a connection to our Inner Being and Source, intent to heal, and a willingness to listen to the energies and intuition.

Before a Client Arrives

Let us say that the appointment has been scheduled, and the client is about to arrive for the healing session. There are a few things you may want to do to prepare the session space and yourself.

Session Space

Once you learn how to do healing sessions for people, there is no limit to the conditions you will be invited to work with to create a healing space. I have performed sessions on kitchen tables, laying on the floor, in chairs, in hospital rooms, and more. Most practitioners, in the optimum conditions, use a massage table with blankets and sheets. Covering a client with a blanket connects them subconsciously with the feelings of getting ready for bed and will help them to relax right away. The blanket can always be adjusted or removed if the client gets too warm.

If you are using another surface, make sure there is some padding underneath the body as the client will be lying down for some time. Place something under the knees like a pillow or bolster to protect the lower back. You may even decide to use a chair if lying down is not comfortable for your client. Work with what you have.

Setting Up the Space for the Intake Interview

I set up two chairs for a pre-session conversation. Next to it, I may have tissues in case the client cries. I also have some paper and something to write with just in case either of us needs to make notes throughout the session. Sometimes I give clients "homework" or practices that they can do after the healing session, and it is important to write the steps down, so they do not forget.

When the client arrives, the lighting should be soft but on the higher side to see. Once we begin the healing session, I lower the lights to help create a relaxing atmosphere. Some people even like eye pillows to help them block out any extra light.

Music

Turn healing music on to bring healing vibrations into the room. Some "spa music" or "healing sounds" are too generic for me and may also be irritating for the client. I personally do not like flute music for some reason and tend to be drawn to more etheric tones like crystal bowls and soft chanting. Find out what your client likes and use those sounds to create a healing atmosphere. Be sure that you are using a system that will not have loud commercials interrupting the session's healing flow. Music will also help to drown out external noise like passing cars or other people. I have even used a "sound machine," a white/brown noise generator, to cancel outside noise. These can be purchased, or you can find pre-recorded white or brown noise recordings online.

Setting the Energy

Clear the room of stagnant or dense energy. You can do this in many ways. Smudge the space by burning aromatic plants, especially in the corners of the room. Open the windows to let the smoke out and fresh air in. Imagine that the walls are made of selenite crystals or that the walls are made of pure white healing energy. If the client is okay with essential oils, you may even diffuse something soothing, like lavender or a calming blend. Many people are extra sensitive to smells, so always ask your client what is appropriate before they arrive. What you may consider essential for a healing environment may not seem healing to another if they are sensitive or triggered. Visualize symbols or images in the space that promote well-being. Invite light beings to tend to the space so that the client feels the love energy right away.

Glass of Water

Get a glass of fresh water to set next to the treatment zone. The client may be thirsty when they arrive or need a drink during the session. I always have a client drink a glass of water after the healing session is complete to wash out toxins and re-lubricate the cells to support the ongoing healing process. You can charge the water with light beforehand to give it extra healing properties.

Hold the glass in your hand and imagine the molecules of water lighting up with golden-white light. Place intentions into the water molecules to support the healing process.

Gridding Up and Self-Treatment

Before the client arrives, connect with Source and ground the energies into Gaia. Begin running the energies and do a short self-treatment to ensure a healing presence when your client arrives. Whether you are aware of it or not, your client has started to tune into the session's healing energies from the moment the appointment was made. Use the time before the client arrives to tune into them psychically through intention and the power of nonlocal consciousness (remote viewing). You can send healing energy to them for their journey to the session. You may also receive intuitive, internal messaging about the client's needs before they arrive. Set the intention and visualize a successful session with lots of love being shared between you and your client. Use your voice to invoke divine healing energies, guides, and Source into the space. You may even want to stretch or do intuitive, flowing movement to lift your mood and open the body's energy channels since you will likely be standing for most of the healing session. Healing sessions should feel like a dance and doing some embodiment practice before the client arrives will help make the session more enjoyable for your body.

The Client Arrives

The moment the client walks into the room, be sure to welcome them and make eye contact warmly. Remember that your eyes, breath, and auric field are already beginning to work on the client's field. Have a feeling of love and welcoming in your energy. You do not have to be overly joyful; this may actually trigger someone who is in a state of agitation. A loving, clear presence is all that is needed.

Subliminal Messaging through the Voice

The tone of your voice should encourage relaxation and feelings of safety. Find ways to subtly suggest to your client that they will be having a deeply relaxing and rejuvenating healing session. Encourage them to let go and unwind and let them know this is a safe space to share whatever is in their heart. Broadcast inner imagery of well-being and joy into the space to connect with the client's Higher Self.

Opening the Field and Establishing Connection

I always start with a simple, short meditation to help both of us feel grounded, centered, and more deeply connected. I ask the client to feel into their heart and set an intention for the session. I want my client to feel a part of the healing process so that they do not rely on me solely for healing. My initial meditation always includes some form of breath awareness, hara line awareness, heart awareness, and an invocation of higher aspects and guides. This also establishes a psychic, empathetic link between myself and the client to receive internal messages and imagery that will help me support the client.

This meditation should be short, lasting between two to five minutes with guidance. Once it is complete, I ask the client what their intention is for the healing session. Then I ask if they have any physical health issues or areas of concern. I ask them what is happening in their life that needs balanced or healed. This conversation serves a few purposes.

- *Connection:* I want the person to trust me and trust the healing process.
- *Understanding:* I want to understand why they are here. I listen to the way they narrate their issues to understand what energy centers are misaligned and some potential focus areas for the laying of hands.
- *Guidance:* While listening to my clients, I often feel their blockages in my own body or receive internal messaging that will help the client and me somehow.

While listening, stay focused on your breathing, connected to your hara line, and gently nod your head at times to show that you understand and that you are listening. You can say "uh-huh," "that's natural," or other short phrases to let your client know that you hear them and that it is okay to be going through whatever they are going through. Many people carry so much shame because they feel that there is no safe space or that their emotions and beliefs are "bad." The intake interview is all about helping them accept themselves and be open to change while also letting them know that I am their unconditionally loving friend and guide.

Inspired Vision

Ask the client what their ideal situation is. Ask them what they want to create if they did not have any of the concerns that they currently have. This helps them start to manifest supportive energies and moves them out of victimhood/fate and into sovereign Divine Creatorship. You may even have them visualize this.

This can be as long or as short as needed for your client's needs and the time allotted. Most of the time, ten minutes covers the basics. Sometimes, clients want to share a bit more. I do not advise this during the interview phase. I simply want to hear what they want to share and help them relax.

Before starting, the client may need to use the restroom. It is a good idea to go anyway since they will be laying down for an hour or more. Once you feel they are comfortable and relaxed, you can begin the session.

The Session: Laying of Hands

Get your client into position for the healing session. Turn down the lights, turn up the healing music, and complete whatever other preparations you need to make. I like to sit for the first part of the session up above the head if my client is lying down. Much of the first part of the session is head-oriented, so having a chair placed above the head before beginning the session is helpful.

Once I have the client in position for the healing session, I take them through a process of breath awareness, unwinding, and intention setting.

Steps to Begin the Session

1. *Gassho:* Ground, center, and activate loving intention.
2. *Reiji-ho:* Welcome in guidance to support the healing session.
3. *Chiryo:* Begin the laying of hands.

There are various ways that a healing session can flow. Each session will be unique and beautiful. Allow yourself to be guided to where the energy is needed. Trust your internal messages. Some people like to stick to a certain set of hand placements. Others like to keep it free-form. I feel that a balance of both approaches is a sign of a proficient hands-on healer.

As I do the stages of grounding, centering, and opening to the healing energies in Gassho, I guide the client to do the same internal process. I guide them through the koshas, going through physical relaxation, life force awareness, relaxing the mind and intellect, and allowing them to rest in the Bliss Body. Progressive relaxation helps to release built-up tension in the physical body, tunes them into subtle energies, and slows down the brainwaves to create internal healing conditions. Doing some gentle breath awareness and breathwork calms the client's nervous system, connects them with their Inner Being, and opens their subtle bodies for healing.

Intention Setting

Intention setting rearranges the client's energy field for optimal healing and anchors the bodymind into coherence. I also tell my client softly that they can remain silent for the duration of the session and simply receive. I let them know that if they need anything, they can ask but that I will be mostly silent for the session. I let them know that they do not need to stay focused on me. They can even fall asleep if they would like! This is their opportunity to fully surrender and tune inward as they receive the soothing energies' benefits.

Invocation of Guides and Healing Energies

While I do Reiji-ho, I ask my client to invite the healing energies and the guidance of those who love and support them. I often say "Let us welcome your team of spiritual beings that lovingly guide and support your healing and evolution. Let us also welcome my team to support today so that we all work together towards harmony and vitality."

Laying of Hands

I like to start by sitting at the client's head and laying my hands on the client's shoulders. This helps them get used to light touch and establishes a connection between my body and theirs. Meanwhile, I lovingly beam Source energy from my eyes into the center of their heart while the energy begins to flow from my hands and entire being into their energetic field.

Practitioner Posture

It is important to keep your posture aligned and open during the session to allow proper flow. Breath awareness will help you keep soft length in the body and keep you focused on the present moment. If you find yourself drifting off with your thoughts, return to your breath, adjust and open your posture, and refocus on running energy for healing. Let the session feel like an intuitive dance. Playfulness helps to keep the spirit up.

Generally, the fingers of the hands should be closed and elongated to ensure the highest surface area is being covered. Thumbs should be connected to the side of the hand. Relax the shoulders and find a position where your body's bones are stacked comfortably. Never force yourself to stay in an uncomfortable position as this will affect the transmission of healing energy. Remember, your ENTIRE energy field is involved in the transmission.

Each hand position should be used for around five to ten minutes, depending on what is needed, and the time allotted for the session. New practitioners often feel like they need to move around or "do" a lot. I recommend "parking it" in a certain hand position for some time and simply running energy. It takes a few moments to feel the chakra open to receive the energy.

Method One: Standard Hand Placements

I do the first five hand placements sitting in a chair above the head of the client:
   1.   Hovering above the face.

2. Hovering to the side of the ears.

3. Under the occipital ridge (back of the head).

4. Hands on the crown with wrists in the center and fingers splaying out towards the ears.

5. One hand to the back of the neck and the other on the high heart. (Never place the hands on the front of the throat. This avoids triggering fear of choking.)

   For the next hand placements, I stand from my chair and walk clockwise around the body. You may choose to stand and do extra work on the heart. I often skip this as I already worked with the heart energies at the beginning of the session with my eyes and in hand placement #5 when I worked on the Throat Center.

6. Solar Plexus — upper abdomen above the navel.

7. Sacral Center — lower abdomen below the navel and above the pelvic bowl.

   For the Solar Plexus and Sacral centers, I place one hand behind the other so that one hand's fingers are touching the other hand's wrist as if I were measuring the width of their torso with my joined hands. Imagine that the torso is separated into four quadrants. The Solar Plexus is made of right and left sides, and the Sacral Center is made of a right and left side. Holding the hands this way ensures that you cover the whole "band" of that chakra's energy.

8. Root Center — Stand with your pelvis parallel to the table, one foot slightly in front of the other, and bring your hands to the outside of the client's pelvis. Use your imagination to visualize the Root chakra at the base of the tailbone.

   I typically skip the knees unless someone has knee problems. Some traditions have people work on the joints of the body. Play with it and see what feels right for you.

9. Feet — I often kneel at the client's feet and beam energy into their soles. You may also stand and hold the base of the feet by wrapping the fingers around the foot. Some people do one foot at a time, and some people do both at the same time. Find what feels comfortable for you.

Optional: Backside

Most of the time, I do not work on the back of the body because the front of the body easily takes an hour or more if I do five minutes or more at each hand position. There are many benefits from working on the back body, especially if the client has neck or back issues. So much gets stored in the spine and "roots" of the chakras that needs to be cleared away and revitalized.

1. Shoulders and Neck — Use the same stacked hand position that you used for the Sacral and Solar Plexus on the front of the body for all four chakra regions.
2. Back of Heart
3. Solar Plexus/Mid Back
4. Sacral Center/Lower Back

If a client begins to have an emotional release, do not interrupt them from their process. Continue holding an illuminated presence and allow them to feel their emotions. If it continues longer than a minute or two, ask them if they are okay and let them know you are here for them.

Method Two: Intuitive Hand Placement Session

Follow the same steps that you would use for a self-healing treatment. Use Reiji-ho to be guided to the places that are needing healing. Trust your guidance. Any time you get confused or are not certain what you need to do, return to Gassho and Reiji-ho to regain connection, clarity, and intuitive guidance.

Method Three: Scanning Method

Follow the same steps that you would use for a self-healing treatment. You may find that the area you are treating can be several feet above or outside of the body.

Method Four: Intuitive and Standard Hand Placements

Begin with the Scanning Method to find the most obvious distortions in the field. Next, you can follow the standard hand placements or do intuitive hand placements. Finish with the Scanning Method to see what else is needed.

Wrapping It Up: Cocooning with Light

Stand a few feet away from the recipient so that you can see their entire body. Stand tall in your connection to Source, face the palms towards the recipient and beam pure, loving Source energy into their entire field. Wrap them in blessings. Imagine them joyfully celebrating their new path. Send gratitude to Source and the guides that assisted in the healing session. You can use symbols to seal and amplify the intentions of the healing session. (*See Channeling Hands Mudra.*)

Finishing the Session

Often clients fall asleep during the healing session or, at the least, have entered a trance state. Take time to bring them back into conscious awareness slowly. The first time you speak should be gentle like you are waking the most adorable infant from sleeping. The client should be able to feel the joy and love in your voice as you awaken them.

Bringing Them Up

Speaking gently and softly, you can guide your client back to full consciousness saying something similar to the following:

1. Begin to gently come back into your body, deepening and elongating the breath. As you breathe, imagine that you are breathing in all the healing energies from the session.
2. Set an intention for your path. Maybe it is to live peacefully or to be loving. Allow your intention to come from your own heart.
3. Begin to gently move your fingers and toes as you take control of the body and begin to wake up now.
4. Begin to hear the sounds around you and the sounds of your body as it moves and you awaken. Become aware of the space and my presence next to you as you wake up now.
5. Almost fully awake now, yawn or stretch as you fully take control of your body.

6. Open your eyes slowly and be here now, feeling refreshed and revitalized.

I like to give the client a few minutes to continue the waking-up process on their own. I tell them that I will leave the room for a few minutes, and they can slowly continue to wake up. I let them know that a glass of water is next to them, and I would like for them to drink it to flush the body. I let them know that I will knock on the door before I re-enter the space.

Once I leave the room, I use the time to do Kenyo-ku, wash my hands, splash cold water on my face, or even shake my bones to get me grounded and centered.

Post-Session Conversation

I spend a few minutes talking with the client about their session to ensure that they are grounded enough to drive. I ask them to tell me about their experience, and I share any insight that may have come to me during the session. Use discernment when relaying intuitive messages and guidance. This is the perfect time to recommend practices to support continued healing.

If you receive inner messaging about serious health issues, please direct them to get proper medical advice from a skilled physician. Be careful to do this in a way that does not generate fear. Disclose that what you received may or may not be true for them, but you are relaying messages you received. Now that we have closed the session, this is the time where I take payment for the session and offer to make a follow-up appointment.

Once They Leave

Use this time for personal and distant healing since you are probably quite charged after the session. Break down the space and clear the energies using smudging herbs or other techniques.

You can also dedicate a self-healing session to another recipient. I love this because both of you get the benefits of the healing session!

Distant & Remote Healing (Enkaku Chiryo)

There will likely be times when you will want to share energy healing with someone you cannot be with physically. We are all connected within the Unified Field of Creation, and distant healing is a powerful tool for us to feel connected with people and places outside of our physical environment through nonlocal consciousness.

Pillars of Distance/Remote Healing

Successful distant healing comes down to three points: **Compassion, Intention,** and **Attention.**

Holding the recipient in your awareness (*attention*) with the *intention* to transmit healing energy links your consciousness to the person, place, or object that you are desiring to support. While meditating on the transmission, continuously renewing a sense of unconditional love amplifies the potency of the transmission.

The Reiki symbols help establish a link by training you to focus on a healing intention but are not necessary for creating a successful and powerful healing transmission across space and time. This ability is given to you through your connection to Source, and the symbols help train you to fine-tune that ability. Many find value in using the symbols at first, then gradually release the tool once they are used to connecting.

Use Gassho and Reiji-ho to prepare the energy for the transmission. Say a declaration to state who you are sending the energy to and where they are in the world. You can also simply pull an image of them into your mind. Keeping an internal image of them or repeating their name mentally or out loud helps strengthen the link and amplify the intentions.

Methods of Remote Healing

Surrogate Method

You can also dedicate a self-healing session to another recipient. I love this because both of you get the benefits of the healing session! When in Reiji-ho, set the intention for the healing to go to whomever or wherever you wish to send healing.

Leg Method

The leg method is effective because you can do a full body session in a short amount of time. This is the method I use the most since my legs and hands are always with me. Find a seated position and dedicate the healing session to a certain person by stating or thinking their name or by bringing an image of that person into your mind. You may also choose to use the Distant Healing Symbol from the Usui System.

Dedicate one thigh of your body to be the front of that person's body, and the other thigh will symbolize the back of that person's body. Starting at the kneecap, symbolizing that person's head, begin to run energy into your thighs, imagining that the person is receiving the energy into their body. After some time, move the hands further up your thighs until you reach your pelvis. You may receive intuitive guidance during the session. Please follow the guidance just like you would for a healing session.

Picture Method

Take a picture of the person, place, or situation you want to send healing to. Hold the photo in your hands or prop the photograph up and beam energy into the picture. Use positive internal imagery and conscious breathing to amplify the intention.

Teddy Bear Method

This is a simple practice where you use a stuffed animal as a stand-in for a healing session. The best stuffed animal to use will have two arms, a head, a torso, and two legs like a human. As you do Gassho, say out loud or state internally that you are dedicating this session to whoever is intended to be the recipient. Continue with the session as you normally would with a client. It will likely be much shorter since your hands cover much of the body.

Starting an Energy Healing Business

For many, starting a business as a healer seems like a natural step in their lives, and for others, it may seem way beyond their edge or comfort zone. I think it is important that there be reciprocation when conducting healing sessions for others. Many healers feel as if they give, give, give, and never have enough energy for themselves and no money to pay the bills. A lot of time and energy goes into developing a healing business beyond the actual healing session. If you are like me, you are working non-stop. I suggest starting with a lower price or a suggested donation price and slowly working your way up until you find the amount that feels good for you to receive and that the clientele you like to work with can afford.

Those who offer healing services often invest a lot of money, time, and energy in fine-tuning their craft and marketing it to the world. This is part of the reason why healers charge for their services. While there is nothing "bad" about charging for healing sessions, we should also make our services accessible to people who need healing and guidance. This can be done in several ways, including bartering, trades, a certain number of donation-based sessions per month, and so forth. Remember, while we do need to earn an income, we can find ways to share our services in a way that is sustainable and accessible to those who need it most.

Attracting People to Share Reiki With (Clients)

There are many ways to manifest or attract others who would be appropriate to work with. I suggest being clear with what you intend to manifest. What type of people do you like to work with? Are they paying or non-paying clients? Do you travel to them, or do they come to you? All these details are important to add to the specifics of what you are calling into your path as a healer.

Meditation for Attracting People for Healing Sessions

1. Take some time to ground, center, and connect with the Light of Source.
2. Visualize the types of beings you want to work with.
3. Imagine that a golden thread is reaching from your heart center and connecting with all those beings to let them know you are available to support them.
4. Imagine how happy they will be to know that someone wants to

help them along their path. Visualize them coming for successful sessions and happily paying or blessing you in some other way because of the benefit of the session.

5. Continue to play with this for a few minutes. Send gratitude out to all the supporting energies for this work.

Group Healing: Many Hands Make Light Work

I highly encourage organizing small or large group gatherings where people share and receive Source-sent healing energies. Someone can guide the group to help everyone synchronize intentions and connect with Source for energy healing. Healing sessions are shorter when done in a group because there are extra hands to cover more areas of the body.

1. Everyone gathers around the person who is going to receive energy healing. Stand a few feet away and begin with Gassho to help them connect with them and to feel the energy of the group.

2. Bring the hands to Reiji-ho to invite higher aspects and guides into the space.

3. Slowly approach the recipient and begin to lay hands wherever you are called to. Feel the power of light moving from the higher realms, through your bodies, and into the recipient. Feel many beings supporting the process and broadcasting their loving vibrations into the group field.

4. When the segment with that client is finished, cocoon the client with light as a group.

5. Use Kenyo-ku to clear and disconnect the energy and prepare for the next client by repeating Gassho and Reiji-ho.

Meditation Script

This meditation script can be read to another person to guide them into meditation, or you can record it yourself to make a guided meditation for your own practice.

Go ahead and move into a comfortable position for seated meditation where you can easily sit with a long spine. You can use pillows, blankets, or any other props to make yourself more comfortable. You can sit in a chair, against the wall, or simply sit up with a long spine. If seated meditation is uncomfortable for you, you can do the practice laying on your back. Soften your gaze or close your eyes and begin to tune inward to the more subtle parts of your experience.

(*Slight pause and allow people to settle in.*)

Notice the physical body and its sensations. Scan through the body to see if you can adjust your posture so that you can sit tall and comfortably. Allow the weight of the pelvis to drop into the ground, stacking each vertebra as you rise up the spine. Gently draw the shoulder blades together to open the chest, allowing the shoulders to open wide as if you were proudly wearing a beautiful necklace. Lengthen the back of the neck by gently drawing the chin toward the chest so that the crown shines towards the sky or ceiling.

(*Pause*)

Notice your breathing patterns and the movement of life force in and around your body. Begin to deepen and elongate the breath. Take long deep inhales to open the body and long, deep exhales to release any unnecessary tension or holding patterns. Use your breath to sweep through and restore all of the energy of your body. Allow yourself to be deeply nourished and revitalized by the breath.

(*Pause*)

As you breathe consciously, notice the mind and the thoughts. Allow the thoughts to drift by like clouds in the sky as you bring your awareness back to the breath and back to the present moment. At any time that thoughts arise, allow them to exist and drift away gently as you bring your awareness back to the breath.

(*Pause*)

Notice the part of you that is observing these experiences, the part of you that witnesses the body, the energy, and the breath. Notice the part that recognizes that "I am meditating." Feel your wisdom body, your ability to understand, and your ability to receive flashes of insight and guidance. If any stories or thoughts arise, allow them to dissolve as you rest in the witnessing part of your consciousness.

(*Pause*)

Expand your awareness and feel your connection to the Universe. Feel yourself expanding in this connection with all of Life. Intend to connect with your inner joy, inner peace, and your willingness to serve the goodness of Life.

(*Pause*)

Imagine that far above your head is a bright star shining with golden-white light. This radiant star symbolizes the Source of All Life, the loving presence of God. As you inhale, invite this pure light to flow down through your central channel, passing through the crown of your head and filling your entire pelvic bowl. As you exhale, send the energy downward anchoring yourself deep into Gaia, Mother Earth. As you breathe in and out, allow light to sweep away any stagnant, unneeded energy and release it into the Earth for composting. Each breath fills you with fresh light. Each exhale anchors you deeply into the Earth.

(*Pause*)

Feel into the core of Gaia. Feel into the loving, evolutionary pulsations of the energy of Mother Earth. As you breathe in, breathe her loving energy up into your own heart center, and as you exhale, send the energy back to Source, back to the star above your head. As you breathe, in and out, bridge the heart of Gaia, your own heart, and the heart of Creation, centering yourself in this Divine Love.

(*Pause*)

Breathing energy from above and from below, from Gaia and from Source, fill your central channel with Love and Light. As you exhale, send that energy in all directions around you, filling your entire auric field with Light and Love. Make your field strong and clear. Notice where your energy ends and where the rest of the world begins. Make your space feel sacred and beautiful.

(*Pause*)

Bring your awareness to your own heart center, to the core of your being, and set an intention for your meditation, a simple intention from the heart. Maybe it is Peace. Maybe it is Love. Maybe it is Presence. Set your intention and allow yourself to settle into your heart, into the spaciousness of love and presence, simple being. If any thoughts arise, notice them and allow them to pass by as you rest in loving awareness. We will be quiet for some time, and I will bring you back after ____ minutes.

(**Meditation**)

The facilitator should be meditating as well as holding space. Set a timer if needed. You can also be sending Light to all who will join the meditation. Clear any dense energy that may arise within you, intending that this also be cleared for the other meditators.

Bringing Them Back

One suggestion to facilitate the gentle return of the meditators is to read them something inspiring such as a quote, a poem, or part of a sacred text. This starts to bring them out of *anandamaya kosha* and back into *vijnanamaya kosha*, the observing part of the consciousness.

You can then address them with loving instructions: Alright, start to come back now bringing all of this awareness, Light, and Love with you.

Keeping the eyes closed, begin to deepen the breath as you become aware of the space you are in. Take deep full breaths as you begin to take control of the body again with a feeling of plenty of time. Begin to slowly stretch the body, enjoying the pleasure of movement as you breathe life into the body.

Let us meet with eyes closed and hands in prayer position at the heart.

Bow the mind to the heart, honoring the wisdom and guidance of the heart. Set an intention for your path. Let it be simple and let it be of love.

(*Pause*)

Bring the prayer hands up to the Brow Center, touching the thumbs against the forehead. Dedicate the fruits of this practice to something beyond yourself. Maybe it is for the liberation of all beings from cycles of suffering. Maybe it is for your family or a loved one. Maybe it is for Mother Earth. Send this love out to all who can benefit from it.

Bring the hands to rest on the lap or bow forward in reverence and gratitude. When you are ready, bring yourself to seated, slowly open your eyes, and allow the Light to come to you as it always has and always will.

Group Prayer and Light Anchoring

There are many ways that a community can come together in prayer to anchor in Light and Love for communal and global healing. For me, the most powerful group prayers honor the Higher Realms, Gaia, the Inner Earth families, and our family from the stars.

1. Sit together in a circle and face inward towards the center of the circle and discuss the focus of prayer for the group. This may be a unified vision or a collection of individual issues. If it is a person that is present and they are comfortable with the attention, you may even place them in the center of the circle to receive.

2. Each member of the circle then connects with their own pillar of Light and sacred heart. This bridges the realms of Light with the Earth. Broadcast a beam of love from the heart towards the center where it is united and merged with the projections from the other group members to create a bright, dazzling star of golden-white light.

3. Welcome guides and spiritual allies to join in the prayer. As the group holds the prayer field in unified intention, visualize the highest potential timelines for resolving what is needed to bring the situation to balance.

4. Amplify the prayer field by singing, toning, or activating Light language together. You may even choose to hold hands and circulate the energy to the left to create a powerful vortex within the prayer field. When holding hands in a circle, I always cue for everyone to turn their thumbs to the left to create balance within the circle.

5. Allow this to continue until the energy subsides.

6. Ground, center, and solidify your own personal auric field once the prayer is complete.

7. Stay in a circle and talk as a community about what insights or experiences may have occurred during the prayer. Share your deepest truths with one another. Join in one heart and witness one another with loving kindness and eternal friendship.

SIXTY-THREE

Manifestation of New Earth Prayer

As we close our journey through *The Illumination Codex* material, let us acknowledge, honor, and celebrate the myriad forms of our Oneself working towards higher harmony and consciousness unity across all times, dimensions, and realities. I wrote this prayer while visiting Glastonbury, UK. It is written in the pagan style and will have different elemental and directional associations if you are used to Native American prayer structure. This prayer is a powerful one to use when opening sacred space and is used now in this book to seal the benefits of reading this material and to open a portal for your next chapter of multidimensional expansion. Bless you all!

We call upon the energies of the East — the direction of the rising sun, birth and rebirth, and the element of air. We honor and evoke the wisdom of winged beings such as the birds, butterflies, and dragonflies who ride upon the air. We honor the cycles of breath, from the personal to the cosmic. We pray for the winds of the Earth to be cleansed and cleared for all generations to be able to enjoy the sweetness of breath. Let us embody the power of renewal and rejuvenation and be reminded of Life's and Spirit's eternal nature and the truth of our immortality.

We call upon the Light Beings and Spiritual Guardians of the East. Let us feel your presence NOW.

We call upon the energies of the South — the direction of the midday sun, the element of fire which burns, purifies, and transforms. We honor and evoke the wisdom of the sacred fire, the magma, and lightning. We call forth this energy to burn away that which does not serve the balance of Life. Purify our hearts and intentions and alchemize our essence so that we may embody our Divine Radiance.

We call upon the Light Beings and Spiritual Guardians of the South. Let us feel your presence NOW.

We call upon the energies of the West — the element of water and the direction of the setting sun. This is a place of endings that lead to new beginnings. A place of reflection and introspection. We honor and evoke the wisdom of the waterways, the lakes, rivers, and oceans, the cleansing rain, and the Living Waters within the Earth. We pray for our waters, both in and outside of our bodies, to be healed and purified in this eternal moment.

We call upon the Light Beings and Spiritual Guardians of the West. Let us feel your presence NOW.

We call upon the energies of the North and the element of Earth — the place of wisdom and rest, the place of our grandparents and ancestral lineages. We welcome the sacred energies and wisdom held within the bones of our ancestors. We honor and evoke the mountains' wisdom, mineral kingdoms, animal kingdoms, elemental kingdoms, crystalline kingdoms, and plant kingdoms. We ask for a special blessing for the healing and rejuvenation of the soil of the Earth. We honor our bodies, given to us by our Earth Mother, as temples for the indwelling of Eternal Spiritual Light.

We call upon the Light Beings and Spiritual Guardians of the North and our ancestors of Light and Wisdom. Let us feel your presence NOW.

We call upon the energies of above and the element of Ether. We invite into our awareness the loving presence of Mother/Father God, Source of our Being. We welcome the loving guidance of our Ascended Self, the Angelic Kingdom, Ascended Masters, Exalted Goddesses, the Elohim, and our star lineages.

We acknowledge the Source of Our Being and invite our Family of Light and our star lineages to be with us as we remember our divinity. Let us feel your presence NOW.

We call upon the energies of below and the love of Mother Gaia. We call forth remembering the wisdom of the Golden Ages of Gaia and the wisdom from our past lifetimes on the Earth. We honor and evoke the wisdom of the Inner Earth kingdoms and our Family within the Earth.

We call upon the Light Beings and Spiritual Guardians of the Below. Let us feel your presence NOW.

We call upon the energies of within, the gateway to the Kingdom of Heaven. We call forth and activate our sacred, crystalline heart and return to the truth of our Oneness, acknowledging the sacredness of all Life. We evoke and dream awake our Ascended Self. Whole. Radiant. And Free. Let us expand this prayer field into all dimensions, all timelines, all universes, and realities so that all of Creation may benefit from our Love.

May it be so! May it be now! And so, it is! OM.

GATEWAY SIX:
ASCENSION LEXICON

I have put together a list of words commonly used in this book and for the topics of awakening, spirituality, and ascension. These are not necessarily defined this way by others but are an excellent way to understand my writings in this book in a more clear and multidimensional way.

-A-

Adamic Form: Original perfected divine human form created for highly developed Light Beings to experience physical creation from within the physical dimension. Fourth Density (4D) body of the New Earth human connecting with oversoul consciousness, higher dimensional beings, and telepathic species.

Agartha: Ancient Inner Earth multi-species civilization with its own sun and ecosystem within the Earth. See *Inner Earth.*

Ain Soph: Kabbalistic term for Source before manifestation into form and translates to "Without Limit" as it is the unlimited creative potential behind all of Creation. Same as "Ineffable" in the Gnostic texts. Can also be written as "Ensof."

Akashic records: Higher-dimensional spiritual records of all experience past, present, and future. Each soul has one. So does each planet and so on.

alchemy: The application of spiritual knowledge to matter to create transformation. This is more commonly known with the Middle Ages' pursuits of turning simple metals into gold. High alchemy being the alchemy of soul/lightbody.

Ancient Egypt: Last golden age of Gaia when many beings held 4th, 5th, and 6th-dimensional consciousness before the descent into lower consciousness (forgetting).

Andromedans: Highly advanced star beings from the Andromeda galaxy assisting humanity's ascension.

Anunnaki: Star beings from the Nibiru system. Sumerian space "gods" who manipulated humanity for personal gain. Now most are in support of humanity's ascension.

apocalypse: 1. Greek word for "unveiling." 2. The dismantling of the mind control matrix and false projections from the controlling forces to reveal to humanity the ugly underbelly and karma of the collective consciousness upon the Earth from this creation cycle which is to be fully reconciled before the planet changes in dimension to Fourth Density New Earth. Not the "end" but a transitionary phase into the next creation cycle.

Archons/Controllers: Term used to describe negatively polarized service-to-self, nonphysical, intelligent beings who siphon negative energy from humanity for their own gain using mind control tactics to keep humanity enslaved through fear and distorted consciousness. The controlling forces behind global institutions. Will be fully dismantled before the shift to New Earth.

Arcturians: Star beings from the constellation of Arcturus assisting Earth with Ascension.

Ascension/ascension: 1. The spiritual maturity process of a soul, moving from an unawakened state of mundane consciousness to multidimensional Source/God-realization described as the movement of the kundalini up the central channel, samadhi, moksha, nirvana, salvation... 2. The movement of Creation into greater states of Glory. 3. The current collective planetary transformation from 3D to 5D consciousness and the New Earth reality.

ascension symptoms: Physical, etheric, mental, and spiritual changes during ascension cycles. Includes headaches, emotional purging, detoxifications symptoms, multidimensional DNA reprogramming, body aches, vivid dreams, and beyond.

Ascended Master: Level of spiritual hierarchy of beings who have ascended in their consciousness enough to no longer need to incarnate in form for spiritual growth but may choose to incarnate to assist the ascension process of a species.

Atman: Divine origin identity, True Self, True Nature, the Witness Consciousness of a lifestream. Same as Brahman. Source Self. Eternally free.

aura: Electromagnetic field of subtle energy that surrounds and pervades the physical body. Contains ever-shifting patterns and geometries of light and vibration that create the template for the physical form.

-B-

biotransducer: organic instrument for transforming energy information for the purpose of manifestation and communication with the universal hologram and divine frequencies. Able to utilize advanced intelligence and spiritual information for the transformation of reality in the human environment.

bodhisattva: Sanskrit term for someone on the path of Buddhahood (ascension) who dedicates their path to the liberation of all beings from cycles of suffering. Able to achieve liberation but delays to assist others in consciousness expansion.

Brahman: The Absolute Reality. Source in impersonal, nonmanifest state. Pure Infinity Existence Consciousness Bliss, *Satchitananda*.

buddhi: the Intellect, reflected consciousness, enlightened consciousness in each person.

buddhic consciousness: enlightened consciousness expressed by *buddhi*, the vehicle for the soul, experienced as profound intuitive insight, unity, and bliss.

-C-

Cabal: Global elite network of negatively polarized service-to-self operatives and organizations working towards complete domination of humanity and planet Earth. See *Archons*.

causal consciousness: the higher mind capacity which utilizes soul memory and intuition to observe and understand manifestation multidimensionally.

centering: Alignment with one's divine nature and inner truth, activating a bridge between Gaia and the Divine through the heart center.

centropy: Regenerative electrification of matter-energy.

chakras: Spiraling transformers of subtle energy with seven primary vortices emanating from the central channel (*sushumna*) which govern our perception of the projected holographic reality and energize our mental and physical processes.

channeling: Opening one's consciousness and vessel as a conduit for subtle energy or other consciousnesses.

Christ: 1. Yeshua ben Joseph (Jesus) in his ascended Lightbody. Forerunner of christ consciousness as part of a divine plan for redemption and restoration of humanity and Earth back to a 4th Density collective. 3. A collective consciousness field that has many emanations and incarnated forms throughout the history of Creation. 4. Title given to one who has achieved consciousness mastery and is "anointed" by Light.

christ consciousness: Also called cosmic consciousness or 5D consciousness. Demonstrated by Jesus of Nazareth in his resurrected 4th Density body.

Christ/Magdalene Lineage: Genetic implantation of higher DNA coding through the offspring of Jesus and Mary. Descendants are worldwide and able to carry a higher light quotient and awaken more easily.

clairaudience: Clear hearing is the ability to hear messages from your Higher Self or spirit beings. This includes hearing the thoughts of other people.

clairgustance: Clear tasting is the ability to receive intuitive information through the sense of taste.

clairesalience: Clear smelling is the ability to intuit information through the sense of smell.

clairvoyance: Clear sight is the ability to perceive information through internal imagery.

clear channeling: Mediumship, or spirit channeling, is the ability to communicate with nonphysical beings and consciousness structures. This can include souls who have passed beyond the veil of physical life or beings that exist in other dimensions.

collective: Representing an entire group, i.e., human collective.

Collective Messiahship: The unification of ascending humanity with the intention of global restoration and ascendency.

cords: Subtle energy attachments that connect us to other beings. Can be negative if developed through limiting beliefs and distorted conditioning.

council: Group of beings joined together with a common focus (i.e., your spiritual council of guides who support your spiritual maturation across lifetimes).

Councils of Light: Groups of advanced spiritual beings that govern the evolution of consciousness and the biological forms of a certain experimental zone to encourage higher states of glory and harmony with the highest being the Universal Council of Light.

-D-

density: 1. Mass per volume. 2. Bandwidth of consciousness reality.

Descension/descension: To go down. The forgetting or falling asleep phases of consciousness. The stepping down of light frequency.

dharma: The noble path of awakening guided through alignment with the Divine through one's True Nature. Exemplified by the life path of beings like Jesus and the Buddha.

The Divine: The frequency emanation that governs and sustains all of Creation across many universes within universes. God Source and the Hosts of Heaven. See *Godhead.*

Divine Androgyny: Harmonic synergy between the divine masculine and divine feminine energetic expressions that results in perfect balance and cohesion.

Divine Creatorship: The birthright of a human to create their life with free-will choice in alignment with their Inner Source.

Divine Feminine: 1. Nurturing creative quality of the Divine 2. Archetypal, spiritual, and psychological ideal of the feminine energetic expression.

Divine Masculine: 1. Administrative quality of the Divine 2. Archetypal, spiritual, and psychological ideal of the masculine energetic expression.

DNA: Genetic blueprint for the development of an organism with both physical and subtle components. Ascended humanity will have 12 fully restored strands.

-E-

Earth Changes: Physical and subtle energetic changes that occur on the planet as it prepares to shift into the next creation cycle. Includes pole shifts, weather changes, seismic and volcanic activity, electromagnetic shifts, and more.

Elohim: First Creation. Creator beings with individual consciousness that work in groups to form Creation. Some created as service-to-all working in unity with Source. Some were created as service-to-self permitted to create in the illusion that they were separate from Source.

empath: Individual who is sensitive to the subtle energy such as thought, and emotional projections of others as they intuitively feel the mental/emotional body of others within their own mental/emotional realm. See *clairsentience.*

End Times: The closing of this current creation cycle where all karma must be balanced, and all shadow revealed so that Earth and spiritually activated humanity can begin the next creation cycle in 4th Density New Earth. See *apocalypse.*

energy: Subtle energy beyond the visible light spectrum ranging from pervasive to neutral to regenerative and life-enhancing. Everything is energy.

energy awareness: Perception of subtle energy in and around one's body.

energy matrix: Geometric organization of subtle frequencies that creates the base structure for the development of form.

entity attachment: Astral debris that has attached itself to a weakened energy system of a host as a source of sustenance and a way to live out "unfinished business." Quite common and easily resolved most of the time by a trained spirit releasement practitioner or energy medicine practitioner.

entropy: Decay and degeneration of matter-energy.

extraterrestrial: From outside of the Earth's biosphere including other planets and universes. There are countless species in our solar system, galaxy, super galaxy, and beyond. Infinite species in infinite realms of creation with many advanced civilizations with histories tracing back trillions of years.

evolution: See *Higher Evolution.*

-F-

false prophets: Teachers and prophets who use spiritual information for service-to-self agendas. Many religious leaders, spiritual teachers, and even those in the ascension community will have their true intentions revealed in the final phases of Ascension.

Family of Light: Physical and nonphysical beings who live their lives in alignment with the Oneness of Creation and the Divine Source. Includes the races of the Star Nations who hold 5D consciousness and higher and the Hierarchy of Light who tend to the many levels of Light Creation.

5D: Consciousness of humans living on the New Earth, can be referred to as christ consciousness or oversoul consciousness.

4D: Awakening stage of ascension bridging mundane consciousness with the New Earth consciousness.

frequency: 1. Rate of vibration measured in hertz (Hz). 2. Higher vibrational rate is likened to positivity and centropy and lower rate towards negativity and entropy.

-G-

Gaia: 1. Sentient Earth 2. Common name for the soul of Earth. Also called Terra.

Galactic Federation of Light: Intergalactic and ultraterrestrial collective of advanced beings who tend to the evolution of consciousness and biological forms throughout the Milky Way. Comprised of advanced scientists, engineers, medical personnel, and other areas of expertise needed to maintain order and balance in the galaxy.

genetic implantation: Seeding of new DNA into the gene pool to evolve a species into higher states of harmony or functionality. Used by the Star Nations and Hierarchy of Light to craft zones of biological experimentation.

gnosis: Direct experience of divine nature through one's own inner being and inner knowing that leads to higher understanding of the nature of the divine reality. See *Knowledge*.

Great Central Sun: Source of all levels of creation in this universe. Brings higher evolutionary coding from Divine Source into other central suns in the universal grid which flow to each solar system evolving each region in accordance with a Divine Plan for Higher Evolution. See *Ishawara*.

Great Divide: The bifurcation of consciousness amongst humanity during the end phases of the planetary ascension process. Includes physical movement across the Earth as humanity moves to be with others of shared consciousness and similar vibration and soul path. Two-world-spit of those who hold negatively polarized, service-to-self consciousness and those of positively polarized, service-to-all consciousness.

Great White Brotherhood: More accurately **Great White Siblinghood**. Ascended Masters, human and non-human, of all gender expressions organized into different orders or councils who tend to the evolution of consciousness and sometimes incarnate to bring new teachings and new energy. Many of these Ascended Masters have aspects of themselves on the planet now to assist the Ascension.

Greys: Extraterrestrial beings from Zeta Reticuli.

God: 1. Supreme Source of Creation 2. Divine Masculine, administrative quality of Godhead, Eternal Mind. See *Ishwara*.

Goddess: 1. Divine Feminine, nurturing, regenerative, creative aspect of the Godhead. 3. Mother God.

Godhead: The Divine Consciousness Source and its various emanations and functions.

Golden Ages: Times of high consciousness and harmony upon the Earth during the Precession of the Equinoxes. (e.g., Avalon, Lemuria)

grounding: The anchoring of one's physical and subtle bodies into the Earth's core through intention, diaphragmatic breathing, and visualization through the Root and Earth Star chakras.

guides: Spiritual beings who assist an incarnated being on their dharmic path towards liberation.

-H-

hara line: Central pillar of light connecting an individual with Gaia and Source.

heart-centered: Action born from inner truth and spiritual ethics through alignment with one's divine nature.

Hierarchy of Light: Various levels of divine consciousness forms, aspects of Source that serve different functions in the evolution of Creation. Ain Soph/Source, Elohim, Archangels, Angelic Realm, Ascended Masters, Ascended Goddesses, Interdimensional Beings, and Restored Humanity in Adamic Form. The Hosts of Heaven.

Higher Evolution: Beyond biological evolution and natural selection, the recoding of experimental zones of the hologram of Creation using divinely encoded frequencies projected through the stellar network which are coordinated by benevolent beings, physical and nonphysical, who serve the evolution of the Divine Plan throughout the Multiverse. Also includes introduction of new genetic expressions into the gene pool, new technologies, and new ideas to be used to evolve the creation into higher order.

Higher Self: 1. The mature part of our consciousness which operates in positively polarized, service-to-all consciousness and is connected to our divine nature. 2. Sovereign self. 3. Harmonic Divine/Human synthesis. 4. Oversoul. 5. Atman.

Holding space: A term used in spiritual growth and self-development circles that means "to hold suffering in an alchemical container of loving awareness so that it may heal."

Holy Spirit Shekinah: The feminine regenerative energy of the Divine. The "presence of God" in the physical dimension. Opening yourself to channel the divine presence begins an alchemical process of light activation that heals and restores all levels of one's being.

-I-

Inner Earth: Ancient and contemporary subterranean civilizations. Many beings went to Inner Earth before the destruction of Lemuria and

Atlantis. See *Agartha*.

intention: Inner resolve to direct one's focus and creative capacity towards a specific goal. *Sankalpa* in Sanskrit.

interdimensional: Existing between dimensions.

intuition: The ability to perceive energy information beyond the five senses before it has become physically manifested in reality. 2. Extrasensory perception.

involution: spiritual consciousness activation that begins as one moves through Ascension and sheds the mind's conditioning.

Ishwara: 1. personal expression of Source. 2. Source in purest manifested form. Commonly called "God" 3. Great Central Sun. 4. Universal Logos.

-J-

Jesus/Yeshua ben Joseph: Master of Light for Earth. Twin flame of Mary Magdalene. Supreme teacher of Divine Love and Ascension. Brought restored DNA and pure Christ Light to the Earth to activate the 4th Density Redemption Plan. Yeshua's cosmic oversoul legacy includes many star systems including the high spiritual schools of Light in the Pleiades and Sirius A and B. His arrival into this dimension of space was the Star of Bethlehem Lightship. His life path was supported by many galactic beings incarnated upon the Earth as well as many extraterrestrials and ultraterrestrial beings. 2. Incarnation of Ascended Master Lord Sananda.

-K-

karma: 1. The sum of a being's actions in this life and in previous existences, both positive and negative actions which influences the soul's path through incarnations.

Knowledge: "Gnosis," divine insight that activates higher consciousness and God-realization. Sanskrit *aparoksha*

kundalini: Serpentine energy originating at the base of the spine that ascends through the sushumna during the awakening process creating ecstatic spiritual expression.

-L-

Lemuria: First advanced human civilization. Often associated with the Pacific Ocean. Destroyed by major flooding and earth changes.

ley lines: Subtle energy pathways that carry evolutionary information across the planetary grid. Also called dragon lines, songlines, telluric lines.

Light: Regenerative divine energy emanations that exist beyond the typical visible light spectrum (Holy Spirit). Different than conventional light from lightbulbs.

Light beings: 1. General term for nonphysical beings of divine origin. See *Family of Light.*

lightbody: 1. subtle body 2. Vital, lower, and higher mind sheaths. 3. Transmigrating soul

Light Conception: The act of conceiving a child directly from the spiritual realms without the need of sperm from a physical being.

Light language: 1. Language spoken through connection to the Divine Presence. Activates multidimensional healing and powerful internal experiences with healing frequencies. Gift of the Holy Spirit, the regenerative creative frequency that quickens and restores all levels of Life. Can be self-initiated or pushed through from the Higher Self and the Divine.

Light Seed: Higher-dimensional, light-encoded genetic material used for Light Conception and altering the genetic composition of a species. Aka *Immaculate Conception.*

Lightship/lightship: Divine craft made by one individual's lightbody/merkaba or a merged merkaba from more than one being for the purpose of interdimensional travel through space-time, stargates, and higher light realms.

Love: Beyond egoic love, unconditional love that is naturally expressed when one develops love for the divine and a service-to-all intention. *Agape* love.

lokas: Sanskrit word for the planes of existence.

loosh: energy of suffering and death harvested by negative human, extraterrestrial, and interdimensional beings which is used to fuel nefarious agendas.

Lyrans: Star beings from the constellation of Lyra. Most commonly known race is the feline beings. First humanoid race in the Milky Way. Original 144,000 oversoul starseeds to bring the human species to Earth.

-M-

magic(k): Use of universal, natural law, and intention to manifest. Can be either service-to-self (dark) or service-to-all (light).

manifestation: The materialization of intention into form.

mantra: Holy names and phrases repeatedly spoken or thought which generate divine thoughtforms to reprogram the physical, etheric, and mental bodies opening one's consciousness to higher perception, divine insight, and union with the Divine. Use of mantra repatterns the DNA, clearing distortion and debris and reprogramming it into higher order and functionality for the projection of divine consciousness light.

Mary Magdalene: Twin Flame and Divine Partner of Jesus. Ancient Egyptian Priestess. High initiate from the Pleiades, Venus, and other high consciousness realms. Arrived at Earth with Yeshua in the Star of Bethlehem Lightship. Gave birth to the offspring of Jesus. This lineage is spread throughout the world.

maya: Illusion. Projecting and veiling power of Source. All that has form and name which tests our ability to see the all-pervasive divine consciousness that supports all manifestations.

meditation: Conscious focusing of the mind on a single object.

merkaba: Divine light vehicle in the auric field that gives one the ability to travel to the higher light realms. Introduced back to humanity through Elijah.

Michael: Archangel who protects and defends all levels of Creation and biological life.

mindfulness: The practice of bringing our life's gross and subtle manifestations into the light of our awareness to observe life in nonduality. Nondual awareness is the ability to see beyond the illusion of duality and see with the eyes of loving awareness.

Mother Mary: Cosmic divine being, a Master soul, who incarnated to give birth to Jesus. High priestess of Ancient Egypt and master teacher of the cosmic priestess arts.

multidimensional: Existing in multiple planes of consciousness, i.e., physical, etheric, mental, and various spiritual dimensions.

Multiverse/multiverse: Universes within universes creating the totality of Creation. What Jesus spoke of when he referred to his "Father's house with many mansions."

-N-

nadis: Pathways of subtle energy in the body. There are said to be 72,0000 that weave in and around the physical body.

New Earth: 1. Higher density light spectrum reality of the ascended Earth. 2. Kingdom of Heaven on Earth.

nirvanic consciousness: liberated consciousness which has transcended suffering, limited egoic identity, and karmic cycles.

-O-

Orion: Constellation with ancient intelligent races with varying levels of consciousness and ranges of polarity. Factions of Reptilian and humanoid beings from Orion fought against Lyrans in the long galactic war.

oversoul: Higher consciousness identity of a soul. Where your individual soul comes from. Collective consciousness of myriad life streams and incarnations. 4th Density/5D Self.

-P-

past life regression: Form of hypnosis or shamanic journeying that evokes information from a client's subconscious mind from previous lifetimes.

Pleiadians: Star beings from the constellation of Pleiades, a highly advanced light consciousness school in our great universe. Cousins of humanity. They implanted upgraded DNA in humanity to open our spiritual connection.

prayer: Approach to the Divine through thought or word which opens the pathways for the living Light to infuse the one who is praying with love and divine insight.

priest: Male devotee of the Divine in service to the illumination of collective consciousness and the ascension of humanity. Administers the will and knowledge of the divine upon the Earth as well as the regenerative, healing presence of the divine feminine.

priestess: Female devotee of the Divine. Often connected to the Goddess. Embodies the wisdom of the divine feminine mothering principle of the Godhead. Matures consciousness in the community into higher states of creativity, sensuality, and grace.

psychic: One who has extrasensory perception. See *intuition*.

pyramids: Sacred architectural sites around the Earth built by various extraterrestrial and ultraterrestrial beings connecting the pathways of vital energy of the Earth with the universal energy grid for the reprogramming of life upon planet Earth. Act as broadcast and receiving systems for information used for planetary evolution.

Prakriti: Manifested reality, transactional reality as opposed to Absolute Reality, maya.

Purusha: Indwelling witness of Creation, Absolute Reality, Brahman, Pure Consciousness. Source Consciousness.

-Q-

quantum: Dealing with the holographic reality and fabric of Consciousness and creation.

quantum consciousness: Holographic consciousness connecting to the matrix of Creation with the ability to focus across time and space through nonlocality and consciousness projection.

quantum healing: Rapid, multidimensional healing that works at the cellular and subtle levels to bring the body's systems into homeostasis. Can be done through psychic processes, shamanic and energy medicine practices, hypnosis, quantum healing technology, star technology, and divine emanations. This is the medicine of New Earth.

quantum mysticism: Emerging evolutionary synthesis between science, metaphysics, and spirituality used to understand Consciousness and the laws that govern Creation.

Qumran: Ancient, multigenerational esoteric Essene community by the Dead Sea in present-day Israel that lived in complete recognition of the Divine through the study and embodiment of divine mystery teachings. Secretive community with advanced star knowledge and superhuman spiritual abilities. Traded knowledge with other global mystery schools and was home and school to Yeshua, Jesus of Nazareth. Yeshua's children studied here as well.

-R-

Reiki: 1. Japanese word meaning spiritual intelligence life force. 2. Intelligently-encoded, divine, redemptive, and regenerative energy from Source. 3. A gift of the Holy Spirit.

Redemption Plan: Cosmic and galactic initiative to restore humanity and Earth back to 4th Density as in the times of Lemuria. Includes genetic implantation, restoration of planetary grid, and operatives incarnating as human to bring new ideas and technologies, broadcasting intelligent and spiritual coding into the biofield of Earth and humanity, and more.

Reptilians: Reptilian humanoid star beings who have had a "negative" influence on Earth who have mostly evolved to positive polarity. Humans have reptilian DNA that gives us our ego mind to assist our perseverance in evolving.

reincarnation: The act of being born again into a new lifestream for the purpose of spiritual growth.

resonance: In spiritual terms, harmonic, synchronous vibrations between two or more objects.

Raphael: Archangel who administers to healing.

-S-

sacred sexuality: Alchemical sexual expression with the intention of uniting with the divine through one's own erotic spiritual nature. Can be practiced alone or with a partner(s).

sacred sites: Holy power spots spread across the planet that form a web of vortex points for subtle energy pathways of the Earth.

samsara: 1. Wheel of Karma 2. rounds and rounds of incarnations on the path of Ascension 3. Suffering mind. 4. Cycles of suffering.

samskaras: Grooves in the mind that create reactive emotions forming our biases, habits, and tendencies. Can be seen as negative or positive.

Self: Divine Self as opposed to the egoic self which is trapped in worldly conditioning.

sentience: The ability to feel, be conscious, or have one's own subjective experience.

service-to-all: Positively polarized, dedicated intention, thought, and action towards the Greater Good and Higher Love as an extension of one's True Self.

service-to-self: Negatively polarized, gives power to false self, ego. Can seem "positive" as intentions can be different than presentation.

sin: Intention, thought, and action that goes against one's inner light that causes an immediate depletion of life force and positive vibration. Serves the egoic self. There is no judgment for this from higher realms. All is for learning and growth. 2. Fear-based judgment system created by religion which connects to belief systems that limit the indwelling of spiritual light by creating perpetual states of fear, shame, and guilt. 3. The fundamental illusion of separation from Source.

Sirians: Star beings from the region of the Sirius A and Sirius B binary star system who have a long, positive history with humanity and are assisting Earth now.

Solaris: Central sun and stargate of our solar system which emanates supraliminal coding for the evolution of the myriad lifeforms in our solar system.

soul: 1. Subtle bodies which transmigrate from one life to the next. See *lightbody*.

spiritual partnership: A relationship that is supported by the desire to assist one another in awakening and healing.

soul contracts: Pre-designed plan and agreements before incarnating for the balancing of karma to propel the path of liberation and ascension. Includes soul agreements between individual souls to play out certain catalyst roles.

soul purpose: Divine intention for a soul for its incarnation encompassing the themes to be explored and lessons to be learned throughout a lifestream. Generally, a soul's purpose is to awaken to Higher Love and Divine Truth.

sovereign: natural consciousness state of the Atman/Self/Inner Source. Human beings embody and reclaim sovereignty through involution and higher consciousness evolution. Able to have agency in all areas of life. Self-regulated. Self-governed.

stargate: Portal used for transportation between long distances and different dimensions.

Star Nations: Space-traveling intelligent species, some positive, some negative, some neutral in relation to humanity and the Earth.

starseeds: Visitors from other schools in the multiverse who have volunteered to live a human life to assist the Ascension of Gaia and humanity. Many of which have experienced ascension mastery in other lifetimes. The best ascension masters from the universe are here on the planet or around the planet in crafts at this time.

substratum: 1. Foundational, base material 2. Source/Brahman/Atman/Pure Consciousness.

superluminal: 1. faster than light

synchronicity: The meeting of two or more seemingly unrelated events or objects that come together in a meaningful way that could even be perceived as divinely coordinated.

-T-

timelines: Pathways of probable events. Infinite potentials and realities fractal out and converge at particular junction points in "time" where choice points exist for the next fractal offshoots of timeline potentials. We are currently moving with multiple timeline potentials for Ascension events that lead to one inevitable event, 4th/5th Density New Earth. Timelines are constantly in flux depending on personal moment-to-moment choices from individuals or the collective meaning the future is never "fixed" but is always in flux. This is the reason why some psychics see different potential probabilities playing out in the future.

3D: Standard human consciousness in its unawakened state, fear/duality-based consciousness which is heavily programmed and hypnotized by the false matrix, the conditioning of the world, and the mind control techniques from the Archons.

Elders: Highest divine council. Progenitors of all cultures in the multiverse.

Twin Flames: Emanations of the same oversoul who assist one another in Ascension. Often uniting at the end of karmic cycles to serve Consciousness. Most commonly thought of as two people in Divine Partnership, but there can be more.

-U-V-W-Y-

Unified Field: The hologram of Creation, the Quantum Field, where all energies and manifestations arise from connecting all through Source Consciousness.

ultraterrestrial: Beings from beyond the physical plane, higher density beings in higher density forms.

vibration: The invisible, subtle layers of matter that form the basic templates for physical reality through repetitive oscillation.

Wisdom: Insight into the Divine Mysteries of Creation and the Godhead that connects us with higher states of divine love and divine grace. See *Knowledge, gnosis.*

walk-in: Exchange of souls during an incarnation. Typically occurs when the original soul consciousness assigned to the body can no longer continue an incarnation from trauma or some other way of vital depletion. A fresh soul consciousness is brought in to accomplish a certain task. Frequently used to bring highly developed galactic beings into the Earth for mission-oriented tasks.

Yeshua ben Joseph: See *Jesus* and *Christ*.

Recommended Reading

The Three Waves of Volunteers and The New Earth by Dolores Cannon

They Walked with Jesus by Dolores Cannon

Jesus and the Essenes by Dolores Cannon

Between Death and Life by Dolores Cannon

Keepers of The Garden by Dolores Cannon

Five Lives Remembered by Dolores Cannon

Return of the Bird Tribes by Ken Carey

Anna: Grandmother of Jesus by Claire Heartsong

Light on Life by B.K.S. Iyengar

The Yoga Sutras of Patanjali (many translations available)

Living Buddha, Living Christ by Thich Nhat Hahn

Reconciliation: Healing the Inner Child by Thich Nhat Hahn

Peace is Every Step by Thich Nhat Hahn

The Path of Energy by Dr. Synthia Andrews

The Seat of the Soul by Gary Zukav

The Book of Knowing and Worth by Paul Selig

The Diamond in Your Pocket by Gangaji

The Magdalen Manuscript: The Alchemies of Horus & the Sex Magic of Isis by Tom Kenyon and Judi Sion

The Kybalion by Three Initiates

Aparokshanubhuti by Adi Shankara

The Upanishads

The Bhagavad Gita

Drig Drishya Viveka

The Keys of Enoch by J.J. Hurtak

Pistis Sophia translated by J.J. Hurtak

The Secret Doctrine by H.P. Blavatsky

Etheric Double by A.E. Powell

The Causal Body and the Ego by A.E. Powell

Regression: Past-life Therapy for Here and Now by Samuel Sagan

Entity Possession: Freeing the Energy Body of Negative Influences by Samuel Sagan

THE ILLUMINATION CODEX

THE ILLUMINATION CODEX
GATEWAY ONE

ASCENSION INITIATION

Keys for Higher Evolution

MICHAEL GARBER

THE ILLUMINATION CODEX
GATEWAY TWO PART ONE

QUANTUM ORIGINS

Keys for Ancient Cosmology

MICHAEL GARBER

THE ILLUMINATION CODEX
GATEWAY TWO PART TWO

COSMIC CHRIST TRANSMISSIONS

The Ministry of Light

MICHAEL GARBER

THE ILLUMINATION CODEX
GATEWAY FOUR

CHAKRA YOGA DISCOURSE

Keys for Higher Consciousness

MICHAEL GARBER

THE ILLUMINATION CODEX
GATEWAY TWO PART THREE

NEW EARTH TRANSMISSIONS

Future Timelines of Gaia

MICHAEL GARBER

THE ILLUMINATION CODEX
GATEWAY THREE

PATH OF AWAKENING

Keys for Transfiguration

MICHAEL GARBER

THE ILLUMINATION CODEX
GATEWAY FIVE

LAYING OF HANDS
REIKI & BEYOND

MICHAEL GARBER

Support Our Initiatives

Ron and I have dedicated our lives to supporting this Grand Transition. We stand alongside all of you as humanity awakens to its True Nature and becomes a People of Light in the heavenly reality of New Earth.

New Earth Ascending is dedicated to assisting people to realize their divinity and manifest that truth in every aspect of their life. For more information about New Earth Ascending or to contact Michael, please scan the QR code below for a list of resources and links, or visit *www.newearthascending.org*. Be sure to check out our courses including the Illuminated Quantum Healing practitioner course.

New Earth Ascending is a registered 508 (c)(1)(a) Self-Supported Non-profit Church Ministry with a global outreach. We greatly appreciate your support as we create new systems, communities, and schools for the development of the New Earth civilization. If you would like to make a tax-deductible donation to support our mission, please go to:

https://donorbox.org/donationtonewearthascending

Scan with a smart device camera for more information including websites, social media, and more! Bless us all!